Credits

Every effort has been made to contact copyright holders for permission to reproduce borrowed material where necessary. We apologize for any oversights and would be happy to rectify them in future printings.

All email correspondence, classroom websites, and hompages used with permission.

Screen shots used by permission from Microsoft Corporation©.

Screen shots from Netscape browser window © 2002 Netscape Communications Corporation. Used with permission. Netscape Communications has not authorized, sponsored, endorsed, or approved this publication and is not responsible for its content.

Screen shots used by permission from Apple Computer, Inc.©.

Screen shots reproduced with permission of Yahoo! Inc. © 2004 by Yahoo! Inc. YAHOO! and the YAHOO! logo are trademarks of Yahoo! Inc.

Chapter 1

ENC Online webpage used with permission of Eisenhower National Clearinghouse for Mathematics and Science.

The Math Forum Problems of the Week webpage used with permission of The Math Forum @ Drexel, an online community for mathematics education (http://mathforum.org/) © 1994-2004, The Math Forum @ Drexel. All rights reserved.

Turn of the Century Child webpage used with permission of Debbie Abilock.

After Reconstruction: Problems of African Americans in the South webpage, from the American Memory website used with permission of the Learning Page of the Library of Congress.

Chapter 2

The Alien Bandstand webpage at the Space Mysteries website used with permission.

Amazing Space Online Explorations webpage used with permission of STScI (Space Telescope Science Institute), Office of Public Outreach for NASA.

Internet Explorer browser image used with permission of Microsoft Corporation.

Netscape website © 2004 Netscape Communications Corporation. Screenshot used with permission.

Safari browser image used with permission of Apple Computer, Inc.

Lewis and Clark's Historic Trail used with permission.

Yahooligans search engine images used with permission of Yahoo!Inc.

KidsClick search engine results used with permission.

Ask Jeeves for Kids search engine results used with permission of Ask Jeeves.

Google™ search engine results used with permission of Google.

All About Tigers webpage used with permission.

Chapter 3 Walking with Dinosaurs webpage from BBC Science Online.

Kids Web Japan webpage used with permission of the Japan Center for Intercultural Communications.

The Particle Adventure webpage used with permission.

Global SchoolNet Internet Project Registry used with permission. Global SchoolNet ©.

Chapter 4 Outlook Express images used with permission of Microsoft Corporation.

Netscape website © 2004 Netscape Communications Corporation. Screenshot used with permission.

Middle-L Homepage used with permission of the Early Childhood and Parenting Collaborative.

Educational Bloggers Network webpage used with permission.

Chapter 5 The Big Myth webpage used with permission.

The Complete Works of William Shakespeare webpage used with permission of Jeremy Hylton.

Imaginary Lands webpage used with permission of Denise Matulka.

Literature Learning Ladders webpage used with permission of Annette Lamb.

New Zealand Writers Window webpage used with permission of the New Zealand Ministry of Education.

Chapter 6 American Memory homepage used with permission of the Library of Congress.

History/Social Studies for K-12 Teachers used with permission.

EdSITEment, sponsored by the National Endowment for the Humanities in partnership with the MarcoPolo Education Foundation, is used with permission of the NEH.

Eartheasy homepage used with permission of Greg Seaman.

The Little Rock 9 WebQuest © 2004 SBC. All rights reserved. Portions of this page have been copied and distributed with the permission of the copyright owner, SBC. SBC is not responsible for and assumes no liability for any loss, injury or damage which may be incurred by persons or entities using this page. Any person or entity using this page does so at its own risk.

Favorites image used with permission of Microsoft Corporation.

Chapter 7 SETI @ Home webpage used with permission.

Mad Scientist Network webpage used with permission.

ENC Features webpage used with permission of Eisenhower Clearinghouse for Mathematics and Science.

Earth Day Groceries Project webpage used with permission of Mark Ahnless.

DNA for Dinner webpage used with permission of William Peace.

Chapter 8

Problem of the Week webpage used with permission of MATHCOUNTS.

Sierpinski Triangle webpage from Fractals by Cynthia Lanius.

The Math Forum homepage used with permission of The Math Forum @ Drexel, an online community for mathematics education (http://mathforum.org/) © 1994-2004, The Math Forum @ Drexel. All rights reserved.

Mega Mathematics webpage used with permission.

Chapter 9

Magical Kingdom webpage used with permission of Magical Kingdom ©.

Ugly Bug Contest image webpage used with permission of the Oklahoma Microscopy Society.

Today Hooray! webpage used with permission of KonnectKids.

Animal Riddles webpage used with permission of Jerry Jindrich, Chateau Medybemps ™.

Mind's Eye Monster Exchange webpage used with permission.

Monarch Watch webpage used with permission.

Chapter 10

México para Niños webpage used with permission of El Balero (http://www.elbalero.gob.mx/).

Portals to the World Homepage from the Global Gatewayused with permission of the Library of Congress.

Activities for ESL Students homepage used with permission of Charles Kelly, *The Internet TESL Journal*.

Project America homepage from Project America.

Windows on the World Showcase webpage from the British Council.

Native Visions of the Natural World webpage used with permission of the Carnegie Museum of Natural History.

Chapter 11

Mysterious Language Riddles webpage used with permission of the Center for Disability Information & Referral. Hounshell, M., & Mercer, M. (1999). Mysterious secret language mystery riddles. Bloomington, IN: Indiana Institute on Disability and Community.

Seeing Disabilities from a Different Perspective webpage used with permission.

Netscape website © 2004 Netscape Communications Corporation. Screenshot used with permission.

American Sign Language Browser webpage used with permission. ©2000 Michigan State University Communication Technology Laboratory. All Rights Reserved.

Kids' Quest on Disabilty and Health webpage used with permission of the CDC (Centers for Disease Control) Office of Communication.

Chapter 12

Netscape website © 2004 Netscape Communications Corporation. Screenshot used with permission.

For our parents who showed us why—
Anne and Don, Charlene and Fran, Rose and Dan.

And for those special teachers who showed us how—
George Bell, Jeanne Chall, Mario DiPonio,
Dorothy Dye, Robert Miles, and Mary Riordan.

Teaching with the Internet K-12: New Literacies for New Times

Teaching with the Internet K-12: New Literacies for New Times

Fourth Edition

Donald J. Leu, Jr. Deborah Diadiun Leu, and Julie Coiro
University of Connecticut

Disclaimer

The authors and the publisher assume no responsibility for errors or omissions in the resources identified in this book. Moreover, the authors and publisher assume no liability for any damages resulting from the use of any information identified in this book or from links listed at sites that are described. As we indicate in this book, the best way to protect children from viewing inappropriate sites or receiving inappropriate messages is to implement a sound acceptable use policy and to carefully monitor student use of the Internet in your classroom, at school, and at home.

We have devoted much time and energy to providing accurate and current information in this book. Nevertheless, in an environment as constantly changing as the Internet, it is inevitable that some of the information provided here will also change. Information provided at one location may move to another, sometimes without any indication it has moved. Updated links are maintained at the companion webpage for this book at **Teaching with the Internet: New Literacies for New Times** (http://www.sp.uconn.edu/~djleu/fourth.html). Here you will also find links to many other resources and an interactive community area where you may share your own ideas about new literacies.

Christopher-Gordon Publishers, Inc.
1502 Providence Highway, Suite 12
Norwood, MA 02062
1-800-934-8322

Printed in Canada

10 9 8 10 09 08

ISBN 10 1-929024-77-0
ISBN 13 978-1-929024-77-3

Library of Congress Number 2004102837

Contents

Preface

We are pleased to share with you this 4th edition of *Teaching with the Internet*. As in previous editions, *Teaching with the Internet* is primarily about good teaching. Our focus on teaching and learning with the Internet is what distinguishes this book from others that tend to emphasize the more technical aspects of the Internet. Each chapter begins with a classroom scenario and continues with several other examples of how teachers are developing classroom communities filled with the excitement of learning and discovery. Throughout this book, we also share stories of how teachers and students are using the Internet in new ways. We show you how to use the Internet thoughtfully in classroom contexts and how to create opportunities for students to share their own expertise with new literacies, enabling you to make a powerful difference in the lives of your students.

Our focus on teaching and learning with the Internet is what distinguishes this book from others that tend to emphasize the more technical aspects of the Internet.

This book is also about saving you time. Teachers wanting to use the Internet in their classrooms tell us that time is their biggest concern. It takes *time* to develop the new literacies that the Internet requires; *time* to locate quality websites; and *time* to weave the Internet into an already overloaded curriculum. Teaching is a profession that demands extraordinary amounts of time and we know you have little to spare as you explore this new context for literacy and learning. This new edition is designed to help you to quickly learn the essentials of teaching with the Internet while locating content specific resources. It will also show you how to weave the Internet into your schedule in ways that actually save time as you integrate the Internet with content area instruction.We realize your time is precious and we seek to help you effectively integrate the new literacies of the Internet into your classroom in the shortest time possible.

One way to save time is to visit the new website for this book, **Teaching with the Internet** (http://www.sp.uconn.edu/~djleu/fourth.html). As you read each chapter, you can follow along on the website, quickly clicking on the corresponding links that interest you. We have also included new opportunities for you to respond to ideas in the book and interact with other readers by posting your comments, lesson ideas, or other insights to an interactive community area on the website. And, because we update this site regularly, you can access additional sites and other great classrooms on the Internet that emerge after the publication of this edition. We invite you to take advantage of this resource and share it with your colleagues as a helpful starting place for weaving the Internet into all areas of your curriculum.

Assumptions That Guide Our Work

Several assumptions have guided our work in this 4th edition. First, an underlying principle of a new literacies perspective (Coiro, 2003; Leu, Kinzer, Coiro, and Cammack, 2004) suggests that *the Internet is fundamentally changing the nature of literacy and classroom instruction in ways that enhance students' opportunities to learn about the world around them.* This book helps you to understand these changes and supports you on your instructional journey. As such, each chapter includes instructional strategies and web resources related to traditional notions of learning within a content or topic area. However, we also guide you through models of how to expand your curriculum to weave in the newer aspects of reading, writing, and communication emerging from new technologies; those that we refer to as "new literacies."

We begin each chapter with a story of a teacher using the Internet in the classroom and then discuss the lessons each of us can learn from this experience.

Second, *we believe that a teacher's knowledge and insight becomes even more important within new literacy classrooms.* Thus, we assume the active role you play in orchestrating experiences with the Internet greatly influences the extent to which your students develop the new literacies they require for learning in academic contexts. Using the Internet most effectively in the classroom requires teachers who can orchestrate more complex learning contexts, knowing what students need to acquire and knowing how to set up social learning contexts to maximize this. We share useful ideas about how best to guide students through these explorations while also taking advantage of the knowledge and experiences they bring with them from outside the four walls of your classroom.

Third, *we assume that understanding something as powerful, complex, and constantly changing as the Internet requires us to work collaboratively while learning from one another. Socially constructed learning is central to success with the Internet.* We believe that those educators who network with other educators, share their expertise and welcome new ideas from others will be most successful in integrating the Internet into their own teaching. Our writing is guided by this assumption in several ways. We begin each chapter with a story of how a talented teacher uses the Internet in the classroom and then discuss the lessons each of us can learn from this experience. These classroom episodes were developed from multiple sources: email conversations we have had with teachers around the world, descriptions of Internet experiences posted on various listservs, ideas posted by teachers at Internet Project sites, classroom observations, and our own experiences as teachers. Each story represents a fusion of multiple sources; no story represents a single teacher's experiences. We feel, however, that each story faithfully represents the many outstanding classrooms we have encountered in our travels on the Internet.

We also include email messages to you from teachers around the world, describing the lessons they have learned while using the Internet. These teachers are the new researchers of the Internet world, exploring these new contexts for teaching and learning and reporting on what works in practical ways. Their insights are critical to your success.

We also include email messages to you from teachers around the world, describing the lessons they have learned from using the Internet.

Each chapter also includes a visit to one outstanding classroom webpage, showing you important lessons we can learn from this classroom and sharing strategies sent directly from the creator of each webpage.

Finally, chapters provide you with access to online communities that put you in touch with other teachers who face the same challenges as you. We all learn from one another in this new electronic environment. We hope to support this learning so that you and your students may benefit.

There is also a fourth important assumption that has guided our work: *We assume that student safety needs to be paramount as we consider the use of this new tool for instruction*. Throughout this book, you will find ideas to ensure the appropriate use of Internet technologies in your classroom. We have been careful to select Internet sites that avoid commercial advertisements whenever possible and to provide strategies for addressing issues such as managing web browsers and ensuring student privacy. Nothing is more important than protecting students while we prepare them for the potential of the Internet and other information and communication technologies.

Changes Appearing In This Edition

This book is also about change. With this edition, you see an important evolution in our own thinking and in the changes taking place in the field. Increasingly, the educational community is beginning to understand that new information and communication technologies (ICT) such as the Internet require new literacies in order to fully exploit their potential (International Reading Association, 2002). For a number of years, we have been developing this perspective, what we call a "New Literacies Perspective," in our own writing (Coiro, 2003; IRA, 2002; Leu, 2000a; Leu, 2002; Leu et al., 2004).

With this edition, we formally integrate this point of view into all of the chapters. We show you how the Internet requires new reading, writing, and communication skills. Most importantly, we show you how to teach these skills while you and your students explore the many exciting learning experiences that the Internet makes possible. This New Literacies Perspective is the most important change we have made to this edition. If you wish to read more about the theoretical foundations of our work on new literacies, these two articles are available online:

We take a "New Literacies Perspective" throughout this book.

- **Reading Comprehension on the Internet: Expanding our Understanding of Reading Comprehension to Encompass New Literacies—**
http://www.readingonline.org/electronic/rt/2-03_Column/
- **Toward a Theory of New Literacies Emerging from the Internet and other Information and Communication Technologies—**
http://www.readingonline.org/newliteracies/lit_index.asp?HREF=/newliteracies/leu

Others appear in our references, a section that now appears at the back of this book.

You will also see other important changes in this 4th edition, many of which were suggested by teachers in their thoughtful email messages to us.

- **A Solid Theoretical Foundation.** The early chapters provide you with an easy to understand theoretical framework that guides your thinking about the three most pressing questions we face in classrooms: *What should we teach?; How should we teach it?; and Why we should teach it?* As educators, each of us will be challenged in new ways to thoughtfully guide students' learning within networked information environments that are constantly changing and increasingly complex. Having this underlying framework from which to design new classroom lessons will aid in making effective decisions about Internet resources, activities, and classroom routines most appropriate for your students.
- **Extensive Coverage of Timesaving Search and Navigation Strategies.** Search engines are often frustrating to new users looking for information. Chapter 2 has been expanded to consider new instructional strategies and electronic tools for weaving elements of Internet navigation, searching, and critical evaluation strategies into classroom instruction. Among many other topics, we introduce new keyword strategies just for teachers, share lessons that model for students how to efficiently read through search engine results, and provide a sneak peek into innovative new search engines on the horizon. We also weave specific search strategies into the content area chapters.
- **Expanded Coverage of Child Safety Issues.** Throughout the book, we point out current policies about Internet filtering, recommend search engines designed for younger children, direct you to sources about student privacy concerns, and highlight strategies for dealing with the growing commercialization of the Internet. Chapter 2 and Chapter 9 have special sections about these important issues.
- **Expanded K–12 Coverage.** We have expanded our coverage to include an even more comprehensive discussion of instruction at all levels. You will find new resources and instructional strategies that immediately apply to your elementary, middle school, or high school classroom. We provide you with an extensive discussion of issues related to multiculturalism and bilingualism in Chapter 10. Similarly, in Chapter 11, we have expanded our coverage of instructional strategies and specific resources for ensuring equity and inclusive educational opportunities for all students. We encourage you to call upon these strategies as you seek to accommodate Internet experiences for students in your class who have been formally identified as requiring special assistance.
- **New Classroom Scenarios at the Beginning of Each Chapter.** As we communicate with teachers around the world, we continually learn new lessons. We share these lessons through new stories about how teachers are using the Internet in their classrooms. Many of their lessons now incorporate new instructional tools like web-based simulations, Flash-animated storybooks, and educational weblogs. Their stories pro-

vide important insights into effective classroom management strategies and the critical decision-making processes involved in designing thoughtful Internet activities for students.

- **Great, New Directories for Content Areas.** Teachers tell us one of their greatest challenges is locating information quickly on the Internet. We have included the best directories from earlier editions and added many new ones to each chapter. By maintaining a companion website, we will continually bring you the most recent Internet resources we believe are useful to the important work you do to prepare students for their future. Chapter 2 also features a table that highlights many of these sites from one easy location. Start your search at one of these locations. Sometimes it is faster than using a search engine.
- **Expanded Discussion of Instructional Models for Teaching with the Internet.** In this edition, we have expanded our coverage of four central instructional models: Internet Workshop, Internet Project, Internet Inquiry, and WebQuest. Since the quality of webquests varies so greatly, we also identify guidelines for how to evaluate a webquest to determine its utility for your classroom. Chapters 5–11 will show you how to begin with easier instructional models and move to more complex and richer models as you feel increasingly comfortable with using the Internet in your classroom. Chapter 4 highlights extensive strategies for using email and other online communication tools for networking, teaching, and learning.
- **Updated Sections on Citing Internet Resources and Plagiarism Concerns.** Often teachers have questions about appropriate ways of teaching students to cite information, images, and resources they have referenced in their school projects. Similarly, there is a growing concern about increasing instances of student plagiarism and how to detect and deter it. Chapters 2, 3, and 6 have updated special sections about both of these important issues.
- **Expanded Coverage of Critical Literacies.** The widespread increase of unedited and uncensored information demands that we help students develop new and more critical stances toward the information they encounter on the Internet. In this edition, we show you how to do this and provide you with the new resources that can support your work in this area. You can find particular sections that address these issues in the context of Language Arts and Social Studies topics in Chapters 5 and 6, respectively.
- **Additional Section on New Literacies.** To parallel the theoretical discussion of our new literacies perspective in the early chapters of this book, we have also added a more practical section toward the end of each content-specific chapter that provides particular examples of how to address these new skills and strategies within your current curriculum. We invite you to explore these sections and to post your thoughts about these new lesson ideas to the interactive portion of our website at http://www.sp.uconn.edu/~djleu/fourth.html. If you are interested, we have also reserved a location for you to submit your own lessons framed around the five components of new literacies. In this way, we

can all join in the spirit of exchanging current and creative ideas with other classroom teachers as new technologies and new literacies continue to emerge.

- **Enhanced Classroom Models for Internet Use.** We believe that the best teacher is another outstanding teacher. The Internet allows us to enter other teachers' classrooms by visiting their classroom homepages. These talented individuals provide excellent models of teachers at all stages of Internet use and can teach us important lessons about how to use the Internet for teaching and learning. They allow us to see the range of Internet resources that other teachers are using and permit us to immediately use these in our own classrooms. Each chapter takes you on an enhanced tour of an outstanding teacher's classroom homepage in a feature called "Visiting the Classroom." In addition to our own reflections of these unique homepage offerings, we have also invited these featured teachers to describe, in their own words, how they use their web-based classroom presence to enhance teaching, learning, and parental support.

The People Who Have Contributed to the Fourth Edition

We could not have completed a complex project like this without the assistance of many individuals. To each, we are profoundly indebted. We would like to thank as many of them as possible.

Many educators shared their experiences with the Internet, providing us with important insights that appear in this book. These include teachers from across the United States and Canada as well as teachers from Argentina, Australia, Ecuador, Finland, Japan, Germany, Great Britain, New Zealand, South Africa, Sweden, and The Netherlands. Most are only known to us through their insightful email messages and the descriptions they shared of their classes. We hope someday to have the opportunity to actually meet each person and personally express our gratitude for his or her important contributions.

Each chapter takes you on a tour of an outstanding teacher's classroom homepage in a feature called "Visiting the Classroom."

We especially wish to thank the following educators who were kind enough to share their insights through the email messages we include in this book: Lisa Brayton, Barbara McInerney, Celia Godsil, Marci McGowan, Maya Eagleton, Carolyn Joiner, Jill Newcomb, Cindy Ross, Beverly Powell, Susy Calvert, Linda Shearin, Susan Silverman, Paula Reber, Jeanette Kenyon, Cindy Lockerman, Debbi Contner, Karen Auffhamer, Susan Hunsinger-Hoff, Gary Cressman, Peter Lelong, David Cognetti, Elise Murphy, Rosemary Salvas, Ruth Musgrave, Leslie Bridge, Jodi Moore, Rob Hetzel, Doug Crosby, Isabelle Hoag, Cathy Lewis, Jack Fontanella, Anne Nguyen, Terry Hongell, Patty Taverna, Nicole Gamble, Fred Roemer, Marylou Balcom, and Heather Renz. As we write this list, each name brings back an important memory of email exchanges with a very knowledgeable educator. We thank each of you for sharing your wonderful lessons with us. Each of you is an outstanding educator, contributing in important ways to our increasingly global community. We have learned from your insights and we know our readers will too!

We also wish to thank our colleagues who have advanced our thinking in important ways: Jon Callow, Dana Cammack, Jill Castek, Karen Costello, Bridget Dalton, Belinha De Abreu, Donna Fochi, Laurie Henry, Lori Holcomb, Paula Johnson, Chuck Kinzer, Michele Knobel, Colin Lankshear, and Diana McMasters

We especially wish to thank our good friends at Christopher-Gordon Publishers, Inc. without whom this 4th edition could not have been completed: Hiram Howard and Susanne Canavan. Hiram and Susanne shared our enthusiasm for this project at the beginning and have given us the freedom to complete this 4th edition in the way we envisioned it. They also picked up our spirits at several important points with their kind deeds and words. Behind the scenes, others at Christopher-Gordon have also contributed to this project in important ways. In addition, we owe a huge thank you to Lori Cavanaugh and Carol Treska for their hard work. Authors could not ask for a more considerate and helpful publishing team.

A very special thank you is due to Julie's two young daughters, Meghan and Sarah and to her husband, Charlie. Writing a book with young children around can be especially challenging, yet Meghan and Sarah eagerly joined in our exploration of the Internet, offering their own insights into effective search strategies and worthwhile resources for young children. Both girls patiently endured many days after school when writing took up so much of Julie's time. More importantly, Charlie's patience, support, and understanding through several months of writing enabled this project to become a reality.

To everyone, our deepest thanks!

Don Leu, Debbie Leu, and Julie Coiro
Ashford and Waterford, CT

1 New Literacies for New Times

Welcome to the 4th edition of *Teaching with the Internet!* So much has happened on the Internet since we wrote the 3rd edition. In this edition, we keep you on top of all of these changes while still maintaining our focus on good teaching and our commitment to saving you time.

With this chapter we begin to think in new ways about the Internet by exploring a New Literacies Perspective (Coiro, 2003; Lankshear & Knobel, 2003; Leu, Kinzer, Coiro, & Cammack, 2004). The Internet is a powerful technology for information and communication but we should remember that the same is also true for books, pencils, and paper. And yet, we seldom think of these particular tools as technologies. Moreover, we never teach the skills required by books, pencils, and paper in a technology class or include them in technology standards. Instead, we teach their use during literacy lessons and within content areas.

A New Literacies Perspective considers the Internet as another important technology for literacy, just like a book, a pencil, or paper. As a result, learning how to effectively use the Internet becomes a literacy issue, not a technology issue.

A New Literacies Perspective considers the Internet as another important technology for literacy, just like a book, a pencil, or paper. Just as literacy skills are required to use book, paper, and pencil technologies effectively, we assume that new literacies are required to effectively use the Internet. In addition, a New Literacies Perspective assumes that we need to integrate these new literacies of the Internet into every content area, just as we do with other information and communication tools. You can see that we believe that learning how to effectively use the Internet is a literacy issue, not a technology issue.

New literacies are especially important to the effective use of content area information on the Internet. They allow us to *identify* important questions, *navigate* complex information networks to locate appropriate information, *critically evaluate* that information, *synthesize* it to address those questions, and then *communicate* the answers to others. These five functions help define the new literacies that your students need to be successful with the Internet and other information and communication technologies (ICT).

New literacies are central to your students' success, but they change so rapidly, as the Internet and other ICT change, that state standards and assessments have a hard time keeping up with them. *You* can keep up, however, since you see these changes every day; important new technologies, requiring new literacies, regularly appear on the Internet. Your insights into these new literacies of the Internet are especially important to your students because it is *you* that your students count on to prepare them for their future. This book will help you with this important responsibility.

After reading this chapter, you should be able to:

1. Identify at least three reasons why the effective use of the Internet is central to your students' success.
2. Explain the advantages of viewing instruction from a New Literacies Perspective.
3. Identify three strategies or skills that you consider most important to the new literacies of the Internet and explain why you chose these.
4. Identify several Internet resources that you explored while reading this chapter and explain how you might use each in your classroom for teaching and learning.

Teaching with the Internet: Venita Rodriguez's Eighth Grade Team

Time! There is never enough time! With new state standards and even more testing this year, Venita Rodriguez and the other members of her eighth grade team wondered how they could accomplish everything in only 180 days of school. They had heard that their representatives were trying to modify the more frustrating aspects of The No Child Left Behind Act. Still, current regulations required state testing in both reading and math for grades 3-8, and in science at least once in the elementary grades and also in the middle school. At the same time, the state had updated standards in history, technology, and other areas. While expectations were increasing each year, time in the classroom certainly wasn't. Sometimes it seemed overwhelming.

During the summer, Venita attended a district academy on teaching with the Internet. She went with her colleague, Yolanda Mathews. Venita taught English for their team and Yolanda taught math. The academy sessions demonstrated impressive instructional resources on the Internet and described effective teaching strategies such as Internet Workshop, Internet Project, Internet Inquiry, and WebQuest.

The academy also framed Internet use around the new literacies that the Internet requires, helping everyone to see the connection with reading and writing and other foundational literacies. Both Venita and Yolanda came back excited about integrating the Internet into their curriculum and the potential it contained for preparing students to excel on the state proficiency exams in English, math, and science.

"Not another thing on top of everything else we have to do!"

Clearly, not everyone on the team agreed. Times were difficult. With no salary increase last year and their contract still being negotiated, it was hard to take on new responsibilities.

"Will this make a difference in students' test scores?"

Venita and Yolanda shared what they had learned when this question came up at the academy. They explained how none of the current state assessments in reading, writing, math, or science included the use of the Internet or other ICT, such as word processors. The state reading test, for example, contained no reading of online material; the state writing assessment did not allow students to use a word processor unless this was formally specified as a modification for students receiving special education services. Moreover, effective email composition was not measured on the state writing assessment. Each test would include these skills eventually, but not until the next revision, at least.

The Internet, however, contained important content resources that would assist students on state assessments. In fact, they pointed out that the Internet contained more content related to the skills and strategies of state assessments than appeared in their textbooks at school. As a result, the Internet was simply too important a resource to ignore.

The Internet contained more content related to the skills and strategies of state assessments than appeared in their textbooks at school. As a result, the Internet was simply too important a resource to ignore.

To illustrate this point, Venita and Yolanda gave everyone a quick tour of several sites. These were ones they had used in the academy. These and many other sites on the Internet directly supported instruction in the skills measured on their state assessments:

- **American Memory**—http://memory.loc.gov/
  This is the U.S. Library of Congress's website that contains a priceless collection of historical artifacts and documents online, making them available to anyone with an Internet connection. More than 7,000,000 items are already online, providing teachers with important primary source documents for reading, writing, and critical thinking in social studies.
- **ENC Online**—http://www.enc.org/
  If you are looking for immediate resources to use in your K-12 math or science classroom, this is the website for you. The Eisenhower National Clearinghouse for Mathematics and Science Education contains a vast array of content for every K-12 topic in math and science. It is a must visit for every math and science educator. Be certain to visit the **Web Links** section of this site (http://www.enc.org/weblinks/) for links to exceptional teaching resources and ideas.
- **The Math Forum**—http://www.mathforum.org/
  An exhaustive collection of hands-on resources for immediate use in K-12 math classrooms. Be certain to visit **Math Resources by Subject** (http://www.mathforum.org/math.topics.html) to immediately find useful resources for your class.
- **Web English Teacher**—http://www.webenglishteacher.com/
  Carla Beard, an English teacher in Connersville, Indiana has created this wonderful resource for English educators. It contains an exceptional collection of online resources to assist you in the classroom.

- **Starfall**—http://www.starfall.com
  Do you have students who need to acquire early reading skills? This exceptional resource contains a series of multimedia, interactive talking story books that teach early decoding skills. You can also request free printed materials to accompany these online resources.
- **The Literacy Web**—http://www.literacy.uconn.edu
  This website offers a great collection of links to literacy education resources, including children's literature, adolescent literature, and writing, that are organized by grade level, K-12.

Every member of their team could immediately see how these Internet resources provided easy-to-use teaching tools to meet state curriculum standards. They could also see how using these resources would better prepare students for the new literacies the Internet required.

The next point that Venita and Yolanda shared was easy to understand: Research showed a consistent increase in motivation by students when Internet and other technologies were used in classrooms (Leu, 2000a; Leu, 2002). And, increases in motivation were almost always associated with increases in learning. They reminded all of the team members that everyone had been noticing a lack of engaged learning and enthusiasm among their students during the past several years as test scores remained stagnant. Both of them were convinced the Internet would bring new enthusiasm to schoolwork that would lead to increases in learning.

Every member of their team could immediately see how these Internet resources provided easy-to-use teaching tools to meet state curriculum standards.

Venita and Yolanda concluded with a final observation they had heard in the academy: "If we know that using the Internet will be essential to our students' future, we cannot afford to wait several years until state assessments catch up with this technology; to do so denies our students the literacies that will be important to their future." There were nods around the table.

What Venita and Yolanda had convinced everyone of the potential of the Internet to increase literacy and learning. Having the school wired two years ago and finding new computers in all the labs and classrooms after summer vacation also helped. So, too, did the technology coordinator's offer to assist them. She wanted this team to succeed and become a model for all of the other teams in the school. She met with them and shared the standards developed by the International Society for Technology in Education (ISTE) at **Standards Project** (http://www.iste.org/standards/). She pointed out that at least 48 states, including theirs, had already adopted these standards. They reviewed ISTE's downloadable brochure (http://cnets.iste.org/pdf/nets_brochure.pdf), especially the classroom scenarios illustrating how teachers were implementing these standards in their classrooms.

With the support of the technology coordinator and with initial direction provided by Venita and Yolanda, the team decided to begin their journey, integrating the Internet and the new literacies of the Internet into all of their classrooms. They planned to carefully evaluate the results at the end of the year. They started the year a bit nervous about the new territory they were entering, but also a bit excited about the possibilities that lay ahead.

Figure 1-1. ENC Online (http://www.enc.org/). This rich site contains links to an extensive set of resources for math and science educators in grades K-12.

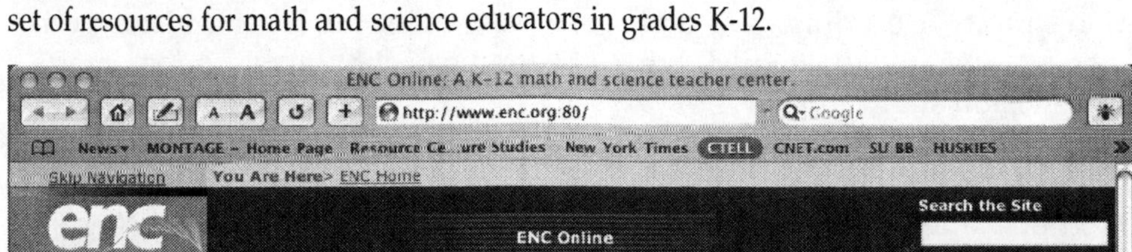

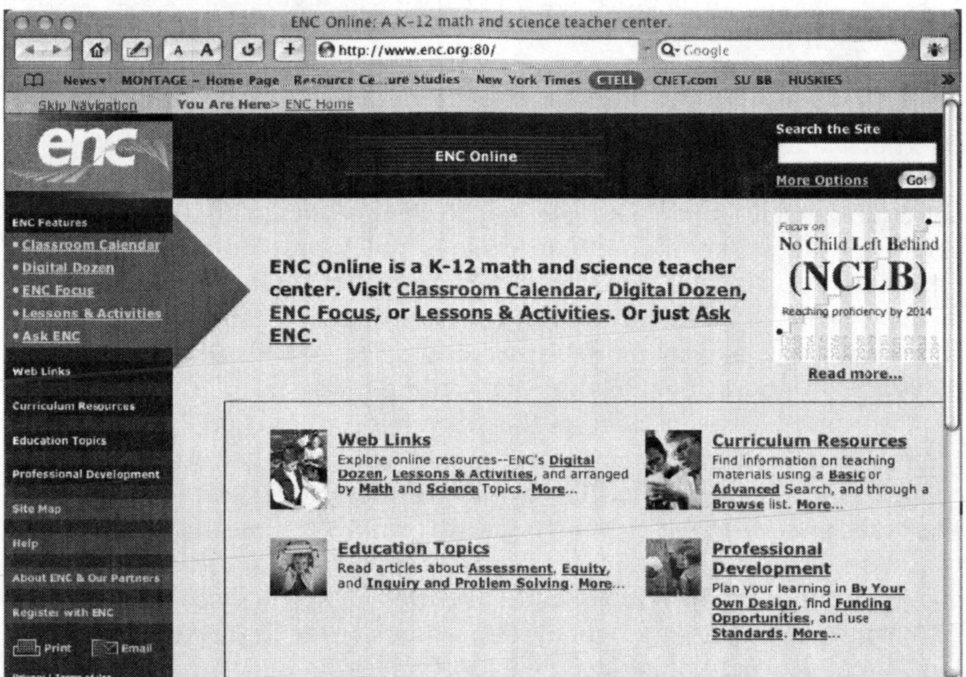

New Literacies in Venita Rodriguez's English Classroom

Tanika and Guy, students in Venita's English class, were typing their critique of a fictional narrative, "Australia 3000," written by Rob Johnson, a student in Melbourne, Australia:

> *Dear Rob,*
>
> *We read the draft of your story about Australia, 3000. It is good, but here is our idea for you. It needs better descriptions. We just don't see it happening in this story. We think you need to help the reader see the city, the people, and the beach better. Use more descriptive adjectives. We have been studying about descriptive adjectives. We used the Descriptive Writing Workshop with Virginia Hamilton and some of us even got our work published. It's at* http://teacher.scholastic.com/writewit/diary/index.htm. *Do you read her books in Australia? We hope you like our suggestion!*
>
> *Tanika and Guy*

Rob was a student in Alan Robeson's English class in Australia. Earlier, Alan had been looking for a class in another country to have revision conferences with via email. He wanted to improve the writing skills in both classes while each class worked collaboratively with students from a different part of the world and learned about using the Internet. Alan had placed a description of his project at the Projects Registry located at **Oz**

Projects (http://ozprojects.edna.edu.au/). Venita Rodriguez had read Alan's project description, asking for a partner classroom for revision conferences. She quickly emailed him to begin the exchange of student drafts and revision suggestions.

Venita knew the attraction of these new technologies to adolescents. She had also learned about an excellent technique during the summer Internet academy: When you introduce a new literacy from the Internet into the classroom, teach it first to a student who is less proficient in foundational literacies and then have that student teach other students. This privileges the weaker student, since she is now literate in something that others are not. This strategy places previously marginalized students into an important classroom position and allows them to regain the excitement about learning that sometimes begins slipping away because of challenges they face with traditional reading and writing tasks.

When you introduce a new literacy from the Internet into the classroom, teach it first to a student who is less proficient in foundational literacies, and then have that student teach other students.

They had viewed a video of this happening in a second grade classroom, where the weakest reader in a class showed the best reader how to complete a center activity with the drawing and writing software, KidPix. The video was at located at **New Literacies** (http://ctell.uconn.edu/cases/newliteracies.htm). This teacher had prepared the weakest reader, a young boy, in the new literacies that KidPix required. You could see the new enthusiasm in his face as he taught the best reader in the class the new literacies of KidPix. The video illustrated an important lesson that could also be applied at every grade level. Venita put it right to work with Tanika and Guy, two of the weaker readers and writers in her class.

When Rob's draft arrived from Australia, Venita worked with Tanika and Guy to read and make revision suggestions. Then she showed them how to use Venita's classroom email account and the spell checker before emailing revision comments to Rob.

The next day, several more drafts had arrived from Alan Robeson's class in Australia via email. Venita's first-period English class divided into small groups to begin reading and critiquing the drafts. Each group read one of the drafts and wrote a short revision message. As these were completed, Venita sent each group to Tanika and Guy who showed them how to use her account's email and spell checker to send their response to Alan's class. She knew this activity would put both of these students at the center of classroom literacy life and would serve as powerful motivation, not just with the new literacies that would be an important part of her class, but also with the foundational literacies they needed for reading and writing with traditional tools. Next week, Venita's class would send their own drafts to Australia and receive revision suggestions from students in Alan Robeson's class.

This collaborative project was an excellent use of the Internet, creating even more powerful and authentic writing experiences than Venita could create solely within her own classroom. She knew that looking critically at someone else's writing would improve her students' writing. She also knew that connecting with a classroom from Australia would be highly motivating. It was a great way to use the Internet to help her students improve their writing. Venita was also confident that revision experiences like this would improve their performance on the state writing assessment that would take place later in the year. Finally, Venita was able to leverage the entry of a new literacy in her classroom to motivate two students whom she was concerned about, helping both of them develop greater enthusiasm for reading and writing.

*Venita's class was also involved in a literature discussion group with classes from New Zealand, Arizona, and Florida using **Book Raps.***

At the same time as this revision project was taking place, Venita's class was also involved in a literature discussion group with classes from New Zealand, Arizona, and Florida. They all used **Book Raps** (http://rite.ed.qut.edu.au/oz-teachernet/) while they read the powerful work of literature, *The Giver*. Students exchanged responses to this book via email each day in a lively series of conversations. These daily messages engaged her students in thinking more deeply about this important work and expanded their literary responses. It also helped her students discover new cultural perspectives and meet students from other parts of the world.

Figure 1-2. Problems of the Week (http://mathforum.org/pow/) at the **Math Forum** (http://mathforum.org/) is a set of challenging math problems for students at all levels. New problems appear each week. Answers are provided and mentoring classrooms are available for assistance with problem-solving strategies.

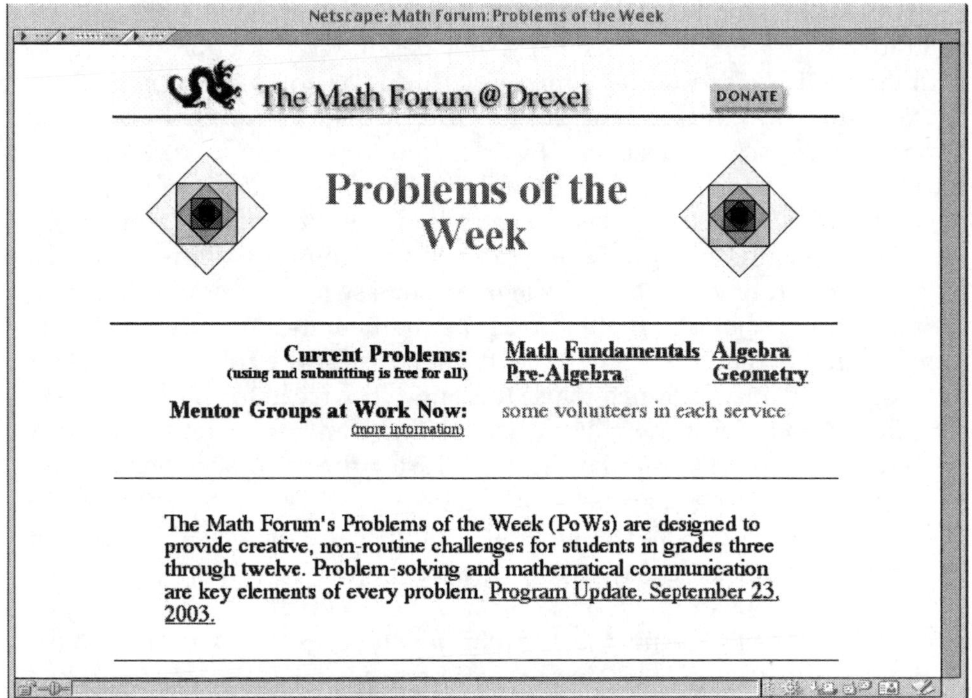

The amount of email traffic was rapidly increasing. In order to save time, Venita appointed Tanika and Guy to print out all of her incoming email messages each morning. That way, Venita could quickly read them during her second-period planning time and prepare them for distribution the next day.

"Ms. Rodriguez, Ms. Rodriguez!" Tanika said from the computer. "Rob liked the ideas we gave him about his story. His teacher wants us to send his class some of our stories so they can give us revision ideas. When can I send my story?"

Guy added, "I want to send my story, too. Ms. Rodriguez, they live in Melbourne. Where's that?"

Venita smiled, knowing her students, including Tanika and Guy, were really on their way this year.

New Literacies in Jackie Thomason's Science Classroom and Yolanda Mathews' Math Classroom

"I know they're gonna be the same. They gotta be. The cylinders use the same size paper so they gotta be the same volume."

Tiffany was explaining her thinking to her group in science class. The problem they were discussing came from a wonderful site, **The Math Forum Problem of the Week** (http://mathforum.org/pow/). Each week, challenging problems were posted for students at every grade level to solve.

This particular problem had students use two pieces of paper that were the same size to make cylinders by rolling one paper lengthwise and the other widthwise. They had to predict if the volume inside these two cylinders was greater in one cylinder compared with the other. They also had to explain the thinking behind their hypotheses and then conduct an experiment to test their predictions. Finally, they had to write a report of their experiment with their results and present it during a short workshop session.

Yolanda, saw this activity on the Internet and showed it to Jackie Thomason, the science teacher. They decided to use it as a team-teaching activity for students in their math and science classes. Jackie was starting the activity in her science class to introduce the method of scientific inquiry at the beginning of the year. Yolanda was going to follow up with a unit on measuring volume. It was a great exercise to get students thinking about both the scientific method and the mathematics of volume. At the same time, it helped integrate the new literacies of the Internet into their classrooms. Yolanda planned to use this site every week for Internet Workshop in her math class, giving her students important opportunities to think systematically about a complex problem during the week and then discuss their thinking during a Friday workshop session. This Internet resource really got her students to think deeply about mathematics and use what they were learning in highly engaging ways.

"Write up your predictions along with your explanation for why you think this will be the result," Jackie told her students. "Make sure you explain your hypothesis clearly because afterwards you are going to conduct an experiment to see if your hypothesis is correct."

"Ms. Thomason? We gonna do science and math like this all year?" Jason asked.

New Literacies in Bob Richter's Social Studies Classroom

As he thought back about the year just winding up, Bob Richter, the team's social studies teacher, recalled that he had been a bit skeptical about the Internet. At least he was skeptical until he saw the resources at **American Memory** (http://memory.loc.gov/ammem/ammemhome.html), an extensive collection of historical documents placed on the Internet by the Library of Congress. Here, he discovered Civil War photos by Mathew Brady, the papers of George Washington, an Abraham Lincoln Virtual Library, as well as extensive collections of online videos, recordings, and documents from all periods of American history. It is an amazing resource for social studies educators, especially with the recent emphasis placed on the use of primary source documents to develop critical thinking and analysis skills. American Memory is a gold mine for the primary source documents of American history. Even more importantly, there are complete instructional units designed by teachers, just waiting to be used in a classroom. Bob had used all of these resources throughout the year, since they provided him with the primary historical documents he needed for his class.

Armand interrupted Bob's memories for the year.

"Mr. Richter, look at this. Remember when we did the unit on the Civil War and all of the pictures by Mathew Brady? Here's my newspaper article. Remember? We shared our work with that class in California. That was cool!"

Armand was cleaning out his locker at the end of the year. His newspaper article made him recall the many exciting experiences in Bob's class with primary source documents.

***American Memory** is a gold mine for the primary source documents of American history. Even more importantly, there are complete instructional units, designed by teachers, and just waiting to be used in a classroom.*

Armand's comment prompted Bob to remember the wonderful lessons and instructional ideas he had discovered that year at a great location within the American Memory site: **Lesson Plans, the Learning Page of the Library of Congress** (http://memory.loc.gov/learn/lessons/index. html).This location got him started with the Internet since it provided everything he needed, from units and lessons developed by teachers, to links to historical documents located at American Memory. During the year, Bob had completed many units:

- **Historian's Sources**—
  http://memory.loc.gov/learn/lessons/psources/pshome.html
  This exceptional resource provides an introduction to the use of primary source documents.
- **Turn of the Century Child**—
  http://www.noodletools.com/debbie/projects/20c/turn.html
  This project, developed by a teacher in California, uses the American Memory resource to study what it was like to be a child in 1900 through the analysis of historical artifacts and diaries.
- **Learning About Immigration Through Oral History**—
  http://memory.loc.gov/learn/lessons/97/oh1/ammem.html
  Here is a project about the immigrant experience through archived oral histories that Bob's class completed.
- **After Reconstruction: Problems of African Americans in the South**—
  http://memory.loc.gov/learn/lessons/rec/rhome.html
  This is an exciting project designed for high school that Bob liked so much he adapted the lessons for his eighth graders. Each site fit in perfectly with his curriculum and provided wonderful opportunities for cross-curricular collaboration with his team members in English, math, and science.

Many of these resources provided opportunities for Bob's class to exchange work and share projects with other classrooms around the world. Throughout all of these experiences, his students acquired many new literacies required by the Internet. They also developed new literacies required to communicate clearly in writing with both word processors and email. And, they had done far more reading and writing than in any previous classes. Yes, it had been a great year with everyone, including himself, learning many new things.

Figure 1-3. Turn of the Century Child
(http://www.noodletools.com/debbie/projects/20c/turn.html) is a lesson developed by Debbie Abilock during a summer workshop with the American Memory group at the Library of Congress. This unit uses primary source documents from American Memory to help students study and understand what life was like in the United States in 1900.

There was so much more enthusiasm for learning this year and everyone had noticed it, especially parents. They were confident the greater engagement in learning had resulted in increased learning.

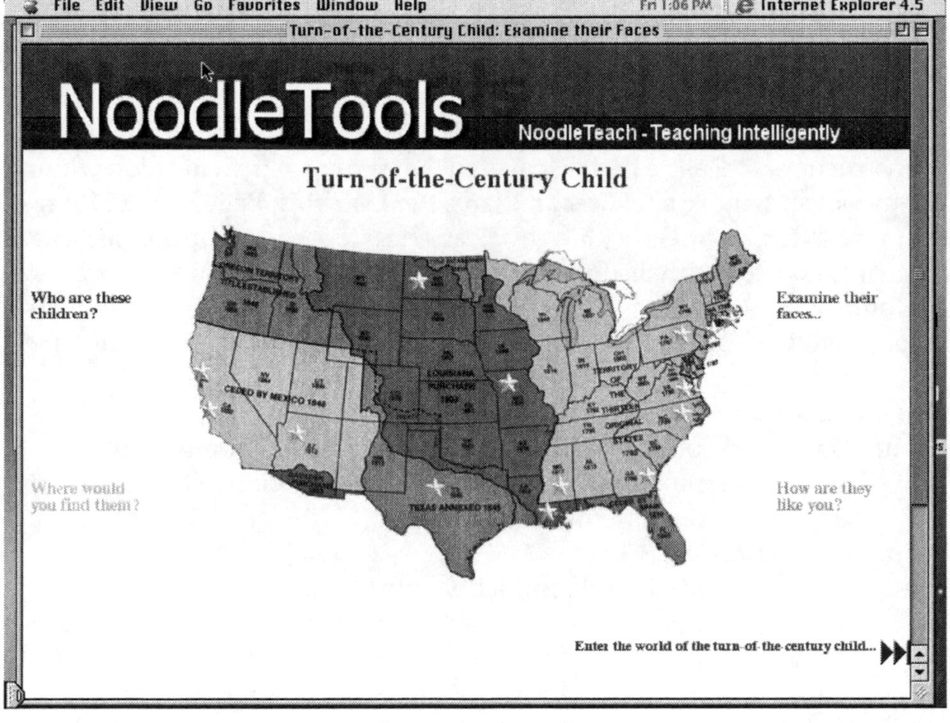

The End of an Exciting Year

The results of the new state testing in reading, math, science, and writing had not yet arrived when Venita, Yolanda, Jackie, and Bob had their final team meeting. Nevertheless, everyone was confident that students in their classes would show important gains. It had been an exciting year with many new lessons for everyone. There was so much more enthusiasm for learning this year and everyone had noticed it, especially parents. The entire team was confident the greater engagement had resulted in increased learning.

They realized, of course, that none of the state assessments measured the skills and strategies their students had acquired with the new literacies of the Internet and other ICT. Their state writing assessment, for example, continued to require students to use paper and pencils, not word processors. This, despite the fact that all of their students were now using word processors for nearly every writing assignment in class and had acquired the important new literacies this technology required. In addition, the state writing assessment did not include the new email skills students had acquired throughout the year from their many collaborative projects. Moreover, state assessments in reading did not measure any of the new literacies their students had acquired, which had improved their reading comprehension on the Internet. The state reading assessment still used short, traditional passages on paper to measure comprehension with multiple choice answers.

Nevertheless, their entire team felt new power and energy throughout all of their classes as they saw students more actively engaged in learning. Most importantly, students were reading far more than ever before. In addition, because everyone was now using a word processor, which made revisions much easier, students were also writing far more than ever before. The team was convinced that state test scores would show an important increase in achievement across the board. Just as importantly, they were proud of the many new literacies students had acquired throughout the year. They knew these new literacies would be essential to their students' future even if they were not yet included on assessments.

It was a year of discovery and renewal for this talented team of teachers, who brought a wonderful spirit of excitement about learning and new literacies into their classrooms each day; everyone discovered new skills and strategies for reading, writing, and communicating with Internet technologies.

The year had been one of learning important new lessons about the Internet and about teaching. It was also a year of discovery and renewal for this talented team of teachers, who brought a wonderful spirit of excitement about learning new literacies into their classrooms each day. Students and teachers both had discovered new skills and strategies for reading, writing, and communicating with Internet technologies. Finally, it was a year in which teachers were able to help several struggling students get back into the center of classroom life by first showing these students several important new literacies. The change was obvious with these students in their new enthusiasm for classroom learning.

As they concluded their final team meeting, there was talk about the summer that lay ahead. Venita and Yolanda were taking a summer course on the use of iChat AV for video conferencing between classrooms around the world. Jackie was taking a workshop on designing classroom webpages and using weblogs or blogs. Bob, the person most cautious about the Internet when they started, had been accepted into the summer fellows program at the Library of Congress. He would be working with another social studies educator from Colorado to develop a unit on the westward migration. Their classes had worked together on this unit during the year after they discovered one another on the Internet. Now they would have a chance to refine their work and post it at the American Memory site for others to use.

Everyone was going to stay in touch over the summer by email so they could exchange the new ideas and the new literacies they were discovering. It really had been an amazing year for them all.

Figure 1-4. After Reconstruction: Problems of African Americans in the South (http://memory.loc.gov/learn/lessons/rec/rhome.html) is a teaching unit available at American Memory, the collection of historical documents being developed for teachers and students by the Library of Congress.

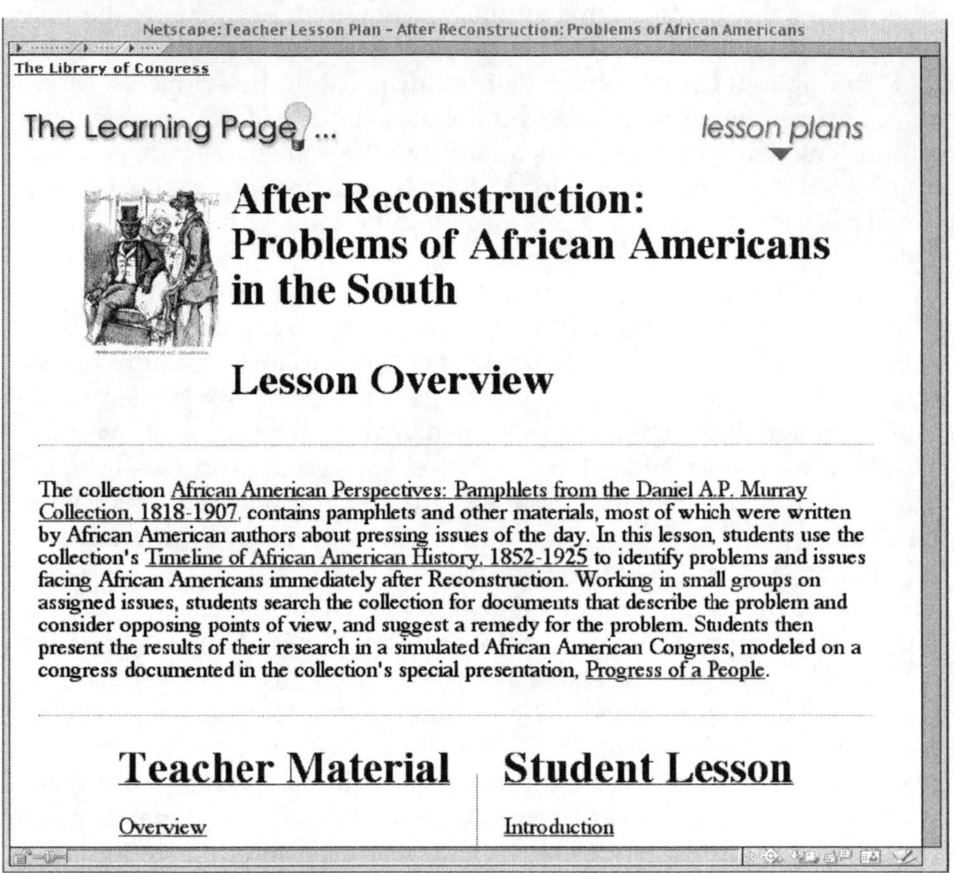

Lessons From the Classroom

Teachers around the world report that the biggest change they see with the Internet is a new enthusiasm and excitement for learning among their students and among themselves.

These episodes illustrate a number of important lessons that will guide us throughout our journey together. First, they illustrate how the many exceptional resources available on the Internet may be used in your classroom to get students excited about learning while they learn essential skills. Teachers around the world report that the biggest change they see with the Internet is a new enthusiasm and excitement for learning challenging content. This is what happened in these classrooms every day. Tanika's excitement about sharing responses to drafts with students in Australia, Jason's new-found enthusiasm for math and science, and Armand's fond memories for the unit on the Civil War are examples of what nearly every student felt that year. Each day, students came early and left late because they wanted to continue their work on the Internet. This same enthusiasm swept across the entire team of teachers. Even Bob Richter, the team member who was least excited about having to use the Internet in his class, ended up being its most ardent advocate. The Internet brings new enthusiasm for both teaching and learning, and this new enthusiasm almost always leads to increases in learning.

The episodes also illustrate a second lesson, one that we hear from nearly every teacher we meet: The Internet opens wonderful new windows to the world for your students. The Internet allows students and teachers to explore new models of collaborative learning that transcend national and cultural borders. Being able to exchange drafts of writing with students in England, Australia, New Zealand, Japan, Canada, and other countries helps students to see the world in new ways. Exchanging responses to *The Giver* and other literary works prompted a deeper understanding of how people in other parts of the world see things from their own cultural perspective. Exchanging solutions to math problems with a mentoring class helped students discover new ways of thinking. And, reading the diaries of children from the early 1900s at **American Memory** enabled students to go back to another period in time and listen to the voices of children their own age.

Looking through the new windows of the Internet develops greater appreciation for the benefits that diversity bestows as others outside our classrooms contribute to the learning taking place within.

Looking through these new windows of the Internet also develops greater appreciation for the benefits that diversity bestows. We develop a new recognition for this important principle as others outside our classrooms contribute to the learning that takes place within. The Internet provides a powerful new tool to access information and then communicate with others about what we have learned. Throughout this book you will find many other sites on the Internet for supporting your students' learning in this fashion. The Internet opens many new vistas for all of us.

These episodes also demonstrate another important lesson, one that will be central to your integration of these new information tools: New literacies are required to effectively read, write, and communicate with the Internet, and it is essential to begin to build these new literacies into your classroom curriculum. This is true for teachers in every subject area, since each content area often uses new literacies that are best acquired within it.

New skills and strategies are required to effectively read, write, and communicate with the Internet and it is essential to begin to build these new literacies into your classroom curriculum.

By viewing these skills as new literacies, we are able to avoid the teaching of the Internet and other ICT as an "add on" to a curriculum that is already far too full. We simply do not have time each day to add a separate class on technology; it is much more efficient to simply integrate these new literacies into our content area classes. This also leads to far more effective learning. Each new literacy is best taught as it is required to facilitate content area learning, not independent of the content that requires it. In addition, we see many more connections to our current literacy programs, connections that help us to better understand how to teach these new literacies and how to integrate them into our classes. If you are a literacy educator, you will see that many instructional models from your current program work nicely with the Internet: activity centers, writing process activities, author chair experiences, thematic units, cooperative learning groups, response journals, jigsaw grouping, and K-W-L, among others. If you teach another content area, we will show you how to use instructional models designed specifically for your class: Internet Workshop, Internet Project, Internet Inquiry, and WebQuest.

The episodes with this team of eighth grade teachers also illustrate another important lesson: Teachers make a profound difference when the Internet enters the classroom; greater even than when the Internet is not in the classroom. Using the Internet effectively creates extraordinarily powerful opportunities for teaching and learning, as we have just seen. This potential is realized with teachers who recognize the new literacies that the Internet requires and who are also familiar with effective instructional strategies to support their development. On the other hand, a teacher who neither recognizes the new literacies nor understands how to integrate them into the classroom can probably do more harm than good. Simply assigning free time at the Internet to students who complete their work early (a far-too-common practice) is likely to create more problems than it solves; advantaged students become more advantaged and struggling learners fall further behind. Teachers really do make a difference when it comes to the new literacies of the Internet.

It is unfair to deny our students the opportunity to learn the new skills and strategies required to use the Internet effectively until we see these skills being included in state assessments.

There is also a fifth lesson in these episodes: We see how the new literacies of the Internet are not yet included in the many new state assessments that are required by No Child Left Behind legislation. As a result, there will be some questions raised as to why we should integrate these new literacies within our classroom programs.

The answer, as these teachers concluded, is that we simply cannot wait. It is unfair to deny our students the opportunity to learn the new skills and strategies required to use the Internet effectively until we finally see these skills being included in state assessments. The new literacies are simply too critical to our students' future to ignore. We must begin to recognize that classroom instruction will always be ahead of assessment in this area (Leu, 2002; Leu, Kinzer, Coiro, and Cammack, 2004). The Internet and other ICTs change at a rapid rate, thus continually generating new literacies required to take full advantage of their potential. The rate at which new technologies and new literacies appear is also far faster than the rate at which we currently revise assessment instruments. As a result, state and other assessments will regularly lag behind the new literacies that we use in our classroom.

Finally, these episodes show how the Internet brings together new communities of learners who engage in socially constructed learning experiences. This lesson is an important one. Many teachers in this team developed collaborative units across curriculum areas during the year, increasing learning opportunities for their students. Equally important, however, is that each teacher discovered the powerful potential of collaborative relationships with other teachers and classrooms beyond the walls of their school. Bob's class became experts in U.S. history when they received inquiries about their work from classes in England and Finland. Yolanda's class was mentored by another class in Wisconsin as they sought solutions to the math **Problem of the Week** (http://mathforum.org/pow/). The next semester, Yolanda's math students volunteered to mentor classes in Hawaii and Oregon. Venita's class joined with several classes during the year to exchange drafts of writing and to share responses to works of literature at **Book Raps** (http://rite.ed.qut.edu.au/oz-teachernet/).

The Internet provides very special opportunities to learn from one another about the world around us.

The Internet provides very special opportunities to learn from one another about the world around us through new models of collaborative learning. We will show you other collaborative models that you may use to assist your students in safely developing new learning communities with Internet resources—an excellent lesson for life.

E-MAIL FOR YOU

From: Lisa Brayton <Lisa.Brayton@MSB.Mat-Su.k12.ak.us>
Subject: Using the Internet at our school

Greetings!

My name is Lisa Brayton. I am a fifth grade teacher at Cottonwood Creek Elementary School in Wasilla, Alaska. Our school has been using technology for a long time. We are making a natural progression to using the Internet in our classrooms. Our principal, Marie Burton, is the visionary!

In just a few years, Cottonwood has gone from having one terminal with Internet access (in our lab) to having a shared line for 4th and 5th grade classrooms, to now having our own free line in each classroom! We also have four lines in the computer lab and one in the library. At this point, our Internet access is unlimited! This has made a positive impact in many ways.

I started this year by entering my class in an Internet contest called **Cybersurfari** (http://school.discovery.com/cybersurfari/) This was an excellent way to teach students how to surf for information. It was, in a sense, a scavenger hunt. Students went from site to site through links, looking for clues. This contest is held annually in October, although you can practice at other times. My students learned navigational skills, neat facts, and felt excited and successful. We also participated in several other great projects at the **Global Schoolhouse** (http://www.gsn.org).

My students also use the Internet as an information tool. During our Colonial study we've gathered historical information about Jamestown, Plymouth, John Smith, Ben Franklin....the list is exhaustive! This is exciting for the students because the information is there to find, and they're very skilled at locating it!

Finally, my students use the Internet as a communication tool. We have key-pals from all over the world. We write to friends and relatives. Our current project is our webpage. Students are now creating their own webpages. We are putting together a Fifth Grade Newspaper, which will be published on our webpage. We hope to inform, entertain, and include links to other sites. Please visit our school's new website (http://www.CWE.Mat-su.k12.ak.us) and send your ideas or comments to us. Talk to you soon!

Lisa Brayton
5th grade teacher
Cottonwood Creek Elementary School
Wasilla, Alaska

Integrating Multiple Theoretical Frameworks Within the Context of the Internet: A New Literacies Perspective

We are still evolving adequate theoretical models to help us understand such a new and transformative tool for teaching and learning as the Internet. Few theories have yet to focus on the Internet itself; instead, most draw upon the Internet as a new context in which to apply theories that were initially developed outside of the Internet. These include theoretical perspectives such as: social constructivism (Snyder, 2001; Vygotsky, 1978),;

distributed cognition (Hollan, Hutchins, & Kirsch, 2001); media literacy (Thoman, 1999); critical literacy (Muspratt, Luke, & Freebody, 1998); and multiliteracies (The New London Group, 2000). We believe that the Internet and other ICT, such as word processors, instant messaging, web editors, video editors, and others are such a powerful, pervasive, and unique set of technologies that they require theoretical perspectives to emerge from the essential nature of their own reality. There are many new realities that define this new technology. Several of the more important realities include:

1. the pervasive and rapid appearance of the Internet;
2. the importance of the Internet; and
3. the new literacies that the Internet and other ICT require.

The Pervasive and Rapid Appearance of the Internet

Developing a theoretical framework emerging from the Internet itself is only necessary if the Internet, a new context for literacy and learning, has become an important fixture of our lives. All of the statistical evidence indicates that this is rapidly becoming a reality at home, work, and school. The Internet is being adopted in all of these contexts faster than any other previous technology, including telephones, televisions, typewriters, and even books (Leu, et al., 2004; U.S. Department of Commerce, 2002).

Consider, for example, the home. The rate of Internet penetration in households is rapidly increasing. Nearly 60% of all households in the U.S. reported that they had Internet access in 2002. Among those who had not previously used the Internet, 47% report that they were somewhat likely or very likely to go online during 2003 (Lebo, 2003). Moreover, the percentage of U.S. households with broadband Internet access has been doubling each year. Most interesting, perhaps, is that Internet users report an increase in time that they spend on the Internet and a decrease in the time that they spend viewing television (Lebo, 2003). Internet users report watching about 10% fewer hours of television per week in 2002 (11.2 hours per week) compared to 2001 (12.3 hours per week). This pattern also holds true for children, where nearly 33% of children reported in 2002 that they are viewing less television than before they started using the Internet; this frequency is up nearly 50% from just one year earlier (Lebo, 2003).

The story is the same for the workplace. In just one year (August, 2000–September, 2001), the use of the Internet at work among all employed adults 25 years of age and older increased by nearly 60%, from 26.1% of the workforce to 41.7% (U. S. Department of Commerce, 2002). If this rate of increase continues in the workplace, nearly everyone in the U.S. workforce will be using the Internet in a few short years. Currently, workers in positions with the highest levels of education report the highest levels of Internet use in the United States. In managerial positions with some professional specialty, 80.5% of workers report using the Internet. But even in technical, sales, and administrative support positions, 70.5 % of workers report using the Internet (U.S. Department of Commerce, 2002).

The rapid diffusion of Internet technologies is also taking place in school classrooms. In only eight years (1994–2002), the percentage of classrooms in the United States having at least one Internet computer went from 3% to 87% (National Center for Education Statistics, 2002). The infusion of these technologies into school parallels what we see in households and in the workplace. Clearly the Internet has quickly become a staple of life in school settings as we prepare students for an information age.

Undoubtedly, you have many feelings about these rapid and pervasive changes. You may be excited, skeptical, nervous, or, like us, you may experience all of these feelings, often simultaneously. We get excited when we discover a site like **American Memory** (http://memory.loc.gov/) and think about how it can be used in the classroom. We become skeptical when we read about politicians who advocate higher standards for student achievement, but disappear when it is time to fund the important new programs in professional development and hardware that are required. We become nervous when we think about the speed of these changes and whether we can ever keep up with all there is to know about the new literacies necessitated by new information and communication technologies. After all, who had even heard of the Internet just a decade ago? And who can tell what new technologies and new literacies will emerge as soon as we begin to understand this one? Yes, the Internet prompts all of these thoughts. To better understand the consequences of the profound changes that are upon us, it is increasingly clear that we require new theories, capturing the essential elements of this powerful new technology.

Today, the new literacies of the Internet and other ICT are required to ensure a fully realized personal and civic life as well as a successful entry into the world of work (IRA, 2002; Leu, et al., 2004).

The Importance of the Internet

One way in which to begin to frame a theoretical perspective that emerges from the Internet itself is to look at why the Internet has become so important. This provides an important starting point if we hope to ground a theory in the reality of the Internet.

Recent literature demonstrates that the Internet has become important because it provides us with information that improves the quality of our personal, civic, and professional lives. Access to this information, however, requires new reading, writing, and communication skills.

In an age of information and communication, being able to read, think critically, and communicate with the Internet has become just as important as being able to read a book and being able to write a letter during an earlier age. We refer to the skills and strategies necessary to read, think critically, and communicate with the Internet as new literacies. Many new reading and writing skills are required to successfully and efficiently use this powerful tool for information and communication. We see, for example, the use of a search engine as requiring a host of new reading skills. So too, does navigating through different websites to locate the information you require. And, of course, email and Instant Messaging require new writing skills.Today, these new literacies of the Internet and other ICT are required to ensure more fully realized personal, civic, and professional lives (IRA, 2002; Leu, et al., 2004).

Consider first how the Internet enables us to lead more fully realized personal lives. People who can use the Internet to define important individual questions, navigate complex information networks to locate appropriate information, critically evaluate that information, synthesize it to address those questions, and then communicate the solutions to others are advantaged in important ways. This might happen while planning a trip, solving a human services problem, advocating for social justice, making important election choices, purchasing books, refinancing a home mortgage, or any one of the hundreds of other tasks important to daily life. Skillful use of these new contexts for information and communication allows each of us more control over what we can do and who we wish to become. Preparation in the new literacies that are required to use the Internet and other ICT enables individuals to have more productive personal lives.

Becoming literate with the Internet and other ICT is also important to the continuation of a civic culture organized around democratic principles. In the United States, Canada, and other democratic nations, the continuation of a civic democracy is based on informed citizens making reasoned decisions at the ballot box. This has led to a widely distributed definition of literacy since it becomes important for all of us to read, think, and debate before making these decisions. It has also led to the establishment of public schools charged with developing citizens who are literate, and through their literacy, might be thoughtfully informed about important national affairs. Our democratic societies survive only if we have informed citizens who make wise decisions at the ballot box.

Preparation in the new literacies required to use the Internet and other ICT helps individuals have more productive personal and civic as well as professional lives.

Democratic principles, however, developed during a time in which our major media outlets included traditionally printed newspapers, broadsides, and pamphlets, owned by many different individuals with many different points of view. In an era of increasing media conglomeration, the Internet has become an important source of additional, independent information about news, candidates, and issues. The Internet requires, however, new skills and strategies to enable us to critically evaluate the information we encounter about current events and political processes. Thus, the new literacies of the Internet and other ICT become essential to enable citizens access to a wider array of voices and to be able to critically evaluate those voices. The functions in which we engage the Internet to more fully realize our civic responsibilities are very similar to those we use to enrich our personal lives. We define important political questions, navigate complex information networks to locate appropriate information, critically evaluate that information, synthesize it to address those questions, and often communicate our answers to others.

Consider, also, the world of work, which is undergoing fundamental change (Mikulecky & Kirkley, 1998; Reich, 1992) as we move from an industrial to a post-industrial economy. Indeed, it is this transformation that prompts many of the changes to ICT and to literacy that we are experiencing, making instruction in the effective use of the Internet critical to the future of students in your classroom.

Because trade barriers are falling and international trade is expanding, many workplaces are undergoing a radical transformation (Gilster, 1997; Mikulecky & Kirkley, 1998). In a global economy in which competition is more intense because competing organizations are more numerous and markets are more extensive, workplaces must seek more productive ways of performing if they hope to survive. Often, they seek to transform themselves into high-performance workplaces that are more competitive, more productive, and more responsive to the needs of their customers. This change has made both effective information use and the new literacies of the Internet essential components in an increasing number of positions in the workforce.

The change from an industrial to a post-industrial economy has recently ocurred in many nations. Previously, a company competed with only one or two other companies producing the same goods or services within national boundaries protected by trade barriers. These traditional, industrial-age organizations were organized in a vertical, top-down fashion in which most decisions were made at the highest levels and then communicated to lower levels. Individuals did what they were told, no more and no less. This wasted much of the intellectual capital within an organization; however, we seldom noticed this loss of important potential because competition was not especially intense.

In a post-industrial, global economy with lowered trade barriers, companies must now compete in a far larger market with tens or hundreds of other companies around the world. This intense global competition requires organizations to abandon traditional command and control structures in order to operate more productively and become more competitive. As a result, information-age organizations seeking to achieve greater productivity are now organized horizontally, with individual units empowered to make important decisions about how they complete their work.

Knowing how, when, and where to locate useful information on the Internet, or an Intranet, will become an increasingly important component of literacy programs, especially since the availability of information resources and search technologies is expanding rapidly, increasing the importance of effective search strategies.

Instead of decisions emanating only from the top, teams within lower levels of organizations are now increasingly empowered to identify and solve important problems that lead to better ways of producing goods or providing services. This takes far greater advantage of the intellectual capital that exists in any organization and results in far greater productivity. Members of these teams must quickly *identify* important questions, *navigate* information resources to locate useful information related to the problems they identify, *critically evaluate* the information they find, *synthesize* this information to solve the problems, and then quickly *communicate* the solutions to others, so that everyone within an organization is informed.

Let's take a quick look at each of these skill sets. First, the change to a high-performance workplace requires organizations to place a premium on people who possess effective problem-identification skills. As collaborative teams seek more effective ways of working, they are expected to ask questions that are important to their unit and to seek appropriate solutions. This has important implications for literacy education since we will need to prepare students to identify important questions, often in collaborative situations.

Having identified important questions, members of high-performance workplace teams must then locate useful information related to those questions. Knowing how, when, and where to navigate and locate useful information on the Internet, or an Intranet, will become an increasingly important component of literacy programs, especially since the availability of information resources and search technologies is expanding rapidly, increasing the importance of effective search strategies.

Having acquired information resources, members of high-performance workplace teams must then know how to critically evaluate that information, sorting accurate information from inaccurate, essential information from less essential information, and biased information from unbiased.

These critical evaluation skills will also become increasingly important elements in literacy programs, especially when we use an informational space such as the Internet, where anyone may publish anything.

The ability to synthesize information that one has gathered will also become increasingly important since the ability to use information to answer questions is the defining aspect of successful performance in a globally competitive information economy. We will need to pay increasing attention to informational synthesis to support this important skill.

Finally, members of high-performance workplace teams need to rapidly and clearly communicate their solutions to colleagues in other organizational units. A decentralized workplace requires communication skills so that changes in one unit are clearly communicated to all other units. Since each unit is empowered to identify and solve problems, one must keep others informed of changes that are taking place and negotiate these changes with others who might be affected by them. We need to support the development of effective communication skills using new communication technologies, such as email and other means, if we wish to prepare individuals for their futures in a world where these skills are crucial.

If we make the correct choices, these new literacies contain important promise, enabling us to ensure that all members of our global society might fully enjoy the potential that life provides in an information age.

Given this analysis of our personal, civic, and professional lives during an age of information, it is not surprising that the Internet and other ICT have appeared and become so prominent. These new information and communication tools empower individuals to lead more involved personal and civic lives as they permit economic organizations to successfully make the changes required to compete in a global economy. At home, at school, and in the workplace, the Internet allows individuals to make greater use of the intellectual capital they possess to lead richer, more fulfilling lives.

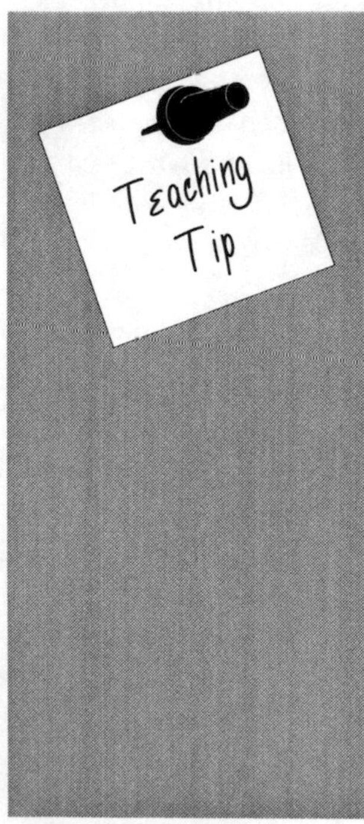

Many teachers find that the most powerful aspect of the Internet is the opportunity it provides them to learn about successful activities and resources from other teachers. Sometimes these are ideas related to Internet use, but more often they are ideas about traditional instructional issues: good works of literature for an upcoming unit, an idea about teaching radicals in mathematics, a great science demonstration on gravitational force, or an upcoming PBS video for social studies. The Internet eliminates traditional barriers that have prevented us from sharing the wonderful things happening in each of our classrooms. In Chapter 4 you will see how to participate in these conversations by using mailing lists, newsgroups, and weblogs. However, to see a preview of the exchanges taking place every day, visit the archives of **RTEACHER** (http://www.reading.org/archives/rteacher.html), a popular mailing list devoted to conversations about literacy instruction. Notice how educators use this resource to ask questions about instructional issues and discover new ideas for their schools and classrooms. The Internet is a very social environment, putting teachers in touch with other teachers so that all students benefit.

This is why the Internet and other ICT are so important to integrate into our classrooms. We need to prepare our students to use these new information and communication technologies because they enable students to fully participate in our society and lead productive personal, civic, and work lives. Nothing is more important for the future of our students. This is the challenge we face as educators in the new world we are all entering.

If we make the correct choices, these new literacies hold important promise, enabling us to ensure that all members of our global society might fully enjoy the potential that life provides in an information age.

INTERNET FAQ

Do other countries have curriculum resources that we can use here in this country?

Yes. In fact, many teachers use the curriculum resources at another nation's directory site for educators. Nations around the world are taking bold policy initiatives to prepare their children for their future with national websites for educators. While each country is responding to the educational challenges of global competition in a distinctive fashion, many nations are developing Internet locations to support the important work teachers do to prepare children for Internet use. Explore some of these locations to find resources to use in your classroom:

- **EdNA** (Australia)—http://www.edna.edu.au/edna/page1.html
- **ScoilNet** (Ireland)—http://www.scoilnet.ie/
- **The National Grid for Learning** (UK)—http://www.ngfl.gov.uk/index.jsp
- **SchoolNet** (Canada)—http://www.schoolnet.ca/home/
- **Te Kete Ipurangi** (New Zealand)—http://www.tki.org.nz

What are the New Literacies that the Internet Requires?

What, exactly, do we mean by "new literacies?" The preceding analysis suggests that our personal, civic, and professional lives are enhanced if we possess the skills and strategies that are necessary to use the Internet to accomplish a common set of functions. Whether we use the Internet for leading more empowered personal lives, more thoughtful civic lives, or more productive professional lives, similar skill sets are required:

1. *identifying* important questions;
2. *navigating* information networks *to locate* relevant information;
3. *critically evaluating* information;
4. *synthesizing* information; and
5. *communicating* the solutions to others.

These skill sets are not new; they have always been a part of our curriculum. Usually they are referred to as higher-level comprehension skills. With the Internet, however, each becomes realized in new ways. Each requires new skills strategies, and dispositions when we use the Internet to accomplish them. Examples of these new literacy skills, strategies, and dispositions appear in Figure 1-5.

E-MAIL FOR YOU

From: Barbara McInerney <bmcinern@freeside.scsd.k12.ny.us
Subject: Using the World Wide Web of the Internet

Hi!

I am really excited about the new doors opening to me as a high school teacher through the use of the Internet. However, that excitement is tempered by some reservations and concerns. One of my biggest concerns is the application of the sources on the Internet. Will I be able to make the use of the Web integrated and meaningful to my students? Will I be able to instruct them correctly and completely in the use of the Web? Will their use of the Internet add to the completeness of the curriculum or just be a casual aside? I feel teachers need to be fully trained and capable in the workings of the Net before attempting to guide students in its use. We do so many "hit and miss" procedures in education, but this technology is here to stay and will be an integral part of their future so students need to learn its use completely and correctly to really enhance classroom experiences.

One of my students, when asked about the feelings they had about our school becoming hooked up to the Internet and what possibilities it presented for them, answered in this manner, "I think it's going to be really cool! I mean, if you are studying, say China, and you could communicate with students in China to really see what it is like there, that would be so cool! Or, if you needed to know some stuff about a topic and all your books were old, then you could go to the Internet and it could tell you new stuff."

Even students with no experience to date on the Internet have a general idea of what they would like to try to do with it—it shows they are thinking about the possibilities, as I am.

I am excited about using this in my class next year!!!!

Barbara McInerney

Figure 1-5. Examples of Skills, Strategies, and Dispositions Required by the New Literacies of the Internet and other ICT

Central Functions During Internet Use	Some of the New Literacy Skills, Strategies, and Dispositions That Are Required
Identify important questions	- Possessing a "problem definition disposition," recognizing that Internet resources are often helpful in order to better understand a problem. As you gather background information about the general nature of the issues involved, the Internet helps you to ask the right question. - Possessing an "ethics of Internet use disposition," recognizing the important ethical responsibilities in using a tool as powerful as the Internet and how this tool needs to be used to identify problems that will make our world a better place for all of us. - Knowing when the Internet is likely to be useful and when it is not for exploring a particular problem. Note: Other new literacies listed below are also used during this phase. As we search, critically evaluate, and communicate information, we continually reframe our initial question, often developing new questions along the way.
Navigate information networks to locate relevant information	- Having a "multiple search strategy disposition," considering multiple search strategy possibilities and quickly evaluating the potential of each one for a given purpose. - Having the disposition to maintain focus on a task and not be distracted by interesting, but irrelevant, information. - Being able to select search strategies that best accomplish a particular task. - When appropriate, selecting the appropriate search engine to use in a search. - Using a search engine effectively to locate relevant information. - Reading and comprehending the results that a search engine produces. - Navigating rapidly through webpages to locate the most appropriate information. - Correctly inferring the contents behind a hyperlink. - Searching through bulletin board or discussion list archives to locate relevant information. - Searching through personal email messages and folders for relevant information. - Using a listserv, email, Instant Messaging, or other communication tools to request and obtain information from knowledgeable others. - Additional searching skills, depending upon the technology.

cont.

Critically Evaluate the usefulness of information that is found	- Having a "healthy skeptic disposition," always evaluating each piece of information that you encounter, thinking critically about information found on the Internet. - Distinguishing relevant from irrelevant information that one encounters during a search. - Using clues at a site to infer who created this information, what "stance" the author takes, and how this stance "shapes" the information that is presented. - Checking multiple sources of information that differ in important ways to evaluate "truthfulness." - Understanding the significance of URL endings in terms of what purposes might be served by information at a site: ".com," ".org," ".edu," and others.
Synthesize information to answer the question or solve the problem.	- Having a "non-linear disposition," seeking out multiple types and sources of information and continually thinking across texts and other media about their meaning. - Bookmarking and organizing bookmarks to save and organize information sources for later retrieval. - Being able to rapidly coordinate and synthesize multiple sources of information from multiple media sources. - Organizing informational elements using a digital mapping tool such as Inspiration.
Communicate the answer to others.	- Having a "communication disposition," knowing that communication with a large number of people can have an important impact if done successfully, efficiently, and ethically. - Using email to communicate the answer or solution to the problem. - Knowing how and when to use Instant Messaging most effectively to communicate information. - Using a weblog to communicate information effectively. - Creating a webpage to communicate information effectively. - Using a word processor and associated functions effectively. - Using video conferencing technologies, such as iSight and others, to communicate with others.

It is essential to also keep in mind that these new literacies build upon foundational literacies rather than replace them. Foundational literacies include those skill sets such as phonemic awareness, word recognition, decoding knowledge, vocabulary knowledge, comprehension, inferential reasoning, the writing process, spelling, response to literature, problem solving, the scientific method, seeing other perspectives, and others that are required for books and other traditionally printed material. These will continue to be important within the new literacies of the Internet and other ICT. While foundational literacies remain important, they will also be insufficient if one is to fully utilize the Internet and other ICT (Coiro, 2003;

IRA, 2001; Leu, 2000b; RAND Reading Study Group, 2002; Spires & Estes, 2002; Sutherland-Smith, 2002). Reading, writing, and communication will take new forms as text is combined with new media resources and linked within complex information networks requiring new literacies for their effective use.

Reading, writing, and communication will take new forms as text is combined with new media resources and linked within complex information networks requiring new literacies for their effective use.

Principles of a New Literacies Perspective

The new realities described in the previous section have prompted us to begin to frame a New Literacies Perspective (Coiro, 2003; Leu et al., 2004). This is an integrated theoretical perspective that helps us better understand both what students need to learn about Internet use and how best to use the Internet in our classrooms to support this development. We have defined the new literacies of the Internet in this fashion:

> The new literacies of the Internet include the skills, strategies, and dispositions necessary to successfully use and adapt to the rapidly changing information and communication technologies and contexts that continuously emerge in our world and influence all areas of our personal and professional lives. These new literacies allow us to use the Internet and other ICT to identify important questions, locate information, critically evaluate the usefulness of that information, synthesize information to solve problems, and communicate the solutions to others. (Leu et al., 2004, p. 1570)

In addition to identifying these five functions that are critical to information use on the Internet, a New Literacies Perspective also identifies a number of principles that are important to recognize as we consider how to integrate the Internet into our classrooms. These include:

1. New forms of strategic knowledge are central to the new literacies.
2. Learning is often socially constructed within the new literacies.
3. Critical literacies are central to the new literacies.
4. New literacies regularly change.
5. Teachers become more important, though their role changes within new literacy classrooms.

A New Literacies Perspective is an integrated theoretical perspective that helps us to better understand both what students need to learn about Internet use and how best to use the Internet in our classrooms to support this development.

If you wish to read more about the theoretical foundations of a New Literacies Perspective, these articles are available online for you:

- **Reading Comprehension on the Internet: Expanding our Understanding of Reading Comprehension to Encompass New Literacies**—
  http://www.readingonline.org/electronic/rt/2-03_Column/
- **Toward a Theory of New Literacies Emerging from the Internet and other Information and Communication Technologies**—
  http://www.readingonline.org/newliteracies/lit_index.asp? HREF=/newliteracies/leu

New Forms of Strategic Knowledge are Central to the New Literacies

You can see from Figure 1-5 that new strategic knowledge is central to the new literacies of the Internet and other ICT. Each technology for literacy contains different contexts and resources for constructing meanings and requires somewhat different strategies for doing so. New technologies for networked information and communication are complex and require many new strategies for their effective use. Hypertext technologies, for example, are embedded with multiple forms of media and unlimited freedom for navigating different pathways. These present opportunities that may seduce some readers away from important content unless they have developed strategies to deal with these seductions. Moreover, the technologies of the Internet will continue to change regularly and rapidly. This will present us with even newer technologies of literacy that demand more (and more sophisticated) strategies to effectively exploit them. It seems clear that the new literacies will be largely defined around the strategic knowledge central to the effective use of information within rich and complexly networked environments.

Social learning plays an important role in the exchange of new skills and strategies needed to interact within increasingly complex and continually changing technologies for information and communication.

Learning is Often Socially Constructed Within the New Literacies

Much recent research suggests that learning is often best accomplished through social interaction in supportive contexts. When students work together, they often are very effective at "scaffolding," or supporting, one another on the way to important insights (Meyer, 1993). Theoretical perspectives established by Vygotsky (1978), Bahktin (1981), and others are often used to explain this process. Method frameworks such as cooperative learning (Johnson & Johnson, 1984), peer conferences (Graves, 1983), jigsaw activities (Aaronson, 1978), literature discussion groups (Leu & Kinzer, 1999), text set activities (Short, 1993), and others are thought to be particularly useful because they create situations in which students help one another to learn important concepts. Socially mediated learning will be central to literacy instruction in the future, and here we highlight three dimensions that are important to recognize within our current framework of a New Literacies Perspective.

First, social learning plays an important role in the exchange of new skills and strategies needed to interact within increasingly complex and continually changing technologies for information and communication. Models of literacy instruction have often focused on teachers whose role was to teach the reading and writing skills they possess to students who lack those skills. This is no longer possible, or even appropriate, within a world of multiple new literacies framed by the Internet and other ICT. No one person can hope to know everything about the expanding and ever-changing technologies of the Internet and other ICT. In fact, today many students possess higher levels of knowledge about some of these technologies than do teachers. For the first time in our history, we have substantial numbers of students who are more literate than their teachers in some technologies of literacy.

As we plan for instruction, we need to recognize that it is simply impossible for one person to have all the new skills and strategies required to be literate in the Internet and other ICT and then to teach these directly to others. Each of us, however, will know something unique and useful to others. You may know how to evaluate a website in order to determine the biases that exist at that site while a student may know a new search engine for locating information that is especially effective in science. You both benefit when you exchange these skills.

Consequently, effective learning experiences will be increasingly dependent upon social learning strategies and the ability of a teacher to orchestrate literacy learning opportunities between and among students who know different new literacies. This will distribute knowledge about literacy throughout the classroom. By orchestrating opportunities for the exchange of new literacies, both teachers and students may learn from one another. Such social learning ability may not come naturally to all students, however. Many will need to be supported in learning *how* to learn about literacy.

On a second dimension, social learning is not only important for how new literacies are developed, but also it often plays a vital role in how information is constructed within the technologies themselves. Much of the information on the Internet is built upon the social knowledge constructions of others (e.g., telecollaborative learning projects, threaded discussions, interactive chats, and collaborative databases). Every day, many new websites are developed and serve to expand the global knowledge base shared through Internet technologies. At home, in the workplace, and at school, the new technologies of literacy allow us to take advantage of the intellectual capital that resides in others, enabling us to collaboratively construct solutions to important problems by drawing upon the expertise that lies outside ourselves.

Social learning is not only important for how new literacies are developed, but it also plays a vital role in how information is constructed within the technologies themselves.

Thus, the construction of knowledge will increasingly be a collaborative, not a solitary, venture within the learning spaces defined by the Internet and other ICT. This is what happened in each of the classrooms described in the opening scenario of this chapter. Corresponding with other students about their drafts, exchanging responses to literature with other classrooms around the world, and working with mentors on challenging math problems are all examples of this important principle. You will find many other examples described throughout this book, including the email messages from teachers who share their insights with you about the lessons they have learned in this new world of the Internet. We will also show you several instructional models that support students learning from one another. With a little encouragement from you, students will be helping one another and discovering new literacies to share with still other students. This can make Internet use an effective tool for community building as well as for learning.

Finally, one might ask, "Does the social nature of learning mean that we should simply turn students loose to construct their own knowledge?" Not necessarily. We believe that teachers have an important role in directing the general, content nature of the learning experience while students (and teachers) often co-construct the new literacies they discover while working on the Internet. The instructional models that we present in this book (Internet Workshop, Internet Project, Internet Inquiry, and WebQuest) allow teachers to define the general nature of content knowledge while students (and teachers) share and exchange the new literacies that they are discovering as they use the Internet and other ICT.

Pioneers, dependent upon others as they built a new world, developed the saying, "Many hands make light work." This saying applies just as well to the pioneering new classroom communities we are building today with the Internet and the new literacies they require. Each of us will need to support others in both developing the new literacies these technologies require as well as using them to collaboratively construct new understandings about the information that they make available.

These new technologies will introduce important new learning opportunities for educators, especially within content area contexts. As the Internet and other ICT bring us closer together, students will need to be prepared for the collaborative, co-construction of new information, and the learning that results (Jonassen, in press; Jonassen, Howland, Moore, & Marra, 2003).

The Critical Nature of New Literacies

As the Internet and other ICT bring us closer together, students will need to be prepared for the collaborative co-construction of new information, and the learning that results.

Another important element of the new literacies of the Internet and other ICT is that they demand new forms of critical thinking and evaluation. In the past, information previously available in textbooks has been edited to fit prevailing cultural norms of what is commonly accepted as accurate or true. In contrast, open networks, such as the Internet, permit anyone to publish anything; this is one of the opportunities this technology presents. It is also one of its limitations; unedited information is much more widely available from people who have strong political, economic, religious, or ideological stances that profoundly influence the nature of the information they present to others. As a result, we must assist students to become more critical consumers of the information they encounter (Alvermann, Moon, & Hagood, 1999; Muspratt, Freebody, & Luke, 1996).Though the literacy curriculum has always included items such as critical thinking and separating fact from propaganda, richer and more complex analysis skills will need to be included in classrooms in which the Internet and other ICT begin to play a more prominent role.

As we develop richer understandings of the new literacies of the Internet and other ICT, we will depend greatly on work from the communities of critical literacy and media literacy, and we will be informed by research that targets higher-order thinking. Multiple, critical literacies populate the new literacies of the Internet, requiring new skills, strategies, and insights to successfully exploit the rapidly changing information and media technologies continuously emerging in our world.

New Literacies Regularly Change

A fourth element of new literacies is that they regularly change as new technologies appear, requiring even newer literacy skills. Consider, for example, the changes experienced by students who graduate from secondary school this year. Their story teaches us an important lesson about our literacy future. Many graduates started their school career with the literacies of paper, pencil, and book technologies but finish having encountered the literacies demanded by a wide variety of digital information technologies: video conferencing, word processors, CD-ROMs, web browsers, web editors, email, spreadsheets, presentation software, Instant Messaging, plugins for web resources, listservs, bulletin boards, avatars, virtual worlds, and many others. These students experienced new literacies at the end of their schooling unimagined at the beginning.

Given the increasingly rapid pace of change in the technologies of literacy, it is likely that students who begin school this year will experience even more profound changes during their own literacy journeys. Moreover, this story will be repeated again and again as new generations of students encounter yet unimagined ICTs as they move through school and develop yet unimagined new literacies. As new technologies appear on the Internet and in other ICTs, new literacies are required to effectively exploit their potential. Thus, each of us is continually becoming more literate as we acquire new skills with new information and communication technologies like the Internet; we can no longer consider a fixed end point to achieving literacy. In fact, because the nature of these new literacies is continually changing with new technologies for information and communication, it may be that learning how to learn new literacies is more important than learning specific new literacies themselves.

Because the nature of these new literacies is continually changing with new technologies for information and communication, it may be that learning how to learn new literacies is more important than learning specific new literacies themselves.

This element of the new literacies creates a particular challenge for assessment. How can we develop valid and reliable assessment instruments when the life cycle for a test is far longer than the rate at which new technologies appear? Multiple versions of Internet browsers, search engines, and other tools for example, will appear within the life cycle of any traditional state assessment for reading. How can we measure the new literacies that these latest technologies make available when they are not included on state assessments? We refer to this as the assessment paradox of the new literacies. We see this today when not a single state currently assesses reading comprehension online; not a single state permits any student who wishes to do so to use a word processor for the state writing assessment. Our assessment instruments are behind the state of our technologies for literacy and learning today, and given the rapid pace of change in the technologies of the Internet and other ICT, they will continue to lag behind the nature of available technologies.

The assessment paradox presents a particular challenge in the classroom. Most of us make certain that we teach the skills that we know will be on any assessment used to measure learning in our classroom. However, if we only teach the skills that appear on assessment instruments, we will always deny our students opportunities to learn the new literacies required of current technologies. But what are these new literacies? You and your students will see them in the classroom before they appear on any assessment instrument or even appear in state standards. Thus, preparing students for the new literacies that they will need in their future will require you to be continually on the lookout for the new literacies that appear in new technologies entering your classroom each year.

E-MAIL FOR YOU

From: Celia <cbmg@MIDWEST.NET>
Subject: You are NEVER too old!

One should never, ever feel lacking when it comes to knowledge about computers and the new literacies of the Internet, no matter how old you are. I say this because, there is so terribly much out there to learn. I sincerely do not believe that any one can know all or even approach knowing all because it is ever changing and growing. I think it is important to liken your quest for knowledge about cyberspace to how a kindergartner or 1st grader must feel when the doors begin to open up to the masses of knowledge one must have in order to be a reader. Or when a child first realizes that there is so much to learn out there about anything and everything. Just think! We give them a minimum of 12 years to learn it! Technology creates that same feeling in us older folks!

My advice is to sit back, relax, and feel good in the knowledge that the cruise ship you are on is full of individuals on the same quest! There are tons of caring individuals out there that are more than willing to help. And just think how exciting it is every time you find out something new!! That "Aha" feeling is really cool. Good luck and keep up the good work.

From a kindred spirit!
Celia Godsil
Title I Teacher
Nielson School,
Galesburg, Il.

Teachers Become More Important, Though Their Role Changes Within New Literacy Classrooms

Internet resources will increase, not decrease, the central role you play in orchestrating learning experiences for your students.

The final element of the new literacies is this: Internet resources will increase, not decrease, the central role you play in orchestrating learning experiences for your students. Teaching and learning are being redefined by the communication technologies that are quickly becoming a part of the information age in which we live. The many resources available on the Internet are the beginning of a radical departure in the nature of information available to you and your students. How we respond to these important changes will determine our students' ability to succeed in the world that awaits them.

Each of us will be challenged to thoughtfully guide students' learning within information environments that are richer and more complex than traditional print media, presenting richer and more complex learning opportunities for both us and our students. Moreover, as we have seen, the new literacies required to use these new technologies will continually change, requiring both us and our students to regularly acquire even newer literacies, learning these new skills from one another. And finally, we need to remember that the risks of integrating the Internet in your classroom are always equal to the rewards that are possible.

You may already have seen evidence of this last element. Left completely on their own, students are sometimes seduced away from reading and thinking critically about a single topic as they discover intriguing links to more and more locations and move farther and farther away from the initial topic. As a result, students sometimes only skim the surface of many, unrelated, pieces of information, never integrating or thinking deeply about any of them.

In this book, we will show you an integrated set of instructional models for teaching with the Internet.

We think this scenario is only possible, however, in classrooms in which teachers do not actively guide the use of Internet resources and, instead, leave decisions about Internet use entirely to students. When students always determine their own paths through this rich and intriguing information resource, there is a powerful tendency to search for what students refer to as "cool," highly interactive and media-rich locations that quickly attract their attention but are unrelated to important learning tasks (Leu, 1996). These often include video, sound, animation, and other elements. As students search for "cool" sites, they are less likely to explore important topics in depth or think critically about the relation of this information to their own lives. Students end up viewing much but learning little.

On the other hand, when students are guided to resources and provided with important learning tasks to accomplish, they quickly focus on important information related to the issue at hand. This is not to say that students should be limited only to Internet resources that you select to complete tasks that only you devise. Clearly, if we wish students to become effective users of the Internet, we want them to develop independent strategies for searching and evaluating information. And, in order to do so we must provide them with learning experiences that they direct. Still, it points to the central role you will play with this new resource as you support their ability to independently acquire and evaluate information on the Web.

In this book, we will show you an integrated set of instructional models for teaching with the Internet. These include: Internet Workshop, Internet Project, Internet Inquiry, and WebQuest. You will see how to begin with easier instructional models and move to more complex and richer models as you feel increasingly comfortable with using the Internet in your classroom.

A central assumption of this book is that your role in orchestrating experiences with the Internet is central to your students' futures.

A central assumption of this book is that your role in orchestrating experiences with the Internet is crucial to your students' futures. Your instructional decisions will determine the extent to which your students gain from this resource. That is why we focus on effective teaching practices while limiting the technical discussion of the Internet to essential basics. It is also why we feature exceptional teachers, who are highly effective at using the Internet in their classrooms, in each chapter.

Visiting the Classroom: Marci McGowan's First and Second Grade Classes in New Jersey

We have seen how the Internet opens new windows to the world for each of us, enabling us to learn from one another in important ways.

If you seek new ideas about integrating the Internet into your own classroom, you might wish to open a window into the classrooms of teachers who are using this tool in exemplary ways. You can do this by exploring classroom homepages and websites that teachers are developing on the Internet to support their instructional programs. Take a look, for example, at Marci McGowan's homepages at H. W. Mountz Elementary School in Spring Lake, New Jersey (http://www.mrsmcgowan.com/index.html). You will note that you will actually find two sets of classroom webpages at this site: one for first grade, which she taught until spring 2003, and another for the second grade class that she started teaching in the fall of 2003. Even if you do not teach at these levels, Marci's classroom webpages contain important lessons for all of us.

If you seek new ideas about integrating the Internet into your own classroom, visit the classrooms of other teachers who use this tool in exemplary ways.

One important lesson is to note the many opportunities she provides for students to publish their work to a worldwide audience. Students are proud to see their writing online and this undoubtedly prompts even more and better writing. Parents and grandparents often visit her site to view the work of their children and grandchildren. Students also love to read the work of other students. The site prompts email messages from others who have read their work, congratulating both Marci and her students on their accomplishment.

A second important lesson is to observe the many exceptional Internet projects Marci and her students have completed with classrooms around the world (http://www.mrsmcgowan.com/projects/index.html). Marci is widely known for developing these collaborative learning experiences, always organized around ISTE standards (http://www.iste.org/standards/). Her students learn important lessons about the new forms of collaborative learning made possible by the Internet and the new literacies they acquire in the process. Visit her class site to see what new projects she is planning each year. Perhaps your class will be fortunate enough to join one of her projects. If so, you will discover how Marci expands the impact of her teaching far beyond the walls of her own classroom.

Marci's webpage also teaches us another lesson: It is important to develop both foundational literacies and new literacies. Take a look at the wonderfully extensive set of resources for developing foundational literacies in her section on reading, writing, and spelling (http://www.mrsmcgowan.com/reading/index.html). These include resources for flash cards, word wall words, a list of Dolch words, reader response journals, comprehension, and much more. At the same time, though, you will also notice many links to resources that develop new literacies including the resources at **SCORE Cyberguides** (http://www.sdcoe.k12.ca.us/score/cyberguide.html) as well as the new literacies developed through her extensive set of Internet projects. This has to be one of the finest collections of links to instructional resources on reading, writing, and spelling that we have seen.

Marci uses her classroom webpage in many ways, but one of the most important lessons it teaches us is how to use a classroom webpage to communicate effectively with parents, forging a tighter relationship between school and home.

Marci uses her classroom webpage in many ways, but one of the most important lessons it teaches us is how to use a classroom webpage to communicate effectively with parents, forging a tighter relationship between home and school. Marci has a special section for parents (http://www.mrsmcgowan.com/1stgrade/parents_teachers.htm). This contains information about herself, the standards for each grade level, the nature of the year's curriculum, her philosophy of teaching, and ideas about how to help their child at home. This classroom webpage communicates an important message to parents about the professional nature of Marci's important work, while also providing guidance on how parents can support their child's development. As more families obtain Internet access, this will be an increasingly important function of a classroom webpage.

By sharing effective resources and strategies on the Internet, we are quickly developing rich curriculum networks that transcend materials previously available for instruction.

Notice, too, that Marci also provides resources for other teachers. Especially useful is an extensive set of links to other first and second grade classroom webpages (http://mrsmcgowan.com/1stgrade/firstsites.html). This is a wonderful resource and shows us how the Internet can connect us with others who share similar professional interests.

Visiting classrooms like this can inform all of us in important ways. Being able to see what teachers are doing around the world has the potential to change our instructional lives, providing us with many new and exciting resources for teaching. By sharing effective resources and strategies on the Internet, we are quickly developing rich curriculum networks that transcend materials previously available for instruction. This is an exciting and potentially powerful development for education. It shows how, once again, we all learn from one another in these new teaching and learning contexts.

Welcome to the new literacies of the Internet!

Figure 1-6. Marci McGowan's Classroom Website for her First and Second Grade Classes (http://www.mrsmcgowan.com/index.html).

E-MAIL FOR YOU

From: Marci McGowan <MarciMcg@aol.com>
Subject: New Literacies in my Classroom!

The Internet provides opportunities for young students to engage in collaborative activities that are meaningful learning experiences using technology. Each year we participate in a 50 States Postcard Project. We share-write a message and send New Jersey postcards telling about our town and school to other classes. In exchange, we receive and read postcards from children all over the country. Teachers take advantage of this pen pal variation by connecting to the project through Internet email.

Similarly, we read our website guestbook messages from far away places, including other countries. Hearing from real people in Colorado is a great motivator to find the state on the map and learn more about that place. Exchanging pets (stuffed animals) with a first grade class in Wisconsin helps us learn about life there. Through email with a class in Australia, we learn that some children ride horses to school instead of taking a bus or walking a few blocks. The Internet really stretches our classroom walls!

Because we use the Internet so much as part of our regular classroom activity, my students think of it as a place to find information and a way to communicate with others—not just a place to play games. Our class website provides students with a safe way to access other webpages. It's the "home base" for all our daily Internet activity.

Students turn the computers on when they arrive, navigate to the Internet and then to our website. The children only go to other websites that I have previewed and saved on our site. A morning weather report, reached from an image link on our homepage, is a good example. Numerous seasonal, thematic, and subject pages are made available through this linking procedure.

Much of our Internet work is done with a partner or in small groups. It's a great opportunity for collaboration and offers a chance for many class members to shine—one student may be very skilled with the use of the mouse and navigating between websites, while another is called on to read unknown words. Both students contribute to the success of the activity. Some of the "New Literacies" at our grade level include using the computer mouse effectively, reading an Internet screen (not an easy task for emergent readers), and navigating between open windows.

The main way we communicate with other classes and the general public is by publishing student work on our webpage. The children love seeing their drawings and writing on screen. So do their families! Some of the most appreciative responses to our website have come from grandparents living far away and parents who travel for their jobs. Knowing that so many people will be seeing their work helps motivate the children to do their best.

Our website also hosts collaborative literacy projects. These projects primarily are designed to provide a rich source of online reading material for young students. The project resource pages stay online as well and can be utilized by other teachers.

I also use the website for pages to extend specific classroom lessons. There are online quizzes for compound words or math riddles and lists of spelling words to drag and drop into ABC order. Some activities I create and others are shared by teachers from all over the country. Our **Month By Month** (http://www.mrsmcgowan.com/1stgrade/monthbymonth.htm) pages and specific subject/theme pages such as the **Ocean Study** (http://www.mrsmcgowan.com/ocean/index.htm) are available as resources for year-round planning.

Finally, our website provides a variety of resources for parents and other teachers. You'll find suggestions for teaching poetry writing with young children, home reading tips, our state standards,

cont.

website building information, links to other teacher websites, math projects, rubrics, book lists, critical thinking questions using Bloom's Taxonomy, holiday puzzles, and more!

New teachers can get started with using the Internet in their classrooms by learning how to do a good search and evaluate websites. Make sure the sites you select have significant alignment with your curriculum and state standards. If you create your own site, keep it simple and focus on content and ease of navigation. Join a mailring or listserv for your grade level or interest, ask for help, and share ideas—learn together!

Best wishes,
Marci
Mrs. McGowan's 2nd Grade 2003-2004
http://www.mrsmcgowan.com/2nd/index.html
Mrs. McGowan's First Grade
http://www.mrsmcgowan.com/index.html

Additional Instructional Resources on the Internet

1st Grade Web sites—
http://www.mrsmcgowan.com/1stgrade/firstsites.html
Marci McGowan has created this webpage with links to an extensive collection of first grade classroom websites.

Education World—http://www.education-world.com/
This is an important online resource for many educators. It has a wealth of information, ranging from news in education to exceptional classroom resources.

Enchanted Learning—
http://www.EnchantedLearning.com/Home.html
A great directory for teachers with a well-organized and extensive set of classroom resources. Pay a visit.

ISTE Standards Project—http://cnets.iste.org/
The homepage for the standards of the International Society for Technology in Education. This contains links to ISTE's standards and also links to the technology standards for most of the states in the United States.

Leading Practice ICT Examples—
http://www.edna.edu.au/edna/page2434.html
Here is an exceptional collection of the best curriculum sites identified by Australian educators. Explore a bit and find some exceptional resources for your classroom.

Mrs. Renz's 4th Grade Class—
http://www.redmond.k12.or.us/patrick/renz/index.html
Heather Renz has one of the best classroom homepages around. Pay a visit to see how new literacies are developed in her classroom.

National Geographic for Kids—
http://www.nationalgeographic.com/kids/index.html
Here is an interactive site for younger students who want to learn about the world around them. You will find many links to resources that you may use right away in your classroom.

New Literacies for New Times—
http://www.sp.uconn.edu/~djleu/fourth.html
This is the online website for this book, containing links to all of the sites mentioned in this book. Just open the screen for each chapter and follow along as you read this text, linking to each site mentioned.

Our children's future: Changing the Focus of Literacy and Literacy Instruction—
http://www.readingonline.org/electronic/RT/focus/
An article in *Reading Online* that explains the many important reasons that we need to broaden our definition of what it means to be literate in an information age.

Pocantico Hills School—
http://www2.lhric.org/pocantico/pocantic.html
Take a look at how this school is creating many exceptional resources, publishing student work and making these available to us all.

Position Statement on Literacy and Technology: The International Reading Association—
http://www.reading.org/positions/technology.html
The leading literacy organization has come out with a thoughtful position statement on the new literacies that will frame our future. A most thoughtful document that explains how and why we need to broaden our view of reading to include the new literacies of the Internet.

2 Navigating the Internet with Efficiency and a Critical Eye

In this second chapter, we examine the new literacies required to critically and efficiently navigate the Internet with students. Traditionally, Internet navigation connotes the process of moving between one link and another through various webpages. However, we look at navigation within the context of a new literacies perspective. We see the act of deciding which path to follow on the Internet as very tightly woven within a complex process of reading and meaning making. Strategies such as querying search engines, critically evaluating multiple forms of information, weaving through search results, and systematically maneuvering within one website are all important and different aspects of moving between links while making sense of information on the Internet.

It is our responsibility as teachers to recognize these important changes in how we think about navigating on the Internet. This chapter will explain how to take advantage of advanced browser tool functions to manage Internet resources in your classroom. You will learn how to locate information using search engines designed for adults and others designed especially for children. We will also explore several important issues related to navigation on the Internet: avoiding excessive commercialism on browsers and web locations; developing child safety policies; and weaving navigation and critical thinking strategies into classroom instruction.

Each of these issues is an important aspect of effective teaching and learning with the Internet. It is not simply about how quickly students can move through this online world, but more about how they decide which information is most accurate, relevant, appropriate, and useful for their purposes. Armed with strategies for these important tasks, we will all be more successful at efficiently navigating the Internet.

After reading this chapter, you should be able to:

1. Name at least three popular Internet browsers and compare and contrast the various features for organizing classroom resources available within each.

2. Describe at least three classroom management strategies for using web browsers with students.
3. Identify several new strategies that are required for students to interact with search engines and informational websites on the Internet.
4. Share at least two Internet search tools designed for teachers and two others designed especially for students. Discuss the similarities and differences across each of these tools.
5. Describe at least three critical reading strategy lessons that can support students in searching for and learning from informational websites.

Teaching with the Internet: Joe Montero's Class

"Hey, cool! Check this out. Space aliens are beaming music down to planet Earth! Look at this!"

"No way!"

"Way! Watch this. There's this X-ray telescope that shows the sound waves that could be from aliens. And over here, there's a video mailbox with tons of video clips to watch."

"Here listen . . . this guy's pretty funny. He's from a recording studio and he wants to make a deal with us if we can prove the music is really coming from space aliens. The class would definitely like this site!"

Julio and Davíd were students who had struggled a bit at school. Actually, they had struggled a lot. They found life outside of school much more interesting than life inside school. As a result, they found themselves further and further behind in reading, math, and other areas. However, this was the start of a new school year and both Julio and Davíd sensed the possibilities for new beginnings that always exist during this special time.

The boys had discovered **Space Mysteries: Alien Bandstand** (http://mystery.sonoma.edu/alien_bandstand/game/htmlout/index.html), an interactive mystery that guides students through an inquiry-based investigation into the source of mysterious sounds coming from outer space (see Figure 2-1). Students use virtual tools, videos, images, and references to help build their case and collect data that supports their conclusions.

"Cool! Let's bookmark this place so we can show everyone else!"

They set a bookmark in Internet Explorer, renamed the link as "Alien Bandstand" and wrote the name of their bookmark on their worksheet.

"So, how do we figure out who sponsors this?" Julio asked.

"Let's try deleting the end part of the URL like Mr. Montero showed us yesterday. That way we can get back to the sponsor's homepage," Davíd answered. They made their way back to the homepage of the **Space Mysteries** site (http://mystery.sonoma.edu/). "You can usually find stuff like this if you scroll down the page." He scrolled down the screen and then explained, "See, it says here at the bottom of the page that it's sponsored by NASA. And . . . look . . . there's the official NASA symbol, so I'm pretty sure Mr. Montero will agree that it's a good site for science."

"Yeah, and look . . . here's a whole bunch of other space mysteries we can show everyone too! Aw, man, we gotta tell Mr. Montero about this one!"

Figure 2-1. The view of the station console at Space Mysteries: Alien Bandstand (http://mystery.sonoma.edu/alien_bandstand/game/htmlout/index.html), the interactive simulation that Julio and Davíd discovered. The video briefings are viewed in the center of the screen. Notice the icons on the bottom of the window. Clicking on any of the icons in the bottom half of the window links to virtual tools like an optical telescope, encyclopedia, video mailbox, x-ray telescope, glossary, and notebook.

They were completing an activity developed by their teacher, Joe Montero, for Internet Workshop (See Figure 2-4). This workshop activity developed Internet navigation strategies as it introduced a unit on space exploration during the first week of school. Joe had always found such great content area sites for kids using the kid's search engines **Yahooligans** (http://www.yahooligans.com) and **KidsClick** (http://www.kidsclick.org). This year he decided to more actively involve his students in locating and evaluating potential websites to include in their space unit. Joe was using this workshop along with a number of reading and writing activities to begin the year.

*Joe had always found such great content area sites for kids using the kid's search engines **Yahooligans** and **KidsClick**.*

"Okay, we bookmarked the page. Now, let's go back and finish the other part of what we have to do before we run out of time." Julio and Davíd returned to the Alien Bandstand webpage, logged in using only their first names (a safety tip Mr. Montero had taught them) but then had trouble getting past the login screen. "Ugh! It says we have don't have Flash on our computers . . . how do we get that? I clicked on the little icon that says 'Get Flash Here' but now what do I do? Where am I now anyway?"

Marcus, another student looking for space sites on the computer next to Julio and Davíd , leaned over to help. "I think you're at the **Macromedia**

homepage (http://www.macromedia.com/). Look for a button at the top that says Downloads, and then you'll see something that links you to Flash. Click on that button there that says 'Install Now' . . . yeah . . . there, I'm sure that's it 'cuz I had the same problem yesterday and after I downloaded Flash from there, the site I was trying to open worked great!"

"Hey thanks, Marcus! You should write that down on your sheet and tell everyone else at Internet Workshop." Davíd and Julio followed Marcus' directions for downloading the Flash plug-in and then logged back into the Alien Bandstand site. They had about 15 minutes left to explore the site to see if it was worth sharing with the class. They listened to the "mission briefing" video and set out to work exploring the virtual set of tools while figuring out which strategies would be most helpful for quickly finding useful information on the site.

They were both a little confused at first by the all the different frames on the screen; it didn't look like the usual format of websites they were used to. Davíd spent a minute trying to figure out where to go first and then said, "Hey, look it. When I put my mouse over the little symbols down here, the name of the tool shows up in the title bar. Let's write that down on our worksheet as a helpful feature we found."

Julio was almost finished writing when Davíd found something else. "You know what else? See this little silver bar here with all the different arrows on it? We should put this down as something that's kind of hard to use unless you know what all those buttons do. Luckily, I do, 'cuz it looks kinda like a computer game I have, but I bet there's some kids in our class that don't know how to use it. I wonder if Mr. Montero would let us show everyone at Internet Workshop."

Rachel and Jenell, two other girls in Mr. Montero's class, had been listening for the last few minutes and leaned over from their searching to see what Julio and Davíd had found. "Hey that looks like a pretty fun site. Wanna see what we found?" Rachel asked. "Watch . . . Jenell . . . show 'em what we did."

"Well . . . okay . . . first, we went looking for pictures of things in space," Jenell eagerly explained, "so we used the AltaVista Image Search from the **Kid's Image Search Tool** (http://www.kidsclick.org/psearch.html) and typed in the keyword 'space'. We skimmed past all these commercial links and then found this site here called **Amazing Space** (http://amazing-space.stsci.edu/). It had the letters 'edu' at the end of the URL, like Mr. Montero taught us, so we figured it was an educational site about space. We clicked on it and we just started clicking the buttons down the left side to see what was on the site . . . we followed this **Online Explorations** link (http://amazing-space.stsci.edu/resources/explorations/) and that's where we found these awesome photos of space and a whole bunch of other activities" (See Figure 2-2). Jenell slowly scrolled down the screen, reading off the titles of some of the activities "*. . . Planet Impact . . . Galaxies Galore . . . Solar System Trading Cards . . . Star . . .*"

Julio's eyes lit up as Davíd interrupted. "Wow, all that stuff would keep us busy for a month! I'm startin' to like this space unit already!"

For the students in Mr. Montero's class, their school year was starting off with a bang!

Figure 2-2. The Amazing Space Online Explorations webpage (http://amazing-space.stsci.edu/resources/explorations/) that Rachel and Jenell found in Internet Workshop for their space exploration unit. It features 10 different interactive explorations and companion materials for teachers too.

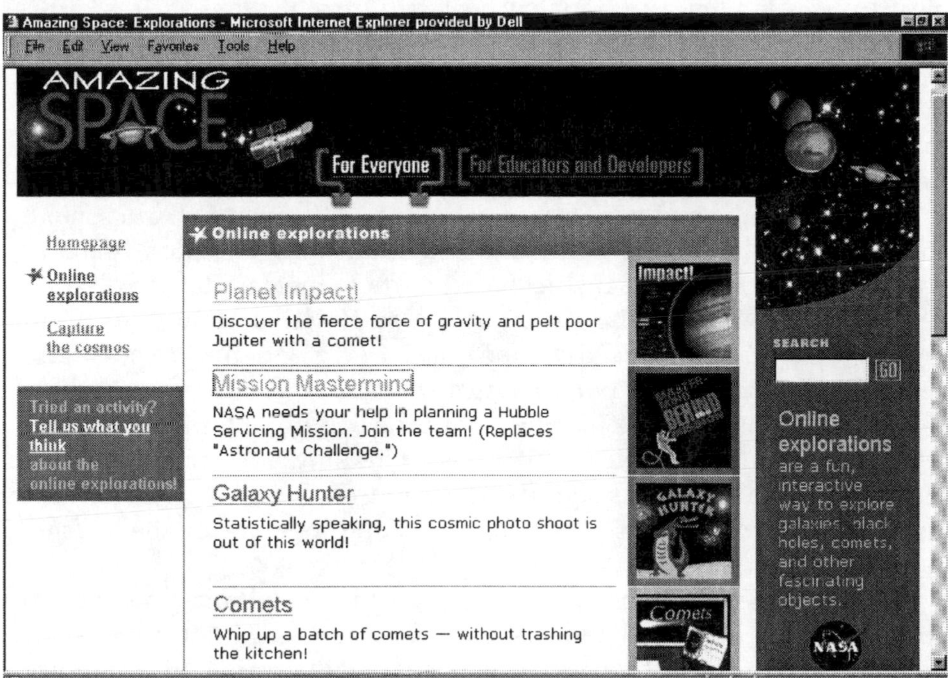

This was the third year that Joe Montero had used the Internet with his students to enrich content area learning. In previous years, he introduced them to the basics of Internet browsers and to a range of different resources. However, recently Joe found that students were more successful at locating helpful websites and synthesizing relevant information when they learned and shared efficient searching and navigation strategies with each other along the way. Taking notes while they were searching kept his students focused on the task at hand and helped them remember what they wanted to share when they met back as a whole group for Internet Workshop.

Recently Joe found that students were much more successful at locating helpful websites and synthesizing relevant information when they learned and shared efficient searching and navigation strategies from each other along the way.

This activity taught several navigation strategies, while introducing important resources for the unit. Because it limited search engine use to two children's search engines that screen sites for appropriateness, the activity also accomplished a third goal: it supported child safety in his classroom. This was important in Joe's district. In fact, the district recently instituted a number of practices as part of its child safety strategy. First, the district used a filter program to deny access to webpages deemed inappropriate for students to visit. Second, each school agreed to have all students obtain an "Internet driver's license" before being given permission to use the Internet. This process required all students to take one of several online interactive quizzes that presented various situations and asked students to make choices about which response would be the most ethical, appropriate, and safe. His district used different quizzes for different age levels, and when students completed the quiz successfully, they earned a license and the right to use the Internet in their classroom.

Another part of the district's child safety strategy was to follow an acceptable use policy. Over the summer, the district had revised its acceptable use policy to more appropriately deal with current issues such as harmful viruses, security of school networks, online harassment, and software piracy. One resource they found especially valuable was the **Educator's Guide to Computer Crime and Technology Misuse** (http://lrs.ed.uiuc.edu/wp/crime-2002/computercrime.htm). Their policy clearly defined "Do's" and "Don'ts" of Internet use, and outlined sanctions for unacceptable use. At the end of the form, there was a location for everyone to sign, indicating they had read and understood the policy: student, parent/guardian, and teacher. The district based parts of their updated policy on the examples found in **The Acceptable Use Policies Handbook** from Virginia's Department of Education (http://www.pen.k12.va.us/go/VDOE/Technology/AUP/home.shtml).

An acceptable use policy clearly defines "Do's" and "Don'ts" of Internet use, and outlines sanctions for unacceptable use.

On the first day of class Joe introduced the computer and the Internet. He went over the acceptable use policy with his students, explaining each item. Then he had students sign the form and take it home to obtain the signature of their parent or guardian, permitting them to use the Internet at school.

As students returned the forms, Joe reviewed the fundamentals of navigation with small groups of students using Netscape Navigator and Internet Explorer, two powerful browsers used to navigate on the Internet. Since his students were likely to encounter both browsers at some point, he reviewed the toolbar and basic features for each browser, leaving time for students to identify the similarities and differences in each. During the first few weeks of school, students were also asked to complete the **Safe Surfin' Driver's Ed Challenge for Kids and Teens** (http://www. safesurfin.com/drive_ed.htm), an online quiz about safe Internet use. Once they could pass the quiz, Joe inserted each student's digital photograph into a driver's license template he created in his word processor. He printed out and laminated a "driver's license" for each of his students and attached it to the signed Acceptable Use Policy statement as a reminder of the importance of safe Internet practice. Finally, he introduced the Internet Workshop activity in Figure 2-4, designed to be completed in pairs.

During his small group lessons, Joe discovered that some students knew more than he did about navigating on the Internet and that others knew very little.

During his small group lessons, Joe discovered that some students knew more than he did about navigating on the Internet and that others knew very little. He wanted students to support one another as they developed basic and higher-level navigation skills. Before they began, he set the homepage location to a classroom search page he had designed with links to kids search engines such as Yahooligans, Ask Jeeves, and Kidsclick. For the first few Internet Workshop sessions, this would always be the first page to appear when students connected to the Internet and started their online activity. He showed students how to bookmark their favorite websites as they discovered them. He also showed them how to organize bookmarks into a separate folder for each new topic, a skill they would practice in Internet Workshop. He reminded students to notice the different features at each website and to pay attention to those features that helped them quickly locate what they wanted as well as those that seemed to pull them off track. He also showed them how to truncate a certain website's URL to trace back to the sponsor of the website and explained how the *About Us* button on a webpage can provide information about a site's creator and its purpose. These were all important new strategies Joe recently learned from a school-based study group session he attended before school began with other teachers from his district.

Figure 2-3. An activity for Internet Workshop used to develop navigation knowledge at the beginning of the year.

Navigating: Beginning our Unit on Space Exploration

Pilot:______________________________ Date:____________

Co-pilot:______________________________

Goals

1. To locate and share at least one great location you found during Internet Workshop that can be used in our space unit.
2. To practice search and navigation strategies on the Internet.
3. To locate at least one helpful feature and one distracting feature of search engines or websites as you navigate the Internet and share them both during Internet Workshop.

Evaluation

1 point	You used a recommended search engine to locate and bookmark at least one great space location.
1 point	You shared your location during Internet Workshop.
1 point	You practiced search and navigation strategies we learned on the Internet.
1 point	You located at least one helpful and one distracting feature on the Internet and wrote each down in your journal.
1 point	You shared the navigational features you observed.
5 points	Total

Exploring Space Resources on the Internet

1. Begin your journey at our class search homepage that starts up when you first open the Internet Explorer browser. Select a search engine, either **Yahooligans** (http://www.yahooligans.com) or **KidsClick** (http://www.kidsclick.org).
2. Use the keyword strategies we talked about to search for and locate at least one great activity or site that we can use in our space unit. If your keyword is not getting any hits, brainstorm a few synonyms or alternative keywords with your partner and try again.
3. Bookmark the website in the Space folder and print out a copy of the page. Below, tell us the name of your discovery, who sponsors the page, and why you think it would be fun to do.

cont.

What I found: ____________________

Who sponsors the page: ____________________

Why it would be fun to do: ____________________

____

What helpful and distracting features did you notice?

1. **Using a search engine**: As you used Yahooligans, AskJeeves, or Kidsclick which features of these search engines were helpful? Which features were distracting or didn't work as you expected?
   Helpful features: ____________________
   ____
   Distracting features: ____________________
   ____
2. **Reading a website**: After you locate and bookmark your favorite site, take a few minutes to explore the pages within this site. Which features of the website help you quickly locate information within the site? Which features are distracting or don't work as you expected?
   Helpful features: ____________________
   Distracting features: ____________________
3. Be prepared to share at least one helpful and one distracting feature you found during Internet Workshop.

If You Have Time: Look through the Hubble Space Telescope (HST) into Deep Space

1. Take a look at deep space with the Hubble Telescope. Select the bookmark for **Hubble Space Telescope Public Pictures** (http://hubblesite.org/newscenter/archive/category/survey/)
2. View some of these pictures from the Hubble telescope. Use the key to help you read the icons that describe each photo. Print out your favorite. Write a description of what you can see on the back and attach it to this page. Bring it to Internet Workshop to share.

At the end of the week, after students completed the space navigation assignment, Joe organized an Internet workshop session with the entire class. Rachel and Jenell shared the online explorations they discovered at **Amazing Space** (http://amazing-space.stsci.edu/) and taught the rest of the class how to download the Flash plug-in from Macromedia. Everyone was excited at the many different activities they could explore in the days ahead. Anthony, another student, proudly showed off the **NASA Quest** site (http://questdb.arc.nasa.gov/content_search_space.htm) that he discovered, explaining how the class could meet real scientists online and learn more about their jobs at NASA. Marcus decided that typing in a keyword could help locate relevant sites faster than using the browsing function of Yahooligans. Another pair of students noticed that their search for "planets" in KidsClick produced far fewer results than the same one in Yahooligans and wondered why this was so.

Perhaps because school success had been rare for them, Julio and Davíd held their surprise until the very end of the workshop session. Finally they told everyone about the Space Mystery simulation they had found. They explained details about the mission and told about their video interview with the head scientist from the Search for Extraterrestrial Intelligence Institute (SETI).

"Let's go over to the computer and you show us what you found," said Mr. Montero.

They all watched while Julio and Davíd gave them a tour of the site, pointing out the NASA symbol that helped them know who sponsored the site. Julio quickly navigated through the multiple frame interface to locate the video interviews and played one for the class. Davíd eagerly showed everyone how to use the silver buttons to replay or pause the video. They explained to everyone how they used the hyperlinks along the left-hand side like a table of contents to find their way around the site, something no one else had pointed out. They even showed Mr. Montero how he could keep an eye on each team's progress by clicking on Exit and then viewing each pair's quiz results, notebook entries, or URL history. Julio and Davíd had become the experts in class with this information, a new position for them at school. It felt good.

Joe was amazed at how much Julio and Davíd had accomplished during their time at the computer—using a search engine to quickly locate such a great site and then staying on task to complete the activity for Internet Workshop.

Joe Montero had not seen this simulation before and was amazed at how much Julio and Davíd had accomplished during their time at the computer—using a search engine to quickly locate such a great site and then staying on task to complete the activity for Internet Workshop. And, these were two of his students that most concerned him. Clearly, the special moments at the computer during that first week of school had opened the school doors for Julio and Davíd and they had jumped right through. Joe was certain this experience was going to be a turning point for them. He could feel it in the confidence they demonstrated as they showed everyone the engaging location they discovered.

As he stood thinking about this, Joe also recalled the words he had heard at a workshop on Internet use in the classroom, "You will become the guide on the side, not the sage on the stage." As he stood watching Julio and Davíd teach his class about these new resources, the meaning of those words was suddenly very clear. His role as a classroom teacher was changing. It was a wonderful start to the new school year. Everyone learned important lessons that day.

Lessons from the Classroom

What lessons might we learn from this episode as we consider navigation issues in the classroom? First is the important lesson of child safety on the Internet. Limiting search engines to those like **Yahooligans** (http://www.yahooligans.com) or **KidsClick** (http://www.kidsclick.org) that screen sites for children helped Joe to ensure his students didn't explore inappropriate locations on the Internet. Also, Joe's district used a software filter to prevent inappropriate sites from appearing on any of the district's computers. The district encouraged all students to earn an Internet driver's

Developing an acceptable use policy heads off a number of problems including the viewing of inappropriate sites, using inappropriate language on the Internet, and receiving inappropriate email from strangers.

license and worked carefully with parents, students, and teachers to update their acceptable use policy for Internet use. Developing an acceptable use policy heads off a number of problems including the viewing of inappropriate sites, using inappropriate language on the Internet, and receiving inappropriate email from strangers. Since it was sent to both students and parents/guardians, everyone received important information about the Internet and how it was going to be used at school. We will discuss acceptable use policies later in this chapter.

A second crucial lesson is how Joe strategically combined three elements within a single lesson: an introduction to the first thematic unit of the year and experiences designed to practice both navigation strategies and comprehension strategies. This type of integrated instruction helps students recognize an important change in how we define the phrase "navigating on the Internet"; a change that will be central to your integration of these new information tools. Traditionally, Internet navigation connotes the process of moving between one link and another on a webpage. However, when we look at navigation within the context of the new literacies perspective, we come to see that the act of deciding which path to follow on the Internet is very tightly woven within a complex process of reading comprehension. Strategies such as querying search engines, critically evaluating multiple forms of information, weaving through search results, and systematically maneuvering within one website are all important and different aspects of making sense of information on the Internet. Joe asked his students to focus their attention on important features of the webpages they visited that supported or detracted from successfully finding information and making sense of it. He, like many teachers, realized that Internet navigation is as much about comprehension as it is about the physical act of moving from one link or website to another.

In the context of this new literacies perspective, it is our responsibility as teachers to recognize these important changes in how we think about navigating on the Internet. More importantly, we must develop instructional models that support student development of the different strategies involved in making meaning as they move through links on the Internet. Like Joe, we must take advantage of the authentic tasks that naturally occur in the content areas and thoughtfully weave efficient navigation and comprehension strategies into each area.

This episode also illustrates a third lesson—the importance of systematically developing a range of navigation strategies at the beginning of the year. Joe's prior experiences with students convinced him that navigational strategies were important; students gather information in a shorter time when they know how to navigate through the Internet. Time was precious in Joe's class and he wanted students to know how to use their time efficiently. Joe also recognized that interactive resources, such as NASA's Space Mystery, demand new strategies to efficiently navigate Internet environments. Unlike traditional texts, information on the Internet is presented in multiple formats of text, video, animated imagery, and virtual tools. Joe wanted his students to first, differentiate these new formats from those found in traditional textbooks and earlier formats of text-based webpages, and second, to identify features of electronic text that enhance and detract from efficiently locating information. He developed a thoughtful plan to accomplish both of these objectives and began by teaching essential navigation strategies through Internet Workshop.

Joe's Internet Workshop at the beginning of his space unit led to many new comprehension strategies while navigating the Internet. One student, for example, had discovered that most websites feature a navigational bar along the top or left margin of their homepage to help guide their path through a website. Another student compared this listing of main topics to a table of contents found in a textbook and explained how understanding each website's organization of these main categories can help to quickly locate a certain piece of information. Yet another student pointed out that the NASA website featured an animated navigation bar and specially formatted words that weren't underlined like traditional hyperlinks. One student explained how he didn't realize at first that these were actually links to other lists of resources and then another shared a strategy for holding the mouse over the words to see if "the little hand tool" showed up to indicate the image indeed linked to a new page. Finally, one pair of students noticed that when they visited the other links at the bottom of **NASA's** homepage (http://www.nasa.gov/audience/forkids/home/), each opened up in a new window. They wondered why webpage designers sometimes did this instead of just having the new page show up in the same window. All these strategies were noted, shared, and discussed. It was a very productive session.

Another lesson is the social learning opportunities that are critical to classroom use of the Internet. Joe used three methods (group introduction, paired learning, and whole class workshop) to teach navigation skills. These worked in a complementary fashion to take advantage of social learning opportunities inherent with Internet use. His initial group presentation explained essential elements for students to practice as they completed the tour in pairs. Working in pairs after the group presentation led to many new learning experiences as students helped one another when they were stuck, discovering new ways of navigating the Internet. Sometimes other students would even stop by the computer to assist a pair having difficulty; this saved Joe time as he worked with students in other areas of the classroom. Finally, having Internet Workshop at the end of the week tied everything together for his class, allowing each student to share new navigation strategies with one another.

As teachers, we need to anticipate the changes in our role. Because Internet technologies are increasingly powerful, complex, and continually changing, our students quickly become more knowledgeable than us in many aspects of information technologies. No teacher can keep up with all of the changes.

Internet Workshop led to other social learning opportunities. In addition to students helping their peers, Joe made time for students to share new information they knew with him, the teacher. Two important points stand out here. First, as teachers, we need to anticipate the changes in our role. Because Internet technologies are increasingly powerful, complex, and continually changing, students quickly become more knowledgeable than teachers in many aspects of information technologies. No teacher can keep up with all of the changes. As a result, our role is changing from being the central source of information in the classroom to becoming a facilitator and guide, putting children together with other children who possess different types of expertise in order to exchange information and solve common problems.

Second, this episode also points out how Internet technologies can create spaces for students who have met with failure in the past. The lesson that Julio and Davíd teach us is important; each child in your room can become an expert on an especially useful aspect of Internet navigation and then share his/her knowledge with others. The Internet opens new paths through which each of your students may succeed, and provides important opportunities to grow and develop in new ways. Anyone may become an expert in some aspect of the Internet, showing us something we did not know before. You will see these opportunities in your classroom, reminding us of the potential in each and every student.

Joe Montero's classroom contains many lessons for us to consider: using child safety strategies; strategically weaving content area knowledge with navigation and comprehension strategies into authentic learning opportunities; the importance of systematically guiding students to develop efficient navigation skills while applying higher-level comprehension strategies; the importance of social learning opportunities for students and teachers using the Internet; and especially the spaces Internet use creates for children who may be struggling in school. Each is important for us to consider.

Some teachers like to use Internet scavenger hunts at the beginning of the year to introduce or review navigation skills. If you are interested in exploring a number of scavenger hunts, visit these locations:

- **Scavenger Hunts: Searching for Treasure on the Internet**—
  http://www.education-world.com/a_curr/curr113.shtml
- **Internet Scavenger Hunts**—
  http://www.aea14.k12.ia.us/technology/ScavengerHunt.html
- **WebHound's Scavenger Hunt**—
  http://www.mcli.dist.maricopa.edu/webhound/hunt.html

Important Tools for Navigating the Internet

Most of us have probably been using the Internet long enough to know the basics of how to open a browser, type in a URL, bookmark a website, and print out a webpage you are viewing. If not, your colleagues are bound to have many tips for using common browser buttons such as Back, Forward, Stop, Refresh, Search, and Favorites. Fewer teachers, we have found, are as comfortable with browser strategies such as organizing bookmarks into folders, exchanging sets of bookmarks with peers, replacing commercial links with school-related links on the toolbar, and saving webpages onto a local hard drive. We will discuss these strategies and a few others after a short description of three powerful Internet browsers. Since we believe that an important component of being literate on the Internet is being able to move between different platforms of software and to flexibly generalize one set of strategies to a new environment, we will briefly introduce each browser separately and then group the three together during our discussion about effective browser practices in the classroom.

Three Powerful Internet Browsers

A browser is the most important tool for navigating the Internet. It is used to locate and view webpages on the World Wide Web and can also be used to organize and manage your favorite Internet resources.

The two most powerful browsers are **Internet Explorer** (available at http://www.microsoft.com/ie) and **Netscape Navigator** (available at http://www.netscape.com), although a new browser known as **Safari** (available at http://www.apple.com/safari/) was recently introduced by Apple and has rapidly gained popularity among Macintosh users. All three browsers are free and easy to download from their respective homepages. Although all three browsers are quite similar, most people have a favorite and tend to use only one when given a choice. For an interesting comparison of the different features offered by Internet Explorer and Netscape Navigator, read through the Browser Comparisons section of the **Finding Information on the Internet Tutorial** (http://www.lib.berkeley.edu/TeachingLib/Guides/Internet/Browsers.html) developed by librarians from the University of California at Berkeley.

A browser is the most important tool for navigating the Internet. It is used to locate and view webpages on the World Wide Web and can also be used to organize and manage your favorite Internet resources.

A Few Thoughts at the Beginning

Before you read the next section, we wish to share three important thoughts with you. The first is that, since our last edition of this book, we have found that word travels quickly in classrooms about the basic fundamentals of browser navigation and that most teachers are familiar with the basic browser tools. As such, in the upcoming description of browsers, we will spend only a brief amount of time highlighting each browser's features and spend more time exploring how to use them quickly and effectively in your classroom. Similarly, we have limited a heavily technical discussion of each browser's features and instead, pointed you to helpful resources and tutorials that provide screen shots and step-by-step directions for each browser. We are sure you have already discovered many useful features and functions of browsers on your own and from your Internet experiences with colleagues and students. New versions of each browser appear often and learning new ways of exploring their features is one of the exciting aspects of the new literacies journey ahead. Take full advantage of these moments. Exploring new features of a browser, email program, or a website is how all of us learn to navigate on the Internet. Be certain, too, to share your discoveries with others. They will appreciate it and share their discoveries with you.

The second issue concerns a developing controversy within the educational community. You will need to decide, perhaps with guidelines from your district, about the amount of advertising to which you wish to expose your students. This happens through the choice and configuration of your browser and the locations you ask students to visit for classroom assignments. Increasingly, browsers use links to commercial sites favoring their products and companies with which they have formed strategic alliances. Increasingly, sites on the Internet include banner advertising along with the information they provide.

Some see this as inevitable and worthwhile. Exposing students to commercial messages helps initiate conversations about how best to critically view information on the Internet. Commercial images are seen as tools for teaching students about the increasingly commercial nature of the information they will encounter in their lives. Others see the intrusion of commercial images as inconsistent with the traditional, commercial-free nature of most educational materials.

We tend to favor exposing students to fewer, not more, commercial images. We believe it is important to engage students in discussions about these matters, but not when we have other educational goals in mind. As a result, we have tried to avoid commercial sites in the recommendations and examples of Internet locations we provide. This is not always possible. Nevertheless, as we have made decisions about which Internet locations to include in this book, we have favored those developed by professional organizations, governmental organizations, non-profit organizations, federally funded sites, and others who limit or exclude advertising at their locations. Some Internet locations we mention do contain advertising or commercially motivated links. In these cases, we decided the information resources were more important than the advertising. You will need to make similar decisions, as it is difficult to be entirely commercial-free in the locations you select for classroom use.

All three browsers described in this chapter have commercially motivated links. Often these appear in subtle ways, ones you would not immediately consider.

This issue also affects your choice of browser in important ways. All three browsers described in this chapter have commercially motivated links. Often these appear in subtle ways, ones you would not immediately consider. Our presentation will show you how to remove most of the commercially motivated links built into each browser, if you so desire. This should enable your students to focus more on the information at a location and less on commercially motivated links that appear as part of the browser.

The final thought is simply a reminder of an important point we made earlier in this chapter about the changes in how we define and teach students about "navigating the Internet." If we are to effectively prepare students for learning with the Internet, we can no longer teach "navigation skills" as isolated technical steps that are separate from critical reading strategies. Many researchers are exploring the notion that comprehension strategies for reading webpages are interwoven with meta-cognitive strategies and navigational strategies (e.g., Burke, 2002; Coiro, 2003; Guinea, Eagleton & Hall, 2004; Leu, Kinzer, Coiro & Cammack, 2004; Schmar, 2003; Smolin & Lawless, 2003; Sutherland-Smith, 2002). Meta-cognitive strategies are used for searching, evaluation, and self-regulation, while navigational strategies are required for moving through multimedia environments with efficiency and purpose. This research reminds us that it is our responsibility to help students realize that it is not only about how quickly they can move through online environments, but also about how they determine the accuracy, authenticity, and point of view of information on the Internet. Because of this, much of our discussion for the rest of this chapter will emphasize strategies to help you support learners to navigate the Internet safely, quickly, purposefully, and with a critical eye.

Internet Explorer: A Powerful Internet Browser

Probably the most well-known and widely used browser for the Internet is Microsoft's Internet Explorer (IE). Available to download from Microsoft's homepage (http://www.microsoft.com/windows/ie/default.asp), it is packaged with free components such as an email program, a newsreader, and an instant messenger tool. The program provides strong technical support for Windows users, yet Microsoft has decided to not continue with new versions for Macintosh users beyond version 6. One negative aspect of Internet Explorer is that it comes packaged with many layers of commercial links on the main Toolbar. You will learn later how to remove these links and replace them with other links more suitable for your students. Also, different versions of the browser are available depending on which Windows operating system you are running. See Figure 2-4 for a view of Internet Explorer's toolbars on a Windows system. For more information on how to use each of its features, you can visit the following sites:

- **Microsoft's How-To's**—
  http://www.microsoft.com/windows/ie/using/default.asp.
  Here you'll find tips for customizing browser features and peer-to-peer discussion boards about Internet Explorer issues and concerns.
- **Internet Explorer (IE) in the Classroom**—
  http://www.actden.com/IE5/
  From here you can explore an interactive tutorial for Internet Explorer from ActDen.

Many teachers are using Netscape Composer to design their classroom webpages; you can read more about this process in Chapter 12.

Netscape Navigator: An Internet Browser with a Companion Webpage Design Program

Netscape Communicator, available to download from Netscape's homepage (http://www.netscape.com) is a suite of several programs that work together. Navigator, the web browser, is packaged with other components such as an email program, a newsgroup reader, an address book, and an Instant Messenger, as well as a very user-friendly webpage development tool called Composer. Many teachers are using Netscape Composer to design their classroom webpages; you can read more about this process in Chapter 12. Like Internet Explorer, Navigator comes packaged with many layers of commercial links on the main Toolbar, although all can be removed. Navigator runs well on both platforms, yet you may notice slight differences in the toolbar on a Windows system (see Figure 2-5) as compared with a Macintosh system. For more information, you can visit **Netscape's Online Help and Support** (http://help.netscape.com/netscape7/index.html) or **Netscape Essentials from UC Berkeley** (http://www.lib.berkeley. edu/TeachingLib/Guides/Internet/NetscapeEssentials. html).

Apple Safari: The New Browser on the Block

Apple's new browser, Safari (http://www.apple.com/safari/), was introduced in 2003 (see Figure 2-6). Although the interface is not packaged with extra tools such as email or newsreaders, it boasts many new browser features. Some of these features include tabbed browsing, which enables switching between multiple webpages in a single window; snapback technology, which returns you to the point where you last typed a URL or selected a bookmark; and a free program that stops pop-up advertisements while you are browsing. If you have used Safari, you will probably have noticed that Netscape powers it, so the homepage looks very similar to the start-up page from within Netscape Navigator. The best location for tips and strategies for using Safari is at Apple's homepage listed previously.

Figure 2-4. The browser toolbar for Internet Explorer 6 on a Windows system (http://www.microsoft.com/windows/ie/default.asp).

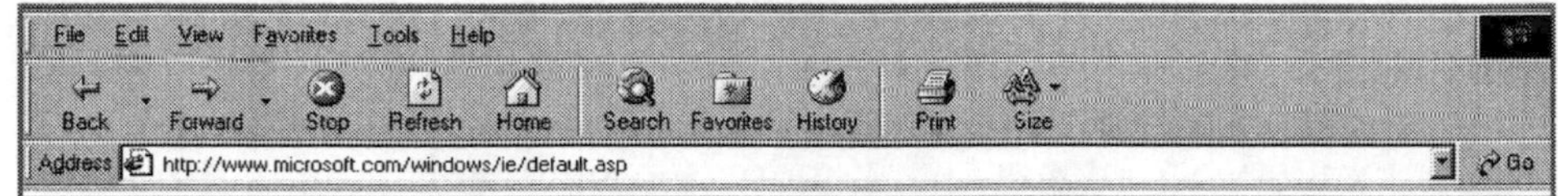

Figure 2-5. The browser toolbar for Netscape Navigator on a Macintosh system (http://www.netscape.com)

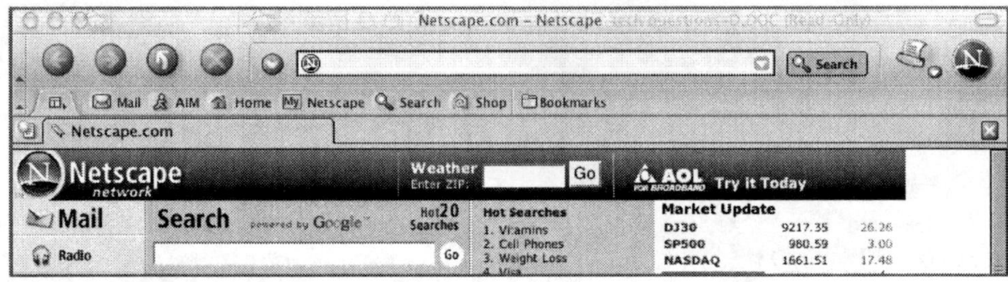

Figure 2-6. The browser toolbar for Apple's Safari browser (http://www.apple.com/safari/) on a Macintosh system.

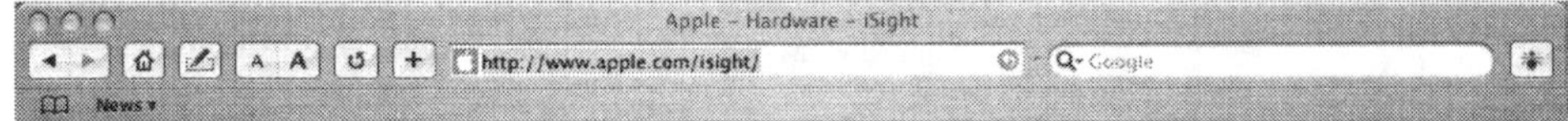

If you are feeling like you would like more information about browsers in general, take a few minutes to explore the excellent resources at **Traveling the Internet with a Web Browser** (http://medlib.med.utah.edu/travel/Start1.html). Here you'll find a step-by-step browser tutorial complete with screen shots and short explanations of the tools and functions available within Netscape Communicator and Internet Explorer on Windows and Macintosh platforms. You can also learn about a few other features and special strategies for using each browser at **Surf the Web: Web Browsers** (http://www.learnthenet.com/english/html/12browser.htm). And finally, if you come across other teachers in your school who are fairly new to the Internet, take time to share strategies that work for you and perhaps encourage them to explore other online resources, such as:

- **WebTeacher For Windows—** http://www.webteacher.org/windows.html
- **WebTeacher For Macintosh—** http://www.webteacher.org/macintosh.html
- **Learn the Net: An Internet Guide and Tutorial—** http://www.learnthenet.com/english/
- **Global Connections Online—**http://www.nsglobalonline.com/

INTERNET FAQ

It takes a long time to repeatedly click the Back button when I need to go back more than one or two locations. Is there a faster way to go back to a site I visited a while ago?

Sure! There are two ways. Either click and hold down the Back button, or find the "Go" menu item and then click and hold it down. In both cases, you will see a list of sites you have already visited since launching your browser. Just highlight a location you wish to return to and you will go there immediately. Internet Explorer will even show you a list of places you have visited many days ago, a nice feature.

Managing Internet Browser Tools in the Classroom

Now that you are able to recognize the basic features of the tools available within the three different Internet browsers, we intend to share a series of higher-level strategies that will work in all three browsers to help you to organize, manage, and share the resources you've compiled with your students and your colleagues. Each of the following strategies is an important new literacy that will foster effective classroom use of Internet browser tools, including:

- Designating a startup page location on your classroom computer.
- Replacing commercial links with educational links on the browser toolbar.
- Organizing bookmarks within folders for classroom use.
- Sharing and exchanging bookmark collections with others.
- Downloading necessary plug-ins and installing them in your browser.
- Saving webpages to your local hard drive, disk, or CD-ROM.

A first strategy that fosters safe and efficient Internet exploration with students is designating a Startup page location for the content your class is studying or for a favorite search engine.

Designating a Startup Page Location for Your Web Browser

A first strategy that fosters safe and efficient Internet exploration with students is designating a startup page location for the content your class is studying or for a favorite search engine.

A startup page location is the page that shows up first on your screen each time students connect to the Internet with any browser. As Joe Montero discovered, this saves time in a busy classroom; students begin immediately with the site you want them to visit first, one with important content for your unit. Although each browser has a series of menu steps in order to change the startup page (sometimes called homepage) location from the one that first appears on your computer, there is a short-cut method that we have found to work in all three browsers. If you look at your address window in any of the browsers, you'll notice a tiny icon just before the URL in the address bar. In Explorer, you'll be looking for a small blue "e" before the URL; in Netscape, it may be a bookmark icon, an @ sign, or the Netscape icon; and in Safari, the tiny icon in the address bar resembles a small blue sphere.

To specify your startup page quickly in Internet Explorer, simply drag and drop this tiny icon on the startup page button (the button with the "house" icon on it) on the Button Toolbar in your browser. You'll be prompted with a window that asks if you want to make this website your startup page, and then the current startup page will automatically be replaced with yours when you start up your browser again or click on the toolbar's Home button. In Netscape Navigator, you'll need to drag this icon onto the Tab Toolbar at the top of your browser. In Safari, you are able to drag a URL to the toolbar and name it Home, but in order to force the browser to start up at this URL each time you open the browser (at least in the version available at this writing), you'll need to follow the older procedu of choosing "Safari" from the top row of commands in the window and then selecting "Preferences." Here, as Joe Montero did for his Internet Workshop startup page, you can enter in the URL for your desired startup page into the box beside "Homepage" and then close this window by clicking on the upper-left reddish X button.

Removing and Replacing Commercially Motivated Links on the Toolbar

You've probably noticed that with each new version of any browser, more and more commercial links seem to make their way onto your personal toolbar. Many teachers have found that it is possible to remove these commercially motivated links without limiting students' ability to navigate the Internet and access resources important to classroom learning projects. The process is very similar to the one described above to set your homepage. If you are concerned about commercial aspects in any of the browsers, we suggest you do the following:

- Set your homepage for an appropriate content page, not the Microsoft, Netscape, or Apple page, by following the directions in the previous paragraph.
- Remove all commercial items from your Favorites toolbar. To delete any links that you don't want from the toolbar, in any of the browsers with a Windows system, simply right click on the icon for the website on the Favorites or Links toolbar and choose Delete from the pop-up menu that appears. With a Macintosh computer, or a mouse with only one button, you'll need to hold down the mouse over the icon until the special menu appears, and then choose Delete.
- If you cannot see your Favorite's toolbar, select View, then Toolbars, and then choose Links. The toolbar will appear near the top of your browser.
- Replace the removed items on your Favorites toolbar with your own favorites for classroom learning. By clicking on the tiny icon in the

address bar, just before the URL, and dragging it to your Favorites toolbar just below the address line, you can fill your toolbar with your own classroom favorites. In Windows systems, if the link's title is too long, right click on the icon, select Rename from the pop-up menu, and type in a shorter name.

Organizing Bookmarks within Folders for Classroom Use

A third strategy that greatly enhances efficient navigation on the Internet is the use of bookmarks or favorites. By now, you've probably explored many useful locations on the Internet and have bookmarked them so that you can use each bookmark to quickly return to a certain location. If not, you can easily set a bookmark for a favorite website by viewing the webpage in your browser and selecting Favorites from Explorer's toolbar and then Add to Favorites, or selecting Bookmarks from Netscape's toolbar and then Bookmark This Page. Bookmarks are useful in a classroom to help students save time in getting to useful Internet locations. Over time, however, too many bookmarks in one long list can overwhelm anyone, especially students cruising along in their search to locate important information for an Internet workshop assignment. Let's say that, for example, over the past few weeks, you had been electronically bookmarking several websites for your upcoming social studies unit on explorers when you came across the excellent collection of resources from **Lewis and Clark's Historic Trail** (http://www.lewisclark.net/index.html). You decided to bookmark this website as well, only to realize after you set it, that this and your previous Internet Explorer bookmarks were scattered in no particular order all through your long list of favorites. You noticed in earlier units that students took way too long to scroll through your ever-growing list of bookmarks to locate the one they needed. The random list of bookmarks makes it difficult for them to quickly visit other related locations on your list.

If this scenario sounds at all familiar to you, it's time to begin using the folders feature in your Internet browser. All three browsers include tools that enable you to manage the organization of your bookmarks by creating folders for different curriculum projects and placing your bookmarks in the appropriate folder. You may also rearrange favorite sites in the window after they've been bookmarked or move items into new folders by simply clicking and dragging them to the desired location. You may also delete items by clicking once on the item and then selecting Clear or Delete from the Edit menu item in each browser.

All three browsers include tools that enable you to manage the organization of your bookmarks by creating folders for different curriculum projects and placing your bookmarks in the appropriate folder.

Since the process of organizing bookmarks looks slightly different in each browser, let's discuss each separately.

Setting Bookmarks with Internet Explorer

While viewing the page you want to bookmark in Internet Explorer, you may begin by selecting the Favorites button from the toolbar to open your list of favorites in a left-hand frame. Next, create a new folder called Explorers by clicking on the Add button at the top of this frame, and then clicking on the New Folder button. Type your new folder name into the box and select OK. Now you may rename the bookmark itself, if you'd like, by typing a new name into the Name box and then selecting OK to create a new Lewis and Clark Trail bookmark in your Explorers folder.

To move your newly created Explorers folder near the top of your bookmark list, simply drag the folder up from the bottom of the left frame and drop it closer to the top, so that students can locate in quickly. Now, when students wish to access your newly organized resources, they can just click on Favorites, click on the Explorers folder and the Lewis and Clark website will be listed inside the folder. Once this folder is created, you can add other bookmarks to this folder or drag bookmarks from your longer list into this folder.

Setting Bookmarks with Netscape Navigator

When using Netscape Navigator to organize your bookmarks, the process is very similar. To create a new folder and save a bookmark in it, select the bookmarks icon from the toolbar and then choose File Bookmark. Click on New Folder, enter the name of your folder, and click OK (see Figure 2-7). Your empty new folder will appear at the bottom of the list of folders and you'll need to click on this folder to open it. Then, select OK and the webpage will be bookmarked within this new folder. To access the bookmark, select Bookmarks from the Browser Menu, highlight the Explorers folder, and the list of links will appear in a new pop-up menu to the right.

For reorganizing bookmarks that you created earlier, select "Manage Bookmarks" from the Bookmarks menu. A new window will open with drag-and-drop features. For specific information about organizing bookmarks in the Navigator window, visit **Bookmark Basics** at (http://www.duneland.k12.in.us/programs/webfun/bookmarks.html) or for a more comprehensive list of tips, try **Bookmark Management** (http://webinstitute forteachers.org/2000/curriculum/homeroommodules/bookmarks/) from the Web Institute for Teachers.

Setting Bookmarks with Safari

Finally, if you wish to create new folders and organize bookmarks in Apple's Safari browser, you may select "Bookmarks" from the top menu and then choose Add Bookmark Folder. To move bookmarks from one folder to another, you may select the tiny book icon on the left end of the toolbar and then drag and drop bookmarks in the right frame of the window into any of the folders in the left frame.

One final thought to consider when managing bookmarks for your classroom is that you may also want to consider the advantages of creating folders labeled with the names of pairs or small groups of students. This practice may provide an easy link to individualized lesson resources while also encouraging students to participate in the process of critically evaluating and marking websites with information that addresses each student's unique questions or interests.

Figure 2-7. Netscape's bookmaring feature enables you to organize groups of bookmarks into folders. Here, Lewis and Clark's Historical Trail (http://www.lewisclark.net/index.html) is being saved in the Explorers folder at the bottom of the list in the smaller window .

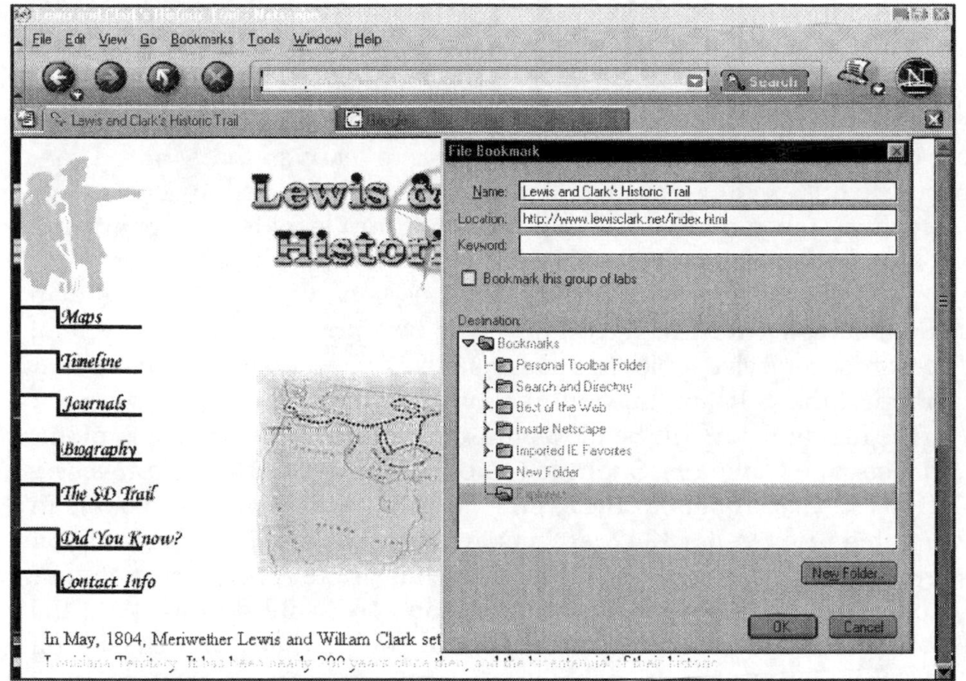

E-MAIL FOR YOU

From: Maya Eagleton <meagleton@cast.org>
Subject: Determining the Relevancy of a Webpage: Edit>Find Strategy

A widely underutilized but extremely powerful tool for helping students determine if a website has the information they seek is the "Edit and Find" strategy. Assuming your students have a clear idea of what they are trying to find (Eagleton, Guinee, & Langlais, 2003) they may select 'Edit' and then 'Find' to search any web page for a specific wod or phrase. For example, one of my 9th graders wanted to know the horsepower of a Camaro Super Sport. Because his reading skills were not strong, and the information was buried in a visually confusing table, I suggested he try Edit>Find, then type the word "horse-power." In seconds, he had information he needed, and I quote, "550 horsepower engine . . . Whoa!" Another nifty use of the "Edit and Find" strategy is to continue pressing "Find Next" to see how many times a keyword appears on a webpage. This can be a speedy method for determining if the website is worth reading more thoroughly, or if the student's focus of interest is mentioned only in passing.

I cannot emphasize strongly enough the value of this EASY, SIMPLE method of evaluating the relevancy of a webpage for students' inquiries. Remind your students to use it often!!!

Respectfully yours,

Maya B. Eagleton, PhD
Senior Research Scientist, Center for Applied Special Technology (CAST)
http://mywebpages.comcast.net/meagleton
Former K-12 Reading Specialist, Title I Coordinator, & Reading Recovery Teacher

Sharing and Exchanging Bookmark Collections with Others

As we mentioned in Chapter 1, one of the principles upon which we've grounded the new literacies perspective is that learning is often socially constructed among a group of peers and often involves new constructions of knowledge. We've found this to be the case particularly in the context of teachers who eagerly share their collections of Internet resources with others. News about great websites for instruction travels fast among the teaching community and there are new literacies to learn so that you can contribute to this exciting exchange. Any teacher who has used the Internet for more than a few months has surely begun to compile folders full of Internet bookmarks to amazing websites for their students. As teachers have less and less time to search for quality websites, a network of teachers who share their collections with each other can be a powerful support system. There are several electronic tools that work in conjunction with your browser to support this collaborative information exchange.

The first tool is a "File Send" feature available in both Internet Explorer and Netscape Navigator. Suppose you come across **SCORE's Connecting California Classrooms to the World** (http://www.score.k12.ca.us/), an incredible resource for K-12 teachers in any major content area, and you want to quickly forward this resource to your grade-level partner at your school. Without leaving your browser, you can easily do this. With the website viewable from the browser window in Internet Explorer, click on "File" from the row of options at the very top of your screen and then select the "Send" option from the pull-down menu that appears. Selecting the "Page by Email" option will paste a working copy of the entire webpage, complete with all of the images, to your email program's new message window. Selecting "Link by Email" will paste a copy of the website's URL into the email message window. In either case, type in the email address of the person(s) you'd like to send the resource to with a short note about the website and click Send from within your email program. It's that easy.

In Netscape Navigator, the process is almost exactly the same. However, when you select "File" from the top row of commands in the browser, you'll notice a separate Send Page and a Send Link option from the initial list of choices instead of in a separate pop-up menu list. Again, selecting either option will open a new email message and copy either the whole page or just the URL into the contents of the message. We'll cover more about sending and receiving email and attachments in Chapter 3.

Another option for sharing resources is to save and export an entire folder's list of bookmarks or even your entire collection of Internet bookmarks!

A second option for sharing resources is to save and export an entire folder's list of bookmarks or even your entire collection of Internet bookmarks! To export your bookmarks from Netscape Navigator, begin by selecting the Bookmarks folder and then, choose the option for Managing Bookmarks. Select the Tools option from the top menu of the bookmarks window and then scroll down to select Export from the pull-down menu. Choose a name for your bookmark file and designate a place to save it on your computer. Once saved, you can email a certain folder of bookmarks or your whole list of bookmarks to colleagues by attaching the exported file to your email message.

To open a saved bookmarks file from within Internet Explorer, begin by selecting File from the top row of browser commands. Choosing the Im-port/Export option from the pull-down menu opens an Export Wizard window that walks you through the process of selecting the folder(s) you want to export and where you want them saved. Again, once you've saved your Favorites file, you can easily share it as an email attachment.

A third way of sharing bookmarks is to publish your bookmark list in a public place on the Internet. In this way, you can build your collection of websites at home, perhaps, and have full access to them from your classroom or from any Internet access point. There are a number of online resources that provide the tools and the virtual space to do this. If this sounds interesting, you may want to explore a few online bookmark managers, such as the following, to find one that's best for you:

- **IKeepBookmarks**—http://ikeepbookmarks.com/
- **MyBookmarks**—http://www.mybookmarks.com/
- **BackFlip**—http://www.backflip.com/login.ihtml

Downloading and Installing Necessary Plug-Ins

OK. You're all set. You've mastered the art of organizing your bookmarks, shared a few collections with your colleagues, and ventured into a large group exploration with your high school American History students using the bookmark you set for **Famous Speeches from The History Channel** (http://www.historychannel. com/speeches/). Everyone is excited to hear President Roosevelt's actual address to Congress the day after Japan's attack on Pearl Harbor and compare it to the numerous earlier drafts you were able to access and print out from another great website, **American Memory** (http://memory.loc.gov/ammem/amhome.html). You locate this famous speech in the database, yet when you click on the link to hear the audio, you discover you cannot hear it without the proper plug-in. You know you've heard audio from other websites; why not this one?

Each location on the Internet may require slightly different tools to read its graphics, audio, and video information. Netscape Navigator, Internet Explorer, and Safari have plug-ins and helper tools that let you access these items.

What is happening is that each location on the Internet may require slightly different tools to read its graphics, audio, and video information. Netscape Navigator, Internet Explorer, and Safari have plug-ins and helper tools that let you access many items. Often, though, you reach a site that uses a multimedia tool you do not have. As a result, you discover you cannot hear the audio or view the video or graphic without adding the appropriate tool to your browser.

When this happens, a message will usually appear directing you to extend your capabilities by adding a new plug-in tool to your plug-in file. You may be directed to a central location for plug-in programs and be encouraged to download the appropriate program. Go ahead and follow these directions, restart your computer, and visit the multimedia site you located earlier. You should then be able to view, read, or listen to the appropriate multimedia element. If you are not directed to a site from which to download the plug-in, you may wish to explore a resource such as **Pearson Education's Browser Tune-up** (http://browsertuneup.pearsoncmg.com/browser_tuneup.html). The tools at this website scan the browser you are currently running and report whether or not your computer has the common plug-ins installed. If you have installed them, you can test each one to make sure it works. If you do not have them installed, you can easily download the plug-in most suitable to run on your computer.

Saving Webpages Onto Your Local Hard Drive, Disk, or CD-ROM

The last strategy we'll share in this section on classroom management strategies for Internet browsers involves a time-saving idea for thinking ahead in case your Internet connection goes down in your classroom. One of the biggest frustrations that teachers have when planning a lesson around a particular website is that often, when they actually get around to visiting the resource with students, the school network has just crashed or the connection is busy or even worse, the website is no longer available. If this has ever happened to you, you know how frustrating this can be! The good news is that all three of the browsers featured in this chapter include a tool that enables you to save a certain webpage onto your local computer drive so that you can access it later without having an Internet connection. This tool can also come in handy when you want to provide access to a website on a computer that is not connected to the Internet or you have a slow connection.

Saving a webpage locally is actually quite simple to do. While using any one of the three browsers to visit the websites you would like to download, select File from the menu bar and then choose the Save As option. A small window will appear, prompting you to name the File. Type a new file name, select the small arrow at the end of the Save As Type text box and choose the option that says "htm html or webpage." From this window, you should also select the location in which to save the page—either on your hard drive, on a floppy disk, or even on a CD-ROM or DVD if it's a large webpage with lots of images and information. Now, just click Save and wait a few moments as your computer saves the entire website, images and all, onto your local drive. Of course, it is important to realize that you have only saved this one page of the website and any time you click on a link to another page, you will get an error message unless you have downloaded that page as well.

To download larger amounts of information such as a website so that all the internal links will be operable, you may want to explore software options (also known as "offline browsers") such as the following:

- **WebStripper**—http://www.solentsoftware.com/ (completely free)
- **WebWhacker**—
http://www.bluesquirrel.com/products/whacker/index.html
(free demo)
- **WebCopier**—http://www.maximumsoft.com/ (free trial)

Of course, you will also need to be aware of copyright issues for saving websites on your computer and for using them with students. We will address some of these concerns later in this chapter.

Knowing how to save a webpage locally means that the next time you are in the middle of a lesson with students and your Internet connection goes down, you can open the downloaded file by clicking on the file icon and it will automatically open in your browser as an .html file, just as if you were connected. The page will load instantly and you can continue your lesson without skipping a beat.

You have now been introduced to six new strategies for managing online classroom resources using your Internet browser program. Take some time to explore these with your colleagues and to exchange favorite websites that have been used successfully with other students. In the next section, we'll review important search tools and navigation strategies that help you make the best use of your time in gathering topical resources for your students.

Internet FAQ

I've heard that some Internet sites use "cookies" to collect information from users. What are cookies and how can I manage them?

Cookies are electronic requests for information from website administrators, which enable them to gather and record information about you from your computer whenever you visit their sites. Sometimes this information is used to direct you to locations you visit most often. Sometimes it's used for statistical purposes, such as determining how many people visit a site. Some users are concerned about cookies, but it's important to remember that occasionally they are useful tools that should not always be disabled. For example, when you enroll in an online course, a cookie enables the server to recognize you as a member of the course, immediately allow you in, and bring you right back to the place you left off during your last session. It should also be noted that some sites block access if cookies are disabled.

All three browsers allow you to manage cookies by setting preferences. Check out your system's options, and choose the level that meets your needs.

Here are the directions for Internet Explorer:

> On the Tools menu in Internet Explorer, select Internet Options. Select the Privacy tab and use the slider to choose the zone that you want to set the security level for. Move the slider up for a higher level of security or down for a lower level. Select "Apply" to register any changes.

Here are the directions for Netscape Navigator:

> Select Preferences under Edit in the menu bar. Click the arrow next to the category called Privacy and Security to reveal the contents of that folder and then select Cookies. Indicate the cookie settings you prefer and click OK.

Here are the directions for Safari:

> Select Preferences from Safari in the menu bar. Then select the Security tab in the window. Select the cookie setting you prefer by choosing among the three options.

Internet Search Tools and Navigation Strategies: Saving Time in Busy Classrooms

As the saying goes, the three most important things in Internet use are time, time, and time. We hear this concern expressed in several ways:

- How do I find the time to learn about the Internet?

- How do I find the time to teach the Internet in addition to everything else?
- How do I quickly locate good sites on the Internet?

The answer to the first question is one each of us must determine in our own way. Clearly, you are taking time out of your busy schedule to learn about the Internet as you read this book. It is important to recognize that we cannot possibly keep up with all the changes taking place by ourselves. We can handle the attempt more efficiently, however, if we organize our classrooms to take advantage of opportunities for each of us to learn from one another. By making Internet Workshop a part of your instructional program, you can help everyone in your class learn from one another. Often, our students will teach us as much about navigation as we will teach them. This is the one of the new realities of life with the Internet. In Chapter 3, we will show you how to use Internet Workshop along with several other strategies to help you learn together with your students.

We believe it is helpful to see these strategies from a teacher's perspective first, and then follow up with a discussion of how and why we need to modify Internet searching for students.

The second question is also important: How do I find the time to teach the Internet in addition to everything else? The answer to this is to be certain you make the Internet a resource, not a subject. The Internet is simply a tool that provides you and your students with information resources. It is no more and no less than a book, a library, an encyclopedia, or a video. The Internet should not become a permanent, separate subject for your students. Except for initial instruction at the beginning, the Internet should not require extra instructional time during the day. Even Internet Workshop should be seen as a time to learn about subject areas, not a time to focus exclusively on the Internet, especially after students develop beginning navigation skills.

The third question is important, too: How do I quickly locate good sites on the Internet? We need to learn to become efficient and more critical in finding useful and appropriate resources on the Internet. We also need to keep in mind that students and teachers often use search engines for very different purposes, and thus, the tools and strategies may be different as well. Teachers planning a unit on simple machines, for example, may search for lesson plans, quizzes, curriculum standards, and assessment measures. Students, on the other hand, would typically look for specific information written on a level they can understand about how simple machines work, what they look like, and how to use them. For this reason, in this chapter we have separated our discussion of search tools and strategies for teachers from those more appropriate for students. We believe it is helpful to see these strategies from a teacher's perspective first, and then follow up with a discussion of how and why we need to modify Internet searching to consider student issues such as child safety, acceptable use policies, and effective practices for students.

Powerful Search Tools and Strategies for Teachers

In this section, we will explore a series of search tools and strategies that can be useful as you strive to locate quality Internet resources to use in your classroom. We will first review strategies for locating information with central curriculum directories and search engines designed for teachers. Then, we will follow up with ideas for locating images and audio files on the Internet, a discussion of copyright issues, and a series of four keyword strategies that work best for locating educational resources on the web. Each of these is an important new literacy for working within Internet learning environments.

Locating Information with a Central Directory

As you begin your journey with the Internet, consider using a central directory. A central directory is a location with extensive and well-organized links about a content area or important subject. Some people may refer to these as "portals" since they are entryways to rich sources of information. Most are located at stable sites that will not quickly change. Most are non-commercial sites. As you explore the Internet, you will discover these well-organized treasure troves of information. They will become homes to which you will often return. We take this approach in this book. Each of the content area chapters will share the best central sites we have found. Set a bookmark or a "favorites" marker and begin your explorations at these central locations. This will save you much time and frustration until you develop effective strategies for using search engines. In fact, you could use only central sites and find almost everything you require for your class.

We have found the locations in Figure 2-8 to be some of the most useful and current central directory locations for different subject areas and interdisciplinary themes. You may wish to visit some of these now and set a bookmark (Favorites) for those you find useful. We will discuss most of these in more detail in upcoming chapters.

Figure 2-8. Central Directories on the Internet for Teaching and Learning.

Area	Central Directories
Teaching and Learning (general)	**ProTeacher—**http://www.proteacher.com/ **Education World**—http://www.education-world.com/
Science (general)	**Eisenhower National Clearance Center—** http://www.enc.org:80/ **Keystone Science Network—** http://www.keystone.fi.edu/index.shtml **Exploratorium**—http://www.exploratorium.com/
Math (general)	**Math Forum—**http://mathforum.org/ **The World of Math Online**—http://www.math.com/ **National Library of Virtual Manipulatives for Interactive Mathematics**—http://matti.usu.edu/nlvm/nav/vlibrary.html **Interactive Math Dictionary for Kids—** http://www.amathsdictionaryforkids.com/
Social Studies (general)	**American Memory—** http://memory.loc.gov/ammem/amhome.html **History/Social Studies for K-12 Teachers—** http://my.execpc.com/~dboals/boals.html **History Matters**—http://historymatters.gmu.edu/ **Library of Congress**—http://www.loc.gov/

cont.

English and Language Arts (all ages)	**Imaginary Lands**—http://www.imaginarylands.org/ **Web English Teacher**—http://www.webenglishteacher.com/ **The Literacy Web**—http://www.literacy.uconn.edu
ESL	**Activities for ESL Students**—http://a4esl.org/ **ESL Study Lab**— http://www.lclark.edu/~krauss/toppicks/toppicks.html
Multicultural Curriculum	**Cultures of the Worl**— http://www.ala.org/ala/alsc/greatwebsites greatwebsitescultures.htm **Multicultural Pavilion**— http://www.edchange.org/multicultural/ **Portals to the World**— http://www.loc.gov/rr/international/portals.html
Early Learning Curriculum	**Enchanted Learning**— http://www.enchantedlearning.com/Home.html
Special Education	**Family Village**— http://www.familyvillage.wisc.edu/index.htmlx
Interdisciplinary Curriculum	**42Explore**—http://www.42explore.com/index.htm **MarcoPolo Internet Content for the Classroom**— http://www.marcopolo-education.org/index.aspx

Locating Information with a Search Engine Designed for Adults

There are countless search engines on the Internet to help you find information you require. A search engine uses a computer program to sift through sites on the Internet and locate items containing the key word(s) you enter. Each search engine seems to have its own style, its own strengths, and its own weaknesses, but good search engines will search through the content on a webpage and not just the page title or keywords designated by the webpage designer. Each search engine has its own internal database of websites, although none search the entire Internet. Some search engines, such as **Yahoo**, provide both a search function (http://search.yahoo.com/web) for specific searches and a web directory (http://search.yahoo.com/dir) that organizes information hierarchically for more open-ended browsing. Other search engines, such as **Dogpile** (http://www.dogpile.com/) and **WebCrawler** (http://www.webcrawler.com/) are called meta-search engines because they compile the results from several search engines into one convenient, yet sometimes overwhelming list. You should become familiar with how each engine searches for information and displays the information it finds. As you use search engines, you will develop a favorite for your work. When this happens, be certain to set a bookmark so that you can return to this search engine whenever you require it.

You should become familiar with how each engine searches for information and displays the information it finds.

We have found that if you are looking for specific information quickly, the best search engine to try first is **Google** (http://www.google.com/). It has a database of over 3 billion webpages that very quickly scans websites and returns to you a list of relevant websites with a short annotation and a link to the webpage. The articles are listed in rank order, with those most popular and relevant at the top of the list. Usually, the list is more than one page, and Google serves up the rest of the list to you in sections. You can navigate to later sections by selecting the next page number in the sequence at the bottom of the search results. However, keep in mind that the goal is to find the most relevant information in the shortest amount of time. If you have not located anything in the first two pages, then it's time to quickly modify your search technique using different keywords. We'll talk more about effective keyword strategies in a moment.

Locating Images and Audio Files

In addition to locating textual information about a topic, many search engines are especially designed to help you locate images, sounds, video, or other types of media that can enhance a lesson you are teaching. You may have noticed that some search engines include a separate image search function. If you have your browser open to **Google** (http://www.google.com/), for example, you'll notice a toolbar of blue buttons directly above the search window. By default, Google searches the Internet for webpages that contain the words in your search term. If you type in the word Jupiter, for example, and click on the search button, you'll get a listing of many websites with information about the planet Jupiter. However, if you click on the second blue tab labeled Images, you'll be pleasantly rewarded with a listing of several images of the planet ranging from clip art to paintings to black and white line drawings.

Two other search engines that feature powerful tools for quickly locating images and other types of media are **Alta Vista** (http://www.altavista.com/) and **All the Web** (http://www.alltheweb.com/). Visit either of these and try typing in phrases such as "Gettysburg Address," "Hindenburg disaster," "Titanic," or "Shakespeare." By clicking on the different tabs for web, images, audio, or video using the same search term, you'll receive a multimedia assortment of resources to spark student interest and build background knowledge about important pieces of history and culture while appealing to various types of learning styles.

If you are searching specifically for specialty sounds or audio files to supplement your classroom multimedia presentations, you may want to explore the subject-specific categories of sounds available from the following audio directories:

- **FindSounds**—http://www.findsounds.com/
- **A1Free Sound Effects**—http://www.a1freesoundeffects.com/
  Click on the option for free sounds.
- **The History Channel's Historical Speeches**—
  http://www.historychannel.com/speeches/
- **Great American Speeches from PBS**—
  http://www.pbs.org/greatspeeches/timeline/

Using Copyrighted Information from the Internet

Of course, it is important to keep in mind that any or all of these images and media clips may be subject to copyright. When using any of these search engines, you can click on one particular image or audio clip to link to its original source. If you'd like to use this piece of media, even for educational reasons, be sure to closely read the terms for usage as you may need to seek permission from the webmaster of that particular website. If this is the case, you'll find a great permission template designed for teachers and students at David Warlick's **Landmarks for Schools** website (http://www.landmark-project.com/permission1.php). For a more comprehensive list of fair use policies for teachers, download the handy chart from **The Educator's Guide to Copyright and Fair Use** (http://www.techlearning.com/db_area/archives/TL/2002/10/copyright.html). As a general rule, it is good teaching practice to encourage students to seek permission when using information, images, or any other type of media found on the Internet.

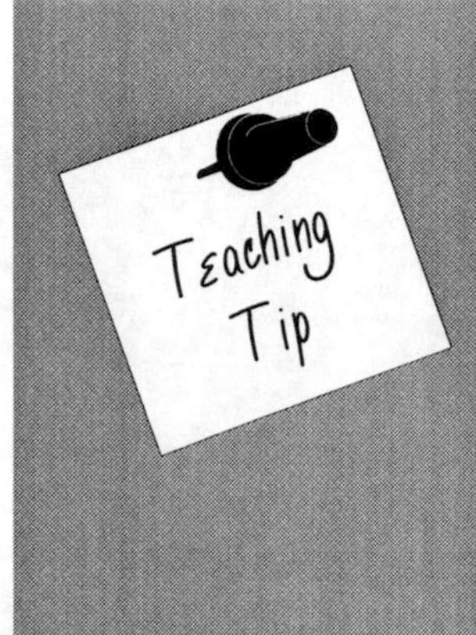

There is growing concern among educators about the increasing instances of student plagiarism and how to detect and deter it. Technology has made it particularly easy for students to locate essays written on just about any topic and copy portions of other people's writing into their own work. There are a number of resources available to help detect Internet plagiarism and others that provide helpful tips for students on how to avoid plagiarism. The easiest method for detecting text plagiarized from the Internet is to enter unique phrases from the paper in question into **Google** (http://www.google. com) to find out if others have used this same phrase. This costs you nothing and results in immediate links to other Internet sources containing this phrase. However, for a fee, you may also use one of several software products or online services to search more extensively. For a summary of these products as well as a 2001 report comparing the results of each service, you may explore the resources at **Downloading Detectives: Searching for On-Line Plagiarism** (http://www2.colorado college.edu/Library/Course/webplag2.html).

Several other resources provide a tremendous amount of information and instructional support in this area, including:

- **Avoiding and Detecting Web Plagiarism Thinkquest—** http://depts.washington.edu/trio/comp/howto/avoid/index.shtml
- **Helpful Tips for Older Students on How to Avoid Plagiarism—** http://www.usm.maine.edu/~kuzma/Ideologies/Plagerism.html
- **Turnitin Research Resources for Preventing Plagiarism—** http://www.turnitin.com/research_site/e_home.html
- **Strategies to Avoid Plagiarism by Bruce Leland—** http://www.wiu.edu/users/mfbhl/wiu/plagiarism.htm
- **Avoiding Plagiarism from the Purdue University Online Writing Lab—** http://owl.english.purdue.edu/handouts/research/r_plagiar.html
- **Issues and Articles for Instructors and Students about Plagiarism—**http://www.web-miner.com/plagiarism

Four Powerful Keyword Search Strategies for Teachers

In the previous section, we mentioned that teachers often use search engines to locate instructional resources such as lesson plans, quizzes, and assessment measures related to a certain topic they are studying. When using a powerful search engine like Google or Yahoo, we have found specific search term strategies that are most effective in helping to quickly locate these specific teaching materials. In this section, we will explore a sequence of four efficient searching strategies that should help you find what you are seeking very quickly. These strategies include:

1. Enclosing phrases with quotation marks.
2. Searching for particular phrases that teachers use.
3. Using a "topic plus keyword" strategy.
4. Using electronic spelling supports.

Why Keywords Are Not Enough: Using Quotation Marks

The first strategy is to perfect your use of certain keywords or phrases in the search window. Let us say that we are searching for information on simple machines for our fifth grade science unit. Using Google, we enter the phrase *simple machines* into our search window and press return. You will notice in the blue line across the top of the page that the search engine returned a list of 2,690,000 results! That is way too many to efficiently sift through to find what you're looking for! What is happening is that the search engine is reading each of the words in your search term as separate searches. This means that, first it locates webpages that have the word "simple" on them and then other webpages that have the word "machines" on them and still more webpages that have the words "simple" and "machines" on them, but not necessarily next to each other, and finally those webpages that have the phrase "simple machines." You will also notice that the search results include many links to college-level articles, advertisements about simple machines, and other resources not necessarily related to teaching students about simple machines. Recently, we have found that popular search engines like Google have become "smarter" and have begun to make inferences from searches without using quotation marks. However, since not all search engines work this way, these are still important strategies to learn. First we will deal with the issue of searching for phrases and then discuss how you can teach search engines to think like teachers.

Recently, we have found that popular search engines like Google have become "smarter" and have begun to make inferences from searches without using quotation marks.

The most effective way to force a search engine to search for a whole phrase and to not separate words is to enclose your search phrase in quotation marks. This works for two-word phrases as well as longer phrases such as the title of a book or the name of an historical event. If you return to your search window in Google and insert a quotation mark at either end of the phrase "simple machines" and then press Enter, you will see that already you have narrowed your list down from 2,690,000 to just 65,800 items . . . still too large to deal with, but a little more realistic. Try it with other phrases you commonly use and notice how quickly you can narrow down the number of items in your search result list.

Teaching Search Engines to Think Like Teachers: Using Keywords

The second step to remember is that a computerized search engine does not realize that there is a teacher sitting at the other end of the connection. In a traditional library setting, a teacher asks the school librarian to help set aside some books for a topic. Librarians typically ask you what grade you teach and then intelligently select books and other educational materials at your grade level. They sift out material that does not apply to classroom learning and make critical judgments about what is appropriate and what is not before setting aside the cart full of materials for your students to peruse. However, computerized search engines are not that smart! They do not readily infer who you are or what you want from them, unless you tell them. In this case, we need to "train" the search engine to think like a teacher and only return search results having to do with specific instructional needs. How do we do this? It's actually quite easy.

By combining keyword strategies with the use of the quotation mark strategy, we can quickly narrow the results of a search. You first need to decide what kinds of teaching materials you are searching for related to a certain topic. Are you looking, for instance, for lesson plans, a quiz, or maybe a simulation or online game? Let's return to our simple machine example again and try narrowing it down even further, remembering to use quotation marks around any phrase with two or more words.

- If we type "simple machine" and "lesson plan," we narrow our search to 2,140 results, and all of the first ten results are exactly what we want.
- If we type "simple machine" quiz, we narrow our search to 3,900. Twelve screens later, we are still finding *only* quizzes about simple machines!
- If we type "simple machine" simulation, we find 2,270 examples.
- If you want to narrow your search even further, try adding the grade level in quotation marks to search for "simple machine" + "lesson plans" + "fifth grade" to narrow your search to 82 lesson ideas for your fifth graders. That is certainly a far cry from the original 2,690,000 results, and you are almost guaranteed to find something useful in the first screen of 10 items! With this strategy, however, be careful to not always limit your search to a certain grade level because often you miss a wonderful resource that may have been developed by a teacher at another grade level which is very appropriate for your students as well.

Using The "Topic and Focus" Keyword Strategy

The third strategy in this search sequence is to narrow down a general thematic topic to focus on one particular aspect instead of pairing up a topic with a type of instructional resource. This is helpful if you are looking for background information about a certain topic you want to teach in class. If you wanted to locate information about the causes of the Civil War, you might use the search strand "Civil War" + causes, or if you wanted to find out more about the mummies of Ancient China, you might use the search strand "Ancient China" + mummies. When you do a search like this in Google, you'll notice the search results include each of the words you searched for in bold letters, so you can easily see how your list of results includes only those webpages with *both* search terms bolded. By beginning with a general topic and then narrowing down your search with a more specific term, you'll spend less time skimming through the list of search results and more time scanning relevant websites to locate the background information you need.

Using Electronic Spelling Supports

The final search strategy we'll discuss in this section builds upon a foundational literacy of being able to spell words correctly. The most common error when searching is misspelling a word. However, this strategy compensates for this mistake with a new literacies support feature found in many search engines. In Google, for example, when you search for a word you have spelled incorrectly or a phrase like "high school" that you mistakenly combined into the one word "highschool," the search engine will reply with the prompt *"Did you mean high school?"* spelled correctly.

Interestingly, many times after this prompt you will still get a list of search results of websites with the same misspelling of the word that you typed, but by clicking on the "Did you mean . . .?" prompt, you'll be linked to pages that include the correct spelling of the word. The new literacy, in this case, involves an awareness of this electronic support system and how it works so that you can use it to help you locate information as quickly as possible. Equipped with this understanding, you can use your best guess of a spelling in a search window, and chances are, the search engine will recognize what you are trying to spell and point you in the right direction.

Child Safety Issues on the Internet: Where to Begin

Now, you have mastered the art of locating quality resources for your students and you are ready for them to begin working on the Internet lessons you have prepared. When you make the decision to use the Internet with children in any type of setting, there are a number of important issues to consider and a number of different options for how you and your school district choose to deal with them. You can take steps to ensure your students' safety on the Internet by doing the following:

- Building awareness of the risks and benefits of Internet use.
- Developing and updating your school's Acceptable Use Policy.
- Using Internet filtering tools.
- Encouraging students to obtain an Internet Driver's License.
- Having students use the Back button when they feel uncomfortable.
- Using search engines designed for children.

Let's explore each of these in more depth.

E-MAIL FOR YOU

From: Maya Eagleton <meagleton@cast.org>
Subject: Selecting Keywords for Searching: TOPIC + FOCUS Strategy

So, you're all set with networked computers, Internet access, and tech-savvy students who are ready to take advantage of the Internet for authentic inquiry projects. What's that, you say? You've noticed that many of your students tend to select inefficient keywords for searching? Perhaps you've seen search engine keyword entries such as "sports" or "whales," or "Who is Bill Gates?" You realize you've got to do some instruction. Here is one strategy that we've found useful based on three years of intensive research with students in grades 6–9, many of whom have learning disabilities (Guinee, Eagleton, & Hall, 2004). We call it the "TOPIC + FOCUS" strategy. Here's how it works.

If there is a common broad research theme for your whole class, let's say, Sports, Animals, or Famous People, allow the students select a topic of high personal interest from within the theme, such as lacrosse, raptors, or Bill Gates. Now, for most research projects, these topics are still too broad to cover in a single semester, or even in a lifetime of doctoral study! Depending on the length of the project, we always direct our students to select one or two focus areas of interest within their topic, explaining that it's impossible to learn and report EVERYTHING about lacrosse, raptors, or Bill Gates in one project. We engage students in a process to identify what it is that they already know about the topic as well as what they really want to know. Research questions are brainstormed, categorized, regrouped, and so on until one or two focus areas rise to the top, those that are of burning interest to the student. The beauty of this method is that more often than not, these focus areas can be instantly transformed into keywords for searching. Here's a wonderful example:

Kevin was interested in lacrosse, but he didn't have very much background knowledge on the topic. After some initial Internet searching using the topic keyword "lacrosse," he quickly found that there are tons of websites about lacrosse! In fact, there were too many! Because he struggled with reading, he used a screen reader program (the *CAST eReader*, available at http://www.cast.org/) with headphones to have portions of a few promising websites read aloud to him. Immediately he learned that lacrosse has a fascinating history, starting with the Native Americans in the Northern U.S. and Canada. He selected "history" as his focus, and used the keywords <lacrosse + history> for the remainder of his inquiry. This brought him directly to websites that covered the history of lacrosse, and eliminated others that would have required wading through mountains of text that were not relevant to his focus.

In the past three years, over 300 adolescents have used the TOPIC + FOCUS strategy with great success. You might want to check out Eagleton & Guinee (2002) or Eagleton, Guinee, & Langlais (2003) for more practical tips about this keyword method, as well as ideas for Internet Scavenger Hunts and authentic Internet inquiry projects. Happy searching!
Warm Regards,

Maya B. Eagleton, PhD
Senior Research Scientist, Center for Applied Special Technology (CAST)
http://myWeb pages.comcast.net/meagleton
Former K-12 Reading Specialist, Title I Coordinator, & Reading Recovery Teacher

Building Awareness of the Risks and Benefits of Internet Use

Being aware of the risks and benefits associated with the Internet is the first step toward successful Internet use. Parents, teachers, and members of your school community need to work together to teach children how to recognize quality online resources as well as how to recognize certain danger signs when using the Internet. We need to provide opportunities for students to safely explore age-appropriate resources while teaching them how to interact responsibly with the many new electronic tools that are evolving in online environments. A number of excellent websites have been developed to support you in this venture. **GetNetWise** (http://www.getnetwise.org/) and **The Educator's Guide to Computer Crime and Technology Misuse** (http://lrs.ed.uiuc.edu/wp/crime-2002/computer crime.htm) may help you make informed decisions about online safety, privacy and security issues. **Netsmartz** (http://www.netsmartz.org) and **CyberCitizenship** (http://www.cybercitizenship.org/index.html) were both designed to teach children and young adults how to stay safe while using the Internet. For a more global perspective, **SaferInternet** (http://www.saferinternet.org/index.asp) outlines safer Internet developments and policies for children within European countries and elsewhere. Be sure to carefully explore and share these resources with your older students and parents of all your students at the beginning of each school year.

Being aware of the risks and benefits associated with the Internet is the first step toward successful Internet use.

Developing and Updating your School's Acceptable Use Policy

Whether your system uses a software filter or not, it is important for your district to develop an acceptable use policy as part of a comprehensive program of Internet navigation. An acceptable use policy is a written agreement signed by parents/guardians, students, and teachers that specifies the conditions under which students may use the Internet, defines appropriate and unacceptable use, and defines penalties for violating items in the policy. All parties need to be aware of the consequences for misusing the privilege of Internet access. Developing an acceptable use policy and then asking all parties to sign it helps to ensure that everyone understands these important issues. Making sure to update and revise your acceptable use policy before the beginning of each school year helps to ensure that you are prepared for new issues that may arise as new tools and opportunities emerge.

What does an acceptable use policy look like? Most contain the following elements: an explanation of the Internet and its role in providing information resources to students; a description of acceptable and unacceptable behavior that emphasizes student responsibility when using the Internet; a description of policies for the proper use of student names and photographs; a list of penalties for each violation of the policy, and a space for all parties to sign the agreement.

You may find out more information, print out sample acceptable use policies, and read about other teachers' experiences by visiting the following Internet sites:

- **Acceptable Use Policies: A Handbook from Virginia Dept. of Education—** http://www.pen.k12.va.us/go/VDOE/Technology/AUP/home.shtml
- **Houston Independent School District's Acceptable Use Page—** http://chico.rice.edu/armadillo/acceptable.html
- **Child Safety on the Information Highway—** http://www.safekids.com/index.html

Some special issues to consider when developing elements of an acceptable use policy for your students include: how to properly use student names and pictures on your website, how much information to divulge in online settings, and how to manage commercial cookies that may be invading an individual's privacy while searching online. Each school community has its own feelings about these issues and different schools handle them in different ways, but the important point is to be sure that everyone is aware of whatever policies are ultimately put into place.

With regard to the first issue, some schools recommend, when referring to students on a webpage, that either their names not be used or only their first names be posted. Others choose to post student work that includes their pictures with no names, but only after teachers get written permission from parents before posting. Still others have opted to use photographs of student work paired with portrait drawings of student's faces so that their real faces are not seen.

Your browser can be set up to not accept any cookies or to notify you when a cookie is required, or students can be instructed to not accept certain cookies without your permission.

With respect to developing guidelines that help students know how much information to divulge on the Internet, you can refer to the tips and tools available from **How Can I Protect My Privacy?** (http://privacy.getnetwise.org/) from **GetNetWise**. The resources here may help your district set new policies in terms of how much personal information students share with online stores, websites, emailers, and chat room members. Similar decisions need to be made when considering policies for managing commercial cookies. Your browser can be set up to not accept any cookies or to notify you when a cookie is required, or students can be instructed not to accept certain cookies without your permission. You can find more information about this in the Internet FAQ about Managing Cookies earlier in this chapter.

Using Internet Filtering Tools

Because the Internet is so powerful, it has the potential for accomplishing wonderful things in the classroom. At the same time, however, this power may be abused. Students may travel to sites that are inappropriate for them to view, send out an offensive email message, or interfere with the running of a computer system. This has led to concerns about child safety. These issues have been profoundly shaped by The Children's Internet Protection Act of 2003. This federal legislation requires each school district in the United States to install an Internet filter in order to receive federal funds. This has helped protect children but has also impeded classroom integration of the Internet in a subtle, but profoundly influential manner.

Here is what happens all too frequently. It is a cautionary tale for us all. A district spends substantial money and energy on professional development in the area of Internet integration, getting teachers excited about the many wonderful possibilities that are now available. Teachers, especially the most dedicated ones, then spend an evening at home checking out Internet resources and planning an exciting lesson for the next day. When they arrive at school, however, several sites they had planned to use in their lesson are blocked by their school district's Internet filter, often for a gratuitous reason. A resource developed by students in the Middlesex School District in Massachusetts, for example, may be blocked simply because of the three-letter ending of the district's name. Other sites are blocked for equally innocuous reasons. As a result, teachers who spent their evening developing a lesson plan are suddenly unable to use the lesson they had developed and have to quickly improvise something else. After one or two frustrating experiences like this, many teachers will stop using the Internet in their classrooms and often the district does not even know why. As a result, their investment in professional development is largely wasted. This is an increasingly serious problem as many districts have been forced to quickly set up a filter system, without being able to take the time to anticipate unintended consequences.

Smart districts, not wanting to waste the effects of their professional development, establish a "Twenty Minute Rule."

Fortunately, filters can be easily overridden or modified by the person responsible for their use. A blocked resource can be made available simply by entering its URL into the system and indicating that this site should be allowed to pass through the filter. Smart districts, not wanting to waste the effects of their professional development, establish a "Twenty Minute Rule." They guarantee every teacher a rapid review, for child safety and appropriateness, of any blocked site that is necessary for a lesson. If a site passes this review, the URL is quickly entered into the system and the site is unblocked within twenty minutes. Teachers need only email any blocked site to the individual appointed by the district to manage the filter for the district. This system is being used in districts that understand the hidden costs that Internet filters place on the classroom integration of the Internet.

Despite intensive efforts, it is impossible to completely protect children from viewing inappropriate sites. Thus, in the long run, it is best to educate children, parents and guardians, and teachers about how to use the Internet safely. This includes developing an acceptable use policy; implement a "Twenty Minute Rule," and supervising student use of the Internet. This is our best insurance for dealing with all child safety issues.

Sometimes parents will come to you for recommendations about filtering software to use at home. There are, of course, many different solutions. You may wish to point parents to the **Tools for Families Database** created by **GetNetWise** (http://www.getnetwise.org/tools/). This very comprehensive database gives you a complete description of each tool, and categorizes its features by those that filter sites, set time limits, or block outgoing content. The database also links you to the homepage for each software tool so that you can download free evaluation copies. Two of the most popular filtering tools include **Cyber Patrol** (http://www.cyberpatrol.com) and **Net Nanny** (http://www.netnanny.com).

Encouraging Students to Earn an Internet Driver's License

One of the most engaging ways to actively involve students in developing their own awareness of important Internet issues is to have them earn an Internet Driver's License before they are allowed to use the Internet without an adult. Students of any age can be introduced to the nature of information on the Internet while learning strategies for safe and appropriate use. Online interactive quizzes present students with various situations in which students make choices about which response is the most ethical, appropriate, and safe. Once each student has answered all the questions correctly, you can print up a student license for each to wear. Young children love to wear a laminated license around their neck. Some prefer to place it next to the computer as a reminder of the rules they agreed to follow when they visit the computer center. Licenses for older students can be worked into the Acceptable Use Policy Contract that they sign before using the Internet without an adult. You may also encourage students to explain the rules of the road to their parents by revisiting an online tutorial at home with other family members to see who knows the rules the best. Explore the following websites to find one most appropriate for your students to visit at school or at home with their parents:

You may also encourage students to explain the rules of the road to their parents by revisiting an online tutorial at home with other family members.

- **PBS Kid's Web License for Young Children**— http://pbskids.org/bts/license/
- **Yahooligans' Savvy Surfing Quiz**— http://www.yahooligans.com/parents/kids/quiz.html
- **Safe Surfin' Driver's Ed Challenge for Kids and Teens**— http://www.safesurfin.com/drive_ed.htm
- **Texas Information Literacy Tutorial (TILT)**— http://tilt.lib.utsystem.edu/
- **Internet Safety Tutorial for Families**— http://familyinternet.about.com/library/safety/blsafety1.htm

Using the Back Button when Students Feel Uncomfortable

One of the most effective Internet safety strategies to implement in classrooms with students of any age, but particularly younger students, is also one of the easiest. When we talk with teachers about what to tell students who inadvertently come across a picture that surprises them or information that seems a little out of the ordinary, many of them quickly share a similar policy that helps keep young children away from trouble. This policy basically states if there is ever a time when you come to anything on the Internet that makes you feel even a tiny bit uncomfortable, the rule is, "Press the back button immediately and tell an adult." This way, you are quickly alerted to any inappropriate situations and you can quickly provide support for a child who has come across information that makes him/her nervous or uncomfortable. This simple rule is easy enough for even the youngest child to understand and apply. It also helps you enforce any policies you may have in place for students who willfully access inappropriate websites on the Internet.

Using Search Engines Designed for Students

Earlier in this chapter, we described a number of helpful search engines for locating interesting content-related websites, multimedia, and useful background information for teachers. However, given the context of the child safety issues that arise when searching on the Internet, a number of exceptional search engines have been designed with the needs and interest of a younger audience in mind. Here, we explore four popular search engines as well as several subject directories and web portals developed especially for students.

The most popular search engine used in many elementary and middle schools is probably **Yahooligans** (http://www.yahooligans.com/). Designed for children ages 7–12, it features a powerful search tool, a comprehensive directory of topics for browsing, and links to popular categories for children ranging from games and animals to news and music. Students can also "Ask Earl," the resident expert, new questions or search the archives of questions that others have asked. This search engine also features a daily survey, joke of the day, and links to a valuable Yahooligans Teacher's Guide and Parent's Guide for safe surfing and Internet literacy.

KidsClick (http://www.kidsclick.org/), a lesser-known search engine, was created by a group of librarians and organizes their handpicked index of 5,000+ websites into more than 600 thematic categories that are organized alphabetically or hidden within the Dewey Decimal System (try the link at the bottom of the page to see what the page looks like through a librarian's eyes). One of the most helpful features of this search engine is that the search results let you know the approximate reading level of each resource as well as whether or not the website contains illustrations. This database of websites is smaller than most search engines, so students will not be overwhelmed by too many search results. It also features one of the best sets of kid-friendly searching tools to help students quickly locate appropriate pictures and sounds from the Internet using a unique collection of general collections and special databases all accessible from one screen. Just click on the link for "Picture Search Tools" or "Sound Search Tools" at the very top of the KidsClick homepage. Be sure to bookmark this set of tools in your Favorites folder!

Ask Jeeves for Kids (http://www.ajkids.com/) is another popular search engine for younger children. It uses a natural-language technology that allows kids to ask questions directly in the search window box instead of using the keyword strategy. This is helpful for younger students, but we have noticed that this process can also confuse older students who may use search engines that work better with keyword searches. The interface for the search results includes pull-down menus to narrow down a search, which is again a different process than other search engines. Instruction for using this search engine should call attention to these differences to avoid confusion when students move between various search engine formats.

TekMom's Search Tools for Students (http://tekmom.com/search/index.html) is a lesser-known search tool, but quite impressive nonetheless. This resource links you to all three of our favorite children's search engines mentioned above as well as to several other subject specific search engines and a helpful reference of examples of how to cite online resources—all from one main webpage. This would be a great website to set as your browser start-up page.

Informational directories are designed to support student investigations into subject-specific areas or aid them in a hunt for help with homework assignments.

Informational directories for students are very much like the central directories that are available to help teachers hone in on a central curriculum area. They are designed to support student investigations into subject-specific areas or aid them in a hunt for help with homework assignments. Often, these directories are designed to suit the needs of particular age groups. We've found it helpful to categorize these resources into those most appropriate for students in Grades K–8 and those for older students in Grades 6–12. Examples of informational directories for students appear in Figure 2-9. Each of these provides an incredible amount of information for students and can serve as a springboard for further Internet exploration. You may want to introduce a new directory to your students at the beginning of each month in the fall by setting each as your browser startup page. After students have practiced using the different directories, you can use Internet Workshop to discuss the benefits of each or to compare the strategies that work best with informational directories with those that are most efficient in more open-ended children's search engines.

Figure 2-9. Informational Directories for Students

Grades K-8	Grades 6-12
Enchanted Learning— http://www.enchantedlearning.com/Home.html **Kids Konnect—** http://www.kidskonnect.com/ **InfoPlease Fact Monster—** http://www.factmonster.com/ **Great Sites from American Library Association—** http://www.ala.org/parentspage/greatsites/	**High School Hub—** http://highschoolhub.org/hub/hub.cfm **Teen Space at the Internet Public Library**—http://www.ipl.org/div/teen/ **The Homework Spot—** http://www.homeworkspot.com/ **Student Navigator for New York Times—** http://www.nytimes.com/learning/general/ navigator/students.html

Instructional Strategies for Developing Student Navigation Skills

Learning how to efficiently and strategically navigate on the Internet is one of the most crucial aspects of instruction for our students. Finding reliable information quickly and then using it appropriately will be central to their future learning success. As we seek to define effective instructional strategies for keeping up with the changing literacies of the Internet, we have found it helpful to recognize that navigating on the Internet is a complex process of three inter-related elements: meaning-making, efficiency, and technical skill.

In Chapter 1, we discussed the overlap of these three elements when reading on the Internet. Each process takes on new and more complex meaning in the context of the other two. On the Internet, traditional text is intertwined with the use of hyperlinks, animated images, scroll bars, and web editors; as a result, making sense of what one reads on the Internet is a much more dynamic process than reading static text. By their very nature, Internet comprehension skills such as inferring the contents behind a hyperlink, inferring the stance of the author and how that shapes the message, and synthesizing information from multiple sources require readers to navigate through various locations while integrating technical skills with higher-level thinking.

Efficient navigating as a process is also complex in new ways. Good navigators on the Internet do more than simply locate the links that will quickly get them from one webpage to another or easily maneuver between multiple windows. They also quickly make inferences, actively make choices, and focus on relevant details while ignoring irrelevant information, all of which combine elements of meaning-making and technical know-how.

Third, any student who is successful at learning on the Internet understands the technical basics of navigating multiple new technologies such as browser tabs and toolbars, threaded discussion boards, and Flash animated menus. More importantly, though, students also need to appreciate the nuances of electronic tools and understand when each is useful and efficient and when it is not.

When designing instruction, then, it is important to recognize that each of these three elements is interconnected, as are many of the other elements required to become proficient in the new literacies of the Internet. Thus, we need to move away from models in which reading teachers see their role as only teaching reading comprehension, content area teachers view their role as only delivering content knowledge, and library media specialists see their role as only teaching search strategies. Students use all of these skills together when interacting within Internet environments and it is imperative that we provide authentic, integrated models and instruction in all three processes within each of our content and specialty areas.

Teachers like Joe Montero realize the complexity of the new literacies for students who are reading, thinking, and learning on the Internet. Joe thoughtfully integrated his new content with some of these new strategies and used the Internet Workshop model to frame time for small group guided discussion, exploration, and sharing. He recognized that some students had more technical expertise than he did in terms of using browsers and multimedia tools, and that technical skills were often acquired informally amidst the social exchanges that took place while completing higher-level learning tasks. He also noticed that very few students took the time to critically examine the reliability of information, recognize new informational text features, or thoughtfully consider the many options available within search engines. He planned meaningful lessons that introduced these new skills and held students accountable for their work in small group activities. There is much we can learn from this episode with Joe as we consider two pressing questions that we often hear from teachers in this area:

- How do I organize instructional time in my classroom to most effectively introduce navigational strategies into my curriculum?
- Are there instructional strategies that foster both navigational efficiency and a deeper understanding of the information presented?

Organizing Instructional Time to Include Navigational Strategies

Setting up a classroom routine for integrating navigational strategies into your regular schedule may initially seem like an overwhelming task. However, by devising a plan that considers central learning objectives, student grouping options, assessment alternatives, and other management issues, you'll be off to a much easier start. If you have only a single computer linked to the Internet, you may begin each week with short, small-group instruction at the computer on an important navigational strategy such as one of the following:

- Comparing and contrasting features of various search engines while searching for a specific piece of information.
- Using directories.
- Selecting helpful keyword combinations.
- Using graphic elements from the Internet in your writing projects.
- Understanding the meaning of addresses on the Internet.
- Helping others effectively.
- Validating information found on a webpage.
- Staying focused.
- Understanding the organizational structure of a particular website.

During this time, show five to six students a new aspect of navigating the Internet. Introduce the strategy, show students why it is useful and when it might be used, and then give one or more students an opportunity to practice it while others watch. As you move through the year, you may wish to turn this responsibility over to the groups themselves. Each week, make a different group responsible for teaching the other groups a new skill they have discovered recently.

Seldom do two students know the same navigation strategies for using the Internet. When students work together, they exchange information and teach each other navigation skills.

During the week, students can integrate the new strategy as they complete content work in one of their subject areas or on a thematic unit. Recall that Joe Montero used Internet Workshop to give students time to locate useful and distracting features of informational text as they explored space-related websites. Keep in mind also, that while some schools may have sufficient computer resources to allow students to work alone on the Internet during the week, it is often preferable to have students work together in pairs since this provides more teaching/learning opportunities. Seldom do two students know the same navigation strategies for using the Internet. When students work together, they exchange information and teach each other navigation skills. Rotating partners each week or so ensures that all students have a chance to learn from every other student in the class. This increases opportunities for sharing information about navigation strategies. An Internet Workshop at the end of each week will help consolidate the navigation strategies you introduced at the beginning of the week and serve as a type of performance-based assessment. It will also raise new navigation issues that you may then explore in subsequent weeks, again in small groups at the beginning of the week, in pairs during the week, and with the whole class at the end of the week.

It is important to note that time used to develop Internet strategies need not be great. Small group sessions at the beginning of the week should take no more than 5–10 minutes. The learning that takes place as students work in pairs occurs during regular content learning experiences. Finally, Internet Workshops need not take more than 15–20 minutes as you share navigational experiences and raise questions that came up during the week. You will find that time devoted to developing navigation skills at the beginning of the year pays rich dividends as your students develop confidence and expertise at efficiently navigating the Internet on their own.

As your students become more experienced on the Internet, you should think about modifying this initial structure for developing navigation knowledge. Spend a little time observing students working together on the Internet, looking for those students who have not acquired some of the navigational strategies you have discussed previously or who may be struggling with foundational reading skills as they move through informational websites. Then, gather these students together in small group sessions at the beginning of each week according to the strategies they need to refine. One group may need additional assistance on selecting useful keywords while a second group may need additional assistance on figuring out where to look on a website to learn more about its creator. This additional small group work ensures that all of your students develop the essential skills of navigation and Internet comprehension. During this time, students may continue to work in pairs on classroom assignments, helping one another. Within a short period of time your students will demonstrate amazing amounts of insight into useful navigational strategies. When this happens, new strategies may be successfully handled during content projects using Internet Workshop, with the entire class sharing ideas they have discovered.

As students develop the ability to navigate on their own, you will find yourself devoting less time to this area and more time on content projects.

As students develop the ability to navigate on their own, you will find yourself devoting less time to this area and more time to content projects. Questions during Internet Workshop, for example, will gradually and naturally move from basic technical issues to higher-level discussions about the reliability of information, the organizational structure of websites, and more efficient ways of locating relevant information with search engines. As you move through the year, you will find less and less time devoted to navigation and more and more time devoted to critically evaluating and creatively responding to information students have discovered on the Internet.

There are wonderful collections of educational games and interactive activities available for times when kids need a break from hard work or when you have some extra time at the end of the day. Many include craft ideas, online board games, puzzles, and fun printables. You can set these up in a center or even use them with one computer and a projector to play a game with the whole class. Be sure to bookmark and organize some of the following in an "Internet Recess" folder in your browser:

- **Bonus.com**—http://www.bonus.com/
- **CBC Kids.net**—http://www.cbc.ca/kids/games/
- **FunBrain**—http://www.funbrain.com/
- **Kaboose**—http://www.kaboose.com/index.html
- **MaMaMedia**—http://www.mamamedia.com/home.html

Instructional Strategies that Enhance Navigational Efficiency and Critical Thinking

After organizing your classroom schedule to gradually integrate navigational instruction into your curriculum, it's important to decide which strategies will elicit the greatest success for your students. In this next section, we will look more closely at seven strategies that increase navigational efficiency while also enhancing critical thinking and content area understanding. For each, we will point you to important online resources that can support your attempts to weave elements of navigation, comprehension, and technical skill into your Internet lessons. Since students are often assigned content-area research tasks when they use the Internet, we have sequenced these seven strategies in a natural progression that loosely parallels the research process, as well as the elements of the new literacies framework: namely, forming good questions, locating relevant information, and evaluating and synthesizing the information from multiple sources. The specific navigational strategies include:

- Understanding searching versus browsing.
- Selecting keywords and appropriate alternatives.
- Making sense of search results.
- Understanding URLs.
- Reading with a critical eye.
- Reading within a website.
- Recognizing and managing advertisements.

We believe that this progression will help you more naturally integrate these navigational strategies into your content-area instruction and the research process.

We have found students to be more efficient at finding what they need when they understand the differences between the searching tools and browsing tools provided within one search engine.

Understanding Searching versus Browsing

When students first start out using search engines or directories designed for children, they do not yet need to use the more complicated search strings we described earlier for use in search engines such as **Google** (http://www.google.com). Most children's search engines work well when students simply type in the topic they are looking for. However, we have found students to be more efficient at finding what they need when they understand the differences between the searching tools and browsing tools provided within one search engine. **Yahooligans**, (http://www.yahooligans.com) for example, as seen in Figure 2-10, provides a list of popular topics to browse down the left-hand column of the window, a more comprehensive directory of categories and subtopics at the bottom of the window, and a search pane in the middle of the window. Interestingly, all the links may eventually bring you to the same place (which some students don't realize), but not all paths are equally efficient.

How can we teach students about these differences? A good place to start is to have them discuss times in their daily lives when they have searched for something they have lost as compared to just browsing in a store. Once students understand that searching is more directed and purposeful, while browsing is more relaxed and often gets you sidetracked, it will be easier to relate these ideas to the use of the Internet. A short lesson such as the following, which illustrates how each tool works and when to use it, should make this point clear.

Figure 2-10. Three different searching processes within the Yahooligans Web Guide (http://www.yahooligans.com). Students can browse through topics using the category boxes in the left margin or the directory listing toward the bottom or use the search function by typing keywords into the search box in the center of the screen.

With a little experience, students will quickly realize that each search engine or directory has it's own unique organization and special features.

Let's say you have a particular research topic in mind, such as *Siberian tiger* or *pilot whale.* By typing one of these phrases into the Yahooligans *search* window, the search engine will quickly provide many relevant resources about this particular animal. However, if you want to explore a little more generally about animals, clicking on the smaller "animals" category button on the left margin will enable you to *browse* through a series of animal guides. Finally, if you want to casually *browse* the entire Yahooligans collection of animal resources, you can do so by selecting the subtopic "animals" below the Science and Nature Directory at the bottom. If you'd like more information about these types of searching and browsing strategies, the **Yahooligans Teacher's Guide** (http://www.yahooligans.com/tg/search.html) is an excellent resource.

With a little experience, students will quickly realize that each search engine or topical directory has it's own unique organization and special features. An Internet Workshop session can provide opportunities for students to explore different directories listed earlier in this chapter in search of these special features. At the end of the week, they can share what they've learned with others while building their repertoire of navigational strategies. In time, students will begin to appreciate the nuances of different searching tools while continuing to critically compare and evaluate the purpose and process behind each new Internet tool they discover.

Selecting Keywords and Appropriate Alternatives

Another area of potential difficulty for students is being able to select appropriate key words or key phrases for their search. Here, we clearly see the overlap between technical navigation success and reading comprehension. In our work with students, we have found that some initially struggle to select the best word from a research question that will help guide their search. Technically, they are able to randomly select words and type them into the appropriate search box, yet their searches are highly inefficient when compared with those of students who carefully consider which words will be most helpful in quickly locating particular types of information. **AskJeeves for Kids** (http://www.ajkids.com), for example, which enables users to type their entire question into the search window, assists students who may have difficulty generating keywords. However, we have found that the interface may also confuse students transitioning back and forth between search engines, since this "whole sentence search strategy" is not always as successful in other search engines. Ultimately, efficient location of information on the Internet requires students to move beyond using pull-down menus to choose from pre-selected categories, to being able to hone in on identifying important words or phrases in a research question.

Students should also practice strategies for generating synonyms or other related alternatives for an important keyword that produces no results. Presented with a task to investigate current alternatives to storing garbage in a dump, for example, students may find little information using the keyword "garbage." However, after a short partner activity to generate a list of synonyms for garbage, students have much more success searching with keywords such as "waste" and "trash."

Strategy lessons such as these can be introduced to elementary and middle school students using ideas from a wonderful resource known as KidsClick's **Worlds of Web Searching** (http://www.rcls.org/wows/). This series of nine tutorials walks students through several basic skills for successful searching using children's search engines and directories, sorted subject guides, and important keyword strategies.

Making Sense of Search Results

A third area that combines navigational skills with comprehension strategies relates to reading and understanding the search results reported back from various search engines. Look closely at Figures 2-11 to 2-14 to examine the search results from the phrase *solar system* using four popular search engines. Clearly, each search engine reports its findings in a very different manner, and each demands new strategies for making sense of them. Yahooligans (Figure 2-11) sorts search results in a three-tiered format that parallels their database of special "inside features," groups of websites sorted by categories and listings of individual websites. KidsClick (Figure 2-12) sorts results in one alphabetical list with longer annotations that describe the creator of the website. KidsClick also includes a coding system to identify sites with many illustrations and appropriate reading levels. AskJeeves for Kids (Figure 2-13) returns a simple keyword search with an interface of pull-down menus and a list of more specific questions for students to answer. And finally, older students using Google (Figure 2-14) are presented with additional coding categories, incomplete annotations ending in ellipses, special indented formats, and sometimes tangential links to a commercial sponsor.

Often, there is very little instruction to support students in these new expository text environments. Although some learners will quickly understand how to interact with these new and varying text features, many will need new strategies for making sense of the unique patterns of information display, layout, and advertising within each new list of search results.

Many students will need new strategies for making sense of the unique patterns of information display, layout, and advertising within each new list of search results.

We have found that the most efficient students are those who are able to quickly scan long lists of annotated results with a critical eye on these important features.

Figure 2-11. Search Results for *solar system* using Yahooligans (http://www.yahooligans.com).

Figure 2-12. Search Results for *solar system* using KidsClick (http://www.kidsclick.org/).

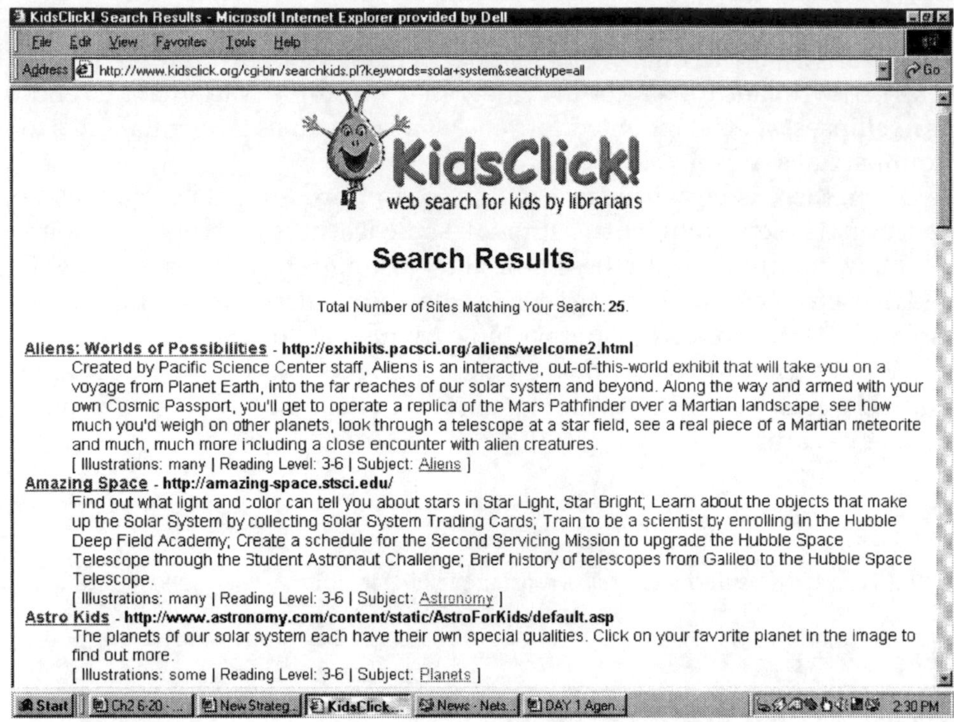

Figure 2-13. Search results for the phrase *solar system* using AskJeeves for Kids (http://www.ajkids.com).

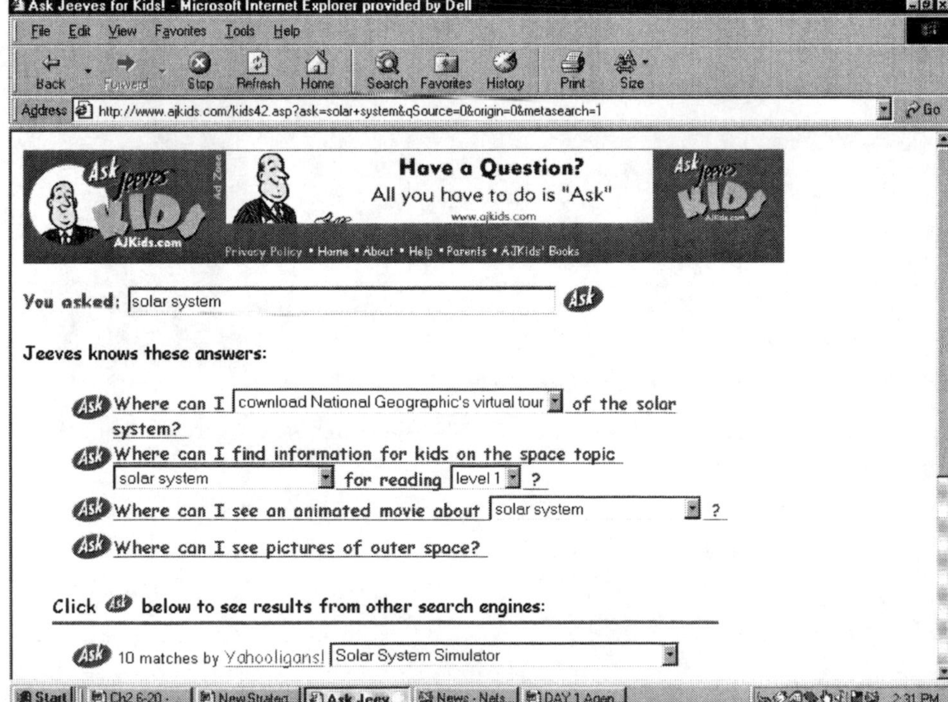

Figure 2-14. Search results for the search term *"solar system"* using Google (http://www.google.com). Notice the ellipses used in the passages after each search result.

Understanding URLs

Another important strategy that weaves elements of navigational efficiency with critical reading comprehension focuses students' attention on the value of understanding the various parts of a website's address. While scanning through a list of search results, for example, there are several context clues that can aid a learner's search for the most relevant and appropriate links. In addition to the descriptors that follow each underlined link, most search engines also list the website's address or "Uniform Resource Locator" (URL). Look carefully again at Figures 2-11 through 2-14 to locate where each search engine identifies a websites' URL in its list of search results. Understanding the parts of this URL can help students make inferences about the credibility of the website's author and may also help locate a page when the link has changed.

Students should have practice breaking down the URL of a particular website. Let's say for example, that during a Google search for help with a math problem they needed to solve, they come across an annotated result for a tool called **WebMath** with the following URL: http://school.discovery.com/homeworkhelp/webmath/. By breaking down the parts of the URL into each section divided by slash marks, much like breaking down a word into syllables, students can learn some interesting pieces of information.

http://—This command tells the browser it is a hypertext document.

.school.discovery—This part indicates the name of the machine or organization that hosts the website; in this case, students may recognize Discovery School as a credible source from a previous science lesson they did with their teacher.

.com—This domain name, .com, indicates a commercial domain.

/homeworkhelp—This is the name of the folder on the Discovery School server.

/webmath—This is the name of a folder inside the "homeworkhelp" folder.

Each backslash and additional folder that may follow this series indicates a path to a folder within that folder. To get a better idea of the types of websites that represent each of the various domains, you may wish to refer your students to the **Understanding URL's Help Sheet** (http://www.clpgh.org/locations/pccenter/helpsheets/urls.html).

Understanding a domain name can provide the first step in determining the credibility of the information found within. In the example above, students have seen other quality resources from Discovery School's website, so they can initially trust that clicking on this link will point them toward a credible resource.

There are at least two other reasons to understand the remaining path of a URL. First, while searching, you'll often come across a webpage that is not the homepage of the site, but rather is stored in a folder several layers down from the homepage. Occasionally, you may notice a tilde (~) in front of a folder's name that indicates you are in a personal subdirectory of webpages hosted on the main computer. By truncating the end of any URL to leave just the domain name, in this case "http://school.discovery.com," you can then explore the homepage for information about the author, the organization's purpose, or get a general overview of the resources available from that website. If none of this is available from the website, this may be a warning sign to question the reliability of information you find.

Making sense of the path of folders in an Internet address can also help with trouble-shooting when you have difficulty accessing a website.

Making sense of the path of folders in an Internet address can also help with troubleshooting when you have difficulty accessing a website. Very often, schools and organizations restructure their websites as they grow larger and move files from one folder to another. When this happens, a website's URL also changes. For example, let's say that Discovery School moved its online math tools to another section of its website. Again, by returning to the **Discovery School homepage** (http://www.school.discovery.com), you can scan the links or do a search for the new location of homework resources or the Webmath tool. Armed with these new strategies for understanding Internet URLs, students can make intelligent and time-saving inferences about what to expect after clicking a certain link and where to find a website whose address may have changed.

Reading with a Critical Eye

Internet technologies raise new issues about our relationship to information. As students scan search results and select particular websites to examine more closely, they'll need strategies for efficiently evaluating the credibility and usefulness of the information they find. In a world where anyone may publish anything, how does one evaluate the accuracy of information one finds? In a world where new juxtapositions of multiple media forms may be created, how do we help children critically evaluate the variety of meanings inherent in the multiple media forms in which messages appear? Clearly, what has traditionally been referred to as critical reading or critical thinking assumes greater importance and new meaning with the introduction of Internet technologies into the classroom.

Open networks, such as the Internet, permit anyone to publish anything; this is one of the opportunities that technology presents. It is also one of its limitations. Information is much more widely available from people who have strong political, economic, religious, or ideological stances that profoundly influence the nature of the information they present to others. As a result, we must assist students in becoming more critical consumers of the information they encounter. They must be skilled at comparing and contrasting the information they find from multiple websites to decide if the information represents two sides of a controversial issue, for example, or rather, that one author is attempting to mislead them with inaccurate information. Such skills have not always been seen as important in classrooms where textbooks and other traditional information resources are often assumed to be correct.

How do we do this? What skills become important when evaluating information on the Internet? We find that helping students to think about five questions provides new, and more critical, insights into the meaning of information at a webpage: Who? What? When? Where? Why? and How?

We must assist students to become more critical consumers of the information they encounter.

- *Who created the information at this site?*
    - o Can you determine the person or the unit that created this site?
    - o What is the background of the creator?
    - o Is this a commercial (.com), organizational (.org), or an educational (.edu) location?
- *What is the purpose of this site?*
    - o Can you locate a link that tells you what this site is about? What does it say the purpose of the site is? How confident can you be that this is a fair statement?
    - o Knowing who created the site, can you infer why they created it?
- *When was the information at this site updated?*
    - o How recently was the information at this site updated?
    - o Is it likely this information has changed since it appeared? How? Why?
- *Where can I go to check the accuracy of this information?*
    - o Are the sources for factual information clearly listed so you can check them with another source?
    - o If not, how confident can you be in the information at this location?
    - o Does the information provided at this site match up with facts located at another website about the topic?
- *Why did this person, or group, put this information on the Internet?*
    - o What is this person, or group, trying to accomplish with the information that they provide?
    - o How can you tell?
- *How is the information at this site shaped by the stance taken by the creator of the site?*
    - o Knowing who created this site and what the stated or implicit purpose is, how does this probably shape the information or the activities here?
    - o What biases are likely to appear at this location?

You will find that many of these questions can also be slightly adapted to facilitate similar types of thinking about more traditional informational sources such as magazines, textbooks, and newspaper articles. Helping students to regularly think about answers to these questions, perhaps by posting them next to your Internet computers and discussing them during workshop sessions, will go far toward supporting their critical evaluation of the information they discover in both online and traditional print environments. There are also a growing number of locations on the Internet to assist you and your students in developing skills for critically analyzing information at websites.

- **Bibliography on Evaluating Web Resources** from the library at Virginia Tech—
  http://www.lib.vt.edu/research/evaluate/evalbiblio.html
- **Critical Evaluation Information** from Kathy Schrock's collection—
  http://school.discovery.com/schrockguide/eval.html
- **ICYouSEE:T is for Thinking**—Guide to Critical Thinking—
  http://www.ithaca.edu/library/Training/hott.html
- **Evaluating Webpages**—A WebQuest for Students—
  http://mciunix.mciu.k12.pa.us/~spjvweb/evalwebteach.html

Finally, you may wish to consider some of these strategies:

- Ask students to always determine who created the information at a website, why they might have created it, and what stance they are likely to take in relation to this information. Answers to these questions often provide insight into how the information at that location has been shaped by the person who created the webpage.
- At the main page of any site, always look for an "About this site" link. This will provide information to help you determine who created the site and why it was created.
- Ask students to provide at least two references for each major idea in their written or oral reports, especially when these come from the Internet.
- Have students type in the name of the author of an online resource in quotation marks in the Google search engine to find out more information about the author's background, credibility, and other texts that the individual has authored.
- Design a classroom bulletin board entitled "Discrepant facts: Who is right?" Encourage students to post copies of material they find containing contradictory information. These may come from the Internet or from printed material. You will be surprised how quickly students will find different spellings, different dates for events, different birth dates for famous individuals, and other information that differs between two sources.
- Discuss this issue in your Internet Workshop sessions and see if students can come up with additional strategies for evaluating the accuracy of information. Strategies might include looking to see if document references are provided, the reputation of the source (an individual you do not know or a source with a commercial reputation to protect), or biases the author may display.

Reading Within a Website

Once students have mastered the art of anticipating successful keywords and critically scanning search results for relevent information, they are then faced with the challenge of reading and meaning within the pages of one website. Informational websites are a new genre of expository text that require new literacies. Readers accustomed to previewing familiar printed text patterns and formats (e.g., textbooks or newspapers) to get the gist of a new text can be taken off-guard by design inconsistencies from one website to the next. Moreover, children who visit new websites are often distracted from the main information by spinning animations, immediate links to unrelated topics and downloads to interactive games that may call attention away from the author's original intention. To read most efficiently, these new text features require new strategies. Instruction can support efficient reading on the Internet by calling students' attention to some evolving patterns in the design and organizational structure of websites. Three useful features common to well-designed informational websites include navigational bars, "about us" buttons, and annotated links. Students' navigational efficiency will increase markedly once they understand how to use these three features to quickly locate the information they need.

First, most students quickly realize that many websites feature some type of navigational bar or row of buttons across the top or left side of each webpage. This navigational system typically stands out from the rest of the text, includes links to the major categories or topics within the website, and remains consistent from page to page (see Figure 2-16). Good readers on the Internet recognize these headings as representative of the underlying structure of the website. They systematically use these main links to anticipate in which category, or behind which hyperlink, they may find the information they are looking for. Inefficient readers, on the other hand, pay little attention to the website structure represented in these navigational toolbars. Instead, they click haphazardly through these links or just follow them in sequence, often getting sidetracked and forgetting the task at hand. These students will greatly benefit from a few short sessions in understanding the purpose of navigational toolbars and how they can be used to more efficiently locate the information they need. For a related Internet Workshop activity, you may have students compare traditional expository text features with those found on a website using a wonderful lesson designed by Sheila Seitz from Syracuse, New York, called **Traveling Terrain: Comprehending Nonfiction Text on the Internet** (http://www.readwritethink.org/lessons/lesson_view.asp?id=98).

Students will greatly benefit from a few short sessions in understanding the purpose of navigational toolbars and how they can be used to more efficiently locate the information they need.

Second, the "About us" or "About this site" button found on most homepages is a great source of information for students working to determine the purpose of an Internet site and the reliability of its information. Be sure to model the use of this resource in a large group exploration of a new website and encourage students to build this standard practice into their own reading routines. By clicking on this button, readers can quickly learn more about the author of the webpage, the intended audience, the site's purpose, and who to contact with questions. If the information seems questionable, or you would like students to verify the author's claims with information from another website, you may want to show students how to enter the author's full name or the topic in question into a search engine such as Google. From here, they can find out what other people are saying about this individual or what other people are writing about that topic.

A third design feature that can help students anticipate where certain links may lead is the use of annotations that follow or surround a hyperlink. Thoughtful web designers include short descriptions of hyperlinked resources to help readers navigate through their website (see Figure 2-15 for an effective use of these short annotations after each link heading in the center of the page). Much like using context clues to help determine the meaning of a certain word in traditional texts, students can use the annotations found around or after a hyperlink to anticipate which links will bring them one step closer to the information they are looking for. New technical skills are often needed here, though, to correctly make inferences from annotations that refer to things such as a .pdf file, a .wav file, or a Quicktime file, as is the case when readers follow the multimedia link from the **All About Tigers** webpage in Figure 2-15. Teaching students to recognize these unique patterns and technical context clues may foster better predictions about where links may lead and where specific types of information may be found. These strategies will, in turn, enhance navigational efficiency and active meaning making on the Internet.

Figure 2-15: The **"All About Tigers"** page of **The 5Tigers Information Center** (http://www.5tigers.org/Directory/allabouttigers.htm). The list of main categories in the left margin is the same on each page as a consistent point of reference. Note the "Who Are We?" button toward the bottom of this list and the short annotations that follow each link in the center of the page.

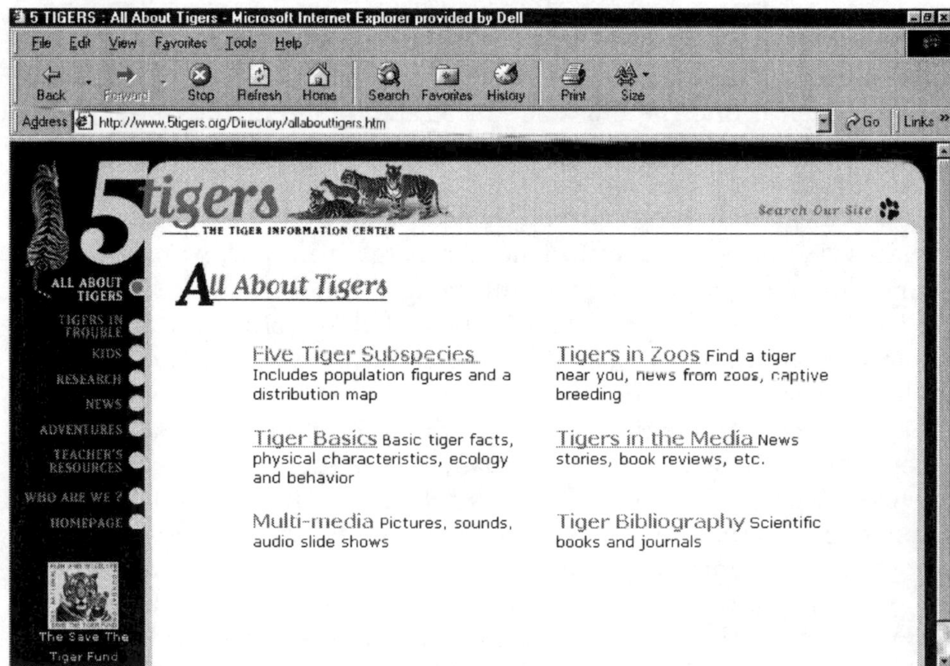

Recognizing and Managing Advertisements

One final suggestion for increasing navigational efficiency and comprehension is to help students recognize and manage the many forms of Internet advertising that they encounter. This instructional strategy will help your students stay on task and avoid being sidetracked while reading on the Internet. For younger students, this means taking time to point out advertisements on the Internet as you explore new sites and helping children differentiate real content from flashing "you have won" boxes and "special offer" banners with enticing requests to "just click here." Even very young students can quickly be taught how and why to ignore these flashing banners by scrolling past them at the top of a webpage or by immediately closing any new advertisements that pop-up in new windows.

If your school allows to you download software onto your computers, you may want to explore some of the free pop-up managers available online:

- **Pop-UpStopper**—
  http://www.panicware.com/popupstoppercompare.html
- **End PopUps**—http://www.endpopups.com/
- **PopThis**—http://www.mathies.com/popthis/
- **Google's Toolbar**—http://toolbar.google.com/
- **Safari's Toolbar**—http://www.apple.com/safari/

Totally avoiding the issue, however, does not adequately prepare older students for the more subtle forms of advertising they will encounter throughout their lives. Lessons such as the **Media Mastery Series** (http://www.teachworld.com/tw_pages/media_mastery.html) can help strengthen students' understanding of how images and language are used as a form of persuasion. Similarly, the **Advertising Lesson** (http://42explore.com/advertis.htm) from Annette Lamb's 42Explore website includes tips for avoiding subtle sales on the Internet and links to several WebQuests about advertising.

Finally, any student who is old enough to visit popular children's websites such as **American Girl** (http://www.americangirl.com) and **LegoLand** (http://www.legoland.com) or even more academic sites such as **Scholastic** (http://www.scholastic.com) and **National Wildlife Federation** (http://www.nwf.org/) should realize that each is guided by certain agendas, both educational and economic, that influence the content on their website. Students should be taught how to recognize the ways in which these websites promote their products and agendas within interactive games, informational passages, student lessons, and consumer surveys. It is our responsibility as educators to help students of all ages approach and process both traditional and new media with a sense of informed skepticism and the critical habits of mind described earlier in this chapter.

Looking to the Future: New Search Engines and New Literacies

One of the biggest challenges of using the Internet and other information and communication technologies is that new navigation and search tools will constantly emerge, presenting all of us with new literacies to be learned. Accepting these changes and learning new strategies is a crucial

New navigation and search tools will constantly emerge, presenting all of us with new literacies to be learned. Accepting these changes and learning new strategies is a crucial element for our personal literacy success.

element for our personal literacy success. As we close this chapter, we'll briefly highlight a few new search tools that reveal some of the new literacies on the horizon.

Kartoo (http://www.kartoo.com/) features a uniquely interactive interface that reports search results in a visual multi-layered web of icons, symbols, and pop-up annotations. It includes an intuitive use of complex queries, requires the use of the Flash plug-in, and provides both a basic and expert version for specialized searching. The option to use this search tool in seven different languages reminds us of the multilingual and global contexts in which these new literacies are emerging. For more information, refer to the help page at http://www.kartoo.net/a/en/aide01.html.

Teoma (http://www.teoma.com/) enables users to do one search and get three different types of responses: ranked results, refined topic suggestions, and lists of specific resources from experts in the field. This tool uses new technologies such as dynamic ranking and advanced algorithms and works by ranking a site based on the number of same-subject pages that reference it, not just general popularity. With this search engine, understanding the purpose of your search is crucial.

Browse3D (http://www.browse3d.com/) searches the Internet and then creates a "room" on your desktop, with your current Web page on the center wall, images of forward links on the right wall, and thumbnails of previously visited pages on the left wall. Efficiently navigating three-dimensional environments will be required to use this new search tool.

Finally, **MicroSurfer 2.0** (http://www.microsurfer.com/) is designed to optimize the time spent searching on the Internet. It lets you select links to preload while you browse the current site, so when you're ready to move on there's no wait.

These new search engines remind us that the Internet represents a learning environment that is diverse, multi-dimensional, and always changing. Take time to explore these new tools with a sense of flexibility and willingness to accept and appreciate the literacy and navigational challenges that lie ahead. Keep abreast of new developments in Internet tools and encourage your students to be actively involved in exploring and sharing new strategies for using these tools most effectively.

Visiting the Classroom: Caroline Joiner's High School Library Webpage in Texas

Regardless of the grade level or the subject you teach, we can all learn important lessons by exploring **Caroline Joiner's High School Library Webpage** (http://www.shschool.org/hslibrary.htm) (see Figure 2-16). Caroline is the librarian at Sacred Heart High School in Hallettsville, Texas. Her well-organized compilation of research resources sends a clear message to students and teachers that learning with the Internet should stress safety, efficiency, critical thinking, and student responsibility.

One of the most impressive aspects of this location is her inclusion of select resources for helping students begin the Internet research process. She begins with reminders about the school's Acceptable Use Policy and step-by-step guides for using important research tools. She then directs students to search strategy tutorials and research freeware. The special sequence of research guides she collected for Mrs. Bladau, the English teacher at her school, demonstrates the power of forging new partnerships between library media specialists and classroom teachers to help integrate navigational and research strategies into the curriculum.

In addition, Caroline provides her students and staff with links to many Internet resources for all of the main subject areas, demonstrating her eagerness to support content-area teachers and other colleagues. Each section of quality links is arranged in alphabetical order with helpful annotations that point users to the best features of each site. Also included in this section are links to topics about computer technology, elementary links, faculty resources, free web translators, librarian resources, and much more.

Finally, Caroline uses her webpages to model appropriate practices for citing sources for the graphics that she uses. Her careful attention to the school's acceptable-use policies are helpful reminders to staff and students of the important rules in place to foster safe and responsible use of the Internet.

This is really an impressive school library homepage. It serves as a wonderful example of the important role that library media specialists play in providing content-area assistance to teachers and instructional support for students as we all practice using effective navigational strategies on the Internet. We invite you to take a look. Be certain, too, to drop Caroline a note and let her know how much you appreciate her contribution.

Figure 2-16: The homepage for Caroline Joiner's **Sacred Heart High School Library** website (http://www.shschool.org/hslibrary.htm), an exceptional example of the important educational contributions made by library media specialists.

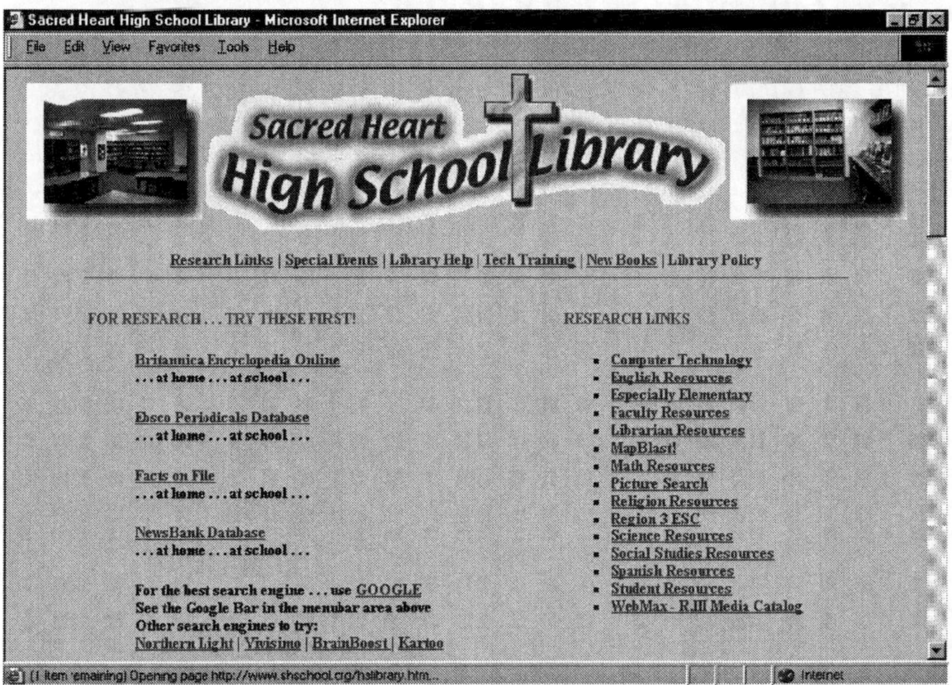

E-MAIL FOR YOU

From: Caroline Joiner (shs@shschool.org)
Subject: Integrating Internet Literacies into the High School Research Process

Since I am the librarian and the technology coordinator for the school, I make sure that each computer shows the high school library homepage when a student accesses the Internet. Teachers encourage their students to use the links there when they begin their research so that they will be directed to educational sites with sound information. Next, teachers advise using the Google search engine, a very comprehensive tool. Additionally, the librarian asks students not to forget the shelved books. Often, browsing the shelves will yield the best results. The Internet can be a slower, more cumbersome process for research if appropriate information is available from the shelf. Lessons in website evaluation and modeling or limiting the selection of topics are steps in the research process that are often overlooked by teachers. Improving the quality of the research process by using shorter, more concise lessons and examining products frequently will yield better results from the students. One page of well-constructed, non-plagiarized research is more desirable than five pages of repetitious and careless work.

Sincerely,
Caroline Joiner
Librarian, Technology Applications teacher, Technology Coordinator
Sacred Heart School, Hallettsville, Texas

New Literacies in Internet Navigation

A common thread weaving through this chapter is that the nature of information on the Internet demands new skills and strategies for how we navigate and construct meaning within informational texts. In this final section, we provide an inspiring model of how a new literacies perspective can be applied to student navigation on the Internet.

Exciting projects are emerging on the Internet as a result of instruction that integrates content-area subject matter with critical literacy skills. The **Internet Detectives Library Media Project** (http://www.madison.k12.wi.us/tnl/detectives/) is representative of at least two principles of the new literacy perspective in action: critical literacies and the social, collaborative construction of new information on the Internet. This project is the result of the actions of middle school students in the state of Wisconsin who joined forces to build a student-generated library of evaluated Internet resources built around content-specific evaluation criteria as a positive alternative to Internet filtering in their schools. Classes begin as groups of Internet detectives in search of websites that answer a question they've asked. Students evaluate a site, describe its contents and features, and recommend it for inclusion in the growing database that is accessed by students all over the world. This project represents an impressive series of critical literacy lessons synthesized into an authentic application. Be sure to visit this resource with your students and find out more. The evolution of this resource over just a few years' time from the original **KIDS Report Web site** (http://www.madison.k12.wi.us/tnl/detectives/kids/) to its current format is an important illustration of the continual changes in literacy that lie ahead.

Additional Navigation Resources on the Internet

4Kids.org—http://www.4kids.org/
From here, among other activities, you can access a weekly KidsQuest for authentic practice with Internet navigation and fact finding. Also, be sure to visit the CoolSpots for a list of well-annotated and unique topical links rated by kids.

Adobe Acrobat Reader—
http://www.adobe.com/products/acrobat/readstep2.html
A plug-in program that you can download for free viewing and printing of files saved in .pdf format, a standard format for reliable document exchange on the Internet.

Amazing Picture Machine—http://www.ncrtec.org/picture.htm
A unique collection of searchable images and many lesson ideas for using graphical resources on the Internet.

Ask.com—http://www.ask.com
Another great search engine for adults and older students from the AskJeeves group.

Childnet International—http://www.childnet-int.org/
This amazing resource sponsored by the Childnet Internet charity features current information for adults and interactive activities for students that focus on Internet safety. Be sure to visit the links to *ChatDanger* for ideas on how to stay safe in chat rooms; *Net Detectives*, an online role program from students using ICT with outside experts; and *Kidsmart*, a portal site that emphasizes five key safety tips and links to wider Internet safety resources in the United Kingdom. Be sure to bookmark this site!

Children's Partnership—http://www.childrenspartnership.org/
Much to read here about forging agendas for youth with regards to equity, digital preparedness, and Internet safety.

Connect Online: Web Learning Adventures—
http://glencoe.com/sec/computered/col/index.html
This is an outstanding interactive guide to the Internet developed as a companion to the book Connect Online by Glencoe. You may think about using this to facilitate small groups of teachers or students interested in exploring the wide range of resources available on the Internet.

CyberSleuth Kids—http://cybersleuth-kids.com/
This kids' search engine organizes information by topical directories and curricular themes. The creators have also developed two free companion website, Classroom Clipart and LessonPlan Central, which support teachers' productivity and instructional needs.

Electric Teacher's Searching the Internet—
http://www.electricteacher.com/search.htm
Compiled by Cathy Chamberlain, a district technology specialist in Oswego, New York, this site links you to countless search engines and directories for teachers and to information about the effective use of search engines with students.

Evaluating Web Information—
http://www.lib.vt.edu/research/evaluate/evaluating.html
Here is a comprehensive interactive tutorial that walks you through checkpoints and strategies for evaluating the authority, objectivity, accuracy, and currency of information on the Internet. The supportive two-framed interface and final practice activities make this a great site to explore during a professional development session or with middle or high school students.

From Now On—http://www.fno.org
This is a free electronic journal with some of the best ideas on using the Internet and other technologies to develop critical thinking, inquiry, and efficient navigation skills in the classroom.

Jackson Creek Middle School Picture Book Clipart—
http://www.mccsc.edu/~kmcglaun/clipart/clipart.htm
Have you been looking for a good collection of appropriate clip art for students? Visit this site to access eight different collections as well as information about copyright protection.

KidzPrivacy—
http://www.ftc.gov/bcp/conline/edcams/kidzprivacy/index.html
This joint venture with the Federal Trade Commission (FTC) features Internet safety strategies for children and adults as well as a list of requirements needed for website operators to comply with the FTC's Children's Online Privacy Protection Rule.

Infopeople Best Search Tools—
http://www.infopeople.org/search/tools.html
Funded by The California State Library project, this is a link to some of the most powerful search engines on the Internet and some helpful how-to guides for other Internet issues.

Internet4Classrooms: Helping Teachers Use the Internet Effectively—
http://www.internet4classrooms.com/index.htm
This one stop website points you to subject area links for K-12 teachers, website for daily use, and on-line practice modules for several teacher productivity tools.

Internet How-Tos—http://oslis.k12.or.us/elementary/howto/
Step-by-step guides created by the Oregon School Library System for elementary students and companion teaching materials to introduce Internet research and navigation. Click on the link at the bottom for a parallel list of resources designed for secondary students and teachers.

Internet Research 9th-12th grade—
http://www.my-ecoach.com/resources/9-12research.html
This site features a set of online research tools and tutorials to help high school teachers develop a simple web-based student activity using one

curriculum site and helpful frames for students collecting information from multiple sites.

Microsoft Design Gallery Live—http://dgl.microsoft.com/

At this location, you may search for, select, and download wonderful collections of free clip art, photographs, and animations that are saved directly into your Microsoft Office applications folder. You can then easily insert them into your presentations, word-processing documents, or student-created projects.

My Reference Desk—http://www.refdesk.com/index.html

Access to news, facts, subject experts, and reference materials galore, all in one easy-to-use location. Be sure to set a bookmark at this one!

Search Engine Watch—http://searchenginewatch.com/

From this site, you can keep a careful watch on new search tools or read current news and reviews of different search engines and their unique features.

SofWeb: Using the Internet—http://www.sofweb.vic.edu.au/internet/

A well-organized introduction from Victoria, Australia to current Internet tools and tips for using them with students. You can also explore discussion groups and links to 27 of their Global Classroom Projects.

Surf the Net with Kids—http://www.surfnetkids.com/

This website features the work of syndicated columnist Barbara Feldman. Although she also uses this site to advertise many of her technology-related products, there are several great free aspects that are too good to miss, including a weekly newsletter of thematic links for kids and free content for your classroom webpage.

White Papers on Technology Use for Educators—
http://lrs.ed.uiuc.edu/wp/

An extensive resource created by graduate students at the University of Illinois, Urbana/Champaign. The papers focus on current issues such as web evaluation, computer crime, access issues, privacy, and commercialism.

3 Effective Instructional Models: Internet Workshop, Internet Project, Internet Inquiry, and WebQuest

How should we teach with the Internet? We will answer that important question in this chapter. Each instructional model we present enables you to support the acquisition of new literacies in your classroom while you also teach important content information. We will share four highly effective instructional models: Internet Workshop, Internet Project, Internet Inquiry, and WebQuest. As you read about each model, you will see immediate connections to your own instructional program.

Do you seek a useful beginning model? Internet Workshop is for you. Would you like to join an exciting collaborative project with other classrooms around the world? Try Internet Project. Perhaps you would like to have students explore independent inquiry projects? Internet Inquiry is what you are looking for. Or, maybe you would like a complete set of online resources for an upcoming unit along with an activity for your students to complete. WebQuest is the model you need. Each of these instructional models will bring new energy and enthusiasm to the lessons you teach every day.

Each instructional model we present enables you to support the acquisition of new literacies in your classroom while you also teach important content information.

As you use these instructional frameworks to integrate the new literacies of the Internet into your classroom, you will thoughtfully guide students' learning within information environments that are richer and more complex, presenting richer and more complex learning opportunities. You will provide important new learning opportunities for your students—opportunities they would not otherwise receive. Moreover, you will provide students with important new literacies that will be essential to their success in an information age.

After reading this chapter, you should be able to:

1. Identify the steps associated with Internet Workshop and develop lessons that use this instructional model in your classroom.
2. Identify the steps associated with Internet Project and develop lessons that use this instructional model in your classroom.
3. Identify the steps associated with Internet Inquiry and develop lessons that use this instructional model in your classroom.

4. Identify several challenges associated with the use of the WebQuest model, then locate several webquest sites on the Internet and describe how you will use these in your classroom.

Teaching with the Internet: Sharee Mendoza's Class

Sharee Mendoza had a hard time sleeping during the first week of school; she was always filled with the excitement of new possibilities, new students, new ideas, and new challenges for her fifth grade class. Often, she would come to school early to work, to plan, and to think. That is what she was doing this morning.

Sharee checked the hamsters' water, looked to see how Felix, their boa, was doing after yesterday's meal, straightened up the science books in the resource center, and checked her email.

Sharee needed to pull things together for the dinosaur unit she was planning. It would start soon. She was gathering resources and ideas from a number of sources: her folder from last year's unit, the school library, and she was trying the Internet, too. Yesterday she posted requests for instructional ideas about dinosaurs at several locations:

- **Dinosaur Mailing List**—http://www.cmnh.org/dinoarch/
  This is a mailing list for educators and others interested in exchanging information about dinosaurs. It is run by The Cleveland Museum of Natural History.
- **MIDDLE-L Mailing List**—
  http://ecap.crc.uiuc.edu/listserv/middle-l.html
  This is a mailing list managed by the ECAP (Early Childhood and Parenting Collaborative) at the University of Illinois.
- **Connected Teacher Email List**—
  http://www.classroom.com/community/email/
  Sharee found this supportive location where teachers post questions about integrating the Internet into their classroom and read to learn what others are doing.

Now it was time to see if her inquiries had brought in any useful ideas.

The most amazing thing to Sharee was not the incredible resources on the Internet; it was the wonderfully supportive teachers she met. Sharee had several email messages in her mailbox with great resources and ideas. None of these teachers knew her but they still took time to write lengthy notes, sharing their experiences and resources. Teachers had responded from California, Oklahoma, Arizona, Alberta, Manitoba, Florida, Washington, Australia, New Zealand, and Great Britain. They provided a number of great ideas for her dinosaur unit.

Develop "Healthy Skeptics" in Your Classroom

A teacher in Texas used this phrase and it seemed to be a good one. She said that the most important new literacies for her were the critical literacies needed to carefully evaluate information on the Internet. She noted that anyone can publish information on the Internet and so one is never certain about the accuracy of material found there. She suggested that students explore **ICYouSee Guide to Critical Thinking** (http://www.ithaca.edu/library/

Training/hott.html) to learn how to critically evaluate Internet information through several guided experiences with websites. She also pointed Sharee to an extensive collection of resources at **Critical Evaluation Information** (http://school.discovery.com/schrockguide/eval.html). She made another suggestion, too: Require students to cross-reference claims from several sources before accepting them as accurate. This Texas teacher showed students how to reference information found on the Web by visiting **Citing Internet Resources** (http://www.classroom.com/community/connection/howto/citeresources.jhtml). Finally, she said that she sometimes used **The Museum of Hoaxes Weblog** (http://www.museumofhoaxes.com/) to prompt discussion about the many hoaxes that appear on the Internet.

Conduct an Internet Workshop Session

A teacher in New Zealand recommended Internet Workshop since it was consistent with more constructivist views of teaching and learning. He liked Internet Workshop since it allowed him to simultaneously teach content information along with the new literacies that are required on the Internet. He really liked having students explore sites related to a unit, as they recorded important information to share with others during a workshop session. He had his class keep a "Digging for Dinosaurs" journal, writing down interesting information about dinosaurs and also indicating the source where it had been obtained. Then, in a workshop session, they shared their findings. He used this activity as an exciting introduction to his dinosaur unit.

He liked Internet Workshop since it allowed him to simultaneously teach content information and the new literacies required on the Internet.

Locate and Bookmark Central Sites for Dinosaurs

Several teachers sent along their favorite sites with extensive and well-organized links to dinosaur resources on the Internet:

- **Walking with Dinosaurs**—http://www.bbc.co.uk/dinosaurs
  There are so many incredible activities and resources for children at this site, developed by the BBC (British Broadcasting Corporation); it is hard to know where to begin. Be certain to listen to the T-Rex and other dinosaurs! Lots of games, puzzles, and activities too. Set a bookmark!
- **Dino Russ's Lair**—http://www.isgs.uiuc.edu/dinos/dinos_home.html
  Here is an amazingly exhaustive set of links developed by a geologist working at the Illinois Department of Natural Resources.
- **Zoomdinosaurs.com**—
  http://www.enchantedlearning.com/subjects/dinosaurs/
  This is a commercial site with banner ads but this site contains exceptional resources for the classroom study of dinosaurs.
- **The Paleo Ring**—http://b.webring.com/hub?ring=paleoring
  Here is a Webring, or collection of sites connected to one another, about dinosaurs.
- **Sue at The Field Museum**—
  http://www.fieldmuseum.org/sue/default.htm
  This is a great location that explains how a new T-Rex is being conserved.

- **Dinosaur Treks**—http://library.thinkquest.org/C005824/
  This is a ThinkQuest award-winning site created by a high school team. Students go on several exciting journeys to study dinosaurs.
- **Dinosaur Eggs**—http://www.nationalgeographic.com/dinoeggs
  This location by National Geographic takes students on a hunt for dinosaur eggs, and then shows how these are "hatched" by researchers who wish to study the embryos inside. Many great stories about today's scientists and their work studying dinosaurs.

Provide Time for Students' Independent Web Exploration

Direct this exploration by setting a bookmark to **Yahooligans** (http://www.yahooligans.com) and limit their search to this search engine. Yahooligans is a directory and search engine for children where information has been screened for child safety. Have students share their search strategies and the information they find about dinosaurs during Internet Workshop sessions.

Figure 3-1. Walking with Dinosaurs from the BBC (http://www.bbc.co.uk/dinosaurs), a wonderful directory for dinosaur study in the classroom.

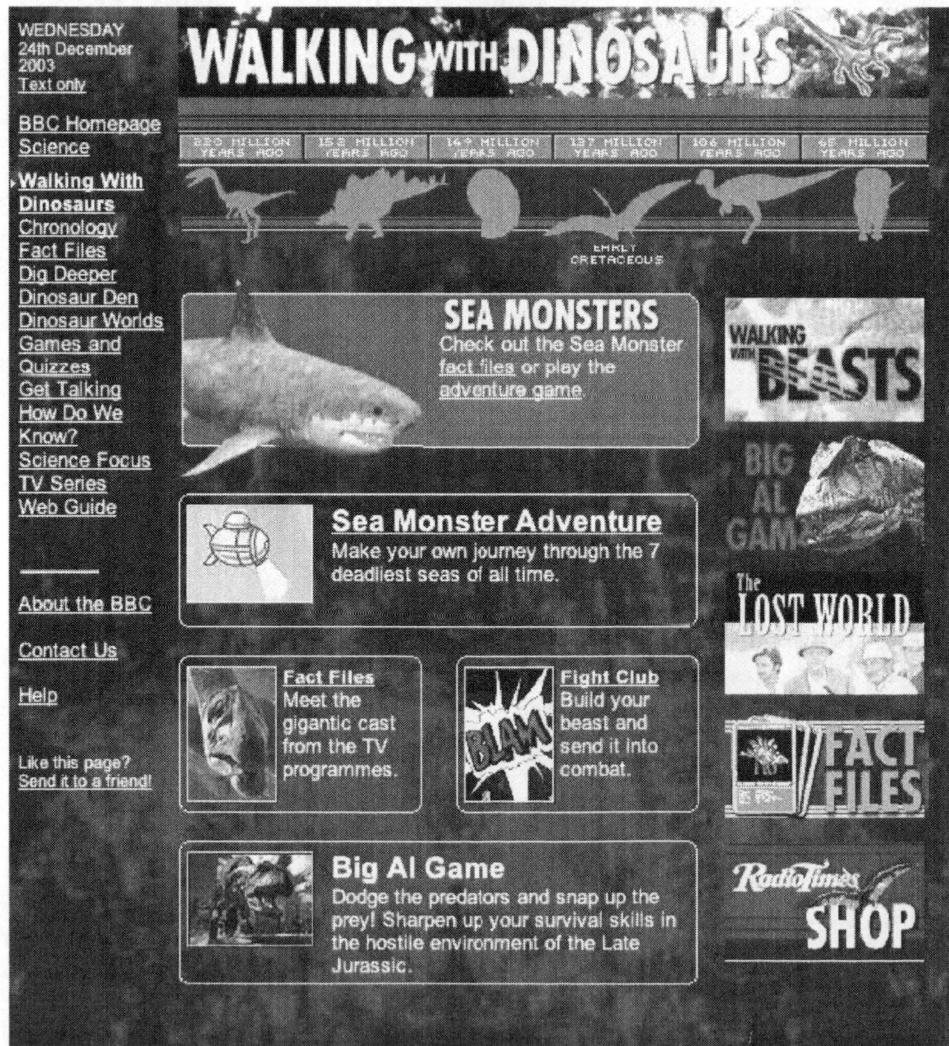

Have Students Complete a WebQuest on Dinosaurs

Webquests are complete lesson experiences on the Internet, usually developed by other teachers following a WebQuest model. Visit webquest locations such as those found at:

- **Here Come the Dinosaurs—** http://its.guilford.k12.nc.us/WebQuests/dino/dinosaurs.html
- **Dinosaur WebQuest—** http://www.lfelem.lfc.edu/tech/DuBose/WebQuest/Vaccarella/WQPS_VV.html
- **Dinosaurs—** http://www.lfelem.lfc.edu/tech/DuBose/WebQuest/reinhardt/dinosaur.html

Ask a Paleontologist Questions about Dinosaurs

Have students visit the **Mad Scientists Network** (http://www.madsci.org) at the University of St. Louis and read answers to previous questions. If their question has not been answered, have them send it via email. A paleontologist will answer it.

Have Students Generate and Exchange Puzzles

One teacher pointed Sharee to **Puzzlemaker** (http://puzzlemaker.school.discovery.com/) at the Discovery Channel site. Here, teachers and students could quickly generate their own word searches, crossword puzzles, as well as many other different types of word games and then quickly print each one out.

Sharee set a bookmark for ***Yahooligans*** *to provide independent exploration time in an area of the Web that would be safe for her students.*

As she read these ideas, Sharee went to her web browser, found each location, and quickly reviewed the contents, determining if they would fit her goals for the unit. First, she made a bookmark for **ICYouSee Guide to Critical Thinking** (http://www.ithaca.edu/library/Training/hott.html). Sharee had decided to begin with an Internet Workshop around the critical thinking skills central to effective Internet use. She also decided to use Internet Workshop with the journal activity, "Digging for Dinosaurs." She set a bookmark for **Walking with Dinosaurs** (http://www.bbc.co.uk/dinosaurs) and for **Dino Russ's Lair** (http://www.isgs.uiuc.edu/dinos/dinos_home.html) for this experience.

Sharee also set a bookmark for **Yahooligans** http://www.yahooligans.com) to provide independent exploration time in an area of the Web that would be safe for her students. One teacher recommended a list of books on dinosaurs so she copied and forwarded this list into an email message to the school librarian. Sharee asked for these books in the school library to be sent down to her room. Then, she set a bookmark for the Puzzlemaker location. This would come in handy during her unit. She planned to show students how to make dinosaur crossword puzzles online.

Sharee liked the idea of having an Internet Workshop session in which students could share the results of their dinosaur research. She would schedule a workshop period for 30 minutes each week. Students could also share information they had acquired and the new locations they had found during their Internet Inquiry explorations. She would do this on Mondays.

The day before, Sharee developed a schedule for students to use with the single computer she had linked to the Internet. Having only a single Internet computer limited access for students but her schedule provided equal access for everyone.

Each week, every student in her class received half an hour alone on the computer and half an hour on the computer with a partner. If students needed more than an hour of Internet access, they would sometimes go down to the media center and use the lab there.

Each week, every student in her class received half an hour alone on the computer and half an hour on the computer with a partner. If students needed more than an hour of Internet access, they would sometimes go down to the media center and use the lab there. While she always wanted more time on the Internet for her students, Sharee noted they quickly learned to use their Internet time efficiently. This appeared to help them develop useful strategies for navigation. You can see Sharee's schedule in Figure 3-2.

Figure 3-2. Sharee Mendoza's computer schedule posted next to her Internet computer.

	Monday	**Tuesday**	**Wednesday**	**Thursday**	**Friday**
8:30–9:00	Michelle	Michelle/Becky	Tanika/Emily	Shannon/ Tiki	Cynthia/ Jennifer
9:00–9:30	Tanika	John/Peter	Jeremy/Dave	Kati	Patti
9:30–10:00	**Internet Workshop**	Ben	Paco	Lisa	Julia
10:00–10:30	Shannon	**PE**	Paul	**PE**	Andy
10:30–11:00	**Library**	Mike	Scott	Faith	Melissa
11:00–11:30	Cynthia	Eric	James	Linda	Sara
11:30–12:30	**Lunch**	**Lunch**	**Lunch**	**Lunch**	**Lunch**
12:30–1:00	Jennifer	Dave	Peter	Tiki	Emily
1:00–1:30	Becky	Jeremy	Ben/Sara	Mike/Linda	John
1:30–2:00	Eric/James	Paco/Melissa	**Music**	Paul/Scott	**Class Meeting**
2:00–2:30	Kati/Lisa		Faith/Andy	Patti/Julia	

Yes, the unit was coming together. Now, if she could find another class on the Internet that would like to do a collaborative Internet project on dinosaurs the unit would be complete. Maybe they could each share the results of classroom inquiry projects. This would help her students develop written communication skills. She would try posting a message again on each of the listservs to see if anyone was interested in joining her for this project experience. Things were coming together nicely as the class entered her room that morning.

Lessons from the Classroom

The episode with Sharee Mendoza provides us with a number of important lessons as we consider effective instructional strategies with the Internet. One important lesson is to recognize how Sharee took advantage of the first principle of a new literacies perspective discussed in Chapter 1. The new literacies are often socially constructed. This principle applies to teachers as well as to students. The Internet requires us to use what we call distributed learning. Increasingly, learning will require us to learn from one another since no single person can be expected to know everything that exists in a rich and complex world like the Internet. Sharee had learned this lesson well. She relied upon other teachers as she gathered ideas for her dinosaur unit. In a very short time, she mined the Internet and came up with many wonderful ideas to include in her unit. Sharee was going to pass along this lesson to her students, too. By doing Internet Workshop, students would learn something special about dinosaurs that they could then share with other students. Internet Project, another instructional model, would also help students develop the collaborative skills essential to distributed learning. By collaborating with another classroom, each class would exchange new ideas and resources and develop new communication skills important for effective information exchange. Sharee was beginning to realize how the Internet was changing the way she taught.

Teachers sometimes describe their change to us as moving from a "sage on the stage to a guide at the side."

Lessons for Teachers

Teachers sometimes describe the changes they experience with the Internet as moving from a "sage on the stage to a guide at the side." What they mean is that their role changes from being the one, and only, expert to being an instructional leader within a classroom community where many members have expertise.

Most of us first see this change when our computer freezes, when the printer isn't working, or when something else fails. Suddenly, a student's expertise becomes visible and critical to our classroom's success. As digital technologies become more important to our classrooms and as they repeatedly change, it is impossible for anyone to keep up with everything taking place. You will see students becoming experts in particular areas that interest them. One child might be an expert in knowing the most useful ways to search for information, another with knowing the best resources about a particular author, another with knowing how to construct a webpage, and still others will become experts in other information areas or other aspects of new literacies. You will need to consider ways to take advantage of the expertise that you find among the students in your classroom.

This change, by the way, reflects the changes taking place in the world of work today. The highly structured and top-down model of business and industry has changed to a far more decentralized model in order for companies to successfully compete in a highly competitive global economy. Nimble, aggressive companies that take advantage of individual employee's expertise survive, whereas inflexible and tightly structured companies that ignore their employees' special talents fail in a world of rapidly changing information and technology. Thus, it is also important that we prepare children for these new worlds of literacy and life-long learning they will experience as adults.

Developing a weekly schedule for Internet use in single computer classrooms helps to ensure that all students receive access to this important resource.

Sharee's story also teaches us a second lesson: Developing a weekly schedule for Internet use in single computer classrooms helps to ensure that all students receive access to this important resource. Sometimes, certain students will tend to dominate access to the Internet and other students will have their time curtailed. It is important to guarantee time for all students to use the resources on the Internet.

Using Internet Workshop was a simple way to integrate the Internet into the curriculum.

Third, Sharee discovered how easy it was to use Internet Workshop. Using Internet Workshop was a simple way to integrate the Internet into the curriculum. Setting a bookmark and then developing a short assignment was easy to do. Moreover, it focused student use of the Internet on important information. Sharee found this simple technique engaged students actively in their learning. She often noticed several students at the computer talking about the information for that week's Internet Workshop experience. It was a great suggestion.

Sharee's story also reminds us how important it is to help students evaluate the accuracy of information they find on the Internet, the second principle of a New Literacies Perspective (see Chapter 1). Since anyone can publish nearly any information they wish on the Internet, it is hard to be certain the information that you find is accurate. We need to help students become "healthy skeptics" if we wish them to become effective consumers of information on the Internet. We also need to show them how to reference the information they use in their writing.

Sharee's story also teaches us a fifth lesson: Internet Project can be a highly engaging and effective instructional model for your classroom. Developing a collaborative project with classrooms in other parts of the world leads to important learning outcomes as information is shared and discussed. Internet Project requires advance planning between teachers, but the rewards are often well worth the additional time.

Developing a collaborative project with classrooms in other parts of the world leads to important learning outcomes as information is shared and new questions are developed.

Note, too, how Sharee provided opportunities for her students to search for information on their own. It is important to provide opportunities for independent navigation through the Internet. This encourages students to discover, and then share, even more useful new literacy strategies for locating information on the Internet. Providing opportunities for independent research, as Sharee did with Internet Inquiry, accomplished this.

It is also important to realize that Internet use may be easily integrated with other instructional practices with which you are already familiar. Sharee's use of a journal for Internet Workshop is one example of this. She also wove in a practice found in many classrooms, the use of an "author's chair." It is important to understand that nearly every instructional activity you currently use in your classroom may also be used with the Internet.

Finally, while the Internet is a tool to support students' learning, it is also a powerful resource for planning instructional activities. In a short session after school, Sharee quickly gathered resources and ideas for an extensive, thematic unit. As you become more familiar with the Internet, you will also develop efficient strategies for using the Internet to plan activities. After a short time, you will wonder how you ever taught without this resource.

E-MAIL FOR YOU

Subject: My Hero Project
From: Jill Newcomb newcomb@voyager.net
Cindy Ross jross@sunny.ncmc.cc.mi.us

For our first experience using the Internet in the classroom, we decided to choose a small group to work on an activity called "Heroes." We used two websites, **My Hero** (http://myhero.com/) and **The Giraffe Project** (www.giraffe.org/giraffe/).

The students first read about well-known heroes described on these websites. Then the students read about local heroes, which were submitted by other students to these websites. The group discussed qualities and characteristics of the heroes using the analytical skills of comparing and contrasting.

Students then choose their own personal hero and wrote an essay about this person. These essays were submitted to the **My Hero** website to be published on the Internet for other students to read.

To further practice writing and communication skills, the students chose a hero from their school or community. Collaboratively they wrote interview questions. After practice and role playing, the students interviewed their hero. The interview was videotaped.

For a culminating activity we held a "Hero Celebration." Students invited their parents and the community hero. At the celebration, the students read their essays, introduced their hero, and all participants viewed the videotaped interview.

Using the Internet was highly motivating for these students. They eagerly shared their findings of heroes with their teachers and classmates. We noticed their enthusiasm carried over to other areas. For instance, when checking out library books, these students now choose biographies over easy-to-read fiction. We are looking forward to other activities using the Internet in the classroom.

Jill Newcomb newcomb@voyager.net
Cindy Ross jross@sunny.ncmc.cc.mi.us
Ottawa Elementary School
Petosky, Michigan

Management Issues in Departmentalized or Self-Contained Classrooms

It is essential to thoughtfully plan how to integrate Internet experiences into your classroom curriculum. Sometimes we abdicate this responsibility when we make Internet experiences available only after students' regular work is completed, providing little direction for what should be done. Using the Internet like this makes it one of several "free choice" activities in the classroom. There are several problems with a "free choice" approach to Internet integration.

First, making the Internet one of several "free choice" activities means that you abdicate your responsibility to prepare students for their literacy and learning futures. It is important for each of us to assume this new responsibility if we seek to adequately prepare our students for a world in which we are all more closely connected to important information resources.

A second problem is that you implicitly communicate that the Internet is an activity for recreation, not for the important work of defining important questions, learning new search and navigations strategies, critically evaluating information that you encounter, synthesizing information that you locate, or communicating your discoveries to others around the world. When you integrate the Internet into your classroom curriculum, you tell students that the Internet is important to their lives and that it needs to be approached with respect and thoughtfulness as well as the interest and excitement it naturally generates.

Finally, equity is an increasingly critical problem. Making the Internet available only when regular work is complete, ultimately results in more advanced students having greater Internet access. This ends up helping the rich get richer and the poor get poorer. Advanced students, who finish their regular work first, become more advanced in their ability to access, evaluate, and use information on the Internet. Meanwhile, weaker students, often last at completing work, are denied these opportunities to improve their abilities. Digital divide issues need to be avoided inside classrooms as well as outside classrooms.

Digital divide issues need to be avoided inside classrooms as well as outside classrooms.

How do we provide all of our students with both sufficient and equal access to the Internet? One of the best solutions for self-contained, single-computer classrooms is the one developed by Sharee and illustrated in Figure 3-2. By developing a weekly matrix with 30-minute Internet periods and assigning students to one 30-minute period by themselves and one 30-minute period with a partner, you can ensure that everyone in your class receives at least on hour of Internet access each week. To do this, however, you must be willing to have one or two students working on their weekly Internet assignments while others in your class receive instruction in another area. Thus, many teachers in self-contained classrooms will assign students who are doing well in math to an Internet session that coincides with math, thinking that these students will be more likely than others to independently make up any missed instruction. Similarly, during science instruction they might assign students to the Internet who are doing well in science.

If you adopt this useful strategy in your classroom, you should keep several additional suggestions in mind. First, be certain that you periodically rotate the assigned times on the computer schedule so that the same students do not miss their time because of regular conflicts with the school's special functions (e.g., regularly scheduled school assemblies, student council meetings, or special activity meetings). It would be unfair, for example, to have a student miss her Internet time on Monday of each week because she had to attend music class. Many teachers will change their Internet schedule once every two weeks.

Second, rotate partners regularly at the computer so that all of your students have an opportunity to work with many different individuals in your class. This increases opportunities for improving social skills while also increasing opportunities to learn new things from other students about Internet use.

Developing a regular schedule for Internet use in a self-contained classroom will help you to manage equity issues during school time. In the future, this problem will be resolved as additional connections are made to classrooms. For now, we need to develop strategies such as this to accommodate our students' learning needs.

Developing a regular schedule for Internet use in a self-contained classroom will help you to manage equity issues during school time.

What about teachers with a single-computer classroom at the middle school or at the high school where instruction is typically departmentalized? Here you will be severely challenged to provide students with equitable access during a single 40- or 50-minute period each day. In fact, most teachers will not even attempt this with only a single Internet computer in their classroom. It is really only possible if you have a cluster of computers within your classroom, unfortunately a rarity, or a lab in your school.

Most teachers in departmentalized programs will schedule time for their entire class in an Internet lab, or provide assignments that are completed in the lab, outside of regularly scheduled class time. In these contexts, it is not always possible to easily set bookmarks for all of the computers in a computer lab. Thus, it is important to provide students with the complete addresses of the sites you wish them to use in each assignment or to provide these at a school or classroom homepage. Developing a classroom homepage is discussed in Chapter 12.

Teaching with the Internet: Effective Instructional Models

When the Internet is used without direction and guidance, it often takes students away from thoughtful navigation, evaluation, and synthesis of information, and other new literacies, in favor of random, unconnected surfing experiences. You will see this pattern, too, in your classroom unless students have a clear purpose each time they sit down to use the Internet. Internet experiences should always have a purpose; they should always be an integral part of your instructional program. This requires you to thoughtfully plan this integration.

How can you effectively integrate the Internet into your classroom? Developing effective instructional strategies with the Internet is not difficult. It should include these models:

- Internet Workshop
- Internet Project
- Internet Inquiry

Internet experiences should always have a purpose; they should always be an integral part of your instructional program.

This sequence of instructional models is developmentally sensitive, so you can begin with Internet Workshop, a model that is easiest to use, and gradually build to more complex and powerful instructional strategies, as you feel comfortable. You will probably find many similarities between elements in these models of Internet use and the instructional strategies you already use in your classroom. This should also make it easier to integrate Internet use into your classroom.

In addition, we will explore an instructional model often found on the Internet, WebQuest. This, too, is easy to use in your classroom and it is made easier since so many teachers have developed webpages containing this model. Thus, you can use their webquests for your own classroom.

Using Internet Workshop in your Classroom

You have just received an Internet connection in your classroom along with a new computer. How do you begin to integrate the Internet into your instructional program? Many teachers start by using Internet Workshop. This is the easiest way to begin using the Internet for instruction. It is a model for conducting research on the Internet that provides opportunities for students to exchange both content information and the new literacies that they find to be most helpful in their work.

Many teachers begin their instructional journeys on the Internet with Internet Workshop.

Internet Workshop has many variations. Generally, it involves these steps:

1. Locate a good site with content related to a classroom unit of instruction and set a bookmark for that location(s) or provide the URL to your students.
2. Develop an activity requiring students to use the site(s).
3. Assign this activity to be completed during the week.
4. Have students share their discoveries, questions, and new literacy strategies at the end of the week during a short workshop session.

The first step is to locate a site on the Internet with content related to the lessons you have planned for that week in your classroom. As you consider which site on the Internet to use, it is helpful to begin your search at a directory site for the topic that you are studying. Directories are locations on the Internet with extensive and organized links about a specific topic. Visiting central directories such as those listed in Chapter 2 will often give you many useful resources for your instructional unit, some of which may be used with Internet Workshop. When you find a location that you wish to use in your activity, set a bookmark.

The second step is to develop an activity related to the learning goals of your unit, using the site that you have bookmarked. Often, teachers prepare an activity page (see Figure 3-4) for students to complete and bring to Internet Workshop.

The third step is to assign the activity to be completed during the week. If you have only a single Internet connection in a self-contained classroom, you may wish to have students work in pairs to complete the assignment. If classes are departmentalized, you could take your class to the computer lab to complete the assignment or you could assign it as work to be completed on their own during the week.

Often, Internet Workshop is used by teachers to develop important background knowledge for a unit.

The fourth step is to have students share their discoveries, questions, and new literacy strategies at the end of the week during a short workshop session. This is a time for the class to get together and share the work that they completed and to ask questions about issues that came up. It is also a time to plan and discuss the next areas to explore for the next workshop session.

Often, Internet Workshop is used by teachers to develop important background knowledge for a unit. At other times, Internet Workshop is used during a unit to explore an idea or an issue that is central to specific curricular goals.

The activity page in Figure 3-4 was developed by two teachers, one in social studies and one in English, to develop background knowledge about

Japan. They developed the activity to begin a unit for an interdisciplinary global studies course they taught as a team. These teachers located **Kids Web Japan** (http://web-jpn.org/kidsweb/index.html) and set a bookmark for this location on the classroom computers. Notice how the tasks on the activity page are open-ended, inviting students to make their own discoveries and then bring these to the workshop session at the beginning of the unit. This is a critical aspect of any assignment designed for Internet Workshop. Open-ended questions invite students to bring many different types of information to Internet Workshop for discussion. If you ask students to find the same factual answers, there will be little to talk about during your workshop session.

Open-ended questions invite students to bring many different types of information to Internet Workshop for discussion.

Figure 3-3. Kids Web Japan (http://web-jpn.org/kidsweb/index.html), a directory site for the study of Japan.

Figure 3-4. A page developed for Internet Workshop to introduce a unit on Japan.

EXPLORING JAPAN

Internet Researcher: ________________________ Date: ________________

Objectives

This Internet Workshop will introduce you to our unit on Japan. You will have an opportunity to explore an important resource on the Internet for our unit. You will also learn about recent news events and the national government of Japan.

News About Japan

1. Go to the bookmark I have set for Kid's Web Japan (http://web-jpn.org/kidsweb/index.html) and scroll down to the bottom of this page. Now click on the button "Monthly News" (http://www.jinjapan.org/kidsweb/news.html) and read several recent news stories from Japan. Find out what is happening in Japan, take notes, and be ready to share what you discovered during Internet Workshop.

   ____

   ____

   ____

   ____

Politics and the Constitution

2. Click on the link "Politics and the Constitution" (http://www.jinjapan.org/kidsweb/japan/j.html) and explore information about the national government. Be certain to read answers to some of the questions at the bottom of this article. Write down what you learned about the politics and constitution of Japan. Be prepared to share this information during Internet Workshop.

   ____

   ____

   ____

   ____

What's Cool in Japan?

3. Now let's explore popular culture among students in Japan who are your own age. Visit "What's Cool in Japan" (http://www.jinjapan.org/kidsweb/cool.html) and find out what students are doing. Take notes about what you discovered and be ready to share this information during Internet Workshop.

   ____

   ____

   ____

   ____

Your Choice

4. Visit at least one of the many other locations at Kids Web Japan. You decide where to go! Write down notes of what you discovered and share your special discoveries with all of us during Internet Workshop. Be certain, too, to bring back new strategies

cont.

that you discovered for both finding information and for critically thinking about the information you found at Kid's Web Japan.

____
____
____
____
____
____
____

Evaluation Rubric:
8 points—You recorded important information for each item (4 x 2 = 8 points).
2 points—You effectively shared important information with us during our workshop session, helping each of us to learn about Japan.

_____

10 points—Total

The workshop session is a critical element of Internet Workshop. The purpose of this session includes:

- supporting students' ability to acquire information from the Internet;
- learning content information about the topic that students are studying;
- thinking critically about the information they, and others, obtain; and
- developing new navigational strategies on the Internet.

The workshop session is a critical element of Internet Workshop.

During the session, students share what they have learned, ask questions, and seek information to guide upcoming work. As such, this time provides the perfect opportunity to make explicit the many "hidden" reading comprehension strategies that we use to locate, critically evaluate, and synthesize information on the Internet. Engaging children in discussions about these new literacies during Internet Workshop should be a central part of your instructional program. It will provide important opportunities for each member of your classroom community to learn from one another.

The nature of the workshop session differs, depending on the teacher and the students who use it. Often, however, it shares several common characteristics. First, it takes place during a regular time period, usually at the beginning or at the end of a week. A regularly scheduled time period allows all members to anticipate the session and prepare for it. Second, workshop sessions provide opportunities for both you and your students to share new literacy strategies as well as content knowledge. This time provides an important opportunity for everyone to learn from one another about the Internet and the information they find. Third, workshop sessions enable you to develop the cooperative learning and critical evaluation skills that will be so important to your students' futures. Praising effective exchanges, modeling useful ways to exchange information, and showing how

Workshop sessions provide opportunities for both you and your students to share navigation strategies as well as content information.

to critically evaluate information resources are important strategies for teachers to use during these workshop sessions.

Teachers usually direct the first few workshop sessions to model what they wish to take place. After students understand the process, teachers turn over more responsibility for the session to students. When you are modeling the first few experiences, workshop sessions might consist of these two steps:

1. What I learned.
2. What I want to learn.

During the first step, what I learned, share with your students something that you discovered while working on the Internet. This might be a new literacy navigational strategy such as how to locate an expert in colonial history on the Internet to answer a question about the Boston Massacre. Or, it might be a new literacy evaluation strategy that you discovered such as checking a webpage to see who created it and what might prompt their interpretation of the information they provide at this location. It might also be a content issue such as information that you discovered about the Boston Massacre. After you share what you have recently learned, invite students to ask questions or share their experiences related to what you have shared.

When you are modeling the first few experiences, workshop sessions might consist of these two steps: what I learned and what I want to learn.

During the second step, what I want to learn, share something that you want to learn but haven't quite figured out. After you share what it is you wish to learn, invite others to respond and see if anyone knows how to do this. If a student does know how to assist you, encourage him/her to share the information. This will allow others to try it out after the workshop session to see if it works. The discussion that occurs during this second step is often the most productive learning time about the Internet that will take place in your classroom.

Often teachers will add a rule for everyone to follow during Internet Workshop: each student may only respond twice until everyone else has had a chance to contribute a response. This rule prevents individuals from dominating the conversation and will encourage quieter students to contribute.

After you model one or two items like this, encourage students to share what they learned and what they want to learn. Gradually, encourage students to assume ownership of Internet Workshop around these two steps. In this way, the class is always focused on items that students find most helpful in their work.

Several types of topics are appropriate for workshop sessions:

- navigation (e.g., "What are the best strategies when using a search engine?");
- content (e.g., "What did you learn about volcanoes.");
- critical evaluation (e.g., "How can I determine how a site might be biased?"); and
- synthesis (e.g., "How can I use an outline or a software tool like Kidspiration to organize the information I have discovered?").

Initially, you may find students more interested in navigation issues. As the year progresses, however, and they become more skilled at navigating the Internet, content issues will dominate. At this point, it will be important for you to introduce critical evaluation issues.

There are many variations to how Internet Workshop takes place.

There are many variations to how Internet Workshop takes place. Some teachers use an activity page like the one in Figure 3-4 and set a bookmark for the site(s) required for the activity. Others, however, ask students to record information in a journal and bring this to the workshop session. This is what Sharee Mendoza did with her "Digging for Dinosaurs" journals.

Still other teachers develop a webpage for Internet Workshop. This is another way to organize this instructional strategy, one that is quickly becoming a popular approach. The advantage of this strategy is that your workshop materials will always be there for you when you wish to use it again next year. You can see an example of this at **Stories from the Titantic** (http://web.syr.edu/~djleu/titanic.html). This is a simulation, organized within an Internet Workshop model, that is designed for middle school students. Students conducted research on a Titantic survivor, learned the story of this survivor, and then presented testimony about what happened to the Senate subcommittee that investigated this disaster.

Figure 3-5. Internet Workshop is as useful for a high school class in physics as it is for a primary grade activity in growing plants. Here is **The Particle Adventure** (http://particleadventure.org/particleadventure/) developed by the Lawrence Berkeley National Laboratory. This is perfect for an Internet Workshop experience for a class in physics.

Would you like to read an online article with more instructional ideas about Internet Workshop and additional Internet resources? Here is an article that has appeared at *Reading Online*, the Internet resource provide by the International Reading Association:

Leu, D. J., Jr. (2002b). Internet workshop: Making time for literacy. Reading Online. [Article reprinted from The Reading Teacher, 55 (5),]. [Online Serial]. Available: http://www.readingonline.org/electronic/elec_index.asp? HREF=/electronic/RT/2-02_Column/index.html

Be certain to read other articles that are located at Reading Online (http://www.readingonline.org).

Using Internet Project in your Classroom

Collaboration, so central to Internet Workshop, can also take place beyond the walls of your classroom. As you use the Internet with your students, there will come a time when you feel confident enough to explore collaborative learning opportunities with other classrooms from around the world. This is an instructional model called Internet Project. Internet Project may take place as you work with another class on a common learning activity, with students and teachers communicating extensively about the topic that both classes are exploring. Internet Project may also take place when many classes contribute data to a common site and then, after the data are analyzed, see how their data compare with others. Often there will also be discussion between participating classes about the meaning of the results and even opportunities to use the data for further analyses. Each leads to rich learning opportunities.

What might Internet Project look like in your classroom? Here is one example you might consider developing. It is called "World Wide Morning Message of the Day." Each day, your class composes a morning email message together and sends it to four other classrooms that have joined you in this activity. Each daily message describes what you are doing in your class, and the important events taking place in your part of the world. Each of these classrooms also sends a similar message to your class and the other participating classrooms. Thus, at the beginning of each school day, you and your students have four morning messages from classes around the world to read, discuss, and respond to. It is an exciting way to begin each day's activities. Moreover, your class gets to compose a message back to the others with new questions and new information. The entire process can be a highly motivating way to engage students in reading and writing. The exchanges will also lead to many research questions to explore together over the Internet (Where is Muhos, Finland? What books are students reading in Finland? What are your favorite movies?). Within a short time, your classroom can form close relationships with students in Australia, Japan, France, Finland, and many other countries in the world.

E-MAIL FOR YOU

From: Beverley Powell (bpowell@ican.net), Ottawa, Canada
Subject: "GrassRoots"—tomorrow's socialization instrument

GrassRoots (http://www.schoolnet.ca/grassroots/e/home/index.asp) is a blossoming feature of Canada's world-class **SchoolNet** (http://www.schoolnet.ca/).

More than 3,000 GrassRoots projects have been jointly funded in Canada's schools by the federal government, provincial/territorial governments, and the private sector. Records of these Internet projects linking pupils in several schools are available through the website. They can therefore be imitated (and improved upon) by any teacher, anywhere.

GrassRoots' goals are to foster skills and employability, integrate communications technology with education and in general help prepare young people for the challenges of what Marshall McLuhan called The Electric Age.

We should be aware that collaborative projects through the Internet offer far more than improved education, in the traditional sense of that word.

As the authors of this book have noted, the Internet can build new bridges between parents and children, using a technology that affects us all. Our globally competitive economy demands high corporate and personal performance. It comes through creative workplace collaboration—not simply following the boss's orders. Our children have to learn how to surf for the best information—much more than merely for their own amusement. And they will need to know to how "mix minds" with many other people.

These learning adventures offer attractive benefits to the socialization process. Young people learn how to plan tasks, work in teams, support each other, develop mutual self-respect, and improve their manners. These are nothing less than the underpinnings of civil society. Notice that they are all independent of the subject matter of the educational collaboration. In this sense, "the medium is the message." Or, to put it more colloquially, "it ain't what you do, it's the way that you do it!"

Marshall McLuhan said that we are driving into the future looking into our rear-view mirror. That was in 1964. Perhaps we are beginning to look through the windshield. One thing is quite clear. If we teachers don't do it, our students will take the wheel and show us the way!

Beverley Powell

Communicating with others around the world on a common classroom project provides special opportunities for your students, opportunities they will not experience without the Internet. You should seek out these opportunities for your students and integrate them into your curriculum for several reasons.

First, communicating with students from a different culture helps students to develop a greater appreciation for the diversity that characterizes our world. Understanding diversity leads children to respect differences; a value increasingly important in a global community.

Moreover, writing takes on a different meaning as students learn how challenging it is to compose messages to audiences from different cultural

Corresponding with other places around the world becomes an exciting way to learn the new literacies of email correspondence.

contexts. Email communication requires meaning to be very explicit; children come to learn this through misunderstandings from poorly written messages. This serves to help them learn important lessons about cultural assumptions, correct spelling, sentence structure, and organization. Each may get in the way of effective communication.

In addition, corresponding with other places around the world becomes an exciting way to learn the new literacies of email correspondence. In fact, all of your curriculum will suddenly come to life when you are able to share your work with students in another location who have similar interests. These special opportunities for communicating and learning from others comprise an important advantage of Internet use. You should seek them out as often as you can.

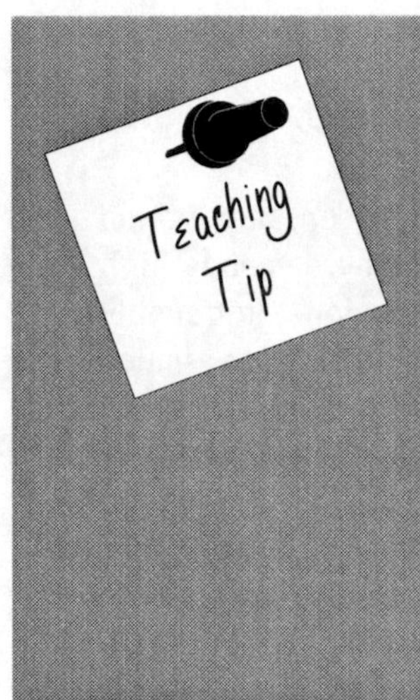

Many teachers who integrate email into their classrooms with Internet Project will have two separate email accounts. One is used for professional correspondence with parents, teachers, and administrators. The other is used for classroom correspondence such as messages from your class to another class. In addition, many teachers include an Email Assistant in their list of classroom jobs that are assigned to students each week. The Email Assistant checks incoming messages each morning in the classroom account (not on your professional account). This person also prints them out and places these messages on your desk to read when you have time. This student also types all messages that go out each day from your class, waiting until you have checked each message before sending it on its way. Assigning a different student to be your weekly Email Assistant helps to develop the new literacies of email.

There are two approaches to the use of Internet Project in a classroom: website projects and spontaneous projects developed by teachers who find one another on the Internet.

Website projects are more permanent projects, coordinated by an individual at a website.

Website projects are more permanent projects, coordinated by an individual at a website. They are a good starting point for teachers new to the Internet because they are often precisely defined with clear directions for participation and a complete package of instructional resources. There is not yet a central Internet site for website Internet projects. You will discover them in your explorations on the Internet. We will describe many of them throughout this book. Figure 3-6 lists several examples of website Internet projects. To participate, you simply need to visit the site and follow the directions.

Figure 3-6. Examples of website Internet projects and their locations

Flat Stanley Project (http://flatstanley.entries asenoreo.on.ca/)	Send a Flat Stanley around the world to collaborating classrooms, collecting journal entries as you go.
NASA Interactive Internet Projects (http://spacelink.nasa.gov/Educator. Focus/Articles/006_Interactive_Projects/)	Discuss issues of physics, engineering, space science, and many other topics with the women and men who make the Space Shuttle go and who are now building the International Space Station. Many other great projects are also at this site including: Women of NASA, Aero Design Team Online, Space Scientists Online, and Personal Satellite Assistant.
Global Virtual Classroom (http://www.virtualclassroom.org/)	This location, for grades K-12, includes great projects for your class, putting you immediately in touch with other classes around the world. Currently, it offers Global Virtual Classroom Clubhouse. Others will appear shortly.
Earth Day Groceries (http://www.earthdaybags.org)	Students decorate grocery bags with environmental friendly messages and distribute these at local grocery stories just before Earth Day. Classrooms report on their experiences. A great social action project for a unit on ecology and the environment.
Human Genetics (http://k12science.ati.stevens-tech.edu/ curriculum/genproj/)	Collect and analyze information to determine which traits are controlled by a dominant gene. Exchange your hypotheses, data, and conclusions with other students around the world.
The Albatross Project (http://www.wfu.edu/albatross/)	A great biology project. Receive an email each day with the coordinates of albatrosses being studied in the Pacific Ocean. Each has a small antenna that is being tracked by satellite. Follow their journeys around this enormous ocean. Plot their travels and formulate and test hypotheses about migration patterns with other biologists.
Global Schoolhouse Projects Registry (http://www.globalschoolhouse.org/pr/ _cfm/index.cfm)	A number of popular projects are located on the left side of this site including Newsday, Geogame, Letters to Santa, and Global Grocery List.
Monarch Watch (http://www.MonarchWatch.org)	Raise Monarch butterflies, tag them, release them, record observations about Monarchs in your area, then watch as your data and those compiled by others are used to track the annual migration of this wonderful creature!
Mind's Eye Monster Project (http://www.monsterexchange.org/)	Useful for primary grade classrooms for language arts. Classrooms and students are matched. Then one student draws a monster and writes a detailed description. The description is sent to the student's partner who must draw the monster from the description. Then, both pictures are posted in the monster gallery. Both reading and writing skills are supported. Much fun!
The International Boiling Point Project (http://k12science.stevens-tech.edu/ curriculum/boilproj/)	Boil water, collect data on several factors, and submit your results to a central database. Then, students can analyze all of the data to reach an answer to the question: What causes a pot of water to boil?
Collaborative Projects (http://k12science.ati.stevens-tech.edu/ collabprojs.html)	One of the best project sites around for science. This one site includes a wide variety of collaborative projects on topics such as water conservation, monitoring water quality, global temperatures, the biology of schoolyards, asteroid watch, and much more.

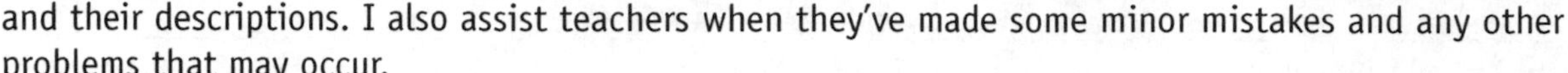

E-MAIL FOR YOU

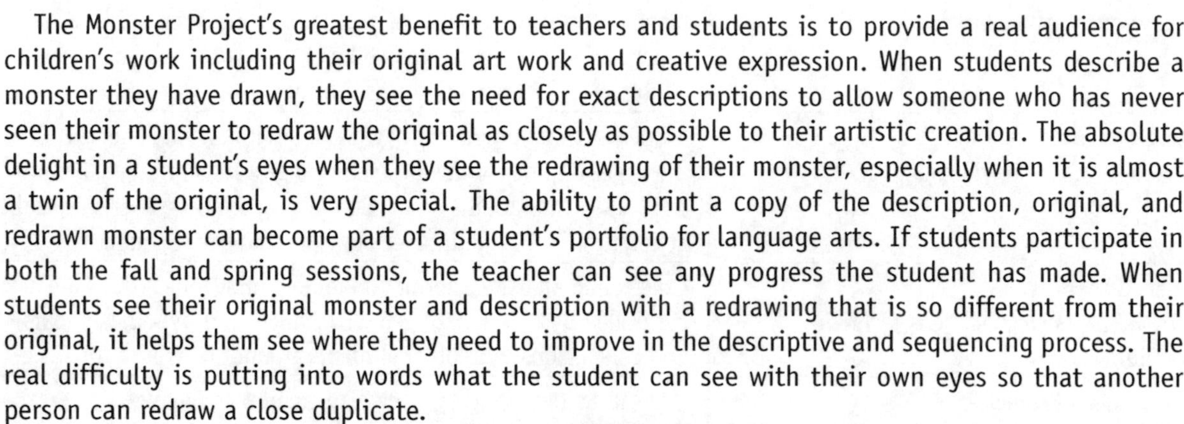

From: Susy Calvert <scalvert@access.k12.wv.us>
Subject: Using The Mind's Eye Monster Project for Language Arts

Hi!

As the administrator for the Monster Exchange Project (http://www.monsterexchange.org/), I am responsible for answering any questions teachers have about the project and helping them out with the entire process for uploading monsters and their descriptions. I also assist teachers when they've made some minor mistakes and any other problems that may occur.

The Monster Project's greatest benefit to teachers and students is to provide a real audience for children's work including their original art work and creative expression. When students describe a monster they have drawn, they see the need for exact descriptions to allow someone who has never seen their monster to redraw the original as closely as possible to their artistic creation. The absolute delight in a student's eyes when they see the redrawing of their monster, especially when it is almost a twin of the original, is very special. The ability to print a copy of the description, original, and redrawn monster can become part of a student's portfolio for language arts. If students participate in both the fall and spring sessions, the teacher can see any progress the student has made. When students see their original monster and description with a redrawing that is so different from their original, it helps them see where they need to improve in the descriptive and sequencing process. The real difficulty is putting into words what the student can see with their own eyes so that another person can redraw a close duplicate.

Other positive aspects of the project include the chance to telecommunicate with students in another country to provide them with real age-level peers who respond to their messages. It's a wonderful Internet activity to incorporate all types of technology, including Internet, email, scanning, digital photos, and uploading files from a webpage and one that doesn't demand an inordinate amount of time. When completed, students are delighted to find their monster descriptions, drawing, and redrawing accessible for everybody to view on the Monster Web Site. Sponsor of the Monster Project, Winstar, provides technical support through email and a chat room for answers to any questions teachers may have. It's wonderful to have a sponsor who provides an excellent student project on the Internet without charge for as many teachers as want to join. Also included on the website is an example of a successful grant written for technology equipment.

The Monster Project is an excellent Internet resource for teachers. It's a very comprehensive site with many features that teachers will truly find as "friendly" and one that promotes the publication of student work. Teachers with have access to the Monster Project will find a perfect project for curriculum integration and lesson planning that they will continue to access every year.

Susy Calvert, Coordinator/Teacher of Gifted Programming
Raleigh County Schools, Beckley, West Virginia
scalvert@access.k12.wv.us

A second type of Internet Project consists of spontaneous projects developed by teachers who find one another on the Internet. Spontaneous projects are increasingly common on the Internet. These projects are created by an individual teacher who then advertises for collaborating classrooms at one of several locations. After teachers express their interest by email, students in each classroom complete the project together and share their work. Spontaneous projects recently developed by teachers on the Internet include:

- **Neighbors to the North and South**
  Posted by a middle school teacher in Illinois, this project sought collaborating classrooms in Canada and Mexico to learn more about each other's country and cultures. Each week, classes would exchange information on one topic: What is your school like? Which holidays do you celebrate and what is the significance of each? What is unique about the economy in your state or province? What are current political issues that people in your state/province do not agree on? How do you spend a typical weekend?
- **Passage to Hiroshima**
  Developed by a teacher in Nagoya, Japan, this class sought other secondary classrooms interested in studying about the importance of peace and international cooperation. They proposed to begin by exchanging useful sites on the World Wide Web related to peace. This class also indicated they would be visiting Hiroshima in November and sought interview and research questions from a collaborative classroom. They volunteered to interview citizens of Hiroshima and then share the results, including photos, upon their return.
- **Culture and Clues**
  In this project for 7–9 year olds, a teacher proposed exchanging boxes of cultural artifacts from the culture where each participating school was located. Students would use these artifacts to make inferences about what life was like at each location and then write descriptions of this culture. These would be exchanged by email and then students would compare how close their guesses were.

Spontaneous Internet projects have many variations. Generally, they follow these procedures:

1. Plan a collaborative project for an upcoming unit in your classroom and write a project description. The description should contain a summary of the project, a clear list of learning goals, expectations you have for collaborating classrooms, and a projected timeline for beginning and ending the project. This step requires you to do some advance planning, at least several months before you wish to begin the project. You need to develop a clear description of the project, a timeline, a list of responsibilities for each participating class, and a list of the learning objectives. A clear description with explicit goals and timelines will make it easier for everyone to understand what will be expected of them.
2. Post the project description and timeline several months in advance at one or several locations, seeking collaborative classroom partners. This should be done in advance so that other teachers have time to find your project. Project descriptions may be posted at several locations, including:

- **Oz Projects**—http://ozprojects.edna.edu.au/
- **Global SchoolNet's Internet Project Registry**— http://www.gsn.org/pr/_cfm/index.cfm
- **SchoolNet's Grassroots Project Gallery**— http://www.schoolnet.ca/grassroots/e/project.centre/index.asp
- **Intercultural Email Classroom Connections**— http://www.iecc.org/

3. Arrange collaboration details with teachers in other classrooms who agree to participate.
4. Complete the project, perhaps using Internet Workshop to work on the project and plan the exchange of information with your collaborating classrooms.

Figure 3-7. An example of a Project Description posted at **Global SchoolNet's Internet Project Registry** (http://www.gsn.org/pr/_cfm/index.cfm)

Project Name: Latitude and Shadow Length
Contact Person: Helen Schrand
Email Contact: schrandh@ride.ri.net

Description: Students will measure the length of the shadow of a 2-meter pole at three times during a school day on three dates over the course of the school year. We would like to receive similar data from schools in other locations so students can compare their findings with those from a variety of places.

How Long: 7 months

Objectives: Students will:

1. learn to use meter sticks to measure accurately.
2. locate places on a world map or globe using latitude and longitude.
3. graph and analyze data.
4. determine the effect of latitude and time of day on shadow length.

Share: We will compile a table of results we receive and email it to participating classes.

Are you interested in discovering more information about using Internet Project in your classroom? Here is an article that has appeared at Reading Online (http://www.readinonline.org), the Internet resources of the International Reading Association:

Leu, D. J., Jr. (2001). Internet project: Preparing students for new literacies in a global village. Reading Online. [Article reprinted from The Reading Teacher, 54, 568-585]. [Online Serial]. Available: http://www.readingonline.org/electronic/elec_index.asp?HREF=/electronic/RT/3-01_Column/index.html

Figure 3-8. Global SchoolNet's Internet Projects Registry homepage, a useful place to find examples of Internet projects developed by teachers around the world (http://www.gsn.org/pr/_cfm/index.cfm).

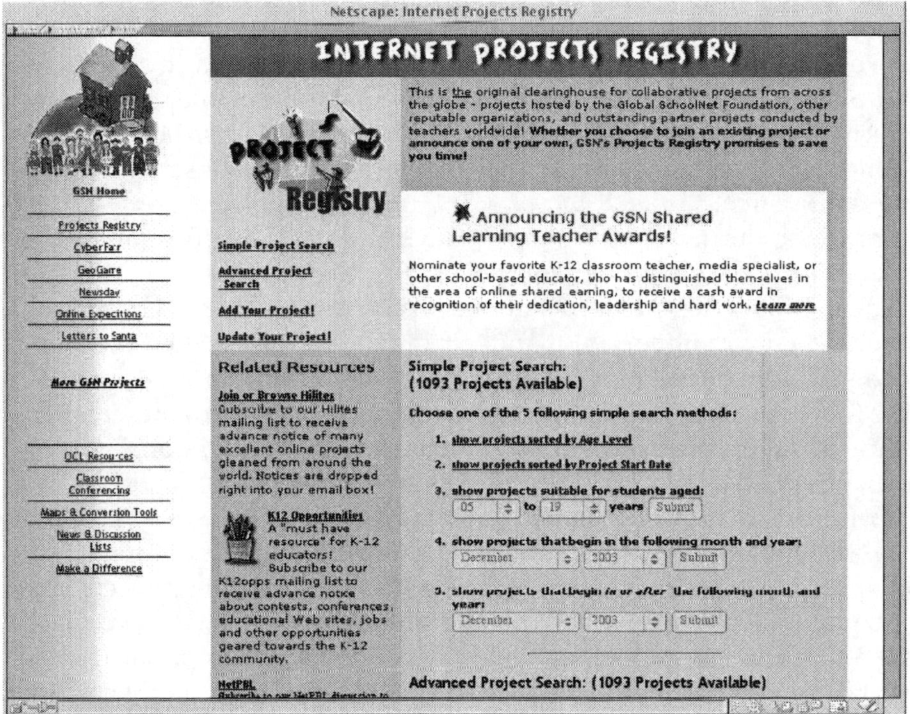

Using Internet Inquiry in Your Classroom

Once your students have become familiar with locating Internet resources, Internet Inquiry may be a useful means to develop independent research skills, develop important critical literacy strategies, and allow students to pursue a question that holds a special interest for them. Internet Inquiry may be developed by small groups or by individuals. Inquiry units usually begin with students identifying a topic and a question they wish to explore related to the current unit. The question may be as specific as "What happened to Benedict Arnold after he betrayed his country in the Revolutionary War?" or as large as "What is it like to live in Japan?" The most important aspect of Internet Inquiry is that the students should conduct research on a question that they find important.

Internet Inquiry consists of these five phases:

1. *Develop* a question.
2. *Search* for information.
3. *Evaluate* the information.
4. *Compose* an answer to your question.
5. *Share* the answer with others.

Internet Inquiry may be a useful means to develop independent research skills, develop important critical literacy strategies, and allow students to pursue a question that holds a special interest for them.

During the question phase, students identify an important question they wish to explore. You can support this phase by engaging in group or individual brainstorming sessions or by setting a bookmark to a central directory for the general topic area and allowing students to explore the area, looking for an issue to explore.

Once students have decided on a question they wish to explore, the second phase, search, begins. Students may search on the Internet for useful information related to their question. Students should also be reminded to use more traditional resources found in their classroom or school library during their search.

During the third phase, evaluate, students should evaluate all of the information they have located and respond to the question they initially posed. Sometimes, this will lead students to address another question they discover to be more important than their initial question. When this happens, they should be encouraged to repeat the search and evaluate phases.

The fourth phase, compose, requires students to compose a presentation of their work. There are many ways to do this including a traditional written report, a poster session, a multimedia presentation, or an oral report.

During the final phase, share, students have an opportunity to share their work with others and respond to questions about their work. Some teachers set aside a regular time each week for sharing the projects students complete during Internet Inquiry. Sometimes this will take place during a workshop session. Sometimes a special science or social studies fair will be held where students have an opportunity to share their work with other classes at school. Sometimes inquiry projects may be shared online.

Internet Inquiry can be an exciting part of your curriculum, allowing students important opportunities to read, evaluate, and write within content areas such as English/language arts, math, science, and social studies.

E-MAIL FOR YOU

Subject: An Internet Project with Thailand
From: Linda Shearin lshearin@bellsouth.net

Greetings Virtual Travelers,

Over the past year my students and I have been engaged in building a webpage with Benchamatheputit School in Petchburi, Thailand. It has been a wonderful experience for us all!

Chumlong Buasuwan, a teacher at Benchama School, has taught me a great deal about his culture and his students. We have worked together to plan the webpage reflecting the commonalities and differences between his school and mine. His students wrote a touching poem celebrating what we share in common that appears on the first page of the website.

What has amazed me most, and my students also, is that the Thai students created all their work on the webpage in English. Although English is their secon d language, and many students don't consider themselves fluent, they have done extraordinary work.

We have faced some challenges over the course of our partnership. Our school calendars are not quite compatible so communication between the students was sometimes affected. Chumlong and I found it challenging to communicate for planning purposes via online chats because Thailand is 12 hours ahead of the US. This time difference also precluded online chats or teleconferences between the two schools.

My students experienced culture shock when they found out that Petchburi has three royal palaces. "What," they said, "do we have in Raleigh, NC that can compare with that?" We had to look more closely at our own community to find aspects of it that the Thai students would find appealing.

Nevertheless, we have all thoroughly enjoyed our partnership. We are planning this year to collaborate on an online newspaper featuring activities at both schools, while we continue to update our original webpage. Chumlong is an outstanding and innovative educator. I am looking forward to learning more from him as we continue our work together!

Linda Shearin
Academically Gifted Resource Teacher
Baileywick Elementary School
Raleigh, NC

Using WebQuest in Your Classroom

A final instructional framework is formally called a WebQuest model. This model means many things to many people. Originally, it was intended to be an activity in which some or all of the information students required came from resources on the Internet. Today, the WebQuest model, developed by Bernie Dodge, usually contains the following sections:

- Introduction
- The Task Definition
- A Description of the Process
- Information Resources
- Guidance in Organizing the Information
- A Concluding Activity

Webquests may be developed by anyone but they are often developed by teachers to provide students in their classroom with an important learning experience using Internet resources.Because they appear on the Internet, they are also available to other teachers.

Because Webquests appear on the Internet, they are also available to other teachers.

The beginning of a webquest usually contains an introduction, orienting students to the learning activity. This explains the purpose of the learning activity in a short paragraph. Next, it usually provides a description of the task students will complete. This will list each of the tasks they are to complete and do this in a manner that is clear to the student. Then, a webquest usually describes the process to follow. This explains how each task should be completed.

The fourth section of a webquest provides links to the information resources on the Internet that will be required to complete the activity. Because these links are provided, students avoid endless searching for information and are able to focus on the activity.

The fifth section of a webquest usually contains guidance about how to organize the information students acquire. This might direct students to answer guiding questions or follow directions to complete a timeline, concept map, or another organizational framework.

Webquests usually end with a concluding statement. This reminds students what they have learned and bring closure to the activity. Sometimes, this will invite students to explore related topics.

A recent addition to many webquest pages is information about how students' work will be evaluated. Often this appears in the form of a scoring chart or a rubric.

The WebQuest model is quickly appearing on the Internet as teachers develop webquests to organize lessons. As a result, you can find many different varieties; some tend to focus on specific learning tasks and do not always include the collaborative aspects found in Internet Workshop. You can find out more information about the WebQuest model at the **WebQuest Page** (http://WebQuest.org/). Examples of webquests for grades K-12 appear at the link to "Top" on this page and at many other locations on the Internet. One of these is the wonderful database of webquests created by teachers in the **Saskatoon (East) School Division in Canada** (http://sesd.sk.ca/teacherresource/WebQuests.htm).

Webquests are quickly appearing on the Internet as popular curriculum resources developed by many teachers.

The WebQuest model can be an efficient way to integrate the Internet into your classroom. However, we encourage you to carefully evaluate each webquest before deciding to use it in your classroom, just as you would any other curricular material. We believe the following questions should be asked before using any webquest:

- *Does this webquest meet my curriculum goals and learning objectives?* How? What do my students learn from this experience? What does it teach? Is this important?
- *How much time will this take for my students to complete?* Is this time well spent or could we accomplish more in less time with another learning experience?
- *Does the webquest require my students to think critically about information and evaluate the information they encounter?* Does higher order

thinking take place during the webquest or are students only required to develop literal, factual knowledge?

- *Has this webquest been developed to accommodate individual learning needs and interests?* Will all of my students be able to benefit from this activity? If not, what must I do to meet individual differences?
- *Is there an opportunity for students to share the results of their webquest with the rest of the class for discussion and additional learning?* How do students share their learning with the rest of the class, enriching everyone's insights about what took place?
- *Do students know, in advance, how their work on a webquest will be evaluated?* Will students know what is important to accomplish in the activity based on how it will be evaluated?
- *Are all of the links in a webquest active and appropriate for my students?* Have I completed the activity myself, and checked each of the links to resources that appear?

Of course, not all webquests match the above goals. As with any activity or resource you use in your classroom, you should carefully evaluate its benefits before using it. Do not simply assume that since it is a webquest that is on the Internet it must be a good experience for your students. Some will be; some will not. Some Webquests will enhance your students' understanding of the content as well as help them to develop new literacies; other sites will merely lead them through fill-in-the-blank exercises that could easily be done with pen and paper.

One of our greatest concerns about Webquests is that they often have students working alone, in pairs, or in small groups without ever getting back together with the entire class to share, exchange, and discuss their experiences.

Also, remember that online sites change incredibly fast—links change, sites move or disappear, and new resources are added continually. Keep in mind that almost anyone can create a website with little or no outside evaluation. Thus, even more than with other curricular resources, you need to evaluate every webquest. The reliability of sites and suitability of activities should not be left to the person who created the activity.

One of our greatest concerns about webquests is that they often have students working alone, in pairs, or in small groups without ever getting back together with the entire class to share, exchange, and discuss their experiences. It is easy, however, to increase the social learning aspects of any webquest by adding a workshop session at the completion of the quest. This way you will have a better understanding of what children learned in order to plan upcoming experiences. You will also have an additional opportunity to shape and support the learning taking place as students explain the meanings they have derived from their experiences. You have an important role to play in the WebQuest model. As always, you know your particular students' needs better than anyone else.

Citation Strategies for Internet References

As students increase their use of the Internet and acquire new literacies, a common question for many of us is how to cite Internet information resources. The question is so new that definitive guidelines for citation style are still evolving. The problem is compounded because so many different types of media sources are available on the Internet: film, video, audio clips, photographs, databases, and many others.

The best information about how to cite Internet resources may be found at the **Learning Page of the Library of Congress: Citing Electronic Sources** (http://memory.loc.gov/learn/start/cite/index.html). This resource provides examples of how to cite the wide variety of media now available to our students. It also contains links to other citation style resources on the Internet. Another location containing links to many different citation guides is located at the Internet Public Library's, **Citing Electronic Resources** (http://www.ipl.org/div/farq/netciteFARQ.html).

The best information about how to cite Internet resources may be found at the ***Learning Page of the Library of Congress: Citing Electronic Sources***

Generally, style manuals favor including the following information in a reference to Internet resources:

> Author's Last Name, Author's First Name. "Title of Document." Title of Complete Work (if applicable). Version or File Number, if applicable. Retrieval date and access path.
>
> For example:
> The U.S. Library of Congress. "The Learning Page of the Library of Congress: How to Cite Electronic Sources." Retrieved January 13, 2004 from http://memory.loc.gov/ammem/ndlpedu/start/cite/index.html

Often the order of this information will change, depending on which reference style manual you use. And, keep in mind these conventions are changing quickly as the Internet itself changes. Regularly checking the citation manuals listed above will keep you current as these styles evolve.

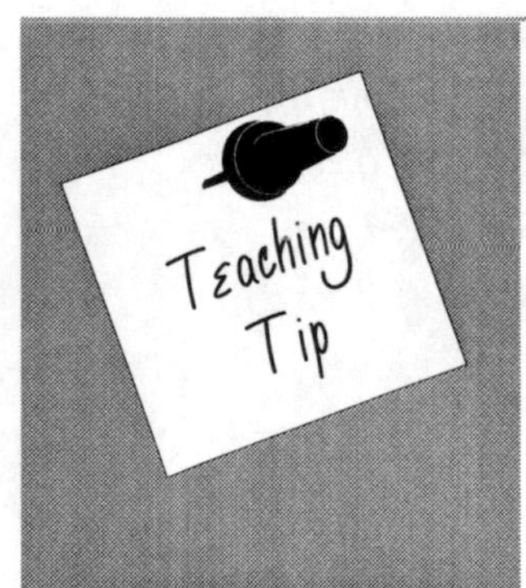

Have your students visit **How to Cite Sources** (http://oslis.k12.or.us/elementary/howto/cited/). They will find an online Citation Maker for developing bibliographic references. Simply enter each type of bibliographic information in the appropriate boxes and the site will provide you with a copy of the complete reference. There is also a useful citation worksheet for students to use, helping them to keep track of each reference as they conduct their research. You will find more information about interactive citation resources and fair use policies for teachers in the New Literacies section at the end of Chapter 5.

Using the Internet to Plan Instruction: Directories for Curriculum Resources

Once you consider these issues, most of your current instructional practices may be easily integrated with Internet resources as you modify Internet Workshop, Internet Project, Internet Inquiry, or WebQuest to meet your own needs. In many ways, the Internet is simply another information resource for your classroom, much like a very powerful encyclopedia. Certainly it also has special potentials, especially in the area of communicating with distant locations, collaborating with others around the world, or discussing issues with experts in the area you are studying. By and large, however, the Internet is simply another information resource for your students to exploit as they engage in classroom learning activities.

Sometimes, though, it is hard to find the resources you require to develop the specific instructional resources you require for a unit. Of course, like Sharee, you may wish to join a mailing list (listserv) and ask others for their recommendations. Alternatively, you could explore the directory sites in specific curricular areas that exist on the Internet, some of which were listed in Chapter 2. You may also wish to visit some of these additional, more general directories as you explore ways in which the Internet may assist you with planning. Here are some outstanding educational directories that exist for teachers interested in using the Internet in their classroom:

- **Blue Web'n**—http://www.kn.pacbell.com/wired/bluewebn/
  This is an outstanding collection of the very best curriculum experiences for students. Each is carefully reviewed before receiving a Blue Web'n Blue Ribbon. There is also a searchable data base so you can find exactly the resource you require.
- **The New York Times Learning Network**—
  http://www.nytimes.com/learning/
  This location has sections for students, teachers, and parents. In addition to great lesson plans for using the free articles at the *New York Times* site in your classroom for current events, this location has a teacher chat area, lesson plan archives, a daily quotation, weekly news quizzes, and links to great curriculum resources in all areas.
- **SchoolNet**—http://www.schoolnet.ca/
  In English or French, this resource from Canada provides educators with an exceptional collection of instructional resources for every area of the curriculum at every grade level. Projects, links to curriculum resources, connections with other Canadian schools, and many more types of support are right at your fingertips.
- **Yahooligans Teachers' Guide**—
  http://www.yahooligans.com/tg/index.html
  Useful for elementary and middle school teachers, this location provides important information about teaching strategies, acceptable use policies, and citation styles. It also contains a limited collection of curriculum resources, but what is here is very good.

Visiting the Classroom: Susan Silverman's Webfolio in New York

If you are interested in exploring the potential of Internet Project, visit the collection of collaborative projects developed by Susan Silverman in New York at **Mrs. Silverman's Webfolio** (http://www.kids-learn.org/). Susan puts together Internet projects with teachers around the world. She has recently become an Instructional Technology Integration Specialist in her district, where she continues her important work. Susan's site tells the story about the exciting potential of Internet Project far better than we can ever hope to accomplish within the pages of this book.

The Webfolio contains links to the many Internet projects Susan's classes have completed as well as projects that she has facilitated for others. These include collaborative projects developed around fall poetry, *Stellaluna*, research about owls around the world, and many more. If you explore some of these sites in depth, you will also discover popular travel buddy projects such as Flat Stanley and Winnie the Pooh. Be certain to visit the links to some of these projects at **Internet Projects** (http://comsewogue. k12.ny.us/~ssilverman/class99/netprojects.html). Each project has linked many teachers, providing students in these classes with exceptional opportunities to develop the new literacies of the Internet and other ICT while they also develop content knowledge.

Figure 3-9. The homepage for **Susan Silverman's Webfolio**, a great location to explore the potential of Internet Project (http://www.kids-learn.org/)

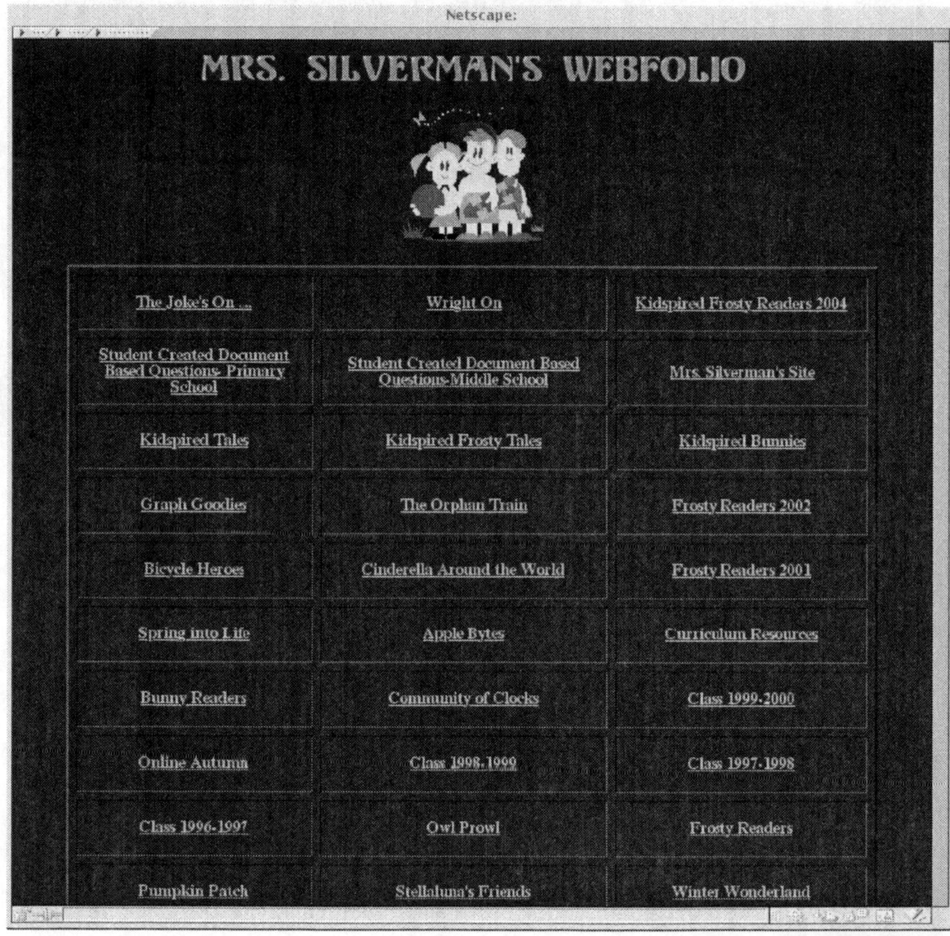

Susan creates projects that are aligned with the curriculum standards of her state, standards that are similar to those found in other states. Then, Susan announces her projects on a number of mailing lists (listservs) and other locations in order to locate teachers with similar curricular needs who are interested in collaboration. In these announcements, Susan carefully defines the purpose of each project, the timeline for completion, and suggestions for how each class might contribute their special talents. You can find an example of a project description by visiting the **About this Project** link for the Online Autumn project (http://comsewogue.k12.ny.us/~ssilverman/autumn/project.html).

The beauty of the Susan's style of Internet Project is that each project results in rich curricular resources developed by classrooms around the world that then become available for all of us to use. Are you interested in having your class read the fall poetry of other primary grade children?

E-MAIL FOR YOU

Subject: The Rewards of Project Based Learning
From: Susan Silverman (susansilverman@yahoo.com)

Looking for a fun, enriching way to integrate the Internet into your curriculum? Consider joining a collaborative project. Your students will acquire online communication skills and meet children from around the world. You will develop creative and technical expertise, discover new educational resources, and have the chance to collaborate with talented colleagues. Your class work will be digitally showcased for parents and administrators to appreciate. And best of all, you only need to have email and Internet access to participate!

My passion for online project based learning began seven years ago when my second grade joined a story-writing project. Several classes from different schools were contributing a paragraph each to a collaborative story. It was so exciting to read the new chapters as they arrived in our classroom every week via email. Finally it was our turn to write a paragraph and the children were thrilled to see the completed project on the Internet. Their writing was especially good and I realized how much pride students take in their work when they are writing for an authentic audience.

After this wonderful experience we joined more collaborative projects and before long I was coordinating my own online projects.

My first project, *An Apple a Day* showcased poetry on apples from second grades. I couldn't wait to post the adorable poems and illustrations from children throughout the US, Canada, and Australia. The experience was so positive that I went on to coordinate projects on seasons, animals, literature, historical documents, famous people, and math! All of these projects have a common thread; educators working together to share their best practices and promote an authentic learning experience for children.

You might think that it would be difficult to find participants from so many geographic areas when teachers need to follow a prescribed curriculum. This has not been a problem at all. The project topics are universal and support state and national standards.

By now you might be wondering where you can find collaborative projects for your grade level. I've compiled a list of places to help you get started.

Where to Find Collaborative Internet Projects http://kids-learn.org/projects.htm

So, what are you waiting for? Sign up for a project today!
Susan Silverman
Instructional Technology Integration Specialist
Comsewogue School District
Port Jefferson Station, New York
http://kids-learn.org

Visit **Online Autumn** (http://comsewogue.k12.ny.us/~ssilverman/autumn/index.html). Is your class doing a unit on apples or pumpkins with your young students? Visit **Pumpkin Patch** (http://www.kids-learn.org/pumpkins/) or **An Apple a Day** (http://members.aol.com/Apples2nd/) to see the wonderful poems, recipes, art work, and other great resources to use immediately in your own classroom, perhaps with Internet Workshop. Pay a visit to this important model for Internet Project and be certain to let Susan know how important her work is for all of us.

Integrating New Literacies within Instructional Models

While several instructional models may be used to help students develop the ability to ask productive questions, Internet Inquiry is probably best at accomplishing this, since students must first determine the question that will direct their inquiry.

We have described the major instructional models that are useful when integrating the Internet and other ICT into content-area instruction: Internet Workshop, Internet Project, Internet Inquiry, and WebQuest. It is important to keep in mind that each model also provides special opportunities for supporting your students in developing the new literacies of the Internet and other ICT. You will recall from Chapter 1 that these new literacies tend to cluster around five important functions:

1. *identifying* important questions;
2. *navigating* information networks to locate relevant information;
3. *critically evaluating* information;
4. *synthesizing* information; and
5. *communicating* the solutions to others.

The Internet and other ICT allow us to accomplish each of these functions, while they demand new skills and strategies in order to do so. The instructional models we have described may be used to help students develop the new literacy skills and strategies in each of these areas.

Identifying Important Questions

Helping students to know how to ask good questions is something that schools have not always considered important. Teachers tend to ask students questions; students tend to answer them. That is how classrooms are often organized. With an informational resource as powerful as the Internet, however, the ability to ask good questions becomes essential to guide any search for information. While several instructional models may be used to help students develop the ability to ask productive questions, Internet Inquiry is probably best at accomplishing this, since students must first determine the question that will direct their inquiry. Especially helpful, here, is to conduct whole class or small group workshop sessions during which you discuss together what defines an important question worth exploring on the Internet. You also may wish to bring students together in workshop sessions periodically during their inquiry projects to discuss how inquiry questions may change, why they might change, and to regularly update one another with the questions each student is pursuing. This will also foster collaboration as students, on their own Internet inquiries, discover new resources that may be helpful to another student's inquiry project. By encouraging this, you will foster the socially supportive environment that is at the heart of a successful new literacies classroom.

Navigating Information Networks to Locate Relevant Information

A second important area is the ability to navigate information networks to locate information. This includes two elements: navigating within a webpage and the more complex new literacy skills associated with effective search engine use. Both were covered in Chapter 2. Which instructional models best support the development of these new literacy strategies?

Many teachers find Internet Workshop and WebQuest to be useful models for developing navigational skills within a particular site. As you use these models, engage students in conversations about why they selected certain links, and not others, to locate resources that were useful. Invite them to share the clues that they use when navigating from one link to another.

Many teachers find Internet Workshop and Webquest to be useful models for developing navigational skills within a particular site.

When you want students to develop the more challenging new literacy skills associated with effective search engine use, Internet Workshop and Internet Inquiry are very helpful. In Chapter 2, you saw an example of how to include search engine strategies within Internet Workshop (see Figure 2-4). Or, you might also wish to conduct an Internet Workshop session solely on search engine use. You could, for example, assign students the task of finding the best set of keywords to locate different types of information and discuss the results that they bring back to the workshop session.

Internet Inquiry is also useful for developing search engine skills. Here, teachers will often conduct a short workshop session at the beginning of each inquiry session to have students share the best search strategies that they have discovered. You might also invite them each day to bring back new search strategies that they have discovered to share with the entire class.

Critically Evaluating Information

A third important skill area in the new literacies of the Internet is the critical evaluation of information that you locate. As we discussed in Chapter 2, we want students to read with a critical eye. You may accomplish this within any of the models that we have presented, but it is especially appropriate with the more independent reading that takes place within Internet Inquiry. Whichever instructional model you use, you might wish to conduct regular, short workshop sessions on critical evaluation that will help your students to think more carefully about the resources they are discovering. You may wish to use the who, what, where, when, why, and how procedure described in Chapter 2, with students bringing back the answers to a workshop discussion organized around questions like these:

1. *Who* created the information at your site? How did you discover this information? What might this tell you about the information at this site?
2. *What* is the purpose of the site? Did you find an "About this site" link? How does this inform you about the type of information that you will find at this location?
3. *When* was the information at this site last updated? Is the information recent or dated?

4. *Where* can I go to check the accuracy of this information?
5. *Why* did this person, or group, put this information on the Internet?
6. *How* is the information at this site shaped by the stance taken by the creator of the site? How is the information presented at the site "shaped" by this person's perspective. All information is "shaped."

Having regular conversations with your students about these issues will help them develop the important new literacies of critical evaluation that are so central to effective use of information found on the Internet.

Synthesizing Information

A fourth important skill area in the new literacies of the Internet and other ICT includes the synthesis of information from many different sources. WebQuest and Internet Inquiry are often very useful when you seek to increase learning in this area, though others may be used as well. The WebQuest model requires students to integrate a limited set of information within a reasonably fixed task. Internet Inquiry presents a bit more of a challenge since the information to be integrated is reasonably unbounded, limited only by the results of a student's search process.

Communicating the Solutions to Others

Finally, communication skills are central to the new literacies of the Internet. Both Internet Project and Internet Inquiry are useful models to support this important skill area. Internet Project provides a slightly more sheltered context in which to develop these skills as you communicate with other classrooms by email. Usually, for example, your class will collaboratively construct email messages. Many other technologies may be used for communication, of course. With Internet Inquiry, you may have students make their presentations on a weblog, on a webpage, or in PowerPoint or another type of presentation software (see Chapter 12).

Each of the instructional models covered in this chapter provides important support in developing the five most important aspects of new literacies. Each will help you teach the new literacies of the Internet while you help students develop important content-area knowledge.

Internet Inquiry is the instructional model that appears to best support the complete range of new literacy skills and strategies required to use the Internet and other ICT effectively.

The Special Potential of Internet Inquiry for Developing New Literacies

We want to make an important observation about teaching new literacies in your classroom. Internet Inquiry is the instructional model that appears to best support the complete range of new literacy skills and strategies required to use the Internet and other ICT effectively. This is true because each of the phases of Internet Inquiry maps to one of the major skill areas of the new literacies. We show this in Figure 3-10.

More than any other instructional model, Internet Inquiry most closely approaches the major functions of the new literacies of the Internet (see Figure 3-10). This requires us to carefully consider the use of this model in our classrooms. We believe, however, that it is often useful to begin with other instructional models in order to prepare your students for the much more independent learning skills required by Internet Inquiry. Thus, you may wish to begin the year with Internet Workshop, Internet Project, and WebQuest, and move to Internet Inquiry as you progress through the year and as your students develop increasing levels of skill and confidence.

Figure 3-10. How the functional areas of new literacy skills and strategies map closely onto the phases of internet inquiry

Major Areas of New Literacy Skills and Strategies	Phases of Internet Inquiry
Identify important questions.	1. Develop a question.
Navigate information networks to locate relevant information.	2. Search for information.
Critically Evaluate the usefulness of information that is found.	3. Critically Evaluate the information.
Synthesize information to answer the question or solve the problem.	4. Compose an answer to your question.
Communicate the answer to others.	5. Share the answer with others.

A Final Word

Earlier we made an important point: It is not the resources available on the Internet, though these are considerable, that will make a difference for your students. Instead, your students' success at life's opportunities will be determined by what you decide to do with these resources. As you begin to incorporate the Internet into your classroom, making it an integral part of teaching and learning, you will develop new ideas and new ways of teaching. We want to encourage you to share these ideas with other teachers who are also learning about this new resource for education. Though we have no evidence, we suspect the Internet will have its greatest impact on teaching and learning through the new ideas that teachers share with one another and the new connections that are formed between teachers and students around the world. For too long, teachers have spent much of their time in school, isolated from other teachers by the walls of their classrooms. The Internet allows us to transcend these walls and learn from one another about best instructional practices. We want to encourage you to take the time to support others and to learn from others as you begin your journey to fulfill the potential the Internet provides for new ways of learning and new ways of teaching.

It is not the resources available on the Internet, though these are considerable, that will make a difference for your students. Instead, your students' success at life's opportunities will be determined by what you decide to do with these resources.

Additional Instructional Resources on the Internet

Busy Teachers' Web Site—http://www.ceismc.gatech.edu/busyt/

Just what it says! If you are busy, stop by. Great locations to wonderful sites organized by subject area. A wonderful resource for teaching ideas and curricular resources.

Civil War Photograph Collection—
http://memory.loc.gov/ammem/cwphtml/cwphome.html

This site at the Library of Congress contains over 1,000 photographs from the Civil War, many by Mathew Brady. Viewing these images makes you feel the national conflict and struggle during this period.

Digital Dozen—http://www.enc.org/features/dd/?ls=fe

Each month the 12 best sites for K-12 math and science are carefully selected by the team at the Eisenhower National Clearinghouse for Math and Science and posted here. One of the finest sites for great ideas on the Web! Set a bookmark! And don't forget to explore Digital Dozen sites from previous months.

Geometry Problem of the Week—http://mathforum.org/geopow/

Part of the exceptional Math Forum site, this location provides you and your students with a challenging geometry problem to solve each week. Use it for a quick Internet Workshop and have a short workshop session at the end of the week to compare solutions.

Global Grocery List—http://landmark-project.com/ggl/

Students share local grocery prices to build a growing table of data from around the world. This Internet Project site allows your students to engage in computation, analysis, and conclusion-building for social studies, science, and mathematics.

Reading Online—http://www.readingonline.org

Devoted solely to teachers, this is the International Reading Association's free electronic journal. In addition to great articles and a discussion forum, this site contains a wealth of resources for teachers, including lists of Internet projects, useful websites, and tips for technology use.

The Biology Project—http://www.biology.arizona.edu/

A central site for all high school biology teachers that is being developed by the University of Arizona. Problem sets and tutorials in: biochemistry, cell biology, developmental biology, human biology, chemicals and human health, and much more. Some sections are also in Spanish.

The Constitution: A Living Document—
http://www.yahooligans.com/tg/constitution.html

A complete unit with lesson plans, activities, and evaluations for students in Grades 6–8 who are studying this important U.S. document.

The Exploratorium—http://www.exploratorium.edu/

A palace of hands-on science learning in San Francisco, this site makes outstanding interactive adventures in science available to the world. A great location for science, fun, and learning.

The ThinkQuest Library—
http://www.thinkquest.org/library/index.html

Here you will find over 5,000 websites created by students from around the world who entered the competitions for web lessons sponsored by

ThinkQuest. Spend some time looking for exactly what you need for your class. Then, consider entering a project from your own school!

The Nine Planets Tour—http://seds.lpl.arizona.edu/billa/tnp/

This is the best tour through the solar system that exists. At each stop, beautiful photographs of each planetary object are displayed along with information about the object. Short sound clips and videos are also available. Many links take you to related sites. A wonderful journey!

The United Nations Cyber Schoolbus—
http://www.un.org/Pubs/CyberSchoolBus/

Is your class studying the United Nations? Visit this site developed by the UN. Take a field trip to the United Nations, explore the mission of this organization, and find teaching ideas. Many classroom activities.

VolcanoWorld—http://volcano.und.nodak.edu

Study volcanoes around the world, talk to a vulcanologist, obtain real-time data on active volcanoes, and many more fun activities for kids and adults.

Online Communities for Teaching with the Internet

EDInfo

Updates from the US Department of Education.
Subscription address: listproc@inet.ed.gov or go to http://www.ed.gov/index and click on Ed Newsletters and check the EDInfo box.
Recent messages: http://www.ed.gov/MailingLists/EDInfo/index.html
Archives: http://www.ed.gov/MailingLists/EDInfo/Archive/index.html

EDTECH

Here is a list with an extraordinarily large (3,500) number of subscribers who discuss K-12 issues of technology use in schools. The list is especially useful if you have questions about new technologies and new literacies that are entering schools. The archives may be viewed from the link to "Discussion Logs" on the homepage.
Subscription address: http://www.h-net.org/lists/subscribe
Homepage: http://www.h-net.org/~edweb/

K12ADMIN

A mailing list for K-12 administrators, but the conversations focus largely on instructional issues. Over 1,000 members.
Subscription address: listserv@listserv.syr.edu
Archives: http://listserv.syr.edu/archives/k12admin.html

RTEACHER

A forum for conversations about literacy in both traditional and electronic contexts. This is a very supportive list and diverse group of educators interested in using the Internet for literacy education. They also discuss non-Internet aspects of literacy education.
Subscription address: listserv@bookmark.reading.org
Homepage: http://www.reading.org/virtual/rt_listserv.html
Archives: http://www.reading.org/archives/rteacher.html

Teachnet T2T

Exchanging ideas, articles, research, experiences, and questions about teaching.

Subscription address: majordomo@t2tforum.com

Homepage: http://www.teachnet.com/t2t/

WWWEDU

A moderated discussion list with over 1600 members from 35 countries. Focuses on the use of the WWW in education.

Subscription: wwwedu-subscribe@yahoogroups.com.

Homepage: http://www.edwebproject.org/wwwedu.html

Archives: http://www.edwebproject.org/wwwedu.html

K12-AUP

Acceptable Use Policies Discussion

Subscription address: majordomo@merit.edu

4 Communicating on the Internet: Email, Mailing Lists, and Other Forms of Electronic Communication

Electronic communication lends itself to various purposes through a variety of activities for both teachers and students.

Not only is the Internet a powerful tool for locating and linking information, but also for linking people. In fact, electronic communication is probably the most familiar use of the Net for most people. It is a quick, cheap, and efficient way to communicate one-on-one with family members, friends, and colleagues both locally and globally. We can also participate in group communication through mailing lists, newsgroups, and weblogs. In addition, real-time (synchronous) communication through programs such as Internet chat and videoconferencing have become popular, especially among students.

In Chapter 4, we will show you how electronic communication lends itself to various purposes through a variety of activities for both teachers and students. For example, teachers can access the expertise and experience of educators around the world while students may conduct peer interviews in another language. At first glance it may seem that Internet activities are no more than renamed older techniques—penpals become keypals, for instance—but take a closer look. The Internet can expand the scope of traditional lessons and activities while leading students toward more independent learning. We will discuss the new literacies necessary to achieve these benefits as well as suggest strategies for incorporating these literacies into your curriculum.

At its best, the Internet offers new ways of learning about and experiencing the world. Most importantly, electronic communication exposes us to a variety of people and a wide range of views from around the globe, with the potential to broaden perspectives and develop critical thinking as we integrate new and diverse ideas with our own experiences. The Internet is not just another tool for getting information; it is an opportunity for students and teachers alike to increase understanding and share their ideas.

After reading this chapter, you should be able to:

1. Manage your email account to communicate successfully with others through individual messages, listservs, newsgroups, and weblogs.
2. Use netiquette and common Internet conventions to promote more effective electronic communication.
3. Be familiar with several strategies for integrating the communicative aspects of the Internet into your curriculum.
4. Identify four types of synchronous communication and share several sites for obtaining additional information about them.

Teaching with the Internet: Marilyn Campbell's Class

Marilyn Campbell was especially excited about the upcoming school year. The first major unit for her social studies class was Latin America. She and the other sixth grade teachers were working together so students could study various aspects of Latin American culture in all of their classes. As in the past, Marilyn was searching the Internet for information related to the unit; in addition, she decided to expand her electronic communication skills by exploring a variety of email uses. It was easier than she had expected.

She started by sending an email message to Gary Diaz, the high school Spanish teacher. Although they lived in different towns, email made it easy to communicate. Marilyn didn't have to call at a certain time or leave messages on an answering machine. In addition, she felt more comfortable asking for help since emailing wouldn't interrupt Gary's schedule in the way that telephoning might have. Gary sent a reply including some of his favorite sites and also suggested that she check out some keypal sites.

Marilyn thought international keypals would be great. The students could ask questions, conduct interviews, and perhaps exchange photos. They could learn a lot about other cultures. When she did a search for "keypals," Marilyn found several sites. She especially liked **Teaching.Com** (http://teaching.com). They offered several services: her students could look for individual keypals, she could request a partner class, and they could link with 50+ aged volunteers for an inter-generational experience. She could read messages on their webpage or subscribe to a list. She decided to subscribe to the K-12 mailing list at **Intercultural Email Classroom Connections** (http://teaching.com/IECC). She then posted an email message introducing herself and her class and asking if there were any teachers from South American countries who might want to partner their class with hers in the fall. It would be convenient to have keypals all from one class and another teacher to share ideas with.

Next, Marilyn sent a message to **MIDDLE-L** (http://ecap.crc.uiuc.edu/listserv/middle-l.html), a mailing list she discovered and then joined during an in-service for the district. Although she had been subscribed to the list for some time, she had never posted a message. She had read many helpful replies to other subscribers, however, so she wasn't surprised when she received many email responses over the next few days.

Several teachers sent information about Latin American sites and Internet activities that their students had done the previous year. One teacher recommended working on a project with a partner class, and mentioned several project sites. He also gave Marilyn the address for a projects mailing list. Another message suggested checking out newsgroups on related topics. Two teachers mentioned how they had used Internet resources to help their students develop research skills and meet required standards. They also mentioned that weblogs were an easy way to publish their data on the Internet. Marilyn was unfamiliar with this term, so she sent a message asking for more information and made a note to look for some example sites the next time she was on the Internet. Another teacher explained how she had arranged for her students to email questions to a professor of Japanese history, and suggested that Marilyn might be able to do the same with an expert on an aspect of Latin American culture.

As Marilyn read her email messages, she began thinking about the best way for her class to present their ideas to a partner class. Just exchanging facts that could easily be found in an encyclopedia wouldn't be very effective. The students would need to learn and develop new literacy skills to make full use of the Internet's capabilities—skills such as effective email writing, evaluation of Internet sources, handling conflicting information, and citations for electronic media. Marilyn and the other teachers would have to develop strategies for teaching and practicing these skills. Perhaps she could get two partner classes from different countries. Then, all the students could get information on specific topics and compare different viewpoints. They might be able to use the data they collected to do some sort of analysis in math class. In fact, maybe their other teachers could also give specific assignments for the students to complete on the Internet. Marilyn kept notes about the best ideas on index cards so that she could share them with the other eighth grade teachers in their planning meetings. She would also share some ideas with her students once school started in order to get their input before final decisions were made.

Marilyn and the other teachers had also been working on a plan to help the students' expand their computer skills and manage their time on the computer. Each classroom had only one computer, but this year, students would have their own individual email accounts. This would be a big change from last year when they had sent their messages from their teacher's account. Last year's teacher had kept an electronic folder for each student in his account, so he could easily monitor what was sent and received. Marilyn would need a different system. She didn't want to print out all the students' messages, but she wouldn't have time to read each one as it was sent either. She decided that she and her students should have a discussion about netiquette (manners on the Internet) relating to themselves and their keypals. Perhaps she could do a workshop and include role plays about how they would feel if they received a mean message. It was a good beginning, and Marilyn was looking forward to the new year, but there was still a lot to do.

Lessons from the Classroom

This scenario illustrates several lessons for using electronic communication effectively. First, Marilyn used email to get suggestions on sites, resources, and activities from other teachers. This is one of the most powerful ways for teachers to expand their knowledge and learn from others' experiences. Mailing lists often have hundreds of members, and newsgroups may have thousands of readers; weblogs provide up-to-date information,

Having email is almost like having access to a personal mentor or an individualized in-service program anytime you need it.

links, and comments on a wide variety of topics. Together, the composite expertise of those who use electronic communication covers almost every subject and point of view. You could say that having email is almost like having access to a group of personal mentors or an individualized in-service program anytime you need it.

Second, Marilyn realized that electronic communication had great power to promote collaboration. Not only was she able to interact with other Internet users and experts, but opportunities for collaborating with the members of her team were also enhanced. She also envisioned numerous possibilities for her students to work together with and communicate ideas to a wide variety of other people.

Third, Marilyn had clear goals and purposes. She did not see the Internet as an end in itself but as a tool whose use could be incorporated into the district's curriculum and her lessons to help students develop certain skills and meet required standards. In this case, electronic communication would improve writing skills, increase understanding of other cultures, provide practice in teamwork, develop critical thinking, and encourage tolerance and respect for others.

Fourth, her students' ages and previous computer experience played a large role in Marilyn's planning. She planned age-appropriate activities that included student participation in choosing activities. This would expand their technology literacy and foster better decision-making, both of which would help prepare them to use electronic communication more effectively and independently in the future.

By planning activities and projects that involved not only obtaining information, but also evaluating and synthesizing it, Marilyn was helping her students develop their critical thinking skills.

Fifth, by planning activities and projects that involved not only obtaining information, but also evaluating, synthesizing, and communicating it, Marilyn knew she would help her students develop the new literacies they would need for effective participation in our information society. Her state's standards emphasized reading, writing, and critical thinking. Electronic communication experiences seemed to fit very well into the program her district was developing to help its students reach specified goals in these areas.

Finally, Marilyn planned lessons on netiquette. As an email user herself, she knew the importance of good Internet manners. With a younger group of students, she would have posted a list of rules. However, because she recognized the eighth graders' developing ability to understand the need for order and safety, she would have them participate in discussions to formulate their own guidelines.

Getting Started with Email

In order to use electronic communication effectively, it is important to integrate Internet knowledge and skills with your own beliefs and teaching practices. You will want to reflect on how various types of communication—email, mailing lists, newsgroups, weblogs, and real-time interactions—fit into your approach to teaching and learning, your state's and national standards, your district's curriculum, and the particular students you teach. If you have not used email before, allow yourself extra time to practice various functions before trying them out with your students in the classroom. Be sure to explore which of the numerous lists, groups, weblogs, and chat groups can best meet your goals; keep in mind that there are vast differences in accuracy and quality among the choices. The more proficient and knowledgeable you are, the easier it will be to anticipate your students' needs and develop effective teaching and learning strategies.

In this next section, we provide an overview of electronic communication from a classroom perspective. Our goal is to help you get started and serve as a launching point for your own future exploration. For some of you, trial and error may be fine. However, we also encourage you to work cooperatively with other teachers, and when necessary, to seek help from technical resource people for more detailed information.

We will begin with email, the basis of electronic communication on the Internet. Once you have a computer and Internet access from a service provider, you need an email account and an email software program. Most likely, these will be provided by your district, or check with your service provider.

Your Email Account

Your email address should include your user name (screen name), your host (service provider, or server), and a domain extension; here's an example:

ddleu@syr.edu

The last part of this address (edu) means that the host (syr) is in the educational domain. Some addresses, especially those outside the United States, are followed by a country code such as .au for Australia.

You will also receive a password with your account. Keep it secret since it provides security for your account, somewhat like a PIN for your bank account. Most programs allow you to change your password, and many providers recommend changing passwords on a regular basis. Unless you are dealing with sensitive material it is probably not necessary to do this. However, if you do choose to change your password, do not select easily guessed words or numbers. In addition, unless you have your own computer in a secure place, it's a good idea to shut it down or at least log off your email account when you leave the terminal. That way, no unauthorized person can read your email or use your account to send messages.

Email Software Programs

There are many different email programs. Some computers come with mail programs already loaded, such as Outlook Express in Microsoft Windows and Mail in Apple OS X; browsers, such as Netscape, Internet Explorer, and Safari, usually include mail readers; there are free web-based programs, such as Hotmail and Yahoo; and you can download programs such as Eudora, free or for-a-fee. Generally, the free programs have fewer options and are less sophisticated than purchased programs. Given the variety of programs available, you may notice differences between your program and our examples; we have tried to use basic terminology, primarily that common to the mail and newsreaders in Netscape Navigator and Internet Explorer, two of the most widely used browsers. You may also see changes among different versions of the same program due to manufacturer upgrades. Usually these differences are not very significant; whichever program you are using, you should be able to follow or adapt the procedures described in this chapter since all programs perform the same basic functions in similar ways.

Identifying Yourself and Setting Preferences

Before you communicate via email, you must let your software program know who you are and where to get and send your mail. This is done by "setting preferences." Most programs offer many options for organizing your mail, but there are only a few that must be set in order to begin sending and receiving messages. Later, when you are more familiar with email, you can customize your system. For now, you will need the information listed below. Contact your technical resource person or service provider for any information you are not sure of.

Your name
Your user ID
Your incoming mail server (host)
Your outgoing mail server (usually the same as the incoming server)
Your reply-to address
Your organization (optional)

Your preferences may have been set when you received your account. If not, however, it is fairly easy to do in most recent programs. Select Preferences, usually in a pull-down menu under either the Edit or Tools button in the main menu. This will open a dialog box with easy-to-follow directions. Simply enter the information above as directed on the screen and you should be ready to start. If you have trouble, check with your technical resource person or a more experienced user.

In earlier editions of this book, we gave detailed instructions on how to use certain email programs. Since that time, however, we have found that many more teachers are familiar with using email. Consequently, the next section only briefly summarizes basic email functions. If you need more information, we suggest checking with a more experienced user or your technical resource person. In addition, most programs include instructions that can be found by selecting Help from the menu. There are also numerous tutorials on the Web. Check the **Google Directory** (http://directory.google.com/Top/Computers/Internet/Email/Help_and_Tutorials/) for a large list.

Reading and Receiving Messages

In order to receive new messages, you must be connected to the Internet. Most programs allow you to work offline, so be sure that you are connected by selecting Work Online from the menu. Depending on your program's default settings, new messages may be downloaded automatically when you log on, or you may have to click the mail icon or select Send/Receive or Get Messages from the toolbar, and enter your password. To read a message, just highlight it and click. Related messages and replies may be grouped together by topic, called "threading." Threads are usually indicated by icons, such as a triangle (Netscape) or a plus/minus box (Internet Explorer). Click the triangle to point down—this reveals all the messages in a thread; pointing right collapses the thread. Or click the box—the minus symbol reveals all of the messages; the plus sign shows only the first message in a thread.

Sometimes messages come with attachments (files attached to and sent with the email). If you want to read the attachment, you need to open it by clicking. However, a caution is in order here. Attached files are one way to transmit computer viruses. Therefore, it is recommended that you not open any attachment unless you know the person who sent it *and* asked that it be sent to you. This is because some viruses can send themselves automatically to everyone in a user's address book without the user's knowledge. There is more information about viruses in the Mailing Lists section later in this chapter.

Figure 4-1. The **Email Message Window** in Outlook Express showing the new users' welcome message and main tool bar.

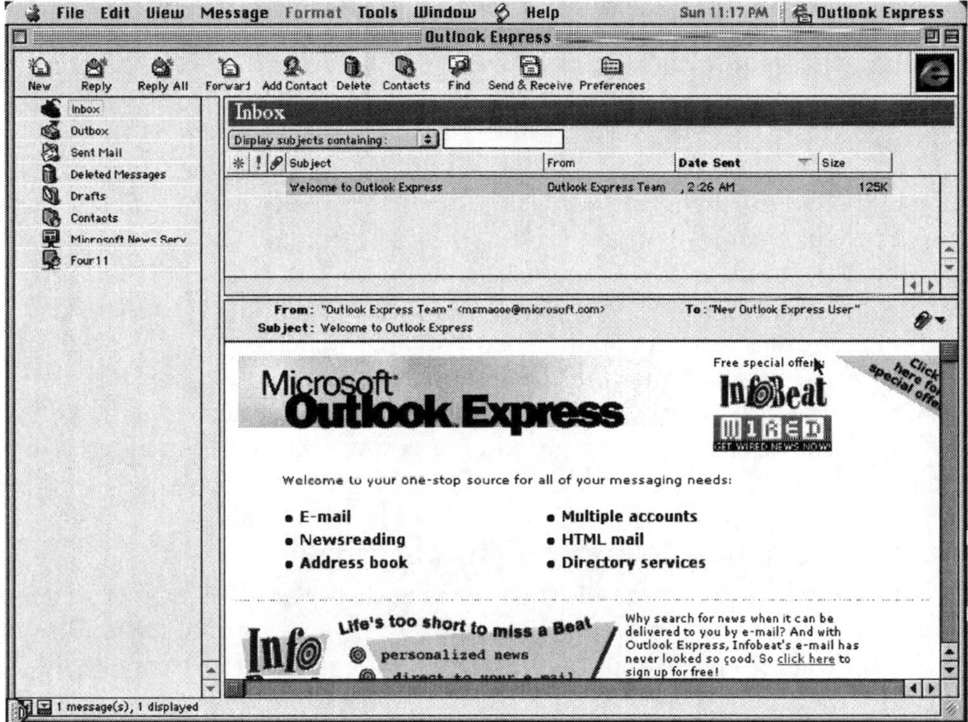

Replying to a Message

After reading a message, you may wish to respond. First, make sure the message you are replying to appears in the message display pane. Then, if the message was sent by one person and has only one address, click the Reply button. If the message contains multiple addresses, *and* if you want to reply to all of them, click the Reply All button. This opens the message composition window. The subject and address will be automatically entered. However, you may edit any entry by moving the cursor to the appropriate box and deleting or adding information. To type your reply, simply move the cursor to the bottom pane of the message composition window and type your message.

INTERNET FAQ

What are the boxes and icons in the toolbar directly below the subject line of the message composition window?

This is the Formatting toolbar. Many programs allow you to use special formatting to customize your email messages. Depending on your program, these word-processing features may be chosen from a toolbar below the subject line of the message composition window or by selecting this feature in a pull-down menu from the main toolbar. When choosing this option, keep in mind that not all email programs support different fonts and layouts. Make sure that your recipient's email software can handle these special features.

After typing your message, it is a good idea to read it over, confirming both the contents and the recipient(s). When you are sure your message is the way you want it, click the Send button. This immediately sends your message to the server if you are working online. If you are not ready to send a message at the end of a session, you can save it by clicking the Save button or selecting Save from File in the main menu. This moves your message to the Drafts folder and holds it until you are ready to finish and send it. When you want to work on your message again, you can retrieve it by clicking the Drafts folder in the left pane folder list. Click Edit Draft to bring up the saved message in the message composition window where you can continue working on it. When you are finished you can send it or save it again for further editing. The Drafts folder can also be used to save messages that you compose while working offline. The next time you are back online, bring up the message, edit it if you want to, and then send it in the usual way.

Including Original Messages with Your Reply

Most software programs allow you to include the original message with your reply by setting a preference or using the Quote button. Depending on the settings of your program, the quote of the original text may be displayed with an angle bracket (>) at the beginning of each line or a vertical line (|) along the left side of the quotation. Some people always include the original message in their replies to provide context for the recipient. Other users prefer not to repeat the original message because it takes up additional Inbox space for recipients and adds extra charges for those who pay for email by the line. Some people prefer to quote only a few important lines. If you prefer not to include an original message, you can delete part or all of it by editing with the cursor while you are working in the message composition window or by changing your preferences.

Forwarding Mail

Sometimes you receive a message that you think would be useful for a colleague. It is easy to share these messages by using the Forward button. If you wish, you may also type a message of your own above or below the quoted (forwarded) message. Before forwarding a message, however, consider whether the original sender would want the message relayed to other people. It is good netiquette to ask for permission. This is especially true if the message is received from a mailing list. The sender would expect the message to go only to list members, so unless explicit permission is given, you should not forward the message. In fact, some mailing lists have specific policies against forwarding messages without permission.

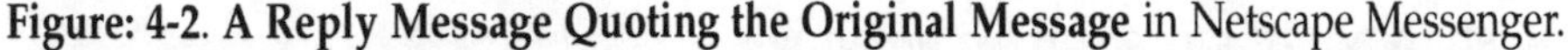

Figure: 4-2. A Reply Message Quoting the Original Message in Netscape Messenger.

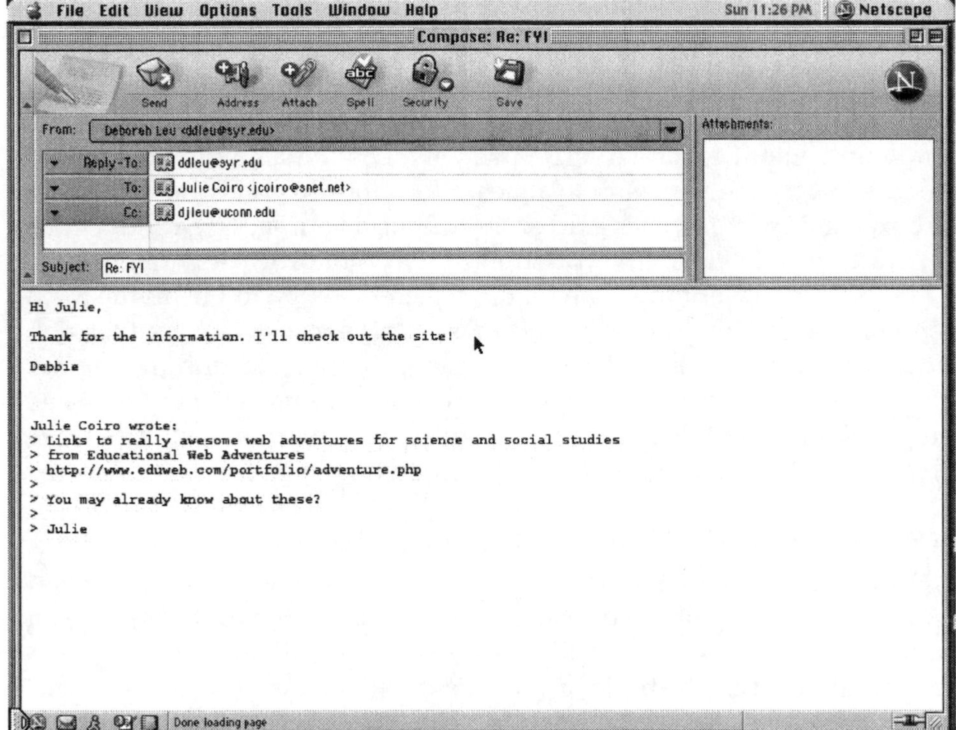

Composing and Sending a New Message

Composing and sending a new message is basically the same as replying. Go to the toolbar and click the New or Compose button. This will open the message composition window, but unlike a reply message, the subject and address boxes will be empty. You must enter the name and email address of the person to whom you are sending the message. You may send your message to more than one person by typing additional names and addresses on succeeding lines. You may also enter addresses for others to receive a carbon copy (Cc) or blind carbon copy (Bcc) by clicking the To button. It is also a good idea to type in a subject (unless you are subscribing or unsubscribing to a listserv, which requires an empty subject box). A subject is not required, but it is considered good netiquette and is helpful for recipients who want to skim their messages in order to prioritize their reading. After entering the name(es), address(es), and subject, proceed in the same way as for a reply message.

Printing

Printing a message is very easy. Make sure the message you want to print is displayed in the bottom pane of the Message window. Then click the Print button or choose File from the main menu and select Print. Although it probably isn't necessary to have paper copies of all your messages, you may want to use this feature on occasion to print out email messages for posting on a classroom bulletin board for the whole class to read (as long as the sender agrees). It is also nice to print out some student messages to share with parents at home or at an open house.

Although it isn't really necessary to have paper copies of all your messages, you may want to use this feature to print out email messages for posting on a bulletin board for the whole class to read or to share with parents at home or at an open house.

Attaching

At times you may want to include additional information such as a Word document or an Internet site with your messages. To attach a file from your computer, click Attach. This will open a dialog box that allows you to select the file you want to attach. When the file you want appears in the box, highlight it and click Add or Open. Finish your message and send it.

To attach an Internet site, you should have your browser window open with the site you want to attach on the screen. Then go to File in the main menu and select Send Page. This brings up a new message composition window with the site included in the message pane. (Depending on your program, you may see only the address, not the page itself in your message composition window, but the recipient will see the page when the message is read.) Finish your message and send the email.

Managing Your Mail and Working with Folders

Now that you understand the basic email functions of receiving and sending, and are familiar with most of the buttons in the toolbars, you can manage your mail by using folders. Most programs initially display several default folders. The basic management folders are:

- The *Inbox*, which stores new incoming messages as well as any old messages that you have not deleted or filed elsewhere.
- The *Sent* folder, which holds copies of messages that you have sent or forwarded.
- The *Deleted Messages* or *Trash* folder, which temporarily holds deleted items until you are ready to remove them permanently.
- The *Drafts* folder, which saves unfinished messages that you intend to work on later.

In addition to these four basic folders, different programs may have other default folders. For example, Outlook Express has an Outbox folder for storing messages when you are working offline (you can view the Outlook default folders in Figure 4-1); Netscape Messenger has a Template folder (see Figure 4-3). Explore the folders in your email program and consider how they can help you organize your messages more efficiently.

Deleting Messages

After you read a message, it remains in your Inbox folder until you move or delete it. As a result, over time your Inbox may become crowded and disorganized, and if it gets too full, you cannot receive new messages.

Therefore, it is a good idea to get in the habit of moving messages out of your Inbox as you read them.

If you do not need to keep a message after reading it, simply click the Delete button in the toolbar. This deletes the message appearing in the display pane and transfers it to the Deleted Messages/Trash folder. If you want to delete any other message, highlight it by clicking its subject header in the listing pane; then click the Delete button. If you have several messages you do not want to save, you can "block delete" them as a group by clicking on each one while holding down the keyboard shift key. This highlights a group of messages. Click the Delete button and the whole group will be removed from the listing pane and transferred to the Deleted Messages/Trash folder.

Figure 4-3. The Default Folders in Netscape Messenger.

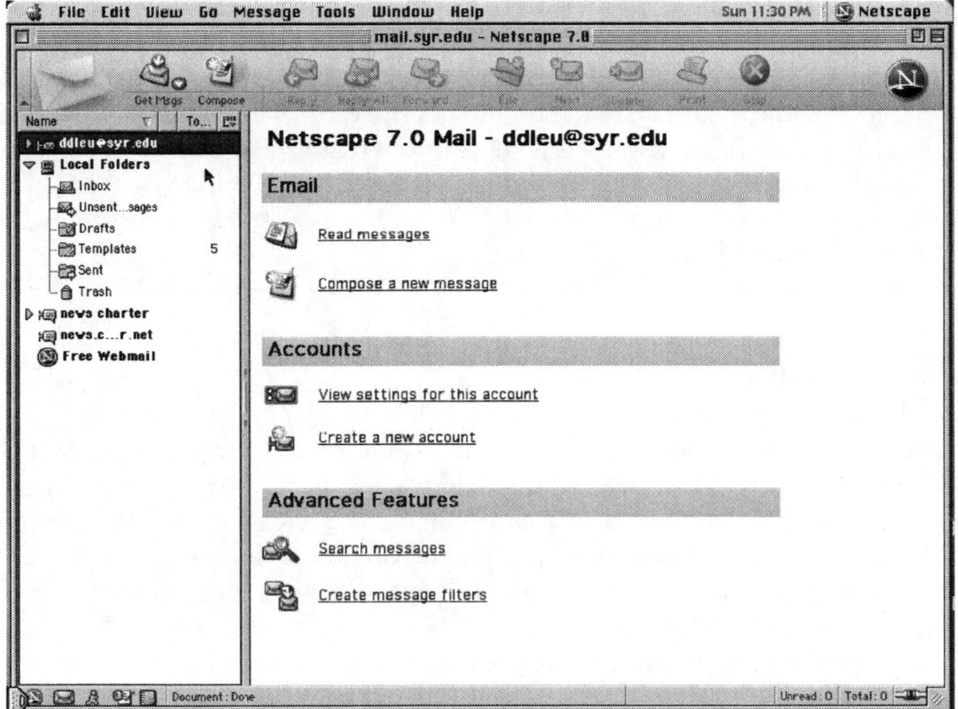

The Deleted Messages/Trash Folder

At this point, although you have deleted your messages, they are not really gone. They are sitting in the Deleted Messages/Trash folder as if you had thrown them in a wastebasket. This can be a convenient feature if you have accidentally deleted a message that you need. To retrieve such a message, click the folder, then highlight the message you want to retrieve in the right listing pane, and drag it to the folder in which you want to save it or use the File button. It is a good idea to then open the folder to make sure that the message has appeared there.

In order to actually remove your deleted messages, you must empty the Deleted Messages/Trash folder, equivalent to taking out the trash. To do this, highlight the Deleted Messages/Trash folder, choose Edit from the main menu, and select Empty. Be careful; once you click, all messages in the Deleted Messages/Trash folder are permanently removed.

Saving Sent Messages in the Sent Folder

Most software programs automatically save messages as you send them in the Sent folder (unless you have changed the default setting, usually located in Preferences or Tools). This provides a convenient record of your messages and allows you to easily re-send a message if necessary. However, this folder can become very large if you are an active emailer. Thus, if you do not need to keep a record of your sent messages, you may want to delete them as explained above.

INTERNET FAQ

How can I use my email account more efficiently?

One of the easiest ways to organize your email is to create additional folders. As you send and receive more messages, your default folders tend to become disorganized and may get filled up. Moreover, they do not offer much flexibility, so it is helpful to create new folders to suit your individual needs. For example, you may create folders to store messages by month, topic, or sender (see the section below to learn how to create folders).

Creating New Folders

The procedure for creating new folders is easy and fairly similar across platforms and programs. Start by selecting File from the main menu and clicking on (new) folder. This usually brings up a dialog box in which you can type the name of your new folder. Then click OK or Finish; the new folder should appear in the list of folders in your email and news window. You can find additional information on creating new folders in the Help section of your particular program.

The easiest way to save a message after you have read it is to drag its subject header from the right listing pane to the folder in which you want to save it.

If you have younger students, or only one computer in your classroom, student mail will probably be sent through your email account. To help manage these mail messages, you may want to create folders labeled with each student's name. Depending on the age of your students, you can keep track of their messages and monitor their correspondence or teach them how to save and delete messages for themselves. In addition, you will most likely want to discuss privacy issues and remind students to read and use only their own folders.

Saving Received Messages in New Folders

An easy way to save a message after you have read it is to drag its subject header from the right listing pane to the folder (in the left pane) in which you want to save it. You can "block save" messages just as you block delete them by clicking each message while holding down the keyboard shift key. Then drag this group of messages to the folder in which you want to save them. The whole group will be removed from the listing pane and transferred to the selected folder. Most newer programs also have a File button in the message window that allows you to shift messages from one folder to another by selecting a folder from a pull-down menu.

Deleting Folders

To delete a folder, highlight it and click the Delete button in the toolbar. Or go to File in the main menu and select Delete Folder. This deletes the folder as well as any messages it may contain. In most programs, the folder is moved to the Deleted Messages/Trash folder, and will not be truly deleted until you empty the trash from the File button on the main menu.

Moving On

We hope that the information we have included has gotten you off to a good start. Now it is time to move on.

Reading about email can get tedious, and like swimming, you don't really know how to do it until you try it. So take some time for hands-on practice.

Reading about email can get tedious, and like swimming, you do not really know how to do it until you try it. So take some time for hands-on practice. Try one or two things at first and work at your own pace. You may check out an online tutorial such as the one from **WebTeacher for Macintosh** (http://webteacher.org/macintosh.html) and **Windows** (http://webteacher. org/windows.html). Or you may wish to work with a partner. If your school does not have a media specialist or technology resource person, try to find someone a bit more experienced who can help out. Remember, everyone was a beginner once and no one knows it all, not even the experts.

As you become more familiar and confident with the basic features of email, you can customize your mail service further. Explore other toolbar selections and choose additional options. Create an automatic signature or a personal address book or reconfigure the mail window.

Using Email for Teaching and Learning

Learning how to use email does take some time, but it is well worth the effort when you consider the many ways it can benefit your students. In particular, it provides opportunities for locating specialized information, working collaboratively in new ways, and communicating ideas to a wider and more diverse audience than their classmates. Many students already use email to communicate with people they know, similar to writing a letter. This activity is easily extended to communicating with new people and can add special excitement to learning as it brings the world into your classroom. It is not surprising then that many teachers begin with and continue to use email activities as one way to integrate the Internet into their classrooms.

Before you begin any email activity, it is important to consider which skills your students will need in order to send effective messages. Many people assume that email is just like any other kind of writing. To some extent this is true; however, the nature of electronic communication means that certain traditional skills need special emphasis and other new skills need to be added to students' repertoires.

Of course, students need the usual composition skills. In fact, we would argue that such skills are even more necessary for effective email communication. Email emphasizes speed, which often leads to "mistakes" such as limited vocabulary, overuse of acronyms, incomplete sentences, and atypical spelling—all of which can lead to misunderstanding. Such problems have no doubt contributed to the blaming of email (and chat) for lowering traditional writing standards. Yet in some circumstances, this informal style of writing is acceptable. The trick is to transfer student awareness of traditional audience and purpose concepts to their email writing. Think, for example, about the differences you would expect between a job application cover letter and a memo to colleagues about a staff meeting. Similarly, consider an email message requesting information from a NASA scientist and an invitation to the class next door to play baseball.

In addition to composition skills, students will need to ask questions clearly, synthesize divergent information, give thoughtful comments, and learn to benefit from constructive criticism. They will also need good keyboarding skills and the ability to use a variety of email programs. It is up to us to provide instruction and practice in these areas. We have found the following suggestions useful for students and teachers:

1. Take time to compose your message carefully so that it is suitable for the recipient and your purpose.
2. Write concisely. Short, to-the-point messages are expected and appreciated in most situations. However, provide enough information to place your message in context.
3. Write explicitly. Words and sentences can often be interpreted in different ways. This is especially true with email, which must be read without the benefit of intonation and facial expressions. Clear and direct messages leave less room for misunderstanding.
4. Be careful when using humor (or simply avoid it). Without the clues mentioned above, a comment may come across as sarcastic or rude. If you mean to be humorous, consider ending your message with a cheery closing so the reader will realize that no bad feelings are intended.
5. Proofread messages before you send them—not only to find mistakes, but also to find words or sentences that could be confusing or misleading.
6. Pay attention to netiquette and the usual conventions of electronic communication.

Netiquette

Internet etiquette, commonly referred to as netiquette, is a very important issue particularly as students begin to use email more independently and extensively. Electronic messages cannot communicate the facial expressions, voice tone, and body language we use automatically in face-to-face communication. Without these paralinguistic features, email messages can more easily lead to miscommunication. Thus, it is very important to help students develop good Internet manners and become sensitive to how their messages might be interpreted and, more importantly, misinterpreted.

We are not talking here about actions that are dangerous or illegal (you can read more about these issues in the section on Acceptable Use Policies in Chapter 2), but about politeness and courtesy. Because the Internet is not run by any single group or government, there are few official rules to teach; moreover, there is no single source of information about what constitutes acceptable behavior. Nevertheless, 7we need to help our students realize that the Internet, as a place of social interaction, has its own traditions and customs. It is important to discuss Internet use as a privilege not a right, and together with our students develop guidelines that encourage tolerance and acceptance of the diversity of people, languages, and viewpoints that exists on the Net.

We need to help our students realize that the Internet, as a place of social interaction, has its own traditions and customs.

People often talk about netiquette in terms of common sense, but common sense varies depending on factors such as age, culture, and experience. Therefore, before you discuss this issue with your students, you may want to get some background information. One often-cited location is **The Net: User Guidelines and Netiquette** (http://wise.fau.edu/netiquette/net). This is a detailed site that provides advice on email, mailing lists, newsgroups, and other areas of the Internet. It includes a question and answer section as well as a bibliography. Depending on the level of your students, you might choose various sections for them to read and discuss. For example, "The Ten Commandments for Computer Ethics" is a straightforward list of "thou-shalt-nots" which would probably be effective with all but the youngest students. Additional information, including a section for system administrators, is available at **RFC 1855—Netiquette Guidelines** (http://www.dtcc.edu/cs/rfc1855.html).

E-MAIL FOR YOU

From: Paula Reber <preber@CSRLINK.NET>
Subject: Keypal project

My class has participated in many Travel Buddy projects with other countries for the past few years and it's been very successful. This year, I wished to try something new. One of my best friends also teaches in my district but at another building (K–3 is in one school, 4–5 in another). My first graders became keypals with her fourth graders. We used a combination of email and the district's LAN server to correspond with each other. In addition to writing back and forth the students also worked collaboratively on some book projects. For example, near St. Patrick's Day my students wrote the first paragraph to a leprechaun story. Each student saved the work on the district server and the fourth grade buddies then finished the stories. After the stories were complete, my students created graphics in KidPix to correspond with the story.

We plan to expand on this next year when I loop to second. We are hoping that the kids will also get to meet next year at some point.

Paula Reber
Visit Reber's Resources for K-6 Teachers
http://www.geocities.com/Athens/8854/

Keypals

In times past, one of the most common ways for students to interact with different people was to write to penpals. Today, the Internet equivalent is emailing keypals, or e-pals as they are sometimes called. This activity can increase motivation, improve writing skills, enhance knowledge, and broaden perspectives. Email's greatest feature, however, is that it reduces the time between messages to just a few seconds or minutes. Because of this speed, students can do much more than simply correspond once or twice a month. Very quickly, they can get many kinds of information by asking questions and conducting interviews with other students or experts, in their own country or abroad; they can share their comments with a variety of people; they can practice a second language; they can even critique each other's homework. And, it is not always necessary to do an elaborate pre-planned project. Close-to-home activities that you set up yourself can also be productive as Paula Reber's email message illustrates.

Directories for Keypals

There are numerous sites for locating keypals and partner classes. Some of them are commercial sites that charge for this service, but many of the best sites are free. The sites included below are ones that we and other teachers have found especially useful for educational purposes. The Internet changes quickly and often, so some of these sites may disappear; certainly new ones will come online. As always, you know which sites will best meet your needs. Therefore, we encourage you to explore these sites as a first step in creating your own list of favorites. (Note that in addition to keypal exchanges, several of these sites are excellent sources for finding and posting collaborative projects. You can read more about Internet projects in Chapter 3.)

- **Intercultural Email Classroom Connections**—http://www.iecc.org/
  One of the oldest keypal sites, originally founded by three teachers at St. Olaf's College, this free site is now located at Teaching.com. It allows subscribed teachers to search for partner classes and projects around the world from the website or by subscribing to any of several discussion groups.
- **Teaching.com**—http://teaching.com/
  This site allows both teachers and students to sign up, but requires parental consent for those under age 13. Currently it has members from 112 countries.
- **ePals Classroom Exchange**—http://www.epals.com/
  Teachers can look for class matches for keypals and projects from many different countries on this site, which emphasizes privacy and safety. Up to 35 free email accounts are available for each registered teacher. Site information is offered in eight languages. Students can also sign up individually with parental consent. This site also offers monitored web-based mail for classrooms or entire schools for a fee.
- **ESD 105**—http://www.esd105.wednet.edu/kp.html
  Sponsored by the Educational Technology Support Center through Educational Support District 105 in Yakima, Washington. This site allows teachers to search for matching keypal classes in the United

States and abroad through free subscription to current K–2, 3–5, 6–8, or high school lists. Announcements of projects may appear as well.

- **Gaggle**—http://www.gaggle.net/
  This site stresses safety in several ways: by monitoring, blocking inappropriate messages and language, and only allowing sign-ups through teachers and schools. However, the free subscription contains ads. Although the ads are screened for student appropriateness, they are still ads. You can pay for an ad-free version if you wish.

Keep in mind that school schedules and levels of commitment to keypal projects may differ. If you are setting up projects in other states or countries, allow for time zone changes and check out semester start and end dates, class session times, holidays, and vacation periods. You may also want to work with more than one other classroom and set up multiple keypals for each of your students. That way, if someone is sick or unable to respond in a timely fashion, your students can still participate in the activity.

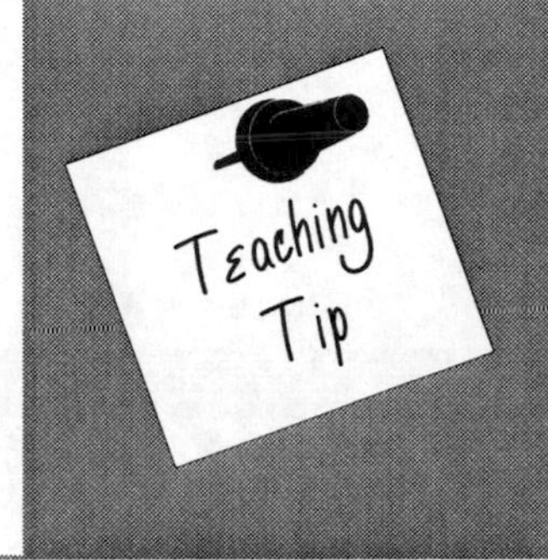

Signing up for keypals and class exchanges is a good way to get started with electronic communication. We hope you are getting excited about its potential for your classroom. However, you may be still be wondering exactly how to introduce this activity, especially if your students have never used email before.

Jeanette Kenyon's message shows how she began simply within the classroom and gradually expanded her class's activities to include the world. Depending on the age and experience of your students, you might want to start out with a message composed jointly by the students, but entered and sent by you. The message and any responses could then be printed out and kept in a binder or put up on a bulletin board near the computer. Later, students could work in pairs or small groups to send their own messages to other students in their school. Then they could move into their community by emailing questions to local businesses and organizations. Finally, they might each have their own international keypal or contact an expert.

Depending on the age and experience of your students, you might want to start out with a message composed jointly by the students, but entered by you.

Ask an Expert

Writing to a keypal who is a real person outside the classroom will be fun and motivating for most students. Communicating about topics of real interest should provide opportunities to improve composition skills and practice the email skills they will need for their futures. Another useful and interesting activity is to have your students send questions to experts in an area they are studying. This can provide excellent opportunities for students to improve critical thinking and collaborate with each other to develop worthwhile questions. You or your colleagues may have developed contacts with people from your community who are willing to work with students. You may also find volunteer experts from mailing lists or newsgroups that you subscribe to. Or check some of these sites:

Directories for Finding Experts

- **Pitsco**—http://www.askanexpert.com/
  This comprehensive site has links to no-fee experts who are interested in helping students and educators. (The site, however, is sponsored by an educational materials supplier and contains a small picture of a Lego block on each page.)
- **CLN**—http://www.cln.org/int_expert.html
  This site is sponsored by the Community Learning Network through Open School of British Columbia, Canada. It is organized by categories and easy to use.
- **Library Spot**—http://www.libraryspot.com/askanexpert.htm
  This site contains fewer entries, but includes some areas not covered by the previous two sites. Check out the individual expert sites, however, because some of them charge a fee.

E-MAIL FOR YOU

From: Jeanette Kenyon (jmkenyon@netzero.net)
Subject: Using Email in Third Grade

Dear Colleague,

One of the first skills I taught to my third grade children after becoming connected to the Internet was email. This seems a logical starting point for teachers as well as students. We began by sending email to the class next door to us. Even though my students have many friends in that class and they see each other daily, the email they exchanged during our Computer lab time became a weekly "event." We composed collective messages where we chatted about what was going on in our room, interesting units we were working on, and general greetings to individuals from their friends. We often included the latest "knock knock" jokes and sometimes posed difficult math problems for the other class to solve.

As the students became more skillful at sending email, we moved beyond our own school and began sending messages to family and friends. Parents love to receive messages at work from their children and far away relatives are thrilled to hear from their young family members. After becoming comfortable with the workings and etiquette of email, the students were confident about sending messages to various people on the World Wide Web. They found that there were experts in almost any field who would gladly answer their questions, and they corresponded with a variety of students around the world whom they had located on the WWW. Many eight and nine year olds are reluctant letter writers but it is amazing how long they will sit at a keyboard painstakingly composing an email message. This is also a great incentive and opportunity to improve keyboarding skills which are also an integral part of our curriculum.

Jeanette Kenyon
Moncure Elementary School
Stafford, Virginia USA

Getting Started with Mailing Lists

In addition to using email for one-to-one communication between individuals, an email address also allows you to participate in one-to-many communication by joining mailing lists—sometimes called discussion lists—and commonly referred to as listservs (a misnomer that comes from the name of one popular software program for managing mailing lists). You can think of mailing lists as a group email somewhat like a newsletter, but you can respond immediately to all the other readers. A message sent to one address is automatically forwarded to a whole group of individuals without the need to make "old-style" photocopies.

There are several thousand mailing lists covering almost every interest area.

This is accomplished by a special computer program that maintains a list of people, the members or *subscribers*, who have joined a particular list in order to discuss a specific topic or interest area. Subscribers participate by sending and receiving email messages, which come directly to their electronic mailboxes. Some lists are moderated by the owner or another designated person who screens and selects the messages that are sent out, but many lists are unmoderated with all messages being passed directly to the list members.

There are thousands of mailing lists covering almost every interest area. Most are intended for a specific audience, but are open for anyone to subscribe. There are some closed lists, however, so your subscription may be denied in a few cases. You may realize after reading some of the messages that a list is not related to the topic you expected from its name, or you may not feel comfortable with the "culture and personality" of a list. If this turns out to be the case, just unsubscribe.

Keep in mind that the amount of list activity varies considerably. Some lists have thousands of members and are very active, while others are quite small and generate only a few messages a month. For busy lists, you might want to receive your message in digest form. (You can find out how to receive messages in digest form from the Welcome Message you receive when you first subscribe to a list.) Digest form means the managing program saves each day's messages and sends them all at once rather than one by one; nevertheless, a busy list may still generate too many messages for you. Therefore, do not oversubscribe. If you join several mailing lists, you may find hundreds of messages per day in your mailbox. Initially, it is probably better to join only one or two lists and try them out. You may want to check with colleagues about their favorite lists and subscribe to one of those. Later, you can subscribe to additional lists as your time permits.

Do not oversubscribe. If you join several mailing lists, you may find hundreds of messages per day in your mailbox.

Subscribing to a Mailing List

In order to subscribe to a mailing list, you need to send an email message to the server that manages the list. It is very important to send your request to the correct address. Mailing lists have two addresses. The first one is the *administrative* address, which begins with the name of the program and server that manages the list. The other address is for *posting* (sending messages to the list members) and usually begins with the name of the list. Make sure you subscribe to the administrative address. Most of these begin with "listserv@..."—the most common server program, or "listproc@..." or "majordomo@..." Occasionally you may see another, independently managed program name. Do not subscribe by sending a message to the address that begins with the name of the mailing list; that will send your message to all of the list members.

Begin by sending an email message to the administrative server of the list. To join the MIDDLE-L listserv, for example, you would first type the administrative address (listserv@listserv.uiuc.edu) in the address box. Leave the subject line blank. Then, in the message pane, type a subscribe message with the name of the list, your first name, and your last name. (Upper and lower case is usually not significant.) Your message should look like this:

subscribe MIDDLE-L Deborah Leu

Do not put any other information, such as an automatic signature for example, in the message pane. Any extra information is unreadable by the server and usually invalidates the request. Some mailing lists have put up their own homepages. These usually allow easy one-step subscription directly from the site and often contain additional information such as the URL for the list archives.

Save the Welcome Message. It contains important information about expectations for members, how to get help, and most importantly how to get off the list.

Figure 4-4. The subscription procedures section of the **Middle-L Homepage** (http://ecap.crc.uiuc.edu/listserv/middle-l.html). Many mailing lists now have similar homepages that provide necessary background information and house their archives.

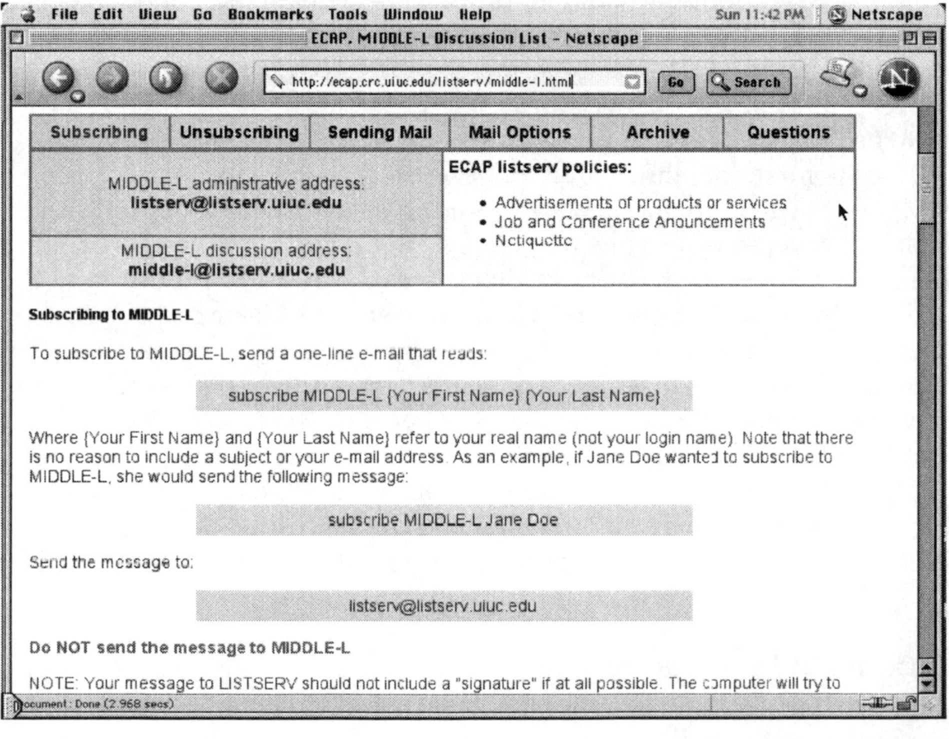

The Welcome Message

Shortly after you send your message, you should receive a return message that welcomes you to the group and details its procedures. *Save this message!* The welcome message contains important information about expectations for members, how to get help, and most importantly how to unsubscribe from the list.

Unsubscribing

You usually leave a list by sending a message similar to your subscription request. Some lists do have special procedures, though, so check the original welcome message if you are having trouble. The general procedure is to type "unsubscribe" and the name of the list. (If that does not work, try "signoff," which is also used occasionally.) It is not necessary to type your name. For example:

unsubscribe MIDDLE-L

Remember to send this message to the administrative address, not the posting address.

INTERNET FAQ

Why do I keep getting messages from a listserv after I've sent an unsubscribe message?

If you have sent your message to the correct administrative address (not the posting address) but are still receiving messages, check the following points. Do you have more than one email account? If so, be sure to unsubscribe using the same account that you originally subscribed from. The server is a computer, not a person, and it cannot recognize you if you try to unsubscribe from a different email address, use a nickname, or spell your name differently.

Occasionally, there can be a problem even if you have only one account. If you use different computers, at home and at work for example, the server may differentiate messages from the two computers, even if the address is the same. Therefore, it is best to try to subscribe and unsubscribe from the same account and the same machine. If you continue to have trouble, send a message to Help at the administrative address as explained in the original welcome message, which should put you in touch with the list manager or another resource person who can take care of the problem.

Posting a Message

When you feel ready to make a contribution to the discussion, you should send your message to the posting (not the administrative) address, which usually begins with the name of the mailing list. For example, the MIDDLE-L posting address is:

middle-l@listserv.uiuc.edu

The address for posting a message to a list is usually included in the welcome message—another reason to save it. If your message is a response to an individual's question, it is often better to send your reply directly to that person rather than to the whole list. However, there are some lists that request that you always respond to the whole list in order to improve the discussion. Again, check your welcome message for information about what is expected, and pay attention to what others on the list are doing to see how they handle responses.

It is easy to reply to either an individual or the group because most email programs give you the option of addressing your reply to either an individual by using the Reply button or to the group by selecting Reply All. It is a good idea to double-check the "reply-to" address of any reply message before you actually send it. Make sure the address box contains the address you want, either an individual's name and address or the listserv name and address. There are a few mailing lists which are configured so that a reply message automatically defaults to the Reply All mode and sends messages to the whole list, even when you click the individual reply button.

In order to get a feel for the culture and "personality" of a list, it is recommended that you "lurk" for a week or two; that is, just read the list for awhile before posting any messages.

Mailing List Netiquette

Netiquette is especially important for mailing list subscribers because their messages may be read by hundreds or thousands of people from all over the world. Remember that not everyone may understand cultural references or colloquial expressions. Try to avoid slang and be explicit rather than implicit. In addition, keep in mind that a mailing list is basically a club where you may run into other members at any time—you do not want to offend someone that you know you will be meeting (electronically) several times a week.

In order to get a feel for the culture of the list it is strongly recommended that you just read the list for awhile without posting any messages; this is called "lurking." It will give you a chance to see how the group operates and find out answers to some of your initial questions. For additional suggestions, refer to previously mentioned netiquette sites: (http://wise.fau.edu/netiquette/net/dis.html) and (http://www.dtcc.edu/cs/rfc1855.html#3). Most group members are tolerant and helpful to beginners. However, the introduction of an inappropriate topic or yet another repetition of a basic question sometimes elicits sarcastic or nasty responses from other members. This is known as "flaming." Observing how list members interact before you begin posting messages will help you avoid problems and ensure that you get the most from your list.

Privacy Issues

The issue of privacy is often overlooked by newcomers to the Internet. Perhaps because we often use email in private, we believe it is private. In fact, it is actually considerably less private than traditional mail. First, just as in the regular mail system, electronic communications occasionally get missent. In most cases, people do not read a letter that is not addressed to them, and will probably try to have it forwarded to the correct addressee. With email, however, the message will be displayed on the screen, and may likely be read before the recipient realizes it is for another person. Although, this does not happen frequently, it is a definite possibility.

Of more concern to many emailers is archiving. Virtually all email messages are archived somewhere, perhaps by the service provider or the school district or the school. Individuals may also save or print messages. Messages can be saved for an indefinite period of time. They are most likely in an out-of-the-way file, known only to a system administrator, so it is unlikely that someone would search through thousands of messages to see what you have written. It is possible, however. Moreover, TV news stories have reported about investigative firms that search email archives to get evidence for various purposes, such as court cases. There is also the **Wayback Machine** (http://www.archive.org/web/web.php) a service that allows visitors to surf previous versions of the Web as it existed on a given date; as of this writing, it contained some 10 billion pages.

Postings to mailing lists are even more accessible and less private than individual email messages since most lists are archived in easily accessed Web locations. Some lists keep their own archives, which may be available only to members, but even that could be a number in the thousands. Many education lists are archived, and are easily accessible through an Internet search. Other lists are posted and archived by various newsgroups. These are read and may be saved or reposted by thousands of people around the world. Finally, there are search engines that can bring up an individual's postings when that individual's name is entered for a search.

We have heard that you should never write anything that would embarrass you if it happened to be announced at your next town meeting. We think this is sound advice.

This information is not meant to alarm you, only to caution you to think about what you write and post. Think of an email message as a postcard, not a sealed letter. We have heard that you should never write anything that would embarrass you if it happened to be read at your next town meeting. We think this is sound advice.

Computer Viruses and Email

You have no doubt heard of computer "viruses"—software programs that can infect a computer with a variety of ills, from small annoyances to destruction of files, major crashes, and even systemwide shutdowns. Students, teachers, and school district administrators are all concerned. But these days, everyone is a potential victim. Even if you do not own a computer, you are likely to experience problems in your dealings with businesses and organizations that do.

INTERNET FAQ

What can I do to avoid viruses?

First, do not open any email attachment unless you have requested that it be sent or have been notified to expect it by the sender. There are viruses that can have themselves sent through an account's address book—unknown to the account owner; thus, merely recognizing the sender's name does not ensure that an attachment is safe.

You should also invest in a good anti-virus software program, and keep it updated to catch new viruses and other bugs as they appear. Pay attention to manufacturer bulletins and news releases on product weaknesses. Download corrective software patches when they are offered. You can find up-to-date information about viruses from various vendors at the U.S. Department of Energy's **Computer Incident Advisory Capability (CIAC)**: (http://ciac.llnlgov/ciac/ciac_virus_info.html).

The good news is that there are ways to reduce the potential for harm. Most Internet service providers and school districts have installed anti-virus software and protective barriers called firewalls to minimize "invasions." These can also be installed on home computers. In addition, individual users can do much to reduce problems by following a few guidelines with their own accounts. Although people often worry about email being a source of infection, viruses are rarely transmitted through email messages themselves. The problem is usually an email attachment containing an infected file that spreads when you open the attachment.

In addition to real viruses, there are also virus hoaxes, which are appearing with increasing frequency. Many times a well-intentioned mailing list member will send out a virus alert that is later found to be a hoax. This overloads inboxes with unnecessary messages and may cause undue anxiety. You can avoid this mistake by checking for hoax information at the **CIAC** (Computer Incident Advisory Capability) website (http://ciac.llnl.gov/ciac/CIACHome.html).

E-MAIL FOR YOU

From: Cindy Lockerman (cklocker@UNCC.CAMPUS.MCI.NET)
Subject: Using mailing lists or listservs

Hi!

I want to share with everyone two experiences using email on the RTEACHER listserv that illustrate an important point: The opportunity to make important connections is useful, informative, and tremendously satisfying as I see concerns and opinions that I hold echoed by voices worldwide. It truly affirms the concept of a shrinking planet! I will try to relate concisely a couple of electronic experiences.

First, I needed some help with a biography on Marie Clay, the New Zealand educator. Clay's work is a mainstay at the school where I teach and so I am quite familiar with her work, but I needed some biographical information for a course I was taking. I posted my needs on the RTEACHER listserv and another member quickly sent me the email address of Professor Yetta Goodman (another prominent literacy educator), suggesting that I ask her for the information. I sent a query and within an hour, she wrote back with biographical information from her personal experience with Dr. Clay. Not only was I able to get information "that inquiring minds want to know," but I was able to converse with Dr. Goodman about literacy issues on a level that would otherwise be impossible.

Second, I recently followed a discussion on RTEACHER concerning the Accelerated Reader computer program. Keith Topping, a professor in Scotland who has done extensive research on this area, shared a number of ideas. After some discussion back and forth with him and some evidence from his research, I decided to do my own research on intermediate proficiency ESL students (grades 4–6). While end-of-grade tests will ultimately tell me if there has been any marked score improvement, I have noted a new enthusiasm in most of my "experimental group" for reading. I have also been able to use the 10-question tests as a springboard to test-taking skill tips. I could probably go on and on, but let it suffice to say that without the discussion and expertise of the listserv participants, I would not have thought to try a program that has been readily available to first language students but untried (in our area) with L2 students.

You may wish to read the archives of this listserv (http://www.reading.org/archives/) or join it yourself (http://www.reading.org/virtual/rt_listserv.html). Good luck!

Cindy Lockerman

Using Mailing Lists for Teaching and Learning

Mailing lists can be very useful in education, especially for teachers. List members have usually subscribed to discuss topics that are particularly important to them and to interact with colleagues. As a result, lists tend to develop a strong sense of community where members get to know one another.

Mailing lists are great places to ask questions, get information, locate resources, share information, and interact with the experts in your field.

Mailing lists are great places to ask questions, get information, locate resources, share information, and meet new colleagues. You may even communicate directly with experts and people who are doing the most up-to-date research in your field. It can be quite motivating and wonderfully surprising to receive an email from the author of your favorite text or the keynote speaker from your most recent professional conference as described in Cindy Lockerman's email message.

Mailing lists can be useful for students as well as teachers; however, some care should be taken when deciding how to use lists in the classroom since there is no way to know in advance what will appear in individual messages. If a list is moderated, obvious problems such as bad language will probably be avoided; however, you may still find topics or viewpoints that not everyone is comfortable with. There are lists especially for children and other education-oriented lists where students can participate with interested adults. Some of the keypal sites mentioned earlier, for example, are similar to a classroom mailing list but they are limited to your students and their partners or to other screened subscribers to their service. Still, most lists allow anyone to join, and even when a list is moderated, the moderator may not screen messages in accordance with what you think is appropriate for your particular students. Thus, it is possible that even a generally appropriate list might sometimes contain postings that are inappropriate for your students. There is also the chance of encountering topics that you consider unsuitable, but that the moderator views as worthwhile, and therefore, allows on the list.

Care should be taken when deciding how to use lists in the classroom because there is no way to know in advance what will appear in individual messages.

Despite these concerns, mailing lists are great resources and many teachers do use them effectively with their students. As always, it is best for you to check out the situation for yourself. One way to do this is to subscribe to a mailing list for at least several weeks before deciding whether and how it might be used in your situation with your students. You can also read a list's archives to get a feeling for the list and review the type of topics that are discussed. Some listservs restrict their archives to members, but many are available on the Internet. To find a list's archives, do a search for the name of the mailing list you are interested in plus the word "archives," for example: ECENET + archives. The search results will give the archive's location if it is available. Finally, check with colleagues for mailing lists that they have used with their students and to find out about any problems they may have encountered on various lists.

Directories for Mailing Lists

It is difficult to recommend mailing lists because of the large number available and since everyone's needs and expectations are different. However, we have included addresses for lists and other online communities related to particular interest areas at the end of the content chapters later in this book.

In the meantime, if you wish to try out mailing lists, the first step is to find the name and email address of a list you want to join. There are thousands of lists, so you might begin by checking with colleagues and professional organizations or looking through journals in your field. There are also many Internet sites containing master lists of mailing lists. Go to one of the sites below, select a list, and follow the subscription directions. Or read on and follow the general steps in the next section, Subscribing to a Mailing List.

- **TileNet**—http://tile.net/lists/
  This very comprehensive site is organized alphabetically. Most entries have descriptions and direct links to their subscription addresses or webpages.
- **Email Discussion Lists and Electronic Journals**—
  http://www.edwebproject.org/lists.html
  This is a smaller list from the EdWeb K-12 Resource Guide, but it focuses only on education, especially K-12 issues, educational technology, and education reform. It also has a little background on mailing lists and an example of how to subscribe. For many lists, you can click here and go directly to their subscription page.
- **The Teacher's Guide**—
  http://www.theteachersguide.com/listservs.html
  Another smaller list that focuses only on education mailing lists. You can subscribe to lists directly from this site.
- **CataList Reference Site**—http://www.lsoft.com/lists/listref.html
  This site is a catalog of listserv mailing lists only. You can search by country or membership size.
- **Global Schoolhouse Mailing Lists —**
  http://www.gsn.org/lists/index.html
  A list of lists from Global Schoolhouse for parents and educators to discuss relevant issues and keep up with projects.
- **Online Forums —**
  http://www.ash.org.au/deliver/content.asp?pid=600
  Forums sponsored by the Aussie School House.
- **Online Educator's Forums —**
  http://www.enoreo.on.ca/schoolnet/forum/e/
  A short but relevant list of forums, some in French and some in English, from Canada's SchoolNet.

Getting Started with Newsgroups

Another popular use of email is reading and posting to newsgroups, sometimes called forums or boards. These are one of the earliest forms of electronic communication on the Internet. The largest network, Usenet, consists of many thousands of newsgroups organized hierarchically by category and topic. More recently, many websites have begun hosting their own groups. These are very convenient for quickly finding topics and other readers in your area of interest. Because they are located directly on a website, there is no need to do a separate search for an on-topic group. Moreover, postings (or articles, as they are sometimes called) tend to be directly relevant to the topic since they are usually made by self-selected site users, not by the general community of readers at large. These forums are also easy to use since reading and posting are done directly from the website with no need for a newsreader software program.

Like mailing lists, both traditional and web-based newsgroups are a one-to-many type of email communication. However, they differ from mailing lists in several important ways. First, access is different. While mailing lists are limited to individual subscribers, newsgroups are available to anyone whose server receives and stores them. Earlier we compared mailing lists to a newsletter being sent to each person on a list. Newsgroups are more like bulletin boards where anyone who is "in the vicinity" can post and read whatever is on the board over a period of days or weeks. The length of time that postings remain on a server varies by newsgroup and server, but many groups also archive their messages for reading at any time. This allows you to browse a large number of messages quickly and read at your convenience rather than having to check your inbox every day.

A second difference is that messages are not sent to individual mailboxes. They are sent and stored on servers around the world, where they can be accessed by other servers. In a way, you can think of your service provider as a kind of subscriber since providers select the newsgroups that they will access and make available to their customers. This means you have access to hundreds or thousands of messages without worrying about subscribing individually or overloading your mailbox.

There is also a different sense of community. Many more people from all around the world participate in newsgroups than subscribe to a mailing list; moreover, they may only read and not respond to messages. In addition, unlike mailing list subscribers, newsgroup readers are not necessarily reading and posting to their major interest groups; they may have been skimming newsgroups and come upon a group that sounds interesting at that moment. After reading a number of messages, they may respond, but often they move on. Even users who are group subscribers may only check messages infrequently. Thus, there is generally less chance to get to know other users well, but there is an incredible variety of topics and viewpoints to be found.

Usenet Newsgroup Hierarchies

Before going on to explore newsgroups, take a moment to look at the format of their names. They may appear confusing at first, but they are actually hierarchical categories and topics, written in lower-case letters separated by dots. It is often easy to figure out the topic of a group by reading its name from left to right as in the following examples:

news.newusers

This group is in the "news" hierarchy and its topic is information for "new users."

k12.ed.comp.literacy

This group is in the "k12" education hierarchy and its topic is "computer literacy." Other hierarchies include:

- alt — alternative (almost any topic, usually from an alternative view)
- biz. — business
- comp. — computers
- humanities — humanities
- misc. — miscellaneous
- rec. — recreation and hobbies
- sci. — science
- soc. — social issues
- talk. — current issues

Newcomer Groups

There are many groups especially for newcomers, such as:

- news.announce.newusers
- news.answers
- news.newusers.questions

Their postings are very useful because they contain information about group expectations and how to participate. They also answer **FAQ**s (Frequently Asked Questions). Many of the messages in these groups are reposted on a regular basis by the group moderator so that they are always available to new users and others for reference. If you have trouble locating these groups on your server, or want to find the FAQ for a particular newsgroup, try a search of the **Usenet FAQ Archives** (http://www.faqs.org/faqs). This site links not only to information for the newcomer groups, but also to FAQs and welcome messages for hundreds of other newsgroups. You may decide to explore a group by lurking—just reading messages and observing how the group operates. However, it is still recommended that you check out the introductory information before posting messages. Experienced newsgroup users often react negatively to such newcomer breaches of netiquette as off-topic postings and redundant questions; more commonly than mailing list member, they may respond by flaming (sending sarcastic or nasty replies).

Other sources of introductory information can be found at Internet glossaries, especially for help with the many acronyms and smileys found in some postings. Smileys, or emoticons, are keyboard symbols used to communicate feelings and attitudes. Usually you can "get the picture" by turning your head to the left. For example, this group of keystrokes **<:-)>** means "smiling" or "happy." A short introduction to smileys can be found at **Learn the Net** (http://www.learnthenet.com/english/html/25smile.htm).

Reading Newsgroups

To get started reading newsgroups you have two choices. The first is to use a web-based newsreader service. These services are easy and convenient since they automatically thread postings (that is, they group messages by topic), and they allow you to read groups directly from the Web without a special newsreader program. Many services charge, but some, such as **Google Groups** (http://groups.google.com/) are free.

The second choice is to use a newsreader program. Fortunately, most browsers come with closely integrated mail and news functions. This means it is relatively easy to explore newsgroups from your browser once you have become familiar with its email program. You can also purchase specialized newsreaders with more functions, but for most purposes, this is not necessary. In order to use your browser's program, be sure that your news preferences are set. Most likely they were automatically set when you entered your mail preferences. If not, go back to the section on setting mail preferences at the beginning of this chapter, and follow the directions.

At this point you are ready to read. In most newer browsers, the list of available newsgroups will be downloaded when you select News from folder list in the mail window. This process may take several minutes depending on the number of groups. If you do not see a list, you may need to select All Newsgroups or a similar heading under View or from a dialog box. When the list is loaded, check to see if the groups are collapsed into threads. This is indicated by an icon—often by boxes with a plus or minus sign or by triangles next to the group names. Just as with email messages, these icons indicate nested or collapsed sub-groups. Clicking the icons will alternately hide and reveal the sub-groups. Next scroll down the list until you find an interesting group.

Subscribing to Newsgroups

If you think you may be interested in reading a particular group's messages, you may want to subscribe. Actually it is the service provider who subscribes by agreeing to carry various groups and providing access to them, but the same word is used when individuals identify specific newsgroups as ones they are interested in and would like to read again. It is convenient to subscribe if you plan to read a newsgroup often. That way, it will appear in the news folder of your mail window. Then, the next time you want to read it, you can simply click the group you want in order to view new postings. This saves considerable time since you do not have to scroll through the entire list. Of course, you can always select all groups if you want to view the whole list again or change your subscriptions. Some programs also let you select a New Groups category, which downloads only groups that have come on since your last reading.

Posting Messages

Composing or replying to a message is very easy since the message composition window is the same for mail and news in most programs. You can refer back to the Reply and Composing New Messages sections earlier in this chapter if necessary. If you are composing a new message, be sure to add an explanatory subject title. This is very helpful for readers who are generally looking for messages in their interest area. There are so many messages on news servers that many readers ignore non-descriptive titles such as "question," so be as informative as possible in a few words. Also, be sure you are familiar with the posting guidelines for the group that you are addressing.

Figure 4-5. A Message from the news.announce.newusers group viewed in the Netscape 7.0 newsreader. There are approximately 25,000 newsgroups available from this account holder's service provider. However, she has subscribed to only 7 groups, which appear in the left pane in her news charter folder. Notice the threaded subject headers in the top right pane.

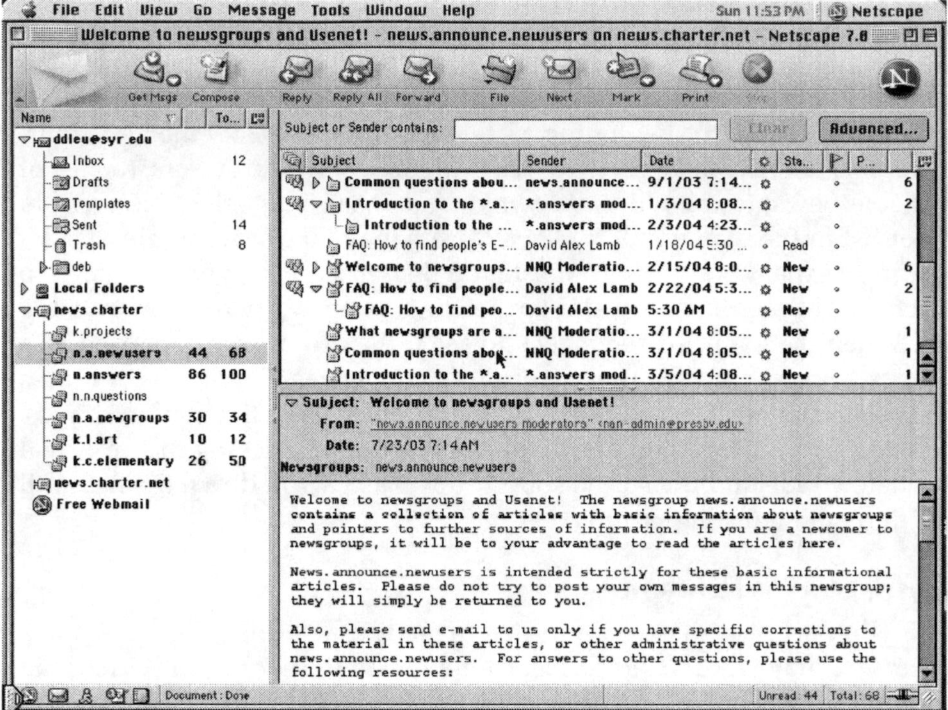

Newsgroup Netiquette

In general, newsgroup netiquette is similar to that for email and mailing lists. You may want to review that section of this chapter or check the newsgroup area of the previously mentioned netiquette sites (http://wise.fau.edu/netiquette/net/dis.html) and (http://www.dtcc.edu/cs/rfc1855.html#3). **Google Groups** also offers good advice on effective postings to newsgroups (http://www.google.com/googlegroups/posting_style.html). In general, you should compose short, well-written, on-topic, and courteous messages. Do not ask newbie questions, or post the same message to multiple groups, and do not overuse acronyms or smileys (some groups prefer none at all). Finally, remember it is always best to lurk until you have a good sense of the personality and culture of a particular newsgroup.

Using Newsgroups for Teaching and Learning

Most newsgroups are unmoderated and encourage postings from a wide open readership with diverse views. This makes them a good source of information that often provides opportunities for teachers and students to broaden their horizons. These same characteristics, however, can cause serious concerns in the classroom since there are sure to be some topics, language use, and discussions that are unsuitable for students. Moreover, several newsgroup categories contain explicit discussions of sex-related topics. These areas may not present problems for you, depending on your service provider. If your provider is your school district or a state network, for example, chances are they will not carry or provide access to controversial groups.

The wide open readership and diversity of views found in newsgroups makes them an excellent source of information. However, they can also be the source of serious concern about topics, language, and discussions that may be unsuitable for students.

On the other hand, even lack of access to certain groups cannot totally guarantee appropriateness because it is still possible for anyone to post to almost any group. Therefore, even seemingly appropriate groups may post inappropriate messages at times. There are some websites that limit their group boards and forums to subscribed members, which can reduce the chance for unsuitable postings. Nevertheless, our experience and many of the email messages we have received indicate that many teachers have reservations about using newsgroups in class with their students. There are some teachers, however, who point out that having older students compare the diverse viewpoints presented in newsgroups can be very helpful in improving critical thinking skills. However, these teachers also stress the need for careful guidance and supervision, and possibly getting permission forms or having discussions with parents.

Perhaps the most common use of newsgroups for many educators is to gather information for themselves, which they can then use or adapt for lessons in their own situations. Researching specific subjects, finding new sources, and discussing topics with experts and more experienced posters are some of the ways teachers recommend using newsgroups. In addition, some teachers have mentioned finding contacts and volunteers for various classroom and email activities, such as presentations or Ask An Expert correspondence.

In short, opinions on newsgroups vary. Groups do provide quick access to large quantities of diverse, up-to-date information. Yet the very quantity of information may make if difficult to find exactly what you need. Moreover, you may be concerned about the appropriateness of some groups for your students, or even for yourself. Therefore, as with all Internet activities, we encourage you to try out a few groups and then make your own decision. You are the best judge of what suits your situation and meets your and your students' needs.

Directories for Newsgroups

As we have said, the newsgroups that are available to you depend on your provider. More and more, however, you can also access groups from individual websites or web-based services. As a result, it is not really necessary to search the Web for newsgroups. However, if you would like to view some master lists, the following sites are good places to start. If you find an interesting site that is not accessible through your service provider, you might ask them to consider adding it.

- **TileNet**—http://www.tile.net/news
  A searchable site listing thousands of newsgroups.
- **Google Groups**—http://groups.google.com/
  A good site for accessing newsgroups from the Web. In addition to reading and posting to many groups, you can also search Google's archives of Usenet groups back to 1981.

- **Usenet Discussion Groups—**
  http://www.edwebproject.org/usenets.html
  A list of groups focused only on education from the EdWeb K-12 Resource Guide.
- **Harley Hahn's Master List of Usenet Newsgroups—**
  http://www.harley.com/usenet/index.html
  A simply organized, easy-to-use site. It includes links to several web-based newsgroup access services (some are for a fee).

Getting Started with Weblogs

Although weblogs, or blogs as they are commonly called, have been around for some time, they are only recently becoming familiar to most teachers. Suddenly we are reading about blogs in newspapers and online journals, hearing about them on TV, responding to them on politicians' webpages, and finding them on school websites. What exactly are weblogs? It depends. Originally, weblogs were just that—websites that contained frequently updated chronological logs of links to interesting sites and news articles from the Web, sometimes containing comments or personal musings from the site's creator —somewhat like an individual's newspaper. More recently, weblogs are often characterized as online journals because they contain personal diary-like entries on almost any topic with no links to news and events. For helpful information and a history of weblogs, check out **Rebecca's Pocket** (http://www.rebeccablood.net/portal.html).

Figure 4-6. The Educational Bloggers Network Weblog
(http://www.ebn.weblogger.com/) showing a typical three-column format.

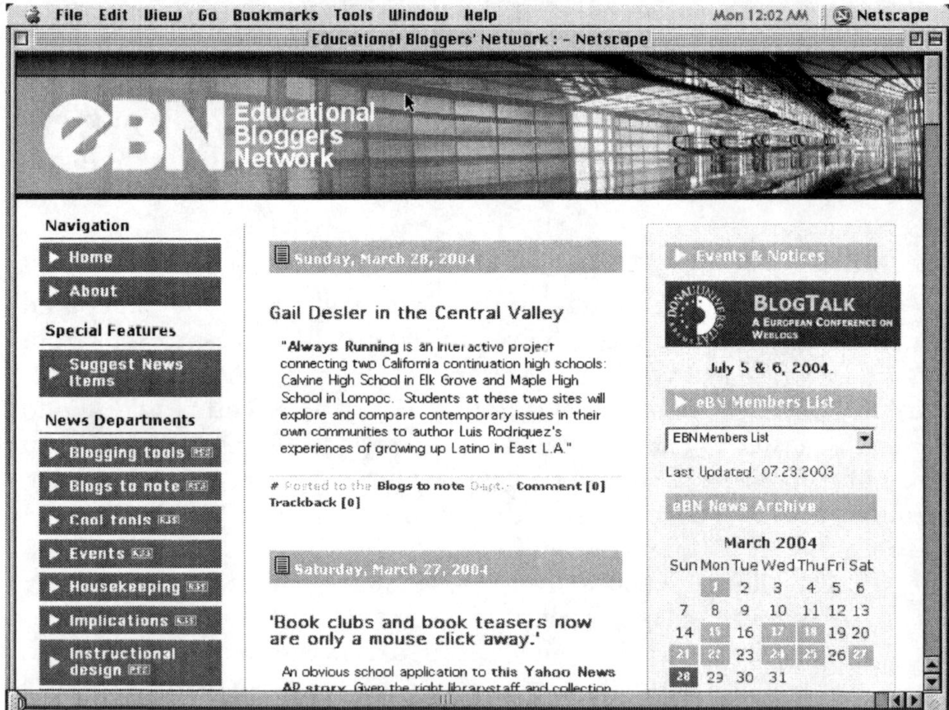

At the time of this writing, "weblog" most commonly refers to an Internet site with frequently updated chronological entries (of news links or personal musings or both) together with related commentary from the author and others who read the blog. Weblogs often include photos and graphics and are easily recognized by their standard two- or three-column template. The widest column usually contains the author's (and perhaps readers') entries in chronological order with the most recent at the top. Most blogs allow readers to respond and track previous messages related to a topic by clicking a button—a bit like email except the comments are automatically posted to the weblog for everyone to read. Many weblogs contain a "blogroll" in one of the columns; this is a list of links to other blogs that the author reads. In this way, bloggers are creating their own networks of people interested in and resources related to the topics that interest them most.

Using Weblogs for Teaching and Learning

The main attractions of weblogs are that they are inexpensive, or free, and easy to use. With web-based software from companies such as Blogger and Manila, authors can create, change, and update their sites with a simple mouse click. Thus, these free or low-cost sites make it possible for even those with no programming knowledge to set up and maintain their own blogs in just a few minutes. There is no need for a webmaster here, or put another way, anyone can now become a webmaster by following a few quick steps.

Weblogs are very popular because they are easy to use and inexpensive or free.

As a result, weblogs offer great potential for those interested in maximizing their use of the communicative aspects of the Internet without investing a lot of time and money in developing specialized skills. Educators have taken notice and are developing a variety of blogs for multiple purposes as this short list of examples illustrates:

- Class blogs such as Will Richardson's **Journalism 1 at HCRHS** (http://weblogs.hcrhs.k12.nj.us/journ1/)
- Teacher news blogs such as Pam Pritchard's **Edublog News** (http://www.edublognews.com/)
- Teacher blogs such as Anne Davis' **EduBlog Insights—** http://anvil.gsu.edu/EduBlogInsights/
- Mentor blogs such as Pam Pritchard's **Entry Year Teacher/Mentor Blog** (http://www.edithere.com/eyt/)
- School blogs such as Tim Lauer's **Merriweather Lewis Elementary School Weblog** (http://lewiselementary.org/)
- Educational blog networks such as the Bay Area Writing Project's **Educational Bloggers Network** (http://www.ebn.weblogger.com)
- School district blogs such as Ohio's **Olentangy Local School District What's New Weblog** (http://www.olentangy.k12.oh.us/whatsnew/)
- Even bear blogs! Jefferson, a bear in Julia Siporin's third grade Oregon classroom has his own site—**The Adventures of Jefferson Bear** (http://jeffersonbear.motime.com/).

Educators are not the only ones using blogs. A large and rapidly growing number of students are also avid blog creators and readers. Several of the blogs above link to student sites.

Blogs can focus on any topic, but many teachers find them particularly well suited to literature and writing courses. Students can put reviews or their own writing on a blog and usually find an eager audience willing to give feedback—on either a restricted classroom site or an open access Internet site. The decision whether to limit access is often based on the age and experience of the students. Teachers say that effort is increased and writing is more quickly revised when students write for multiple readers giving immediate feedback. One interesting example of using blogs in composition classes is **The Year of the Blog** (http://www.bgsu.edu/cconline/barrios/blogs/index.html).

In other content areas, such as science and social studies, blogs can be used to keep track of observations and record results of experiments. Math students can work on difficult problems by entering questions and sharing possible solutions. Teachers at all levels are using weblogs to give homework assignments, publish student reports, and update parents on class activities. Blog sites and networks also provide opportunities for teachers to share ideas with colleagues on almost any topic or concern. The communication possibilities of blogs seem limitless and well suited to educational purposes. Here are a few sites to get you started, but you may want to do your own search for additional sites since this is a rapidly growing section of the Internet.

Directories for Weblogs

- **Eaton Web Portal**—http://portal.eatonweb.com/
  A very large directory for all types of blogs.
- **Google Directory of Journal Hosts**—
  http://directory.google.com/Top/Arts/Online_Writing/Journals/Resources/Hosts/
  A large and growing list of places to find blog software and hosting sites. Some charge fees.
- **Blogger.com**—http://new.blogger.com/
  A blog software site for creating and hosting your own blog. Free and pay versions available.
- **Diaryland**—http://www.diaryland.com/
  A free site for creating and hosting your own blog.
- **Movabletype**—http://www.movabletype.org/
  Software for creating and hosting your own blogs. Free (donations accepted) for non-commercial users. Donations are requested for additional services.
- **Userland Software**—http://www.userland.com/
  Many blogs are created with Manila and Radio software from this company. For a fee, but many users say it is worth it.

Getting Started with Real-Time Communication

Email, mailing lists, newsgroups, and weblogs are non-synchronous forms of electronic communication. There are, in addition, several types of real-time communication available on the Internet. These include listening to radio broadcasts; reading and writing simultaneous messages through chat (Internet Relay Chat) or instant messaging (IM); or "conversing" with other visitors as you "move around" text-based virtual locations in MOOs (Mud [Multiple User Dimension] Object Oriented); and audio and video conferencing. We have heard and read about several positive experiences with real-time communication, but it is also a frequently debated topic on lists and forums, and among teachers and parents. Therefore, as with other Internet activities, we recommend that you explore the possibilities and decide for yourself whether they are useful and appropriate for you and your students. We have provided a list of resources at the end of this section to help you get started.

Real-time interaction is getting easier as various sites offer easier software with step-by-step instructions and click-on capabilities for participants.

As you try out these new types of communication, keep in mind that in addition to their benefits, many teachers have expressed concerns about using synchronous communication in the classroom. One problem is that many of these applications require additional software, equipment, or special access, which can be expensive. Nevertheless, real-time interaction is getting easier as various vendors and organizations offer web-based programs that can be accessed directly from a browser.

Another concern is the time that may be needed to learn a program. Some programs are confusing at first, especially for beginners, or take a great deal of practice to become proficient. Again, however, web-based programs are making programs easier by including step-by-step instructions and click-on capabilities for participants. In addition, many schools have technical support people who can help you set up what you need. There are also many students who already know how to use certain programs—especially chat and IM—and do so on a daily basis for their own purposes. These students can become your class experts and gain confidence in the process. This can be especially beneficial for students who struggle with foundational literacies but who really know how to navigate chat and IM environments.

Many teachers, especially those with one-computer classrooms, express concerns about scheduling time for every student to participate in real-time interactions. Chat, for example, usually entails one student in a cycle of typing and reading messages with an Internet partner over the course of several or many minutes. In contrast, using email, one student types a message and then moves on, making the computer available for another student. Nevertheless, some teachers feel that the excitement and motivation created by chat make it worth using. They also say it is a great way for students to improve keyboarding skills since if they want to be active participants, the best way to keep up is to type faster. Other teachers say trying to keep up can create its own problems, however. They point to the numerous acronyms, abbreviations, non-standard spellings, and sentence fragments that are typical of chat and question whether this style of writing has any value. Some teachers blame IM for lowering language arts skills among their students.

Perhaps the biggest concern about real-time applications is safety. We have all seen and read reports on the dangers of meeting the wrong type of people on the Internet. Keep in mind, however, that problems such as the use of concealed or false identities for malicious purposes can be found with all types of Internet communication. Just as you would choose safe sites for keypals or explore newsgroups before having your students participate in them, you can explore various ways to use real-time applications safely. For example, create your own chat room at an educational site that screens members, or make sure that IM buddy lists include only students from your classroom. Use only educational MOOs that you have explored. Or try video conferencing—you choose the other participants and can be in the room with the students.

As we have stressed with all Internet activities, the real challenge is to consider whether and how they can best contribute to our teaching and learning goals, and then to develop successful ways to integrate them into your own classroom settings. In the end, you are the best judge of which programs and activities will bring the most benefit your students. Check out the sites below to begin your explorations:

Chat

- **Chat Magazine**—http://www.chatmag.com/index.html
  A very comprehensive site that explains what chat is and the basics of IRC (Internet Relay Chat). Includes good information on chat safety, netiquette, and different types of chat programs. Useful for teachers new to chat.
- **e-Pals.com**—http://www.epals.com/chat/
  A safe and secure site to join existing chat rooms or set up your own password-protected room. For teachers and students.
- **Kidlink.org**—http://www.kidlink.org/english/general/irc.html
  A good site for students with chat rooms in several languages.
- **Tapped In**—http://ti2.sri.com/tappedin/index.jsp
  This site provides chat and discussion boards for its "international community of educators" to share and discuss a variety of education topics.
- **Teacher.Net**—http://www.teachers.net/chatboard/
  A large variety of topics can be found at this site for teachers.
- **IRCLE**—http://www.ircle.com/
  The homepage for a very popular IRC software program for Macintosh.
- **mIRC**—http://www.mirc.co.uk/
  The homepage for a very popular IRC software program for Windows.

Instant Messaging

- **AOL Instant Messenger**—http://aim.com
  A site for downloading AOL's Instant Messaging program. It is free and you can use it even if AOL is not your service provider. Several newer versions of browsers now come with this software already installed.

- **MSN Messenger**—http://messenger.msn.com/Mac/ or http://messenger.msn.com/?client+1
  The sites for downloading MSN Messenger's programs for Macintosh and Windows.

MOOs

- **Moosetracks**—http://www.cc.gatech.edu/elc/moose-crossing/
  This fun site is a MOO designed especially for 9–13 year olds, but anyone can try it. Adults must be identified as "rangers." It has links to the free software needed for both Mac and Windows users.
- **Educational MOO Resource List**
  http://www.bridgewater.edu/~rbowman/CICconf2000/edMOO resources.htm
  A good site for book suggestions, websites and links to information about MOOs.
- **Rachel's Super Moo List Educational Moos**—
  http://moolist. yeehaw. net/edu.html
  A list of educational moos for all levels including university students.

Video-Conferencing

- **SBC Knowledge Network**—
  http://www.kn.pacbell.com/wired/vidconf/index.html
  A nice introduction to the topic with examples, strategies, and a glossary. You can also join their mailing list to discuss video conferencing issues.
- **Digital Bridges**—
  http://www.netc.org/digitalbridges/vc/index.html
  Digital Bridges is a project of the Northwest Educational Technology Consortium. This well organized site has examples of current project schools and links to videoconferencing resources.
- **Videoconferencing Advice Sheet—**
  http://stage.ncte.ie/ICTAdviceSupport/AdviceSheets/Video Conferencing/
  Basic information from Ireland's ScoilNet about using classroom videoconferencing.
- **iSight**—http://www.apple.com/isight/
  A new camera from Apple for videoconferencing with iChatAV. It is easy to use and relatively inexpensive.

Visiting the Classroom: Mrs. Contner's Fourth Grade Class in Ohio

Mrs. Contner's site (http://home.earthlink.net/%7Econtner/firstpage.html) illustrates many ways teachers can use a website to communicate with students, parents, other educators, and anyone else who is interested. Mrs. Contner is a fourth grade teacher at Maineville Elementary School in Warren County, Ohio. For students, she posts spelling lists, vocabulary words, and homework assignments along with links to online homework help resources. Not only is this useful for students who miss class, but it also provides practice with many of the new literacies in an Internet context: students identify a problem with their homework, locate useful resources, and synthesize information to solve a problem or answer their questions. Her site also features a class weblog where students publish their book reports and other writing assignments. Visitors can also read about the students social studies units here.

Another interesting feature is the class's guest book. A click takes visitors to a map where they can place a virtual flag to mark their location and leave a message for the class. This provides another communication opportunity for the students.

E-MAIL FOR YOU

From: Debbi Contner (contner@earthlink.net)
Subject: A Classroom Website for Communication

Dear Colleagues,

Over the years I have noticed that having a website for my classroom greatly increases the communication between school and home. As more and more homes have computers with internet access, logging onto the classroom site becomes routine. The parents know that the current week's spelling words, vocabulary words, and assignments will be listed. It takes the guess work out of trying to find out what your child needs to know and do for school. Students who are used to using the excuse of "My teacher didn't tell me what I was supposed to do!" find that it no longer works. Parents can check the site to see important announcements that students may forget by the time they get home.

I also have several weblogs that are part of the site. These are used to post student writing and to share educational ideas with parents and other educators. My class communicates with people from around the world by way of our weblogs. Anyone can become a member of our weblogs and send us comments about what we post. Our site also serves as a beginning spot for research. By following the links provided, students can research without searching in unnecessary sites.

Having a classroom site makes communication between the teacher, student, family, and colleagues easier.

Debbi Contner
Hamilton Maineville Elementary School
Maineville, Ohio

For parents—in addition to viewing the students' work—there are announcements, a newsletter, and links to the school's weblog, the Little Miami School District site, and the Ohio State Board of Education. Mrs. Contner's site also includes her own weblog with thoughts on blogs in education among other topics. Her blogroll links to other educators' blogs and useful educational sites, which is helpful for other teachers who visit her site. And of course there is a link emailing Mrs. Contner. Be sure to visit this great site!

Figure: 4-7. Mrs. Contner's Fourth Grade Class Homepage
(http://home.earthlink.net/%7Econtner/firstpage.html). This site incorporates several types of electronic communication: email, a newsletter, weblogs and links to other relevant sites.

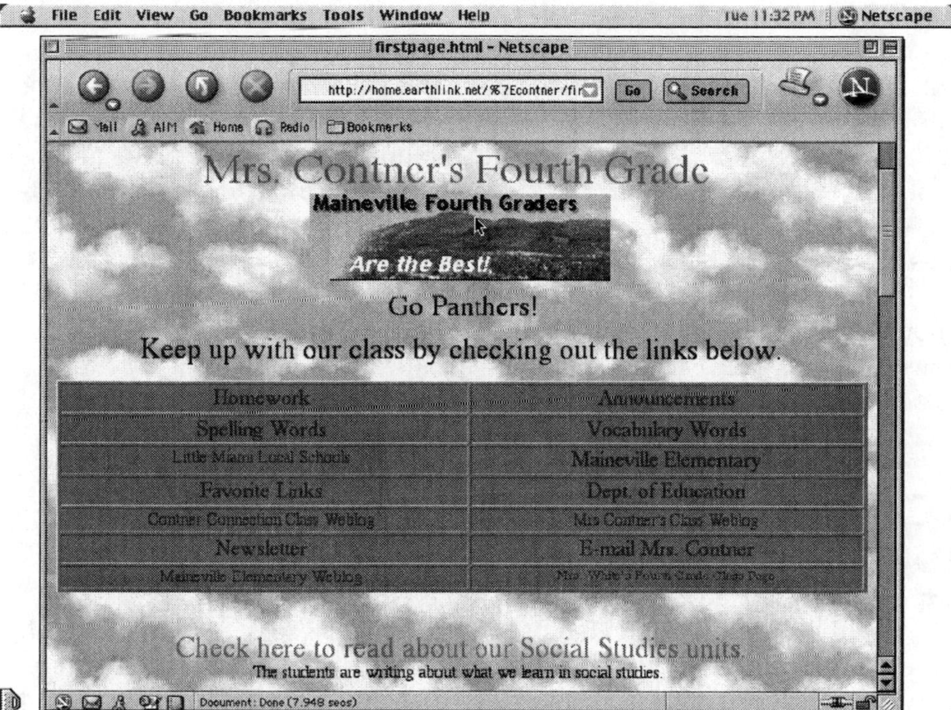

New Literacies in Internet Communication

Throughout this chapter we have discussed many ways the Internet can be used for quick and easy communication both locally and around the world. Of course, foundational literacies play an important role in using the programs and tools we have demonstrated. But if students and teachers want to achieve the maximum benefit from Internet communication, they must be skilled in the new literacies as well. As discussed in Chapter 1, these literacies relate to the basic functions of identifying problems and then locating, critically evaluating, synthesizing, and communicating information about solutions to those problems. Obviously, students and teachers need skills directly related to the communication function. At the very least, they will need to use and manage email accounts, and they will also benefit greatly from knowledge of and participation in mailing lists and newsgroups. They may need IM or videoconferencing for real-time interactions. And if they want to communicate and receive feedback easily from a wide and diversified audience, weblogs may be the way.

If students and teachers want to achieve the maximum benefit from Internet communication, they must be skilled in new literacies as well as foundational literacies.

It may not be so obvious, however, that for truly effective communication, students and teachers will also need to develop new literacies related to the other functions. For example, they will need to identify important problems, questions, and issues to include in their messages. An ethical disposition toward Internet use will help their communication be useful and appropriate for their receivers.

Students and teachers looking for information will need excellent navigation skills in order to locate appropriate people, groups, and lists for askingquestions and sharing their solutions.

In both sending and receiving communications, students and teachers will need to critically evaluate the relevance, accuracy, and suitability of information for themselves and their readers. Bloggers will use this same ability to make decisions about what to include on their sites. Being able to synthesize information from a variety of disparate and sometimes conflicting sources will be even more necessary for composing clear and concise messages.

In short, communicating successfully on the Internet requires broad knowledge and a wide variety of skills—as any mode of communication does. Students and teachers need both foundational and new literacies. We hope the information in this chapter has given you much to reflect on and many strategies for successfully communicating on the Internet.

Additional Communication Resources on the Internet

Beginners Guide to the Internet—
http://205.146.39.13/linktuts/bgtoc.htm

A well-organized guide to most of the topics discussed in this chapter: email, mailing lists, newsgroups, videoconferencing, and several more. Other locations at the site have classroom activities, resource links, and a glossary.

Edublog Webring—
http://alterego.manilasites.com/stories/storyReader$138

A webring for teachers, technologists, and librarians who are interested in integrating weblogs into the classroom. Also for teachers who are using blogs in their classrooms.

Education Web Logs—
http://www.techlearning.com/story/showArticle.jhtml?articleID=12803462

An informative article with basic background information on weblogs and links to examples.

Email: A Guide to Using It in Bristol Schools—
http://www.bristol-lea.org.uk/teaching/pdf/email_guide.pdf

A comprehensive guide from Bristol, England that includes a lot of background information on using email as well as some suggestions for classroom activities. Most appropriate for primary and middle grades.

An Introduction to Weblog Terms for Weblog Readers—
http://www.gyford.com/phil/writing/2003/01/05/an_introduction_.php

Just what it says. Not specifically for educators, but an easy to understand introduction from Phil Gyford.

Online Netiquette—http://www.onlinenetiquette.com

A great site to find information on Internet manners. It includes definitions, Netiquette 101, forums, a newsletter, and links to related sites.

A Practical Guide to Blogging—
http://www.writerswrite.com/journal/jul02/gak16.htm
This great one-page summary comes from *Writers Write—The Internet Writing Journal*, but contains useful material for everyone. It has many links to related resources.

Teacher Mailrings—http://teachers.net/mailrings/
A network of 50,000 teachers around the world from the Teachers.Net site. Mailing lists are organized by grade level, subject, and special interests.

Ten Tips for a Better Weblog—
http://www.rebeccablood.net/essays/ten_tips.html
Tips from Rebecca Blood, author of the *Weblog Handbook*.

weblogg-ED—http://www.weblogg-ed.com/
Another blog from Will Richardson. See the idea file, read the FAQs, and check out the blogroll for links to other informative blogs.

Weblog Ethics—
http://www.rebeccablood.net/handbook/excerpts/weblog_ethics.html
An excerpt on weblog ethics from the *Weblog Handbook*.

West Loogootee Elementary School—
http://www.siec.k12.in.us/~west/edu/chat.htm
A site for teachers with basic information on email safety and mailing lists, a chat room list, and resource links.

5 English and the Language Arts: Opening New Doors to Literature and Literacy

The essence of both reading and writing has always been change. Reading a book or writing a story changes us forever; we return from the worlds we inhabit during our literacy journeys with new insights about our surroundings and ourselves. Moreover, teaching students to read and write is also a transforming experience; it opens up new windows to the world, creating a lifetime of opportunities. Change has always defined our work as literacy educators. By teaching students to read and write, we change the world.

Internet technologies create new literacies, which are required to effectively exploit their potentials. Traditional definitions of reading and writing will be insufficient if we seek to provide children with the futures they deserve.

Today, reading and writing are being defined by change in even more profound ways. Internet technologies create new literacies, which are required to effectively exploit their potentials. These technologies also make possible new instructional practices to help children acquire the literacies of their future. Traditional definitions of reading and writing will be insufficient if we seek to provide children with the futures they deserve.

The Internet opens new doors to literature and response, creating new opportunities for the English/language arts curriculum. Your students can participate in an electronic discussion about Shakespeare, view a video of a favorite author explaining her writing process, read reviews of books posted by students from around the world, join a global discussion group via email, quickly search online versions of Bartlett's *Quotations* and Roget's *Thesaurus*, or engage in many other wonderful experiences as you open new doors to literature and literacy.

C. S. Lewis understood what happens when you open new doors to new worlds. In *The Chronicles of Narnia*, Lewis leads us through the secret door of a wardrobe, opening a magical world full of exciting new opportunities. We believe the Internet is another door, opening new worlds for you and your students with many exciting opportunities to explore in literature and composition.

After reading this chapter, you should be able to:

1. Identify at least three resources that contain online collections of works of literature and another three resources that provide extended lesson ideas related to literature and language arts.
2. Discuss various options for students looking for writing support and opportunities to publish their writing via the Internet.
3. Develop and share an original idea for Internet Workshop or Internet Project related to literature and language arts, using the lesson ideas in this chapter as a springboard.
4. Discuss ways of integrating instruction about citing sources and copyright issues into your language arts curriculum.

Teaching with the Internet: Tricia Abernathy's Class

It was Friday afternoon in Tricia Abernathy's fifth grade class. Her class was in the middle of a workshop session. Not an Internet Workshop session, just a regular workshop session; one she had learned from reading *In the Middle* by Nancie Atwell.

Tricia had developed a cross-curricular thematic unit around the advantages diversity creates. Her goal was to increase students' appreciation for diversity as they studied math, science, social studies, reading, writing, speaking, and listening. In math, she had activities for students to explore number systems from several ancient civilizations, including a study of systems using bases other than 10. These included several great activities she had found at **The Math Forum** (http://mathforum.org/). In science, she was using the unit on biodiversity she had developed in a summer workshop at the university last year. In social studies, she developed experiences for students to better understand the cultures of both Native Americans and immigrants. In language arts, Tricia had planned experiences around "pourquoi tales," creation myths that exist in every traditional culture. Pourquoi tales explain sources of natural phenomena such as how people obtained fire, why mosquitoes buzz in people's ears, where the moon came from, or why rivers run into the ocean.

Tricia had developed a cross-curricular thematic unit around the advantages diversity creates.

Tricia was just beginning to use the Internet in her classroom. She and her students only used it for research or for printing out materials. Others at her school were using the Internet for instruction, but Tricia was the careful type. She was moving gradually into the new worlds that the Internet opened, being careful not to misuse this powerful new tool.

Tricia had introduced the concept of a pourquoi tale at the beginning of the unit by engaging the class in read-aloud response journal activities (Leu & Kinzer, 2002) with several examples of this genre: *The Fire Bringer* by Margaret Hodges and *Star Boy* by Paul Goble. Then she had students work in one of three literature discussion groups. Each group had a large set of pourquoi tales to read. One group read and discussed tales from the Americas, another read tales from Asia and Australia, and a third read tales from Africa, Europe, and the Middle East. She used book club activities suggested by McMahon, Raphael, Goatley, and Pardo (1997); text set activities suggested by Short (1993); and response journal activities suggested by Hynds (1997).

Tricia gave each group this assignment:

"Make a class presentation about one culture using only the information in the pourquoi tales for your region. Infer aspects of that culture from the stories you read, indicating what you inferred and the evidence supporting your inferences. Also explain why the cultural patterns you found are useful. You may use the Yahooligans search engine, as well as any books in the library."

Individuals chose different books to read from the classroom and library collections. Students also discovered and shared stories they found on the Internet during their scheduled time on the classroom computer. They liked to print out copies of each story and exchange them with others in their group.

Members of each group got together twice a week to share their literary experiences in a student-led discussion organized around a "grand conversation" (McGee & Richgels, 1990). During their grand conversations, each group discussed the pourquoi tales they were reading and what each suggested about the cultures they were studying. They also made plans for their class presentation. Once a week, the entire class came together to share the work they were doing in groups and to plan new work.

Marcus had waited a long time to make his contribution during the whole-class, workshop session.

"I was using Yahooligans and I did a search for pourquoi stories like we're reading and I found a cool site!"

Marcus was one of those students who thrived in an organized class that also provided opportunities for individual exploration. He liked to find out things on his own.

Marcus continued with his contribution to the workshop session, "You know our group has Africa and I found this place called **The Big Myth** (http://mythicjourneys.org/bigmyth/index.htm). It has a lot of cool legends. And then we also found a place where some kids wrote their own pourquoi tales and posted them online (see **Pourquoi Tales for Third Graders** at http://www.sme.k12.nf.ca/pourquoi_tales/index.html). Ms. Abernathy, could we do an Internet Project like this class? You know, make a place like that with all kinds of creation stories from different countries. We could even add some new ideas like have other kids email us from where they were in the world. . . like from Japan, and Indonesia, and Amsterdam. Ms. Abernathy, could we . . . you know . . . ask kids to email us pourquoi tales from their countries? Then we could . . . we could put them on our class homepage so other kids could read them. It would be cool to put all the stories on our homepage."

"Yeah. Cool!" A chorus of thoughts emerged from the class.

"Did you set a bookmark, Marcus? Can you show us?"

Knowing she would ask this question, Marcus had done precisely that. First, he showed the class one of the pourquoi stories from **The Big Myth** (http://mythicjourneys.org/bigmyth/index.htm). It was created with Flash technologies that read the story out loud and the kids were pretty impressed. Next, he linked to **Pourquoi Tales for Third Graders** (http://www.sme.k12.nf.ca/pourquoi_tales/index.html) and scrolled down to show the range of different stories the students had written.

Then, with a telling gleam in his eyes, Marcus also showed Ms. Abernathy the homepage for **Ms. Hos-McGrane's 5th-6th Grade Class at The International School of Amsterdam** (http://www.internet-at-work.com/hos_mcgrane/). Marcus knew Ms. Abernathy's ancestors came from the Netherlands and he had saved this Internet location for last. He took her to the wonderful project this class had completed: **Creation Stories and Myths** (http://www.internet-at-work.com/hos_mcgrane/creation/cstorymenu. html). It was a collection of pourquoi tales from around the world they had written and collected from others. It was this site that gave Marcus the idea for the Internet Project he had suggested. As Marcus showed Ms. Abernathy and the class this great resource, he knew she would give them the green light for Internet Project.

"Marcus, "she said, "you certainly know how to convince me. This is wonderful! We'll see what we can do."

In this class, a "We'll see" from Ms. Abernathy was almost as good as gold.

"Yes!" several students said simultaneously, pumping their arms.

Tricia Abernathy smiled. Everyone was excited about the possibility of doing an Internet Project and using their new classroom homepage to publish stories from around the world.

Figure 5-1. One of the African pourquoi tales with Flash technologies available from **The Big Myth** (http://mythicjourneys.org/bigmyth/index.htm).

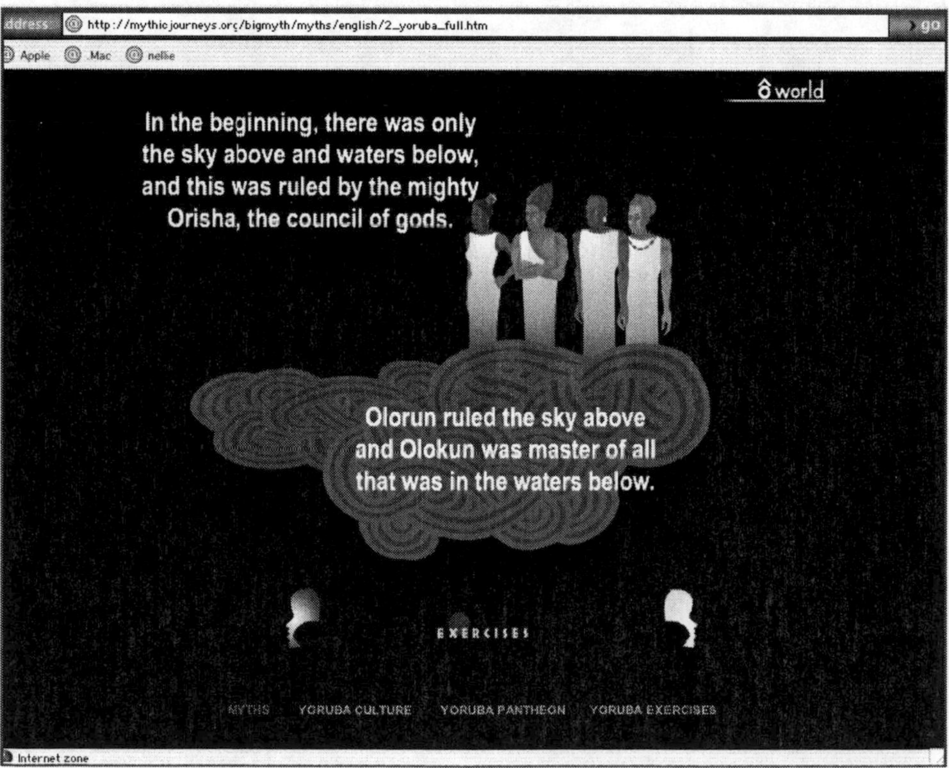

After school that day. Tricia started thinking. She had to do some quick planning as she went over to the classroom computer. She had heard about the projects a few of the teachers were doing at her school so she talked briefly with Patty Bolin who gave some ideas and useful locations on the Internet. Returning to her classroom, Tricia visited a wonderful tutorial at OzProjects called **Getting Started with Online Projects** (http://ozprojects.edna.edu.au/support/started.html). Here, she studied how to develop collaborative projects on the Internet. She quickly linked to a number of useful resources that told her exactly how to set up a project, announce it to others, and post her announcement.

Returning to her classroom, Tricia visited a wonderful tutorial at ***OzProjects*** *called* ***Getting Started with Online Projects.***

In just a few minutes, she had posted an announcement at a number of different locations, explaining the project and asking teachers and students from around the world to contribute pourquoi tales from their cultures. By exchanging stories, they would each develop a deeper appreciation for differences and for important aspects of other cultures. She posted her project at the following locations from around the world:

- **The Internet Projects Registry** of the Global Schoolhouse (http://www.gsn.org/pr/_cfm/index.cfm)
- **Collaborative Learning Project Center** (http://www.2learn.ca/Projects/projectcentre/projframeb.html), a location in Alberta, Canada
- The **Projects** Location at the Australian National site, **EdNa** (http://www.edna.edu.au/edna/go/pid/747)
- **Intercultural Email Classroom Connections** (http://www.iecc.org/)
- **Global Classroom in Australia** (http://www.sofweb.vic.edu.au/gc/projects.htm)

Tricia also went to the webpages for several mailing lists, joined each list, and posted her project announcement. She went to the webpage for **RTEACHER** (http://www.reading.org/virtual/rteacherdirections.html), **the Discussions List** site (http://serv1.ncte.org/lists/) for English educators organized by the National Council of Teachers of English (NCTE) where she joined the **NCTE-middle** mailing list; and the homepage for the **CHILD_LIT** mailing list (http://www.rci.rutgers.edu/~mjoseph/childlit/about.html), a list for educators interested in children's literature. She posted a description of her project on each of these mailing lists, inviting other classrooms to join in her collaborative classroom project.

By the end of the week, Tricia had received messages from eight different schools from cities around the world: Darwin, Australia; Bristol, England; Haifa, Israel; Kyoto, Japan; Newberg, New York; Dublin, California; Rapid City, South Dakota; Beaumont, Texas; and Clearwater, Florida. Each had promised to collect traditional myths from cultures in or near their location and share these in two weeks via email with all of the collaborating classrooms. It was a simple project, but one Tricia felt certain would open new doors for her classroom.

Tricia had also heard from a high school English teacher in her district that was teaching a special course in storytelling. Tricia had mentioned their project to him. He wanted to know if his students could also participate, working with her students to research each story and its cultural traditions and helping her students develop storytelling performances for several of the stories. Tricia thought this would be a great way to introduce her class to this wonderful craft. It would also provide important support for the students in her class who experienced important challenges with reading and writing.

As Tricia announced the results of her work to the class the next day, everyone was full of new ideas. Each group, they decided, would work with schools from their part of the world: the Asia and Australia group would coordinate work with the schools in Darwin and Kyoto; the Americas group would work with schools in the United States; and the Europe, Middle East, and Africa group would work with schools in Bristol and Haifa.

Their unit would be celebrated at the end with a storytelling concert for the entire school with performances put on by her class and students from the high school.

Also, each group now had a new assignment, to uncover explanatory myths from cultures in their own community so that they could share these with their partner schools on this project. This would take some work interviewing parents and relatives to see what they could find. Then they would draft versions of these stories and work to revise them. Afterward, they would polish off the final version using an editing conference with peers in class before sending it to their partner schools. And throughout this process, they would work with the high school class to develop performances for some of the stories.

Their unit would be celebrated at the end with a storytelling concert for the entire school with performances put on by her class and students from the high school. Tricia's class was humming with excitement as each group set to work.

Lessons from the Classroom

There are several important lessons we can learn from this experience in Tricia Abernathy's class. First, this story illustrates how important it is to learn from one another about the Internet. Marcus showed Tricia new ideas for Internet use, ideas that Tricia discussed with a colleague. Tricia also visited several classroom homepages, discovering wonderful models for Internet use from other teachers. In addition, Tricia relied on colleagues from the RTEACHER, NCTE-middle, and CHILD_LIT mailing lists to help develop her project. And, the collaborative relationships her class formed with other classrooms, including the storytelling class from the high school, also led to many new learning experiences. Clearly, we all learn from one another as we discover the many possibilities the Internet provides.

This story also demonstrates how exciting new curriculum resources, tested in the reality of classrooms around the world, are being developed by teachers and children and posted on classroom webpages.

This story also demonstrates how exciting new curriculum resources, tested in the reality of classrooms around the world, are being developed by teachers and children and posted on classroom webpages. As Tricia discovered these resources she was amazed at how many teachers were creating these instructional resources that other classrooms were using.

In other work, we refer to this exciting potential as "The Miss Rumphius Effect," (http://www.readingonline.org/electronic/RT/rumphius.html) after the title character in *Miss Rumphius*, a book by Barbara Cooney. At a young age Miss Rumphius is told by her grandfather, "You must do something to make the world more beautiful." When she grows up, Miss Rumphius travels the world, accumulating many adventures. Eventually, however, she returns to her home by the sea and discovers a way to make the world a better place by planting lupines, beautiful wildflowers, wherever she goes. The story illustrates how a committed individual can envision a better world and then act on that envisionment, transforming all of our lives.

Just as Miss Rumphius made the world a better place by planting lupines wherever she went, teachers and children are enriching our instructional worlds by planting new visions for literacy and learning on the Internet, transforming the nature of this new technology. Other classrooms then use these instructional resources, making our students' worlds richer and more meaningful.

The story of Tricia's classroom also illustrates how Internet Project may be used to integrate the language arts and other subject areas into your classroom curriculum.

In fact, shortly after Tricia Abernathy's class completed their project and published it at the classroom homepage, they received the Miss Rumphius Award for their work. This award is presented by members of the **RTEACHER** mailing list (http://www.ira.org/publications/rt/rteacher directions.html), a mailing list of literacy educators run in conjunction with *The Reading Teacher*, a journal of the International Reading Association. The Miss Rumphius Award goes to teachers who have developed exceptional curricular resources on the Internet and share these with others, making all of our instructional worlds better. If you are interested in visiting curriculum resources developed by these teachers, visit the site for **The Miss Rumphius Award** (http://www.reading.org/awards/rumphius.html).

The story of Tricia's classroom also illustrates how Internet Project may be used to integrate cross-cultural perspectives into your classroom curriculum.

By creating this project and connecting with other classrooms, her students also discovered many new cultural experiences. These cross-cultural insights connected immediately with her activities in social studies and science. Internet Project provides exceptional possibilities for cross-curricular integration and multicultural understanding.

This story also illustrates another lesson: The Internet provides wonderfully authentic opportunities for supporting literacy learning by connecting reading, writing, speaking, and listening. The Internet provides natural opportunities for your students to communicate about their work. This has important benefits for your students.

This story illustrates how important it is to learn from one another about the Internet.

Reading, writing, speaking, and listening are similar processes. Supporting students in one area leads to gains in the others. In busy classrooms, we need to seek ways in which to combine subject areas that have traditionally been viewed as separate and that benefit from being combined. This is possible when we connect all four of the language modalities in learning experiences with the Internet.

After she announced the project, Tricia's class read, wrote, spoke, and listened as they had never done before. Students worked hard in the ensuing weeks to gather explanatory myths from the Vietnamese, Cambodian, African American, Italian, Iroquois, and Chinese cultures in their own community. They wanted very much to have good stories to share with these classes in distant places. Not only did students communicate more because of this experience, but they also communicated better because their interest was so high and members of their literature discussion group supported them. In addition, important new writing opportunities opened up as students collected stories from their community and carefully drafted, revised, and edited these before sending them to other schools. And, as students shared the stories they found, one often saw students helping other students read them together.

Her students were especially fortunate to connect with the high school storytelling class since this added nicely to the speaking and listening experiences in this project. Listening and speaking experiences evolved naturally out of this project, as students exchanged information and planned their presentations. The Internet can be an important tool for supporting the English-language arts by connecting reading, writing, speaking, and listening.

This story also illustrates another important lesson: Teachers consistently report to us that publishing their students' work on a classroom homepage provides many important benefits for classroom instruction. One of the greatest benefits is that students learn very quickly how important it is to revise and revise and revise their work until it is presentable to the world. When a student receives an email message pointing out a spelling mistake or other evidence of writing that was quickly completed, it has a galvanizing effect. Students want to be certain their work is the best they can make it before it gets published. As one teacher wrote to us,

> Never before have I seen my students so concerned about the revision process. This used to be completed in a mechanical fashion with little apparent concern. Now, my students have 4 or 5 others read their work looking for parts that could be written more clearly. Going public with their work helps everyone to see the importance of clear writing for clear communication.

Finally, this story also illustrates another lesson: While the Internet contains many original works of literature for students to read, it is especially useful to enrich the literary experiences of students as they read books away from the computer. Using the Internet almost always means your students will read more books, not fewer. Immediately after Tricia announced the project, each group read much more than they had read before. While some of these stories were gathered from the Internet, many more were discovered in the school library. Virginia Hamilton's *In the Beginning: Creation Stories from Around the World* was a favorite. As one student said, "We want to be ready when we start to get our stories from Japan and Australia." As students brought their stories back to each group, many discussions took place as they shared ideas about each culture. These experiences enriched the literary potential of the initial assignment by taking students beyond their set of books and into their local community, their library, and even the rest of the world through the Internet. Many opportunities to enrich children's literary experiences may be developed by integrating the Internet into classroom instruction.

Internet FAQ

Sometimes, I try to reach a location on the WWW and I get an error message indicating that the server is not accepting connections or that the server may be busy. What can I do?

This usually is caused by one of two conditions. First, the computer on which this site is located may be down for servicing. Second, too many people may be trying to get into the server at the same time, something that occasionally happens with popular educational sites during the school day. A strategy we use is to try to contact the same location three times before we give up on a busy server. Sometimes we can sneak in, even if many people are trying to reach this location at the same time. Move your cursor to the end of the address in the location bar, click, and then press your return key. Your browser will try again to connect to this location. If, after three tries, we still cannot get in, we usually give up and try again later.

Directories for Literature

Directories are well-organized collections of links to important resources in a particular area. There are a number of great directories for literature:

- **The Complete Works of Shakespeare**— http://the-tech.mit.edu/Shakespeare/
- **Carol Hurst's Children's Literature Site**— http://www.carolhurst.com/index.html
- **Imaginary Lands**—http://www.imaginarylands.org/
- **Literature Learning Ladders**— http://www.eduscapes.com/ladders/index.html
- **WebEnglish Teacher**— http://www.webenglishteacher.com/index.html
- **Cyberguides**—http://www.sdcoe.k12.ca.us/score/cyberguide.html
- **The Reading Zone of the Internet Public Library**— http://www.ipl.org/div/kidspace/browse/rzn0000/
- **ALA's Language and Literature**— http://www.ala.org/parentspage/greatsites/lit.html

If you have an interest in Shakespeare, students at MIT have developed a marvelous directory for your classroom needs, **The Complete Works of Shakespeare** (http://the-tech.mit.edu/Shakespeare/) (see Figure 5-2). This amazing resource contains all of the works of Shakespeare, an electronic glossary for locating the meanings of archaic terms, discussion groups in which your students can ask questions and share ideas, and much, much more. Be certain to pay a visit and explore this location. There are many opportunities for classroom activities to bring Shakespeare alive for your students.

Figure 5-2. The Complete Works of Shakespeare homepage (http://the-tech.mit.edu/Shakespeare/), a directory for Shakespeare study.

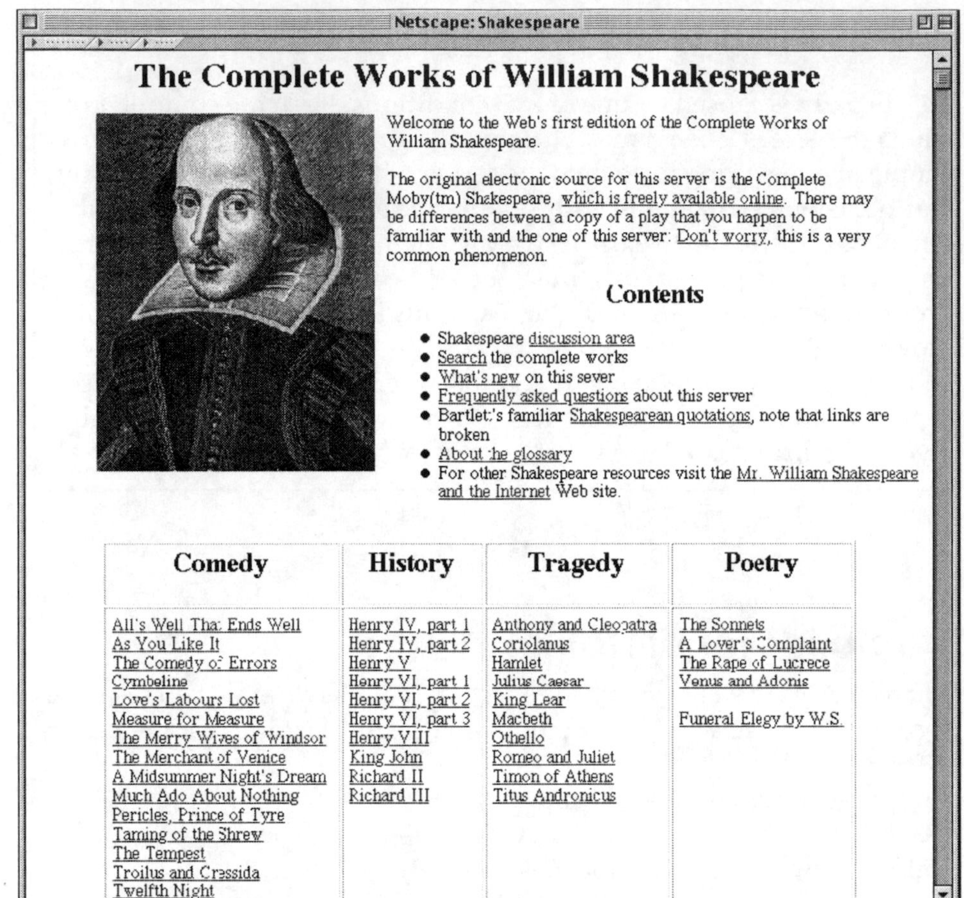

Carol Hurst's Children's Literature Site (http://www.carolhurst.com/index.html), is a treasure trove of book reviews, classroom lesson ideas, and technology-related extension ideas sorted by theme, curriculum area, or grade level. This site is updated often with a newsletter and is a great place to start searching for literature related to a certain classroom theme.

An impressive directory for young adult and children's literature is **Imaginary Lands** (http://www.imaginarylands.org/), a site maintained by Denise Matulka, a youth services librarian. The three parts of this amazing location remind us of the multiple and global nature of new literacies. The first section, "Passport: International Children's Literature," introduces the concept of international literature as compared to multicultural literature and reminds us of our need to learn to evaluate books from other countries. Literature resources are organized by continent, and within each you can peruse links to information about literary awards, book fairs, booksellers, grants, journals, online resources, literacy organizations, and book publishers.

The second section, "Children's Literature Navigator," directs you to literary resources from such perspectives as art, music, picture books, poetry, traditional literature, and TV/radio. From here, students can also learn more about how books are created, parents can link to reading resources that encourage family literacy, and everyone can learn more about puppetry, illustrators, favorite book characters, and much, much more.

Figure 5-3. Imaginary Lands homepage (http://www.imaginarylands.org/), a directory for children's literature.

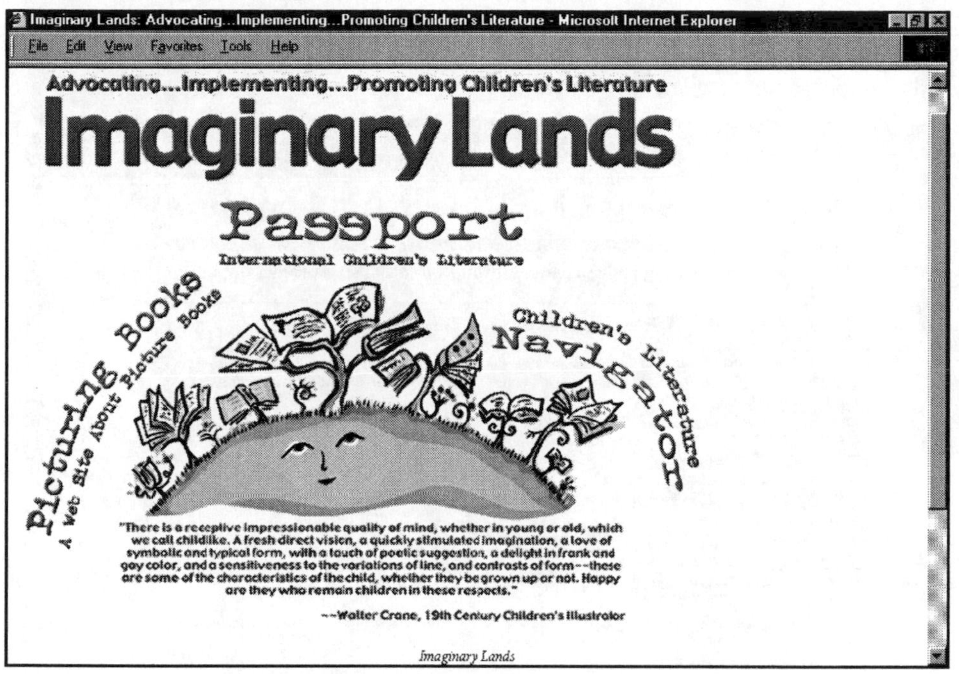

The third, and perhaps most unique section, entitled "Picturing Books," features several thematic guides to selecting and evaluating picture books, a comprehensive overview of the "anatomy of a picture book," and useful collections of information about artistic media and style used in picture books. Resources at this location are designed to enrich your students' literary experiences without taking them away from books. If you are serious about literature in your classroom, you should explore this site, set a bookmark, and incorporate its many resources into classroom learning projects.

Is your class reading specific works of literature and you need some quick ideas for Internet integration, perhaps even some ready-to-go Internet activities? Be certain to visit another popular site for K-12 literature: **Literature Learning Ladders** (http://www.eduscapes.com/ladders/index.html). This wonderful location, being developed by Annette Lamb and Larry Johnson, is a great location we have found for the immediate integration of exceptional books. Caldecott or Newbery Award winners, as well as other popular children's and young adult literature, are paired with discussion questions and most are also linked to current web resources that can extend, expand, or enhance particular topics or themes from the book. Literature selections at Literature Learning Ladders are nicely organized by title, author, and theme. The website also features resources for literature-related collaborative projects, thematic literature circles, ideas for web-based thematic units and the new Naturescapes web projects that provide multi-level, informational readings, resources, and activities related to nature. Set a bookmark today! And don't forget to drop an email message to Larry Johnson and Annette Lamb, telling them what wonderful work they are accomplishing for all of us.

Figure 5-4. The homepage of **Literature Learning Ladders** (http://www.eduscapes.com/ladders/index.html), which was developed by Annette Lamb and Larry Johnson to facilitate active reading through book-technology connections.

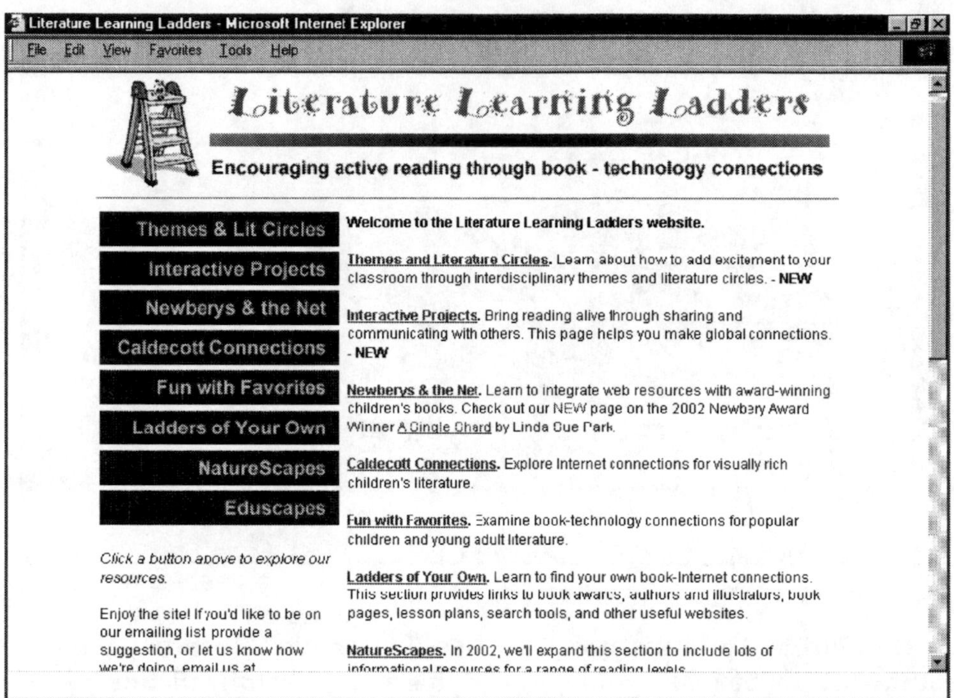

There are several types of online literature collections: older classics with expired copyrights, traditional tales, works of literature written by children, and original works published on the Internet.

In addition to these central directories, there are many directories containing online works of literature for your classroom. While we tend to prefer real books for most literary experiences, it is often useful to read works on the Internet, especially if they are related to books that you use in class. It is especially nice to know that any work you find online may be printed out so that students may read it in the class or take it home to share with their family and friends. There are several types of online literature collections: older classics with expired copyrights, traditional tales, works of literature written by children, and original works published on the Internet.

You will find many older classics with expired copyrights on the Internet. Because their copyright has expired, these works may now be published on the Internet without violating copyright law. Older classics often are used by teachers to provide additional literary experiences for students who have read one work by an author and are interested in reading others, especially when your library's holdings are a bit thin. The problem with these classics is that they usually appear in a text-only form without illustrations. This sometimes takes away from the literary experience. Some of the best locations for classic works of literature include:

- **Project Gutenberg**—http://promo.net/pg/
  This voluntary project publishes an average of one e-text every day and it currently has about 6,200 e-texts! Here you will find the complete texts of many classic works by authors such as Louisa May Alcott, Jane Austen, Aesop, O Henry, Victor Hugo, Charles Dickens, and many others. Set a bookmark!
- **International Children's Digital Library**—http://www.icdlbooks.org/
  This collaborative project from the University of Maryland and The Internet Archive is celebrating it's first anniversary of working toward building a digital library of 10,000 international children's books in at least 100 languages that is freely available via the Internet. You can currently read 324 books online using a Flash-based zoom function and you can search in multiple languages by category, author, title, or region in the world.
- **The Academy of American Poets**—http://www.poets.org/
  This searchable database includes more than 1,200 poems by over 450 American poets organized in a national poetry map. You can also access biographies, photos, and other information about each poet or hear their poems read aloud in the listening booth.

Traditional tales are another form of online literature. These include folktales, fairytales, myths, and legends. Because so many were published some time ago and their original copyrights are out of date, many are now in the public domain and available online. Usually these exist in text-only versions. Occasionally, you will find illustrated versions.

Because traditional tales come from an oral tradition, there are many different versions for most stories. The richness of the Internet allows us to share multiple versions of the same story with students. This leads to wonderful opportunities for critical analysis as students evaluate how the versions differ, consider the types of response each provokes in readers, or determine what characterizes a "typical" traditional tale.

The richness of the Internet allows us to share multiple versions of the same story with students. This leads to wonderful opportunities for critical analysis as students evaluate how the versions differ, consider the types of response each provokes in readers, or determine what characterizes a "typical" traditional tale.

Some of the best central sites for traditional tales include:

- **The Encyclopedia Mythica**—http://www.pantheon.org/
  This is an encyclopedia devoted to myths, folklore, and legends. An outstanding place to begin research in this area.
- **Tales of Wonder**—
  http://members.xoom.com/darsie/tales/index.html
  This is an extensive archive of folk and fairy tales from around the world—a must for any cross-cultural unit or for a unit on this genre. Set a bookmark!
- **American Folklore**—http://www.americanfolklore.net/
  This unique collection of American folktales, Native American myths and legends, tall tales, weather folklore, and ghost stories from each of the 50 United States makes a great addition to thematic study of multicultural folktales.
- **Aesop's Fables**—http://www.aesopfables.com/
  This website indexes over 655 of Aesop's fables, many with an accompanying audio component, in a well-organized table that includes a motto for each. This site also features a discussion board to read and respond to lesson plan ideas and original mottos for the

fables as well as links to a dictionary and a tool that plays soothing music while you read along to your favorite fable!

Other directories for literature contain children's voices, literature written by children. These sites are great to motivate the writers in your class and show them what is possible. Some of these locations include:

- **KidPub**—http://www.kidpub.org/kidpub
  A wonderful collection of more than 42,000 stories written by children and maintained by a father in Massachusetts who initially just wanted a place for his daughter to publish her work. Many great stories are located here and great writing activities, too.
- **Cyberkids**—http://www.cyberkids.com/
  This is a quarterly online magazine written by kids for kids ages 7–11. It includes articles and stories by young writers.
- **Global Storytrain**—http://storytrain.kids-space.org/
  This is an illustrated, collaborative writing project for creative children from all over the world. Children are invited to build one car, or chapter, of each three-part storytrain with their own writing and illustration and then watch it grow as others from more than 100 countries add to it. With over 2,200 stories already written, this site will surely inspire students to try their hand at creative writing.
- **Stone Soup—**http://www.stonesoup.com/main2/listen.html
  This webpage is a companion to the *Stone Soup* children's magazine, which is made up entirely of the creative work of children, ages 8–13. From here, children can listen and read along to recorded stories that were accepted for submission into the printed magazine.

Internet FAQ

Are there any sites where children can listen to stories?

New technologies for multimedia continue to appear on the Internet. Sound and video technologies are ones that are changing especially rapidly. There are several locations with stories that are read aloud for younger students. A few of these include:

- **Children's Stories**—http://www.childrenstory.com/
- **Steven Cosgrove's BookPop—**http://www.bookpop.com/
- **Alfy's Fairy Tales—**
  http://www.alfy.com/teachers/teach/thematic_units/Fairy_Tales/Fairy_1.asp

Reading a great story is one of the better experiences we can provide students. Often, though, our students' experience with a story is limited by knowing little about the author. Learning about an author helps students to better understand the work they are reading. This helps to contextualize the literary work and provides important information to students about why an author wrote a story, what experience in their life prompted the story, how they write, other books the author has written, and issues the author often writes about. Knowing this information enriches children's literary experiences. There are many sites on the Internet that will provide your students with this information.You may, of course, use one of the search engines to locate information about authors. Keep in mind, though, that most author locations (not all) have been developed with commercial interests in mind. Some of the best central directories for author locations include:

- **The Author Corner**—http://ccpl.carr.org/authco/index.htm
  This non-commercial site provides an extensive set of links to popular authors and illustrators, K-12. Hear their voices; access a list of their books, short biographies, and their mailing address too!
- **The BBC Web Guide**—
  http://www.bbc.co.uk/webguide/schools/index.shtml
  A great resource from the BBC in the United Kingdom. Go to this site and select "English." Then search for the name of a specific author or search using the more general term "authors."
- **Authors and Illustrators**—
  http://www.eduplace.com/kids/hmr/mtai/index.html
  Although this location features only those authors and illustrators in Houghton-Mifflin's Reading series, it contains information about a number of popular authors including David Adler, Avi, Paul Fleischman, Jean Fritz, and Gary Paulsen, and includes photos of the authors, a biography, and lists of other books by the author.

There are many sites on the Internet that will provide your students with information about popular authors.

- **Author Studies Homepage**—
  http://www2.scholastic.com/teachers/authorsandbooks/authorstudies/authorstudies.jhtml
  This site is another commercial resource, yet the offerings are too good to pass up! Over 200 authors are featured here, with biographies, photos, interview transcripts, and links to their website. From here, students are invited to share what they are reading or review student reviews of favorite books, attend real-time online author and illustrator interview sessions or visit several online writing workshops featuring tips from successful authors.

Some of these locations are quite impressive, containing extensive information about the author and his/her life. Some even have listservs or bulletin boards to discuss the author's works. Some contain curriculum materials for using the author's works in your classrooms. A few of our favorites include:

- **Charles Dickens**—http://www.helsinki.fi/kasv/nokol/dickens.html
  This location contains all of the works by this important author as well as extensive information about his life and about London during the time when he was writing. The perfect site for your study of this author.
- **Into the Wardrobe: The C.S. Lewis WWW Site**—
  http://cslewis.drzeus.net/
  This is the one of the best author sites around. Many rich resources including a biography, an album of photographs, recordings of the author's voice, many links to other Lewis sites, a listserv address, a usenet address, and even a live chat location.

- **The L.M. Montgomery Institute**—http://www.upei.ca/~lmmi/
  The official institute's site for Lucy Maud Montgomery, the author of *Anne of Green Gables* and other works. The location includes information about her life, additional links to related sites, information for subscribing to a listserv about her books, and sites on Prince Edward Island, her home.
- **Knowing Edgar Allan Poe**—
  http://knowingpoe.thinkport.org/default_flash.asp
  This website was created and developed by Maryland Public Television to introduce learners to Poe's work from many perspectives and to guide students as they explore his writing and the facts of his life. Be sure to visit the Classroom Connections portion for critical reading lesson ideas, an online video of "The Raven," and much more!
- **Magic Treehouse Homepage**—
  http://www.randomhouse.com/kids/magictreehouse/
  If your younger students enjoy Mary Pope Osbourne's popular *Magic Treehouse* series, this is the place for you! This site features book summaries, links to related websites for further study, online writing opportunities for students, teacher's guides, and a chance to email the author questions to answer online.
- **Charles' George Orwell Links**—
  http://pages.citenet.net/users/charles/links.html
  This site celebrates the life and writings of George Orwell, with extensive links to biographical information, reviews of his work, and many resources to extend the reading of *Animal Farm* or *Nineteen Eighty-Four*.

E-MAIL FOR YOU

From: "Karen Auffhammer" <kauffhammer@msn.com>
Subject: Maniac Magee

Hello!

I have recently read the story "Maniac Magee" by Jerry Spinelli and it is by far one of my favorites. I was so excited to see a site on the WWW on this story. Here's the URL: (http://www.carolhurst.com/titles/maniacmagee.html).

Check it out!! It provides a brief summary of the story, character descriptions, things to discuss with your class, activities and related books. From here you can click to see other popular books that have been reviewed.

Karen Auffhammer
Curriculum Consultant
Central Square Intermediate School
Central Square, NY

Central Directories for Writing

The Internet also opens new doors to authentic writing experiences as students communicate with other writers from around the world. Students may correspond with experts about their writing, publish their work and invite comments from others, read responses to their writing, and write messages back to others. These opportunities make the Internet a wonderful resource to support student writing at all levels. There are two types of central directories in writing: those that provide a wide range of support for student writers and those that provide opportunities for students to publish their work.

The Internet provides wonderfully authentic opportunities for supporting literacy learning by connecting reading and writing.

Locations On The Internet That Support Young Writers

There are a number of central sites on the Internet for young writers. These locations are often important sources of support for students who are serious about their writing. Explore these locations, set a bookmark, and invite your students to take advantage of the many resources at each location.

- **Writer's Window**—
  http://writing2.richmond.edu/writing/wweb.html
  This site features a Writer's Workshop that guides students through writing stories, poems, reviews, and essays with various exercises and writing tips. Students can also peruse the showcase of writing from young writers ages 5–18 to inspire their own creativity, join or read an archive of unique continuous stories, or exchange questions and writing interests on the discussion board. Be sure to link back to the English Online homepage to access the fully resourced writing units at each grade level.
- **Writer's Web**—http://writing2.richmond.edu/writing/wweb.html
  This is an excellent handbook designed by students and faculty from the University of Richmond. It explores topics by the stages of the writing process. Guides, tips, and strategies are offered for older students for getting started, writing first drafts, focusing and connecting ideas, analysis and argument, editing, using sources effectively, and writing online. A great resource for high school students!
- **Poetry Express**—http://www.poetryexpress.org/
  If your students need some support for creative writing, this site walks them through the poetry writing process and provides 15 different types of poems to get them started.
- **Biography Maker**—
  http://www.bham.wednet.edu/bio/biomaker.htm
  This series of writing guides students through the stages of questioning, learning, synthesis, and story telling as part of the process of writing an engaging biography.
- **High School Journalism**—http://www.highschooljournalism.org/
  This is the best compilation of resources we have found in this area, created to support and inspire teen journalists and their teachers.

Figure 5-5. The homepage of New Zealand's **Writers' Window** (http://english.unitecnology.ac.nz/writers/home.html) leads to a variety of opportunities for students to read, share, and respond to creative writing with others around the world.

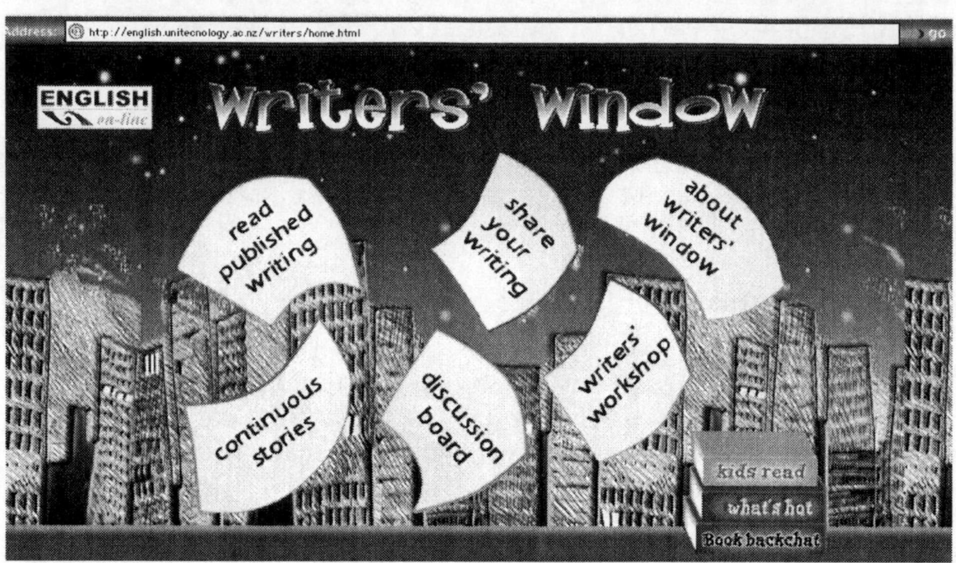

The Internet provides new and exciting opportunities to publish your students' work. You may also publish student work at many locations on the Internet devoted especially to this purpose.

Publishing Student Work on the Internet

The Internet provides new and exciting opportunities to publish your students' work. You may publish student work on a classroom weblog or homepage (see chapter 12). You may also publish student work at many locations on the Internet dedicated especially to this purpose. You can take advantage of these locations to engage students in comprehensive writing process activities, which include prewriting, drafting, revision, editing, and publishing. When a student's work is prepared, think about submitting it to one of these locations:

- **International Kids' Space**—http://www.kids-space.org
  A great location for children to share their works of art, short stories, and music with others.
- **Storyteller from EdByDesign**—
  http://www.edbydesign.com/storyteller/index.html
  Students can add to the compilation of more than 32,000 stories and have their writing rated by an experienced team of editors.
- **Kids Newsroom**—http://www.kidsnewsroom.com/
  Kids news and stories written and posted by kids. A weekly news magazine featuring news, games, information, and submitted articles from kids and schools from around the United States.
- **Telling Stories with Wildlife Art—**
  http://www.wildlifeart.org/ArtTales/index.html
  This site represents a unique twist on publishing with opportunities to frame stories around online wildlife art through the eyes of a frontier explorer, field guide writer, or museum curator.

- **Midlink Magazine**—http://longwood.cs.ucf.edu/~MidLink/
  This site is home to the award-winning student's digital magazine for students ages 8–18. It invites submissions based on classroom projects that reflect the creative learning process.
- **Kids on the Net**—http://kotn.ntu.ac.uk/index.htm
  Submit creative writing pieces, access writing tips from successful authors, and explore an interesting guide and models to writing in new online media formats.

There are many bookstores on the Internet now such as **Amazon.com** (http://amazon.com/) and **Barnes and Noble** (http://www.barnesandnoble.com/). These locations provide opportunities to publish a review of any book your students have read and quickly see it posted. As students complete independent reading projects, invite them to write a review. Have them read the initial draft of their review during Internet Workshop and seek suggestions for revision. After the review has been revised, help students to use the search engine at a bookstore to locate their book. Then, have them post their review at this location. For an example, visit **PS 116 Student Book Reviews** (http://www.ps116pta.org/kids/spotlight_pages/book_reviews/book_reviews.html).

Grammar on the Internet

Grammar on the Internet, you ask? Yes, indeed. There are many interactive and creative resources for grammar experiences on the Internet. If you take just a few minutes, you can discover the informative and engaging manner in which some locations present this information. Though the content is the same, grammar sites on the Internet present this information in a manner that is certainly different from the way we learned.

There are many interactive and creative resources for grammar experiences on the Internet. If you take just a few minutes, you can discover the informative and engaging manner in which some locations present this information.

- **Guide to Grammar and Writing**—
  http://webster.commnet.edu/grammar/index.htm
  This excellent central directory has been developed by Professor Charles Darling at Capital Community College in Connecticut. It features interactive quizzes, information on the principles of composition, grammar logs about English grammar and usage, and much, much more! Be sure to set a bookmark here!
- **Hacker Handbook Resources**—
  http://www.bedfordstmartins.com/hacker/exercises/
  Flash-animated interactive lessons engage students in constructing grammatically correct sentences. Also includes a companion site with student and instructor resources for composition.
- **Traditional Grammar: An Interactive Book**—
  http://www.engl.niu.edu/dhardy/grammarbook/title.html
  This provides your students with a step-by-step guide through 12 text-based modules, each followed by a series of interactive quizzes.

- **Wacky Web Tales**—http://www.eduplace.com/tales/
  Younger students will love applying their understanding of grammar and parts of speech at this interactive online equivalent to Mad-Libs. Geared for Grades 3 and above, students can choose from many original tales or create their own for their online peers to complete.

Keeping It Simple: Using the Internet Workshop

There are as many good ideas for enriching literary experiences with the Internet as there are creative teachers with a few moments to plan a new Internet Workshop experience. We can not be exhaustive here. We can, however, provide some examples that might serve to inspire you to think of your own creative ideas for developing Internet activities that integrate new and foundational literacies.

There are as many good ideas for enriching literary experiences with the Internet as there are creative teachers with a few moments to plan a new Internet Workshop experience.

- **Linking Fiction and Non-Fiction**: Refer to the compilations of quality literature-based websites to help build lessons that foster text-to-world connections between the characters and settings in popular children's literature and real people and issues of today. After reading the beginning level chapter book *Twister on Tuesday*, for example, younger readers can explore the links already gathered for this book and many others at **The Magic Treehouse** (http://www.randomhouse.com/kids/magictreehouse/books/). From here, in small groups or with a partner, students can witness the real devastation caused by recent tornadoes, learn how experts tame a tornado, and find directions for creating their own tornado in a soda bottle. You can also use Internet Workshop to invite older readers to make these text-to-world connections. If you set a bookmark to **Annette Lamb's Newberys on the Net** (http://eduscapes.com/newbery/new.html), students can explore the "Classroom Connections" section of informational links paired with award-winning titles such as *Holes, Island of the Blue Dolphins*, or *The Watson's Go To Birmingham*. After, have students share the connections they made between fiction and non-fiction during Internet Workshop discussions. This type of workshop can be repeated throughout the year with a discussion of new titles and new understandings of the connections between literature and real life.
- **Lord of the Flies**—After reading William Golding's *Lord of the Flies* about a group of young boys who are isolated on a desert island, visit **Personality and The Lord of the Flies** (http://www.ops.org/lang-art/lord-of-the-flies.html), an excellent example of how to integrate character analysis, critical thinking, written response, and just one website into your Internet Workshop. In this lesson, students review personality types of famous people as described at **Kiersey's Four Temperaments** (http://keirsey.com/matrix.html) and then associate characters from *Lord of the Flies* with the personality types listed. For their written response, students compare and contrast two of the characters in the novel from the perspective of each individual's temperament.
- **Julius Caesar Unit**—Take advantage of the activities developed at **Cyberguides** (http://www.lausd.k12.ca.us/lausd/resources/shakespeare/caesarwebguide.html) to add to your unit on Shakespeare's *Julius Caesar*. This site contains resources and directions to help students com-

plete four compositions about this classic work: an opinion/comparison-contrast essay, an expository essay, a statement of opinion, and an argumentative essay. Use Internet Workshop to share works in progress as well as completed works. This will prompt conversations about the play and about students' different interpretations of character, plot, and theme.

- **Fairy Tale Character Studies**—Engage your class in a study of Cinderella tales from around the world. Nearly every culture has its own version of this classic tale. Compare and contrast different versions to infer what these differences might suggest about the culture associated with each story. Begin with beautifully illustrated versions from your library such as *Mufaro's Beautiful Daughters* by John Steptoe. Then have students explore the Internet for other versions. They may wish to start with **Ten Cinderella Stories from Around the World** (http://www.geocities.com/Athens/Academy/6064/cinderella.html) or D.L. Ashliman's collection of **Cinderella Stories** (http://www.pitt.edu/~dash/type0510a.html). Then have students begin exploring the Internet using various search engines for even more versions. For a collection of other fairy tales with many versions to explore, set a bookmark to **The SurLaLune Fairy Tales Site** (http://www.surlalunefairytales.com/).
- **Studying Indigenous Peoples' Literature**—If you engage students in a project studying Native Americans or other indigenous peoples, be certain to set a bookmark for **Indigenous Peoples Literature** (http://www.indigenouspeople.net/), an outstanding site developed by Glenn Welker, or the **Native American Lore Index Page** (http://lehua.ilhawaii.net/~stony/loreindx.html), which indexes over 150 Native American stories. Have students explore these sites to find out information about the culture behind each of the books they read. Have them share the information they find during Internet Workshop.
- **Jan Brett's Stories**—If you and your class are reading one of many excellent stories by Jan Brett, invite students to visit the **Jan Brett Home Page** (http://www.janbrett.com/), and then share what they have discovered during Internet workshop. A similar activity could be done with any author page. This is especially useful to build background knowledge about the author and his/her works.

Many teachers organize learning experiences around collaborative, Internet projects with other classrooms around the world. Project-based learning experiences are especially useful to integrate the language arts; students naturally engage in reading, writing, speaking, listening, and viewing experiences during the course of a project.

Using Internet Project

Traditionally, classrooms organize learning around separate subject areas. Recently, many teachers have explored an alternative, taking a thematic approach to organize learning. Some teachers are now beginning to take a third approach as they seek to capitalize on the learning opportunities available on the Internet. These teachers organize learning experiences around collaborative Internet projects with other classrooms around the world. Using Internet Project can be a very powerful way to develop learning experiences for your students. Project-based learning experiences are especially useful to integrate the language arts; students naturally engage in reading, writing, speaking, listening, and viewing experiences during the course of a project. One sees in these classrooms a rich interplay between content learning and English/language arts activities, often combining Internet experiences with more familiar method frameworks including: cooperative group learning, response journals, readers' theater, process writing, inquiry projects, and other highly effective techniques.

E-MAIL FOR YOU

From: Susan Silverman
Subject: The Ultimate Online Collaboration

What started out as a simple collaboration between two fourth grade classes from New York, ended up as a project that included a high school class, a fourth grade class from Missouri, a media specialist, an Orphan Train rider from the early 1900s, and the daughter of an Orphan Train rider.

Students read the historical novels *Orphan Train Rider* and *A Midnight Train Home.* For each book they created a multimedia slide show with Kid Pix software. Their work was showcased on a website along with student created interactive quizzes, graphic organizers, poetry, and reflections. As we all know, a good unit of study includes an assessment piece. To our delight the authors of both novels evaluated the slide shows and emailed their comments to the students. Here's a perfect example of writing for an authentic audience!

You may wonder how a simple project turned into a learning experience that has touched the hearts of children and adults throughout the nation. I was trying to get permission to use an Orphan Train image for our project. The person I contacted was working with a group of fourth graders from Missouri on the same topic. Before long, a very enthusiastic fourth grade class joined our project.

Our Missouri partners were able to contact Shirley Andrews, the daughter of Irma Craig, an Orphan Train rider. We emailed the Orphan Train Society and they were able to help us find Orphan Train rider Bill Oser. Eighty-year-old Mr. Oser drove his sports car forty miles to tell his story to us and the Missouri class by a video-conference in our school media center.

Some of the comments on our guest book are from children whose parents were Orphan Train riders. Their feedback is a testimonial to our project. The ingredients in our success are quite simple: All you need is great literature, technology, and collaboration!

The Orphan Train (http://comsewogue.k12.ny.us/~orphantrain/)

Sincerely,
Susan Silverman
Instructional Technology Reading Specialist
Comsewague School District
Port Jefferson Station, New York
Come view my website at http://www.kids-learn.org

Examples of Internet projects that emphasize the language arts include:

- **Flat Stanley: A Travel Buddy Project**—http://eduscapes.com/flat/
  There are many variations of this project, but in its most basic form, students begin by reading the story *Flat Stanley* by Jeff Brown. They learn that Stanley is squashed flat by a falling bulletin board and then he visits his friends by traveling in an envelope. Students get involved by making paper Flat Stanleys, pack him up with a beginning journal and send him to primary grade classrooms around the

world. When Flat Stanley arrives, he has to keep a journal describing his adventures, the cultures he visits, the sites he sees, and the people he meets. Other activities such as calculating mileage and locating Stanley on the map are also used to integrate social studies, science, math, and language arts. To see different examples of this Flat Stanley project, visit **Doing A Travel Buddy Project** at http://eduscapes.com/tap/topic1h.htm or **Flat Stanley Visits Asia** (http://eduscapes.com/flat/). For specific ideas about other projects like this, visit **Travel Buddies from Oz-TeacherNet** (http://rite.ed.qut.edu.au/oz-teachernet/projects/travel-buddies/).

- **SchoolWorld Endangered Species Project**—
http://www.schoolworld.asn.au/species/species.html
In this ongoing project, students from around the world research and report on an endangered or threatened mammal, reptile, insect, or plant and then submit their work to this online database for others to read. Unique collections such as this illustrate the power of students collaboratively constructing age-appropriate knowledge bases of information that can then serve as references for others. Science, geography, and language arts are integrated within this learning unit.
- **Middle School Student Created Document Based Questions**—
http://comsewogue.k12.ny.us/~ssilverman/documents/index.htm
The purpose of this collaborative project designed by Susan Silverman and Melissa McMullen from Port Jefferson Station, New York, is for students to evaluate primary and secondary documents as intelligent consumers. Students locate one or two primary documents that relate to change, progress, or power issues in their curriculum and then create two questions for each document. Documents and questions are posted on the website and other students are invited to submit their answers for publication. You could design a similar project based on other concepts such as persuasion or propaganda. A similar project for students in Grades 2–4 can be found at **Primary Student Created Document Based Questions** homepage (http://comsewogue.k12.ny.us/~ssilverman/dbq2003/index.htm). These projects integrate critical thinking, visual literacy, social studies, and language arts.
- **Monster Exchange Project**—http://www.monsterexchange.org/
This very successful Internet Project is entering it's eighth year and still going strong! Classrooms are paired with other classrooms from around the world. Each student designs an original monster, draws a picture, and writes a description. The classes then exchange descriptions via email and students are challenged to draw their partner's monster from the written description. This project integrates reading comprehension, writing and revising skills, creativity, and teamwork.
- **Newsday Project**—
http://gsh.lightspan.com/project/newsday/index.html
Eager to find authentic expository writing opportunities for your students? Why not have students publish newsworthy articles about

The special advantage of Internet Project is its potential to create very powerful learning opportunities, especially in English and language arts. Communicating with students in other locations motivates your students in ways you probably have not seen in your classroom and opens the door to important cross-cultural understandings.

current local, national, and global issues. In this project, one of many sponsored by Global Schoolhouse, students learn the ins and outs of newspaper production by collaboratively designing the paper's appearance, writing articles, assembling them into a finished project, and uploading them to the Internet. Writing workshop is used to teach lessons about summarizing, sequencing, and targeting a particular audience. This project integrates current events, language arts, and careers in the humanities.

The special advantage of Internet Project is its potential to create very powerful learning opportunities, especially in English and language arts. Communicating with students in other locations motivates your students in ways you probably have not seen in your classroom and opens the door to important cross-cultural understandings.

Done correctly, Internet Project can be the cornerstone of your English/ language arts program.

How do you get started? You may wish to visit several locations where teachers register collaborative projects for other teachers to find. Reading about other projects will give you ideas for your own Internet project. These sites were listed in Chapter 3.

Initially, you may wish to join someone else's project. After several experiences, though, you could develop your own project, post it, and see if you can get other classrooms to join you.

If you are interested in using Internet Project in your classroom but anxious about how to get started, simply join one of the online communities listed at the end of this chapter devoted to English and the language arts. Then, post a message asking others to share their experiences with this approach. Ask for suggestions that would be helpful to a person who is first attempting Internet Project. You will receive many great ideas from your colleagues. Others, too, will benefit from the suggestions colleagues share on the mailing list in response to your question.

Using WebQuest

Webquests can be found on the Internet for just about any curriculum topic imaginable. When searching for webquests in the area of language arts and literature, many focus on particular genres or pieces of literature, but you'll also find that many content area webquests in social studies and science integrate critical reading, writing, and response into their online tasks as well. Below we describe a range of webquests that can enhance your language arts curriculum.

- **Solving Mysteries: Canine Sleuth Training—**
  http://edservices.aea7.k12.ia.us/edtech/teacherpages/cruff/crime.html
  This web-based activity would be a great introduction to a genre study on Mysteries! Students build background knowledge about

what it takes to be a good detective as they seek to gather information about a crime, the surrounding scene, shreds of evidence, and potential suspects in order to solve the Mystery challenge. The mystery itself is actually one of a series of 30 mysteries archived at **MysteryNet's QuickSolve Mysteries** (http://kids.mysterynet.com/quicksolve/). After solving this mystery and graduating from the Sleuth Training Academy, students are prepared to read and solve other forms of "chillers," "magic tricks," and "solve-its" available from this website before trying their hand at writing their own mystery to enter into the growing compilation of "Mysteries by Kids."

- **The Samurai's Tale—**
  (http://edtech.suhsd.k12.ca.us/inprogress/act/dfickett/japan/samuraistale.htm).
  This middle school webquest was developed by California teacher Dan Fickett to enhance his students' reading of Eric Haguard's novel *The Samurai's Tale*. Assuming the role of investigative reporter, part archeologist, part detective, and part psychologist, students report historical, cultural, and thematic discoveries and interpret their meanings with respect to characters and events in the novel. They apply reading strategies that focus attention to important details while also learning more about inferencing and characterization. All of the strategies that we describe as new literacies are integrated in this student quest to draw connections between themselves and the past sons of samurai.
- **EGallery of Tragic Heroes in Literature and Life—**
  http://www.teachtheteachers.org/projects/JZarro2/index.htm
  In this webquest, high school students are challenged to immerse themselves in an authentic task to design a website for an I-Zine to teach others about the archetypical pattern of the tragic hero during their unit study on Greek mythology. There is a separate Teacher's Resource page and a comprehensive rubric evaluation that make this webquest an exceptional one for use in high school English classes.

Inquiry approaches require students to engage in self-directed reading and writing projects as they explore issues of personal interest. The intensive reading and writing experiences required in inquiry projects provides students with authentic literacy experiences in which they learn much about critical thinking, comprehension, and composition.

Using Internet Inquiry

Inquiry approaches to the Internet are also valuable to support learning in language arts and literature. Inquiry approaches require students to engage in self-directed reading and writing projects as they explore issues of personal interest. The personal nature of these inquiry projects motivates students in exciting ways, helping them to accomplish tasks they might have thought impossible to accomplish. The intensive reading and writing experiences required in inquiry projects provides students with authentic literacy experiences in which they learn much about critical thinking, comprehension, and composition.

Often teachers combine Internet Workshop with Internet Inquiry to provide special opportunities to learn from one another. Combining these methods will help you capitalize on these special opportunities. Here are several ideas and examples for using Internet Inquiry with Internet Workshop as you engage students in Language Arts and Literature:

- **Why Does the Caged Bird Sing?**—
  http://edweb.sdsu.edu/wip/examples/cagedbird/index.htm
  This literature inquiry project is an example of an open-ended inquiry project that follows a "spiral path of inquiry" designed at San Diego State University. The stages of asking questions, defining procedures, gathering and investigating data, analyzing and manipulating data, reporting findings, and reflection mirrors the central functions of new literacies we describe in this book. In this project inspired by Maya Angelou's poem "I Know Why the Caged Bird Sings," students are encouraged to ask their own questions and are given strategies for searching and locating various types of information on the Internet instead of being directed to specific tasks and related links. Project ideas and assessment examples are described, but again, the focus of each inquiry remains in the hands of the learner. When their projects are complete, encourage students to share the challenges they encounter and the final results during Internet Workshop.
- **Living Museum of Literary Authors**—
  Invite students to complete Internet Inquiry on the author of a work they are reading. Have them conduct research using some of the author resources described earlier in this chapter to discover everything they can about their author. Then, invite them to dress up as the author and prepare a display, sharing information they discovered about this person. Have students pose in their costumes as other classes visit your living classroom museum of literary authors reading the displays and viewing the authors. Your students may enjoy a visit to the **American Writers: Journey Through History** (http://www.americanwriters.org/index_short_list.asp) before they begin this project to gather ideas about how author information can be organized for visual presentation.
- **Going Beyond the Letters: Creating New ABC Books**—
  If you have younger students who are not quite ready for high levels of open-ended inquiry, you can still engage them in an exciting project that integrates each step of the inquiry process as they explore a common theme to create an original ABC book. Rich, informational websites designed for developing readers of all ages such as **Enchanted Learning's Zoom Units** in geography, animal science, space, and geology (http://www.enchantedlearning.com/school/) or **Ben's Guide to Government for US Kids** (http://bensguide.gpo.gov/) can be an incredible inspiration for thematic ABC books on so many different topics. Students can be assigned a certain theme to explore within one of these websites or use a children's search engine such as **Yahooligans** (www.yahooligans.com) or **KidsClick** (www.kidsclick.org) to seek examples beginning with each letter of the alphabet. With a small bit of scaffolding, each student or pairs of students can locate the information they need, synthesize their findings into a summary paragraph about that particular topic, and

share his or her individual contribution to the alphabet book in Internet Workshop. This project integrates reading, writing, and navigational skills into the content-area. Many classes extend their project to create an ABC book published on the Internet. Some web-based examples of student-created ABC books include:

- **Rainforest ABC Book—**
  http://www.ed.uri.edu/SMART96/ELEMSC/CyberForest/rainfr.html
- **Beanie Baby ABC's in 4th Grade—**
  http://www.towson.edu/csme/mctp/StudentProjects/BeanieBabyABC/TitlePage.html
- **Surfing for ABC's—**
  http://www.siec.k12.in.us/~west/proj/abc/index.html
- **Children's ABC View of Earthquakes Facts and Feelings—**
  http://pasadena.wr.usgs.gov/ABC/index.html

Do you use literature discussion groups in your class? Here is a way to do the same thing on the Internet between classes reading the same work of literature (K–12). Visit some of the sites below to learn how children from around the world engage in literature discussion groups about common works of literature they have read, exchanging insights about the world from a variety of cultural perspectives. You can adapt literature discussion groups to the Internet by posting the works of literature your students will be reading to see if other classes would be interested in reading the same work(s) and exchanging responses. For more information about participating in book discussions in traditional sessions as well as in new online environments, you may wish to explore the following sites:

- **Nancy Keane's Booktalks: Quick and Simple—**
  http://nancykeane.com/booktalks/
- **Book BackChat—**
  http://english.unitecnology.ac.nz/writers/home.html
- **BookChat—**http://www.cgps.vic.edu.au/bookchat/home.htm
- **BookRaps—**
  http://rite.ed.qut.edu.au/oz-teachernet/projects/book-rap/index1.html
- **Reading Scene from Eduplace—**
  http://www.eduplace.com/readingscene/

Comparing responses to literature on the Internet will provide many opportunities for integrating the language arts while opening windows into the diverse opinions and perspectives of students around the world.

Visiting the Classroom: Germantown Academy's Fifth Grade Classes in Pennsylvania

The four fifth-grade teachers and their students at Germantown Academy in Fort Washington, Pennsylvania, explore the world of the Internet and then share their work with the rest of us through the results of their wonderful interdisciplinary classroom projects. Their thematic activities, called "Interdisciplinary Journeys with Technology," incorporate reading, writing, math, researching, geography, history, mapping, graphing, science, sociology, art, and music. (Read more in Susan Hunsinger-Hoff's "Email for You".)

The four fifth-grade teachers and their students at Germantown Academy in Fort Washington, Pennsylvania explore the world of the Internet and then share their work with the rest of us through the results of their wonderful interdisciplinary classroom projects.

Take a few minutes to explore their **Fifth Grade Homepage** (http://www.ga.k12.pa.us/academics/ls/5th/homepg5.htm). It highlights student writing projects including dragon poetry, Native American myths, scary stories, student-designed webpages, creative writing samples of an Endangered Earth unit, and much, much more. Their **Fifth Grade's Back to School Page** (http://www.ga.k12.pa.us/academics/ls/5th/BTS97/btsindex.htm) introduces students to the year ahead, reminding them of summer reading tasks and pointing them to pertinent Internet resources for future homework assignments.

Be sure to pay a visit to their ever-growing collection of book reviews for kids written by fifth graders and compiled at **GA Super Readers** (http://www.ga.k12.pa.us/academics/ls/superreader/index.htm) (see Figure 5-6). This collection serves as an inspiration to other teachers searching for authentic activities that integrate reading, writing, appreciation of literature, and electronic publishing. It also serves as a model of how students are successfully infusing new literacies with more traditional forms of literacy and communication.

Finally, a link back to Germantown Academy's school-wide **Curricular Technology Plan Implementation** site (http://www.germantownacademy.org/curtech/techplan/implemen.htm) provides an excellent example of how teachers are designing instruction that addresses curriculum standards and school-wide technology competencies while engaging students as active and purposeful learners. Clearly, their vision to "contribute to critical thinking, problem-solving, collaboration, and to the creative process, essential skills for today's education and tomorrow's global job market" inspires us all as we move into the future.

E-MAIL FOR YOU

From: Susan Hunsinger-Hoff (shunsin@germantownacademy.org)
Subject: Successfully Integrating Technology Into An Interdisciplinary Curriculum

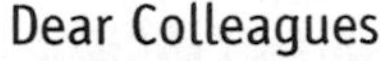

Dear Colleagues,

The key to the success of our fifth grade program at Germantown Academy has been our determination to integrate technology into an already existing, strong interdisciplinary curriculum. We have discovered technology's potential to help teachers address the multiple intelligences and diverse learning styles of our students. We have also avoided the pitfalls of attempting to squeeze technology into a full curriculum as an add-on, or separate "subject." Finally, we have sought ways that the new technologies would reinforce, enhance, and enrich the teaching/learning process. Strategically placing computers, projection systems, scanners, printers, digital cameras, CD burners, etc. in the fifth grade classrooms, easily accessible during every lesson every day, has made all the difference in the world. Technology has become an integral part of most classes throughout the day, from brainstorming, word-processing, editing, and publishing in the writing process; to pre-reading activities, virtual experiences, and sharing literature in the reading process; to collecting facts, note-taking, organization and analysis of data, and presentation of multimedia research reports in our thematic interdisciplinary units. We teach students skills to utilize the powerful tool technology has provided.

We begin with a general introduction to the computer, where students are taught navigating the desktop efficiently, finding and saving documents, file sharing and accessing their server accounts to keep their work organized, and opening and closing various applications. Then, we guide them through keyboarding, word processing, problem solving games and simulations, multimedia presentations, and research applications and strategies for exploring the World Wide Web.

We found that in order to integrate Internet research effectively and to enable our students to understand what they were reading on various sites, our activities had to be as carefully planned as any other directed reading lesson. Lessons on netiquette are introduced early in the year. Curriculum related video-conferencing sessions (such as our yearly visit and chat with the curator of The Museum of Radio and TV, part of our interdisciplinary study of the 20th Century, in which we discover the impact that media had on the Civil Rights Movement) complement students' other interdisciplinary studies throughout the year, as do our collaborative projects that connect students with their peers and with the world beyond the classroom.

Our **Fifth Grade Webpage** (http://www.germantownacademy.org/academics/ls/5th/homepg5.htm) was initially designed as a means to publish student work. As it developed over the past eight years, it has become a treasure chest of fabulous creative and expository writing, multimedia research projects, photography, artwork, and more! In addition, our webpage has become a means to communicate with people around the world, to connect our children with other youngsters in faraway places, and to share our lesson plans and ideas with a wider community of educators, including home schoolers. Onramps such as the one created for our interdisciplinary study of **"Endangered Earth,"** (http://www.germantownacademy.org/academics/ls/5th/Earth/eeonlineonramp.htm), have provided students and teachers with current web resources for use at home and school, helping the children stay on track with their studies. Programs like **"Super Readers"** (http://www.ga.k12.pa.us/academics/ls/superreader/index.htm) (see Figure 5-6) enable students to use email to submit their reviews for editing and to publish their book reports for others to enjoy and use for selecting books they might like to read. This invaluable resource, extending to a community of learners far beyond our campus, is the result of collaborative efforts from our reading specialist Betty Grant, our librarian Bridget Flynn, our web

cont.

director Andrea Owens, fifth grade teachers Phy Chauveau, Charlotte Dean, Ellen McMichael, and myself.

I also designed a course for fifth graders entitled "Acquiring a Sense of Metaphor" using "Blackboard." (http://www.blackboard.com/). Now our students are involved in online distance learning that enables them to participate in class lessons related to the novel, *The Lilith Summer*, even when they are not in class because of illness or weather-related cancellations. Students are able to submit assignments, download handouts distributed in class, and preview questions for future discussions as they read their novel at home.

We develop electronic portfolios with, and for, the students as the year progresses. Samples of text, graphics, multimedia presentations, and web design may be included, with emphasis on reflection, self evaluation, and the decision-making process as to which artifacts best reflect the individual's intelligences, styles of learning, and achievements.

In summary, the ability to access data from the Internet and to communicate with others through the World Wide Web has revolutionized our fifth grade program. We wish you the best of luck with your own classroom Internet endeavors.

Susan Hunsinger-Hoff
Fifth Grade Teacher and Divisional Technology Coordinator
Lower School, Germantown Academy, Ft. Washington, PA

Figure 5-6. The **Title Index** page at **GA Super Readers** (http://www.ga.k12.pa.us/academics/ ls/superreader/title/index.htm), a website containing book reviews for kids written by Fifth Grade Students at **Germantown Academy in Fort Washington, Pennsylvania**.

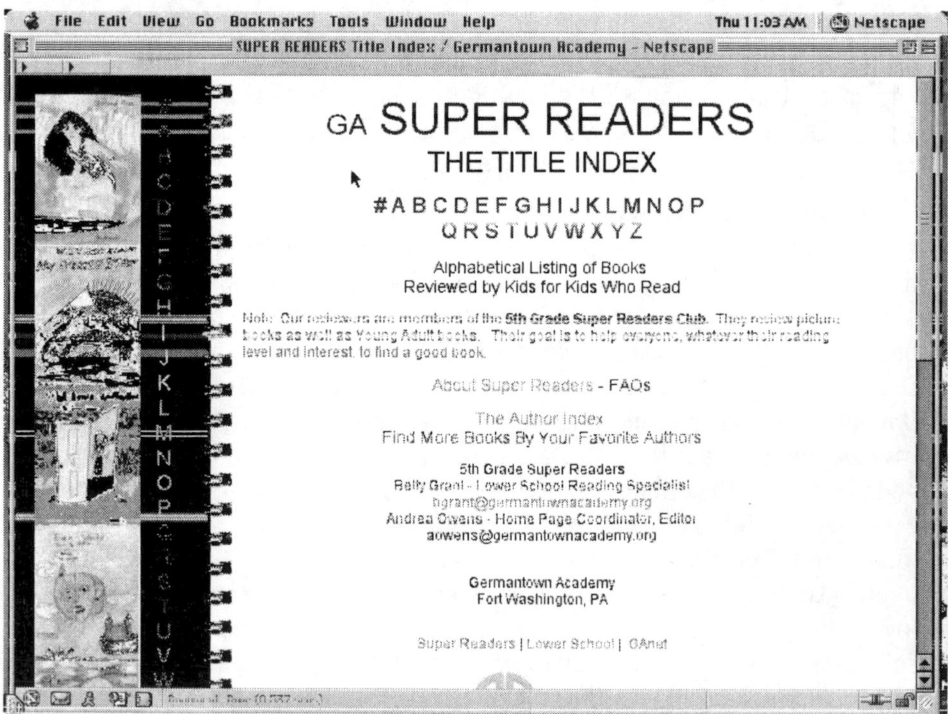

New Literacies in English and Language Arts

A new literacies perspective suggests that instruction in the effective use of the Internet needs to be systematically integrated into the curriculum. Students should have many opportunities across disciplines to identify important questions, locate information, critically evaluate that information, synthesize information to solve those questions, and communicate the solutions to others. With respect to English and the language arts, as more and more information is accessed electronically, strategies for citing electronic resources and getting the appropriate permissions to publicly share these resources with others become increasingly important.

Interestingly, the Internet functions as both the source of new challenges in this area as well as the source of excellent instructional supports. The fact that text, images, video, and audio can so easily be downloaded, copied, adapted, and uploaded again to another source makes it difficult for students to truly appreciate the notion of intellectual property and copyright. Freedman (1998) argues "teachers and officials themselves, not students, may be most responsible for the growth of plagiarism in schools and on campuses, by not anticipating and preparing for it, not recognizing it, or excusing it when they do uncover it." In Chapter 2, we briefly mentioned some of the challenges associated with plagiarism. To learn more about these challenges, you can read the helpful explanation of **Copyright of Fair Use in the Classroom** (http://www.umuc.edu/library/copy.html), provided by University of Maryland or explore the **Copyright Cyberbee** website (http://www.cyberbee.com/copyrt.html) for access to an interactive copyright quiz, a comprehensive copyright lesson for middle school students, and other informational pieces. For further explanation of fair use policies for educators, **Technology & Learning's Online Educator's Guide to Copyright and Fair Use** (http://www.techlearning.com/db_area/archives/TL/2002/10/copyright.html) is a very helpful guide. The "handy chart" from this website can be printed out and posted in your classroom as a reference for you and your students.

The Internet also provides a host of web-based tools to support your students' efforts to gather and share information correctly. **David Warlick's permission templates** for students (http://landmark-project.com/permission_student.php) and teachers (http://landmark-project.com/permission1.php) are designed to help appropriately and efficiently seek permission for using information retrieved online. For assistance with citing informational resources, you can choose from many resources to locate one that best supports your needs:

- **Long Island University's Citation Style for Research Papers—** http://www.liunet.edu/cwis/cwp/library/workshop/citation.htm
- **David Warlick's Citation Machine—** http://landmarkproject.com/citation_machine/cm.php

  This site has an electronic form that students can fill in to quickly generate a citation in either MLA (Modern Language Association) or APA (American Psychological Association) format. Once generated, the citation can easily be cut and pasted into any word processor or electronic document.

- **Oregon School Library's Citation Maker and How-To Guides for Elementary Students**—http://oslis.k12.or.us/elementary/howto/cited/) and **Secondary Students**—http://oslis.k12.or.us/secondary/howto/cited/
  The citation maker at the above two sites automatically generates formatted citations and enables you to maintain a list of citations to save and print out later.

By helping students to be aware of these important issues and by integrating opportunities for practice with new electronic supports into the language arts curriculum, we will be better preparing our students for their literacy futures with multiple information and communication technologies.

A Final Thought

Probably one of the most powerful uses of the Internet for the classroom is the potential that exists to support English and language arts. The Internet permits rapid, written communication between people around the world, quickly fulfilling the dream many have of a global village. It brings new meaning to the traditional saying, "It takes an entire village to raise a child." As a result, you have a very special tool to support literacy learning in your classroom. As you work with the Internet in your classroom, you and your students will discover many new ways to exploit this potential. Be certain to share your successes with others by posting Internet Project ideas for others to join or describe your successful experiences on a mailing list, inviting others to learn from your successful experiences.

Additional Language Arts and Literature Resources on the Internet

A+ Research & Writing for High School and College Students—
http://www.ipl.org/teen/aplus/

This page of the Internet Public Library will show your students how to write the perfect research paper.

Aaron Shephard's Readers Theater Page—
http://www.aaronshep.com/rt/

This site contains readers theater scripts you can print out and use in your classroom. It also links to ideas for writing and publishing, parents resources, and storytelling. If you use this instructional method in your class, this is the location for you!

African-American Biography Resources—
http://www.germantownacademy.org/academics/ls/4/online/laafambios.htm

This collection of biographies and primary source documents all centered around Black History and prominent African-Americans is sure to encourage an appreciation of diversity within your language arts curriculum.

American Writers II—The Twentieth Century—
http://www.americanwriters.org/
This is the product of a C-SPAN initiative to bring together writers, scholars, historians, and actors to examine the lives and work of selected twentieth-century American writers who have influenced our nation's history. From here, you can also access C-SPAN's American Writers: Journey Through History.

Animal Diaries K-6—
http://www.tesan.vuurwerk.nl/diaries/
Home to a worldwide K–6 Internet project developed in the Netherlands in which students write stories about animals (endangered or otherwise) from that animal's point of view. Participants include students from countries like Brazil, Denmark, Sri Lanka, Puerto Rico, Japan, and the United States.

BarbWired—http://english.unitecnology.ac.nz/barbwired/home.html
Set up in New Zealand so that young people between the ages of 12 and 19 can contribute and read articles about their issues and interests. This great model of online student publishing also provides links to resources to help start your own online classroom newspaper.

Bartleby Great Books Online—http://www.bartleby.com/index.html
All the great ones are here for free from Agatha Christie to Emily Dickinson, from W. E. B. Du Bois to T. S. Eliot, from F. Scott Fitzgerald to Robert Frost. Read away!

Bartlett's Familiar Quotations—http://www.bartleby.com/100/
Who first coined the phrase "Snug as a bug in a rug?" Using this classic work of famous quotations will quickly tell you it was Benjamin Franklin. This online resource is a tremendous source for great quotations. It contains a wonderful search engine with cross links to famous authors. Set a bookmark!

The Bulwer-Lytton Fiction Contest Home Page—
http://www.bulwer-lytton.com/
"It was a dark and stormy night . . ." Here is the homepage for the whimsical literary competition that challenges entrants to compose the opening sentence to the worst of all possible novels each year. It's great fun and an energizing assignment to any writing class tired of the same old, same old.

The Children's Literature Web Guide—
http://www.ucalgary.ca/~dkbrown/index.html
This site contains a comprehensive and organized array of links to literature resources including online works of literature, resources for teachers, locations about movies developed from literature, resources for parents, resources for storytellers, discussion groups about literature, lists of award winners, information about authors, and much more!

Do The Right Thing—
http://www.gridclub.com/have_a_go/english/right_thing/index.shtml
Sponsored by the Grid Club, this is part of England's official Department for Education and Skills website for 7–11 year olds. It features unique interactive word games involving imagery, idioms, and favorite sayings as well as links to reference materials. Be sure to check out the "Grown-Ups" link.

Electric Soup—http://homer.hcrhs.k12.nj.us/esoup/index.html
A very interesting online world created in New Jersey that accepts submissions of student writers of all ages. There are currently 17 volumes of writing, which when read in order, illustrate the progression of new literacies developed as they become more adept at collaboration and communication using the Internet and other ICT.

Electronic Text Center Collection—
http://etext.lib.virginia.edu/uvaonline.html#conditions
Home to more than 70,000 electronic humanities texts in 13 languages and an awesome collection of over 1,800 free e-books, all compiled by the University of Virginia. Check it out!

English: BBC Education Web Guide—
http://www.bbc.co.uk/webguide/schools/subcat.shtml?english/ks12/0
The URL may look intimidating but this is a set of links for the English curriculum in the United Kingdom, right from the BBC. Learn English from the English. What a novel idea!

English Online—http://english.unitecnology.ac.nz/
Educators will find over 150 fully resourced and downloadable teaching units, professional readings, selected links, and discussion forums.

Face To Face—http://www.itvs.org/facetoface/flash.html
December 7, 1941 and September 11, 2001: two days that changed the world forever. Face to Face explores what it means to be an American with the face of the enemy. These are real stories of fear, anger, hatred, loyalty, and trust. Respond on the discussion list or complete an activity.

Favorite Poem Project—
http://www.favoritepoem.org/thevideos/index.html
A collection of 50 short (and free) video documentaries that showcase individual Americans reading and speaking personally about poems they love.

Five Paragraph Essay Wizard—
http://www.geocities.com/SoHo/Atrium/1437/index.html
For students needing practice with this measure of writing proficiency, this site provides great models of expository, narrative, and persuasive writing, and tips for mastering essay writing.

Garbl's Writing Resources Online—
http://garbl.home.comcast.net/writing/
This resource is maintained by Gary Larson in Seattle, Washington, who has over 30 years of experience as a writing instructor, an editor, and coordinator of media relations. This site does contain some commercial messages but it is a comprehensive annotated directory to resources on the writing process, tips for writing persuasively, a list of online writing experts, and an interactive message board to discuss questions and interests about writing with others.

Gifts of Speech: Women's Speeches from Around the World—
http://www.giftsofspeech.org/
This site is dedicated to preserving and creating access to speeches by influential contemporary women from around the world. It's a great resource for expanding biographical studies with links to speeches that have never before been published in print-based texts.

Information Please—http://www.infoplease.com/

A one-stop online reference for students and teachers including a dictionary, encyclopedia, atlas, and almanac. Also includes a link to FactMonster for younger children.

Kathy Schrock's Citation Guides—
http://school.discovery.com/schrockguide/referenc.html#copyright

Needing more information about copyright issues in the K–12 learning environment? Look no further than this huge compilation of online references and tools.

Kids Newsroom—http://www.kidsnewsroom.com/

Kids news and stories written and posted by kids. A weekly news magazine featuring news, games, information, and submitted articles from kids and schools from around the United States.

KidStack Collections of Children's Literature—
http://www.utm.edu/vlibrary/docust5.shtml

This incredible collection compiled by librarians at the Andy Holt Virtual Library at the University of Tennessee-Martin links to hundreds of online children's classics in English, Spanish, and French. Four other collections of literature for readers of all ages are also housed here, linking you to nearly a million and a half online documents!

Literacy Web—http://www.literacy.uconn.edu/

Created at the University of Connecticut, this resource is designed to promote the use of the Internet as a tool to assist classroom teachers in their search for best practices in literacy instruction, including the new literacies of Internet technologies. You can locate information sorted by grade level, literacy topic, or level of research.

Lynch Multimedia Shakespeare—
http://www.lynchmultimedia.com/shakespeare.html

Simplified prose versions of six of Shakespeare's plays—great for introducing children to his work. There are RealAudio additions to add to the experience as well as a separate classroom version to facilitate group reading.

Magazines—
http://search.yahooligans.yahoo.com/search/ligans?p=Magazines

This is a central site with links to many outstanding online magazines for kids. A treasure trove of resources.

Moving Words—http://www.open.ac.uk/crete/movingwords/

Explore this inspiring example of how new interactives forms of text (e.g., hypertext, animation, video) and diverse perspectives can change our notions of literary response.

Multicultural Resources—
http://falcon.jmu.edu/~ramseyil/multipub.htm

Here you will find articles about multicultural children's literature as well as reviews and a host of literature selections organized by cultural groups. It is a real treasure for teachers serious about multicultural literature.

Online Poetry Classroom—http://www.onlinepoetryclassroom.org/
Sponsored by the Academy of American Poets, this website contains instructional materials, teachers' forums, and a searchable database of 450 poets and more than 1200 poems to support high school language arts teachers with free online poetry resources.

Paradigm Online Writing Assistant—http://www.powa.org/
Here is a great resource to help your high school writers polish their writing skills with a variety of formats including: informal essays, thesis/support essays, argumentative essays, and exploratory essays. It also helps students to document their sources appropriately.

Poetry Aloud: A Directory of Poetry Readings on the Internet—
http://www.dc.peachnet.edu/~shale/humanities/composition/handouts/poetryaloud.html
Looking for a way to entice students into the world of poetry? Invite them into a virtual listening booth by encouraging them to explore these online links to audio files of various poetry collections.

Reading Online—http://www.readingonline.org/
This is the free electronic journal of the International Reading Association, the best online journal currently found on the Internet. It contains a wealth of resources including sections on the electronic classroom, new literacies, and an international forum. Special features include the use of many multimedia resources and discussion forums where you may comment on articles you read. Set a bookmark!

Read, Write, Think—http://www.readwritethink.org/
This site, sponsored by the International Reading Association, National Council of Teachers of English, and MarcoPolo, leads you to an ever-growing very current list of standards-based lesson plans for all areas of language arts and reading instruction. Set a bookmark to this one for sure and consider submitting your own lesson plan!

Resources for Writers—
http://owl.english.purdue.edu/handouts/index2.html
Here you can find all the handouts for spelling and grammatical work developed by the Writing Lab at Purdue University.

Stories from the Web—
http://www.storiesfromtheweb.org/sfwhomepage.htm
Managed by the Birmingham libraries in the United Kingdom, this site has grown from a research grant project to stimulate reading, writing, and creativity among 8–11 year olds to an interactive online resource for 8–14 year olds to read, write, and respond to stories and poetry.

TALK: Technology Assisting Literacy Knowledge—
http://teach.fcps.net/talk/
Explore this Classroom Literacy Guide to find model lessons that integrate software, the Internet, and best literacy practices. Select Language Arts Content Area lessons to get started.

TeenLit—http://www.teenlit.com

This interactive site administered by two secondary teachers in Michigan publishes poetry, short stories, essays, and book reviews from teen writers. Authors can also visit the writer's workshop for writing tips, join the very active writing discussion boards to critique others' writing or receive feedback on their own.

The Doucette Index—http://www.educ.ucalgary.ca/litindex/

Are you looking for websites that have teaching ideas for a particular work of literature or a particular author? Here's the site for you. This index is a search engine limited strictly to children's and young adult literature. It will find instructional resources on the Internet related to your literature needs.

The Reading Zone of the Internet Public Library—
http://www.ipl.org/div/kidspace/

This is a good central site for literature with many opportunities for your students. Developed at the University of Michigan, your students can read answers to questions from authors such as Virginia Hamilton, Timothy Gaffney, Shonto Gegay, and others, read biographies and view photos of many more authors, discover links to many authors' homepages, read original stories or listen to them being read aloud, enter a writing context, see the book recommendations of other students, and much more. Set a bookmark!

Write Site Homepage—http://www.writesite.org/

An interactive language arts and journalism project for middle school students in which students take on the role of journalists—generating leads, gathering facts, and writing stories—using the tools and techniques of real-life journalists.

Writing with Writers: Scholastic Series—
http://teacher.scholastic.com/writewit/index.htm

Don't miss this one! Students get advice from real authors of 10 different genres as they are walked step-by-step through the brainstorming, writing, and publishing process. Teachers' guides and extended resources are available for each writing unit.

Online Communities for English and Language Arts

American Association of School Librarians

Several electronic discussion lists to support the exchange of ideas and curricular resources with library media specialists.
Homepage: http://www.ala.org/Content/NavigationMenu/AASL/Professional_Tools10/Electronic_Discussion_Lists2/Electronic_Discussion_Lists.htm

CHILDLIT

A list devoted to discussion and critical analysis of children's literature.
Subscription address: listserv@rutvm1.rutgers.edu
Homepage: http://www.rci.rutgers.edu/~mjoseph/childlit/about.html

Childrens-Writing

A discussion list for children's writers and illustrators, and anyone interested in writing or drawing for kids.

Subscription address: majordomo@lists.mindspring.com

Folklore

A folklore discussion list.

Subscription address: listserv@tamvm1.tamu.edu

KIDLIT-L

A listserv on children's literature.

Subscription address: listserv@bingvmb.cc.binghamton.edu

RTEACHER

A forum for conversations about literacy in both traditional and electronic contexts. The archive for these conversations may be found at http://listserv.syr.edu/archives/rteacher.html

This is a very supportive and diverse group of educators interested in using the Internet for literacy education. We also discuss non-Internet aspects of literacy education.

Subscription address: listserv@bookmark.reading.org

Homepage: http://www.reading.org/virtual/rt_listserv.html

Archives: http://www.reading.org/archives/rteacher.html

STORYTELL

A discussion list for those interested in storytelling.

Subscription address: STORYTELL-REQUEST@venus.twu.edu

TAWL

A listserv discussion group on teaching from a whole language perspective.

Subscription address:
listserv@listserv.arizona.edu

6 Social Studies: A World of Possibilities

We believe the Internet provides more new possibilities for social studies education than any other content area. Why? There are several reasons. First, the Internet permits our students access to extensive collections of primary source documents. By helping our students analyze primary source documents, we develop the critical thinking and interpretive skills crucial to students' futures. Critical evaluation is a central part of the new literacies and social studies is a wonderful venue in which to develop this with primary source documents. Second, having the Internet in our classroom enables students to experience different cultures through the communication experiences they have with students in other parts of the world. This is a special and very powerful potential for social studies education. Finally, there are simply more information resources for social studies education than any other subject area on the Internet.

We believe that the Internet provides more new possibilities for social studies education than for any other content area.

These new opportunities, though, also present important challenge to teachers and students: How do you quickly find useful primary source documents, and how do you support the critical analysis so important with these new resources? How do you develop exciting cross-cultural projects that are now possible with Internet technologies? How does one locate necessary and relevant information when so much is available? In this chapter, we will share solutions for each of these challenges.

Most importantly, we will describe effective strategies throughout the chapter, enabling you to immediately integrate the Internet into your social studies curriculum. Using the Internet opens up a world of possibilities for you and your students in social studies education.

After reading this chapter you should be able to:

1. Identify at least four outstanding social studies directories that contain resources and lesson plans for some of the topics covered in your curriculum.

2. Design a series of three Internet Workshop sessions for your students to complete based on an informational site you have selected from one of the social studies directories in this chapter.
3. Log on to at least two Internet project registry sites and identify several collaborative projects that would be useful and appropriate for your class to join.
4. Use Internet Workshop to help your students design individual student-to-student activities that might follow the completion of Internet Inquiry projects.
5. Identify at least three websites that you can use for the development of lessons that will enhance your students' critical evaluation capabilities.

Teaching with the Internet: Miguel Robledo's Class

It was the beginning of a new year for Miguel Robledo, his second using the Internet in his American History classes at Del Rio High School. He sat at his desk in the morning light, enjoying his coffee and thinking back to his early experiences with this new tool for teaching. He smiled a bit remembering how intimidated he had felt by all of the information on the Internet for social studies. He recalled wondering how he was going to remember everything without getting lost. He hadn't known about bookmarks or making a webpage with links to favorite sites.

Miguel had started simply that first year. He was a cautious person when it came to change. Initially, he had developed scavenger hunts to develop navigational skills for his students using resources at **Internet Scavenger Hunts** (http://homepage.mac.com/cohora/ext/internethunts.html) and **Education World** (http://www.education-world.com/a_curr/curr113. shtml). These scavenger hunts had students find information about the unit they were studying, but did not ask them to do any critical evaluation of the information. He quickly discovered, though, that his students already possessed many of these skills required for navigating the Internet, so he developed other types of learning experiences. Each week, he set up a single Internet Workshop for students to complete based on the many resources available at **History/Social Studies for K-12 Teachers** (http://members.cox. net/dboals/boals.html). He set a bookmark for the best location for each week's topic and developed several critical thinking questions for his students.

*Each week, Miguel set up a single Internet Workshop for students to complete based on the many resources available at **History/Social Studies for K-12 Teachers** (http:// members.cox.net/ dboals/boals.html).*

Each workshop activity required students to think critically about the information at a site related to their current unit. During one week of the colonial period, he had students complete an Internet workshop activity where they had to search for information about Benjamin Franklin and draw a conclusion about his most important achievement. They also had to bring back information to the workshop session about how they concluded that the site they used in this task was one that provided accurate and reliable information. Many new strategies for evaluating the accuracy of web resources emerged from this simple activity. At the end of the week, during a short Internet Workshop session, students had a chance to compare their ideas and discuss their conclusions. The discussion had really made the totality of Franklin's life come alive as students described his many accomplishments and debated which accomplishment was most important.

In the middle of the year, as he felt more confident and knowledgeable about Internet resources, Miguel had decided to use Internet Project, connecting with other classrooms around the world. He wanted his students to see how people in different cultural contexts interpreted the same historical event. He had posted a project to compare perceptions of World War II (WWII) of students from several different countries at **The Global SchoolNet Projects Registry** (http://www.gsn.org/pr/_cfm/index.cfm).

During the middle of the year, as he felt more confident and knowledgeable about Internet resources, Miguel decided to develop an Internet Project, connecting with other classrooms around the world.

After studying this event in their individual classrooms, students in each class wrote an essay describing the significance of WW II to their country. These essays were exchanged by email between each of the participating classes so that students could see how history is often interpreted differently by different societies. Each student then wrote a second essay describing what they had learned from reading the essays of students in the different countries. Classrooms from Japan, Russia, Germany, England, Italy, and Canada participated in the project.

Also as part of the project, participating classrooms read stories from people who lived during the 1940s. They found all of this wonderful information at the homepage for **Memories** (http://atschool.eduweb.co.uk/chatback/english/memories/memories.html). They also subscribed to the mailing list located there, also called **Memories** (listserv@maelstrom.stjohns.edu). This is a mailing list in which participating classrooms can exchange email messages with survivors of WW II. This was an especially important experience for everyone involved as students asked questions about different events and received information from people who had actually lived through the war era. For Miguel and his students, studying about history had fundamentally changed. History was no longer just something they read about; it was the people they were talking with over the Internet and the experiences they shared. History had become human.

Miguel's project was a tremendous success. It provided a powerful experience for each of the classrooms, making history come alive for everyone as students learned how to communicate effectively across cultural divides, learning from one another about each other's cultural context. Some classes in the project continued exchanging information throughout that year. Each teacher promised to get together again the next year so they could repeat the project.

For Miguel and his students, studying about history was fundamentally changed. History had become human.

As the end of last year approached, Miguel had decided to try Internet Inquiry. Students identified a question in American History that they wanted to explore on their own using resources on the Internet and in the school library. Before they started their projects, Miguel set up individual bookmark folders for each student on his classroom computers so that students could keep track of good locations and not get these mixed up with those of other students. He also conducted several Internet Workshops on how to critically evaluate information at websites.

Miguel had students complete the planning form in Figure 6-1. This helped to focus their efforts and provide a road map for their initial work during Internet Inquiry. After one week, he held individual conferences with students to check their progress and make revisions to their project if necessary.

Figure 6-1. The Internet Inquiry Planning Form Used in Mr. Robledo's Class.

Planning for Internet Inquiry

Directions: Use this form to plan for Internet Inquiry, keep you on track as you complete your work, and help you evaluate your work when you finish. Please fill in each item as completely as possible and then schedule a conference with me to discuss your planning.

Name(s): ______________________________ Date: ______________

Title of my (our) Internet Inquiry: ______________________________

The project will be completed on: ______________________________

The purpose of my (our) project is: ______________________________

____

____

____

As I (we) planned my (our) project, I (we) used the following resources: ________

____

____

____

I (we) will do the following during this project: ______________________

____

____

____

I (we) will evaluate the project in the following manner: ________________

____

____

____

I (we) will begin by using the following Internet sites or by using the following words/phrases with a search engine: ______________________________

____

____

____

I (we) had a conference with Mr. Robledo about this project on the following dates:

______________ ______________ ______________

At the end of their Internet Inquiry projects, Miguel had used an activity called Student-to-Student. In this activity, each student was asked to develop a learning activity related to the inquiry they had just completed and then create a poster advertising this learning experience. Students provided the Internet address, explained the learning activity they had developed for this site, and advertised the virtues of completing their activity. Miguel required each student in his class to participate in at least three of these activities during the last two weeks of school. At the end of each week, he conducted a workshop session where students shared the results of their Student-to-Student activities. It was a nice way to wrap up their study of history during the year.

Then over the summer, Miguel attended a workshop on using primary source documents on the Internet in the social studies classroom. He picked up some great strategies to try out in his class this year. He was using one today.

His students were just beginning their study of American history, so he had designed an early activity with primary source documents to orient them to the Internet and to the critical thinking he would be expecting from them. His class would work in small groups. Each group would have a set of historical documents, books, and artifacts with information from one time period in American history. The activity called for them to use their materials to frame questions about history that they would explore in upcoming weeks. Miguel designed this activity to whet his students' interest in history and introduce them to the historical analysis of primary source documents. The activity would also develop important background knowledge that would help his students throughout the year.

Each group would have a single day to explore one of four sets of materials and develop questions about the time period of their materials. The next day, the groups would rotate to the next set of historical materials. On Friday, they would share their questions and their discoveries in a whole-class discussion during Internet Workshop. Miguel planned to organize their questions around the different time periods covered during the year, introducing themes and issues they would explore in upcoming units.

One of the first lessons Miguel learned with the Internet was that students often spend their limited time at the computer just "surfing" for information, moving quickly from site to site trying to find something interesting.

During part of each day, three groups would work at their desks while a fourth group would work in pairs at the three Internet computers in his classroom, locating and analyzing original documents from the 1900s that they found in cyberspace. Each day a different group would complete an activity at the computer cluster, trying to develop important questions from the primary source documents they found during their session.

One of the first lessons Miguel had learned during his first year of Internet use was that students often spend their limited time at the computer just "surfing" for information, moving quickly from site to site trying to find something interesting. Often his students' time at the computer would run out before they had an opportunity to really read and learn anything. Or, they would sometimes end up at sites that were inappropriate for their work.

To combat that situation this year, Miguel had set the startup page location on all three computers to **American Memory** (http://memory. loc.gov/) as soon as his students connected to the Internet (see Figure 6-2). This outstanding resource from the Library of Congress contains a wonderful collection of original documents, photos, motion pictures, maps, and sound recordings for social studies education. Here, students can find all kinds of great resources including: original documents from the Continental Congress, a collection of 350 pamphlets providing insight into the African American experience from 1818–1907, audio recordings of famous speeches, a collection of over 1,000 photographs from the Civil War, and much, much more. This was one of the important directories he had discovered during his summer workshop. Setting the homepage to a site like this saved valuable time in a 40-minute class period.

Figure 6-2. American Memory (http://memory.loc.gov/), developed by the Library of Congress, contains an extensive collection of primary source materials including documents, photos, motion pictures, maps, and sound recordings. A good site for a classroom computer's startup page.

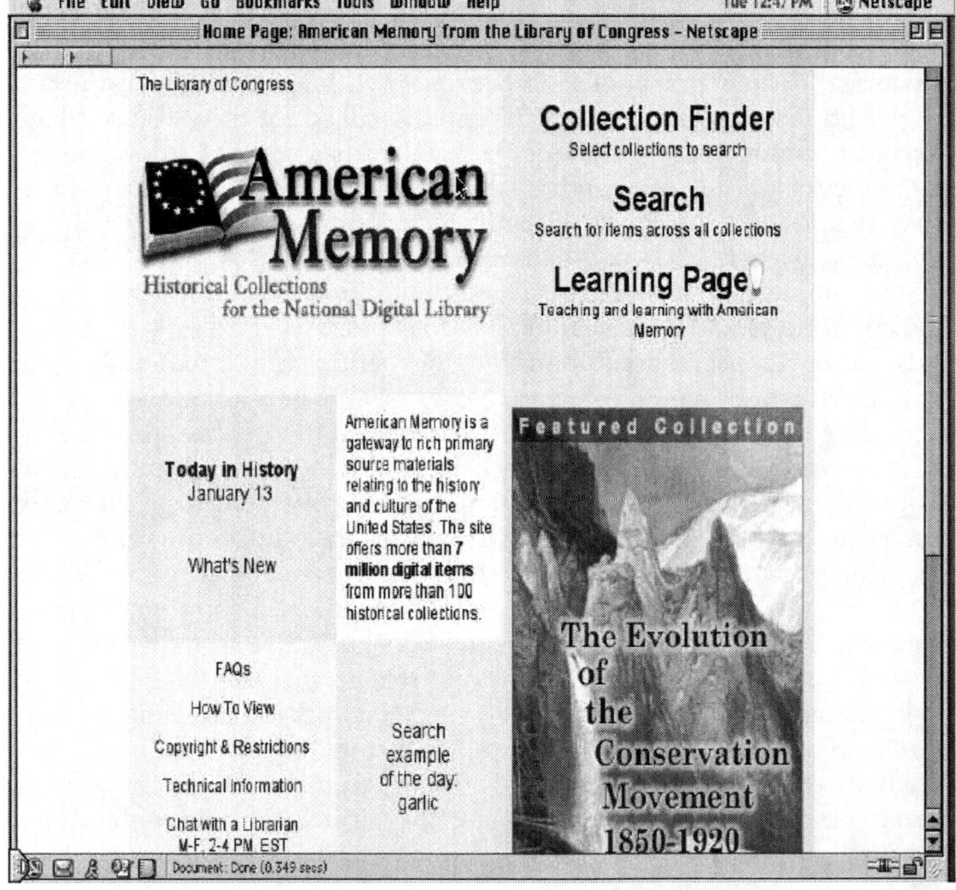

Miguel knew that students often taught one another about the Internet faster than he could teach them. Among other strategies, he set aside a portion of the bulletin board next to the computers for students to post information about the Internet. Students listed useful sites and shared other information about their current work. Some students used the word pro-

Miguel knew that students often taught one another about the Internet faster than he could teach them. Among other strategies, he set aside a portion of the bulletin board next to the computers for students to post information about the Internet.

cessor on the computer to type these notes, so word processing skills were supported, too.

Miguel's thoughts were interrupted as his students came in and took their places. Sarah and her partner Vanita clicked on a site at American Memory that someone had described on the bulletin board. The site, called **"Votes for Women" 1850–1920** (http://memory.loc.gov/ammem/vfwhtml/vfwhome.html), contained a collection of photographs and documents about the women's suffrage movement in the United States.

"Hey, check it out ... sisters marching," said Vanita as an image of women marching appeared on their screen. Both girls chuckled. Then they started reading **One Hundred Years toward Suffrage: An Overview** (http://memory.loc.gov/ammem/vfwhtml/vfwtl.html), developing a greater appreciation for the struggles women have faced.

"Look, Seneca Falls. That's where they had the first women's rights convention. Cool! I went there last year," said Sarah.

At the next computer Jonathon and his Internet partner, Josh, were working. "Hey, look! Jackie Robinson. We can study the history of baseball?" Jonathon, had found a great source: **Jackie Robinson and other Baseball Highlights, 1980's–1960's** (http://memory.loc.gov/ammem/jrhtml/jrhome.html). They started reading about Jackie Robinson and viewing the extensive set of documents about this famous American.

"They got Larry Doby?" asked Jonathon. Clearly, Jonathon knew his baseball history.

At the third computer, Mircalla and Jessica had found the movie section. "Hey, it's a movie about San Francisco and the earthquake. I was born there but I never saw anything like this before," noted Mircalla.

"Don't forget to write down questions you want to explore in class this year," Tanisha reminded everyone. "We're going to have Internet Workshop on Friday."

The groups at the Internet computers got together quickly to list their questions:

- Why didn't people want women to vote?
- Who were some of the important women? What did they do?
- What were the Negro Leagues like and who were some of the best players?
- What was racism like for Jackie Robinson?
- What was San Francisco like before the earthquake?
- How did they put the fire out in San Francisco?

Jonathon typed their questions at the computer as the others dictated them. Then they printed their questions for Mr. Robledo on the classroom printer.

Before they went back to their desks, Mircalla and Jessica typed and printed out a short note which they then posted on the bulletin board next to the computer. It said:

See the FANTASTIK movie about the San Francisco earthquake on the Internet. It's at:

http://memory.loc.gov/ammem/papr/sfhome.html
Look in Mircalla's bookmark folder.
Click where it says "list the film titles."
—Mircalla and Jessica

Lessons from the Classroom

Miguel Robledo's experience illustrates a number of important lessons about integrating the Internet into your social studies classroom. First, it demonstrates the benefit of starting simply, perhaps with activities such as scavenger hunts. If your students already have basic navigation skills, beginning with Internet Workshop is an easy way to use the Internet and develop their skills further. Workshop experiences provide many opportunities for you to integrate the Internet into your classroom. Reading about the history of the Negro Leagues and then viewing a short movie about Jackie Robinson made this information come alive for Jonathon and Josh. They talked about it all day with other students and even shared this information at home. And, of course, they talked about this during Internet Workshop. The same was true for Sarah and Vanita about the suffrage movement, and for Mircalla and Jessica about the San Francisco Earthquake. Internet Workshop provides a powerful strategy for you and your students to gather information and then communicate with others about what you have learned. In addition to discussions on social studies content, workshop sessions provide an excellent opportunity for students to share problems and solutions related to the new literacies they are discovering.

Using Internet Workshop is often the easiest way to begin using the Internet in your classroom.

Second, we again see the power of Internet Project for bringing classroom learning alive. Collaborative experiences with students at other locations around the world motivate classes in important ways as they learn important lessons. Internet Project can be an especially powerful way of organizing classroom learning experiences in social studies; it enables students to better appreciate the power of different cultural experiences, and understand how people in different parts of the world view historical, political, and social events. Participating in the Memories mailing list and sharing thoughts about WWII with other students around the world fundamentally changed the nature of historical study in Miguel's classroom.

Third, Miguel's experience shows how the Internet provides many opportunities for students to work with primary source documents in their social studies curriculum. These original documents provide you with important instructional opportunities to help students develop critical thinking, synthesis, and evaluation skills. All of these skills will become increasingly important as our students enter the workforce in an age of information.

Fourth, Miguel's experience shows how instructional strategies like Student-to-Student may be used to support social learning, a new literacy necessary for getting the most from the Internet and for successful operation in the information world of their future workplaces. This activity is also a good way to wrap up a unit in your classroom, allowing students to teach one another about what they have learned.

The Internet provides many opportunities for students to work with primary source documents in their social studies curriculum.

In addition, Miguel's planning encouraged his students to help one another as they searched for information. The bulletin board told others where useful information was located on the Internet. Miguel had encouraged all of the students to do this when they came across something they thought others might be able to use. He also used workshop sessions in which students could both share their discoveries and seek assistance. Social learning opportunities abound with Internet resources, and Miguel's encouragement for students to assist one another on the Internet helped develop a very supportive classroom community. We will show you other ways in which you can assist your students to help one another with Internet resources, an excellent lesson for the world after school, too.

Finally, Miguel's experiences demonstrate how extensive the resources on the Internet are for social studies. It will benefit students tremendously if you help them sort through these many resources to find those that are most useful. It is also helpful to provide assistance with using various search engines to locate information. You may also want to develop individual bookmark folders so that students can keep track of their own favorite sites.

Internet Project can be an especially powerful way of organizing classroom learning experiences in social studies since it enables your students to understand how people in different parts of the world view historical, political, and social events.

Internet FAQ

There is so much information and so many sites for social studies. How do I find what I need?

The easiest strategy is to visit one of the social studies directories mentioned in this chapter and begin to explore the resources there. These sites are usually organized by topic and easy to navigate. Many of them include an internal search engine that searches only within their site.

If you are looking for specific information on a certain topic, do a keyword search using one of the search engines described in Chapter 2. Remember, keyword searches usually work best if you use descriptive words that are likely to be on the pages you are seeking. For example, to search for something about the pyramids of Giza in Egypt, simply type in "pyramids Giza Egypt." Avoid function words, such as "the," "of," and "in."

Another successful strategy is to join a mailing list or forum and ask other teachers for their recommendations—both for sites and on how to locate them. There is a list of online communities focused on social studies at the end of this chapter. (You can review mailing list subscription procedures in Chapter 4).

Directories for Social Studies Education

Because there are so many Internet resources for social studies education, using directories is often a useful strategy for quickly locating resources directly related to your learning goals. Fortunately, there are several exceptional directories available for social studies education. We divide them into two basic groups: directories for social studies resources and directories for social studies teaching.

Directories for social studies resources contain extensive collections of links to great social studies resource sites for your classroom. Resources are systematically organized under various topics to make it easier for you to find the information you and your students require. While these sites may have links to actual teaching units, we have listed them here as outstanding sites for locating primary source documents and secondary sources that provide background information and explore various aspects of the social studies curriculum.

Directories for Social Studies Resources

The best directories that we have found for general social studies resources include these locations:

- **The Library of Congress** —http://www.loc.gov/

  There is probably no better location for multimedia access to primary source documents about the United States. Your students can view items ranging from the original draft of the Declaration of Independence in Thomas Jefferson's handwriting to the Vietnam War POW/MIA database. It is a most impressive resource for your social studies program. Included in separate sections are: **Thomas** (http://thomas.loc.gov/), the official source of legislative information for the U.S. Congress; **Exhibitions** (http://lcweb.loc.gov/exhibits/), a collection of recent exhibitions at the Library of Congress; **Using the Library** (http://www.loc.gov/library/), providing you with access to the extensive catalogs of the Library of Congress and many others; and **The Library Today** (http://www.loc.gov/today/), containing information about the most recent information and events at our nation's library.

- **History/Social Studies for K-12 Teachers—** http://members.cox.net/dboals/boals.html

  This is one of the best single locations we know. The homepage for this location only hints at the many resources it contains. Pay a visit to this site and explore the variety of topics. You will find an amazingly exhaustive set of resources organized in an easy to understand hierarchical structure.

- **History Matters**—http://historymatters.gmu.edu/

  A wonderful joint effort from City University of New York and George Mason University for secondary and university teachers. It has links to primary source documents by "ordinary" people, syllabuses, and web-based lessons. Don't miss the sections on making sense of evidence—guides for understanding and using various types of primary sources such as oral histories; past meets present—articles pointing out links between past events and current situations; and secrets of great history teachers—a set of interviews with many helpful suggestions.

- **Learning Resources**— http://www.schoolnet.ca/home/e/resources/index.asp

  A directory for Canadian resources that is part of SchoolNet. See, especially, the link to social studies. A wonderful collection of all things Canadian.

- **Nebraska Department of Education Social Science Resources Homepage**—http://www.nde.state.ne.us/SS/

  This location developed by the State of Nebraska contains resources for social studies education organized under history, civics, economics, and geography.

- **Best of History Web Sites—**http://besthistorysites.net/

  The links are organized by historical time periods. There are also links to online sites for maps and research.

Figure 6-3. A very extensive directory for social studies resources: **History/Social Studies for K-12 Teachers** (http://members.cox.net/dboals/boals.html).

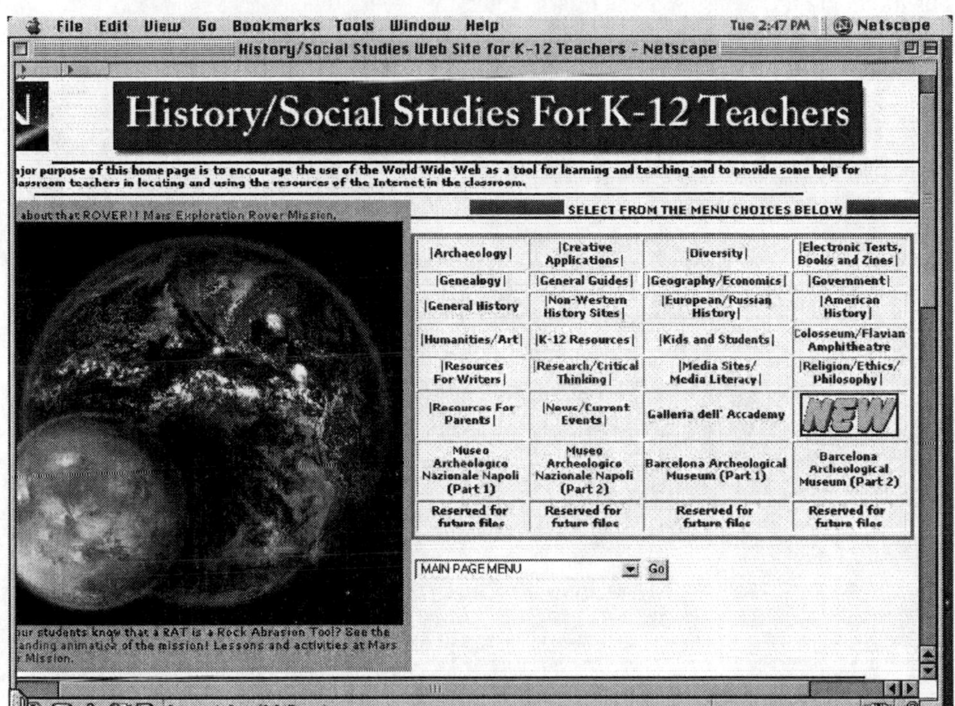

Directories for Social Studies Teaching

Directories for social studies teaching provide specific tools for instruction including Internet units and lesson plans as well as other resources. Some of the best we have found include:

- **Blue Web'n Applications: Social Studies**—
  http://www.kn.sbc.com/wired/blueWebn/contentarea.cfm?cid=8
- **CEC**—http://www.col-ed.org/cur/index.html
- **Digital History** — http://www.digitalhistory.uh.edu/
- **EDSITEment History and Social Studies Lesson Plans**—
  http://edsitement.neh.gov/tab_lesson.asp?subjectArea=3
- **Lesson Plans and Resources for Social Studies Teachers**—
  http://www.csun.edu/~hcedu013/index.html
- **National Park Service Teaching with Historic Places—**
  http://www.cr.nps.gov/nr/twhp/
- **PBS Social Studies Teaching**—
  http://www.pbs.org/teachersource/soc_stud.htm
- **S.C.O.R.E. History/Social Science**—http://score.rims.k12.ca.us/
- **The Learning Page: American Memory—**
  http://memory.loc.gov.learn
- **The Peace Corps World Wide Schools**—
  http://www.peacecorps.gov/wws/educators/index.html
- **Thinkquest Winners**—http://www.thinkquest.org/library/index.html

Figure 6-4. EDSITEment History and Social Studies Lesson Plans (http://edsitement.neh.gov/tab_lesson.asp?subjectArea=3), a great collection of lesson plans for all grades, covering many topics. Check out their other subject areas, too. Sponsored by the National Endowment for the Humanities in partnership with the Marco Polo Education Foundation.

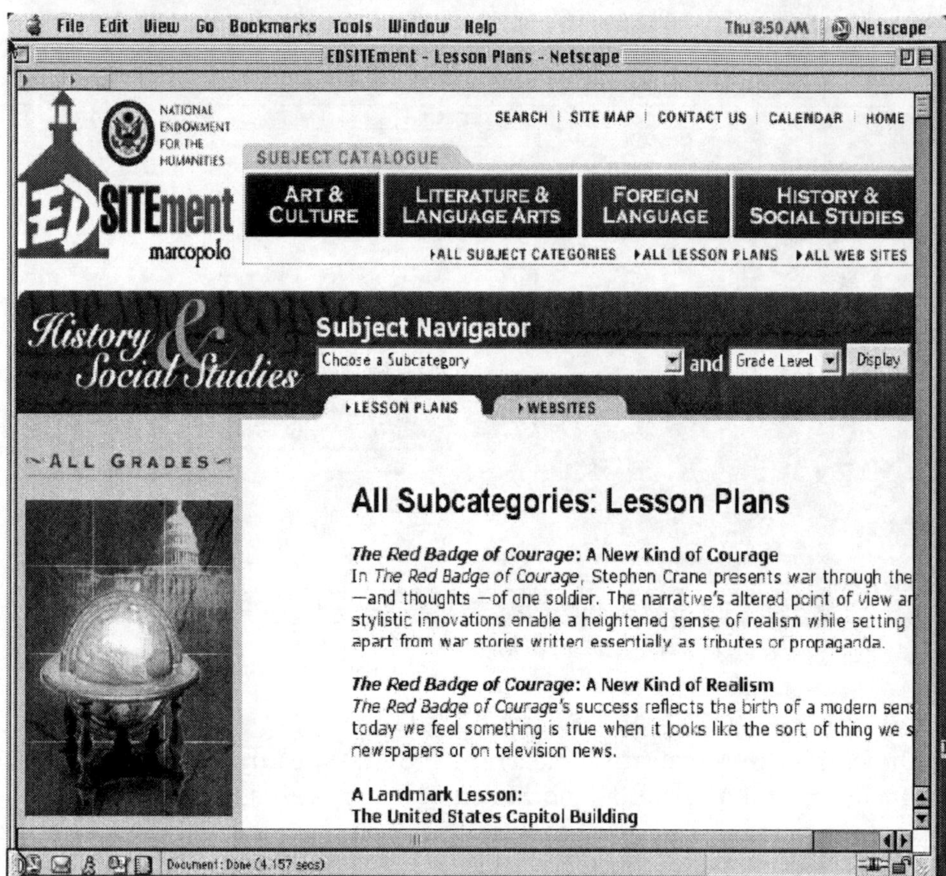

Keeping It Simple: Using Internet Workshop

It is often easiest to begin Internet use in your classroom with Internet Workshop. This may be especially useful as you begin to explore the extensive resources available on the Internet in social studies. Simply locate a site on the Internet with content related to the learning objectives in your classroom and develop an activity that encourages students to explore that site, then have them bring what they've learned to the workshop session for sharing and discussion. The easiest way to find a good location is to visit one of the directories for social studies education identified in previous sections of this chapter. Then develop an activity related to that site and assign this activity to your students. They can complete it during their weekly time at the computer. Afterwards, discuss their experiences during a short workshop session.

Nearly any set of good resources from the previously listed directories might be used in this fashion. For secondary students, if you are studying the Civil War, for example, you might set a bookmark for **The Civil War Letters of Galutia York** (http://www.morrisville.edu/library/local_history/civil_war/), and invite students to read the letters of this Union soldier, taking notes in a journal about this soldier's view of himself and his country. For the same workshop session, you might also set a bookmark for **The Timeline of the Civil War** (http://memory.loc.gov/ammem/cwphtml/tl1861.html) in the **Selected Civil War Photograph Collection** (http://memory.loc.gov/ammem/cwphtml/cwphome.html). Have your students read about and view the pictures, printing out one picture and then doing research about the battle to determine its significance. Post these photos and descriptions on a bulletin board in your classroom for everyone to see. During Internet Workshop, have students share their observations of this diary and photos. Use your students' observations to draw conclusions about the Union soldiers of that era and how they felt about their country. These activities could serve as a powerful introduction to the human side of the Civil War.

Setting up Internet activities in your classroom is a good way to ease yourself and your students into simple projects before attempting the richer, but more complex, experiences that are possible with Internet Project and Internet Inquiry.

Invite fifth or sixth grade students who are studying Benjamin Franklin to visit a series of activities located at the SCORE Cyber Guides site (http://www.sdcoe.k12.ca.us/score/ben/bentg.html). Have them complete any one of the activities and bring their work to a workshop session to share as you read together the book *Ben and Me* by Robert Lawson.

For younger students studying Abraham Lincoln, set a bookmark for the wonderful resource developed by Tammy Payton, a first grade teacher in Loogootee, Indiana: **Abraham Lincoln Classroom Activities** (http://www.siec.k12.in.us/~west/proj/lincoln/class.htm). Have students complete as many of the activities as they can and then share their work during an Internet Workshop session.

Setting up Internet activity assignments such as these in your classroom is a good way to ease yourself and your students into simple activities before attempting the richer, but more complex, experiences that are possible with Internet Project and Internet Inquiry. Several Internet activities are described in Gary Cressman's Email for You.

E-MAIL FOR YOU

From: Gary Cressman (cressman@inspire.ospi.wednet.edu)
Subject: America the Beautiful Lesson

Here is a set of Internet activities I do with my 8th graders. It takes about 3 weeks. I'm sure it could be modified for other classes. You can get the entire lesson on my website (http://www.learningspace.org/socialstudies/soc_st_subjects/lessons.html). Click on the folder called Tour of America.

The basis for this lesson is: What places in America can you identify as truly American? What places would you take immigrants to in order to show them what our country stands for? For example, you might think of America when you see the Statue of Liberty or Mount Rushmore.

I start by having students list 13 or more examples of things that seem truly American to them, things that are recognized as being only in America. After a few minutes, I have the kids pair up and generate one list of 10 places.

We go to the computers next to do Internet research. Using a search engine of your or their choice, have them find one picture of each place on their list. This leads to much debate as to which is the best picture. Have them save their picture and its source in a folder. This is a good time to discuss copyright issues and online citation styles.

Students will do a slide show for a final presentation, and explain why each picture was used and how it represents America. I use Graphics Converter on my Mac because it makes a slide show really easy. Students also make one map of the US to put on the bulletin board to show where each place is.

Next, student teams fill out an expense account spreadsheet on the computer for a trip to these places, and have to stay within the budget given. They have to figure mileage between each place they visit, and show its latitude, longitude and elevation. There is a website (http://www.indo.com/distance) where they can find these numbers. Of course, students have to buy a car, so I send them to Kelley Blue Book (http://kbb.com/) to check out new car pricing. They really begin to understand gas mileage, and there are lively discussions as students pick their vehicle carefully. They have to get rooms at Motel.com (http://motel.com), and plan their meals. I give them this hint: on Google, if you type the city name plus food, you will find some good information - for example: "Seattle food." All expenses are then indicated on their spreadsheet.

Gary Cressman
Chair, History Department and Computer Resource Teacher
Enumclaw Junior High
Enumclaw, Washington

Using Internet Project

Previous chapters have described the important role Internet Project can play in your classroom. We have also identified locations such as the following where you may search for Internet projects that other teachers have developed or post your own:

- **The Global SchoolNet Projects Registry—** http://www.gsn.org/pr/index.cfm
- **Intercultural Email Classroom Connections—** http://teaching.com/IECC/

- **KIDPROJ**—http://www.kidlink.org/KIDPROJ/
- **Oz Projects**—http://ozprojects.edna.edu.au/
- **SchoolNet's Grassroots Collaborative Learning Projects Gallery**—http://www.schoolnet.ca/grassroots/e/project.centre/project-search.asp
- **Telecollaborate!**—http://telecollaborate.net/
- **Windows on the World**—http://www.wotw.org.uk/

Internet projects are especially useful in social studies since they allow your students to compare their experiences and views with those of students in other cultures. Often, communicating with a class in another part of the country or world will make your study of that area and culture come alive as you exchange information about experiences. This is what happened in Linda Shearin's class as she describes in her email message.

E-MAIL FOR YOU

From: Linda Shearin <lshearin@bellsouth.net>
Subject: Canada Comes Alive!

The Internet is a great tool for making Social Studies come alive for students. In North Carolina, 5th grade students engage in a comparative study of peoples and regions of the Western Hemisphere. When I was working at Lead Mine Elementary School, I located **Canadiana** (http://www-2.cs.cmu.edu/Unofficial/Canadiana/), a treasure trove of information on Canada.

From Canadiana I located Canadian school homepages for each province in Canada. I then emailed the schools to see if there was a class who would be interested in engaging in a short term research project with our students. Fifth grade classes brainstormed questions they would like answered about homes (types of building materials, size, cost) and schools (schedules, subjects, homework) in the Canadian communities. It is difficult to find current and detailed information on these particular topics in print materials.

The first year we did this, it was evident our students were stuck in the "Age of Exploration," assuming Canadians still lived in log cabins and cooked over open fires. What a wonderful opportunity this presented to correct some misconceptions about lifestyle. This worked both ways since our students were amazed at the Canadian students asking if all our students were "wanded" for weapons before entering our school. A great discussion ensued about how the Canadians might have developed this impression.

When the responses arrived from the Canadian students, our 5th graders were surprised to find out that there were many similarities between themselves and their Canadian counterparts. They also enjoyed comparing the various school descriptions to our school.

The 5th graders used the correspondence and information gathered from other Canadian sources on the Web and in print to write a research paper in the form of a narrative based on a trip to their chosen province. In addition to being able to include information from the Internet they learned how to properly cite Internet sources.

In order to plan for a future literature connection we also solicited a list of best books, fiction and non-fiction, by Canadian authors to add to our school Media Center.

Simple but effective communication made our neighbors to the north more real to us, and us to them.

Linda Shearin
Academically Gifted Resource Teacher
Baileywick Elementary School
Raleigh, North Carolina

If you are just beginning to use Internet Project, it is often easiest to find projects posted by other teachers and seek to join a learning experience that seems appropriate for your class.

If you are just beginning to use Internet Project, it is often easiest to find a project posted by another teacher that seems appropriate for your class to join. Then, as you develop more experience with Internet Project, you will have a better sense of how to develop a project that others will be interested in joining and know where to advertise for cooperating classes. We encourage you to visit the sites listed above and explore the many opportunities available for your class through Internet Project. Here are a few examples of previous and ongoing projects:

- **Menus of the World was p**osted by a middle school teacher in Washington, this project sought collaborating classrooms around the world to learn more about each other's culture through their food. Each week, classes exchanged email messages containing a typical daily menu from their part of the world for four people, plus the estimated cost for each item in the meal using the local currency. The menu was used as a spring board for classrooms to ask questions about the cultural meanings for different food items: what unusual items were, how food was obtained, who prepared the food, how the meal was served, and how the meal was eaten. Each meal's cost was also converted into the currency used in each classroom to compare costs of common foods as well as the average cost for each meal.
- **Books on Tape** (http://booksontapeforkids.org/) is a wonderful project developed by two teachers in Rhode Island. It helps students understand the importance of community service and caring about others. The goal of this project is to send at least two packages with books on tape to two hospitals in each state. Each package contains a children's book, an audio tape of a student reading it aloud, illustrations, and letters from the students. The class has attracted several sponsors to support their important work.
- **Geo Game** (http://www.globalschoolhouse.org/project/gg/) is actually a contest. Each participating class completes a questionnaire about their own location including information about latitude, typical weather, land formations, nearest river, time zone, points of interest, direction from the capital, population, and other items. These are then mailed to the project coordinator who removes the name of the location and then returns the questionnaire items to participants. Participants try to locate the city for each set of items using maps, atlases, and reference materials on the Internet.

Internet Project has many rewards, but careful planning is necessary to gain maximum benefits and avoid disappointments. For example, if you are studying a country around the world and want to include communication with classrooms there in your project, you need to take into account different schedules, vacation periods, and time zones. Peter Lelong emphasizes the importance of good planning in his email message.

E-MAIL FOR YOU

From: Peter Lelong (lelongp@fahan.tas.edu.au)
Subject: Internet Project Challenges

The greatest challenge many of us have when we contemplate a collaborative project is in finding a partner school to work with that shares the same goals. Unlike our first experience back in 1986 when locating any school to communicate via electronic mail was difficult, today's classrooms in many schools have access to a wealth of educational sites such as the Global School House (http://www.gsh.org) and the Aussie School House (http://www.ash.org.au). A variety of projects, such as the highly successful Travel Buddies (http://rite.ed.qut.edu.au/oz-teachernet/) [click on Projects], all aim to stimulate ideas that will encourage students to dip their toes into the world of electronic communication.

The relationship that develops between the coordinating teachers has always been crucial in any of the projects I have been involved with. As teachers we share via email our aims and objectives prior to commencing work with the students. Our topics for each week are planned ahead through regular email contacts, and a promise is made to communicate on set days if possible so that our students can expect responses to any questions asked in a timely fashion.

Such planning has always been of importance to the success of a project. Not only does it provide teachers with a chance to become acquainted and plan a series of lessons together, but it also ensures that the students, because of this prior contact between the teachers, will not become disappointed through lack of interest or poor planning by either party to a project.

Peter Lelong
Fahan School
Fisher Avenue
Sandy Bay
Tasmania 7005
http://www.fahan.tas.edu.au
http://www.fahan.tas.edu.au/indonesia/indo.html

Using Internet Inquiry

Internet Inquiry helps students develop independent research skills and critical thinking through the exploration of topics and questions that are personally important to them. Inquiry projects may be developed by individuals or small groups, and usually include these phases: developing a question, searching for information, evaluating the information, composing an answer, and sharing the answer. You may wish to review Chapter 3 for additional information on developing and using Internet Inquiry in your classroom. You can also find examples of inquiry projects at several online locations. One of the best is **Web Inquiry Projects** (http: / / edWeb.sdsu.edu/ wip/), a site hosted by the Educational Technology Department at San Diego State University.

When setting up Internet Inquiry for your students, and when evaluating inquiry projects developed by others, keep in mind that the more open-ended an inquiry is, the more opportunity there will be for students to develop their research skills and critical thinking. This does not mean, however, that only totally open-ended projects have benefits; it may be very appropriate to use teacher-generated questions and restricted resources for young students or as early inquiry lessons. However, if students are to develop the new literacies they require for their future success, Internet Inquiry must also lead to student-generated questions and open-ended use of a wide variety of Internet and traditional sources for locating information. You are the best judge of which kinds of inquiry activities are most suitable for your students.

An example of a relatively open-ended project is **Woman's Suffrage in Twentieth Century America** (http://edweb.sdsu.edu/wip/examples/suffrage/index.htm). It may be suitable for your students as is, or you can easily adapt it. For example, the activities can be narrowed by providing specific questions and a more limited list of resources. There are also several ways to make this project more open-ended. For example, initial "boundary" questions are provided in the first step, but students could be encouraged to modify these or add their own. For locating information, a list of websites is provided and students are asked to search within those sites, but students could be challenged to locate additional sites and resources. To share their findings, students in this project are asked to discuss interesting facts and create a KWL (Know, Want to Know, Learned) chart. However, students could be given the opportunity to explore other options for communicating their results. Many projects end with the sharing results phase, but this one includes another chance for students to consider "possible additional questions," and suggests that these might serve as the basis of a new inquiry.

One of the best ways to learn something is to teach it to someone else. This is the idea behind Student-to-Student.

As your students become successful with teacher-planned inquiries and are able to manage more open activities, consider having them design an Internet Inquiry of their own, either individually or in small groups. You may wish to point them to ThinkQuest (http://www.thinkquest.org/). This site contains over 5,000 collaborative projects done by teams of students who have created and entered them into a worldwide competition. It is a great source of ideas; you and your students may even want to enter the competition.

Combining Internet Inquiry with Internet Workshop is a very effective strategy. While working on their inquiries, students or groups can share what they have learned in their research as well as discuss any roadblocks they have encountered and solutions they have discovered. These conversations not only enrich the study of your unit but also help your students develop necessary skills in the new literacies.

Student-To-Student Activities

One of the best ways to learn something is to teach it to someone else. This is the idea behind Student-to-Student activities. As your students use the Internet during a unit, consider adding this type of activity to the end of the unit as you summarize and review the learning that has taken place. During a student-to-student activity, students first identify a useful online location related to their project or studies. Next they develop a learning experience for other students to complete using that website.

Student-to-Student is a great way to culminate Internet Inquiry. Set aside at least one day at the end of a unit for students to share their work. Start by discussing some examples with them during Internet Worksop. Then, have each student develop a short Internet activity based on what they've learned from their inquiries. Next, create a webpage listing all of these Internet activities and invite your students to complete as many as possible. An alternative to listing these activities on a webpage is to have students design a poster, advertising their website and describing what students will be required to do. These poster advertisements can then be displayed around the room so that everyone can read them and select the sites they wish to visit.

When students complete an activity designed by another student, have them obtain the signature of the student who developed the activity along with a brief evaluation. This is an especially nice experience if you have access to an entire lab of Internet computers. Each student can set up an individual station. Have half of the class visit the student stations and the other half share their Internet activity at a computer. Then rotate groups.

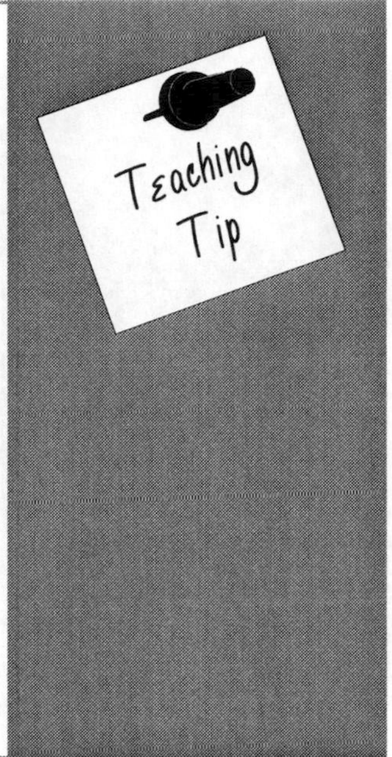

Here are some examples of student-to-student activities:

- After her class completed a unit on the Civil War, a student discovered a multimedia experience on the Underground Railroad developed by the National Geographic Society. This student set a bookmark for **Underground Railroad** (http://www.nationalgeographic.com/features/99/railroad/) and asked her classmates to take this journey. After their journey, students wrote a message describing their feelings in a journal that would then be read by other students as they began their journeys. The entire journal was then displayed at Back to School Night for parents to read.
- Another student, after completing a unit on sustainable agriculture, invited his classmates to visit **Eartheasy** (http://eartheasy.com/homepage.htm). He asked them to read the ideas suggested there, and then list their three choices for the easiest ways they could help sustain the environment in their community. The students' choices were added to a continuously updated graph using a spreadsheet program on the computer so that everyone could see which suggestions were most popular.
- Another student, completing a unit on ancient civilizations, invited classmates to explore **The Ancient Olympic Games Virtual Museum** (http://devlab.dartmouth.edu/olympic/), a wonderful site, and then write an imaginary letter home to their parents in Athens describing what they saw.

Student-to-Student is useful for consolidating learning experiences during the final weeks of an Internet Inquiry, or other type unit, in your classroom. It may be used, of course, in all subject areas but because there are so many resources on the Internet for social studies, it is especially useful in this area.

Figure 6-5. The **Eartheasy Homepage** (http://eartheasy.com/homepage.htm), where students can get suggestions for treating the environment gently. A good resource for student-to-student activities.

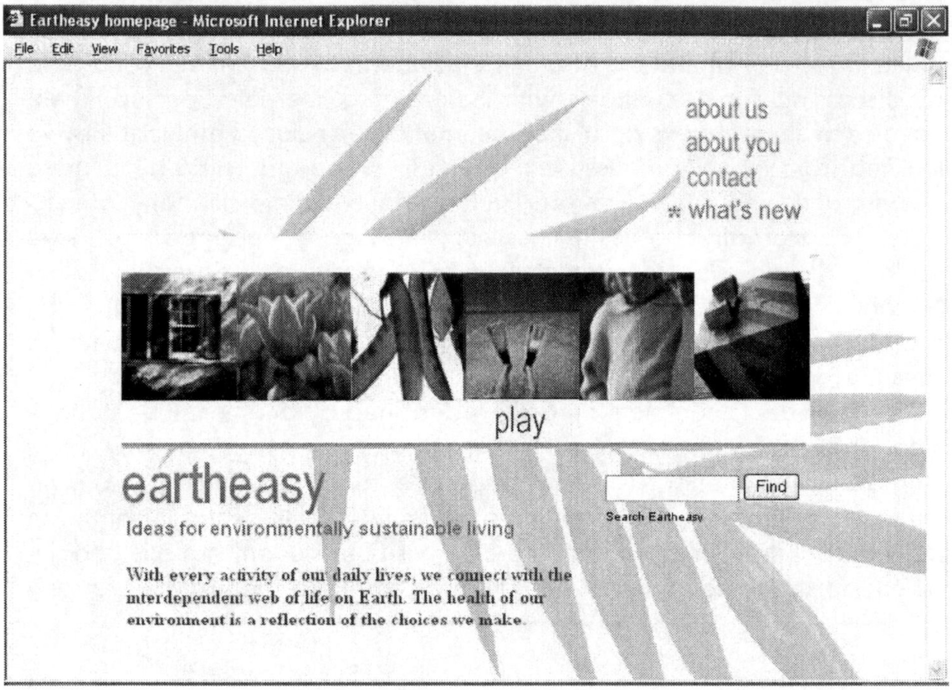

Using Webquest

Webquests offer the possibility of an immediate solution to the problem of how to integrate the Internet into your classroom. However, as with any curricular material, you should carefully evaluate any quest to determine its suitability for your particular students.

Webquests continue to increase in popularity among many teachers. Providing ready-to-use plans for a lesson or a unit on a variety of topics at any grade level, webquests offer the possibility of an immediate solution to the problem of how to integrate the Internet into your classroom. However, as with any curricular material, you should carefully evaluate a webquest to determine its suitability for your particular students. There is a detailed discussion of webquests in Chapter 3, including suggested questions for evaluating them. You can also visit **The WebQuest Page** (http://webquest.sdsu.edu/) for an overview and FAQs (frequently asked questions) about WebQuests, and **the WebQuest Portal** (http://webquest.org), which contains links to sites that have been evaluated and found to be good examples of the original WebQuest model.

Webquests can be an efficient way to integrate the Internet into your classroom, and the best ones may provide some of the learning opportunities of an inquiry project. When you find a good one, we suggest doing a check for broken links and outdated material before assigning it to your students. Even some of the best sites are not updated. Here are some of our favorite social studies webquests. You may want to evaluate them for possible use with your students. Other quests may be found in many of the directories for social studies teaching that were listed earlier in this chapter.

- **Battle of the Battlefields**—http://score.rims.k12.ca.us/activity/battle/
  Which of many revolutionary battlefields should receive money for a museum to commemorate its historical significance? Your team

must decide which of several battles was most important in the Revolutionary War and should receive this money.

- **Searching for China**—
  http://www.kn.pacbell.com/wired/China/ChinaQuest.html
  What actions should the United States take in its policy toward China? Your team develops a group report that contains a three-point action plan. Team members assume roles as various experts and contribute information from their special perspectives focusing on business, culture, religion, human rights, the environment, and politics.
- **To Hunt or Not to Hunt?** —
  http://rhem.spschools.org/specialprojects/webquest/Webquest.html
  Using a balance of Internet and offline resources, your group will gather background information, then choose a role—Inuit hunter, animal protection activist, or environmental protection agent, and make a presentation explaining the issue from that point of view. After the presentations, your class will discuss the question and try to reach consensus. The follow-up is a choice of real-world activities such as writing to your congressional representative.
- **The Little Rock Nine**—
  http://www.kn.sbc.com/wired/BHM/little_rock/
  Using historical resources, information about previous solutions, and an exploration of the situation in their own community, students work in a group in order to answer the question, "What, if anything, should be done to racially desegregate U.S. schools?

Figure 6-6. Little Rock 9 WebQuest (http://www.kn.sbc.com/wired/BHM/little_rock/).

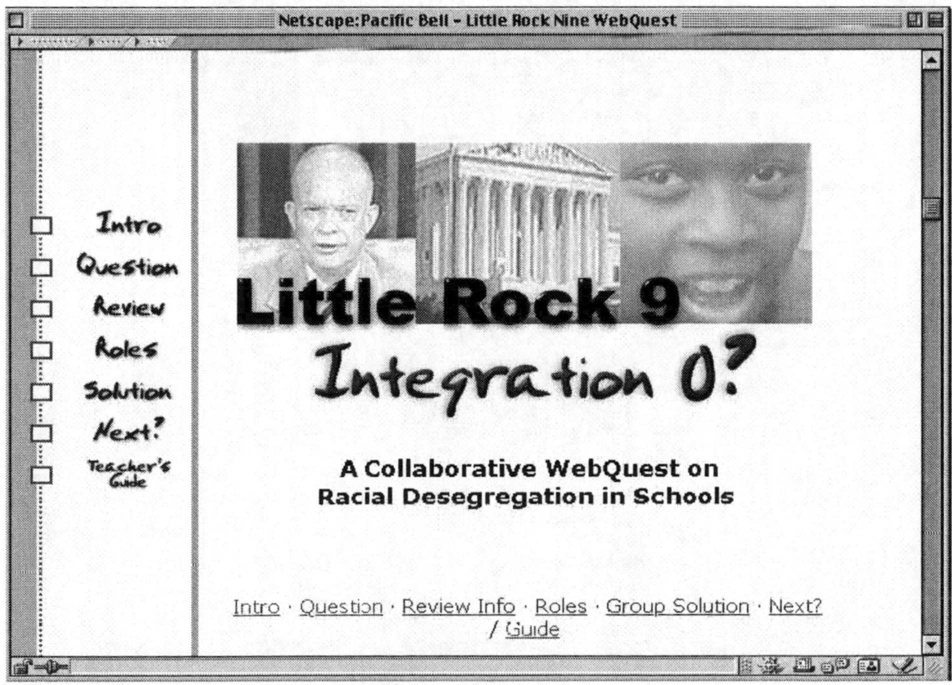

Using Individual Bookmark and Favorites Folders

You may face a challenge when you have an entire class doing Internet Inquiry with many individuals setting bookmarks or favorites (as they are called in Internet Explorer browsers). In a single computer classroom, your list of bookmarks will almost certainly become lengthy and confusing. Recent versions of most browsers allow you to solve this problem by making a separate bookmark/favorites folder for each student in your class. Below are brief descriptions of creating individual folders in Internet Explorer and Netscape. For specific information on your platform, select "Help" from your browser's menu and check the index or search box for managing or organizing folders.

You may face a challenge when an entire class does Internet Inquiry with many individuals setting bookmarks or favorites. Recent versions of most browsers allow you to solve this problem by making a separate folder for each student.

To make individual folders with Internet Explorer, go to the main menu item "Favorites" and click "New Folder." This adds a folder to the Favorites sidebar. Type in the name of a student. Repeat this procedure for each student in your class and you will have a Favorites window that looks similar to Figure 6-7

Now that you have a folder for each student, you will need to show them how to keep their folders organized. Each time a new favorites location is added by clicking "Add Page" from the main menu, it will be added to the end of the Favorites list. Remind students to open the Favorites window and then drag and drop their new sites into their own folder. In more recent versions of Internet Explorer, students may also be able to select their folder name from the list that appears in a dialog box. It might be helpful to cover this information in an Internet Workshop session.

Figure 6-7. An example of **Individual Favorites Folders** in Internet Explorer.

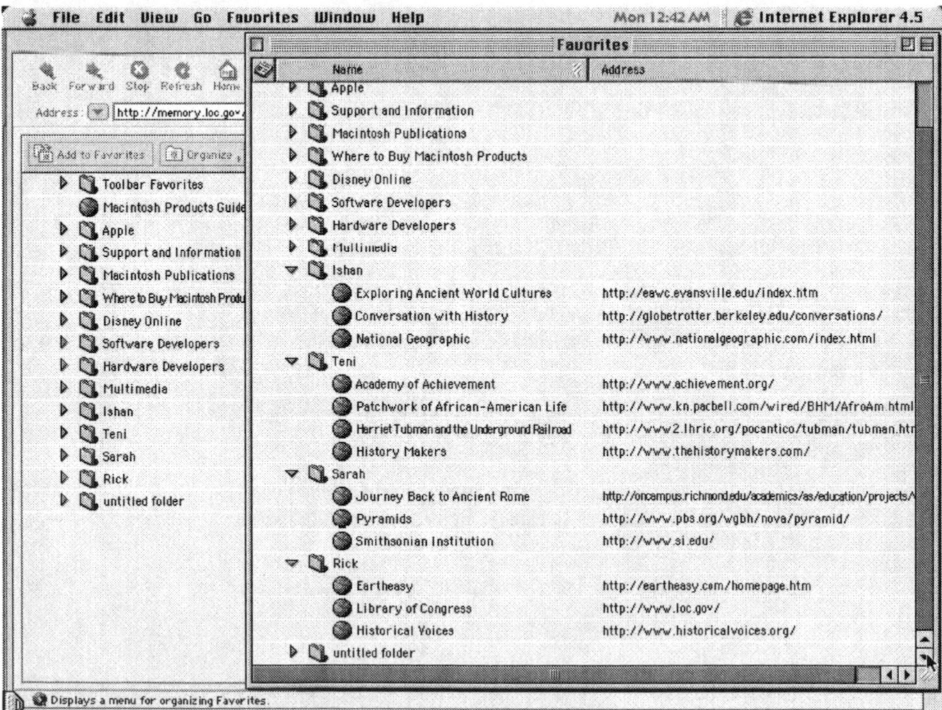

In Netscape, the process is similar. To make individual bookmark folders, click "Bookmarks" from the main menu. Select "Manage Bookmarks." This will open a separate window where you can select "New Folder." A window will then open asking you to name this new folder. Simply type in the name of a student and then select OK to close the window. Repeat this procedure for each student.

You will need to show students how to put items in their own folders and not one belonging to someone else. To bookmark a page to an individual folder, have the student select "Bookmarks" from the Navigator menu. Then click "File Bookmark." This will bring up a window showing the various folders. Have the student scroll through the list and then highlight his or her folder and click "OK." The bookmarked page will be put in that folder. You may wish to cover these procedures during an Internet Workshop session.

Projects and writing papers have always been a big part of social studies classes. The new technologies of the Internet make it easier than ever to find wonderful resources for completing these tasks. However, as always with this powerful tool, there is another side. It has also become easier to for students to just copy information and even whole papers from the Web. Audio and video images abound as well.

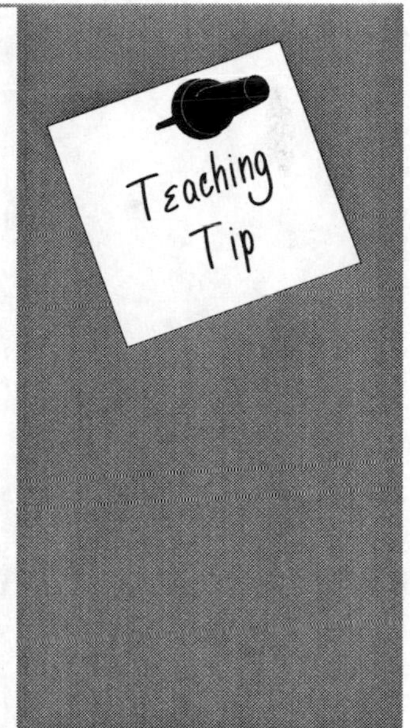

Copyright law and online citation forms have become an issue in most social studies classrooms. For a good overview, visit these sites:

- **Copyright and Fair Use in the Classroom, on the Internet and the World Wide Web**—(http://www.umuc.edu/library/copy.html)
- The **Columbia Guide to Online Citation**—(http://www.columbia.edu/cu/cup/cgos/idx_basic.html)
- **Plagiarism: What It is and How to Recognize and Avoid It**—(http://www.indiana.edu/~wts/wts/plagiarism.html).

You may also refer to the Using Copyrighted Materials section in Chapter 2 for additional information and related links.

Visiting the Classroom: David Cognetti's Social Studies Classes in New York

There are a number of great social studies resources available on the Internet. As we have seen, students can learn a lot by exploring directories and participating in projects. Closer to home, a great class website can be another good resource.

Mr. Cognetti's Homepage (http://www.watervilleschools.org/education/staff/staff.php?sectiondetailid=2037) is such a site for his eighth grade social studies students at Waterville Middle School in Waterville, New York (Figure 6-8). From his opening day PowerPoint presentation, to his photo album, to extra credit for pumpkin projects, students know they will be in for a good time.

The site is not all fun and games, however. One of the really great features of Mr. Cognetti's page are his links to DBQs. These are Data Based

Questions, related to the New York State Standards, which students must respond to by writing essays on standardized tests. Parents can link to the NY Standards site, as well as Parent Information and FAQs on these questions. Students can download sample essays and get inspired by a cool hamburger graphic that represents the elements of a good essay.

Other helpful study aids are a link to the New York State 8th Grade Test Prep site and Vocabulary Flashcards. These cards can be downloaded and printed out for students to study words and concepts from their assignments. There is also a Projects page with links to WebQuests and other projects the class has worked on.

There are links to all the pages in the website at the top and bottom of each webpage. This makes it quick and easy to find and get to the information you want.

There is an interesting "About Mr. Cognetti" page which includes some unusual photos. You can also find his mission statement with his goals for his students' learning—a somewhat unexpected, but great feature for any teacher's homepage. And don't forget to check out the **?????** link. As Mr. Cognetti says, "Believe it or not, sometimes questions get asked in class that I can't answer." But after doing some research, he posts the answers here.

One final point about the navigation of this site. There are links to all the pages in the website at the top and bottom of each webpage. This makes it quick and easy to find and get to the information you want without using the back button.

Figure 6-8. Mr. Cognetti's Social Studies Classroom Homepage
(http://www.watervilleschools.org/education/staff/staff.php?sectiondetailid=2037).

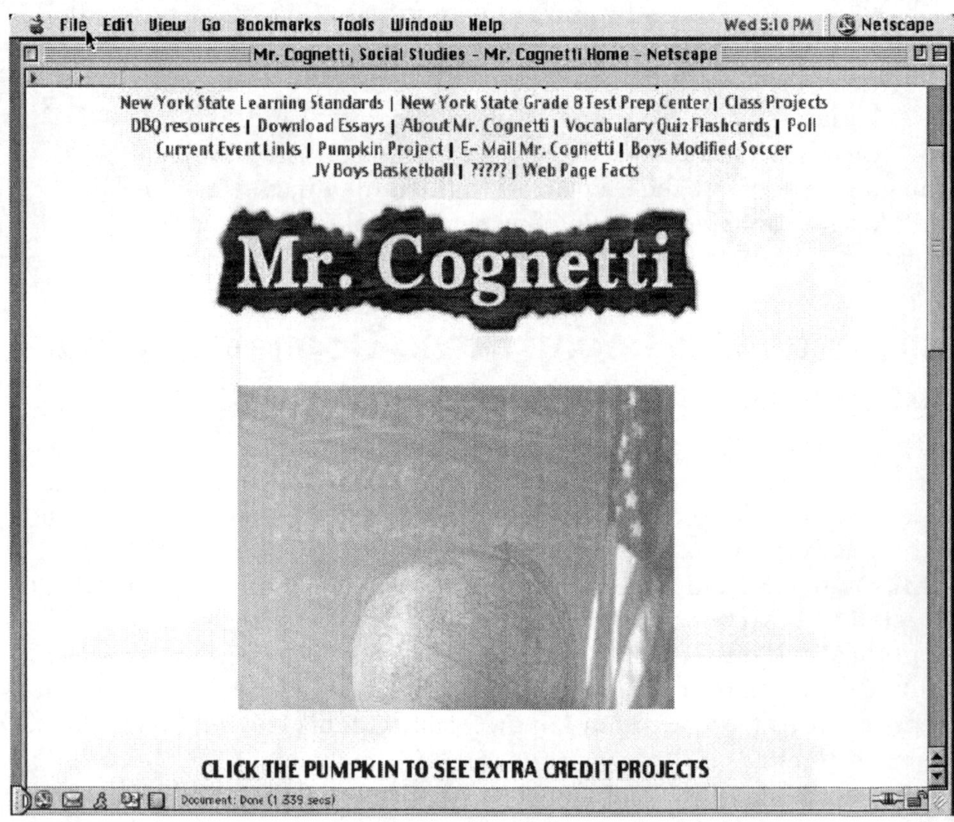

E-MAIL FOR YOU

From: Dave Cognetti (DCOGNETTI@watervilleschools.org)
Subject: My Social Studies Website

When I built a website for my 8th Grade Social Studies classes, I had two goals in mind: to enhance instruction and to promote better study skills and habits. By completing WebQuests and virtual tours on the Internet, students visit swebsites useful in the study of American History. These sites provide students with access to high quality digital images of photographs, paintings, political cartoons, and other primary source documents. The Internet also allows students to create in-depth projects that could not be done using pen and paper. Students feel a sense of accomplishment when their completed work is displayed on my classroom homepage.

Students can also utilize their computers as a study tool. I regularly update "electronic vocabulary flash cards" which can be made using Microsoft PowerPoint. These slides can be downloaded from any computer and provide students with an easy way to study their notes.

Another important function of the webpage is to keep parents informed. Both students and parents can access New York State curriculum guides and assessment test information. Parents are also encouraged to use the webpage link to email me with any questions or concerns that arise during the year.

Bringing the Internet into the classroom has broadened students' resources and provides them with the most up-to-date information available. In the process, learning has become a more enjoyable experience for the students and myself.

New Literacies in Social Studies

From our perspective, it is clear that effective use of the Internet should be integrated throughout the curriculum since students need many opportunities in all content areas to fully develop the new literacies necessary for success in an information society. Moreover, teaching new literacies as they are actually required in various content areas is more effective and efficient than having students learn them in isolated exercises.

The widespread increase of unreviewed information on the Internet makes it more important than ever that we teach our students how to evaluate information critically.

In the past, we relied on traditional information sources: newspapers, magazines, and books that were scrutinized by editors and publishers, and required sizable sums of money for mass production and distribution. In contrast, the open world of the Internet and new technologies such as weblog software make it possible for almost anyone to publish almost anything for a wide audience with little or no support from reviewers or bankers. This widespread increase of unreviewed information makes it more important than ever that we teach our students how to evaluate information critically.

The social studies classroom provides an especially rich environment for us to do this. Teachers have always focused on analysis and critical evaluation in traditional print environments; students have had to separate fact from opinion and support their positions with credible, reliable evidence as they discussed current events, debated public policy, and considered controversial issues. We need to help them develop this same critical disposition in the context of the Internet. But how can we do this?

We start by having students ask five basic questions, which we believe help them develop new insights and more critical awareness about the sites they visit:

- Who created the site?
- What is the purpose of the site?
- When was the site created?
- Where can I check the accuracy of this site's information?
- How will the information at this site be shaped by the stance of the site's creator and sponsors?

You can find a more detailed discussion of these questions along with strategies for evaluating websites and the information they contain in the Reading with a Critical Eye section of Chapter 2. This section also includes locations of online sites to help develop critical evaluation skills.

If you are interested in preparing your own lessons on this topic, especially for use with secondary students, these additional sites may be helpful:

- **Evaluating Webpages: Links to Examples of Various Concepts**—http://www2.widener.edu/Wolfgram-Memorial-Library/webevaluation/examples.htm

  This site offers a conceptual approach to website evaluation with links to many examples.
- **Evaluating Webpages: Techniques to Apply and Questions to Ask**—http://www.lib.berkeley.edu/TeachingLib/Guides/Internet/Evaluate.html

  This site focuses on various techniques, in addition to following a checklist, for evaluating webpages and the information they contain.
- **Evaluating Websites: Criteria for the Classroom**—http://www.lesley.edu/library/guides/research/evaluating_web.html

  A lot of information, including links to seemingly authentic sites that are actually hoaxes.
- **The Good, the Bad, & the Ugly or Why It's a Good Idea to Evaluate Web Sources**—http://lib.nmsu.edu/instruction/eval.html

  This site has a good bibliography as well as links to example sites illustrating various points on the checklist.
- **Thinking Critically About Discipline-Based World Wide Web Resources**—http://www.library.ucla.edu/libraries/college/help/critical/discipline. htm

  This site includes questions on website structure and appropriateness for specific disciplines. Also visit its companion site **Thinking Critically About World Wide Web Resources** (http://www.library.ucla.edu/libraries/ college/help/critical/index.htm).

Following the suggestions and using information at the sites above should lead you and your students to sites that are reliable and suitable for your purposes. Occasionally, however, even after careful evaluation, you may find sites that appear to fulfill all the right criteria, but are actually misleading or even fraudulent. Some of these sites may be parodies or hoaxes meant as jokes. Others are promoting hidden agendas, as may be the case at sites sponsored by hate groups. Many of these sites do an excellent job of camouflaging their true origin and intent, and even experienced Internet users may be fooled initially.

The topics covered by these sites often relate to social studies areas such as civil rights, historic events, and famous people. Especially for older students, lessons built around these questionable sites can be very instructive. An excellent source of additional information and ready-made lesson plans is the **Media Awareness Network** (http://www.media-awareness.ca/). This outstanding site from Canada can be read in English or French. It has a wealth of information for teachers and parents on developing critical awareness towards all kinds of media and advertising. Click on Teachers to search their free downloadable plans, and be sure to check out the Web Awareness for Teachers section. **Teaching Zack to Think** (http://www.media-awareness.ca/english/resources/educational/handouts/internet/teaching_zack.cfm) is an especially effective lesson that points out telling words and offers tips for double checking a site that appears genuine. Do a search for "Zack" on their site to avoid typing the long URL.

The Internet provides myriad resources for social studies education, but as with any tool, we must know how to use it, and we must help our students learn to use it wisely and safely.

The Internet provides myriad resources for social studies education, but as with any tool, we must know how to use it, and we should help our students learn to use it wisely and safely.

Additional Social Studies Resources on the Internet

Academy of Achievement—http://www.achievement.org/

An outstanding online "museum" with exhibits on achievers from all walks of society. It includes the achievers' profiles, biographies, and online interviews available as text or with audio/video. Student Materials and teacher facilitation guides, mostly for Grades 7–12, but some materials for Grades 3–6 as well. Visit Steps to Success to see and hear quotes from well-known people on topics such as vision, integrity, and courage.

Adbusters: Culturejammers Headquarters—
http://www.adbusters. org/home/

A location to help your middle school and high school students develop critical media literacy insights about the commercial world around them.

American Cultural History—
http://kclibrary.nhmccd.edu/decades.html

A series of web guides to the decades of the 20th century. Basic facts and photos as well as guides on areas such as art, fashion, education, music, and events.

American Experience—http://www.pbs.org/wgbh/amex/

An excellent site related to the PBS series. Contains teacher sections, including guides for using the programs in class, as well as archives for information and materials on past programs.

American Presidents Life Portraits—
http://www.americanpresidents.org/

A companion site to C-Span's TV series. This site contains presidential biographies, important events of each presidency, presidential places, and references. Teacher guides, lesson plans, and video clips make this a very useful site.

Ben's Guide to U.S. Government for Kids—http://bensguide.gpo.gov/
A guide for students, teachers, and parents. Organized by grade level. Includes links to many U.S. government sites. Also includes information on getting and using documents from the Government Printing Office.

Contacting the Congress—http://www.visi.com/juan/congress/
Use this location to quickly send any of the members of the U.S. Congress an email message about your concerns. It may also be used to request information for units you are planning.

Conversations with History—
http://globetrotter.berkeley.edu/conversations/
Read or view (with streaming video) this series of unedited interviews with distinguished men and women from around the world, produced by the Institute of International Studies at the University of California at Berkeley. You can search for interviews by name, topic, or year. This site also has information on CWS—Connecting Students to the World, a program designed to increase collaboration between UCB and other educational institutions.

Cybrary of the Holocaust—http://remember.org/
This is an incredibly extensive cyber library of resources for individuals wishing to study the Holocaust. Audio interviews from survivors, written recollections by survivors, works of literature, images, and a wide array of resources depict this dark period in history.

The Early American Review—http://earlyamerica.com/review/
An online journal on the people, issues, and events of eighteenth-century America. A wonderful scholarly resource for high school students in an American history course.

Exploring Ancient World Cultures—
http://eawc.evansville.edu/index.htm
This location consists of "an introductory, on-line, college-level 'textbook' of ancient world cultures, constructed around a series of cultural pages consisting of: The Ancient Near East, Ancient India, Ancient Egypt, Ancient China, Ancient Greece, Ancient Rome, Early Islam, and Medieval Europe." The site contains an anthology, chronology, essays, maps, and an interactive quiz for each of the cultures.

First Gov for Kids—http://www.kids.gov/
An excellent directory from the government's Federal Citizen Information Center. Organized by topics, including Global Village, Careers, History, Money, Arts, and many more. Also includes a scavenger hunt. Many sites are suitable for younger students.

Free Federal Resources for Educational Excellence—
http://www.ed.gov/free/index.html
ED.gov's link to free resources, sorted by topic and with a featured site of the week.

Harriet Tubman and the Underground Railroad—
http://www2.lhric.org/pocantico/tubman/tubman.html
Designed by students in a second grade class, this site includes a timeline, a quiz, character sketches, and crossword puzzles about Harriet

Tubman. Also included are activity ideas for incorporating the content into the classroom as part of an interactive lesson plan.

The History Makers—http://www.thehistorymakers.com/

An oral history archive dedicated to preserving African American history. This site also includes photos and text and features history makers in areas such as business, civics, education, entertainment, and style.

Historical Voices—http://www.historicalvoices.org/

As they say, "a rich set of both online exhibits and educational curricula, utilizing audio files as a key component of these resources." Includes various galleries of speeches, interviews, and audio versions of events. An excellent section on teaching with audio clips.

Infonation—http://www.cyberschoolbus.un.org/infonation/info.asp

This site allows you to view and compare statistical data for all United Nations member states.

Journey Back in Time to Ancient Rome—
http://oncampus.richmond.edu/academics/as/education/projects/webquests/rome/frames.html

A WebQuest intended for upper elementary and middle school students using a jigsaw approach. Students use teamwork and the Internet to explore Ancient Rome and learn about daily life, myths, and government. Each person on the team learns one piece of the puzzle and then comes back together to get a better understanding of the topic.

Just for Teachers—http://www.ed.gov/teachers/landing.jhtml

ED.gov's site for educational resources including links to government documents, 30,000 lesson ideas, and reports and readings for teachers.

Letters Home from an Iowa Soldier in the Civil War—
http://www.civilwarletters.com/home.html

These letters home bring to life the struggles of a country and the experiences of an individual. Nice primary source documents for the study of U.S. History. Lesson ideas are included.

My Hero—http://myhero.com/home.asp

This site for elementary and middle school students allows you to read about heroes, many of whom come from history, and submit your own stories. These heroes can be famous individuals or parents. Step-by-step instructions are listed at the site.

National Council for History Education—
http://www.history.org/nche/

A non-profit organization for promoting history in schools and society. Click their history file and resources links to visit related sites. Also contains archives for their newsletter, "History Matters."

National Council for Social Studies—http://www.ncss.org

Many excellent sources and resources for teachers, organized by the ten themes of the Curriculum Standards for Social Studies. Visit the **Standards** page (http://www.ncss.org/standards/teachers/vol1/home.shtml), tpp.

National Geographic Society Homepage—
http://www.nationalgeographic.com/main.html

The homepage of the National Geographic Society provides a wealth of information for students related the programming and books of this to organization. Within the site is a great location (http://magma.national geographic.com/education/index.cfm) for lesson ideas on geography, an area of the curriculum that is often neglected. Also located at this site are maps that may be printed out by students for reports.

Nova Online/Pyramids: The Inside Story—
http://www.pbs.org/wgbh/nova/pyramid/
Take a guided tour inside the great pyramids of Giza, read about the history of these magnificent wonders, share the recent discoveries of archeologists, and come away with a new appreciation for the accomplishments of this ancient civilization. A great site for any class studying ancient Egypt.

Oddon's The Fascinating World of Maps and Mapping—
http://oddens.geog.uu.nl/index.html
Search for online maps, find resources for buying paper maps, or browse Oden's Bookmarks for maps and other resources by country.

Our Documents—http://www.ourdocuments.gov/
This government source has links to primary source documents, special features, tools for teachers, and a news and events link. Be sure to visit their Related Resources for links to other excellent sites.

Oyez: U.S. Supreme Court Multimedia—
http://www.oyez.org/oyez/frontpage
Listen to over 2,000 hours of audio recordings from the Supreme Court. This includes all audio since 1995 with some selections from previous years. Check out the tour of the Supreme Court Building.

Patchwork of African American Life—
http://www.kn.sbc.com/wired/BHM/AfroAm.html
This exceptional site contains six separate resources for the study of African-American issues: a hotlist of links to important resources on the Internet, an interactive treasure hunt, a subject sampler, a WebQuest on the Little Rock 9, a WebQuest on the Tuskegee Tragedy, and a video conference.

The Smithsonian Homepage—http://www.si.edu/
The Smithsonian Institution calls itself "The nation's treasure house for learning." This site certainly does it justice. Many outstanding links to the wonderful resources of this fine institution.

Stately Knowledge—http://www.ipl.org/div/kidspace/stateknow/
From the Kidspace section of the Internet Public Library. Facts, information, and a map of every state. Also a quiz on state capitals.

Treasures—http://www.bl.uk/collections/treasures/digitisation.html
The British Library's site of digitized "treasures." It contains a limited number of documents at this time, but fascinating primary material such as the Gutenberg Bible and Leonardo's Notebook make this site worth a visit.

The White House for Kids—http://www.whitehouse.gov/
Click on Kids to take a tour, find out about holidays, and "meet" the presidents and first ladies.

World Gen Web—http://www.rootsweb.com/~wgwkids/
A good place for students to begin exploring genealogy and family roots.

Online Communities for Social Studies

GEOGED

Geography Education List
Subscription: listserv@ukcc.uky.edu

H-HIGH-S

A mailing list for high school of social studies teachers. Their homepage contains a nice list of resources and links to members' webpages.
Subscription address: LISTSERV@H-NET.MSU.EDU
Homepage: http://www.h-net.org/~highs/
Discussion Logs: http://h-net.msu.edu/cgi-bin/logbrowse.pl?trx=lm&list=H-High-S

H-Net Discussion Networks

This webpage contains links to the homepages for many mailing lists in social studies.
Homepage: http://www2.h-net.msu.edu/lists/

MEMORIES

This listserv allows students to talk with survivors of World War II.
Subscription address: listserv@maelstrom.stjohns.edu
Archives: http://maelstrom.stjohns.edu/archives/memories.html

NCSS Discussion Board

The Instructional Technology Committee of the National Council for the Social Studies has established this listserv for interested Internet users to share information and ideas about social studies education in grades K–12 and in teacher education.
Homepage: http://databank.ncss.org/index.php?topic=discussion

TAMHA

Teaching American History (TAMHA) is a list for American History teachers to ask questions, share tips, and discuss issues.
Subscription address: LISTSERV@LISTS.WAYNE.EDU
Archives: http://lists.wayne.edu/archives/tamha.html

7 Science: Using the Internet to Support Scientific Thinking

Science education is not just about learning facts. At its core, science education helps students to think scientifically. This means helping them to ask questions and seek logical answers through observation, reading, writing, and critical analysis. As noted in the **National Science Education Standards** (http://stills.nap.edu/html/nses/), science education needs to provide both a "hands on" and a "minds on" experience. It is essential that we prepare each of our students to think scientifically if we hope to provide them with the futures they deserve.

Thinking scientifically also includes the use of new literacies. Developing the new literacies required by the Internet and other ICT provides access to exciting demonstrations of scientific principles, scientists who are willing to answer students' questions about their research, ongoing scientific studies in which students may participate, and much more. The Internet also provides listservs and bulletin boards on the teaching of science in which you may obtain valuable ideas to bring to your classroom and lesson plans to help you with your science teaching. Certainly, the Internet provides you and your students with resources right at your fingertips that have never before been available.

It is essential that we prepare each of our students to think scientifically if we hope to provide them with the futures they deserve.

Some teachers lack confidence about their ability to teach in this area. Approached from the proper perspective, however, science education can become the center of every classroom as you use it to integrate language arts, math, social studies, and other subject areas. Each of us needs to help our students in this area, even if our primary teaching responsibility is not in science education.

After reading this chapter, you should be able to:

1. Identify your favorite directory in science, one that provides you with the best resources on the Internet for immediate use with Internet Workshop and other instructional frameworks.
2. Locate at least two Internet projects in science that allow your students to gather data, analyze the results, and draw conclusions.

3. Locate at least three webquests that you can use in your classroom science program this year.
4. Design a unit with Internet Inquiry that includes the use of workshop sessions and Student-to-Student activities.

Teaching with the Internet: Anne Miller's Class

As her fifth grade class completed the beginning activities on their first day of school, Anne wrote this word in big, bold, capital letters: SETI. Next to it she wrote: http://setiaathome.ssl.berkeley.edu

Over the summer, Anne had discovered an exciting science project on the Internet, called ***SETI@Home****.*

"Here's a new word for us this year," she said. "Has anyone ever heard of this?"

She heard murmurs: "It's a website."

"The Internet? Cool!"

"That's right," she said. "It's on the Internet and 'SETI' stands for these words."

Next to SETI, Anne wrote: Search for Extraterrestrial Intelligence.

"You know what 'Search' means and you know what 'Intelligence' means. Now how about this word, 'Extraterrestrial?'"

"Is it a new search engine?" Meghan suggested tentatively.

"Outer space," announced Narita. "It means outer space. It was in the movie 'Contact' with Jodie Foster. She looked for radio signals coming from people in outer space . . ."

Over the summer, Anne had discovered an exciting science project on the Internet, called **SETI@Home** (http://setiathome.ssl.berkeley.edu). This project allows anyone with an Internet computer to participate with the research team in searching our galaxy for radio signals from intelligent life. Initially funded by the National Science Foundation, and now run by a private foundation, this project uses the enormous radio telescope in Arecibo, Puerto Rico to collect radio signals from outer space. These signals are sent to the University of California, Berkeley and then passed on the SETI@home site for analysis. Anyone with a computer can download a program that regularly analyzes a small portion of these radio signals for patterns indicating intelligent life.

Several million desktop computers around the world automatically receive packets with radio data, process these radio signals, and send the results back to the project headquarters over the Internet. Much of this work takes place at night while people leave their computers on but do not use them.

The program uses a screen saver that automatically picks up new data from the SETI Institute and conducts the analysis. It shows the results of each computer's SETI analysis in a continuously changing graph and results page. When it has completed the analysis, the results are sent back to the Institute over the Internet and new data is acquired for additional analysis.

By harnessing millions of desktop computers, this project can analyze far more data than it could ever hope to analyze with a single, large computer; there simply isn't a computer large enough to keep up with the data. This creative project distributes the workload to all of the participating computers around the world. It follows the traditional adage, "Many hands, make light work." Distributing work like this ends up being a far more efficient a way to accomplish complex tasks.

You may download the screensaver software from the **SETI@home** site (http://setiathome.ssl.berkeley.edu). It is an exciting new way to conduct rescarch.

"Just think of it," Anne said to her class. "If our computer discovers a signal from outer space, we will be on TV and in all of the newspapers. Everyone will recognize you as the kids who discovered life in outer space."

That brief introduction served to inspire Anne's students throughout the rest of the year. They were scientists, doing important work on their computer over the Internet.

Her class sat for a moment thinking about this. Very quickly, they started firing questions right and left to Anne.

"You mean we can really see if there is a message from space?"

"How do we know if we found a signal?"

"I'm gonna tell my sister about this."

"We'll be famous!"

That brief introduction served to inspire Anne's students throughout the rest of the year. They were scientists, doing important work on their computer over the Internet. Every morning, her students wanted to check the overnight results. The local newspaper even printed a story about their work.

Figure 7-1. SETI@Home (http://setiathome.ssl.berkeley.edu) provides a screen saver that allows you to search for radio signals from intelligent life outside our solar system. The project is available to anyone with an Internet computer.

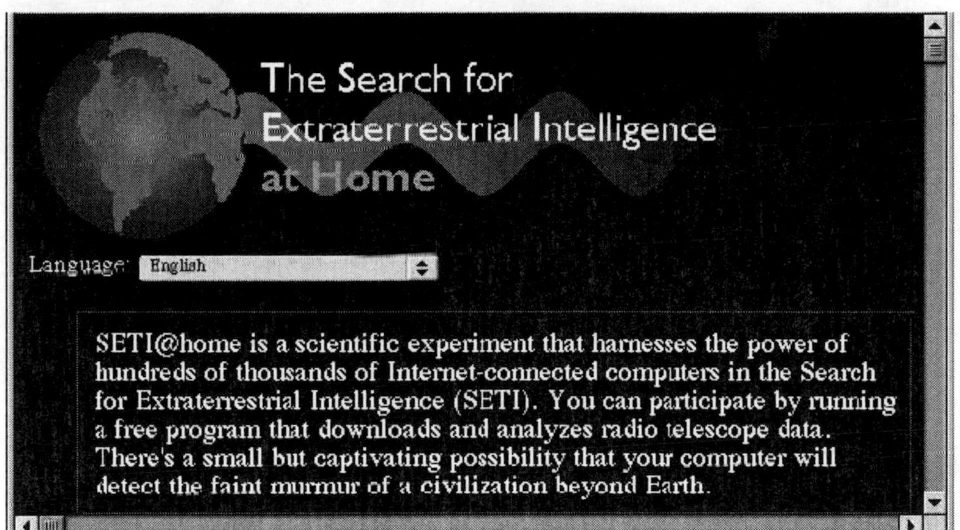

Anne's year included many other important experiences with their single Internet computer in her classroom. They corresponded by email with other students around the world who were also analyzing SETI@home signals. This led to the development of several Internet projects. One consisted of evaluating the quality of stream water at each location, comparing the results each class obtained, and then exchanging ideas for action they could each take to improve water quality at their location. They even used iSight video cameras (http://www.apple.com/isight/) along with iChat AV software and held video conferences with their partner classes once a week in the spring. This allowed them to compare their work on different streams as they held video conferences with classrooms in France and Canada. The video conferences helped each class to better understand the cultural context and the political realities that existed in each country. It was also great fun as they actually got to see students with whom they had been emailing.

They even used iSight video cameras along with iChat AV software and held video conferences with their partner classes once a week in the spring.

Her class also completed a unit on the solar system with integrated language arts experiences by reading *This Planet has No Atmosphere* by Paula Danzinger and *A Wrinkle in Time* by Madeleine L'Engle. She created links at their classroom homepage for **Journey to Mars** (http://www.exploratorium.edu/mars/index.html), the **Mars Exploration** program, (http://marsprogram.jpl.nasa.gov/), **The Nine Planets Tour** (http://seds.lpl.arizona.edu/billa/tnp/), and **the Hubble Space Telescope Site** (http://hubblesite.org/). Her class had followed the work of the scientific teams directing several Rovers that landed on Mars during the winter. They also viewed live webcasts from Mars team scientists who were right in the middle of their discoveries. Anne developed several short Internet Workshop assignments for students to complete at these locations. She also monitored several online communities for science educators, following the conversations to see if she could get additional ideas for her class. One of these conversations mentioned the **National Standards for Science Education** and gave the URL for this document (http://www.nap.edu/readingroom/books/nses/html/). She explored this site and its links, learning about the national standards for science, getting several useful ideas, especially the concept of science as inquiry.

Over a holiday break, Anne discovered the location for **NASA Quest** (http://quest.arc.nasa.gov/index.html), a wonderful site with opportunities for her students to work directly with the men and women scientists at NASA. From here, she located a number of free curriculum materials and activities for her class to complete.

Toward the end of the year Anne decided to try Internet Inquiry with cooperative group science projects. Students worked in groups of twos and threes to identify an important scientific question. Then they used the Internet and their school library to try to discover the answer. Workshop sessions twice a week seemed to really help students on their inquiry projects. More importantly, however, Anne used these to facilitate the exchange of new literacies that each student was developing. The best search engine strategies were shared as well as ways to critically evaluate information that they found on the Internet. At the end of the unit, the class held a science fair with each group setting up a poster session describing their question, their work, and what they had discovered. Each of her students also developed a Student-to-Student activity. Every student had to complete at least five of the Student-to-Student activities.

Tyronne and Alex completed one of the inquiry projects. Both of them had been interested in the ant farm Anne had brought into the classroom after the winter holidays. They were fascinated by the continuous activity of these insects. The question they wanted to answer in their Internet Inquiry was "Do ants ever sleep?" When they shared this question during a workshop session, other students had all kinds of suggestions. They could check in the library for books about insects. They could check on the Internet by doing a search with one of the search engines for "ants" and "sleep." Someone also gave them the URL for **The Mad Scientist Network**, a place on the Internet where they could ask a scientist this question (http://www.madsci.org/). And, someone else suggested that they mark one ant and watch it for 24 hours to see if it ever stopped moving and actually slept. The idea of staying up all night caught their attention and they pleaded with Anne to take the class ant farm home over the weekend. She finally relented and, after they selected one ant, "Hooty," and marked him with a non-toxic marker. Anne dropped the ant farm off at Alex's house Friday after school.

Tyronne and Alex made observations every 15 minutes in their science journal for an entire day and through the night. They concluded that Hooty never stopped to take a rest or stopped working. They found other information on the Internet suggesting that ants might rest, especially during colder weather when some species hibernate. They concluded that Hooty didn't sleep because it had been warm inside all night. They even took some pictures for their poster session at the science fair. They created a wonderful poster that presented all of their work. It included photos, a written report describing their research, and the conclusions they reached. They also included the email message in Figure 7-2 from a scientist in Australia. They were pleased they had figured out a way to answer their question using a method that even the adult scientist had not considered.

They were pleased they had figured out a way to answer their question using a method that even the adult scientist had not considered.

Figure 7-2. The response (http://www.madsci.org/posts/archives/dec96/841965056.Zo.r.html) to Tyronne and Alex's message from an Australian scientist on the **Mad Scientist Network** (http://www.madsci.org).

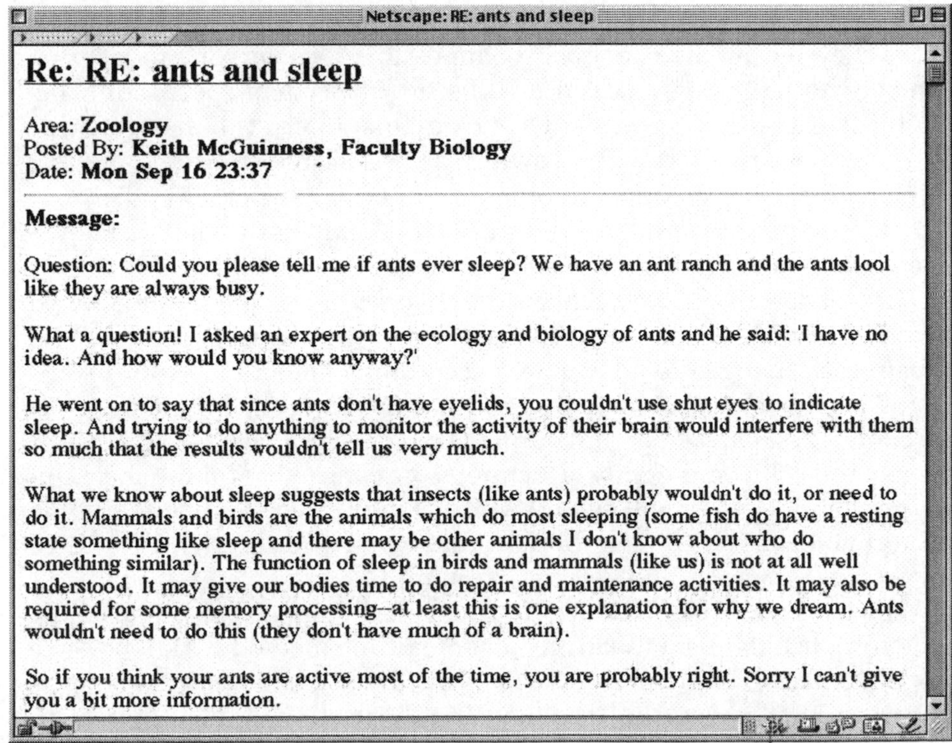

Netscape: RE: ants and sleep

Re: RE: ants and sleep

Area: **Zoology**
Posted By: **Keith McGuinness, Faculty Biology**
Date: **Mon Sep 16 23:37**

Message:

Question: Could you please tell me if ants ever sleep? We have an ant ranch and the ants lool like they are always busy.

What a question! I asked an expert on the ecology and biology of ants and he said: 'I have no idea. And how would you know anyway?'

He went on to say that since ants don't have eyelids, you couldn't use shut eyes to indicate sleep. And trying to do anything to monitor the activity of their brain would interfere with them so much that the results wouldn't tell us very much.

What we know about sleep suggests that insects (like ants) probably wouldn't do it, or need to do it. Mammals and birds are the animals which do most sleeping (some fish do have a resting state something like sleep and there may be other animals I don't know about who do something similar). The function of sleep in birds and mammals (like us) is not at all well understood. It may give our bodies time to do repair and maintenance activities. It may also be required for some memory processing--at least this is one explanation for why we dream. Ants wouldn't need to do this (they don't have much of a brain).

So if you think your ants are active most of the time, you are probably right. Sorry I can't give you a bit more information.

That year, many new worlds opened to Anne's class through the exciting experiences with science and the Internet. A number of students announced they were now going to become scientists. It had been a very productive year.

Lessons from the Classroom

This story from Anne Miller's classroom has several important lessons for each of us to consider. One of the most important lessons comes from the **SETI@Home** project (http://setiathome.ssl.berkeley.edu). This project vividly demonstrates the power of distributed work—distributing a complex task among many people who accomplish small parts of the larger activity. Distributing work among many different people will be a central aspect of our future in a world of networked information resources. A parallel notion, distributed learning, will exist in our classrooms with the Internet. The notion of distributed learning is a powerful one to consider.

An important aspect of new literacies within a world of distributed learning, is that sometimes students are literate in a new literacy while their teacher is not.

Distributed learning, however, only takes place if students in your class have acquired the new literacies of the Internet and other ICT and can effectively use the powerful information resources that are now becoming available to them. Using email and iSight video conferencing with students around the world, as Anne's class studied water quality, was just one example of how new literacies became important in her classroom. There were many others.

An important aspect of new literacies within a world of distributed learning is that sometimes students are literate in a new literacy while their teacher is not. Most of us first see this change when we have students in our classroom who begin assisting us when our computer freezes, when the printer isn't working, or when something else fails. Suddenly, a student's expertise in new literacies becomes visible and critical to our classroom's success. As digital technologies become more important to our classrooms and as they repeatedly change, it is impossible for everyone to keep up with everything taking place. You will see each student specializing, becoming an expert in a particular technology that interests him or her. One child might be an expert with knowing the best search strategies, another with email techniques, and still others will become experts in other new literacies. We need to develop strategies for making this distributed knowledge about new literacies accessible to everyone in our class.

This change, by the way, reflects the changes taking place in the world of work today. The highly structured and top-down model of business and industry has changed to a far more decentralized model in order to successfully compete in a highly competitive global economy. Nimble, aggressive companies that take advantage of individual employee's expertise will survive; inflexible and tightly structured companies that ignore their employees' special talents will fail in a world of rapidly changing information and technology. Thus, it is important that we prepare students for these new worlds of literacy and life-long learning.

Which teaching methods help us to achieve this goal? Workshop activities accomplish this better than any other teaching method we know. Anne took advantage of workshop sessions, both within Internet Workshop as well as during the workshop sessions that she used with Internet Inquiry.

During these workshop sessions, she invited students to share their new literacies as well as their developing knowledge about particular content. This served to support students as they developed both new literacies and new dimensions of content area knowledge. The class learned new search strategies, new ways of critically evaluating information, and many more important lessons. This is what Internet Workshop accomplishes.

Another important lesson we learn from Anne's class is that the Internet provides many helpful resources to assist you in developing an exciting and dynamic science program in your classroom, a program consistent with the National Science Education Standard's emphasis on thinking scientifically through inquiry. The Internet facilitates scientific thinking as you develop important domain knowledge in science.

The Internet provides many helpful resources that can assist you in developing an exciting and dynamic science program in your classroom, a program consistent with the National Science Education Standard's emphasis on thinking scientifically through inquiry.

This additional lesson is also clear—Internet projects are a powerful way of helping your students to think scientifically as they work collaboratively with others to gather data and interpret the results. Working with other classrooms around the world provided Anne's students with an exciting and authentic science experience. They learned much about this special way of looking at the world.

Finally, Anne's class also demonstrates how Internet Inquiry is an excellent instructional framework as you develop a science-as-inquiry program in your classroom. Tyronne and Alex learned what scientific work was like through their experiment and their conversation with a scientist in Australia. Science is as much a verb as it is a noun. Having students identify questions they wish to answer and then helping them to develop techniques for answering their questions is important in preparing students who not only *know* science but also *do* science.

Directories for Science Education

There are a number of outstanding directories on the Internet for science education. These provide a well-organized array of links to useful curricular resources in science education with ready-to-go instructional activities, locations for Internet projects, resources for Internet Inquiry, webquests, ideas for science demonstrations, lesson plans, and other resources for your classroom. These directories will be useful as you plan your science education program.

If you only have time to visit one directory, pay a visit to the **Eisenhower National Clearinghouse for Mathematics and Science Education** (http://www.enc.org). This federally funded project provides K–12 teachers with the best online source of information on mathematics and science education, linked to national standards. It now provides five different ways to quickly locate links to important resources for your class: Classroom Calendar, Digital Dozen, ENC Focus, Lessons and Activities, and Ask ENC. Links to these areas are located at the top of the site so they are easy to find.

The **Classroom Calendar** (http://www.enc.org/features/calendar/) provides links to topically organized resources for science education. The **Digital Dozen** (http://www.enc.org/features/dd/) provides you with the twelve best sites found on the Internet that month for math and science education. Clicking on **ENC Focus** (http://www.enc.org/features/focus/) provides you with links each week to a new topic for your class. **Lessons and**

Activities (http://www.enc.org/features/lessonplans/) gives you a traditional directory of instructional links to math and science topics. If none of these great resources provide you with exactly what you need, just select **Ask ENC** (http://www.enc.org/features/ask/) and direct a question to the talented experts at the Clearinghouse. They will reply promptly and point you to great standards-based resources for your class. Clearly, this Internet location is of tremendous utility as you seek to use the Internet to improve your classroom science program. Set a bookmark!

Figure 7-3. The **Lessons & Activities** page (http://www.enc.org/features/lessonplans/) at the **Eisenhower National Clearinghouse for Mathematics and Science Education** (http://www.enc.org/), an outstanding directory for science education.

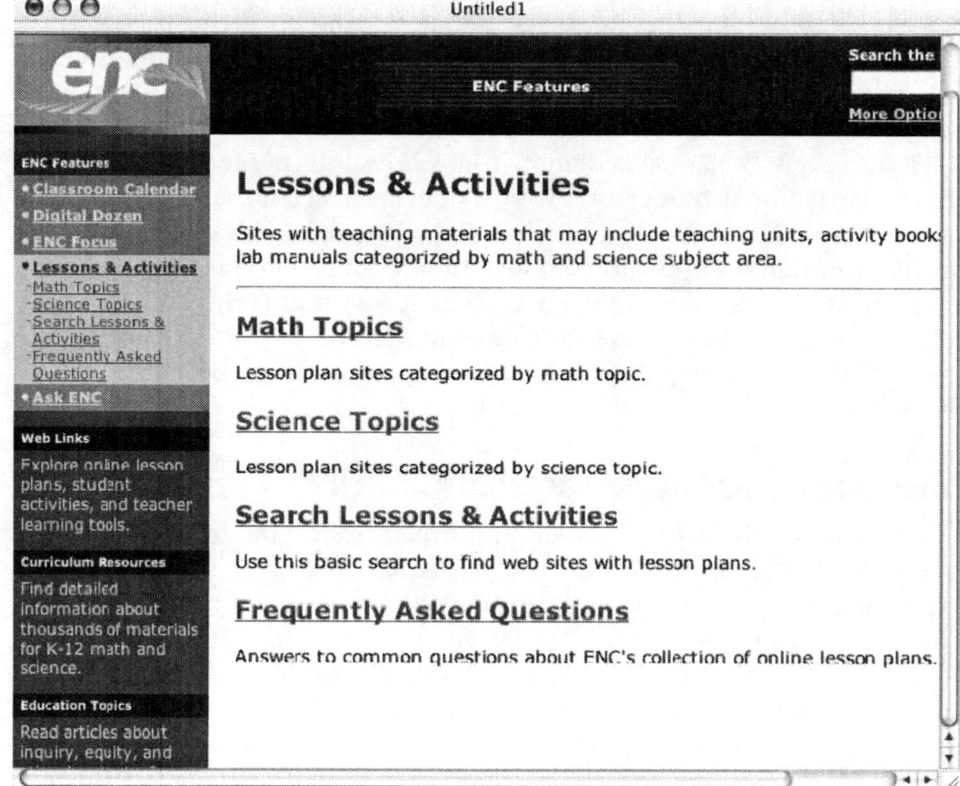

A second useful directory in science is the National Science Teachers Association's **Science Websites** (http://www.nsta.org/main/sciencesites/). This location provides links to useful science sites that have been recommended by members and organized by area. You may also make a recommendation of your own.

You should also visit the directory for science in the United Kingdom organized by the British Broadcasting Service, **Science** (http://www.bbc.co.uk/science/). This location contains many interactive resources using Flash and Shockwave technologies. It also contains links back to a more general directory in education that is organized by age level, **Schools** (http://www.bbc.co.uk/schools/).

Another site to use as a jumping off point is **Frank Potter's Science Gems** (http://www.sciencegems.com/). Though it now has become a commercial site, this resource contains over 14,000 links to outstanding science resources on the Web. What is especially nice about this location is that resources are organized by science area (e.g., Physical Science, Earth Science, Life Science, etc.) and by topic within each area (e.g., within Earth Science there are locations for measurement, earth, solar system, astronomy, atmosphere, land/oceans, and natural resources). Each topic is also organized by grade level. The organizational scheme used at this site allows you to quickly find resources for your class.

Teachers often use demonstrations to catch students' interest and get them to think scientifically. There are a number of useful directories on the Internet with demonstrations to illustrate scientific principles. One location with exciting demonstrations is **Whelmers** (http://www.mcrel.org/whelmers/). Developed by Steven Jacobs, these demonstrations catch students by surprise and get them to really think about physical principles. Each is aligned with the National Science Education Standards.

Demonstrations, such as those found at **The Exploratorium Science Snackbook** (http://www.exploratorium.edu/publications/Snackbook/Snackbook.html) provide a wonderful way to catch the attention of even your most reluctant young scientist. These activities are usually simple things that you can do in the classroom to demonstrate a scientific principle and get your students thinking like scientists. A useful idea is to conduct a demonstration, engage students in a discussion about what they see happening, and then send them off on an Internet Workshop activity, using a search engine to locate more information about the principle you have just demonstrated. Have them share what they discovered during a short workshop session the next day or at the end of the week.

Keeping It Simple: Using Internet Workshop

Internet Workshop is a good way to begin using the Internet in your classroom for science education. Internet Workshop assignments are easy to set up and require minimum navigation knowledge by either you or your students. Locate a site on the Internet with content related to your science unit, perhaps by using one of the directories described above, and set a bookmark for this location. Next, develop a thoughtful activity that requires students to use the information at the site. Then, assign the activity to your students to complete during the week. Finally, share your experiences during a workshop session.

Internet Workshop assignments may be developed from resources located at outstanding science museums around the world.

In addition to using directories such as the **Eisenhower National Clearinghouse for Mathematics and Science Education** (http://www.enc.org/), Internet Workshop assignments may be developed from resources located at outstanding science museums around the world. These place many of their displays online, provide exciting simulations, demonstrations, or science puzzles for students. By developing appropriate Internet Workshop assignments, you can engage your students in important scientific thinking related to national or state standards as they travel the world, visiting the very best science museums.

A good place to begin is **Try Science** (http://www.tryscience.org/), a great resource with links to an exceptional collection of activities, live web cams, and science museums around the world. You might also visit the **Science Learning Network** (http://www.sln.org/), another directory for museums and science education around the world. Their **Explore Our Resources Page** (http://www.sln.org/resources/index.html) contains links to outstanding, highly interactive, science activities. These range from a virtual cow's eye dissection for a unit on optics to a visit to Leonardo da Vinci's workshop. Or, click on the link to **Visit Our Museums** (http://www.sln.org/museums/index.html) to travel to the several science museums this location monitors. Stop by and explore this important location supported by the National Science Foundation.

The best science museum we know for students is San Francisco's Exploratorium.

The best science museum we know for students is San Francisco's Exploratorium. It used to be that only Bay Area students were fortunate enough to access the many exciting and informative science exhibits there. Now, anyone with an Internet connection can participate. Be certain to pay a visit to the **Exploratorium Home Page** (http://www.exploratorium.edu/). You won't regret it. There are so many exceptional science resources here that we cannot list them all. You can even have your students participate in a host of webcasts with streaming video from locations around the world as scientists share their most recent work.

Here are several examples of Internet Workshop assignments that might be developed for science units.

- **Virtual Fish Tank—**http://www.virtualfishtank.com

  This is pretty special! Have your elementary or middle school students build their own fish by selecting different types of qualities. Then, turn the fish loose in the aquarium at the Boston Museum of Science or the St. Louis Science Center and see how long each survives. Graph the results. Have students conduct research on the qualities of fish that survive longer. Have students share their data during a workshop session so that you can all see patterns and then develop new hypotheses to go out and test at this site. Truly exceptional!

- **The Science of Cycling—**
  http://www.exploratorium.edu/cycling/index.html

  Invite your students to visit this location to gain a scientific view of a common activity—cycling. Use a jigsaw grouping technique and assign small groups to different aspects of the science of cycling: the wheel, braking and steering, frames and materials, aerodynamics, and human power. Have each group explore their section, completing the interactive simulations of items such as braking distance under different conditions, and then prepare a short presentation during Internet Workshop to discuss their results.

E-MAIL FOR YOU

From: Elise Murphy <emurphy16@cox.net>
Subject: Enhancing Content Area Learning with the Internet

Hello! My students use the Internet quite often to enhance our social studies and science curriculum. Students research topics such as rocks, minerals and communities. This research provides students with current, real life experiences for learning about these topics. For instance, in researching rocks, students can search for rock types that interest them as well as locate certain rocks that can be found in their own communities with the touch of their fingertips. Two great places to start are the **Yahooligans Rocks, Gems and Minerals directory** (http://yahooligans.yahoo.com/Science_and_Nature/The_Earth/Geology/Rocks__Gems__and_Minerals/) or the **Rocks and Minerals Slide Show** (http://volcano.und.nodak.edu/vwdocs/vwlessons/lessons/Slideshow/Slideindex.html) from Volcano World. There is also a very nice collection of educational sites and lesson ideas compiled by Jerrie Cheek from Kennesaw State University in Georgia called **Rocks and Minerals** (http://edtech.kennesaw.edu/Web/rocks.html). Students gather around the computer and guide the teacher in seeking out information or they team up to search in pairs. The reasoning skills required to specify and target fruitful searches is often just as important as the content. My favorite kid-friendly search sites include **Yahooligans** (http://www.yahooligans.com) and **Enchanted Learning** (http://www.enchantedlearning.com).

Students then present the information gathered. They work in teams to create multimedia presentations that display their learning. They incorporate graphics, sound, text and animations to bring a topic "to life." Many graphics come from informational sites that students download from the Internet for their presentations. Credit is always given to the sites that graphics are downloaded from.

Essentially, the Internet provides valuable learning opportunities for students that would otherwise not be possible.

Elise Murphy
Third Grade Teacher
Michael D. Fox Elementary School
Hartford, Connecticut

- **A Virtual Dissection of a Cow's Eye—**
  http://www.exploratorium.edu/learning_studio/cow_eye/
  If you are doing a unit on optics or physiology, you may wish to set a bookmark for this location. Here students are taken step-by-step through the dissection with supporting glossary terms for the parts of the eye; RealAudio sound clips from the Exploratorium staff explain what is taking place. This location also contains a program students can download to your computer that will help them learn the physiology of a cow's eye. Have students explore the entire web location in order to draw an accurate illustration of a cow's eye with each of the important parts labeled. On a separate page, have them explain how this important body part works. Post these next to your computer as they are completed. Afterwards, have them ask an expert from the Exploratorium via email a really great question about how a cow's eye works. Post questions and answers.

Internet Workshop assignments such as these will enable you to support science units with Internet experiences that require little preparation time yet provide important experiences for your students.

- **Scientific Thinking with Literature—**
http://www.accessexcellence.org/AE/mspot/
Reading mysteries that revolve around the study of health and science is an exciting way to make science come alive. Visit this location and have students choose to read different interactive mysteries. During your workshop session, have students share the problem in the story they have read to entice others to read it. Ask them to write up and turn in their solution to the mystery so as not to spoil it for others.
- **Snowflake Study—**
http://www.enc.org:80/features/calendar/unit/0,1819,171,00.shtm
Have your students visit this exceptional location with many links to activities and information about the science of snowflakes. Have students bring their discoveries to share at each workshop session. During your study, you might also read the award-winning book, *Snowflake Bentley*, about a scientist in Vermont who spent his life studying and photographing snowflakes.

Internet Workshop assignments such as these will enable you to support science units with Internet experiences that require little preparation time yet provide important experiences for your students.

Using Internet Project

Internet Project is useful in science for several reasons. First, it creates situations in which students help one another discover important concepts. Internet Project takes natural advantage of opportunities for socially mediated learning—opportunities that are powerful within the Internet for science education.

Second, Internet Project provides natural opportunities for curricular integration with science and other subject areas. Internet Project requires students to engage in language arts experiences as they communicate with others via email. These experiences also lend themselves to social studies as students learn about different parts of the world and the social and cultural characteristics that define those locations. In addition, Internet Project often requires students to engage in math experiences. A project comparing weather patterns in different parts of the world, for example, will require students to record rain amounts, wind speed, and temperature and calculate the means for these over an extended period of time. Students may also have to compare and perhaps graph meteorological data reported from other locations. Thus, Internet projects in science contain inherent possibilities for curricular integration, an important concern for busy teachers who have to continually squeeze new additions to the curriculum within school days that do not expand.

Finally, when Internet Project is designed appropriately it can foster scientific thinking. Thinking scientifically involves developing and evaluating best guesses about why things are the way there are. This can be an important part of any Internet project in science. Classes in different parts of the world often see the same issue in different ways because of different cultural traditions.

Internet projects in science allow students to question one another, decide on appropriate ways of evaluating competing hypotheses, gather information, and evaluate that information to reach conclusions that are agreed to by all parties.

As you begin to consider Internet projects around science topics, be certain to visit the locations for this approach described earlier to find examples of Internet Project: **Global SchoolNet's Internet Project Registry** (http://www.gsn.org/pr/index.cfm), **Oz Projects** (http://ozprojects.edna.edu.au/), the **CIESE Online Classroom Projects** (http://k12science.stevens-tech.edu/currichome.html), **Kidlink** (http://www.kidlink.org/), or the **SchoolNet's Grassroots Project Gallery** (http://www.schoolnet.ca/grassroots/e/project.centre/index.asp). Examples of projects posted at these locations previously (many continue to run each year) include:

Internet projects in science allow students to question one another, decide on appropriate ways of evaluating competing hypotheses, gather information, and evaluate that information to reach conclusions that are agreed to by all parties.

- **International Boiling Point Project**—
  http://k12science.stevens-tech.edu/curriculum/boilproj
  This Internet project site has your students gather data, contribute your results to a common forum, and then analyze related data from around the world. A great Internet project for any class.
- **Earth Day Groceries Project**—http://www.earthdaybags.org/
  Each year participating classes obtain grocery bags from local supermarkets, decorate them with environmental messages, and then return them to be used at the grocery store by customers. Students share photos and reports of their accomplishments at a central site. A teacher at the Arbor Heights Elementary School in Seattle, Washington has developed this wonderful environmental awareness project. Over 1,200 schools around the world participated last year, distributing over 500,000 grocery bags decorated with messages about the environment.
- **The Global Water Sampling Project**—
  http://k12science.stevens-tech.edu/curriculum/waterproj/index.html
  Are you interested in having your class study the water in your community? Here is an Internet Project for middle school and high school students to gather and share data about the water quality of a local river, stream, lake, or pond with other fresh water sources around the world. Projects run in fall and spring. This project is coordinated by the Center for Improved Engineering and Science Education (CIESE) located at Stevens Institute of Technology in Hoboken, New Jersey.
- **Monarch Watch**—http://www.MonarchWatch.org/
  Here is a wonderful opportunity to participate in science studies of the Monarch butterfly, sponsored by the Department of Entomology at the University of Kansas. The site contains an extremely comprehensive set of resources for studying Monarchs and sharing your observations, especially of their migration through your area. Find out about migration patterns, join one of several science projects, learn how to raise and release Monarchs in your classroom, learn how to start a butterfly garden near your classroom, and communicate with scientists who study these beautiful creatures. Set a bookmark!

- **The Journey North**—http://www.learner.org/jnorth/
  Over 250,000 students from all states in the United States and provinces in Canada participate in this annual tracking of migrations and changes in daylight, temperatures, and all living things. Students share their own field observations with classrooms across the Hemisphere. In addition, students are linked with scientists who provide their expertise directly to the classroom. Several migrations are tracked by satellite telemetry, providing live coverage of individual animals as they migrate.
- **Measuring the Circumference of the Earth**—
  http://k12science.stevens-tech.edu/noonday/index.html
  Have your students repeat this means to measure the Earth that was first discovered by Eratosthenes using simple tools and the shadow of a stick at noon. This exceptional resource has a guide for teachers, a location to post your data and use data from other classrooms in your calculations, reference material, a discussion area, and an "Ask An Expert" feature. A wonderful project for your students.
- **Worldwide Weather Watch.** A first grade teacher from Macedon, New York and second grade teachers from Mound, Minnesota posted this science project and attracted classrooms from the United States; Canberra, Australia; and Tasmania. Primary school students around the world compared global weather conditions by sharing monthly email reports about their weather, what they wore, and what they did outside. Students learned about different temperature scales, seasonal change in different hemispheres, measurement, math, cultural variation, and language arts.

Figure 7-4. The Earth Day Groceries Project (http://www.earthdaybags.org/), a great environmental awareness project site, developed by a teacher at Arbor Heights Elementary School in Seattle, Washington.

E-MAIL FOR YOU

From: Rosemary Salvas <rsalvas@groton.k12.ct.us>
Subject: Journey North

Over 400,000 students from the USA and 7 Canadian Provinces are participating in the Journey North Program this year. Journey North is a free online educational service which engages students in a global study of wildlife migration and seasonal change. In my classroom, my students learn about these science topics through reading, writing and data exchanges with students all over the world. In the Fall's Journey South, my fourth grade students learn about Monarch Butterflies and their migration to Mexico. Journey North has excellent organized lessons, activities and information that any grade level teacher can use to plan students' activities.

Students also plan and plant a tulip garden that becomes the official announcement of Spring in our area. Using the Internet, students across the Northern Hemisphere follow the emergence and blooming of tulips and the wave of spring as it moves northward. Many math and science skills are involved in this study. The Journey North website has an excellent rubric that shows how this study supports National Science Standards.

In the fall, we also track the Whooping Crane migration from Wisconsin to Florida. The wonderful informative emails that are sent each week describing the cranes' progress were thoroughly enjoyed by all my students last fall. We also follow the fall migration of Monarch butterflies. We incorporate art and cultural diversity into this study by making symbolic paper butterflies, which are then sent to Mexico with our brief messages (written in Spanish) attached. These paper butterflies are displayed at the Children's Museum in Mexico City or sent to the areas where the butterflies spend the winter. In the spring, we receive back paper butterflies from many different areas in USA or Canada, just as the real butterflies return. This activity can develop into a friendship circle exchange of email or letters.

In the fall and spring, students become phenology data collectors. My students exchange data with a partner class, and working in groups they have to use phenology clues to identify partner school's location.

Beginning in February, many different migratory animal species are tracked. Students become field observers and share with other classes. In addition, students are linked with scientists who share their expertise directly with students. Some animals are even tracked with satellite telemetry, providing live coverage of individual animal migrations.

Journey North was established in 1991 and has been always funded by the Annenberg Foundation/CPB. The website is very well organized and has many resources and support pages for teachers. There are many different studies and activities to choose from. As a first time user, I would suggest that teacher begin at this location: http://www.learner.org/jnorth/tm/.This is one of first places teachers should look.

Rosemary Salvas
Mary Morrisson School
Groton, Connecticut

Using Internet Inquiry

Internet Inquiry is a perfect vehicle for helping your students think scientifically, critically, and carefully about the natural world. Students have so many questions about the world around them and there are so many resources on the Internet to engage them in careful study of natural phenomena that Internet Inquiry should be an important part of your science program.

Children have so many questions about the world around them and there are so many resources on the Internet to engage them in careful study of natural phenomena that Internet Inquiry should be an important part of your science program.

You will recall that Internet Inquiry usually contains five phases: question, search, evaluate, compose, and share. In the first phase, *question*, students identify an important question they wish to answer, related to the unit you are studying. You can support this phase by participating in group brainstorming sessions or by conducting an Internet Workshop around the topic of important questions that might be explored. In addition, you may wish to brainstorm individually with students who are having difficulty identifying an intriguing question. Another useful strategy during this phase is to set a bookmark for science museums or other science directories and encourage students to explore these locations for an interesting question to address.

During the second phase, *search*, students look for information and/or perform experiments to address the question they have posed. They may search the Internet for useful resources, experiments, and demonstrations. Students should also be encouraged to use more traditional resources that may be found in their classroom or school library.

Internet Inquiry often leads students to other interesting questions and ideas about the issues they study. When students develop an especially intriguing question during their work, invite them to discuss it with an expert via email. Communicating with experts via email can be very helpful to students and brings them into the real world of scientists who are also exploring interesting questions. Be certain, however, that students only use these resources when they are unable to discover an answer on their own. People at ask-an-expert sites do not like to do homework for students who should really do it on their own. You can help by conducting an Internet Workshop session on how to ask the best question possible. Here is a list of email addresses and web locations where students may contact experts in science:

General Locations for Contacting Experts in Science

- **Ask an Expert**—http://www.askanexpert.com/
  This is a general site with links to a wide range of experts.
- **Ask a Mad Scientist**—http://www.madsci.org/
  This wonderful resource will put you in touch wid a wide range of scientists around the world.
- **Ask a Science Expert**—
  http://www.sciam.com/askexpert/_directory.cfm
  Obtain answers from experts in many scientific fields from the experts at the journal *Scientific American*.

During the third phase, *evaluate*, students critically evaluate all of the information they have in order to respond to the question they initially posed. Sometimes this phase leads to a straightforward answer derived from several supporting lines of evidence: the results of an experiment, a graph of data, an email response from a scientist, documentation from several books or Internet locations, or an email message from another student studying the same question. Often, the evaluate phase may be supported by peer conferences during which students share their results and think about their meanings. Or, you may wish to use Internet Workshop to support students' critical evaluation skills.

The fourth phase, *compose*, requires students to compose a presentation of their work. This may be a written report, a poster board display, or an oral report with displays of evidence. You may wish to follow process-writing procedures to support this phase by engaging students in drafting, revision, and editing conferences.

The final phase, *share*, is an opportunity for students to share their work with others and respond to questions about their investigation. Some teachers set aside a regular time one day a week for sharing Inquiry Projects as they are completed. You may wish to use a variation of an Author's Chair in your classroom by designating a Scientist's Chair for use during presentations of inquiry projects. Alternatively, you may wish to have a science fair in your classroom at the end of each unit where students may display their work and answer questions as students circulate around, visiting each of the presentations. Or you may wish to conduct a Student-to-Student activity as described in Chapter 6.

Internet Inquiry can be an exciting aspect of your classroom and your science program. It provides independent explorations of the scientific world, opportunities to contact real scientists about important issues, and opportunities to support the development of scientific thinking.

E-MAIL FOR YOU

From: Ruth Musgrave <seamail@whaletimes.org>
Subject: Using Ask-an-Expert Sites Effectively

"Dear Jake, the SeaDog, I'm doing a report and need to know...."

One of the most popular portions of our website **WhaleTimes SeaBed** (http://www.whaletimes.org/) is "Ask, Jake, the SeaDog." Kids and adults from all over the world have written Jake to ask about whales, dolphins, sharks, penguins and other ocean animals. Other experts have also opened the door to their world and knowledge via their website or an "ask an expert" site. This, of course, is one of the extraordinary capabilities of the Internet—allowing students to ask questions direct to the expert. Such interaction is the essence of the World Wide Web.

Here are some tips to help your students work with "ask an expert" sites:

Be specific. "How long is a whale shark?" is easy to answer because it is specific. Some questions, though, are a little vague, like, "...I need to know everything about whales..." Some seem dangerously close to asking us to write their report, "...list three shark adaptations and describe how they're used...." WhaleTimes responds to all requests. We can provide specific facts, general information, even help with the vocabulary words which may be

cont.

slowing a student down from discovering the answer on their own. Not all "expert" sites respond to questions in the same way or same time frame. Some reply with a list of links or books, others may post answer on the website rather than a personal reply. You may want to try a few to see the kinds of responses you receive.

Plan ahead. When the email says, "...and I need it in an hour..." somebody may be disappointed. Although we try to answer within 48 hours, we may take as long as a week. Other sites may take longer to respond. If part of your assignment requires students to ask an expert questions, you'll need to allow them time to receive a response.

Be realistic. Getting an answer about fish should be easy, right? Maybe not. There are 25,000 different kinds of fish. So asking for a list of all of them isn't realistic. Sometimes finding information on some topics is a challenge, even for the expert. Experts are happy to supply basic information, but generally are unable to spend hours researching a student's project.

Be polite. Student's need to remember, experts are taking time out of their day to help them. "Please" and "thank you" are always appreciated.

Whether asking "Jake, the SeaDog" about whales or a race car driver about cars, interacting with an expert is an excellent way for students to learn about careers, motivate them to learn more, make homework more personal, and hopefully, make a lasting impression on the satisfaction of discovering something new.

Best wishes on your journey!
Ruth Musgrave, Director <seamail@whaletimes.org>
WhaleTimes SeaBed (http://www.whaletimes.org)

Using WebQuest

As you consider the use of WebQuest in your classroom, it is important to keep in mind that each should be evaluated in terms of the questions listed in Chapter 3 before deciding to use it in your classroom. When a webquest is able to meet each of these concerns, you have discovered a powerful tool to support the critical thinking, evaluation, and careful reasoning that is at the heart of any effective program in science education.

When a webquest is able to meet each of these concerns, you have discovered a powerful tool to support the critical thinking, evaluation, and careful reasoning that is at the heart of any effective program in science education.

If you teach biology, for example, you might wish to have your students complete the webquest called **DNA for Dinner?** (http://www.vsb.cape.com/~peace/dna.htm) This experience challenges your students to evaluate the appropriateness of eating genetically engineered foods. At the beginning, students gather and evaluate current information about the genetic engineering of food crops, discovering how genes in plants can be changed, why they are changed, and what the possible side effects might be, if any. Then they draft a law to guide what should be done to label genetically engineered products. This law is presented to the class and debated. Finally, your class emails government officials to tell them what type of legislation should be enacted. This is a wonderful teaching resource to get your students thinking critically about the scientific and the legal questions surrounding this issue.

Figure 7-5. DNA for Dinner (http://www.vsb.cape.com/~peace/dna.htm) is an example of a webquest for science education that challenges students to gather information, think critically, and then act on that information in a socially responsible manner.

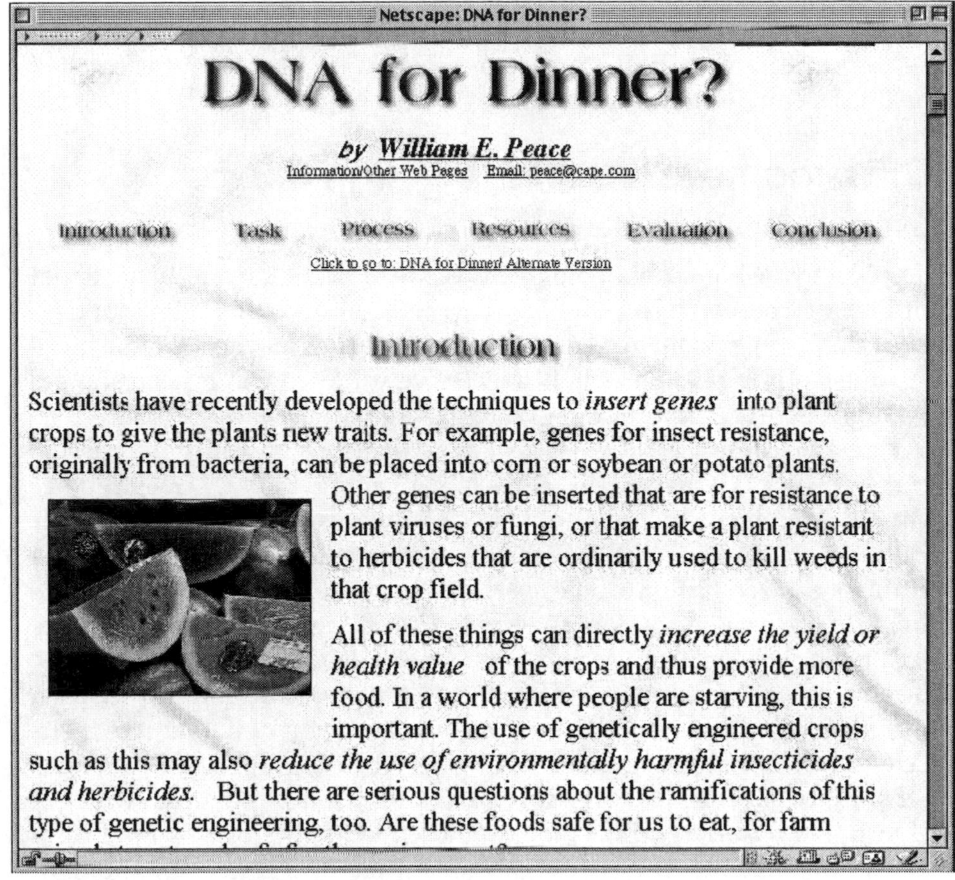

If you teach physics, you might have your students complete the webquest called **How Far Does Light Go?** (http://kie.berkeley.edu/KIE/web/hf.html). In this debate project, prepared at the University of California at Berkeley, your students are challenged to examine the scientific properties of light using evidence from the Internet. Then they take a position about one of two competing theories. After gathering information and taking positions, groups present their arguments and respond to questions from other students.

If your class is exploring ecology, you might wish to explore the webquest called **Conflict Yellowstone Wolves** (http://www.powayschools.com/projects/mt&r/ConflictYellowstoneWolf.htm). This requires students to investigate both sides of the issue surrounding the reintroduction of wolves into the Yellowstone ecosystem. After they decide on their position, they use the information resources they have gathered to write a group letter to important public policy individuals asking them to support or reject the reintroduction of wolves to Yellowstone.

These and many more webquests may be used to bring important energy and enthusiasm to your science program as you engage your students in critical thinking about scientific information and application to real-world issues and action.

If you are interested in additional webquests for your science classroom, be certain to stop at the science section of **Blue Web'n** (http://www.kn.sbc.com/wired/blueWebn/).

Visiting the Classroom: Leslie Bridge's High School Biology Classes in New Jersey

Exploring the high school biology website of Leslie Bridge, a teacher at Point Pleasant Beach High School in New Jersey, one immediately notices the work of a very organized, dedicated, and caring teacher. You also notice an outstanding example of how to effectively integrate Internet resources into a high school curriculum, regardless of subject area.

The biology class website of Leslie Bridge is an outstanding example of how to effectively integrate Internet resources into a high school curriculum, regardless of subject area.

At Leslie's **Biology Index Web Pages** (http://www.ptpleasantbch.k12.nj.us/bridge/), you will find links to her general biology class and her Advanced Placement biology class. Each provides students with a clear description of the course proficiencies, assignments, lecture notes, and a carefully organized outline of the topics covered in each class. Within these outlines, Leslie provides links to web resources that will assist her students in understanding each topic she covers as they develop the new literacies required to read and learn on the Internet. These links are carefully chosen to provide exactly the support students might require, whether it is a virtual cell simulation for an understanding of cell biology, practice problems in genetics, or links to the **Mendel Web** (http://www.mendelweb.org/) for additional information on the life and experiments of this important biologist. Assignments are neatly organized by marking period and thoughtfully constructed.

Leslie uses Internet resources to expand on her class lectures; they are not used to take students away from essential learning with flashy animations or sound. Each site has been carefully selected to closely fit the learning goals for that session. One imagines students exploring these great resources, drawing a better understanding of the information she presents in class. It is a wonderful example for all of us to consider for our own classes.

Figure 7-6. Leslie Bridge's **Biology Index Web Pages** (http://www.ptpleasantbch.k12.nj.us/bridge/), an outstanding example of how to incorporate Internet resources into the high school science program.

E-MAIL FOR YOU

Subject: Using a Classroom Webpage in Biology
From: Leslie Bridge <lbridge@ptpleasantbch.k12.nj.us>

It has been several years now since posting my first Biology home page on the Internet. Since then, I have been building upon it and have expanded it to well over 100 pages of assignments, labs, lecture notes and other information. It has become one of the most comprehensive and extensive high school Biology sites I have found on the Internet. I still view it very much as a work in progress.

For me, the most taxing thing is keeping the pages current. Updating assignments, due dates, and keeping the notes current are difficult while teaching a full class schedule during the day. I don't work on it every day, but when I do sit down to tackle it, it can take up large chunks of time, usually after school or from home in the evening.

I have also found that keeping my links to outside websites current can be a troublesome issue. I have cut down somewhat in that area (linking) because other people's pages move around too much.

I have slowly increased the number of assignments (labs and worksheets) posted, which definitely helps those students who are absent for extended periods of time, as well as those who may "misplace" their homework the night before it's due. Students can print out many of my lab activities and

cont.

other assignments from their home computers. I am working on the premise that I could eventually create a virtual online course for those very motivated students who may be on home instruction. I also offer "perks" like extra credit assignments on my website in an effort to get more kids to use it effectively. We are fortunate in our district to have no shortage of classroom computers as well as two separate computer labs, so all students have the chance to access the Internet regardless of their situation at home.

My site also gives students a chance to print out my lecture notes, with diagrams, ahead of time so they can pay more attention to LISTENING to me in class instead of scrambling to write down every word I say.

On the other hand, I have found that some students use the information on the site as a "crutch", choosing to do little in class, thinking they can catch up at home using the site as their only resource. BIG MISTAKE. It doesn't usually work.

Both students and parents have expressed nothing but positive feedback. I have even received emails from high school students as far away as Florida and California who have been using the pages to help them get through their biology courses.

Parents tell me that they have found the webpages quite useful in checking up on their sons/daughters. Parents can see what assignments are due and when to stay on top of "problem" students. I have found that it is an excellent tool to help shift accountability back to the students and the parents. I try to emphasize that educational responsibility exists outside of school as well.

Good luck!
Leslie

New Literacies in Science

There are two important goals in science education: (1) teaching the content domain knowledge in the various disciplines of science; and (2) developing scientific thinking. The Internet is an important new tool to help you accomplish both of these goals. As we engage in Internet Workshop, Internet Project, Internet Inquiry, and WebQuest, we will see new enthusiasm for learning and new levels of understanding. However, this will only happen for *all* of our students if we support each of them in developing the new literacies the Internet requires. This requires us to integrate the development of new literacy skills as we teach science.

We should not engage in assumptive teaching about new literacies, assuming that students already have these new literacies in place or will naturally acquire them. Instead, we should observe carefully to see who is skilled in their use and who is not. This will be obvious as you notice that some students know how to quickly use a search engine to find precisely what they require, while others do not. Or, you may notice that some students are able to critically evaluate the information they encounter, always questioning what they find and seeking to establish its validity, while others simply accept what they find as fact.

How do we observe in classrooms to evaluate the nature of new literacy development? It is really quite easy. Just keep in mind the five central functions that define the new literacies of the Internet:

1. *identify* important questions;
2. *navigate* information networks to locate information;
3. *evaluate* information;
4. *synthesize* information; and
5. *communicate* information to others.

As you integrate the Internet into your science curriculum, keep a keen eye out for students who struggle with any of these functions. When you see this, be certain to spend time during workshop sessions to discuss the challenge you observed and have others in your class demonstrate the strategies that they use to solve the problem. Be certain to also encourage this type of strategy exchange throughout the day so that it also happens when students are working together.

In addition, keep an eye out for students who discover novel strategies on the Internet. These strategies are important to distribute as widely as possible within your classroom. Then, make time during workshop sessions for students to share their very powerful and novel strategies for using the Internet. It may be something as simple as how to download a pdf file to your desktop or as complicated as inserting video files into a webpage students are constructing. In either case, if it is important and new to your classroom context, you should take advantage of the new literacy knowledge that you see and encourage that it be shared with others.

Thus, new literacies are both a means to scientific thinking and a set of skills that require scientific thinking themselves to acquire.

It is also important to recognize that acquiring new literacies also requires scientific thinking. Scientific thinking means asking questions and seeking logical answers through observation and analysis. This is precisely what takes place each time that a student attempts to figure out a new technology or critically explore the information located at a new website. They engage in hypothesis testing as they form questions and seek answers about how each new technology might be used or as they evaluate the appropriateness and validity of information that they encounter.

Thus, new literacies are both a means to scientific thinking and a set of skills that require scientific thinking themselves to acquire. In science, new literacies are both a means and an end to greater understanding.

Additional Science Resources on the Internet

AeroNet—http://library.thinkquest.org/25486/
Interested in the physics of flight as well as the history of aviation? Here is the site for you. A ThinkQuest award winner. Amazing visuals and demonstrations.

Air Travelers—http://www.omsi.edu/visit/physics/air/
For the upper elementary grade levels, this great resource provides an introduction to the basic principles of buoyancy, the properties of gases, temperature, and the technology involved in hot air ballooning. It includes activities, teacher background information, and a gallery of photos.

Critical Issues Forum—http://set.lanl.gov/programs/cif/
The Los Alamos Nuclear Labs invite you and your students to participate in the study and articulation of public policy about how best to address issues and circumstances involved in safeguarding nuclear weapons. You will find challenging curricula in five areas focusing on the nuclear world. High school teams prepare and present a final posi-

tion paper of their conclusions and recommendations to a panel of scientists at Los Alamos National Laboratory, thus giving them a say in decisions regarding our nuclear future.

El Niño or El No No—http://www.powayschools.com/projects/elnino/

Students in this webquest initially gather background information in order to become more familiar with the phenomenon know as El Niño. Then they analyze both historical and real time data from a buoy at the equator as well as in San Diego to construct a model to determine if we are currently in an El Niño cycle. They write a speculation paper on the possible effects of El Niño and submit their work to a local community leader in San Diego.

Ewe 2—http://powayusd.sdcoe.k12.ca.us/ewe2/

This inquiry-oriented activity explores the science and ethics of cloning. It ". . . places students in the position to ask great questions, seek out the answers, develop new relationships, and take a stand on a current hot issue: cloning." This case study approach to webquests includes warm-up activities, instructions for teachers, forums, and grading rubrics.

The Franklin Museum Science Institute—http://www.fi.edu/

This is one of the finest science museums around, devoted to helping children think scientifically and explore the fantastic world around them. There are so many great experiences for students it is hard to know where to start. Perhaps with the science of thrill rides? Maybe an interactive exhibit on the workings of the heart? Or maybe explore the adaptations of animals to urban environments? You may even follow the life of a high school biology classroom. Wonderful. Set a bookmark!

General Chemistry Online—
http://antoine.frostburg.edu/chem/senese/101/

Looking for a directory for your chemistry class? Here it is with everything you and your students need to supplement your classroom work. A great resource!

The Great Plant Escape—
http://www.urbanext.uiuc.edu/gpe/index.html

This series of mystery adventures from the Illinois Cooperative Extension Service is designed for 4th and 5th grade students who are asked to "help Detective Le Plant and his partners Bud and Sprout unlock the amazing mysteries of plant life." The site combines web activities with hands-on experiments. It includes six cases, a glossary, links, and a guide for teachers. In Spanish, too!

The Jason Project—http://www.jasonproject.org/

Each year, the JASON Foundation for Education sponsors an amazing scientific expedition with curriculum developed for Grades 4 through 8. Students participate in the expedition through live, interactive programs.

NatureShift—http://www.natureshift.org/

This exceptional resource is loaded with wonderful multimedia programming, and great lessons and activities for students, all organized around a fine instructional model. A truly exceptional site. Do not miss it!

Of Mind and Matter: The Mystery of the Human Brain— http://library.thinkquest.org/TQ0312238/cgi-bin/view.cgi

The brain is one of our most amazing organs. Turn it loose at this amazing site to learn all about it. Many excellent animations and interactive tools help you understand the human brain.

Physics 2000—http://www.Colorado.EDU/physics/2000/index.pl

From the University of Colorado, this site introduces principles of physics in an interactive and friendly manner with interactive simulations. Subjects range from electromagnetic waves and particles to microwave ovens to classic experiments in atomic physics.

Rainforest Web—http://www.rainforestWeb.org/

If you are engaged in an ecology or rainforest unit, here is a great location to find out about the latest efforts to preserve these important parts of our ecosystem. Many links for those who are serious about preserving our planet and its systems.

Science: The Interactive Body—http://www.bbc.co.uk/science/humanbody/body/index_interactivebody.shtml

This exceptional resource is an important tool when studying health issues. Developed for the BBC in the United Kingdom, it contains a number of highly interactive learning features on senses, organs, the nervous system, muscles, and many other links. It includes a very useful section on puberty, so be certain to follow guidelines about this topic developed by your district.

The Science of Hockey—http://www.exploratorium.edu/hockey/

Why is ice slippery? How can you make a puck fly 100 mph? Are you fast enough to stop a puck? Developed with the assistance of the NHL's San Jose Sharks, this site explains the science behind hockey. It includes RealVideo and Audio interviews with top scientists and NHL players and coaches.

Skateboard Science—http://www.exploratorium.edu/skateboarding/

Want to get your skateboarding students interested in science? Here is the place. Wonderful resources to explain how skateboarders perform all their tricks. From the talented folks at the Exploratorium Museum in San Francisco.

Virtual Frog Dissection Kit—http://www-itg.lbl.gov/vfrog/

An outstanding demonstration of the potential of the Internet for science education. Think of all the poor frogs that will be saved! This site, developed by the Lawrence Berkeley National Laboratory contains a great dissection experience in which students learn about a frog's internal organs and systems. Videos are also available. At the end, students may also play the Virtual Frog Builder Game, where they try to put a frog back together. Set a bookmark!

Virtual Labs and Simulations— http://home.stlnet.com/~grichert/applets.html

If you are looking for a way to demonstrate different scientific phenomenon with virtual modeling and simulations, here is the place for you. A wonderful set of simulations including things such as Galileo's Law of Falling Bodies, Newton's First Law—Inertial, Hooke's Law, Kinematic Friction and Kinetic Energy, and much more. If you recognize any of these, be certain to pay a visit. Great examples for your classes to see.

VolcanoWorld—http://volcano.und.nodak.edu/

Here is a wonderfully interactive location to explore volcano science. View maps of active volcanoes, talk to vulcanologists, view videos of the most recent eruptions, and explore a host of educational links. This is a tremendous resource for a somewhat unusual, but very exciting, topic.

Webcytology: An Exploration of Unicellular Life—
http://library.thinkquest.org/27819/

Designed for students in Grades 5–12 interested in exploring unicellular biology. The site contains an amazing interactive simulation where "... users create their own species of life and then put it to the test in a virtual Petri dish where it will both respond to varying environmental conditions and interact with other people's organisms." Create your cell and see how it survives.

The Why Files—http://whyfiles.org/index.html

Funded by the National Science Foundation and located at the University of Wisconsin, this location provides you and your students with science information behind recent news stories. What evidence is there of life on Mars? Does a climatologist study changes in the Earth's climate? What causes Mad Cow disease and how do humans catch it? How does amber preserve DNA? These and many more questions are answered here along with related links to other sites on the Web.

Online Communities for Science

Goddard in Your State

Keep up to date with Goddard Space Flight Center and learn about events and programs in your state as well as keep up with science curriculum issues.
Subscription procedures: majordomo@listserv.gsfc.nasa.gov
Homepage: http://education.gsfc.nasa.gov/pages/listserv.html

K-1 Earth Science Listservs

Here is a directory of many listservs that are available for teachers of Earth Science. A nice collection.
Homepage: http://dlesecommunity.carleton.edu/k12/listservs/

The National Science Teachers Bulletin Board

This location contains a number of forums for science educators including bulletin boards discussion areas for elementary, middle school, and high school science.
Homepage: http://www.nsta.org/main/forum/

PHYS-L

This list is dedicated to physics and the teaching of physics. Traffic varies from 0 to 60 messages per day with an average of about 10 messages per day. There are about 700 members from 35 countries.
Homepage: http://physicsed.buffalostate.edu/PHYS-L/index.html
Archives: http://lists.nau.edu/archives/phys-l.html

8 Math: Thinking Mathematically on the Internet

Since 1989, when the National Council of Teachers of Mathematics (NCTM) first published *Curriculum and Evaluation Standards for School Mathematics* (http://standards.nctm.org/), a change in the way that we view mathematics education has been taking place. We see it in school classrooms where teachers increasingly engage students in critical thinking and communication through math experiences. These require basic skill knowledge, of course, but they also emphasize mathematical insight, reasoning, and problem solving. Increasingly, students are being prepared to understand that math is a sense-making experience, as they become active participants in defining problems, creating knowledge, and communicating that knowledge to others. These changes continue today in the latest set of standards developed by the NCTM (See http://www.nctm.org/standards/).

Increasingly, students are being prepared to understand that math is a sense-making experience, as they become active participants in defining problems, creating knowledge, and communicating that knowledge to others.

Integrating new literacies and the Internet into your math program can help you to realize the potential all children have for thinking mathematically. There are many useful sites to engage your students in important math experiences and to help them communicate with others about what they are learning. We were certainly surprised to find such an active and exciting math community on the Internet. The National Science Foundation has supported the development of several outstanding directories. In addition, there are sites with intriguing puzzles, software to download, weekly math challenges, biographies of famous women in math, mathematicians who answer your students' questions, lesson plans, a homework center for students, and even ol' **Blue Dog** (http://www.forbesfield.com/bdf.html) who will answer any four-function math problem your primary grade students throw his way . . . by barking out the answer! We hope you enjoy all of these locations.

After reading this chapter, you should be able to:

1. Identify the best directory that you have discovered for math and explain why this one is better than others for your particular classroom needs.

2. Develop two Internet workshop activities that are designed to meet the needs of students at your grade level.
3. Review the many registry sites for Internet Project and locate at least two projects that would meet your instructional needs.
4. Search and locate three webquests that meet your students' needs using the evaluation criteria identified in Chapter 3.

Teaching with the Internet: Elissa Morgan's Class

"I want to show you our Web Math." It was Open House Night at Washington Middle School. Clarissa pulled her mom over to the Internet computer in her math classroom. They sat down to see what Clarissa had been talking about every night during dinner. Clarissa had her mom come early so they would have the Internet all to themselves. "See, here is what we do each day at the beginning. We read about the number for today."

Since today was the first of the month, they read a portion of the page for the number one at **Numbers** (http://richardphillips.org.uk/number/Num1.htm) a site located at Nottingham University in England:

> An ace is number one in playing cards. French playing cards are marked '1' instead of 'A'. A cyclops is a creature with one eye and a dromedary is a camel with only one hump. There is only one of lots of things. There is only one President of the United States, there is only one Atlantic Ocean and there is only one you. All of these are unique.

"Ms. Morgan has a quiz to see if somebody knows the new vocabulary words when we go home. I print the number page out for my group so we all know it," Clarissa said.

"Today she asked us what a dromedary was and we knew the answer in my group," Clarissa said proudly.

"See, now here we got the Problem of the Week . . . These are to tease our brains and make us smarter and we got to work together 'cause that's the best way to learn Ms. Morgan says. Julie and me, we always figure it out, but sometimes we ask our mentors to help. See, all we need to do is send them an email message and they give us good clues. It was easy this week. See?"

Clarissa had selected the bookmark for **Problem of the Week,** a link at **Math Counts** (http://mathcounts.org/), a site with new math problems each week that really challenged students to think. This was a regular, weekly assignment in Elissa Morgan's room.

Elisa also drew problems from a series of different sites located at **Math Word Problems** (http://emints. more.net/ethemes/resources/S00000474.shtml). Often there would be a group of students at the computer talking about a problem and trying to figure out the best strategy to solve the answer. Usually she didn't mind since she wanted her students to learn how to learn together. Sometimes, though, she had to tell them to be a bit quieter when they got too excited and noisy. This was a good noise, though. She could usually hear them arguing about how to solve the problem as they learned from one another.

"See, and here's what I'm doin'. It's a report on famous women in math and it's about Hypatia. She discovered parabolas but she was killed in Egypt 'cause they thought she was a witch. She was just smart. I'm putting my report on our class webpage. Ms. Morgan's helping me." As she spoke, Clarissa showed her mom some of the locations that she had used in her research, **Past Notable Women of Mathematics** (http://www.cs.yale.edu/homes/tap/past-women-math.html) and **History of Mathematics** (http://www-groups.dcs.st-and.ac.uk/~history/index.html). I used **Google** (http://www.google.com) and did a search for 'Hypatia famous math women.' Ms. Johnson said to choose key words carefully and I did."

"And here is where we did our fractals project," Clarissa said as she showed her mom the site called **Fractals** (http://math.rice.edu/~lanius/frac/). "Fractals are cool! Here is the Sierpinski Triangle we made when we did this. We had to measure and find all the midpoints in our triangles." Clarissa pointed to the bulletin board and the large fractal made from students' separate fractals. It is a tenth generation fractal. They put our picture at the website. That's sweet! See!"

Figure 8-1. An example from the **Problem of the Week** site located at **Math Counts** (http://mathcounts.org/). Each week a series of challenging math problems appear for middle school students about contemporary events. Answers appear the following week.

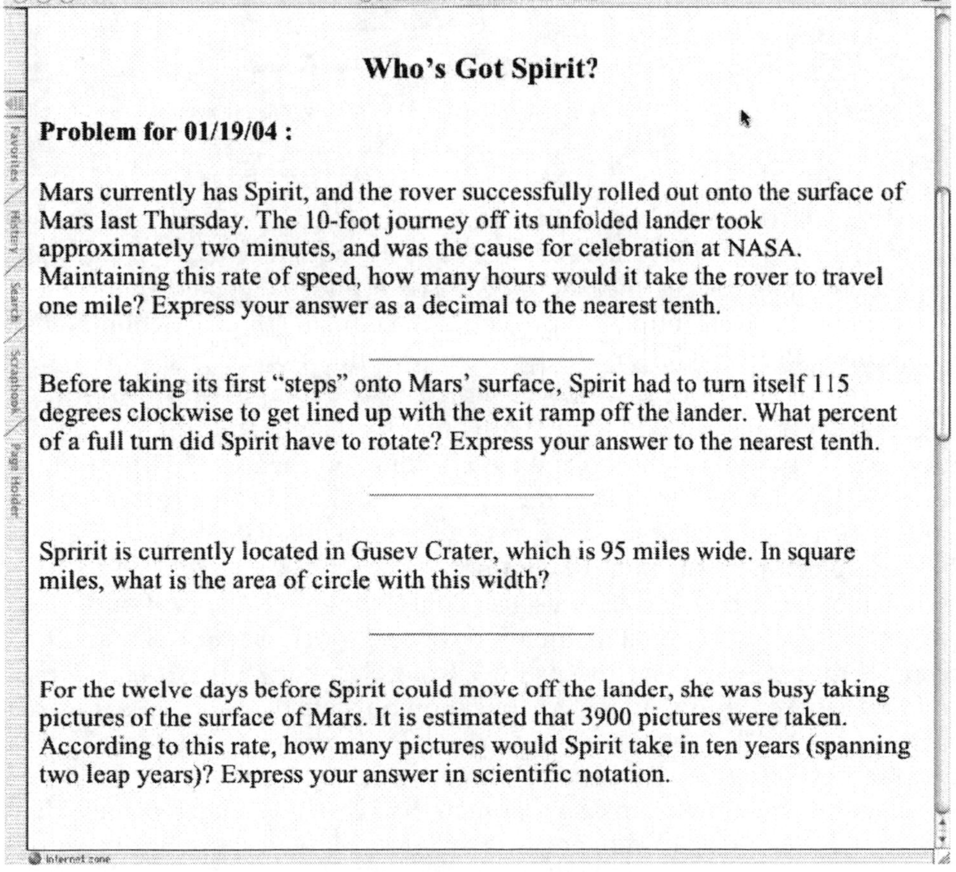

Figure 8-2. The Sierpinski Triangle, a location at **Fractals** (http://math.rice.edu/~lanius/frac/)

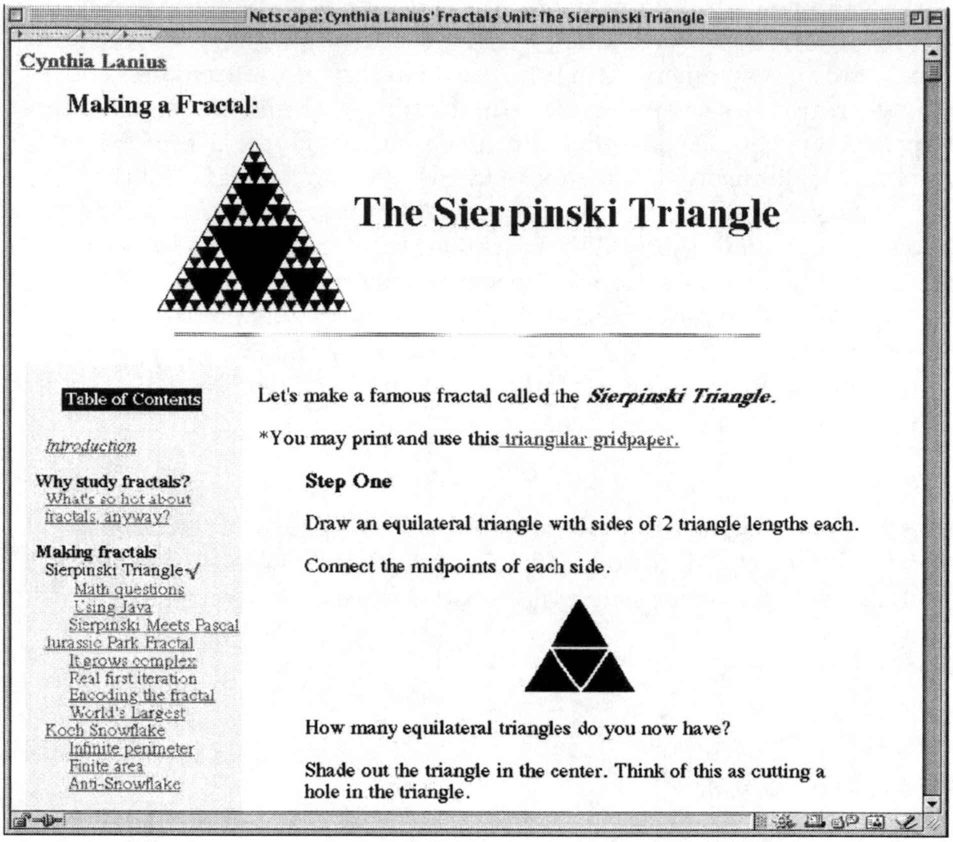

Netscape: Cynthia Lanius' Fractals Unit: The Sierpinski Triangle

Cynthia Lanius

Making a Fractal:

The Sierpinski Triangle

Table of Contents

Introduction

Why study fractals?
What's so hot about fractals, anyway?

Making fractals
Sierpinski Triangle√
Math questions
Using Java
Sierpinski Meets Pascal
Jurassic Park Fractal
It grows complex
Real first iteration
Encoding the fractal
World's Largest
Koch Snowflake
Infinite perimeter
Finite area
Anti-Snowflake

Let's make a famous fractal called the ***Sierpinski Triangle.***

*You may print and use this triangular gridpaper.

Step One

Draw an equilateral triangle with sides of 2 triangle lengths each.

Connect the midpoints of each side.

How many equilateral triangles do you now have?

Shade out the triangle in the center. Think of this as cutting a hole in the triangle.

Then, Clarissa took her mother over to another location in the room where there was a display called "Food Prices Around the World." It showed the results of their recent Internet project. Their class had posted an Internet project at **Oz Projects** (http://ozprojects.edna.edu.au/) and at **SchoolNet's Grassroots Project Gallery** (http://www.schoolnet.ca/grassroots/e/project.centre/index.asp). It was designed to compare the price of a Big Mac, regular fries, and soda, along with other food items, around the world. Each class reported on the price for each item and then used the average hourly salary for their country to calculate how long it took to earn each food item. The participating classes shared the results with one another so they could compare the price of common food items in each of their countries. Each participating class was also completing a unit on statistics. Together they had discovered the many resources for classes at **What are the Chances** (http://www.enc.org/features/calendar/unit/0,1819,44,00.shtm) and had worked through most of the common statistical concepts: mean, median, mode. "See we need to work 11 minutes for a Big Mac," said Clarissa. "And in Russia they have to work 2 hours."

The participating classes shared the results with one another so they could compare the price of common food items in each of their countries.

Clarissa's mom was thinking that math had certainly changed since she went to school. She had a conversation with Ms. Morgan about this because she wasn't certain how she could help Clarissa at home. Ms. Morgan gave her a copy of an article she had printed out from the U.S. Department of Education website called **Helping Your Child Learn Math** (http://www.ed.gov/pubs/parents/Math/index.html). It contained all kinds of useful ideas for parents to do at home to assist their children. "Yes," Clarissa's mom thought to herself on the way home, "Math certainly has changed."

Lessons from the Classroom

Clarissa's story from Elissa Morgan's classroom illustrates several useful lessons for us to consider as we look at the Internet for math education. First, the Internet profoundly changes the possibilities for math education in fundamental ways. The availability of extensive resources on the Internet enriches the nature of mathematics education and changes it as much as when school textbooks first appeared for elementary students during the eighteenth and nineteenth centuries.

E-MAIL FOR YOU

From: Linda Shearin <lshearin@bellsouth.net>
Subject: Enhancing communication between school and home

Hello fellow educators,

Much has been written about using the Internet and the WWW to communicate with others around the world in order to bring a variety of virtual experiences into our classrooms. I have found the Internet to be very useful in this way.

However, we can also use the communication opportunities available via the Internet to connect with our students and parents in new and different ways that strengthen the relationship between school and home.

I have provided my students with my email address so that they [and their parents] would have another avenue for communication. My homework assignments are posted online weekly. The website I use also has an email option. I will admit that initially I did have reservations. Would I get a lot of prank email? Would parents and students take advantage of the 'easy' access?

To date, my initial concerns have been unfounded. Parents and students both have readily taken to this new dimension in communication with the teacher. All of us have found email communication to be invaluable. When a student is absent they can more easily be kept up to date with assignments. It is easier for me to respond to parent concerns, and provide feedback. We even use email to set up appointments such as a phone conference or school conference at a mutually agreeable time thus reducing time spent on phone tag.

But what I find most exciting in expanding my communication options is the opportunity the Internet provides me for mentoring my students. Being available to my students via the Internet helps me to provide timely instruction as and when it is needed. Questions can be addressed outside of the normal school timeframe.

While not a perfect solution, realizing that all students do not yet have Internet access, enhancing communication between school and home via the Internet is a powerful tool in helping students achieve success.

Linda Shearin
Academically Gifted Resource Teacher
Baileywick Elementary School
Raleigh, North Carolina

The Internet allows teachers and students to study mathematics in important, new ways that are consistent with the recent standards adopted by the National Council of Teachers of Mathematics and the emphasis on mathematical insight, reasoning, and problem solving. As with other content areas, we will see that Internet Workshop, Internet Project, Internet Inquiry, and WebQuest are all important instructional models for math education. Each may be used to integrate the learning of math with other subject areas and with the new literacies of the Internet.

In addition, the Internet provides a wealth of mathematical data which may be used to help students learn more about themselves and the rest of the world. Just as Clarissa's class developed new insights about living standards around the world, your class may use the Internet to reach new conclusions based on data available through the Internet.

Finally, the Internet provides opportunities for students to communicate their developing insights and to compare them with those of other students, in their class, and around the world. This puts them in regular touch with the new literacies the Internet requires. Increasingly, math lessons ask students to communicate their insights about patterns they see in the world around them. The Internet provides important opportunities to accomplish this.

Directories for Math Education

You can use a number of directories for a jumping off point as you begin to explore the Internet for math education. These have well-organized collections of links that will quickly take you to locations designed to support your math program. Directories may also contain links to lesson plans and locations where you can share ideas with other teachers about math education. A few will contain links to publications that allow you to keep up with developments in math education.

Usually directories are more permanent and stable locations; they will be less likely to move to another location, disappear, or turn into a subscription service that will require a fee.

Usually directories are more permanent and stable locations; they will be less likely to move to another location, disappear, or turn into a subscription service that will require a fee. They are often supported by a state or federal unit or by a non-profit organization or university. We encourage you to begin your explorations at one of the following directories.

- **Eisenhower National Clearinghouse for Mathematics and Science Education** —http://www.enc.org/
  There are many great locations in this directory. We especially like **Math Topics** (http://www.enc.org/weblinks/lessonplans/math/) since it is neatly organized around the topics of math education. Other key locations include:
  - **Digital Dozen** (http://www.enc.org/features/dd/),
  - **Classroom Calendar** (http://www.enc.org/features/calendar/),
  - **ENC Focus** (http://www.enc.org/features/focus/), and
  - **Lessons and Activities** (http://www.enc.org/features/lessonplans/).

  Be certain to begin your exploration in math at the Eisenhower National Clearinghouse for Mathematics and Science Education. It will save you substantial time with locating resources to use in your classroom.

- **Math Forum @ Drexel**—http://mathforum.org
  Another great directory funded by the National Science Foundation. The goal of this location is to ". . . to build a community that can be a center for teachers, students, researchers, parents, educators, citizens at all levels who have an interest in mathematics education." They have done an exceptional job by providing many useful resources for teachers, students, and others. In addition to links to useful math sites on the Web, the Math Forum maintains chat areas and listservs/mailing lists for students and teachers to share ideas and questions about math. **Dr. Math** (http://mathforum.org/dr.math//) is also on call to answer questions from you or your students. The Math Forum is an exceptional site on the Web. Be certain to explore the many resources here.
- **Math Archives**—http://archives.math.utk.edu/newindex.html
  Located at the University of Tennessee, this site has an especially good collection of interactive math experiences and free software to download and use in your classroom. The Math Archives provide resources for mathematicians at all levels, not just K–12 educators. There is also a nice collection of links to web resources for math in the section **Topics in Mathematics** (http://archives.math.utk.edu/topics/). You will find a visit to this location well worth your time.
- **Math Section of Learning Resources**—
  http://www.schoolnet.ca/home/e/resources/index_cur.asp
  This is a section of **Canada's SchoolNet** (http://www.schoolnet.ca/home/e/) and is useful as you begin to explore links to math resources. The directory contains links to a number of math sites. At the present time, this list is not organized by topic or grade level but SchoolNet is quickly evolving and it looks like this will be an important resource.
- **Mathematics**—http://www.ohiorc.org/browse/mathematics/
  The fine educators in Ohio are developing another growing directory. It allows you to browse math resources by topic and grade level. All items are linked to the standards of Ohio, which do not substantially differ from other states, since most are derived from the national standards. We especially like the grade browser since this saves tremendous amounts of time by organizing links by grade level. All of the sites at this location contain resources you can use immediately in your classroom. It appears to have been developed by people who really understand teachers' classroom needs.
- **Math Virtual Library**—
  http://www.math.fsu.edu/Virtual/index.php
  This site from Florida State University provides a collection of exceptional links to math resources. While it is neither topically nor developmentally organized, it contains highly useful resources for math educators.

The Internet provides many helpful resources that can assist you in developing an exciting and dynamic science program in your classroom, a program consistent with the National Science Education Standard's emphasis on thinking scientifically through inquiry.

Figure 8-3. The homepage for **The Math Forum @ Drexel** (http://mathforum.org/) an important central site for math education.

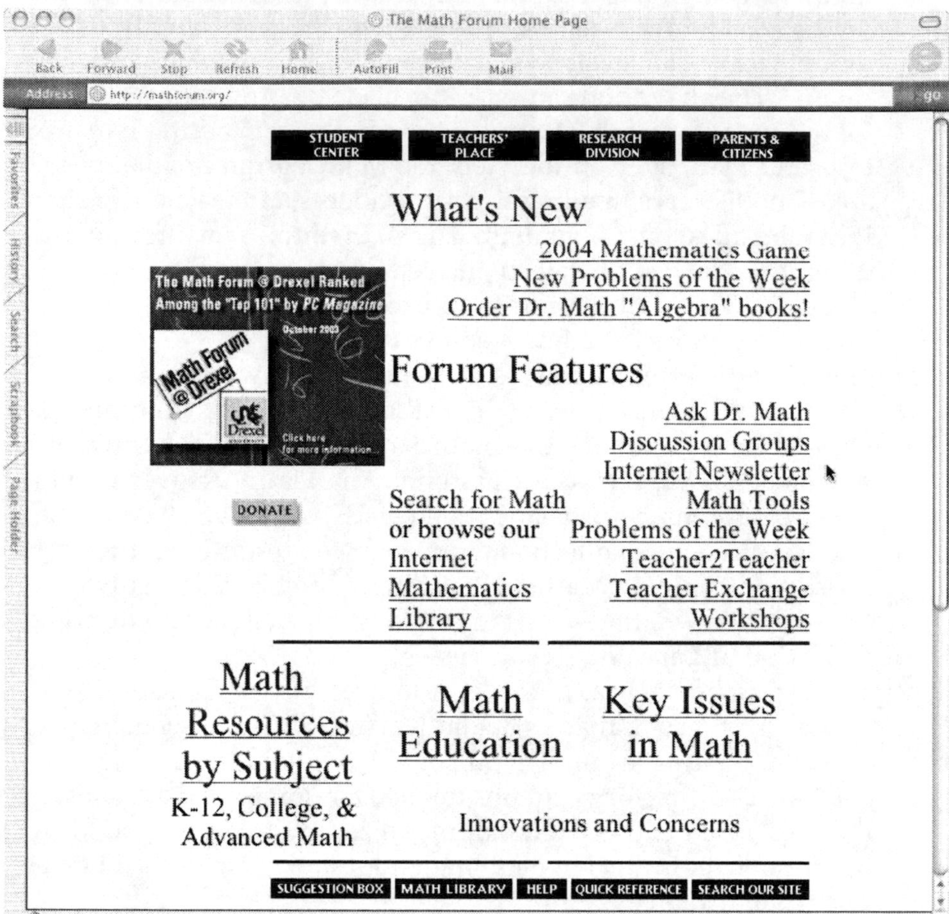

Finally, you may wish to participate in one of the online communities for math educators located at the end of this chapter. Join in and share your questions, concerns, and insights or just follow the conversations taking place.

Keeping It Simple: Using Internet Workshop

If you explore some of the directories described above you will quickly find many exciting locations related to the units in your math program. These are great places to use as you develop assignments for Internet Workshop, the fastest way to bring the resources of the Internet into your classroom for math and other areas of your curriculum. Developing an assignment for Internet Workshop is easy. Locate a site on the Internet with content related to your math unit and set a bookmark for this location. Then develop an activity that requires students to use that site. Assign this activity to your students to complete during the week. Some teachers will develop a number of different activities related to the site and then ask students to complete as many as possible during their computer time. Work completed during the week may be shared during a weekly workshop session.

If you explore some of the directories described above you will quickly find many exciting locations related to the units in your math program. These are great places to use as you develop assignments for Internet Workshop.

Many teachers will develop assignments for Internet Workshop from one of several locations on the Web that provide challenging math problems for students that require careful thinking to solve. Alternatively, some teachers will just print out this math problem each week and duplicate copies for their students. One location with weekly problems for students is **Brain Teasers** (http://www.eduplace.com/math/brain/), which is sponsored by Houghton Mifflin Publishing. Each week, a new problem is presented by grade level. If students require it, they may click on a "Hint" or a "Solution" button. There is also an archive of problems used in the past.

If you work at the middle school level, you may wish to use problems that appear on Japan's Junior High math tests to see how your students compare. Visit **Japanese Math Challenge** (http://www.japanese-online.com/math/). Or, pay a visit to **Ole Miss Problems of the Week** (http://www.olemiss.edu/mathed/contest/), a site featuring a weekly prize.

When you use Internet Workshop with problem of the week sites you want to make certain that students share the answers they get, but even more importantly, that they share the different solutions they used to solve the problem. You will find there are usually multiple ways to solve any of these problems. During workshop sessions, be certain that students share the strategies they used to solve the problem.

Internet FAQ

I have heard that each time I visit a site, there is something called a cookie that captures information about me. What is a cookie? What can I do to prevent a website from obtaining personal information about me?

Cookies are requests for information from website administrators who record and request information about you whenever you visit their site. Internet Explorer and Netscape Navigator may be set to warn you when a cookie is being requested. In Internet Explorer, go to the Edit menu item, click on "Preferences. Look for the button to "Cookies." Check the box that says, "Warn before accepting cookies." In Netscape Navigator, go to the Options menu and click on "Advanced." Check the box that says "Warn me before accepting a cookie." In Safari, select Preferences, and Security. Then just click the appropriate button for managing "cookies."

Other sites, too, may be used for Internet Workshop. These may be found by exploring some of the directories for math education described earlier and creating activities related to your units of study. Here are just a few ideas to get you started with your own Internet workshops:

- **NRICH**—http://nrich.maths.org/public/

  This site at Csmbridge in England provides an exceptional collection of math problems and puzzles for your students. Assign one each week for Internet Workshop. Or, have a different student select the problem for the whole class to work on and solve. This is an excellent starting point for Internet Workshop in math.

- **Biographies of Women Mathematicians—** http://www.agnesscott.edu/lriddle/women/women.htm
  This site contains a developing set of biographies. The group that created this site is looking for others to research famous women mathematicians and submit additional biographies. Invite students to read about one of these favorite women and bring their stories to Internet Workshop. Or, better yet, have them do research on a new person, share their work during Internet Workshop, and then send it to the manager of this site to be posted.
- **MacTutor History of Mathematics archive**— http://www-groups.dcs.st-and.ac.uk/~history/
  Extensive links to sites with information about the history of math. A nice location to set up a weekly question related to math history that will help students develop a richer understanding of math concepts.
- **The Fruit Game**—http://www.2020tech.com/fruit/index.html
  A simple interactive game, originally called Nim, with a hidden trick. See if your students can explain the trick in writing. Share your best guesses during Internet Workshop.
- **Interactive Mathematics Miscellany and Puzzles**— http://www.cut-the-knot.org/content.shtm
  Forget the title. Check this site out! It has an incredible list of links to games, activities, and puzzles that will keep your class busy all year with Internet Workshop! Set a bookmark!

Using Internet Project

While it may take more time and planning in math, Internet Project is an important instructional tool for several reasons. First, Internet Project supports cross-curricular learning experiences. Language arts is almost always a part of any Internet project in math since projects require students to communicate with others about their thinking. In addition, social studies and science are also frequently a part of these projects. An insightful teacher will plan to take advantage of these natural opportunities for cross-curricular integration. The new literacies of the Internet are often best developed in math through the cross-curricular opportunities provided by Internet Project or Internet Inquiry.

In math, Internet Project is important because it encourages students to work together to develop the ability to think mathematically.

In math, Internet Project is important because it encourages students to work together to develop the ability to think mathematically. Part of thinking mathematically is being able to communicate problem-solving strategies to others and to listen as others describe different approaches to proofs. This is supported when classrooms are communicating with one another, modeling their approaches to solutions and explaining their answers.

E-MAIL FOR YOU

From: Jodi Moore (jmoore@ms.spotsylvania.k12.va.us)
Subject: Using the Internet for Math

Hi! The Internet is a tool that will motivate and excite all your students, especially in math. There are countless websites available to entice even the most reluctant learners. I print a problem for my class each week from **Brain Teasers** (http://www.eduplace.com/math/brain/) or **The Elementary Problem of the Week** (http://mathforum.org/elempow/). The problems provide an avenue for healthy competition as well as practice and discussion within the classroom.

My students also frequent various websites that provide useful information for research and reference on mathematicians and related mathematical topics such as the **MacTutor History of Mathematics Archive** (http://www-groups.dcs.st-and.ac.uk/~history/). This information enhances classroom instruction and helps math takes on a new and exciting face. Enlivening the classroom environment with the real world is motivating. Students display confidence locating information readily and they are able to apply the knowledge they have collected.

Lastly, students in my class have been able to integrate history and math by joining seven other schools from the U.S., Newfoundland (Canada), Germany, Saudi Arabia, and Australia in an Internet project. During a three-month period we all agreed to write four different articles with information about our school and the history and geography of our area. After composing each short research project, students at each school wrote five math problems based on the research. This was then sent using email to the other six schools. Students in the participating schools solved the problems and sent back their answers. We were able to check the solutions as well as analyze any errors. It was especially interesting to listen as students decided if it was a computational error, an error in writing the problem, or a misinterpretation of the data. My students also benefited from the submissions of the other six schools. Each of the teachers in the project often collaborated to "lead" the problems in a particular area to provide appropriate practice and subsequent mastery.

I thoroughly enjoy the opportunities the Internet allows me to provide my students. Just like any other new toy, limits must be set and specific rules must be devised. Still, this powerful tool will literally make all the difference in the world with students. I can honestly say I am glad technology has arrived!

Jodi Moore
7th grade
Freedom Middle School
Fredericskburg, VA 22407

There are several examples of Internet Project in math that run continuously and have a site on the Internet. **Down the Drain** (http://k12science.ati.stevens-tech.edu/curriculum/drainproj/) is a project that connects both science and math. It has students measure the amount of water they use each day and then compare their use with others around the world. It is a real eye-opener to how we treat water.

Graph Goodies (http://comsewogue.k12.ny.us/%7Essilverman/graphs/) is another wonderful Internet Project developed by that amazing Susan Silverman. Designed for K–2 students, it provides an early introduction into the power of numbers and analysis. Take a look and you will find many ideas that you can use right in your classroom.

The Noon Day Project: Measuring the Circumference of the Earth (http://k12science.stevens-tech.edu/noonday/noon.html) is a project also used in science. It has students recreate the classic experiment conducted by Eratosthenes over 2,200 years ago to determine the circumference of the Earth. Collaborating with students from other schools throughout the world at roughly the same time, classes measure the length of a shadow cast by a meter stick, share this data electronically, use scale drawings and a spreadsheet to make comparisons, and use this information to estimate the circumference of the earth.

Another project site for mathematics is **The Global Grocery List Project** (http://www.landmark-project.com/ggl/index.html). This project invites your students to enter grocery list data from their location and then conduct a variety of analyses using a worldwide database of prices and foods contributed by other classes around the world. It is an outstanding way to integrate social studies with mathematics.

Other projects may be joined by reviewing projects posted at the traditional locations on the Internet such as **Global SchoolNet's Internet Project Registry** (http://www.gsn.org/pr/index.cfm), **Oz Projects** (http://ozprojects.edna.edu.au/), **SchoolNet's Grassroots Project Gallery** (http://www.schoolnet.ca/grassroots/e/project.centre/search-projects.html), or **Intercultural Email Classroom Connections** (http://www.iecc.org/). If you see a project that matches your instructional needs for an upcoming unit, be certain to join.

Alternatively, you may wish to work with your class to develop an Internet project in math that you post and invite others to join. Be certain to plan this far enough in advance that you can attract enough participants and develop communication links. Examples of projects that you may wish to post for others to join include:

- **Problems for Problem Solvers.** Invite other classrooms to join you in exchanging interesting math problems to solve together. Appoint one class each week to be the lead class on a rotating basis. The lead class is responsible for developing five problems or puzzles that are sent to participating classes who then have a week to return the answers. The lead class is also responsible for responding to each class and the solutions they suggested. Each week, another class becomes the lead class and circulates five new problems or puzzles for everyone to solve.
- **Heads or Tails?** Here is a simple probability project for younger students. Invite other classes to flip a coin from their country ten times and record the number of times that heads turn up. Repeat this ten times. Then have them send the results to your class. Record the data, write up the results, and send back a report with the percentage of times heads turns up during a coin toss. You may wish to invite par-

ticipating schools to exchange the coins they flipped so that young children become familiar with different currency systems.

- **Graph your Favorite**. This project was completed several years ago by students in Grades 2, 4, and 6 classrooms in Michigan, Minnesota, Canada, Australia, and California. Students in eight participating classes voted each week on their favorite item in one category: pets, holidays, sports, school subjects, and food. The data was calculated separately for boys and for girls. Participating classes sent their data to the project coordinator who compiled the results each week and emailed it to everyone for further analysis. Students used the data in raw form to make their own spreadsheets, both manually and by computer. They also made computer bar graphs and pie graphs as well as manually drawn bar graphs. Then they analyzed the graphs and drew conclusions using the graphing website **Create a Graph** (http://nces.ed.gov/nceskids/Graphing/).

Here is a project for middle school or high school students who are exploring statistics. Invite a group of participating classes to join you in working through the experiences at **Statistics Every Writer Should Know** (http://www.robertniles.com/stats/) and **What Are the Odds** (http://www.teacherlink.org/content/math/interactive/probability/home.html). After completing these experiences, have each class develop group projects to analyze and report comparative statistics from their country, state, or nation on some category where numerical data is kept. Use the site **Finding Data on the Internet** (http://www.robertniles.com/data/) to obtain these data. Then share the reports that were developed and provide responses to each report.

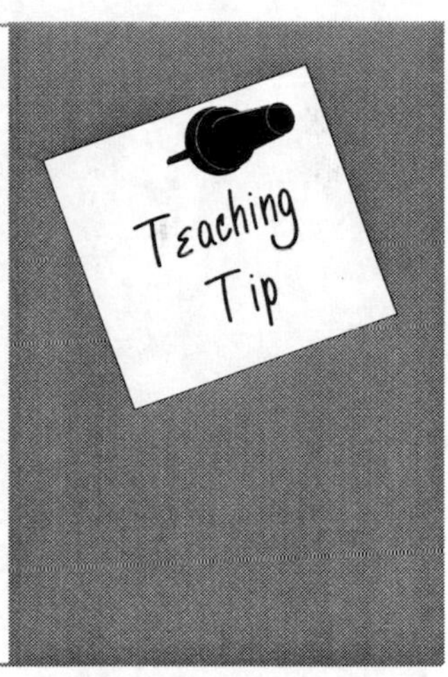

Using Internet Inquiry

Part of thinking mathematically involves identifying questions that are important to you and then seeking answers to those questions. Internet Inquiry allows you to support these more independent experiences among your students.

Part of thinking mathematically involves identifying questions that are important to you and then seeking answers to those questions. Internet Inquiry allows you to support these more independent experiences among your students.

You will recall from the previous chapters that Internet Inquiry usually contains five phases: question, search, evaluate, compose, and share. Students identify an important question they wish to explore, search for resources to help them understand the information related to this question, evaluate the data they have obtained, compose a presentation of their work, and then share their work with others. These steps may also be used to structure Internet Inquiry in mathematics. Sometimes, it is possible to organize Internet Inquiry around interesting sites that already exist on the Internet. Examples include the very rich sites that exist for the following:

- **Kids Count Data Book**—http://www.aecf.org/kidscount/databook/
  Your students can explore this exceptional database with all types of demographic information on issues that may concern them. Their explorations will lead to important questions that all of us need to think about. It includes exceptional tools for displaying results in

graphs, maps, rankings as well as raw data files. Use this in your social studies classroom, too!

- **NationMaster**—http://www.nationmaster.com/
  Here is a site to parallel the Kids Count Data Book. It provides students with important demographic statistics by nation, allowing them to compare countries around the world on a number of different variables (over 900!). It also provides graphing and presentation tools. Set a bookmark for Internet Inquiry!
- **Pi Mathematics**—
  http://www.ncsa.uiuc.edu:80/edu/RSE/RSEorange/buttons.html
  Have students read about the history of pi, view a video, complete several different activities, calculate the best deal on several pizzas, and share their favorite pizza topping with students around the world. Have them write up a report on their experiences and share them with others. Soon, you will have to have a sign-up list for this site during Internet Inquiry.
- **A Fractals Lesson**—http://math.rice.edu/~lanius/frac/
  Have students explore this site during Internet Inquiry, making a fractal, learning how fractals are related to chopping broccoli, and viewing fractals on the Web. Then have them prepare a poster session on fractals for the class including examples they printed out from sites on the Web.
- **Mega Mathematics**—http://www.c3.lanl.gov/mega-math/
  There are so many wonderful Internet Inquiry possibilities at this site it is hard to know where to begin. From a seemingly simple coloring problem that has perplexed cartographers for centuries, to the mathematics of knots, to issues of infinity, to graphs and games, this site has enough intriguing issues to keep any student thinking mathematically for a year. Point students to this site and stand back. Set a bookmark!

Another approach to Internet Inquiry is to encourage students to explore sites containing links to many different topics in mathematics. As students explore these sites, encourage them to explore and define a project they wish to complete. You could direct them to any of the central sites described earlier in the chapter or you could direct them to some of these locations:

- **Knot a Braid of Links**—
  http://www.cms.math.ca/Kabol/knotlinks.html
  Here is a great math location for students searching for an Inquiry project. Each week a new site is selected in math. Previous links are available so that you can go down the list until you find something really interesting. It won't be hard at this location.
- **Interactive Mathematics Miscellany and Puzzles**—
  http://www.cut-the-knot.org/content.shtml
  Have students do Internet Inquiry on one of the puzzles or problems at this site. Be certain to encourage them to report on the history behind the problem as well as the problem itself. They may wish to visit some of the history sites mentioned earlier to gather information.

Figure 8-4. The homepage for **Mega Mathematics** (http://www.c3.lanl.gov/mega-math/)

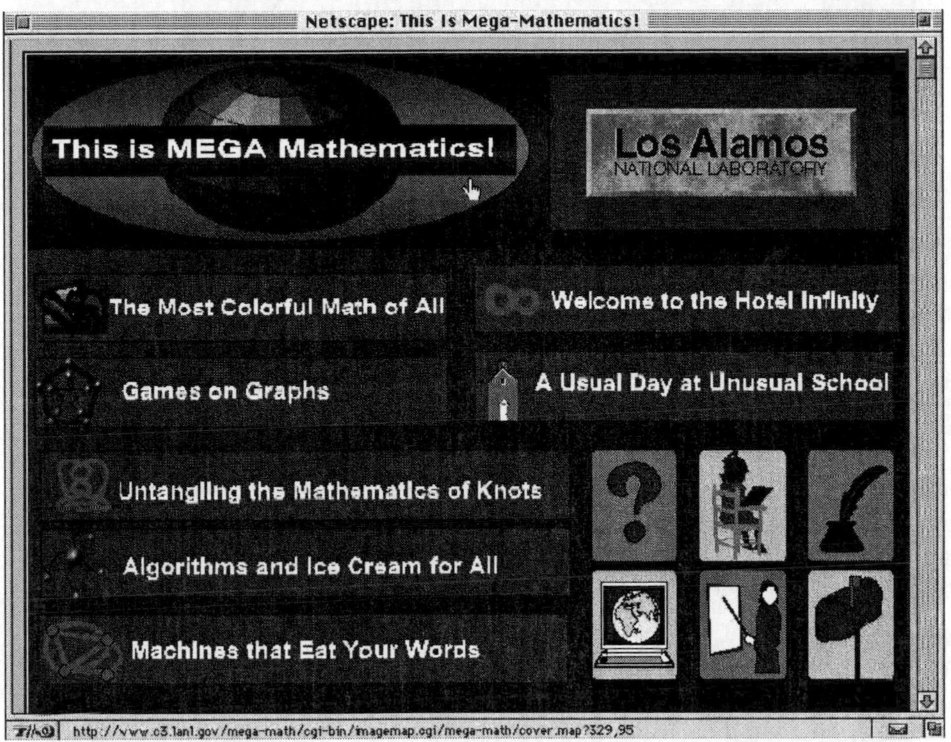

As you do more and more inquiry activities with your students consider having a Math Fair where students present their projects in a poster session. If you can, schedule this at a time when parents can attend so that they can witness all the wonderful things you are doing with your students.

Using WebQuest

For some reason, webquests are not as frequently found on the Internet for math compared to other subjects. Nevertheless, a little searching will uncover a number of webquests that might be appropriate for your classrooms. All you need to do is pay a visit to your favorite search engine, such as **Google** (http://www.google.com) and type in key word strings such as: webquest, math, and [X] grade. When we conducted a search (webquest math 6th grade), we found many resources. Alternatively, you could conduct a search by topic: webquest, geometry, and [X] grade. Either way, be certain to screen all your webquests using the guidelines we shared in Chapter 3.

If you teach middle grade math students you might wish to explore **A Creative Encounter of A Numerical Kind** (http://studenthome.nku.edu/~Webquest/gabbard/index.htm). This humorous webquest will send your students on a voyage of number systems, determining which system would be best.

Perhaps you would like your students to calculate the current cost of building a pyramid using modern materials and ancient methods. Take a look at **Mr. Pitonyak's Pyramid Puzzle** (http://wcvt.com/~tiggr/index.html).

If you teach math in Grades 4–8, you might be interested in using **Best Weather** (http://www.wfu.edu/~mccoy/NCTM99/weather.html), a webquest for which you must develop a definition of good weather and then evaluate the weather statistics in several cities, making graphs for each, as you present the case for which city has the best weather. Student presentations are then displayed for Open House Night.

If you teach Grades 6–12, you might wish students to complete **World Shopping Spree** (http://www.wfu.edu/~mccoy/NCTM99/shopping.html). In this webquest, you find four common objects for sale in four different countries. Then, converting each cost into dollars, you determine which country has the best buy for each item.

If you teach at the high school level and are looking for a webquest on statistics, you might find **Baseball Prediction** (http://www.wfu.edu/~mccoy/NCTM99/baseball.html) useful. In this experience, students must analyze statistical correlations between a team's winning percentage and several performance indicators in order to make a recommendation to management about which type of player to acquire: a home-run hitter, a high-average hitter, a hitter who bats in more runs, a base stealer, or a pitcher with a low earned-run average. If you have any baseball fans, this would be a big hit.

A final example of a math webquest is **Titanic: What Can Numbers Tell Us About Her Fatal Voyage** (http://asterix.ednet.lsu.edu/~edtech/Webquest/titanic.html). In this activity students evaluate several data bases containing statistical information on survivors and deaths from this tragedy. Students use these data in the construction of spreadsheet tables, with appropriate graphics, to illustrate specific statistical conclusions.

Visiting the Classroom: Rob Hetzel's Math Classes in Wisconsin

"Life is good for only two things, discovering mathematics and teaching mathematics."

Rob Hetzel quotes Simeon Poisson at his home page telling us all what he considers important: "Life is good for only two things, discovering mathematics and teaching mathematics." You can see the true meaning of this quote by paying a visit to his excellent homepage (http://www. madison.k12.wi.us/okeeffe/math/index.htm). Rob teaches Connected Math and Algebra at Georgia O'Keeffe Middle School in Madison, Wisconsin. His site contains all the elements of an excellent homepage. It is unusual to see one that is so nicely developed in this area. Like any good math solution, it is simultaneously simple and elegant. One of its distinguishing features is a wonderful weekly problem of the week that he creates each week. His students, or anyone else, may visit the weekly problem and submit a solution to Rob via email. This is a feature others should think about including at their own home pages. We can imagine the enthusiasm for math it must bring out in students. In essence, it is an online Internet Workshop since we imagine that Rob provides time each week for a discussion of the solution.

On the main page, Rob celebrates two outstanding math students each week. This is a nice way of honoring outstanding work. We assume that he must obtain permission from parents and students to do this with a standard permission form. He also has links for each of the classes that he teaches. For each, he provides the following: a listing of the week's assignments, a table of assignments completed by each student, a syllabus for the class, and information about himself. The syllabus contains elements such as the materials that are required, the grading system, and a note to parents and guardians.

Rob also has a link on his main page to a resource section, containing links to many of the sites that we have shared in this chapter. He also has a link to student work that has been completed, often in geometry.

Rob's home page is highly functional and easy to navigate. As he notes in his email message, he has designed it to only take about 30 minutes a week to update, a real advantage for busy teachers. This is an excellent example of a home page for middle school math.

Figure 8-5. The Problem of the Week at the homepage of Rob Hetzel, an 8th grade math teacher at Georgia O'Keeffe Middle School in Madison, Wisconsin (http://www.madison.k12.wi.us/okeeffe/math/index.htm).

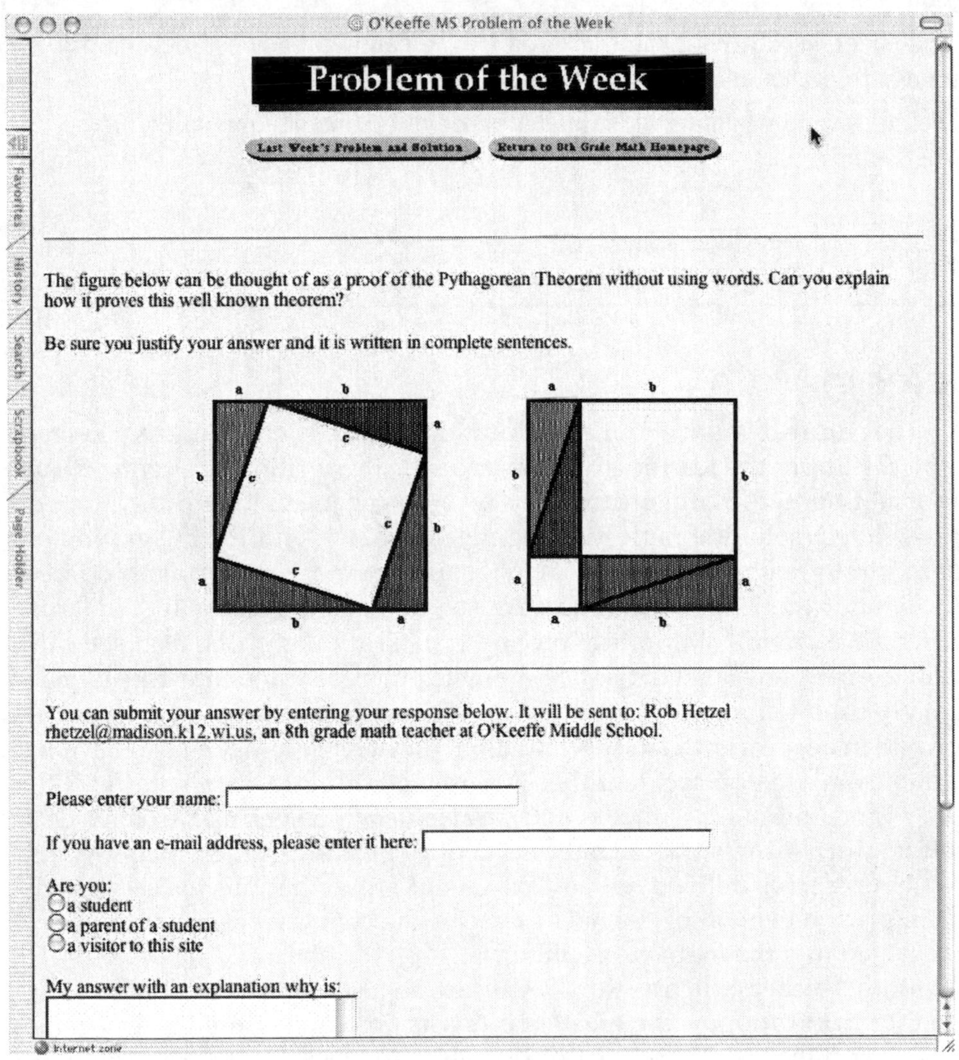

E-MAIL FOR YOU

From: Rob Hetzel (rhetzel@madison.k12.wi.us)
Subject: Using a Classroom Webpage in Math

The 8th Grade Math Homepage at O'Keeffe Middle School in Madison, Wisconsin is available to anyone with access to the Internet. It has several components, linking pages that provide information and resources for both students and parents.

Creating the webpages for our math program was done during the summer several years ago. Our district offers an excellent course on web design and publishing. After participating in the course, I saw an opportunity to address the needs of parents seeking current and updated information regarding the curriculum, grading, class expectations, and their child's progress in class.

It was also an opportunity to impact student learning. Positive attitudes toward learning are reinforced by recognizing students through the Outstanding Math Students page and the Student Work page. A calendar of weekly assignments provides students with an additional resource to help them stay current with class assignments.

I maintain and update the pages weekly. With the framework of the pages already established, it takes approximately 30 minutes to author and publish the weekly changes.

Our webpage has been well received by families as a wonderful use of technology providing information and resources for their child's class.

Good luck on your journey!
Rob Hetzel (rhetzel@madison.k12.wi.us)

New Literacies in Math

The nature of math and math education is rapidly changing. No longer is math simply the learning of algorithms or the writing of proofs. In an information age, with profoundly new connections being developed through technology, a rapidly changing workplace, and the integration of math throughout our daily life, new goals are emerging for math classes throughout the K–12 continuum. We see this change in math standards that now include communication and critical thinking. We also see this change in the new label that is beginning to emerge, numeracy. This term is usually used to broaden traditional notions of mathematics to include information acquisition, critical evaluation, problem solving, and communication. And, it is no accident that we are beginning to see the terms "literacy" and "numeracy" linked in federal legislation such as No Child Left Behind. Increasingly, mathematics is taking on some of the broader goals that have always defined literacy. We would argue that this lexical change is simply a reflection of the new literacies that we see being increasingly integrated into the math curriculum.

In an information age, with profoundly new connections being developed through technology, a rapidly changing workplace, and the integration of math throughout our daily life, new goals are emerging for math classes throughout the K-12 continuum.

Many teachers, such as Rob Hetzel, are beginning to take advantage of the Internet to support the greater emphasis on critical thinking and communication that is at the heart of the new literacies. Recall, for example, that Rob has a problem of the week at his online homepage that not only requires critical thinking to solve but also online communication to submit the answer. Clearly Rob is preparing his students for some of these new literacies.

You have also seen in this chapter how the basic instructional frameworks that we use in this book fit into the changing nature of mathematics and numeracy. Internet Workshop, Internet Project, Internet Inquiry, and WebQuest all work to support your instructional program in math by engaging students in the new literacies of the Internet while they also help them to think more deeply about essential mathematical ideas and practice basic skills. The Internet is an exceptional tool for helping our students to think mathematically as they develop the new literacies that are quickly becoming part of our evolving definition of mathematics in a world in which math, information, critical thinking, problem solving, communication, and the Internet are all converging.

Additional Math Resources on the Internet

100th Day of School Celebration—
http://www.siec.k12.in.us/~west/proj/100th/

As you approach the 100th day of school each year in your primary grade classrooms, here is a series of great activities to celebrate the magic behind the number 100. Send and receive a hundred emails, see how hundreds of jellybeans can make hundreds of thousands, and many more great, quick projects for your class.

Additional Resources—http://score.kings.k12.ca.us/additional.html

This is a teacher friendly collection of great math resources for your classroom. Many useful links for teaching and learning. Set a bookmark!

ArithmAttack—http://www.dep.anl.gov/aattack.htm

How many basic math problems can you solve in one minute? This non-commercial site challenges you and your students. Set a bookmark and see how much each student can improve his or her scores for addition, subtraction, multiplication, and division during the year. A great location for the elementary grades. You may even download this software for free.

Arithmetic Software—
http://mathforum.org/arithmetic/arith.software.html

Do your students need new and fun ways to master basic arithmetic? Here is a central site for great freeware and shareware you can download right to your classroom computer. Set a bookmark!

Blue Dog Can Count!!—http://www.forbesfield.com/bdf.html

A classic! Blue dog answers all your basic math problems by barking out the answers. A fun site and especially useful in the primary grades for practicing basic math skills.

Explorer: Mathematics—
http://unite.ukans.edu/explorer-db/browse/static/Mathematics/index.html

The Explorer is a collection of educational resources including instructional software, lab activities, and lesson plans for K–12 mathematics and science education. A nice collection for busy teachers to obtain very useful resources. Set a bookmark!

Finding Data on the Internet—http://www.robertniles.com/data/

Here is the place to get nearly every piece of statistical data on states, countries, cities, and other geographical and political units. A treasure trove for data snoopers and a great place for older students to explore during Internet Inquiry. If you work with high school students, set a bookmark!

Flashcards for Kids—http://www.edu4kids.com/math/

This location offers a set of flashcard experiences for your students for addition, subtraction, multiplication, and division at several different levels of difficulty. It also lets you run flashcards in a timed or untimed mode and keeps your score for you. A great resource for students learning their basic facts.

Geometry Classroom Materials—
http://mathforum.org/geometry/geom.lessons.html

Are you looking for a range of Internet resources for your course in geometry? Here is your answer, a great collection of teaching tools from the Math Forum.

Great Graph Match—
http://earthobservatory.nasa.gov/Laboratory/Biome/graphindex.html

If you work with graphs, here is a great location for an Internet Workshop assignment. It may be set to make it harder or easier for your students as they work to solve the problems.

Macalester College Problem of the Week—
http://forum.swarthmore.edu/wagon/

If you are looking for math challenges for your high school classes, here is a wonderful site. Use each week's problem to run a brief Internet Workshop on Fridays to see if anyone has come up with the solution.

Math Hunt—http://teacher.scholastic.com/mathhunt/skill.asp

Have your students complete a series of treasure hunts that help them to solve a math problem. A great Internet Workshop resource.

Numbers in Search of a Problem—
http://score.kings.k12.ca.us/junkdrawer.html

Looking for real-world statistics for problems in your class? Here is a great site with statistics on everything from sports to population to the stock market.

Practical Algebra Lessons from Purplemath—
http://www.purplemath.com/modules/index.htm

A series of wonderful tutorials and then interactive Try-Its. A great set of assignments for Internet Workshop.

Statistics—http://www.learner.org/exhibits/statistics/

Learn about central statistical concepts as you follow a fictional race between two candidates by reading news bulletins. Discover what a random sample is, what "margin of error" means, and why polls aren't always right.

Online Communities for Math

Math Forum Newsletter

An electronic newsletter from Drexel University.
Homepage: http://mathforum.org/electronic.newsletter/
Subscription address: majordomo@mathforum.org
Mailing Lists and Newsgroups list: http://mathforum.org/discussions/

Mathedcc

This list is intended for anyone interested in technology in math education.
Subscription address: listserv@vm1.mcgill.ca
Archives: http://archives.math.utk.edu/hypermail/mathedcc/

Mathsed-L

A discussion on mathematics in education.
Subscription address: listserv@deakin.edu.au

MATHWEB-L

A general math discussion area.
Subscription address: mailserv@hcca.ohio.gov

NCTM-L

National Council of Teachers of Mathematics. Discussion of mathematics teaching and the national standards.
Subscription address: majordomo@mathforum.org
Archives: http://mathforum.org/epigone/nctm-l

Math and Science Board

This is a community from ProTeacher
Homepage: http://www.proteacher.net/cgi-bin/dcforum/dcboard.cgi?az=list&forum=science

9 Special Ideas for Younger Children: Using the Internet in the Primary Grades

The primary grades are aptly named. In these grades (K–3), children receive their primary learning experiences, experiences that will last a lifetime. If you are a primary grade teacher, you are already aware of this issue. You are concerned about the start that you provide for your students and you have shouldered this additional responsibility because you believe that you have something special to contribute to their young lives. Thoughtful Internet use becomes especially important at these grade levels. The decisions you make about Internet use in your classroom are critical to children's success in later grades. Especially important will be how you respond to child safety issues and the growing commercialization of the Internet.

This episode from Sarah Shanahan's classroom demonstrates how the Internet contains many fine resources for the very youngest learners at school.

You will find in this chapter a number of ideas to assist you with these responsibilities and a number of websites that are especially useful when working with young children. New multimedia technologies and plug-ins are providing many exciting resources for young children. Talking storybooks, electronic coloring books, web-based microscopes, a guided tour of the White House, and a number of other resources are all available to assist you. We expect you and your students will enjoy these experiences as you make new discoveries about the world around us.

After reading this chapter, you should be able to:

1. Design and share a series of three short Internet Workshop activities for young children to complete using one of the informational websites recommended in this chapter.
2. Log on to at least two different online Internet Project registries to locate three examples of telecollaborative projects appropriate for young children that you might be interested in joining. Identify the timeline, learning objectives, student products, and evaluation methods used in each project.
3. After visiting at least three of the webquests for young children featured in this chapter, make a judgment about how well each provides emergent readers with an opportunity to learn within web-based environments.

4. Describe at least three instructional strategies and two Internet resources designed to foster young children's understanding that certain agendas, both educational and economic, influence the content on websites.

Teaching with the Internet: Sarah Shanahan's Class

Dominique, Juan, and Mika were working together at the Internet computer in their kindergarten classroom.

"Let's listen to *The Lion and the Mouse*. Ms. Shanahan said we could listen to that story. She said it was a good one," Mika said.

They clicked on the link to this story and waited a moment for the Shockwave plug-in to load. Earlier, Sarah had downloaded the **Shockwave and Flash plug-ins** from http://www.macromedia.com/shockwave/download/ onto her classroom computer. These new plug-ins opened an entire world to her kindergarten class. They enabled her students to listen to storybooks that were read aloud and many more engaging experiences with multimedia. Wonderful animations, video, and speech enabled her young students to engage in important learning experiences on the Internet. Today, her students were listening to an outstanding read aloud, *The Lion and the Mouse*, housed within a collection of interactive stories in the "More Animal Stories collection" from **The Magical Kingdom** (http://www.magicalkingdom.co.uk/story.htm).

Dominique said, "We got to write down a word from the story and draw a picture. That's what Ms. Shanahan said. Where's that word "lion?'"

"Listen," Juan said, pointing to the word "Lion." "That's it right there. See, the person just read it. It starts with L."

"And we got to draw a picture of that lion, too," said Mika. "Stop the reading. I want to draw that picture just like the book."

Juan and Mika wrote down the word "Lion" and drew a picture to share during Internet Workshop. Being the individual she was, Dominique wrote down the word "Mouse" and drew a picture of this character instead. They started listening again to the story as soon as they finished. As they listened, they also added to their drawings.

At the end of this beautiful story, Mika said, "Look, Ms. Shanahan says we gotta read the Swahili book today, too." "Go to the Swahili book. Click there. Go to the Swahili book."

They clicked on the link to an **alphabet book in Swahili** (http://www.beavton.k12.or.us/greenway/leahy/99-00/swahili/) that a class in Oregon had developed. The children in David Leahy's class had recorded their pronunciations for each word, many of which came from the book *Jambo Means Hello* by Muriel Feelings. Mika and his friends listened to the class in Oregon reading words in Swahili. They talked about the words and the pictures as they listened to the words being pronounced.

"We gonna write them an email," said Mika. "Ms. Shanahan said we can write them an email in Workshop today."

Each morning, Sarah read a morning message to the children. Each morning message mentioned an Internet Workshop activity for her children to complete. She knew their interest in this new classroom resource would mean that many would try to read this part of the message on their own. Today the message was:

Wednesday, May 10

It is a rainy day.

Today we will have music.

Please listen to the story on the computer, "The Lion and the Mouse."

Listen to the Swahili Alphabet Book, too.

Shall we send them an email message?

Ms. Shanahan

"My turn," announced Kevin as he walked over to the computer corner. He pointed to the clock. "The big hand is on 12 and Ms. Shanahan said it's my turn when the big hand's on 12. You gotta stop now. My turn."

Figure 9-1. The read-aloud storybook *The Lion and the Mouse* from BBC's **The Magical Kingdom** (http://www.magicalkingdom.co.uk/story.htm) that Sarah Shanahan's kindergarten class listened to with their Internet computer.

Each week, Sarah selected a picture from files at a scanning electron microscope site and had students draw a picture of the object and then write a description of what they thought it was.

Dominque, Juan, and Mika moved over for Kevin and watched as he clicked on a picture of a strange microscope image (see Figure 9-2) available from the **Oklahoma Microscopy Society's Ugly Bug Contest** (http://www.uglybug.org/), a site with many strange-looking photographs taken with a scanning electron microscope. Each week, Sarah selected a picture from the files at this location or from **What is it?** (http://www.uq.oz.au/nanoworld/whatisit.html), **Nanoworld** (http://www.uq.oz.au/nanoworld/nanohome.html), or **Scanning Electron Microscope** (http://

There are many locations on the Internet for supporting young children as they learn important lessons about the world around them

www.mos.org/sln/sem/index.html), and had students draw a picture of the object and then write a description of what they thought it was. It was always great fun to have students share their pictures and read their invented spelling for this activity during a brief Internet Workshop.

"Cool. It's a monster."

"No, it's a dinosaur."

"It's a monster bug."

Ignoring all of these suggestions, Kevin carefully drew his picture of the strange shape and wrote below his picture:

KEVIN

I THK S A KRB

"What you say?" asked Justin.

Proudly, Kevin read his work, "I think it's a crab."

Figure 9-2. An image taken with a scanning electron microscope (http://www.uglybug.org/images03/bug16.jpg) submitted to the **Ugly Bug Contest** at the **Oklahoma Microscopy Society** (http://www.uglybug.org/). These images can be used in writing activities for young children.

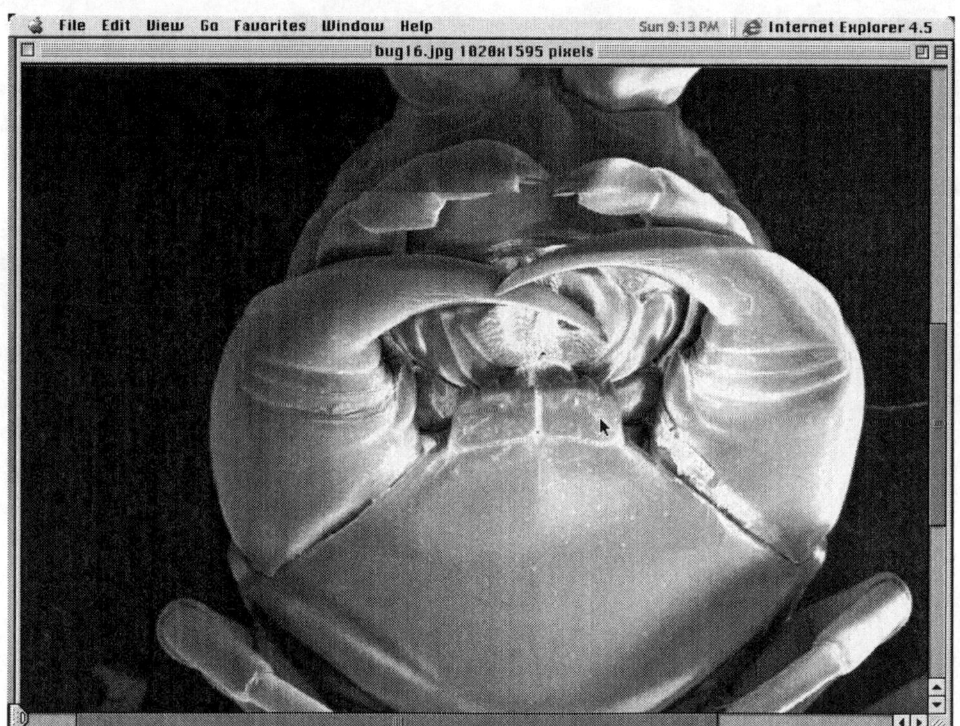

Lessons from the Classroom

This episode from Sarah Shanahan's classroom demonstrates how the Internet contains many fine resources for the very youngest learners at school. In a short time, her students had many important experiences with stories, letters, writing, and listening skills. There are many locations on the Internet for supporting young children as they learn important lessons about the world around them.

The episode also illustrates how thoughtful teachers can integrate Internet Workshop into their instructional practices. In this class, Sarah always began each morning with a "Message of the Day." She read this with her children as a Language Experience Activity, exposing her children to print and showing them how to use print to obtain information. After taking a course on teaching with the Internet, Sarah began to include Internet Workshop in her "Message of the Day" for the class. She found that students paid particular attention to the activities she wrote in the morning message and would refer to them often throughout the school day. Children would come up to the message and point to each word as they tried to read it. Others would point to it from the computer as they reminded others of what they were supposed to do.

Sarah began to include an Internet activity in her "Message of the Day" for the class. She found that students paid particular attention to the Internet activity she wrote in the message and would refer to it often throughout the school day.

The episode in Sarah's class also illustrates a third lesson; it is important for lower grade classrooms to receive the very best technology possible. Sarah had one of the few color printers in her school and a powerful multimedia computer, capable of playing speech, animation, and sound very quickly. The color printer helped her children to quickly acquire color names when they printed out their color drawing with KidPix software. The multimedia computer allowed her children to listen to many things on the Internet with Shockwave and RealAudio technologies. A favorite right now was listening to classic folk and fairy tales read aloud over the Internet.

Last year Sarah wrote a memo to her principal. She pointed out her kindergarten always had the oldest computer in the school and this limited her children's learning opportunities. She suggested that younger children really deserved the very best technologies so they could benefit from having stories read aloud to them on the Internet, so they could learn color names faster, and so they could view the memory-rich, multimedia resources available on the Internet. She pointed out that older students could read text but that her students needed the new speech technologies to assist with learning to read and write. She also noted that a color printer would ensure her children learned color names. Apparently, her arguments were compelling; at the beginning of the year she found a multimedia computer and color printer in her classroom. Sarah would take full advantage of their potential to support her young children.

Sarah made judicious choices in her selection of sites to use in the classroom, avoiding those with the most blatant of commercialism that pervades Web sites for young children.

There is also a final lesson in this short episode. Sarah made judicious choices in her selection of sites to use in the classroom, avoiding those with the most blatant of commercialism that pervades websites sites for young children. She had a rule in her class never to use a site with banner ads. For this reason, she continued to search long and hard after finding a version of *The Lion and Mouse* story at a location in which it was surrounded by advertisements. Eventually, she came across **The Magical Kingdom** (http://www.magicalkingdom.co.uk/story.htm) website and was able to find one with no commercial logos nearby. She decided to use the one without the banner ad since it was still early in the year and there had not yet been time to discuss these issues with the children. Later in the year, however, once she had taken the opportunity to teach students the difference between advertisements and information pertinent to the lesson, there were times when the quality of the resource outweighed the appearance of a commercial logo or an advertisement around the border of a webpage. Sarah had learned that it was hard to make simplistic decisions about commercials, such as never to use a .com site in her class. Some .com locations didn't overtly sell products or services while some .org and .edu locations did. Sarah had learned that these decisions needed to be made carefully and each location needed to be explored thoroughly. She did this with each site she used in her classroom.

E-MAIL FOR YOU

From: Doug Crosby (kiwi@digisys.net)
Subject: First Grade Projects In Our Class

Hi all!

In a previous year I was involved with two new major projects that you may want to take a look at. The first is an exciting ongoing collaboration project that my first graders did with our local nursing home. We visited the residents throughout the year, reading to them and enjoying their company. Our final project was for each of my students to interview a resident, find out their family backgrounds, likes etc. and then to write a book about their partner either in fiction or non-fiction form. The culminating activity was to present these books to the residents at the end of our school year. This was a tremendously rewarding activity both for my kids and the residents, some great friendships formed. We reported our activities on our class home page where you can see photos and a write up of the project. Take a look at: http://www.digisys.net/cherry/nurshome.html

The other interesting project was a collaboration between our school and Lockheed Martin, the company that puts together the space shuttles. They selected our school as one of five from each state to be part of their Student Signatures in Space Program. On Space Day we celebrated space by having the whole school sign a poster which was then sent back to Lockheed where the signatures are scanned onto disk and flown aboard a space shuttle flight. We reported on the event at: http://www.digisys.net/cherry/spaceday.html. This is a great ongoing project and the kids are really excited about the fact that their signatures are space bound.

We have also continued to email on a regular basis to a class in New Zealand. There are so many possibilities for using the Internet - we have a lot of fun thinking up new ones!

Hope this is useful, all the best.

Doug - The Kiwi at Cherry
Cherry Valley School
Polson, Montana
http://www.polson.k12.mt.us/cherry/teachers/crosby/crosby.site/index.html

General Issues for the Primary Grades

There are several issues that require special attention if you are fortunate enough to work with children in the primary grades: ensuring child safety, supporting emergent navigation skills, and seeking supportive technologies for your children. Each is essential to keep in mind as you work with young children on the Internet.

Child safety is a critical concern for young children unfamiliar with the Internet. As a teacher you are responsible for your students' physical safety in the classroom. You are also responsible for new safety issues that now arise because of the Internet. Chapter 2 described the nature of software filters and acceptable use policies. These help to establish rules for the appropriate use of the Internet and prevent young children from viewing objectionable locations. Chapter 2 also described several locations on the Internet where all links are screened for child safety, another important strategy if you work with young children.

Child safety is a critical concern for young children unfamiliar with the Internet.

Primary grade teachers will need to pay particular attention to child safety on the Internet. We have always discussed fire safety and traffic safety in primary classrooms. Now we must begin to discuss Internet safety. You may wish to discuss issues of Internet safety as they arise in your class within an Internet Workshop framework as described in Chapter 3.

Teachers in the very youngest grades (K–1) will often limit children's use of the Internet to sites they have bookmarked or locations with links on their classroom home page. This limits the viewing of inappropriate locations. Others develop a rule similar to the "Four Click Rule" developed by Isabelle Hoag for her young students in Amsterdam (See her email message about Child Safety in this chapter). This, too, limits exposure to inappropriate locations.

Internet safety also applies to email. Increasingly, school districts require that all incoming and outgoing email messages for primary grade students go through the teacher's email account. This way, you may monitor the email communication of your students and help to ensure their safety.

Should you find any inappropriate messages from strangers, immediately report the incident to your principal or another designated person in your district. You should also respond to the message, indicating that you have reported it to a supervisor.

Should you find any inappropriate messages from strangers, immediately report the incident to your principal or another designated person in your district. You should also respond to the message, indicating that you have reported it to a supervisor.

Several resources have been developed recently to teach even very young children about Internet safety. In addition to the safety resources we shared in Chapter 2, take time to explore the following to find one that best meets your needs:

- **CyberSmart Curriculum—**
  http://www.cybersmartcurriculum.org/home/
  This website provides extensive curriculum ideas at each elementary grade level with the mission of empowering students to use the Internet safely, responsibly, and effectively. The non-sequential curriculum known as "Be Cybersmart" is aligned with the National Educational Technology Standards (NETS) and encompasses elements of Internet safety, manners, advertising, research, and technology. Lots to explore here!
- **Privacy Playground: The First Adventure of the Three Little Cyberpigs—**
  http://www.media-awareness.ca/english/special_initiatives/games/privacy_playground/index.cfm
  The purpose of this game, developed by The Media Awareness Network, is to teach children ages 7–9 how to spot and avoid online marketing ploys, as well as threats to their personal safety. There is

an accompanying teacher's guide with background information and lesson ideas to try with your children as well.

- **NetSmartz Kids**—http://www.netsmartz.org/KIDS/indexfl.html
  This interactive educational resource developed collaboratively by the National Center for Missing and Exploited Children and Boys & Girls Clubs of America consists of a 3-D online environment, student activity cards, safety pledges, and much more for kids in Grades K–2, 3–6, and older students (so you can share with your colleagues)!
- **Safekids.com**—http://www.safekids.com/
  From this site, you'll find lots of ways to involve your students' families in the effort to reinforce safe Internet practices at home with resources such as a newsletter, family safety contract, guidelines for parents, and an online safety quiz.

E-MAIL FOR YOU

From: Isabelle Hoag (hoag@euronet.nl)
Subject: Child Safety

I was both nervous and excited when my class got hooked up to the Internet! I asked several people for their ideas about having the kids surf around and about making my own page. They sure helped me. I hope my ideas help you, too.

First, I was worried my third graders might find a site I would not want them to see for some reason. To guard against this, I made up the "Four Click Rule." My students must first ask to use Netscape. Then, they must start with a site I have saved on our list of "favorites" or "bookmarks." They can follow four links from that starting point but then they must return or start with another bookmark. They can also show me sites they would like to add to our bookmarks.

Next, I was worried that they kids would buy something or download a virus or sign up for something. There are many attractive blinking icons that scream "click here!" and children are being taught to follow instructions! So my class has strict instructions to never, ever write their name or give out any information when they are surfing. They must come and get me if they are asked for information.

Finally, when setting up my own pages, I wrote a permission slip similar to the ones I use for field trips. Only photos, work, and first names of children for whom I have permission slips are used. I only use first names and never identify children in photos.

This is a new technology and, if treated with respect and caution, it is a valuable resource in the class! Have fun!

Isabelle Hoag, Primary School Teacher
The International School of Amsterdam

Another important aspect of Internet use in the primary grades is to help children learn basic navigation strategies. Learning about hyperlinks, bookmarks, mouse skills, and other emergent navigation strategies are important for the very youngest learners. You should not assume your students have these skills, but rather, plan systematically to support their development. Working with partners during computer time, using Internet Workshop, and developing very simple scavenger hunts for your young students are all ways to support this aspect of Internet use.

An exciting way to introduce very young children to the concept of navigating through the Internet is by having them explore online web-based alphabet books. You can find alphabet books on many topics (try typing *any topic + alphabet book* into a search engine). Quickly, children begin to understand that each time you click on a letter, you are brought to a new page with new ideas. Some great beginning alphabet books that also cover early elementary themes include the following:

- **Space ABC's**—http://buckman.pps.k12.or.us/room100/abcspace/
  Developed by first graders in Oregon.
- **ABC Hurricane Experience**—
  http://avocado.dade.k12.fl.us/projects/hurricaneabc/a.html
  Created by elementary students in South Florida after experiencing Hurricane Andrew.
- **Rainforest ABC Coloring Book—**
  http://www.ed.uri.edu/SMART96/ELEMSC/CyberForest/alphabet/A.htm
  From here, you can even print out and color individual alphabet pages.
- **Dinosaur Alphabet Book**—
  http://www.EnchantedLearning.com/dinoalphabet/
  This one is slightly more complex, introducing students to previous and next page buttons.

Once your young students understand the concept of hyperlinks, they are ready to begin exploring one of the very best online dictionary resources for young children. It is called **Little Explorer's Picture Dictionary from Enchanted Learning** (http://www.EnchantedLearning.com/dictionary.html). Here, they will quickly learn the art of scrolling up and down webpages in order to view the enormous collection of pictures and links here. Best of all, children can select words from the dictionary in ten different languages! This site even offers a number of thematic alphabet quizzes for young children that provide practice with navigating between webpages while learning more about the alphabet. See for example the **Find It! China Quiz** (http://www.EnchantedLearning.com/classroom/quiz/china.shtml). Be sure to bookmark this site!

Simple scavenger hunts that students complete in pairs or small groups are also a useful introduction to the non-linear nature of the Internet.

Simple scavenger hunts that students complete in pairs or small groups are also a useful introduction to the non-linear nature of the Internet. Scavenger hunts have students search for information at various locations on the Internet and then share their results with the rest of the class during a workshop session. These develop the new literacy strategies required to locate information as students also practice functional reading and writing tasks. To view the variety of formats for online hunts available, try, for example, **The Animals Scavenger Hunt** (http://www.pasadenaisd.org/gardens/ClassWebs/FarmHunt_Teacher.htm) for kindergarten students; **The Martin Luther King Scavenger Hunt** (http://users.rcn.com/tstrong.massed/Martin2000.html) for second graders, or **The Thanksgiving Scavenger Hunt**

If you find yourself teaching in the primary grades without a computer capable of using the multimedia technologies at websites, consider Sarah Dye's approach—take your concerns to your principal, explaining the greater need young children have for the latest technologies.

(http://www.iss.k12.nc.us/schools/scavenger/kmhunt/thanksgi.htm) for third graders. Here is another suggestion for the very youngest children: When you ask students to write down an answer during a scavenger hunt, look for words that are displayed on the screen so that they may copy them onto their worksheet. This will make it easier for children to successfully complete this experience as you help to develop early literacy skills.

Finally, we want to speak up in support of primary grade teachers seeking and receiving supportive technologies to assist the youngest learners. Often, school districts follow a "hand-me-down" policy with computers. In these districts, primary grade classrooms receive the oldest computers that are passed down from the high school, to the middle school, and finally to the elementary school. This is unfortunate since the youngest learners benefit the most from the latest technologies and the most powerful computers. Children who struggle with decoding may play audio clips to support their reading experiences. Newer, multimedia computers also provide animations and other supportive technologies to explain challenging concepts. In order to take full advantage of these types of Internet resources, you will require a computer with a fast connection to the Internet and enough memory to run the latest versions of Netscape or Internet Explorer with multimedia plug-ins while you also run word processing and other software. If you find yourself teaching in the primary grades without a computer capable of using the multimedia technologies at websites, consider Sarah Shanahan's approach—take your concerns to your principal, explaining the greater need young children have for the latest technologies.

Directories for the Primary Grades

As you look for directories for young children, it is important to keep in mind child safety concerns. One place to begin your search is at **Yahooligans** (http://www.yahooligans.com/). This is one of the largest collections of useful sites for children with links that are screened for child safety before being accepted. As with all lists, though, one can never guarantee the contents of links that move away from these sites. Thus, you must still monitor student use. You may wish to set a bookmark for Yahooligans and allow students in the older primary grades access to this information. For younger students, you may wish to preview locations, set bookmarks, and only allow children to use the bookmarks you have set.

Probably the best central directory screened for child safety is ***Great Sites****. This resource has been developed by the American Library Association and includes over 700 outstanding locations for children.*

One of the best central directories screened for child safety is **Great Sites** (http://www.ala.org/greatsites). This resource has been developed by the American Library Association and includes over 700 outstanding locations for children. Be certain to explore the wonderful resources here.

There is also an excellent, but lesser known directory for young children located at **KidsKonnect** (http://www.kidskonnect.com/) (see Figure 9-3). These sites have been screened and compiled by educators into well-organized tables and are organized alphabetically or by subject. Some special features include the collection of U.S. state pages, children's reference sites, and the popular **Today Hooray!** (http://www.kidskonnect.com/TodayHooray/TodayHooray.html)—a compilation of jokes, questions, information, and games for every day of the year!

Figure 9-3. A portion of the daily activities available at **Today, Hooray!** (http://www.kidskonnect.com/TodayHooray/TodayHooray.html), a favorite link from the KidsKonnect directory. This is an exciting gateway into the range of daily activities available for children to share with their friends during Internet workshop as well.

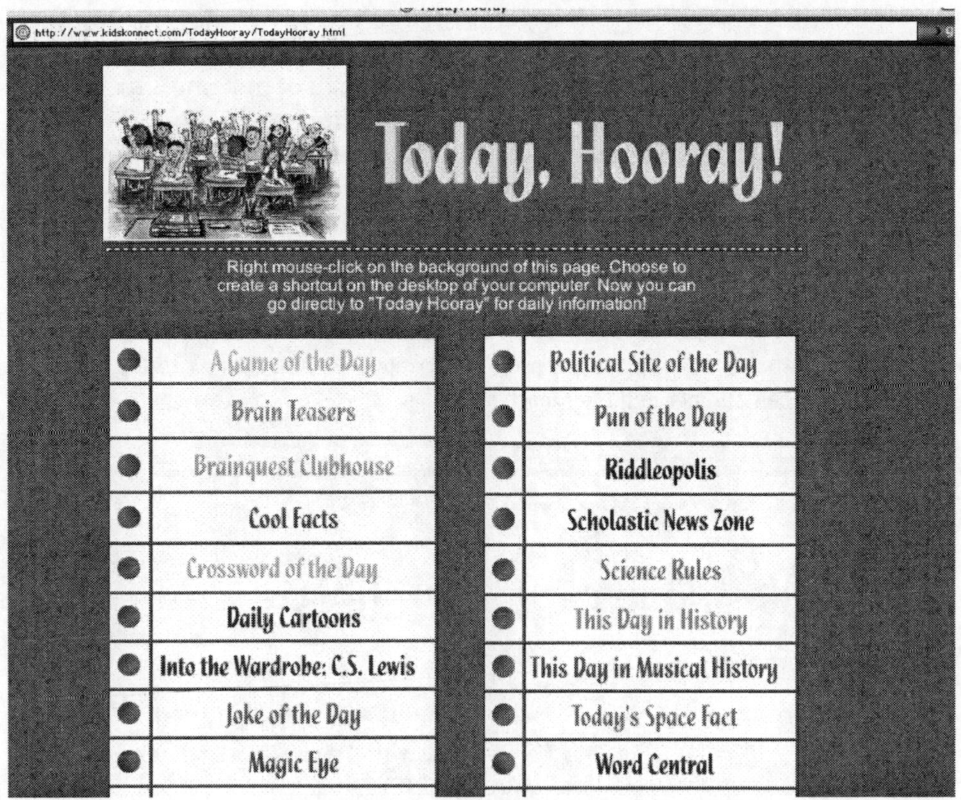

INTERNET FAQ

Should I be concerned about using commercial sites in my classroom? How can I tell if a location on the Web has commercial intentions if there aren't any advertisements?

As you consider which directories for young children to use, you should pay attention to why a site was developed. Many directories for young children are located at commercial locations. These can be identified by the ".com" at the end of their URL. Commercial sites sometimes seek to exploit the marketing potential available when many young children visit their location. Of the directories identified in this chapter, only the one developed by the American Library Association is not a commercial site.

Keeping It Simple: Using Internet Workshop

As you visit directories for the primary grades you will quickly find many locations that fit into Internet Workshop. These may include coloring books, alphabet books, and stories, some of which are read aloud. They will also include activities in all of your content areas: language arts, math, science, and social studies.

The Internet provides many opportunities to support your younger children in the classroom, especially with the use of Internet Activity.

The Internet provides many opportunities to support your younger children in the classroom, especially with the use of Internet Workshop.

As you have already discovered, Internet Workshop is easy to develop. Simply find a location related to your classroom curriculum, set a bookmark for it, develop a brief activity, and then have your students complete this activity during the week. You may want to develop several activities for your students to explore during the week instead of just one. Often, it is useful to include a writing activity with the assignment to support young children's developing literacy ability. Children can keep an Internet writing journal throughout the year and then share their writing during a workshop session at the end of each week. This is a great way to track writing development and record new facts they learn with each new theme or unit.

Figure 9-4. A screen shot of **Animal Riddles**, one of several activities available from **Chateau Meddybemps** (http://www.meddybemps.com/index.html), an interactive learning page for young children, their parents, and their teachers.

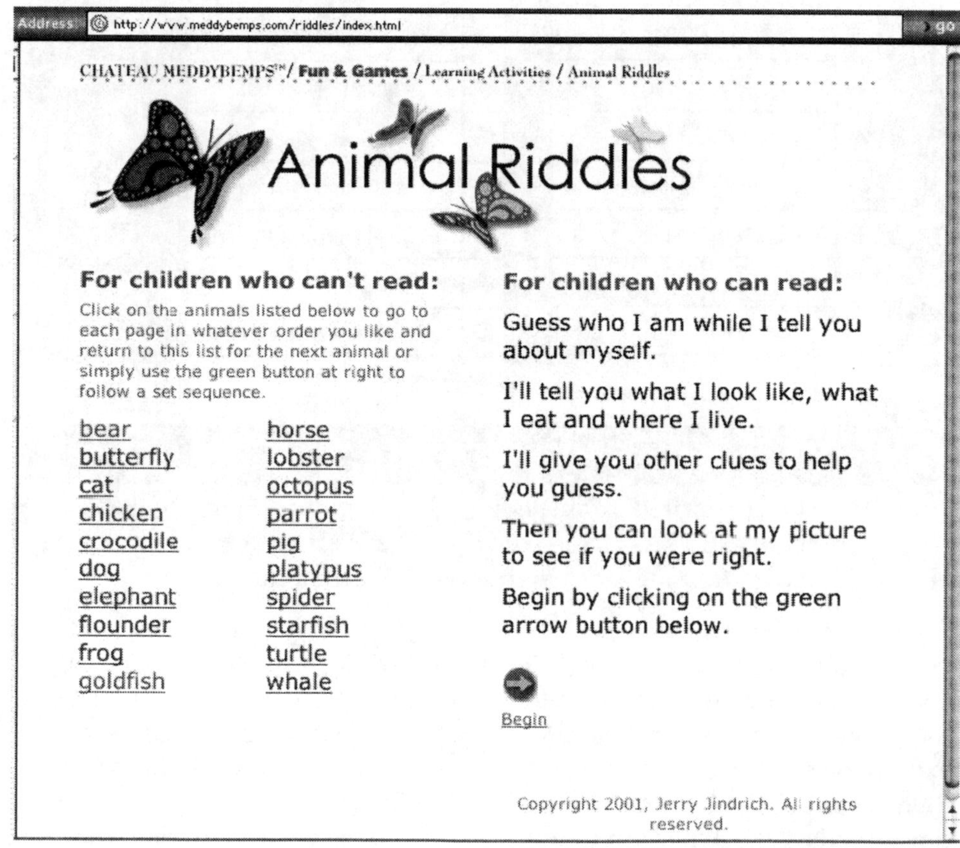

Here are some examples of Internet Workshop that might be used with students in the primary grades:

- **Chateau Meddybemps**—
  http://www.meddybemps.com/index.html

  Lots of places to explore and creations to share at workshop time! Among the many activities at this site, budding writers will love the opportunity to visit the **Young Writer's Workshop** (http://

www.meddybemps.com/9.700.html) and print out their favorite thematic story starter as a background for their writing or the chance to solve a few interactive **Animal Riddles** (http://www.meddybemps.com/riddles/index.html) (see Figure 9-4). Have children carefully copy their favorite riddle and illustrate their own picture before adding it to an Animal Riddle Bulletin Board in your classroom.

- **Building Language for Literacy** —
http://teacher.scholastic.com/activities/bll/index.htm
Kindergarten students needing a little more practice with early literacy skills can explore these three research-based activities sponsored by Scholastic to reinforce their knowledge of oral language, phonological awareness, letter knowledge, and concepts of print. Students can bring their journal to the computer table and jot down favorite pairs of rhyming words or their favorite adventure setting and then share this in their workshop session or small group language activity. This site comes with a comprehensive teacher's guide as well.
- **Poem Pack**—
http://www.bbc.co.uk/education/wordsandpictures/longvow/poems/fpoem.shtml
A wonderful location for working on long vowel patterns in phonics containing ten cute poems with animations and audio. Have students listen to the funny poems and complete other exciting activities located at **Long Vowels** (http://www.bbc.co.uk/education/wordsandpictures/longvow/index.shtml). Then, have students bring to your workshop session at least two words containing long vowel sounds. As they read their words, make a list for the entire class to see. Part of the many exciting resources at the BBC site in the United Kingdom. Uses Shockwave plug-ins.
- **Alex's Scribbles—Koala Trouble**—
http://www.scribbles.com.au/max/bookmain.html
This site from Australia features an extensive collection of wonderful stories about Max, the koala bear, by Alex Balsom (five years old) and his dad. It is quickly becoming a classic on the Internet for young children. The stories contain hyperlinks within the illustrations; these require children to click on the correct location in the illustration in order to move forward in the story, thus supporting reading comprehension. Have children draw a picture of Max and write their own story after reading one of these delightful adventures. Then have them read their stories during Internet Workshop.
- **Boowa and Kwala**—http://www.boowakwala.com/
This location was originally for our very youngest students, ages 3–6, but there is a new section devoted to slightly older students, ages 6–10. There are so many different possibilities here for Internet Workshop. Visit different countries, learn new songs and play interactive games. This site uses Flash and has lots of music, sounds, and animations. Available in both English and French.
- **Hangman at Kids Corner**—http://kids.ot.com/cgi-local/hangman/
Here is a fun site for this traditional game. Children select letters as they try to guess the spelling of a word. This is a great place for kids to develop their decoding and spelling talents as they complete an

Internet Workshop activity. Invite students to print out their successful work and share it during the workshop session. Set a bookmark!

- **A+ Math.com**—http://www.aplusmath.com/
  Lots of opportunities for children to apply their math skills during a few free minutes at the computer. They can choose from flashcards, interactive games such as Math-0 (like Bingo) and Concentration. Children can even use the online flashcard maker to create their own math games to bring to workshop and stump their friends! Speedy math fact solvers may also want to try their hand at **ArithmAttack** (http://www.dep.anl.gov/aattack.htm), to see how many math problems they can solve in one minute.
- **Whiskers' Corner** —
  http://www.weeklyreader.com/kids/grade2/whiskers_corner.asp
  Each week, select a few children to log on and read a new question posted by Whiskers, the cat, encouraging them to solve authentic problems about getting along with others, treating people with respect, and acting responsibly. At the end of the week, student responses from around the world are posted for all to read. Invite students to print out and bring along their own response as well as one from another child who solved the problem differently—great discussions about alternative problem-solving strategies may result during Internet workshop!

Each week, select a few children to log on and read a new question posted by Whiskers, the cat, encouraging them to solve authentic problems about getting along with others, treating people with respect, and acting responsibly.

In addition to these traditional uses of sites for Internet Workshop, it is also possible to use your computer without requiring any navigation at all by your students. This is a very safe experience for your children since they only view an image you have bookmarked on the computer. For example, find an unusual image each day to display on the screen and encourage your students to draw a picture of this image and then write down what they think it is. A few great sources of mystery images or photos include:

- **Nanoworld Image Gallery**—
  http://www.uq.oz.au:80/nanoworld/images_1.html
  You find images taken by an electron microscope.
- **Junior Master Gardener**—
  http://www.k2demo.com/jmg/index.k2?did=5337§ionID=2016
  Has microscopic images of items in nature.
- **Bugscope 3D Gallery—**
  http://bugscope.beckman.uiuc.edu/diversions/3d/
  Has incredible full-color microscopic photographs of insects and spiders.
- **Weekly Reader's Weekly Contest—**
  http://www.weeklyreader.com/kids/grade2/contests.asp
  Provides a link to mystery puzzles, captions, photos, and sounds; each one changes weekly.

Sometimes images will contain the label for the item. This is also useful for students who may wish to copy the word down as they write a sentence describing the picture they see. This can easily be set up as an Internet Workshop for kindergarten classrooms with children's pictures and writing shared during a brief workshop session at the end of the day.

E-MAIL FOR YOU

From: Cathy Lewis (clewis@mail.orion.org)
Subject: Being Careful with Young Children on the Internet

When children are little we tell them to stay away from hot stoves. "HOT" should convey danger. On the other hand little ones also see GOOD things coming from the stove and hunger surpasses the urge to touch. It is just like this with the Internet for grade school students. It's "HOT" but they are also hungry for information.

At the beginning, I believe students should be guided to websites that answer their questions. Goals and objectives should be determined before they begin and the students should have some type of assessment to be sure they learned what they needed.

Picking up the Internet is like thumbing a regular book. There are times you just want to thumb through and enjoy the pictures and at other times you NEED TO KNOW SOMETHING. Students will need time for both, but in schools our time is so limited that goals and objectives should be determined that enhance the curriculum and not leave young minds bewildered with "thumbing through the pages."

The Internet has HOT items so let's be sure we are cooking with fire and not explosives. Both will do the job but the latter will end in disaster.

Cathy Irene Lewis
Reading Specialist
St. Mary's School, Grades 3-4
Pierce City, MO

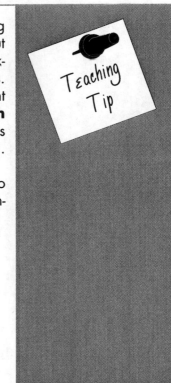

There are a number of coloring books on the Internet for very young children to enjoy. Have children print out their work and then write about their picture. They can read and share their work during Internet Workshop. Be careful, however, about screening sites for commercial messages. Interactive coloring books provide opportunities to color illustrations right on the screen. A nice, non-commercial, example is **Draw Your Own Picture** http://www.coloringpage.org/drawing.htm) and another is **Kendra's Coloring Book** (http://www.isoverse.com/colorbook/). Shockwave is required for these sites.

Non-interactive coloring books contain black and white illustrations to be printed out and then colored. Some examples related to early elementary subject areas include:

- **The Happy Earth Day Coloring Book** from the EPA— http://www.epa.gov/region5/publications/happy/happy.htm
- **Smokey's Coloring Book**— http://flame.doacs.state.fl.us/Fp/color.html
- **Federal Emergency Management Agency (FEMA) Coloring Books**— http://www.fema.gov/kids/games/colorbk/index.htm
- **Ivy Joy's Coloring Page Search Engine**— http://www.ivyjoy.com/coloring/search.html

Using Internet Project

Permanent sites for Internet Project in the primary grades are beginning to appear on the Internet. One of the many great project locations is **The Mind's Eye Monster Exchange Project** (http://www.monsterexchange.org/) (see Figure 9-6).. This site puts classes together that wish to participate in a collaborative language arts project. Students begin by drawing a picture of a monster and writing a description of their monster picture. Paired classes exchange their descriptions and attempt to draw a picture of what they think the other students' monsters look like. Finally, the images of all monsters are posted at the Monster Exchange Project so that classes may see the originals and compare them with the descriptions that were written. Many lesson plans and extension ideas are also listed at this location for teachers. For instance, monsters can be drawn using only geometric figures to enhance math skills or the types of media can be limited to pastels or watercolors or collage materials to focus on more artistic media awareness. This is a wonderful Internet Project idea for any primary grade classroom. The opportunities for language arts experiences, as students communicate about their monster images, are exceptional.

Figure 9-5. The homepage for the **Mind's Eye Monster Exchange** (http://www.monsterexchange.org/), an outstanding Internet project location for primary grade children.

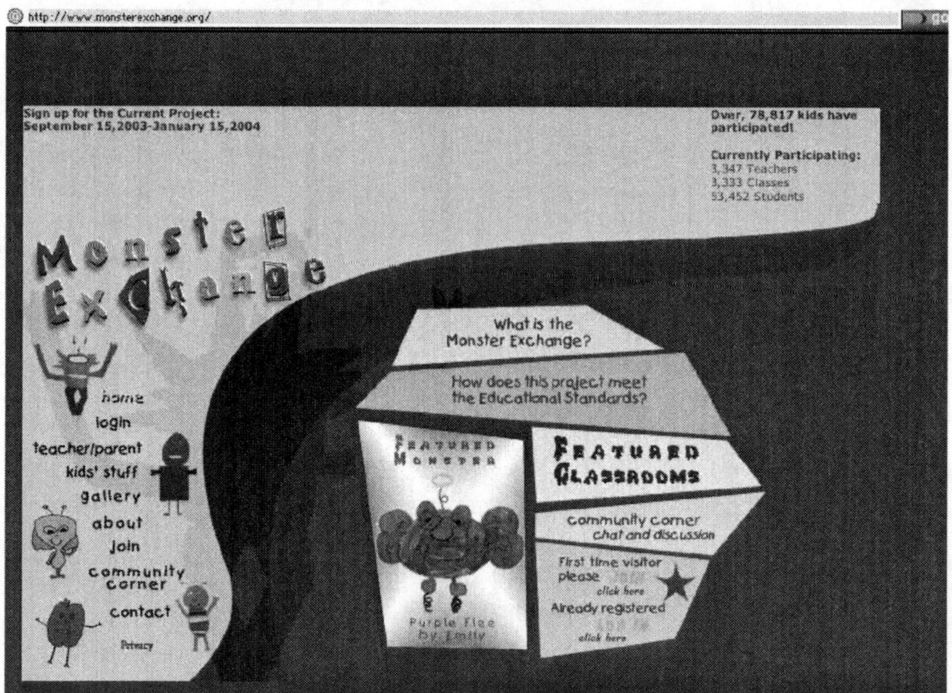

Another permanent project location on the Internet is **Monarch Watch** (http://www.MonarchWatch.org/) (see Figure 9-6). If you wish to plan a project around this beautiful species of butterfly, this is the place for you. The location contains an amazingly extensive set of resources designed for children and teachers to learn more about butterflies. Your students can raise butterflies, band them, release them into the wild, and track their progress as reports come in from observers around North America. Pay a visit to this excellent resource.

In addition to permanent sites such as these, you should also visit locations on the Internet where less permanent Internet Projects are described, inviting you and other teachers to join in classroom interchanges. Or, you may come up with your own idea for a great project and invite other teachers to join you by posting it at one of these locations. Locations where teachers post projects and invite others to join them have been described in other chapters. Most allow you to search by age level, grade level, project type, content area, or theme. They include:

- **The Global SchoolNet Projects Registry**— http://www.gsn.org/pr/index.cfm
- **SchoolNet's Grassroots Collaborative Learning Projects Gallery**— http://www.schoolnet.ca/grassroots/e/project.centre/project-search.asp
- **Oz Projects**—http://ozprojects.edna.edu.au/
- **KIDPROJ**—http://www.kidlink.org/KIDPROJ/

Another permanent project location on the Internet that provides an amazing set of resources for your children is ***Monarch Watch.*** *If you wish to plan a project around these beautiful creatures, this is the place for you.*

Figure 9-6. To develop an Internet project about Monarch butterflies, be certain to visit **Monarch Watch** (http://www.MonarchWatch.org/).

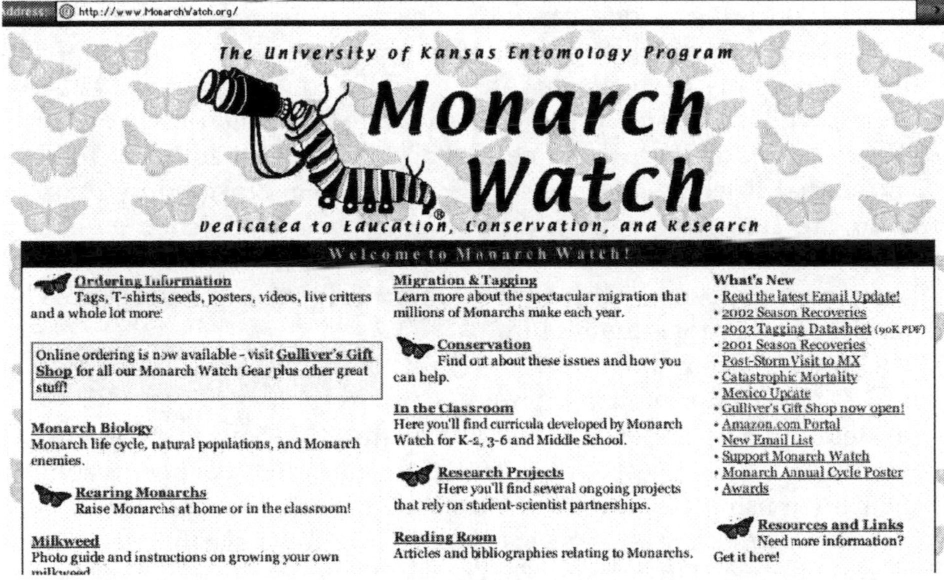

Examples of projects you may wish to consider joining or developing for primary grade students include:

- **The Eric Carle Book Club.** Invite other classes to read works by Eric Carle (or another popular author). Then, using writing process activities, share children's written responses to these works with each classroom. Also, consider polling each class about their favorite books by this author and sharing the results with other classes. When all of the results are in, have each class develop a graph to display the results. Send the results of your work to the author and see if he/she responds. The **Eric Carle Homepage** (http://www.eric-carle.com/) has a link to his email address. An example of this type of activity can be found at **The Eric Carle Project** (http://www.netxroad.com/ECPS/index.shtml).

- **Kindergarten Potluck Project—**
  http://home.earthlink.net/~gbnewman/Potluck.html
  This well-organized literature based project from Pensacola, Florida is a simple, yet elegant example of how the Internet opens up new worlds for young children. After reading the children's book Potluck with her students, Mrs. Neuman was inspired to make an "online recipe book" by kindergarten students, for kindergarten students. What results is a well-organized alphabet book of recipes and photographs for students to explore, with each recipe connected to another book to share. Your students can simply explore this online resource, or better still, it can serve as an inspiration for your own Internet project. With an email connection and a few basic web design skills that you can learn in Chapter 12 , you can quickly be on your way to creating a similar project with your own primary school children!

Playground chants are part of every child's culture no matter where they go to school. Have your students write these down carefully and exchange them with classes at other locations around the world.

- **Playground Chants Around the World.** Playground chants are part of every child's culture no matter where they go to school. Have your students write these down carefully and exchange them with classes at other locations around the world. Communicate with classes to find out the meanings of chants that are unfamiliar to your students. This is a wonderful way to support reading and writing in your primary grade classroom and to discover important aspects of other cultures. To get you started, listen to some hilarious examples from **Playground Chants from the United Kingdom** (http://www.bbc.co.uk/cbbc/music/make/index.shtml) or read others available from **Streetplay.com's Jumprope Rhymes** (http://www.streetplay.com/thegames/jumprope/jumproperhymes.html).
- **My Town is Important—**
  http://www.mrsmcgowan.com/town/index.html
  Students in kindergarten through fourth grade join forces in this telecollaborative project to write and illustrate individual poems about their town using the format of Margaret Brown's *The Important Book.* Students also share a class poem on the project Web page that describes special features of their town. This project fits well with a unit on communities, neighborhoods, or even poetry writing.
- **Wright On!—**
  http://lakelandschools.org/edtech/WrightOn/home.htm
  Primary school students celebrate the 100th anniversary of the Wright brothers' flight by joining this collaborative research project. Students' showcase what they learned through bar graphs, concept maps, poetry, original stories, P.E. activities, and much, much more!

- **Flat Gingerbread Project—** http://myschoolonline.com/page/0,1871,24742-145616-27-3271,00.html This idea was originally created by Pam Elliott, a second grade teacher in Maine, to help her students learn more about their own state and other states. Students are asked to decorate flat "gingerbread" boys or girls to depict the state that they live in and then mail them to be displayed on a common Web site. Students may use this resource to access the bears and compare/contrast facts, weather, customs, and more about each state. Several examples of these bears can be viewed from this Web page.
- **Teddy Bears Travel the World.** Have each participating class purchase a small teddy bear and send it to one of the other classrooms. In each class, the teddy must go home with a different child each night. Each child must then write a description of the what they did, where they went, and what it was like at their location. These should be developed with the parent/guardian and returned to school. Each day, these messages go out to each participating class to be read by the students. A map can be marked to show where each Teddy is in the world. At the end, teddy bears can be mailed back to the home classrooms with souvenirs from its host classroom. You may join a huge project with over 2600 classes from around the world at **I-EARN's Teddy Bear Project Exchange** (http://www.iearn.org.au/tbear/) or view a much smaller-scaled project between two primary classes at **The Teddy Bear Project** (http://www.iol.ie/~manister/teddy.html).

Visit Susan Silverman's model for Internet Project. Susan Silverman is a technology integration specialist in the Comsewogue School District, in Port Jefferson Station, New York. She has developed a wonderful model for Internet Project for young children located at **Mrs. Silverman's Webfolio** (http://kids-learn.org/) that all of us could use in our classrooms. Many projects are centered around popular children's literature, elementary curriculum, and sometimes incorporate children's software tools such as *Kidspiration* and *Kid Pix* into the finished products. Younger children really enjoy reading original versions of favorite stories created by children just their age from around the country. Take a look back at the end of Chapter 3 to read more about the exceptional projects she has developed with other classrooms around the world. Lots of great ideas to try out in your own classroom.

Using Internet Inquiry

Internet Inquiry occurs less frequently in the primary grades than it does at other grade levels. Part of the reason for this is child safety. Parents are often reluctant to have their young children independently explore resources on the Internet. As a result, school boards often will place limits on children's independent Internet use at these younger levels. A more common reason, however, is that children at this age are still developing navigation skills. Because these skills have yet to be completely developed, it simply takes too long for many students to acquire useful information about a topic or project that interests them. Finally, the speed of obtaining information on the Internet is also impeded by young children's emerging literacy ability. Even when children do find resources that are related to their inquiry project, they are not always able to understand the information. Thus, independent inquiry projects are less common in the primary grades than at older grade levels.

Recently, however, a few exemplary models of primary school students engaged in inquiry have emerged. Several of these do not require much reading or navigating, per se, but rather serve as a web-based source of inspiration for student inquiry by providing access to new technologies.

Recently, however, a few exemplary models of primary school students engaged in inquiry have emerged. Several of these do not require much reading or navigating, per se, but rather serve as a Web-based source of inspiration for student inquiry by providing access to new technologies.

- **Bugscope**—http://bugscope.beckman.uiuc.edu/
  As a class, with some guidance from a teacher, young children can design their own experiments by shipping their own "bugs" to the Beckman Institute for Advanced Science and Technology at the University of Illinois at Urbana-Champaign, and then, scheduling a session to have their bugs imaged in full-color high magnification using a remote Web-based scanning electron microscope! You can view an example of this from elementary students at **Benjamin Franklin Elementary School in Illinois** at http://bugscope.beckman.uiuc.edu/members/2003-002/. They collected 100 images and added them to the institute's online database to share with others around the world. Similarly, you can see how second-grade teachers at **Yankee Ridge Elementary School** (http://www.inquiry.uiuc.edu/action/bugscope/bugscope.php) extended the unit with student projects like Insect Alphabet books, HyperStudio projects, and an online survey about adult and hatchling crickets. This is truly an example of how new technologies can empower young children and their teachers.
- **Spider Inquiry Project**—
  http://avocado.dade.k12.fl.us/projects/spiders/
  This collaborative science inquiry project from Avocado Elementary School in Miami, Florida is a wonderful model of how hands-on inquiry based science and technology can be used effectively with young children. This site walks you through the progression of their unit, beginning with examples of initial student inquiry questions; idea clusters about living things in their schoolyard; student notes and drawings from their "field observations"; and ending with samples of student "research projects" after they built spider vivariums and observed/recorded the behavior of the spiders that lived in these environments. You may want to try using this model to develop your own student inquiry project!
- **Researching Organisms of the Seashore**—
  http://www.euro-cscl.org/Members/Marjaana/Idea.2003-05-19.0541
  Here, you can read the reflections from a teacher in Finland who used web-based inquiry with her third-grade students for the first time. Although there is no link to any student products, this is certainly evidence that inquiry with elementary students can be suc-

cessful. This example also reminds us of the progress that educators in other countries are making with regard to integrating new literacies into their curriculum. We expect many more examples of Internet inquiry with young children to be available in the next few years.

INTERNET FAQ

I have seen hundreds of locations on the Web but I never know if I am looking at something "good." How can I tell if I am looking at an "outstanding" Website?

The definition of an outstanding website is, of course, subjective. You may, however, wish to review the criteria the American Library Association uses to define outstanding websites. They organize an extensive criteria list around these elements: authorship/sponsorship, purpose, design and stability, and content. Take a look and see if you agree. Their **Selection** page is located at http://www.ala.org/parentspage/greatsites/criteria.html.

Using WebQuest

Webquests are especially important to evaluate in the primary grades since some of your students will be less independent at reading directions and less familiar with navigating the Internet effectively. Thus, it is essential to provide opportunities for students to work together on these experiences so they may benefit from the natural support that comes from working together. Given the concerns about webquests mentioned earlier and these special concerns for the primary grades, you may wish to consider using webquests in your classroom.

It is essential to provide opportunities for students to work together on webquest experiences so they may benefit from the natural support that comes from working together.

An exceptional source for primary grade webquests may be found at **The WebQuest Portal** at http://Webquest.org/. To locate examples of what are considered top or middle level WebQuests, select "Top" or "Middle" from the left menu and then choose from the K–2 subject area links in the Webquest Matrix. Other WebQuests may be located by using a search engine—simply visit **Google** (http://www.google.com), type in < *your topic +Webquest +grade level* > and you'll be on your way! Here are examples of some of the fine activities available for you to use in your classroom:

- **The Animals are Lost: Help Bring Them Home**—
  http://aldertrootes.wcpss.net/farmanimalsa.html

  This is the perfect introduction to webquests for young children. After learning about animals that live on the farm and those that live in the zoo through images, sound, and small bits of text, children are tasked with returning each animal to its proper home. Easy for beginning readers to navigate and understand.
- **I Like Books**—
  http://www.sdcoe.k12.ca.us/score/books/bookssg2.html

  In this webquest for Kindergarten and first grade, students read this work by Mark Browne and then complete several activities,

helping them to identify their favorite genre, contributing one page to a class book about their favorite reading selections, and then write a story themselves.

- **Konnichiwa: Welcome to My World—** http://score.rims.k12.ca.us/activity/konnichiwa/index.html
  This webquest was designed for first grade but is probably more appropriate for second or third grade. Students work together to write a book to help a new student from Japan feel welcome at your school. They read and research comparisons between life in the United States and in Japan and then each student creates one page to be included in a class book for the new student.
- **Meeting in the Mitten**—http://projects.edtech.sandi.net/grant/mitten/
  After reading *The Mitten* by Jan Brett, children explore selected links while learning more about the author, characters, and setting of the story. Their quest culminates when the class uses what they learn to perform a play based on the story.
- **Snakes Alive—**http://www.thematzats.com/snakes/index.htm
  In this webquest, students assume the role of Junior Herpetologists, using the Internet and other sources to gather information about snakes (e.g., habitat, life cycles, eating habits) in order to construct a snake exhibit that shares their learning with others.
- **Digging Up Dinosaurs Webquest—** http://mywebpages.comcast.net/saponaro/dino/dinowebquest.html
  After reading several dinosaur books written by Aliki, students are invited to become a member of a well-respected dinosaur expert team. Each team, consisting of a worker, paleontologist, draftsman, and photographer, is asked to go on a dig in a location believed to have many remains of dinosaur teeth . In the end, they present what they have learned to the museum's board.
- **In Search of Stellaluna's Family—** http://projects.edtech.sandi.net/chavez/batquest/batquest.html
  This webquest is based on the book *Stellaluna* by Janell Cannon. Students are asked to teach Stellaluna, a baby bat, more about being a bat after she realizes she is not a baby bird like her friends. They explore sites with breathtaking photos of bats, learning about how they behave, what they eat, and how they communicate using echolocation. After becoming a bat expert, there are plenty of games, quizzes, and extension activities to satisfy any child's curiosity about these unique creatures.

In the past few years, we have observed the rapid commercialization of educational resources on the Internet.

Commercials in the Classroom: The Commercialization of Educational Sites on the Internet

In the past few years, we have observed the rapid commercialization of educational resources on the Internet. We see this as new e-companies appear, developing educational resources to attract teachers and children and then selling banner ads to generate income. We see this as children's authors and their publishers develop websites containing instructional materials to promote their work and sell more books. We see this as teachers themselves begin to develop their own .com sites, directing others to these

E-MAIL FOR YOU

From: Doug Crosby (kiwi@digisys.net)
Subject: Early literacy and the Internet

Dear Friends,

How things change! Just three years ago we had just one dial up account to the Internet, now with lots of hard work we have high speed connections in all our classrooms and our teachers are finding new projects every day.

I would like to tell you about two ways in which we have integrated our school's strong emphasis on early literacy development with technology through our school website. Quite a number of years ago we moved away from using a basal reading program because we realized that all our students were at different places on theliteracy continuum. In its place, we have developed a centralized reading resource for all students, kindergarten through fourth grade.

In order to do this we have leveled over 1000 books for instructional reading and entered them onto a database which we have made available to other schools through our school website. Teachers can request a copy and we send it out via email attachment. You can see photos of our reading resource at http://www.digisys.net/cherry/CentRR.htm.

Another way we have shared our celebration of literacy is through the use of a digital camera during our annual literacy week. During this week, each classroom decorates their door like a book cover and on one day we all dress up as our favorite storybook characters. Last year we used the digital camera to record these events for the making of class books and for posting at our website. This proved to be very popular particularly with out of town relatives who could see what their grandkids, nieces and nephews were up to at school. The book covers and teacher characters can be viewed at http://www.digisys.net/cherry/literacyweek.html.

The Internet is a wonderful resource and we are have just as much fun creating for the Internet as we do visiting other sites.

Doug :-)} - The Kiwi at Cherry
Cherry Valley School
Polson, Montana
http://www.polson.k12.mt.us/cherry/teachers/crosby/crosby.site/index.html

commercial locations with links from their classroom homepage. Since writing the previous edition, the most significant change we notice on the Internet is the growing commercialization of educational resources.

We worry greatly about this trend. Never before has there been such a direct pipeline into the classroom from companies interested in developing brand recognition and loyalty among future consumers. The Internet permits this and the commercial world is keenly aware of the potential for profit in having this direct access to an important and relatively uninformed consumer group, the young children in our classrooms.

Should teachers play a part in this new effort to have commercials in the classroom? We think not. Our role should be to avoid exposing our students to as many of these commercials as possible as we educate them about how to critically understand the nature of this information.

As educators, we need to seriously consider the new challenges we face with commercials in the classroom that enter over the Internet.

Some organizations have been concerned about commercials in the classroom, especially with the increased access to the Internet. A few resources to explore with more information about this include the following:

- **Educators Guide to Commercialism—** http://lrs.ed.uiuc.edu/wp/commercialism/Commercialism.htm
- **Commercialism in the Classroom—** http://www.pta.org/ptawashington/issues/commercial.asp
- Commercialism in Education Research Unit's Annual Report— http://www.asu.edu/educ/epsl/CERU/CERU_Annual_Report.htm

As educators, we need to seriously consider the new challenges we face with commercials in the classroom that enter over the Internet. In the next few years, districts will be developing their own policies about the use of commercials in the classroom with Internet technologies. We suspect it will become an increasingly important issue for all of us. As we all think carefully about these new developments, here are several thoughts that we have about this issue:

- Wherever possible we should select Internet resources that do not have banner ads or pop-up windows selling products. These locations should only be used if they are central to learning an important aspect of the curriculum that may not be acquired in another, commercial-free manner.
- We should develop lessons and teach students to critically evaluate the commercial aspects of the Internet so that they may make informed decisions about overt commercial messages and covert data gathering procedures as they visit various Web sites.
- We should make every effort to avoid hosting our classroom homepages on commercial sites that provide free space for webpages in return for banner ads and pop-up commercials. We should encourage our districts to place our classroom pages on their servers so that we do not need to resort to these commercial alternatives.
- We should tell students in primary grade classrooms not to click on a banner ad or pop-up window, should these appear.
- We should teach all students to never provide their names or email addresses to anyone without first seeking permission from their parents.
- We should avoid making links on our classroom webpages to commercial sites including award images that, when clicked, actually take the viewer to a commercial location. Many of the awards given to teachers for their good work are actually links to commercial sites.
- All that we do should ensure that our students are thoughtfully protected from commercial interests at the same time we educate them in understanding both the overt and the hidden aspects of commercialism that appear on the Internet.

INTERNET FAQ

How can I begin to teach younger children to understand the difference between advertisements and relevant information on a website? Is this aspect of new literacies instruction appropriate for primary school children?

In Chapter 2, we stressed the importance of children understanding that certain agendas, both educational and economic, influence the content on websites. In our opinion, as soon as children are old enough to use the Internet (or even watch television), they are old enough to receive instruction on critical "habits of mind." In the early grades, you can begin by providing guided opportunities for children to practice locating advertisements embedded within otherwise "safe" informational websites. For example, **Funschool** (http://www.funschool.com/) features a wide range of entertaining and educational games worth exploring with children. However, advertisements are splashed around the border of the activity menu and pop-up boxes sometimes appear. These may potentially distract children from their assigned activity, but these also serve as important opportunities for critical literacy instruction. This website can be displayed on one computer using a projector, while the teacher facilitates discussion about which links lead to an educational game and which links lead elsewhere. Children can practice predicting and verifying their predictions. This will lead to a discussion of how different web-based context clues might help you make better choices about where to go next while reading on the Internet.

Other websites embed commercial messages in more subtle ways, by including their logo on all the pages and or by featuring free web-based games or related links centered only around products that they sell. Some examples of these include **American Girls** (http://www.americangirl.com/), **Lego** (http://www.lego.com/eng/), and **Scholastic** (http://www.scholastic.com/kids/home_flash.asp). Take time to explore these sites with your students in large or small group guided discussions, sharing thoughts about why certain toys or books are featured on each website and how the ".com" in each URL can help to identify commercial sites. These are important first steps toward helping young children think more critically about media and information in general—you will be amazed at the new critical insights that emerge.

Some believe that kindergarten classes do not need a classroom webpage. They say that children at this age are just too young for the Internet. Jack Fontanella proves how wrong this view is.

Visiting the Classroom: Jack Fontanella's Kindergarten Class in Alaska

Some believe that kindergarten classes do not need a classroom webpage. They say that children at this age are just too young for the Internet. Jack Fontanella proves how wrong this view is. Take a look at his wonderful classroom homepage (http://www.jsd.k12.ak.us/hbv/classrooms/Fontanella/fontanejhbvHome.html) in the Juneau School District (See Figure 9-7).

Looking through his classroom pages, one sees a teacher who cares deeply about the children in his classroom and a teacher who understands the needs of parents with children who are just beginning their school journey. If you spend a few minutes exploring his classroom webpage, you will also see the outstanding work he does to display his student's accomplishments, communicate important information to parents, and explore the many professional resources on the Internet for early childhood educators. You will also see the connections he has made to many other kindergarten teachers around the world.

Jack is clearly an outstanding educator. You see it in the photos of students at work on projects in the classroom, you see it in the important information he provides to parents, you see it in the art work his students complete, and you see it in the links to professional resources he has discovered on the Internet. If you are a teacher in the primary grades, this section alone is worth a visit.

Take a close look at the extensive information he provides to parents at the "Welcome to Kindergarten" page and at the "Parent's page" (read more at Jack's Email for You message). All of the important information about classroom policies and procedures are here, as well as links to many other resources that parents of kindergarten children might wish to explore.

Figure 9-7. A page from **Jack Fontanella's kindergarten class website in Juneau, Alaska.** It features some of his students' art work created on the computer. (http://www.jsd.k12.ak.us/hbv/classrooms/Fontanella/fontanejwork.html).

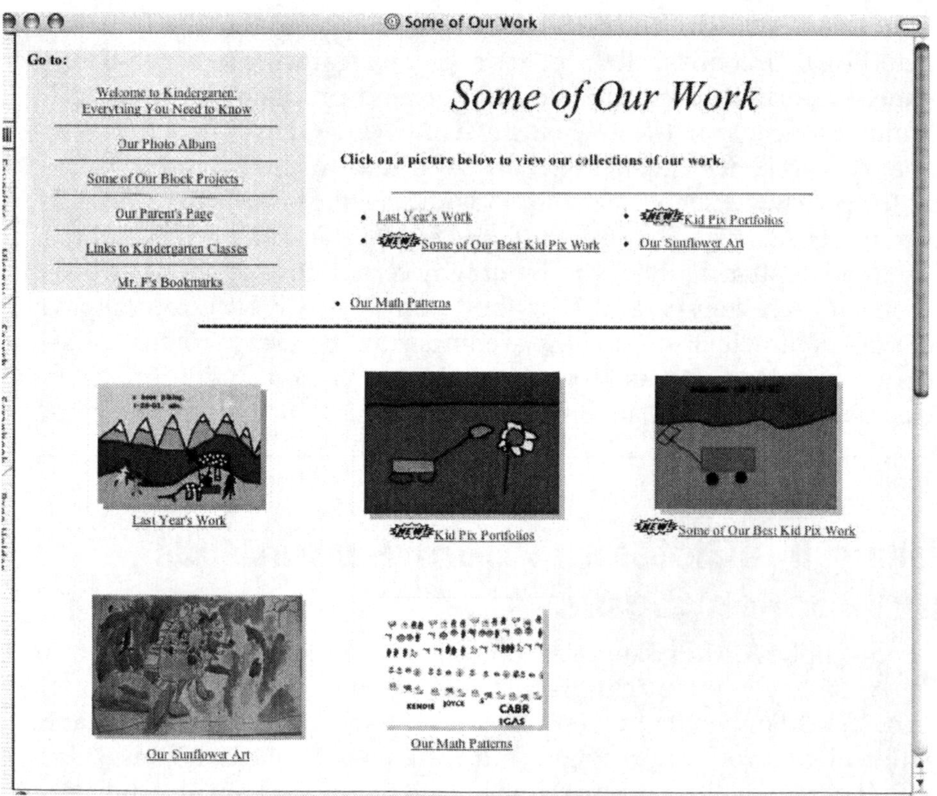

Don't neglect a visit to the many art projects students complete in Jack's class. Take a careful look at the KidPix artwork his students constructed in making an Internet alphabet book. And look at their holiday cards as well. There are some very talented children in this class exploring their special views of the world around them.

Finally, notice how Jack has developed a webpage with links to many other kindergarten classrooms on the Internet. Visit as many as you can and develop an understanding of the new communities of educators coming together through the work of outstanding educators such as Jack Fontanella.

Kindergarten teachers will come away from a visit to this location thinking of the many new possibilities the Internet provides for constructing connections with parents and guardians, children, and other kindergarten teachers. Classroom homepages not necessary for kindergarten classes? Not a chance!

E-MAIL FOR YOU

From: Jack Fontanella <fontanej@jsd.k12.ak.us>
Subject: How has the Internet changed my teaching?

Dear Colleagues,

In my kindergarten classroom, I do not use the Internet to teach with, per se. I use it as an important source of information when planning lessons and units. I use listservs to keep up with what is happening and have found many important resources this way. The number one way I use the internet is as a communication tool. I use my webpage to post things such as our classroom newsletter; pictures of what we have been doing in class; exceptional student work, especially projects that have turned out especially well; and all student work that is completed in the lab, since this saves quite a bit of paper.

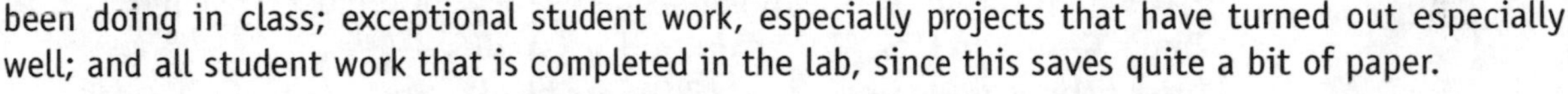

I post all of this on the world wide web in an attempt to bring parents and extended family into the classroom to get a closer look at their child's education. I also use e-mail to communicate at least weekly with parents. I currently have 90% of my families on my e-mail list. Technology for me is an important and potent form of communication that enables me to stay in close contact with parents and extended family members.

Sincerely,
Jack Fontanella, Kindergarten Teacher
Juneau, Alaska

New Literacies for Young Children

During our Internet travels for this chapter, we came across an excellent example of how a single curriculum-based project can provide the opportunity for young children to practice and apply strategies that encompass the five elements that frame the five dimensions of new literacies.

In the activity **Be a Web-Site Sleuth** (http://www.yorkville.k12.il.us/Webquests/Webqwagner/Webqswagner.html), first and second grade children pair up as detective partners, like favorite book characters Cam Jansen and Nate the Great. They set out to explore great book and author websites, vote on their favorite using a simple rating sheet, and construct a bar graph that communicates their results to others. This activity invites students to (1) consider important questions pertaining to what makes a good website about a book or an author; (2) locate relevant information within four different websites; (3) critically evaluate the information they find, judging its quality with a simple rubric; (4) synthesize information from multiple sources using a numerical tally system and a bar graph; and finally, (5) use oral and visual literacies to communicate their findings to their classmates with an oral presentation to accompany their bargraph. You may wish to build in similar strategies in your Internet experiences to help students acquire these important new literacies. Armed with these strategies early on, these young children will be well prepared for the new literacies of today's information and communication technologies.

Additional Resources on the Internet for Young Children

A World of Kindergartens—
http://www.coe.iup.edu/worldofkindergarten/

This is an incredible resource for kindergarten teachers! From here, you can quickly locate ideas for books, Web sites, songs and poems, recipes, and student activities related to almost any kindergarten theme imaginable. Much of the information here is compiled from ideas and resources shared through educational listservs for Kindergarten teachers.

Ben's Guide to U.S. Government for Grades K-2—
http://bensguide.gpo.gov/k-2/index.html

This is one of our favorite sites for introducing the world of government to young children, featuring simple descriptions of information and colorful images related to our nation, our government, local communities, and U.S. symbols. It also includes a hyperlinked alphabet book, a multi-leveled interactive map game, and an online coloring book. A great addition to your social studies curriculum!

BIG Ideas in Beginning Reading—http://reading.uoregon.edu/

Developed by the Institute for the Development of Educational Achievement (IDEA) at the University of Oregon, this Web site focuses on providing teachers and parents with research-based information on how to teach and assess the five "Big Ideas" of early literacy: phonemic awareness, alphabetic principle, fluency, vocabulary, and comprehension. You'll find a link to the research-based standardized assessment called the Dynamic Indicators of Basic Early Literacy Skills (DIBELS).

Billy Bear's Internet Post Office—
http://www.billybear4kids.com/post/office.htm

Young children love to send letters to their friends, their teachers, and their family! From this site, they can safely select from a wide range of traditional greeting cards or age-appropriate thematic e-cards, add their own music, message, and stamp and then email them off to their favorite person. A great writing activity to introduce students to electronic forms of communication.

Children's Books Online: The Rosetta Project—
http://www.childrensbooksonline.org/index.htm

This site houses a unique collection of over 300 antique children's books published in the early nineteenth and twentieth century. Viewed in full color and one page at a time, many texts have been translated into several world languages, providing a special opportunity for young children to access a wide range of children's titles. The Rosetta Project hopes to one day be an online library for all the world's children.

CIERA—http://www.ciera.org/

The Center for the Improvement of Early Reading Achievement is a federally funded effort to study and improve early reading. This location has many important resources for any primary grade educator interested in early literacy.

Chucky's Concentration—
http://www.pappyland.com/games/chuck.htm

A memory game for young children based on the classic Concentration game. Uses Shockwave. Rich in sound and animations.

Draw and Color with Uncle Fred—http://www.unclefred.com/

These simple step-by-step lessons from cartoonist Fred Laswell can boost children's confidence in drawing and coloring while also teaching them about cartoon drawing techniques.

Early Childhood Technology Literacy Project—
http://www.mcps.k12.md.us/curriculum/littlekids/

The Montgomery County Public Schools in Rockville, Maryland developed this comprehensive resource to share information about how to integrate technology into instruction and increase early childhood students' skills in reading and writing. You'll find great lesson plans, examples of student work, a list of recommended software, and technology tips to download.

Early Connections: Technology in Early Childhood Education—
http://www.netc.org/earlyconnections/index.html

From here, you can learn about the five dimensions of early development and learning from birth to third grade and how technology connects to each of those essential learning skills.

Family Literacy Backpack Project—
http://www.buddyproject.org/backpack/default.asp

This Web site provides everything teachers need to work with library media specialists to create theme-based backpacks filled with materials and activities for use at home. Follow links to theme-related backpacks and read reviews by teachers who have used them. Downloadable teaching materials and related Web site accompany each backpack theme. A great way to involve families!

Federal Emergency Management Agency (FEMA) Games for Kids—
http://www.fema.gov/kids/games1.htm

These quizzes, puzzles, and games about hurricanes, tornadoes, lightning storms, earthquakes, and other weather emergencies would go along perfectly with a unit on weather or to stimulate interesting discussions about what to do in an emergency.

Fred Penner's Jukebox—
http://games.funschool.com/game.php?g=1649&t=s&w=504&h=304§ion=g1

Very fast-loading, full-length popular songs for kids sung by Fred Penner, all accessible through an online interactive jukebox. Great for building oral language skills and listening for enjoyment!

Games for Children Ages 1 to 5—
http://www.kidspsych.org/oochy2.html

Don't let the name fool you. You simply must visit this site to see the wonderful THINKING activities for young children. The use of a Shockwave plug-in provides new levels of sound and animation in these very creative thinking activities for young children. Set a bookmark!

Games for Children Ages 6 to 9—
http://www.kidspsych.org/oochina.html

More great thinking activities and games for your students using a Shockwave plug-in. Set a bookmark!

GeoQuiz—http://www.lizardpoint.com/fun/geoquiz/index.html

Students can test their geography knowledge of country locations around the world using this interactive quiz that gives you three tries before it provides an answer. The maps are easy to read and, by clicking on help, children have access to a "cheat'" sheet that could be printed out for a nice matching activity with very young children.

Giggle Poetry—http://www.gigglepoetry.com/

Kids of all ages can read funny poems, enter a poetry contest, perform poetry plays, answer rhyme-time riddles, and learn how to write funny poems with tips from popular children's poet Bruce Lansky.

Hatching Emus—http://www.siec.k12.in.us/~west/proj/emu/

This picture gallery was designed by second graders in Indiana as they incubated four emu eggs in their classroom. Fun for kids to explore and a great model of how you can use digital photographs to record and share special events in your classroom that happen over time.

Jigzone.com—http://www.jigzone.com/

Any photo can be uploaded and transformed into a online interactive puzzle ranging from 6 to 240 pieces! Race against the clock to solve a puzzle already in their database or upload your own photo to be added to the collection. Kids will love the opportunity to email their photograph puzzles home or to a favorite relative to share an event that perhaps happened at school that day. Great fun!

Just for Kids from University of IllinoisExtension—
http://www.urbanext.uiuc.edu/kids/index.html

This is an amazing collection of ten interactive, Web-based informational resources about insects, plants, trees, gardening, and good health. Each is available in both English and Spanish. Although the developers indicate that much of the content was originally created for children in upper elementary school, the potential for fostering background knowledge about science topics for younger students was too much to pass up.

Kaboose Network's Shockwave Games—
http://www.kaboose.com/index.html
A great collection of activities for young children using Shockwave. You should screen these to select ones that actually lead to supporting your classroom program but many are quite useful. Also note the large number of pop-up boxes associated with this resource; you may want to set your browser to block pop-up ads.

Karaoke Song Corner for Kids—
http://www.geocities.com/EnchantedForest/Cottage/3192/
Kids will have a ball with this one! Hundreds of children's songs with lyrics and fast loading. Some favorites include Drunken Sailor, Never Smile at a Crocodile, and Take Me Out to the Ballgame. You may want to print out the lyrics and even use them as part of your guided reading group!

Little Fingers Shockwave Parlor Index—
http://www.little-g.com/shockwave/loading.html
Here is a set of great activities to practice important early learning skills including alphabet name knowledge, telling time, counting numbers, counting change, and much more. Uses Shockwave.

Hunkin's Experiments—
http://www.HunkinsExperiments.com/default.htm
Lots of safe cartoon experiments for kids with food, light, sounds, clothes, and more. May need an adult to help read the directions.

Minutes from ME—http://sln.fi.edu/qa96/meindex.html
A series of columns from a primary grade teacher, Margaret Ennis, who is a fellow at the Franklin Museum. Her articles contain many great ideas for working with very young children on the computer. Each one contains very practical ideas and lesson ideas to use immediately in your classroom. A newer section discusses issues related to young readers and the World Wide Web.

National Wildlife Federation KidZone—http://www.nwf.org/kids/
The National Wildlife Federation has developed this site for kids interested in animals and the environment. It contains interactive games for the youngest users, riddles and jokes for older students, and even articles from past issues of Ranger Rick and Backyard Buddies. Many articles also appear in Spanish. A nice location during units on animals and the environment. Set a bookmark!

NASA For Kids—
http://www.nasa.gov/audience/forkids/home/index.html
Your young science buffs will love to explore the interactive simulations, games, space stories, and much more. This is a great way to build background knowledge about space in a fun, engaging manner. A super idea for Internet Workshop within a space unit.

Online Autumn—
http://comsewogue.k12.ny.us/~ssilverman/autumn/index.html
Susan Silverman, a second grade teacher on Long Island, is a master of Internet projects. She has acquired an international reputation for her outstanding work. If you are doing work on seasonal change in the fall with your primary grade classroom you simply must visit this loca-

tion. It contains links from around the world to projects by other classrooms where children wrote poetry, stories, and art about autumn. Set a bookmark!

Outline Maps from Education Place—
http://www.eduplace.com/ss/maps/

Ever looking for a quick map to highlight the setting of a book or a current news event for your younger students? This site provides one click access to clear, black and white downloadable maps of all the major countries as well as regions in the United States. Great for coloring and labeling.

PBS Between the Lions—http://pbskids.org/lions/

Grounded in a research-based comprehensive literacy framework, this companion Web site to PBS' television series for children ages 4–7 is a wonderful multimedia addition to your early literacy curriculum. The site features interactive games, printable games and coloring sheets, video clips, songs, a 200-word illustrated speaking glossary, and 70 online stories, each paired with a set five other books with similar themes.

Pocantico Hills School—
http://www2.lhric.org/pocantico/pocantic.html

This school, in Pocantico Hills, New York, features one of our very favorite compilations of primary classroom Web-based projects for you to explore. From the homepage, select 'Class Pages' from the left menu and save plenty of time to peruse through each teacher's classroom Web page in kindergarten through third grade. A few teachers have six or seven years of Web-based environments to share with you, each proudly displaying the evolution of new literacies for young children.

Pook in the World—
http://www0.un.org/cyberschoolbus/pook/index.asp

Join Pook, a small character who wants to save the world, in an animated learning adventure for children ages 6 and up developed by the United Nations CyberSchoolbus. Each mission introduces young children to a different global issue through colorful characters and animation. Flash is required for this site.

Reading A-Z—http://www.readinga-z.com/newfiles/preview.html

If you're in need of a few leveled fiction and non-fiction books that children can take home and share with their families (without the fear of losing them), then you'll love this site. Although most of the resources are reserved for paying members, from this page you can download up to 30 free books, in English or Spanish, at different levels, as well as activity sheets that accompany each title.

Scholastic's Games and Quizzes—
http://teacher.scholastic.com/scholasticnews/games_quizzes/index.asp

Here you'll find a series of interactive educational games that changes weekly. Choose from learning games like Write the Caption, Build Your Own Caterpillar, Construct a Food Web, Interactive Weather Maker, Mapman, and Hangman.

Smokey Bear's Official Home Page—http://www.smokeybear.com/
Here is a great location for an Internet activity during Fire Safety Week. Kids can play several games about fire safety, take a quiz and see how they do, and even email Smokey. Set a bookmark! Sponsored by the USDA Forest service.

Stage Hands Puppets Activity Page—
http://www3.ns.sympatico.ca/onstage/puppets/activity/index.html
If you are interested in using puppets in your classroom here is a site for you! Puppet activities are a wonderful way to support language development in the primary grades.

Starfall Early Reading Games—
http://www.starfall.com/n/level-a/index/load.htm?f
Your emergent readers will love to explore the online storybooks here, each with animation, audio, sound effects, and more, and all focused on building beginning reading skills. These activities would make great center activities. Be sure to have headphones available for your little ones!

Technology and Young Children's Interest Forum—
http://www.techandyoungchildren.org/index.shtml
This forum is sponsored by the National Association for Education of Young Children (NAEYC). It shares research findings, demonstrates best practices, and fosters collaboration among those using technology with children aged birth through eight years.

The Future of Children—http://www.futureofchildren.org/
This Website, funded by the David and Lucille Packard Foundation, provides research and analysis to promote effective policies and programs for children. It features a seasonal journal and interactive conversations about current issues. Check out the Fall/Winter issue on Children and Computer Technology.

The White House for Kids—
http://www.whitehouse.gov/kids/presidentsday/index.html
Have your children take a tour of the White House. A fun activity for your students to complete as an Internet Activity. Your students can even write a letter to the president. Set a bookmark!

Webbing Into Literacy—
http://curry.edschool.virginia.edu/go/wil/home.html
A great collection of activities for supporting early literacy instruction in your classroom. Also a number of nice ideas for assessment of emergent literacy.

Weekly Reader—http://www.weeklyreader.com/kids/index.asp
Sponsored by the creators of *Weekly Reader* magazine, this Web site features interactive contest, games, and activities at each grade level. Grades 2 and up include a section on fantastic facts, a writing corner and a weekly online poll.

Online Communities for the Primary Grades

ECENET-L
"The place where parents, teachers, representatives of professional associations and government agencies, faculty and researchers, students and teachers, librarians, and anyone else interested in early child-

hood education come together to share ideas, resources, problems, and solutions."
Subscription: listserv@listserv.uiuc.edu
Homepage: http://ecap.crc.uiuc.edu/listserv/ecenet-l.html
Archives: http://ecap-sun.crc.uiuc.edu/listarchives/ecenet/old/

ECEOL-L

Early Childhood Education On-Line mailing list. Hosted by the University of Maine.
Subscription: listserv@lists.maine.edu
Homepage: http://www.ume.maine.edu/ECEOL-L/
Archives: http://lists.maine.edu/archives/eceol-l.html

ECL-DL

This low-volume listserv exchanges related to the research, development, and implementation of early childhood literacy programs.
Subscription procedures: http://www.topica.com/lists/earlyliteracy/
Archives: http://www.topica.com/lists/earlyliteracy/read

EC-PEN

Members share information about a child's early years of life sponsored by the Early Childhood Public Education Network in Alaska.
Subscription procedures: http://www.alaskafamily.org/blurbs/01/04/09/2313210.shtml

European Council of International Schools (ECIS) Early Childhood List

This group is sponsored by the United Kingdom but has members all over the world.
Subscription: listserv@listserv.ecis.org
Homepage: http://www.ecis.org/Committees/early.htm
Archives: http://listserv.ecis.org/archives/early.html

P3—Preschool to Year 3 Education Queensland (Australia) Mailing Lists

Subscription: http://education.qld.gov.au/listserv/subscribe.html
Homepage: http://education.qld.gov.au/listserv/
Archives: http://education.qld.gov.au/archives/p3.html

PROJECTS-L

A group interested in using a project approach in early childhood education.
Subscription: listserv@listserv.uiuc.edu
Homepage: http://ecap.crc.uiuc.edu/listserv/projec-l.html

RTEACHER

A discussion group to support literacy learning in the elementary classroom sponsored by *The Reading Teacher*, a journal of the International Reading Association.
Subscription: listserv@bookmark.reading.org
Home page: http://www.reading.org/virtual/rt_listserv.html
Archives: http://www.reading.org/archives/rteacher.html

10 Using the Internet to Increase Multicultural Understanding

We are excited by the opportunities the Internet provides to increase multicultural understanding and appreciate the diversity that defines our lives. The United States and Canada, for example, are home to over 100 different linguistic groups, numerous religions, and countless ethnic and cultural groups. The United States has the greatest variety of multi-ethnic households in the history of the world. In the Los Angeles School District alone, more than 80 different languages are used. Such societies only survive if their individual members develop a common commitment to respecting the rights of others and the cultural contexts they come from. This is not something that should be left to chance. We need to actively support multicultural understanding and appreciation of diversity at every chance. The Internet and other ICTs are special tools that can aid these efforts.

We need to actively support multicultural understanding and appreciation of diversity at every opportunity.

This chapter will discuss ways that these technologies can draw us closer to others who come from different cultural contexts. We will suggest resources to help students gain a better understanding and deeper appreciation for diversity and professional resources to assist teachers in incorporating a multicultural approach in their classrooms. Understanding and appreciating other cultures has long been an important goal. It is increasingly important in the global society that is developing. We should all take advantage of the opportunities that new technologies provide in our efforts to build a better world. As teachers, it is our responsibility to make sure that our students develop the new literacies that are necessary to successfully access and fully benefit from the Internet and other ICT.

After reading this chapter you should be able to:

1. Visit several online directories and identify at least four sites containing background information or lesson plans that you could use to prepare activities for increasing multicultural understanding and appreciation of diversity in your classroom.

2. Design a series of Internet activities using at least three websites from this chapter that you could use to foster your students' appreciation of other cultures and diverse ways of viewing the world.
3. Explore at least one Internet Project Registry that connects students with peers or classes around the world, and consider strategies you could implement to avoid or reduce typical problems that may occur in these electronic relationships.
4. Identify at least one Internet resource that could be used to support students from each cultural group commonly represented in your school and community.

Teaching with the Internet: Cheryl Chan's Class

"But I don't understand why we can't write to Native American students," said Desmon. "I don't understand why it hurts their feelings when we say we are studying their culture."

The students were doing Internet Inquiry in a unit designed to increase multicultural understanding and build classroom community. Studying different cultural traditions helped to accomplish these goals.

Desmon was reporting during an Internet Workshop session in Cheryl Chan's social studies class. The students in her class were doing Internet Inquiry in groups, working on projects in a unit designed to increase multicultural understanding and build a classroom community. Studying different cultural traditions helped to accomplish these goals.

Each group had selected a different culture to explore. One group had selected a Latin American theme and was reading literature and studying about many different Latino cultures. They had found many useful locations on the Internet by beginning their study at the **Latin American Network Information Center LANIC** (http://www. lanic.utexas.edu/), especially the site for **Primary and Secondary Education** (http://www.lanic.utexas.edu/la/region/k-12/). They also found the site **México para Niños** (http://www.elbalero.gob.mx/) and its English version **Mexico for Kids** (http://www.elbalero.gob.mx/index_esp.html). (This site also has French and Italian versions). The students were trying to determine who developed these sites, why they developed them, and what this suggested about the information located here. Cheryl had introduced the unit with an activity on critical literacies and this group was putting the information to good use. During this exploration they noticed some differences between the Spanish and English versions.

"Hey—what's this?" asked Rob. "The English site only has five links over here, but the Spanish site has nine. I guess *historia* means history, and maybe we can match up some of the other ones by their colors, but what's this mean? *Fondita*?"

"We can ask Orlando," suggested Lee. "Orlando, can you help us a minute?"

A little later, Cheryl saw Orlando, Rob, and the rest of the group talking back and forth as Orlando was trying to explain the links. This project was certainly building community in her classroom. The group was getting extra information about the site, and very importantly, she could she that Orlando had a sense of pride in his ability to speak and read Spanish. Last year, speaking Spanish had often been seen as having liability.

This year, with the Internet in the classroom, there were opportunities to use other languages, and Orlando's linguistic ability was seen in a very different light. Being fluent in Spanish was now an asset that was much in demand, especially after Cheryl established connections with a Spanish-speaking classroom in Argentina. At the same time, working on the translation helped Orlando develop a better understanding of English. Listening to their conversation as they worked together showed Cheryl that each student was learning much about the other's language.

This year, with the Internet in the classroom, there were opportunities to use other languages, and being fluent in Spanish was now an asset that was much in demand.

Figure 10-1. The El Balero **México para Niños** homepage (http://www.elbalero.gob.mx/) that students in Cheryl Chan's class evaluated.

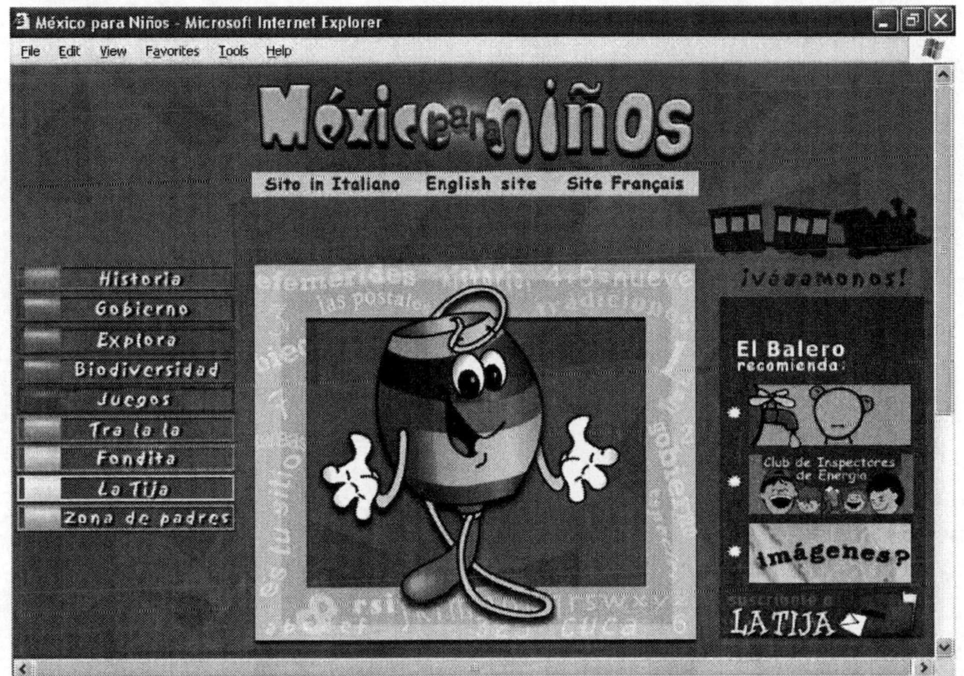

Another group had picked an African American theme and decided to focus on the connections they saw between the poetry of Langston Hughes and the actions of Rosa Parks and Martin Luther King, Jr. in the civil rights struggle. They had located a wonderful model of a webpage, **Timeline of the American Civil Rights Movement** (http://www.wmich.edu/politics/mlk/), they were going to follow as they put their report together. Two members of the group knew how to make webpages so they were all hard at work gathering information and exploring the connections they found between the poetry and the civil rights movement.

Other students had picked a Japanese theme and were studying the literature and cultural traditions of this culture. Using **Internet E-mail Classroom Connections** (http://www.teaching.com/iecc/) Cheryl had helped this group link up with a class in Kyoto. In addition to their Internet research, the students were exchanging email messages and participating in online chat, discovering many important insights about each other's cultural traditions.

Desmon's group was studying Native American literature and cultures, especially the common respect they all expressed for Mother Earth. His group had developed a growing respect for the traditions, struggles, and views of Native Americans by reading many prayers, poems, and stories from Internet sources. Cheryl had bookmarked suitable selections from sites such as **Indigenous Peoples Literature** and **Native Web Resources** (http://www.nativeweb.org/resources/literature/). In addition, the group had read a number of books from the library including: *Thirteen Moons on Turtles Back*, by Bruchac and London, *Giving Thanks: A Native American Good Morning Message* by Chief Jake Swamp, *Ceremony—In the Circle of Life* by White Deer of Autumn, *Buffalo Woman*, by Gobel, *Chief Sarah: Sarah Winnemucca's Fight for Indian Rights* by Morrison. They had also been exploring some of the many Native American sites on the Web.

The students were excited when they found a site with a place for posting messages. They wanted to link up with Native American students who might be interested in becoming keypals. But then they saw a message from the author of the site, which said:

> Non-Indians: teachers, kids, please do not say "studying Native Americans and want to correspond with some." This is offensive, racist. This service is primarily a way for Indian kids to get in contact with each other, not a method of providing specimens for study by your class or students.

The discussion in Cheryl's class was useful in developing greater respect and sensitivity for others, issues at the heart of effective cross-cultural communication and understanding.

Desmon was sharing his question with the rest of the class during their regular workshop session. "I didn't know that I was being racist," he said. "And I don't want to hurt anyone's feelings. I just want to understand more about their culture."

This event prompted a lively discussion in Cheryl's class. Some students could not understand the reason behind the website message, but then Michelle asked how they would feel if someone wrote: "We are studying girls, or Latinos, or African Americans, or boys, and we want to correspond with some."

"It makes you feel like a thing, not a person," she noted. "And, there are many different Native American cultures, not just one." This made many students think about how the person who developed this website must have felt when reading messages such as this.

The discussion in Cheryl's class was useful in developing greater respect and sensitivity for others, issues at the heart of effective cross-cultural communication and understanding. It increased students' awareness of the power of words and how the words one uses in a verbal or email message may unintentionally hurt people. It also helped students develop greater sensitivity to different cultural traditions and how one must be respectful of cultural differences on the Internet as well as in daily life.

Toward the end of their conversation, Cheryl pointed out how important it was for all students to have a space to communicate with others from their own cultural background, and that others needed to respect this right. However, she also noted that some Native American students were interested in communicating with students from non-Native cultural traditions. Cheryl had recently discovered **Cradleboard** (http://www.cradleboard.org/main.html), a project of the Nihewan Foundation founded by Buffy St. Marie. This outstanding site offers many free curriculum resources as well as materials for sale. Cheryl was not certain if the site's Cradleboard Teaching Project was open to her class, but she would send a message to get more information. She would also revisit **A Line in the Sand** (http://www.hanksville.org/sand/). This site presented Native American views on cultural property and helped Cheryl understand why many Native Americans objected to the way their cultures and sacred traditions were widely distributed over the Internet. Perhaps she could develop a follow up activity for their next workshop.

Lessons from the Classroom

These episodes from Cheryl Chan's classroom have several important lessons for us to consider as we think about using the Internet to increase multicultural understanding. First, it is clear the Internet provides special opportunities to help everyone better understand the unique qualities in each of our cultural traditions. No other instructional resource available in your classroom is as rich in its potential for developing an understanding of the diverse nature of our global society and for helping each of your students to walk in someone else's footprints.

It is clear the Internet provides special opportunities to help everyone better understand the unique qualities in each of our cultural traditions. No other instructional resource available in your classroom is as rich in its potential for developing an understanding of the diverse nature of our global society and for helping each of your students to walk in someone else's footprints.

Using the Internet to celebrate the diversity that exists in our country and our world accomplishes many goals. Bringing this information into your classroom sends an important message to your students about the respect and dignity that should be accorded to every human experience. The Internet makes it easier than ever before to integrate numerous authentic resources from different cultures into your curriculum. Through working with resources that represent their culture and reflect a familiar world view, students feel pride in themselves and their culture. Moreover working with these resources from the Internet helps *all* students appreciate and value the variety of cultural experiences that create a rich and vibrant society. In addition, students develop a richer appreciation of the historical forces that have shaped our societies and the contributions made by different cultural groups. And, the Internet allows all students to explore issues of social justice. Exploring these issues is essential to preparing children for citizenship in a diverse society in which equal access and opportunity are fundamental to our collective well being.

Cheryl sought to take advantage of these potentials. Each group in her class defined and completed an Internet Inquiry project celebrating a particular cultural group. Cheryl provided several guidelines for each group to follow: each project had to treat the culture with respect; it had to include literature and Internet experiences; and each group had to develop a learning experience for the rest of the class based on something they had learned from that culture. In addition to acquiring content knowledge and a better understanding of other cultures, students developed new literacies: finding the best search engines to locate answers for their questions; critically evaluating the sites they found using online checklists; and synthesizing information presented in various media from those sites. In addition each group had to communicate its findings to the rest of the class. They used a variety of formats and a combination of new and foundational literacies to share their results. One group was building a learning center in their classroom that included a PowerPoint presentation of cultural artifacts. Another group was planning a poetry reading and a readers' theater presentation, followed by completion of an online survey they had developed. Another group was developing a reading corner with both books and an Internet scavenger hunt for everyone to complete.

A second lesson comes from the episode with Orlando. An Internet connection in your classroom coupled with well-designed activities such as those developed by Cheryl, helps build classroom community among all students, and leads everyone to think differently about linguistic diversity. Instead of viewing a student as English language deficient, fluency in another language becomes an asset when you create opportunities to utilize this skill in activities with classes around the world. Orlando's ability to speak and read Spanish became a special talent that was valued by other members of his class when Cheryl recognized its potential use on the Internet. Orlando's sense of self-worth increased greatly as he became a central member of his classroom community. Moreover, Orlando acquired English more rapidly as he interacted with his classmates, while they were learning new concepts and words in Spanish. Everyone gains when teachers orchestrate positive multicultural experiences such as this in their classrooms.

An Internet connection in your classroom coupled with well-designed activities helps build classroom community among all students and causes everyone to think differently about linguistic diversity.

Cheryl's class teaches us a third lesson: online communication experiences may be very useful when you use the Internet to increase multicultural understanding. Email and other forms of electronic communication allow students to immediately communicate with people from different cultural traditions in order to learn more about their unique heritage. This opportunity has never before existed in school classrooms; it enables your students to engage in powerful and immediate cross-cultural experiences with authentic feedback that may be used to develop understanding and respect for others.

Such communication is a two-edged sword, however, for developing multicultural understanding. On the positive side, online communication, particularly email, removes many of the visual trappings that often impede conversations between members of different cultural groups; we are unaware of physical differences and focus instead on considering the ideas and experiences of the people with whom we communicate. This is what the students who studied Japanese cultural traditions experienced in Cheryl's class. On the other hand, when we bring stereotypes about a cultural group to our conversations, these stereotypes often appear, even if unintentionally, between the lines of our messages and may be hurtful to the recipient. This is what happened when students in Cheryl's class left messages for Native American keypals. Online communication, particularly email, between different cultural groups requires sensitivity toward the recipient and an ability to anticipate how any message might be interpreted or misinterpreted as you compose it. Often, it forces us to confront stereotypes we may have but may not realize. These are good lessons for all of us to think about.

Directories for Multicultural Resources

Many locations on the Internet provide a comprehensive set of resources to help your students appreciate and understand different cultural traditions. There are also sites that support students from particular cultural, ethnic, and linguistic groups. You may wish to review the resources at these sites as you develop Internet Workshop, Internet Project, and Internet Inquiry with your students. Some locations also contain webquests.

It is possible that some of the directories identified in this section contain links that eventually lead to locations where issues of sexual orientation are considered. While we believe these issues are important for older students to consider, we recognize that a number of teachers and communities may feel uncomfortable allowing younger students to access these sites. We mention this so that you may make informed judgments about the locations you make available to your students.

Many locations on the Internet provide a comprehensive set of resources to help your students appreciate and understand different cultural traditions.

Some of the best directories for increasing multicultural understanding include:

- **African American History and Culture—** http://www.si.edu/resource/faq/nmah/afroam.htm
  A useful collection of resources from the Smithsonian Institution.
- **Asian Americans—** http://newton.uor.edu/Departments&Programs/AsianStudiesDept/asianam.html
  An award-winning site with collections of resources on aspects of the Asian American experience as well as links to East and Southeast Asia resources.
- **Cultures of the World—** http://www.ala.org/ala/alsc/greatwebsites/greatwebsitescultures.htm
  A site with many extensive resources selected by the American Library Association as appropriate for children from preschool to age 14.
- **Humanities Interactive**—http://www.humanities-interactive.org/
  An interactive site from the Humanities Council of Texas, featuring virtual exhibits of art and information on many cultures around the world. With teacher guides, lessons, games, and essays, this site is also great for teachers.
- **Index of Native American Resources on the Internet—** http://www.hanksville.org/NAresources/
  The most comprehensive site of Native American Resources we've found. Useful for teachers too.
- **Language and Culture Links for Limited English Proficient Students—** http://www.ncela.gwu.edu/links/langcult/toplangs.htm
  Educational, linguistic, and cultural online resources for the top languages/language groups of English learners in U.S. schools.
- **Latin American Network Information Center—** http://www.lanic.utexas.edu/
  A great location with many sites and resources devoted to the study of Latin America. The education area is especially useful. Some of the locations are in Spanish.
- **Portals to the World—** http://www.loc.gov/rr/international/portals.html
  This site from the Library of Congress provides a wealth of information on most of the countries of the world. Especially useful for secondary students.

- **Yahooligans: Around the World**—
  http://yahooligans.yahoo.com/around_the_world/

  One of the best sites for classrooms in the elementary grades exploring cultural diversity. Especially useful is the section on cultures, but all areas will have links to resources that may be immediately used in the classroom.

Figure 10-2. Portals to the World (http://www.loc.gov/rr/international/portals.html), an excellent site from the **Library of Congress Global Gateway** (http://international.loc.gov/intldl/intldlhome.html).

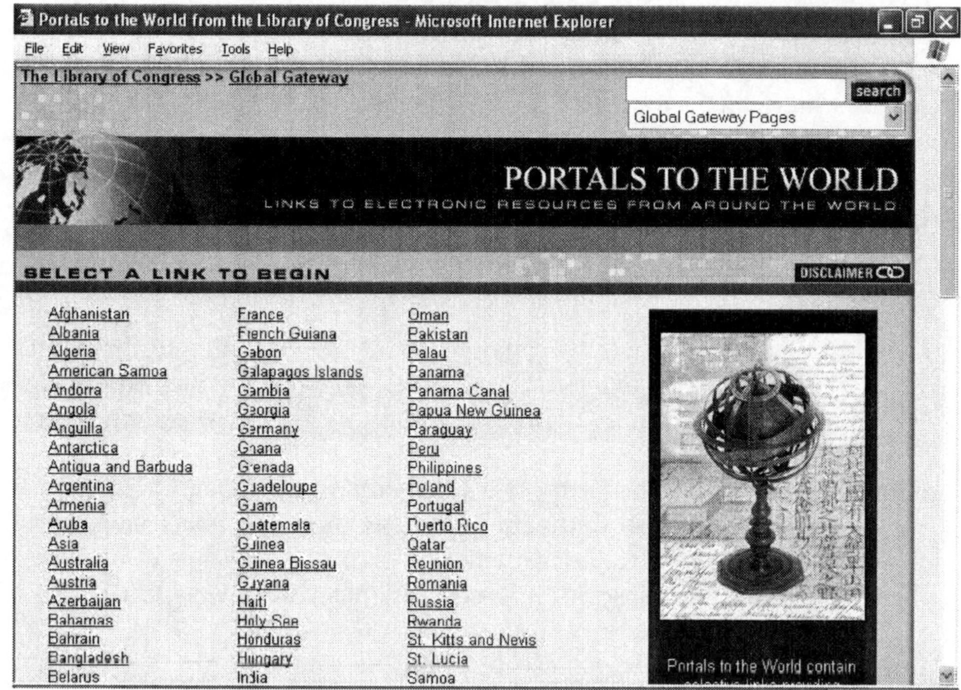

Directories for Teaching Multicultural Awareness

The directories above offer rich resources for students. In addition, there are excellent directories for teachers that often provide lesson plans as well as information. Here are some of the better directories for teachers that we have found:

- **Asia on the Web**—http://www.isoplucla.edu/eas/Resource.htm

  A very extensive set of resources from the Center for East Asian Studies at UCLA. Be sure to check the K-12 Curriculum resources (http://www.isop.ucla.edu/eas/web/curric-web.htm).
- **Asia for Educators**—http://afe.easia.columbia.edu/

  An excellent resource from Columbia University. Includes information on DBQs (data based questions for NY state assessments).
- **Five Dimensions of Digital Equity: Cultural Relevance**—
  http://digitalequity.edreform.net/

  This site from the Education Reform Network has an eclectic list of resources representing the cultural relevance dimension of digital

equity, one of the five fundamental dimensions of its equality criteria list. Sites range from ESL activities to an archive of African American music to an assessment rubric.

- **Hot List of Sites in ¡Español!**—
  http://www.kn.pacbell.com/wired/fil/pages/listspanish.html
  A great list of resources in Spanish from the SBC Knowledge Network.
- **K-12 African Studies**—
  http://www.sas.upenn.edu/African_Studies/AS.html
  A variety of resources of links from the African Studies Center at the University of Pennsylvania. Check their General Resources category for country pages and K–12 resources.
- **Native American Sites**—
  http://www.nativeculture.com/lisamitten/indians.html
  A variety of links including the home page of the **Native American Library Association** (http://www.nativeculture.com/lisamitten/aila.html).

Opportunities for English Language Learners

As we have seen, the Internet can provide special opportunities for English language learners (ELL) in your class. Using Internet Project with schools that use the same language as students in your room who are learning English as a second language (ESL) is a wonderful method for supporting linguistic development. Having ESL students assist with translations gives them a valued role within the classroom's activities. If you have your second language learners work with other students on the translations, both native and non-native speakers will develop a better understanding of one another's language. To find a school with students who speak the language of ESL students in your class, you may wish to pay a visit to **IECC** (http://www.iecc.org/), **Kidlink** (http://www.kidlink.org/), or **Windows on the World** (http://www.wotw.org.uk/). Locate several possible schools and send them an email message with a list of projects you would be interested in completing together.

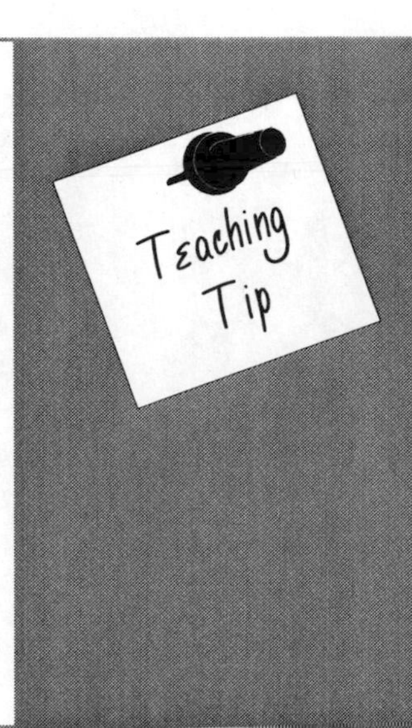

Using online translation sites seems like a great idea. But it is probably better not to depend on them for serious work since they tend to convey the gist of a message rather than an exact translation. They do best with simple language and common words, but even then you can end up with some strange phrases or sentences. "Fun recipes" might come out as "amused prescriptions," for example. It is also better to use longer sections of text for translation since a very short message can be hard to follow if it has two or three incomprehensible sentences. In a longer message, you will probably get the idea even if it contains a similar number of wrong sentences.

Here are three sites to try. Be sure to click the free electronic translation button unless you want to pay for a human translator!

- **Babelfish**—http://babel.altavista.com/tr
- **Free Translation**—http://www.freetranslation.com/
- **World Lingo**—http://www.worldlingo.com/products_services/worldlingo_translator.html

If you have an ESL student whose English ability is insufficient for translating project information, you may wish to try another approach. Pair the student with a native speaker in your class. Give them a usual Internet activity assignment related to the country or culture from which the ESL student comes. Students can search for information in their native languages and then share what they have found. To help you find Internet resources about a particular country or culture, visit one of the directories mentioned above such as Portals to the World or Yahooligans. Follow the links to the country you wish to visit. The country's major newspapers should be especially useful as they contain many interesting news items in the first language of your student. You can find links to international newspapers at the **Internet Public Library** (http://www.ipl.org/div/news/).

Many students will find it exciting to listen to radio stations around the world with the Internet, especially if they have a partner with whom to exchange the information.

In addition, you may wish to have your students listen to a radio station in the country or from the culture from which the ESL student comes. This can be done by visiting the **Stations Guide** location at **RealAudio** (http://radio.real.com/) and searching for radio stations by the student's geographical region. Alternatively, you could visit **Yahoo's Live Radio** site (http://dir.yahoo.com/News_and_Media/Radio/By_Region/Countries/) and search for online radio stations in a target country. Many students will find it exciting to listen to radio stations around the world with the Internet, especially if they have a partner with whom to exchange the information.

Conducting an Internet activity about the English Language Learner's (ELL) country will engage both students in conversation about something familiar to the ELL student. This will motivate both students and make conversation easier for the ELL student. Including a reading or writing task as part of the Internet activity can further foster collaborative second language learning between the two students.

Another option is to direct the two students to develop their own Internet activity. For the first week, for example, you might ask the two students to visit some sites in the student's country of origin and create a list of Internet activity assignments they want to complete. Then use this list to guide work during subsequent weeks. You might rotate partners every few weeks to allow the ESL student to meet and work with all members of the class. If you conduct an Internet Workshop session each week, you may wish to have the two students report the results of their assignment to the class. This provides a nice opportunity to support oral as well as written language development.

Do not forget to take advantage of any new literacies that English language learners might have. For example, in many countries online chat is extremely popular. An ESL student in your class may be able to help other students set up individual chat accounts through an organization such as IECC, and follow up by helping them learn the ropes. Many ESL students are proficient at navigating or have experience creating a webpage; this is other knowledge that could be shared with classmates, or the teacher!

Figure 10-3. Activities for ESL Students (http://a4esl.org/) from the *Internet TESL Journal* (http://iteslj.org/), a great location for ESL learning experiences.

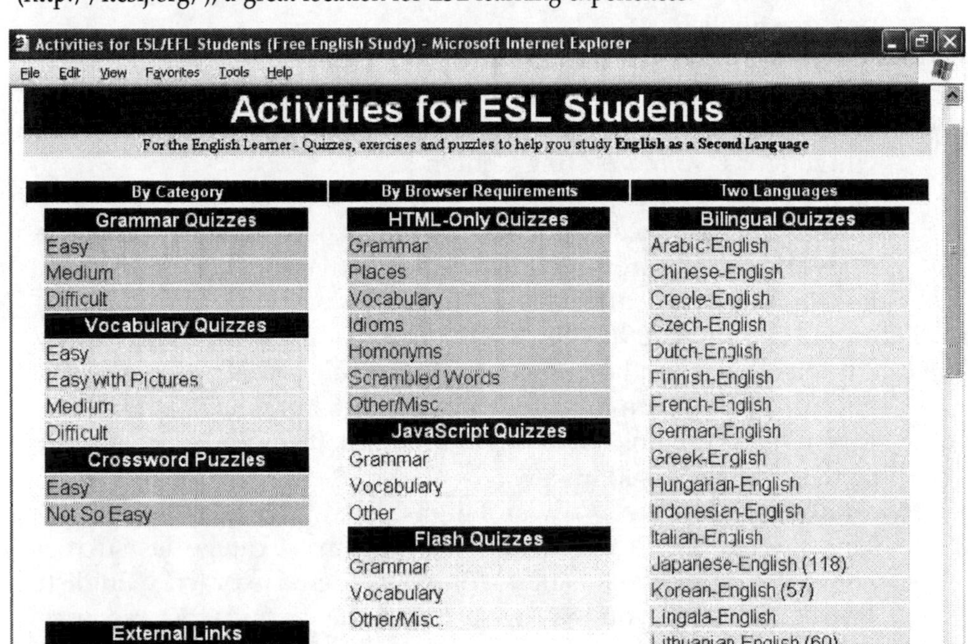

Useful Sites for English Language Learners

Here are additional Internet resources that you may find useful for supporting English Language Learners in your class:

- **Activities for ESL Students**—http://a4esl.org/
  A great site from the *Internet TESL Journal*. This site has links to numerous exercises and quizzes. It also includes links to bilingual puzzles in several languages.
- **Dave Sperling's ESL Cafe**—http://www.eslcafe.com
  This is one of the most popular general sites for ESL. It has ads and more commercial links than it used to, but it's still a good site for teachers and older students. It offers bulletin boards and chat as well as activities and resources.
- **ESL Independent Study Lab**—
  http://www.lclark.edu/~krauss/toppicks/toppicks.html
  Links to many activities and games. Organized by ability level.
- **E. L. Easton: Materials For Teaching English**—http://eleaston.com
  Here is another excellent directory with ESL links for a variety of levels and purposes, as well as to other related sites such as flags of the world.
- **IATEFL Young Learners Special Interest Group**—
  http://www.countryschool.com/ylsig/
  A site for teachers from the International Association of Teachers of English as a Foreign Language. This is a list of resources for English Language Learners according to age: very young, primary, and secondary.

- **Interesting Things for ESL Students**—http://www.manythings.org/
  A variety of games, puzzles, proverbs, and other enjoyable ways to practice English.
- **OWL ESL Resources, Handouts and Exercises**—
  http://owl.english.purdue.edu/handouts/esl/
  Excellent site for middle and high school students from Purdue University's Online Writing Center.
- **Randall's ESL Cyber Listening Lab**—http://www.esl-lab.com/
  One of the best sites! Students can practice listening to conversations and lectures from a wide range of native speaker voices. Easy, medium, and difficult levels, with quizzes.
- **TESL, TEFL, TESOL, ESL, EFL, ESOL LINKS**—http://iteslj.org/links/
  Another site from the *Internet TESL Journal*, this is one of the best ESL directories with links for teachers and students. It's non-commercial and contains no frames or graphics. It's updated frequently, so there are few dead links.
- **Tower of English**—http://towerofenglish.com/
  This site offers an extensive list of sites (in 34 categories such as animals, comics, and business) for ESL students to practice English. There are ads, so you may wish to use this as a teacher resource. Ads appear in a relatively unobtrusive side bar, however, so check it out and decide if it is appropriate for your students.
- **The University of Victoria's English Language Centre Study Zone**—
  http://web2.uvcs.uvic.ca/elc/studyzone/
  This site offers a variety of activities and explanations regarding grammar and reading for students at various levels.

E-MAIL FOR YOU

From: Anne Nguyen (cnguyen742@aol.com)
Subject: Supporting ESL Students through Email

Hi!

I'm sure it's obvious, but I had a wonderful experience with some of my former students recently. I have 2 email addresses—one through my district that I had not used in 4 weeks because of the summer holidays. Then I went to school and checked my district account. I had about 12 messages—all from my students from last year. I poured over each and every one of the messages and laughed in amazement. I was amazed at what they had to say. Students seemed more willing to share personal information with me in this format and asked readily for advice too.

These are ESL students and I realized what a good method this was to practice not only their writing skills, but also reading—by reading the replies they would receive—and those from teachers or American students would most likely have correct grammar and spelling—a good model! But I think the best thing is the ease with which a teacher can touch base with ALL students.

This experience has cemented an idea I have for my students next year. I am going to make sure all my students get email addresses at the beginning of the year and are able to use them to communicate with each other as well as with me.

Anne Nguyen, ESL Teacher
Syracuse City School District
Syracuse, NY

Keeping It Simple: Using Internet Workshop

Exploring links at the multicultural directories and ELL sites mentioned earlier should give you several ideas for an Internet Workshop activity designed to increase multicultural understanding. Some teachers like to devote a weekly Internet Workshop activity to this topic as a regular part of their curriculum, each week exploring a different cultural experience on the Internet and discussing this experience during a workshop session. When setting up Internet activities to increase multicultural understanding, try to provide opportunities for students of different backgrounds to work together on an activity. This creates opportunities for important exchanges to take place that raise awareness about cultural issues. This almost always leads to conversations that are important in developing greater respect and sensitivity for other cultures, especially if you establish this value in your classroom.

Here are some examples of Internet Workshop that could be used to support multicultural understanding:

Some teachers like to devote a weekly Internet Workshop activity to increasing multicultural understanding as a regular part of their curriculum, each week exploring a different cultural experience on the Internet and discussing this experience during a workshop session.

- **On the Line**—
  http://www.oxfam.org.uk/coolplanet/ontheline/index.html
  See how people in eight different countries on the meridian line from Europe through Africa share the same time of day but lead very different lives. Have students select one country and come to the workshop session with a presentation on the culture of that country. Although the project has finished, the information is still available in English, Spanish, and French on line.
- **Mancala**—http://imagiware.com/mancala/
  This strategy game from Africa is often found in classrooms. Here it is in a virtual form. Students can play this game against the computer as you study African or African American cultural traditions. It contains clear directions, and the program will even give you hints if your game is not going very well. Students can share strategies at Internet Workshop. There is also information about how Mancala is celebrated and the meaning of the important symbols. Have your students read the information and then come to Internet Workshop prepared to share what they have learned.
- **Chinese Calendar**—
  http://www.fi.edu/fellows/fellow1/apr99/calendar/index.html
  The Chinese Zodiac is a 12-year cycle in which each year is named after an animal. People born in a given year are said to have that animal's characteristics. Have your students visit this Chinese calendar activity developed by students at Loogootee Elementary School. Have them find the animal that corresponds to the year of their birth and read about the characteristics of people born in that year. They can share their information and discuss its accuracy. If you teach older students, have them read the more extensive information available at the **Chinese Culture Center's Zodiac Page** (http://www.c-c-c.org/chineseculture/zodiac/zodiac.html) and complete a similar activity.

It is important to study different cultural experiences in order to better understand the diversity that defines our world. At some point, students may want to move from understanding to social action. If this is feasible, seek ways with your students to engage them in community action projects, either in your own community or through the Internet. Students have used the Internet to support efforts in famine relief at locations such as **The Hunger Site** (http://www.hungersite.com/), or to support the purchase of rain forest habitat at locations such as **Rain Forest Care** (http://rainforest.care2.com/).

If you are working at the high school or middle school level, **UNICEF's Voices of Youth** (http://www.unicef.org/voy/index.php), is a great resource for getting started; its Explore, Speak Out and Take Action sections provide background information, suggestions for choosing a project, and ways to make a difference. You might also seek social action or volunteer projects in your community by visiting **Project America** (http://www.project.org/index.html). This resource, originally developed by two high school students, puts you in touch with organizations in your area who are seeking volunteer assistance with a number of projects, many of which permit your students to act in positive ways while also developing their knowledge and experience of diversity.

Figure 10-4. Project America (http://www.project.org/index.html) puts people in touch with organizations in their area that are seeking volunteer assistance.

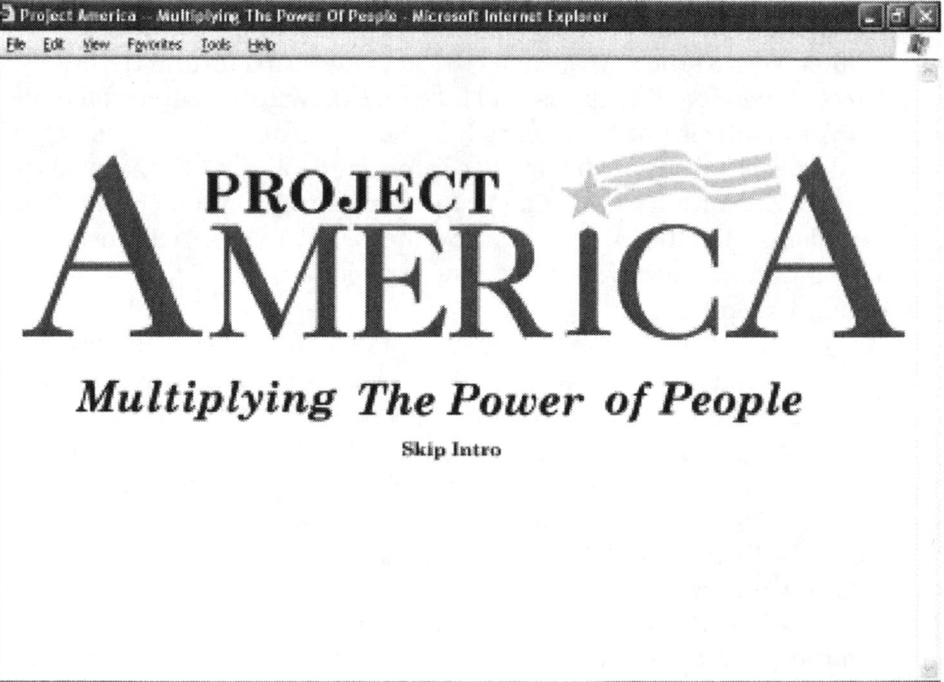

Using Internet Project

Internet Project is, perhaps, the best method for developing multicultural understanding among your students. When your students communicate with students from another cultural context, many important insights are shared about how we all are alike and how we are different.

For older students, information and experiences gained through online interaction and collaboration with students from other cultures or ethnic groups can bring out awareness of stereotypes and cause students to reevaluate their opinions. Younger students can also gain from online interactions. They often have a way of cutting right through social trappings to share essential information with one another. Their queries, which might be perceived as offensive to an adult, are often appreciated for what they are by other youngsters—an honest attempt to understand the world around them. Guiding both older and younger students into these new types of cultural interchanges on the Internet can do much to increase their understanding of cultural differences. The Internet Project information and sites described in Chapter 2 may be useful as you seek out projects with classes from different cultural contexts.

Internet Projects are perhaps the best method to develop multicultural understanding among your students. When your students communicate with students from another cultural context, many important insights are shared about how we are all alike and how we are different.

- **The Global SchoolNet Projects Registry**—
  http://www.gsn.org/pr/index.cfm
- **Intercultural Email Classroom Connections**—
  http://teaching.com/IECC/
- **KIDPROJ**—http://www.kidlink.org/KIDPROJ/
- **Oz Projects**—http://ozprojects.edna.edu.au/
- **SchoolNet's Grassroots Collaborative Learning Projects Gallery**—
  http://www.schoolnet.ca/grassroots/e/project.centre/project-search.asp
- **Windows on the World**—http://www.wotw.org.uk/

You may also want to visit **iEARN** (http://www.iearn.org.au/collab.htm) the International Education and Resource Network in Australia. This is another collaborative projects site, but one that tends to stay away from unstructured keypal exchanges in favor of projects which "involve students in discussions of issues, production of materials, and creative efforts, and seeks to engage students through commitment to meaningful work with others." Another difference is that iEARN projects often use a range of ICT, such as newsgroups and video-conferencing, instead of only email.

Sometimes extra effort is needed to find partner classrooms from other cultural contexts. If working through project registry sites is not successful, you may be able to find a contact through an Internet search in the way that Cheryl Chan found Cradleboard. Another strategy is to initiate contact directly with individual teachers and schools. You could email a teacher whose website you admire or the principal from a school whose population you would like to collaborate with. Or you might join a listserv or read an online bulletin board created for members of the cultural group you hope to work with. Allow enough time to just read the messages and get a feel for the culture of the list before posting a message. Then make your request in an appropriate way. Certainly, not everyone will respond, but usually there is enough response to make this strategy worthwhile. We encourage you to try it because the rewards can be substantial.

Figure 10-5. The **Showcase** page (http://www.wotw.org.uk/showcase/index.html) from the British Council's **Windows on the World** (http://www.wotw.org.uk/intro/index.html) has links to examples of partner classes and descriptions of their projects.

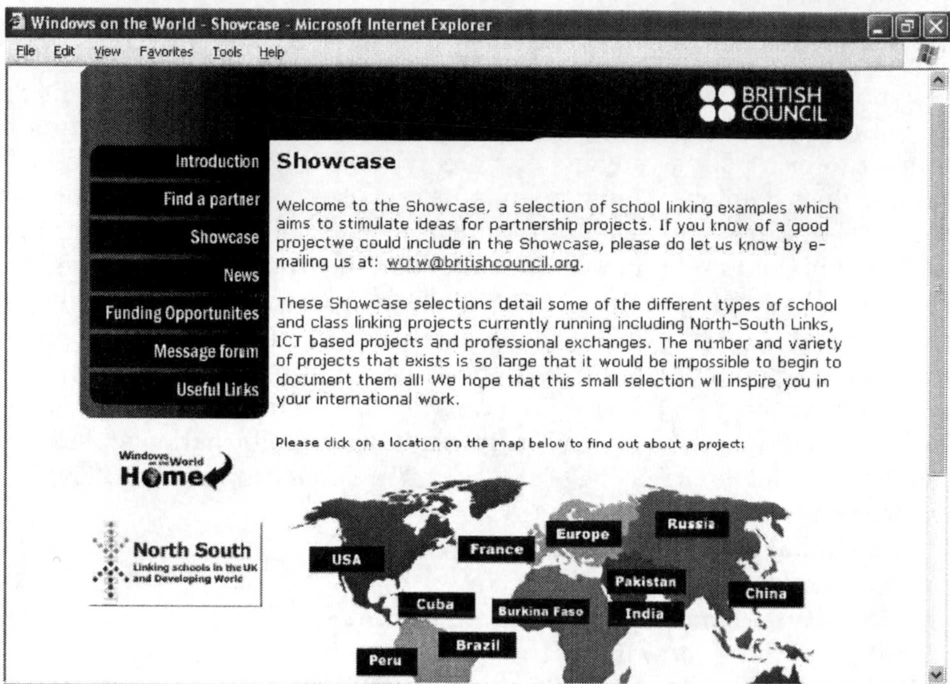

Examples of projects you may wish to consider joining or developing to increase multicultural understanding include:

- **Breaking Bread Together.** Breaking bread together is a traditional way to begin a cultural exchange about important matters. Invite several classes from around the world to participate in an email collaborative project as you exchange foods from your countries and eat a common meal on the same day. Each class sends a small package of culturally significant foods to participating classes along with directions for their preparation. If this is not possible, you may be able to get a list from the partner class and purchase the foods in your own country, or online. Before the common meal and on the day of the celebration, classrooms exchange information via email about each type of food and its significance within their culture. Differences in time zones may prevent immediate back and forth of email messages, but some classrooms schedule their event on a weekend day or in the evening so they can communicate in real time. Other classrooms have their email exchange take place during the following days. Great fun and very important insights always result from this activity.
- **Who are our Heroes?** Invite classes from several different cultural contexts to participate in a heroes project. Each student in participating classes can write a description of their greatest hero, explaining what it is about this person that makes them admirable. Classes

then exchange these essays in order to understand who students in different cultural contexts admire. Then, provide an opportunity for students to ask questions of one another about their essays, especially information that may relate to their culture. Use Internet Workshop to share essays and discuss the qualities each hero shares. These essays and conversations provide an ideal opportunity to discover important aspects of different cultures. This project could be extended to include heroes in different categories: parent/guardian heroes, teacher heroes, sports, politicians, and so on.

- **Weekly News from Around the World.**
  Invite classes from around the world to contribute two or three news articles each week from their classroom about local events. Have one class collect these articles via email and distribute a weekly world newspaper to each of the participating classes. Writing about local events for students in another cultural context forces students to develop greater sensitivity to the needs of their readers from different cultural contexts. Use Internet Workshop to plan new articles and read those contributed by others. Discussing these events develops a better understanding of the cultural context in different parts of the world.
- **Explanatory Myths from Around the World.** Every culture contains a set of explanatory myths that explains the creation of natural elements—why the sun comes up each day, where fire came from, how a mountain or lake was created, or where the face in the moon comes from. Invite schools from different cultural contexts to have students research, write, and share these stories with students from different cultural contexts. Read these stories during Internet Workshop and discuss what each may say about the culture from which it came.

Individual students often have an interest in a particular cultural context, either their own or one with which they have a special connection. Exploring these interests with Internet Inquiry is an effective approach since learning focuses on questions that are personally significant to the student.

Using Internet Inquiry

Individual students often have an interest in a particular cultural context, either their own or one with which they have a special connection. Exploring these interests with Internet Inquiry is an effective approach since learning focuses on questions that are personally significant to the student. Moreover, it helps students develop independent research skills. You can refer back to Chapter 3 for a detailed discussion of Internet Inquiry. You can also visit **Web Inquiry Projects** (http://edweb.sdsu.edu/wip/), hosted by the Educational Technology Department at San Diego State University, for examples. This excellent site also contains an overview explaining the concept of Inquiry as well as templates you can use for creating inquiry projects on your own.

An example of an Inquiry dealing with discrimination can be found at **Stamping Out Injustices** (http://www.biopoint.com/traversecity/stand_up2.htm). This project includes the usual question, search, evaluate, compose, and share phases. The students' task is to recommend an outstanding individual who has worked against discrimination for inclusion in a series of postal stamps. To do this, students must answer the basic question, "Which American leader had the biggest and most lasting impact on the fight against prejudice and intolerance in America?" The project begins with a list of background questions for students to answer about five well-known American activists; students are also given suggested resources on each individual's life and contributions. After searching these sites and evaluating the information they find, students select one of the candidates. They then share their results by designing a stamp, writing a proposal, and making a presentation supporting their choice.

As you use Internet Inquiry with your students, be sure to include opportunities for them to pose their own questions. This crucially important function is often overlooked as teachers and ready-made online inquiries provide all the questions to be researched. Initially, you might try having students identify questions for further research at the end of their projects. Or for students who are successful with teacher initiated questions, create a more open-ended inquiry experience such as the one in **Digital Divide** (http://www.thirteen.org/edonline/lessons/digitaldivide/). This lesson plan for Grades 7 to 12 helps students understand issues of equal access to technology by comparing them to similar issues that have been raised within other divides such as gender, race, and poverty. Finally, you may want to encourage students to create their own Internet Inquiry from start to finish, using the patterns and new literacies they have developed during previous inquiries.

Using Internet Inquiry together with Internet Workshop can be especially powerful in developing multicultural understanding, especially if you keep the following points in mind. First, where appropriate, encourage your students to form group inquiries. When students work in groups, they often share new insights, interpretations, and resources. This leads to important new directions as students pursue related questions. With support, these groups may be able to conduct their own group Internet Workshop sessions focusing on both their topic and the new literacies that they have discovered along the way.

Using Internet Inquiry along with Internet Workshop to share and exchange learning experiences can be especially powerful in developing multicultural understanding.

Second, be certain to have students share their multicultural learning in an Internet Workshop with the whole class on a regular basis, even if they also have a group workshop. When many students share their new learning and questions about a variety of cultural contexts everyone gains new insights about the diversity that exists in our world. Moreover, discussing these matters openly reveals and potentially helps remove stereotypes, while sending your students a powerful message about the respect we should accord each culture.

Combining Internet Inquiry and Internet Workshop in this way allows all students to share what they have learned and discuss any roadblocks they may have encountered. These conversations can be truly productive since they not only foster a multicultural view and enrich the study of your unit but also help students acquire and develop the new literacies they need to function in our diverse global society.

Figure 10-6. Native Visions of the Natural World (http://www.carnegiemuseums.org/cmnh/exhibits/north-south-east-west/index2.html) from the Carnegie Museum of Natural History, is one of the resources used in the **Native Americans in the Natural World WebQuest** (http://its.guilford.k12.nc.us/webquests/native/native.html).

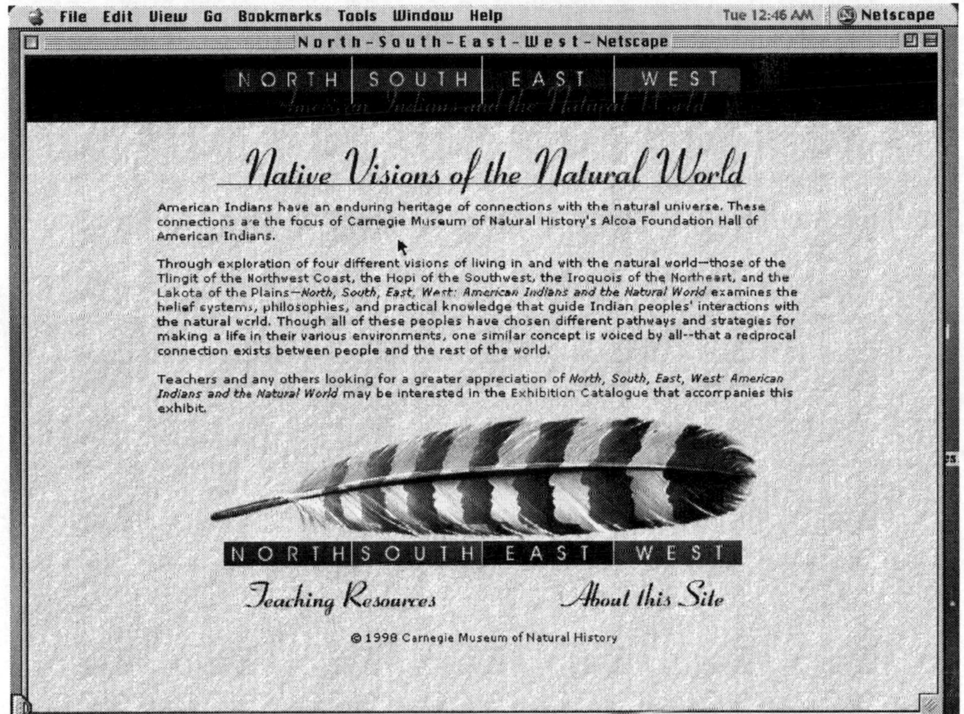

Using WebQuest

Using WebQuest for developing multicultural understanding seems natural. Collaboratively exploring issues of difference within a heterogeneous grouping can have a powerful effect in developing a greater appreciation for the diversity that defines us. Unfortunately, however, good webquests in this area have been somewhat slow to appear on the Internet. This is not to say that we lack models for exceptional quests that promote a greater understanding of cultural diversity. They do exist, but you may need to do a bit of searching to find one that fits your goals and meets your students' needs. (Refer to Chapter 3 for information on evaluating webquests). You may wish to evaluate the following quests to see if they are suitable for your students.

- **Six Paths to China**—
  http://www.kn.pacbell.com/wired/China/#WebQuest

  This outstanding collection of activities includes both a full WebQuest **Searching for China** (http://www.kn.pacbell.com/wired/China/ChinaQuest.html) and a number of other, more focused WebQuests. As a complete package, it is the perfect place to begin your exploration of this diverse and fascinating culture.

- **Tuskegee Tragedy**—
  http://www.kn.pacbell.com/wired/BHM/tuskegee_quest.html
  An outstanding WebQuest for secondary school students, enabling them to explore the tragedy of Tuskegee, compare it to other events such as gun control, abortion, and the use of internment camps, and then determine whether Tuskegee was a unique event or one that we must continually guard against. At the end of their research, students write letters to the authors of articles they have read and researched on the Internet, sharing their opinions. A powerful WebQuest with equally powerful learning outcomes. One of the many fine resources at **Blue Web'n** (http://www.kn.pacbell.com/wired/bluewebn/).
- **Native Americans in the Natural World**—
  http://its.guilford.k12.nc.us/webquests/native/native.html
  Many students (and others) share the belief that all Indians are the same. This WebQuest has students explore a number of resources in order to compare four different Indian cultures and lifestyles: the Tlingit, the Hopi, the Iroquois, and the Lakota. After completing their research, each group does a five-card Hyperstudio presentation.
- **Black History: Exploring African-American Issues on the Web**—
  (http://www.kn.pacbell.com/wired/BHM/AfroAm.html)
  An excellent collection of resources at Blue Web'n permitting you and your students to study a number of important issues related to many African American experiences. Included are a **Black History Hotlist** (http://www.kn.pacbell.com/wired/BHM/bh_hotlist.html) with links to many sites on the Internet, an **Interactive Treasure Hunt and Quiz** (http://www.kn.pacbell.com/wired/BHM/bh_hunt_quiz.html), a series of short explorations called **Sampling African America** (http://www.kn.pacbell.com/wired/BHM/bh_sampler.html), and a full WebQuest on racial desegregation called **Little Rock 9 Integration 0** (http://www.kn.pacbell.com/wired/BHM/little_rock/).
- **Stomp Out Stereotypes**—
  http://www.kn.sbc.com/wired/fil/pages/webstompoubr.html
  An excellent WebQuest designed to help Russians and Americans break down their stereotypes of each other. This quest may be appropriate for your students, but even if it is not, check out the many activities and resources for ideas that could be useful in creating your own webquest dealing with multicultural understanding issues.

You might also develop your own webquests using some of the suggestions from Janet Kenyon's Email for You.

E-MAIL FOR YOU

From: Jeanette Kenyon (jmkenyon@netzero.net)
Subject: Creating WebQuests

I have found WebQuests to be an effective way to quickly engage students in a hands-on learning activity that presents a large amount of specifically selected material in a short frame of time. In addition to helping teach content reading for meaning by going over questions first, and then scanning, filtering, and searching for specific information, it promotes cooperative learning and problem solving. I have successfully constructed WebQuests for a variety of learning situations. My school has a Science and Technology Club composed of students in Grades 2 to 5. In a very short amount of planning time, I was able to build several WebQuests that:

1. presented a specific body of information (that correlated with other club activities).
2. could be easily tailored to meet the abilities of all age groups.
3. empowered students to become actively involved in their learning.

The steps I followed to construct these WebQuests:

1. Decide on your "target information"—what specific facts do you want to present?
2. Search the Internet using "key words."
3. Copy and paste web addresses of sites that contain the information you are seeking in age appropriate context.
4. Prepare a list of questions from your list of sites.

I wrote and saved both the list of links and the questions as HTML documents (using Netscape Composer or some other HTML editor) and then they were posted on our school server. I also provided the students with a hard copy of the questions on which they would fill in the answers. Because of the large number of students involved, they usually worked as partners (helpful for those who might have trouble working independently). In addition, we added an element of competition by awarding small prizes for those teams who completed the questions first.

By posting as much information as possible on our local server, students were able to begin the activity quickly, zero in on specific information, and complete the task within a specified amount of time (usually an hour). For "quick finishers" additional links were added for further exploration.

Of course, WebQuests can be used as a starting point or integrated activity for larger, more involved projects. You may also use a "ready made" quest from the Internet and tailor it for your own situation. I have included a list of links that cover the basics of WebQuest construction (some are quite extensive) as well as a few that have a large number of WebQuests created by teachers.

- **WebQuests for Learning**—http://www.ozline.com/webquests/intro.html
  A very good "how to" page explaining the reasoning and strategies of WebQuests. This site deals in depth with the "new literacies" that are emerging in the field of technology.
- **WebQuest**—http://sesd.sk.ca/teacherresource/webquests.htm
  A comprehensive site that includes sample projects covering all areas of the curriculum, put together by a teacher.
- **WebQuests**—http://www.techtrekers.com/webquests/

cont.

A **very** extensive collection for all grade levels and areas. Virginia Standards of Learning numbers are noted in red.

- **Understanding and Using WebQuests**—http://midgefrazel.net/lrnwebq.html
  An all encompassing site that includes tips, information, and many links to WebQuest pages.
- **WebQuests from the Spartanburg, PA school district**—http://www.spa3.k12.sc.us/WebQuests.html
  Loads of information and many "ready made" quests.
- **A list of quests from California schools**—http://www.itdc.sbcss.k12.ca.us/curriculum/webquest.html

Good luck and Happy WebQuesting!
Jeanette Kenyon, Grade 2 teacher
Anne E. Moncure Elementary School
Stafford, Virginia

Visiting the Classroom: The Harriet Tubman Page Developed by Terry Hongell and Patty Taverna in New York

We can learn many important lessons from a visit to **Harriet Tubman and the Underground Railroad** (http://www2.lhric.org/pocantico/tubman/tubman.html), a wonderful resource developed by Terry Hongell and Patty Taverna. There are, of course, the many lessons we can learn about the life of this famous African American and the important work she accomplished. You will discover these as you explore the many links and resources created by these two, very talented teachers and the students with whom they work. Visit the timeline of Harriet's life with art and text from the students in Patty's class and then try out an interactive quiz they developed. Read the short biographies they have developed and gain a greater appreciation for the life Harriet led. Read the poems this class wrote and print out the crossword puzzles they developed after conducting inquiry projects about Harriet's life. Finally, explore the marvelous links they have placed at their page, taking you and your students to new locations with new information resources about Harriet Tubman. Yes, there are many lessons we can learn from this remarkable woman and this location will help our students to understand them.

The collaboration between the classroom teacher, Patty, and the technology teacher, Terry, is a model that all of us might seek to follow.

There are also lessons at this location to remind each of us of our own journeys as Internet users. The collaboration between the classroom teacher, Patty, and the technology teacher, Terry, is a model that all of us might seek to follow. By combining the instructional insights of Patty and her students with the technology insights of Terry, they are able to achieve much more than the sum of their individual parts. Most importantly, by posting these curricular resources on the Internet, they are allowing all of us to benefit from their work.

As networked information resources become more extensive and complexly structured, and as the Internet continues to change, no one person can be expected to know everything there is to know about teaching with the new technologies of literacy; these technologies will simply change too quickly and be too extensive to permit any single person to be literate in them all. Each of us, however, will know something useful to others. This will distribute knowledge about how to best use the Internet in the classroom. Each of us needs to be open to new collaborative ventures with other teachers and colleagues as we each seek to improve instruction in our own classrooms. Terry and Patty show us how this can be done and the exciting resources that can result.

As networked information becomes more extensive and complex, no one person can be expected to know everything there is to know about teaching with the new literacies of technology. Each of us, however, will know something useful to others.

Figure 10-7. Harriet Tubman and the Underground Railroad (http://www2.lhric.org/pocantico/tubman/tubman.html), a wonderful site for cultural diversity developed by Terry Hongell and Patty Taverna.

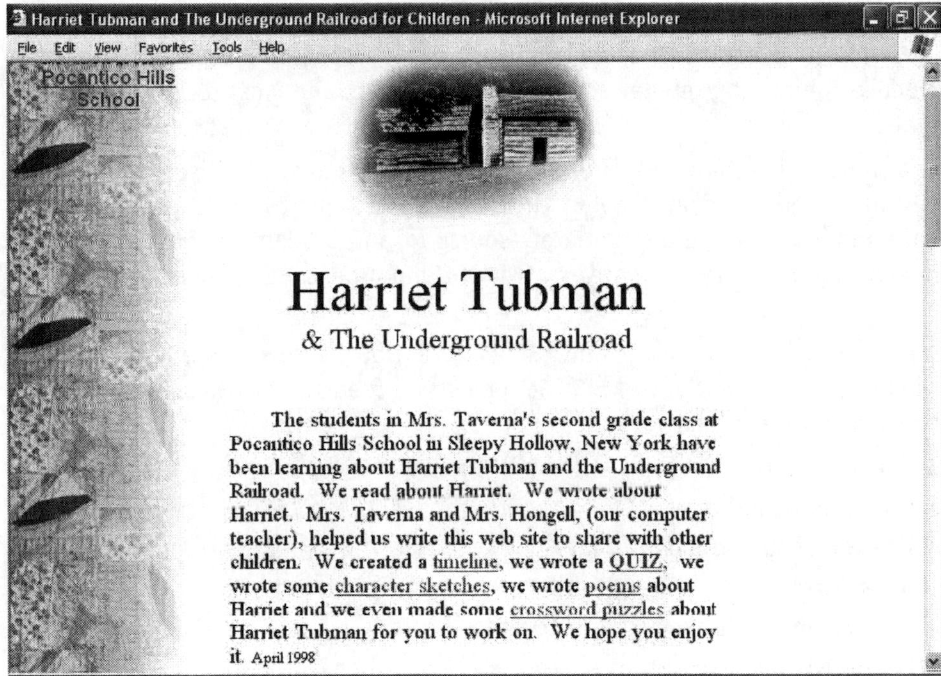

E-MAIL FOR YOU

From: Terry Hongell (thongell@attglobal.net)
Patty Taverna (taverna@pocantico.lhric.org)
Subject: Our Websites

Six years and 2,000,000 visitors ago a group of our second graders created a website about Harriet Tubman and the Underground Railroad. Little did we know then that the site would attract so many visitors! The students (now 8th graders) still get excited reading the email we continue to receive. Each year a new group of students is introduced to Harriet and adds a piece to the site to keep it current.

We create at least one new site each year. Often the inspiration for the student's web work is a piece of literature. After a month long study, another group created a website about the classic *Charlotte's Web* by E. B. White. When the inspiration for a website is based on rich literature, the outcome can be impressive. The story *Angel Child, Dragon Child* by Michele Maria Surat is about a young Vietnamese girl who comes to the United States with her family. The children found this story very powerful and poignant. All of us wanted to learn more about this distant country. Our research led to the creation of *Vietnam: A Children's Guide*. Much of our second grader's work is biographical. Use of primary sources has helped us to introduce John D. Rockefeller, Sr., Benjamin Franklin, and most recently, The Wright Brothers to our students.

The creation of a website is the culminating piece of our classroom study, but it often serves as a beginning for others who are interested in learning about the same topic. Our goal is to make the website an authentic showcase and a useful and appropriate resource for our students as well as for others. The work involved in creating each site generates excitement and a genuine commitment on the students' part.

The students are not the only ones learning. Our technical skills have grown and so has our vision. Sometimes we look back and chuckle at our early work, but it serves as a roadmap of where *all of us* have been on our continuing journey as learners.

- Pocantico Hills School Homepage (http://www.pocanticohills.org/pocantic.html)
- Harriet Tubman and the Underground Railroad (http://www.pocanticohills.org/tubman/tubman.html)
- A Children's Guide to Vietnam (http://www.pocanticohills.org/vietnam/vietnam.htm)
- Charlotte's Web (http://www.pocanticohills.org/charlotte/index.htm)
- John D. Rockefeller, Sr. (http://www.pocanticohills.org/rockefeller/jdr.htm)
- Benjamin Franklin: A Man of Many Talents (http://www.pocanticohills.org/franklin/franklin.htm)
- Meet the Wright Brothers (http://www.pocanticohills.org/wright/wright.htm)

New Literacies in Multicultural Understanding

New literacies permit new understanding and new appreciation of the diversity that exists in our world. The Internet is shrinking the world we inhabit in a significant way. Suddenly, without leaving our desks, we can visit a school or museum in Viet Nam or South Africa; instantly, without picking up a phone, we can communicate with students or experts in Helsinki or Brazilia. Our perception of how close we are to one another is fundamentally altered by this special technology and the new literacies we must acquire to use it.

As we draw closer together in a shrinking world, we will experience both important opportunities and difficult challenges.

Our opportunities will be defined by newfound abilities to more easily bring diverse perspectives to whatever problems we face. Having multiple ways of looking at an issue is always advantageous since there is a wider array of interpretations and possible solutions to choose from. Greater variety of choice makes it more likely that we will find good solutions for the complex issues that face us. However, we can only take advantage of this variety if we are open to new ways of thinking and able to synthesize information from diverse perspectives. This is why it is essential that we actively work to support multicultural understanding and to develop a deeper appreciation of diversity in our classrooms. The Internet together with the new literacies it requires allow us a chance to gain a more powerful understanding and a deeper appreciation of diversity than most of us have ever before experienced. In a world in which problems are quickly becoming more complex and seemingly intractable, mastering the new literacies is crucial; they will allow us to take full advantage of the opportunities that diversity provides.

The new literacies of the Internet provide us with the means by which we can prepare our students for the increasingly diverse world that awaits them.

Our challenges will be defined by our ability, or inability, to seek out these benefits and understand the value of having diversity represented in problem-solving tasks. It is all too easy to respond to a shrinking world by reverting to older and more parochial ways of looking at the world, rejecting the opportunities presented by culturally different ways of knowing and problem solving. It is much easier to stereotype people who appear different or who come from different cultural backgrounds than it is to recognize that that they have something valuable to share. This is our challenge.

In this chapter, we have seen how new literacies provide us with the means by which we can prepare our students for the increasingly diverse world that awaits them. We have also learned how to take advantage of this diversity through the use of several instructional models. Internet Project, in particular, is a powerful tool to use with students and classrooms around the world. As we seek to support an enhanced appreciation of diversity through the new literacies of the Internet, we help our students value difference and see its advantages in a world with complex problems requiring collaborative resolution.

Additional Resources on the Internet for Multicultural Understanding

The African American Mosaic—
http://www.loc.gov/exhibits/african/intro.html

An online exhibit from the Library of Congress exploring Black history and containing many primary source documents.

Africa Online: Kids Only—
http://wus.africaonline.com/AfricaOnline/coverkids.html

A nice location for your students to learn about Africa. They can read *Rainbow Magazine*—a Kenyan magazine for kids, play African games and decode messages, learn about the over 1000 languages in Africa, meet African students on line, find a keypal, or visit the home pages of schools in Africa. In English and French.

Alaska Native Knowledge Network—
http://www.ankn.uaf.edu/index.html

An online site for "compiling and exchanging information related to Alaska Native knowledge systems and ways of knowing."

Albleza—http://www.ableza.org/index.shtml

A Native American arts and media institute. Also see the section on appropriate methods for teaching about Native Americans (http://www.ableza.org/dodont.html).

Amazon Interactive—http://www.eduweb.com/amazon.html

A wonderful site for learning about Amazonia and the people who call this beautiful place home, including the Quichua people. Many exciting learning activities appear here.

American Indian Education—
http://www.cde.ca.gov/iasa/indianres.html

A variety of resources from the State of California for those who teach Native Americans.

American Indian Resource Directory—http://indians.org/index.html

Includes a tribal directory and links to Native American Literature; from the American Indian Heritage Foundation.

American Indian Sports Team Mascots—
http://www.aistm.org/1indexpage.htm

Articles, quotes, cartoons, comments, and information on the issue of using Indians and elements of their culture as sports team names and mascots.

Anthropology Outreach—
http://nmnhwww.si.edu/anthro/outreach/outrch1.html

A site for teachers from the Museum of Natural History. Contains bibliographies, leaflets, and teacher packets on a variety of topics.

Art History Resources on the Web—
http://witcombe.sbc.edu/ARTHLinks.html

Photos of artifacts from every part of the world, ancient to contemporary. Has links to many of the world's art museums.

Asia Source—http://www.asiasource.org/

Links to various aspects of Asian culture: arts and culture, business and economics, government and policy and social issues. Sponsored by the Asia Society.

Asian Nation—http://www.asian-nation.org/index.shtml

Information on history, political issues, the arts, and many links to other Asian American sites.

Ask Asia—http://www.askasia.org/

A collection of K-12 resource from the Asia Society.

Circle of Stories—http://www.pbs.org/circleofstories/

A PBS site that uses documentaries, photos, art, and music to celebrate Native American storytellers.

Center for Applied Linguistics—http://www.cal.org/

A national center for language study and application with many links to a wide variety of ESL resources.

Center for Educational Technology in Indian America—
http://www.ldoe.org/cetia/
A site that provides professional development and technical support for Indian educators, schools, and communities.

CivilRights.Org—http://civilrights.org/
An excellent site for information dealing with all types of civil rights issues.

Cultural Quest World Tour—
http://www.ipl.org/div/kidspace/cquest/
Another site from the Internet Public Library's Kidspace. Click on a region to visit various countries and learn something about their cultures. Games, museums, and recipes are some of the topics you may find out about.

Evaluating Native American Web Sites—
http://www.u.arizona.edu/~ecubbins/webcrit.html
Suggested guidelines for identifying websites with accurate information about Native Americans.

The First Americans—
http://www.germantown.k12.il.us/html/intro.html
A great project developed by the 3rd graders at Germantown Elementary School in Illinois, providing us all with a new resource for our study of native Americans.

Cranes for Peace—http://www.cranesforpeace.org/
Cranes for Peace began as a project to collect paper cranes to be sent to Hiroshima for the 50th anniversary of the bombing as a wish for peace. Based on the book *Sadako and the 1,000 Cranes,* this ongoing project continues to celebrate peace each year by sending cranes to be placed at the memorial to Sadako in Seattle or to the peace shrine in Hiroshima. Visit this location to find out more about this wonderful book and the many Internet projects for peace it has sparked.

A Critical Bibliography for North American Indians, K-12—
http://nmnhwww.si.edu/anthro/outreach/Indbibl/bibliogr.html
A site for teachers from the Smithsonian Institution that annotates a number of books on Native Americans. Organized geographically.

The First Americans—
http://www.germantown.k12.il.us/html/intro.html
A great project developed by the 3rd graders at Germantown Elementary School in Illinois, providing us all with a new resource for our study of Native Americans.

For Students of Languages—
http://www.geocities.com/~oberoi/language.html
A collection of useful sites for students learning one of five languages: English, French, German, Italian, and Spanish.

"I" Is Not For Indian—
http://www.nativeculture.com/lisamitten/ailabib.htm
A site for teachers that has a selective bibliography and guide for evaluating how Native Americans are portrayed in books for young children.

Jewish Culture and History—
http://ddickerson.igc.org/judaica.html
One of the more extensive sites on the Internet on Jewish culture with many links to other locations including links to Virtual Jerusalem and the Tour of Israel. More appropriate for older students.

Kids from Ka-na-ta Project—
http://www.kidsfromkanata.org/~kfk/home.html
This is a Canadian national telecommunications project linking urban and rural First Nations and non-Native students and teachers via the Internet.

KIDPROJ'S Multi-Cultural Calendar—
http://www.kidlink.org/KIDPROJ/MCC/
Here is another wonderful resource for your classroom developed by KIDLINK, a non-profit organization. This location contains a great database of celebrations taking place around the world together with ideas for connecting the calendar to your curriculum.

KUMC Calendar: Valuing our Differences—
Celebrating Our Diversity—http://www3.kumc.edu/diversity/
Another list of religious, ethnic, and cultural holidays from around the world. Many days on the list link to sites with further information about the special day.

Kwanzaa Information Center—http://www.melanet.com/kwanzaa/
Kwanzaa is the African American spiritual holiday initiated by Dr. Maulana Ron Karenga in 1966. Today it is celebrated in an increasing number of homes. This location at Melanet provides a rich set of information resources about this holiday.

Latin American Children's Resources—
http://www.zonalatina.com/Zlchild.htm
From Zona Latina, this location contains links to a number of children's resources from Latin America, including many in Spanish.

Martin Luther King, Jr.—http://www.seattletimes.com/mlk/index.html
A great site designed for teachers and students to reflect on the legacy of this famous American. Developed by a newspaper in Seattle, this location includes an interactive timeline of his life and contributions, audio clips of important speeches, reflections on his life from many individuals, a photo tour of the civil rights movement, and information about the national holiday in the United States.

Micositas—http://www.miscositas.com/
Organized by a K–12 certified language teacher in New York, this site contains 40 virtual picture books, in English, Spanish, and French. Also some games and curricular suggestions. A commercial site, but there are no ads on the main pages. You only find the catalog if you click on the shopping bag icon.

NAME—http://www.nameorg.org/
The home page for the National Association for Multicultural Education. Contains position papers and information on conferences.

National Civil Rights Museum—
http://www.civilrightsmuseum.org/gallery/movement.asp
The home page for this museum. Take the interactive tour of the exhibit to learn about this continuing struggle.

The New Americans—http://www.pbs.org/newamericans/
The companion site to the PBS series on immigrants and refugees seeking the American Dream.

Newswatch Style Guide—http://newswatch.sfsu.edu/guide/
From the Center for Integration and Improvement of Journalism at San Francisco State University. See the style guide for links to help journalists accurately and fairly cover people and communities who have been the victim of biased reporting or ignored by the news media. For secondary students.

Oyate—http://www.oyate.org/
This organization evaluates texts, resource materials, and fiction by and about Native peoples. See their list of non-recommended books for children.

SARAI—Southeast Asia Resource Access on the Internet—
http://www.columbia.edu/cu/lweb/indiv/southasia/cuvl/
Excellent source of links and resources for southeast Asian countries including India, Pakistan, Tibet, Bangladesh and Nepal.

Say Hello to the World—http://www.ipl.org/youth/hello
From the Internet Public Library. Learn to say hello in over 35 languages including Braille and Sign Language. Requires Real Audio if you want to listen as well as read the pronunciation guide.

The Simon Wiesenthal Center—
http://motlc.wiesenthal.com/index.html
The home page for this organization with links to thousands of important resources covering the Holocaust and other issues of Jewish struggle.

Talking Leaves—http://www.wisdomkeepers.org/talkingleaves/
This site provides lists of books, newspapers, e-zines, and other resources that present Native American concerns.

Teaching Diverse Learners—
http://www.lab.brown.edu/tdl/index.shtml
A site for helping all teachers learn to work with English Language Learners in their classrooms.

Tolerance.Org—www.tolerance.org/teach/index.jsp
An online project from the Southern Poverty Law Center. Sections for parents, teachers, kids, and teens with news and information on fighting hate and promoting tolerance.

U.S. Women's History Workshop—http://www.assumption.edu/whw/
Online resources and curricular modules on women's studies and United States history for use in history, English, and social studies courses, grades 3 through 12.

WWW Resources for Foreign Language Teachers—
http://www.cortland.edu/flteach/flteach-res.html
A good collection of links to language teaching resources for teachers put together by members of the Language Teaching Forum. Includes general resources as well as language-specific resources for Chinese, French, German, Italian, Japanese, Latin, Portuguese, Russian, and Spanish.

Online Communities for Increasing Multicultural Understanding

CULTUR-L

A discussion group on cultural differences in the curriculum.
Subscription address:
listserv@vm.temple.edu

FLTEACH

Foreign Language Teaching Forum
Subscription address: listserv@listserv.buffalo.edu
Homepage: http://www.cortland.edu/flteach/
Archives: http://listserv.buffalo.edu/archives/flteach.html

MCPavilion

A list for discussing equity, social justice, and multicultural education. Your subscription must be approved by the list moderator. Archives are available only to subscribers.
Subscription procedures:
https://list.mail.virginia.edu/mailman/listinfo/mcpavilion.

MCPavilion Bulletin Boards

Homepage:
http://www.edchange.org/multicultural/pavboard/pavboard.html

MULTC-ED

Sponsored by the National Association for Multicultural Education, the University of Maryland-College Park, and George Mason University. Discussion on multicultural curriculum, teaching, or research in pre-K–12; colleges and universities; other educationally related agencies; and parents.
Subscription address: listserv@umdd.umd.edu

MULT-CUL

Discusses theoretical and practical aspects of multicultural education.
Subscription address: listserv@listserv.acsu.buffalo.edu.

MULTICULTURAL-ED

Discussions of multicultural education.
Subscription address: listproc@lists.fsu.edu

NAME-MCE

The mailing list of the National Association for Multicultural Education.
Subscription address: listserv@listserv.umd.edu
Homepage: http://www.nameorg.org/listserv.html

S-L Lists: The Student List Project

Discussion forums on a variety of topics for English Language Learners, with separate groups for university and adult learners, immigrants, and teens. Teachers can enroll entire classes and track their messages in order to provide feedback or progress.
Homepage: http://sl-lists.net/

TESL-L

Classroom issues related to teaching English to non-native English speakers around the world.
Subscription address: listserv@cunyvm.cuny.edu
Homepage: http://www.hunter.cuny.edu/~tesl-l/

WORLD-L

Discussions on teaching non-Eurocentric world history.
Subscription address: listserv@ubvm.cc.buffalo.edu

11 Including All Students on the Internet

Internet equity has become an important issue within the educational community. It is important to provide more equitable access and ensure that we do not leave any members of our society behind. Most of this discussion, though, has focused on how to ensure equal Internet access between schools and school districts. This is one important aspect of Internet equity. Another is to do everything we can to ensure equal Internet access *within* individual classroom communities. This aspect of equity has gone largely unnoticed.

An important aspect of Internet equity is to do everything we can to ensure equal Internet access within individual classroom communities.

Sometimes, for example, a few students in a classroom become so excited about electronic learning that they tend to dominate the use of limited electronic resources, inadvertently excluding others in the process. At other times, students who fall behind in navigational skills at the beginning often fail to take full advantage of their computer time because they are uncertain about how to accomplish tasks and are too embarrassed to ask for assistance. At other times, challenged students do not always participate in Internet experiences for any of a number of reasons. This chapter recognizes each of these issues as it seeks ways to ensure equitable Internet access for each child in your class.

After reading this chapter, you should be able to:

1. Describe at least three ways that classroom teachers can orchestrate classroom environments to ensure equitable access to the Internet for all students.
2. Explore at least one of the web-based communities that have been created to foster interaction among students who have similar or unique educational, social, or medical needs and then reflect on the advantages and potential drawbacks of establishing these types of electronic relationships.
3. Design a series of three Internet Workshop activities using two or more of the websites in this chapter that could be used to foster a class's appreciation of the academic and social challenges that students with special needs face at school.

4. Explore Internet resources for professionals related to the inclusion of all students in the regular classroom and identify three instructional strategies offered by other educators who have successfully incorporated inclusion practices in their classroom.
5. Identify at least one assistive technology that increases access to information on the Internet for each of the following populations: students who are visually challenged, students who are hearing challenged, and students who are otherwise cognitively challenged.

Teaching with the Internet: Monica Ashburn's Class

As Monica Ashburn looked around her sixth-grade classroom, she noticed a pair of students who were very excited about what they had just discovered on the Internet. "Cool . . . look at that!" they shouted. Earlier that morning, she had downloaded the free version of **ReadPlease** (http://www.readplease.com/rpfree.php) to assist two of her students who had trouble decoding portions of the text on **Joke-A-Rama** (http://www.whatalulu.com/index-4Jokes.html), one of the websites she had bookmarked for them to explore as part of their creative writing unit on Riddles, Jokes, and Poems. Jeffrey and Eric, two students who often struggled to read on grade level, were working together at the computer and they had just figured out that all they had to do was cut and paste the text from the website page into the ReadPlease window, and each riddle would be read out loud in a voice and pace of their choice! Finally, they could have access to the same jokes and information that their classmates had been reading and having so much fun with earlier in the week. She was so pleased with the enthusiasm these students experienced about learning as they used the Internet.

Two students who had earlier struggled to read on grade level could now have access to the same jokes and information that their classmates had been reading and having so much fun with earlier in the week.

As she glanced around to a second computer set up in her classroom, she realized, however, that Maya, one of the quieter members of her class, was missing her scheduled time at the computer. She had noticed Maya reluctant to claim her computer time, when others, because of their excitement, did not leave the computer according to the classroom schedule. Maya was so shy she missed her computer time several times last week. Monica was determined not to let this happen again. She encouraged the group at the computer to quickly finish their work and allow Maya her full turn on the Internet.

"Can I help Tora when I am done?" asked Maya. Tora was a student with limited vision. Tora and Maya often worked together.

"That would be great," said Monica, "And could you change the font size to 48 like I showed you?" Changing the font to this larger size in the web browser enabled Tora to read the information on the screen. "Oh, you may also want to see how the slider bar works in the Read Please program . . . it'll make the text a little bigger so Tora can see too and follow along as you both listen."

"Okay, Ms. Ashburn . . . we'll check it out and let you know!" said Maya. Tora and Maya went to work, busily exploring another site that Monica had bookmarked called **I Spy: Write a Riddle Online** (http://www.scholastic.com/ispy/make/riddle.asp). They spent the first half of their scheduled time listening to riddles that other students their age had posted in the monthly contest and then decided they'd try their hand at writing their own riddle. Thanks to the free CloseView Screen Magnifier program that Monica downloaded from **The Screen Magnifiers Homepage** (http://www.magnifiers.org/links/), the screen image was greatly enlarged and Tora was able to join Maya in viewing the online I Spy images and locating objects to integrate into their I Spy Riddle.

"Hey, I spy a curly metal ring, right up here in the corner. Do you see it Tora?" Maya asked, as she pointed to the image on the computer.

"Oh yeah, let's put that in our riddle!" Tora grinned proudly, glad to be able to see the same things that her friend Maya could see on the computer. "I don't think anyone else mentioned that yet! Hey, since you found it, I'll start writing." Monica smiled, realizing all the wonderful opportunities being provided with new technologies.

Finally, on the third computer station in Ms. Ashburn's classroom, Peter, Janell, and Ryan were busy trying to solve the first two riddles (see Figure 11-1) at the **Mysterious Secret Language Mystery Riddles** (http://www.iidc.indiana.edu/cedir/kidsWeb/mysteryp.html). Peter, a student who had a younger brother with a significant hearing loss, had introduced his group to this site since it had to do with riddles and he thought that maybe he could use it as a way to help his friends practice using Fingerspelling so that they could talk more with Peter's brother at recess. Half way through the riddles, they realized they'd soon be over their scheduled computer time, so Janell asked, "Mrs. Ashburn, can we add this fingerspelling riddle site to our bookmarks so we can come back to it tomorrow?"

New technologies such as speech readers, screen magnifiers, and interactive Web sites provided exciting opportunities to level the playing field among the students in her classroom. Individual differences were being recognized and celebrated.

"Sure, it does tie in pretty nicely with our creative writing unit!" Monica answered. "Go ahead . . . and Janell, will you show Peter and Ryan how to bookmark this site so it gets saved in our Riddles, Jokes, and Writing bookmarks folder?"

"We're on it, Ms. Ashburn!" Janell replied confidently, as she began guiding the boys through the bookmarking process.

"Hey!" Ryan added excitedly, "maybe next time, we could even try to write our own riddle, using the fingerspelling symbols on this site!"

"Hey, yeah . . . that'd be really cool. My brother would LOVE that!" Peter exclaimed.

Again, Monica smiled, thinking that each of these Internet activities were especially nice since they accomplished several things at once. Each group discovered new forms of creative writing and each was working collaboratively, respecting his/her own unique abilities and differences in the process. New technologies such as speech readers, screen magnifiers, and interactive websites provided exciting opportunities to level the playing field among the students in her classroom. Individual differences were being recognized and celebrated. Each student was learning so much about the different ways people interact with the world and with each other and everyone was able to share in the excitement of learning with the Internet! It was certainly a wonderful experience to observe.

Figure 11-1. Two of the riddles from the **Mysterious Secret Language Mystery Riddles** (http://www.iidc.indiana.edu/cedir/kidsWeb/mysteryp.html), a great site for students to learn more about the fingerspelling symbols that individuals with hearing difficulties often use to communicate with each other.

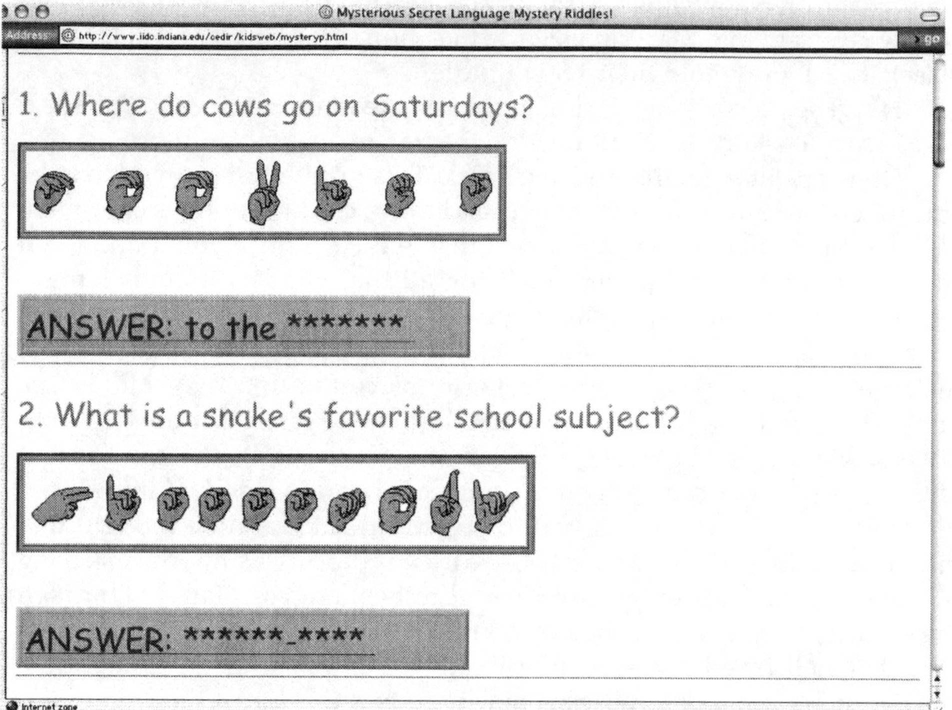

Lessons from the Classroom

This episode from Monica's classroom illustrates an important lesson for all of us to consider: the sensitive orchestration of classroom environments by an insightful classroom teacher can help to support Internet access for all students. Just having a computer connected to the Internet does not guarantee equity of access for each of your students. You must work actively to ensure equity in your classroom.

The sensitive orchestration of classroom environments by an insightful classroom teacher can help to support Internet access for all students.

One element of this active orchestration is being sensitive to times when students' enthusiasm for their work on the Internet impedes others' access to this important resource. Having a regular schedule for Internet use, as suggested in Chapter 3, provides a certain level of equity in your classroom. In addition, however, you will have to carefully monitor student use as Monica did, watching for those moments when students become so enthusiastic they lose track of time and prevent access by others.

Another important element in the active orchestration of equity is to be certain you are aware of ways to accommodate the unique learning needs of each child in your classroom. Adjusting the font size and locating a free screen magnifier for pictures for Tora enabled her to access the world of text and visual information available on the Internet. Previously, she had been limited to large-print books and an expensive electronic magnifier that her parents could not afford at home. The Internet permitted Tora to access an enormous amount of information, simply by enlarging the size of the browser font on Netscape Navigator or Internet Explorer and providing the option of using a speech reader and/or screen magnifier.

Similarly, providing access to a speech reader that reads text from a website enabled Jeffrey and Eric to laugh with their peers while reading along with text that was previously too difficult for them to read. These opportunities gave both boys a tremendous sense of satisfaction as they found themselves becoming active participating members of their classroom community of readers and writers. Everyone gains when the unique strengths and abilities of all students are included in classroom communities by teachers who know how to orchestrate equity.

Teaching Tip

Many webpages are inaccessible to students with various disabilities because of the way they are designed. The American Library Association recommends sites be compliant with the Americans with Disabilities Act as much as possible and provides a link to the **World Wide Web Consortium (W3C)** (http://www.w3.org/), an organization that promotes the accessibility of websites to people with disabilities. Other organizations such as the **Center for Applied Special Technology (CAST)** (http://www.cast.org) and the **National Center for Accessible Media** (http://www.wgbh.org/wgbh/pages/ncam/) have developed criteria that may be used to evaluate the degree to which a website meets basic principles of universal design. If a website meets these basic design principles, it will display a visual certificate such as those below. Look for these certificates as you make decisions about which Internet resources to use in your classroom. If you wish to evaluate the extent to which your classroom website meets principles of universal design and access, be certain to visit **Bobby** (http://www.cast.org/bobby/). Here you can have your website evaluated online. You will automatically receive a report indicating any accessibility and/or browser compatibility errors found on your page. If the report indicates your site meets the Bobby standards, you are entitled to display a Bobby

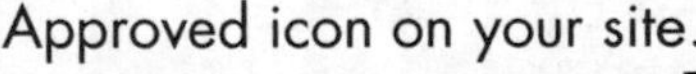

Approved icon on your site.

A final lesson we can learn from Monica's classroom is how eagerly students take on new roles as peer assistants and as teachers of new literacies. A new friendship between Maya and Tora had been facilitated through collaborative tasks at the computer and both girls now had many opportunities to appreciate each other's abilities. Early in the year, Monica had several discussions with her students about how each brought new understandings about the Internet into their classroom community, and her efforts were paying off as Maya helped to adjust the font size for Tora in the new screenreader interface. Similarly, Peter felt confident about recommending new Internet websites to his peers that blended in with their classroom learning goals and Janell was more than happy to share her knowledge about bookmarking websites, leaving Monica available to work with other students who needed assistance in other areas. Truly, this social collaboration and teamwork was paying off as each of these students, including those who are visually or cognitively challenged, was building his/ her confidence about using and sharing new literacies.

Orchestrating Equity in your Classroom

Truly, this social collaboration and teamwork was paying off as each of these students, including those who are visually or cognitively challenged, was building his/her confidence about using and sharing new literacies.

Chapter 3 described several strategies for orchestrating equity within Internet classrooms. Posting a schedule for all students to follow, rotating assigned computer times to avoid regular schedule conflicts, and rotating partners at the computer in a one-computer classroom are all useful strategies. In addition, however, there are several important issues for you to consider. These will require you to make subtle adjustments that happen moment to moment in your classroom as you seek to individualize learning experiences for each of your students.

Monica experienced one of these issues when she noticed a group of children at the computer excited about what they had discovered for their creative writing unit. As enthusiastic as they were, Maya was losing important time on the class computer because this group had forgotten their obligation to turn the computer over to the next person on the schedule. This is a common event in most classrooms and requires you to periodically monitor the computer schedule you establish for your class, reminding students when it is time to turn the computer over to the next person. You may also wish to bring this concern up during Internet Workshop and remind students why it is important to provide everyone with an equal amount of time on the Internet.

A few online resources that include recommendations from other teachers who have successfully managed their students' use of one computer in the classroom include:

- **Jan Scaplen's list of Classroom Management Techniques—** http://www.stemnet.nf.ca/~jscaplen/integration/english/prep2.html
- **Linda Burkhart's Classroom Management Tip Sheet—** http://www.lburkhart.com/elem/tip4.htm) and
- **Ideas for Teaching with One Computer—** http://www.lburkhart.com/elem/strat.htm

Another issue occurs when individual students fail to develop efficient navigation strategies for Internet use. Falling behind in this area prohibits students from acquiring as much useful information as other students who have become proficient at navigating the Internet. There are several techniques to help you to minimize this problem. First, observe carefully. Pay exceptionally close attention to the navigation strategies students develop or fail to develop as they work on the computer. You may refer back to Chapter 2 for a discussion of the various new literacies required while searching and reading on the Internet. Second, pair students who have not picked up important strategies with others who have acquired these strategies. Provide opportunities for these students to work together on the Internet. Many useful strategies can be acquired in this manner but be certain to also provide individual time for students to practice new skills on their own. Often, when you pair a proficient navigator with a less proficient one, the former dominates navigational decisions. Third, provide short tutorial sessions for students who are weak in navigation strategies. You may choose either a small group or an individual format. In either case, focus on a central strategy you have noticed that students lack. Finally, be certain to use discussions during Internet Workshop to both evaluate and teach navigation strategies. This is a perfect time to listen to students describe how they use the Internet and, at the same time, support students who have failed to acquire these skills.

Be certain to use discussions during Internet Workshop to both evaluate and teach navigation strategies. This is a perfect time to listen to students describe how they use the Internet and, at the same time, support students who have failed to acquire these skills.

It may also be the case that gender differences exist with respect to Internet use. While we have no hard data on this phenomenon, we have noticed that boys will sometimes dominate Internet use in a classroom and that some girls may express less interest in using this resource. You should watch for this in your class to see if it exists. Sometimes, communication experiences on the Internet are especially engaging for girls. You may wish to consider ways to exploit this interest by developing an Internet Project with communication opportunities between members of different classes or by creating opportunities for girls to visit such sites as **Club Girl Tech** (http://www.girltech.com/), which includes links for boys to visit too! This may equalize any gender differences you see in your classroom.

A final issue to consider is how to support challenged students in your class who have been formally identified with special learning needs. In some cases, technology may be able to adapt to these students' needs as was the situation with Tora, Jeffrey, and Eric in Monica's class. In all cases, there are resources on the Internet to provide useful information about accommodations you can make in your classroom to help each student reach his/her full potential.

A few additional resources that may prompt your thinking about equity issues and technology in the classroom include:

- **Digital Equity: It's Not Just About Access Anymore**—
  http://www.techlearning.com/db_area/archives/TL/2002/04/equity.html
- **Excellence and Equity Through Technology Network**—
  http://www.rmcdenver.com/eetnet/default.htm
- **Closing the Equity Gap in Technology Access and Use: A Practical Guide for K-12 Educators**—http://www.netc.org/equity/

At the beginning of the year, develop an Internet Workshop session around the ThinkQuest resource **Seeing DisABILITIES from a Different Perspective** (http://www.thinkquest.org/library/site_sum.html?tname=5852&cid=2&url=5852/) (see Figure 11-2). A very simple way to do this is to have your class explore this wonderful resource and bring to the workshop session three ideas to share that they learned about disabilities explored at this important resource. It is an important way to begin the year, bringing issues of diversity and difference to your entire class. Note that this site was developed by students in Grades 4–6 at Sherwood Elementary School in Illinois as part of the **ThinkQuest Junior annual competition** (http://www.thinkquest.org/). Consider developing a project for this contest or the ThinkQuest contest with your students.

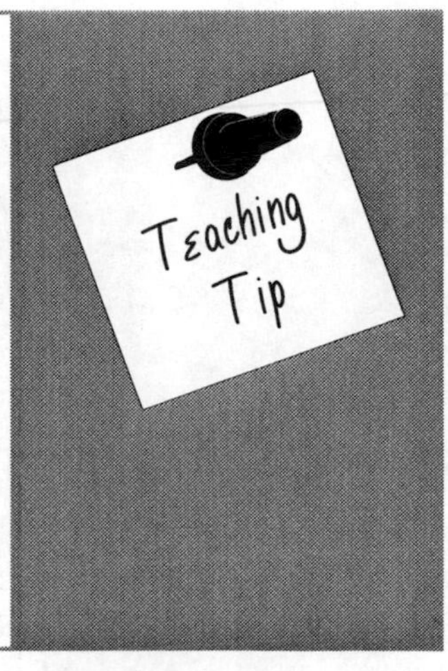

Figure 11-2. Seeing DisABILITIES from a Different Perspective (http://library.thinkquest.org/5852/homepg.htm), a great resource to help your students become more sensitive and knowledgeable about differences. This is an award winner in the Junior ThinkQuest competition.

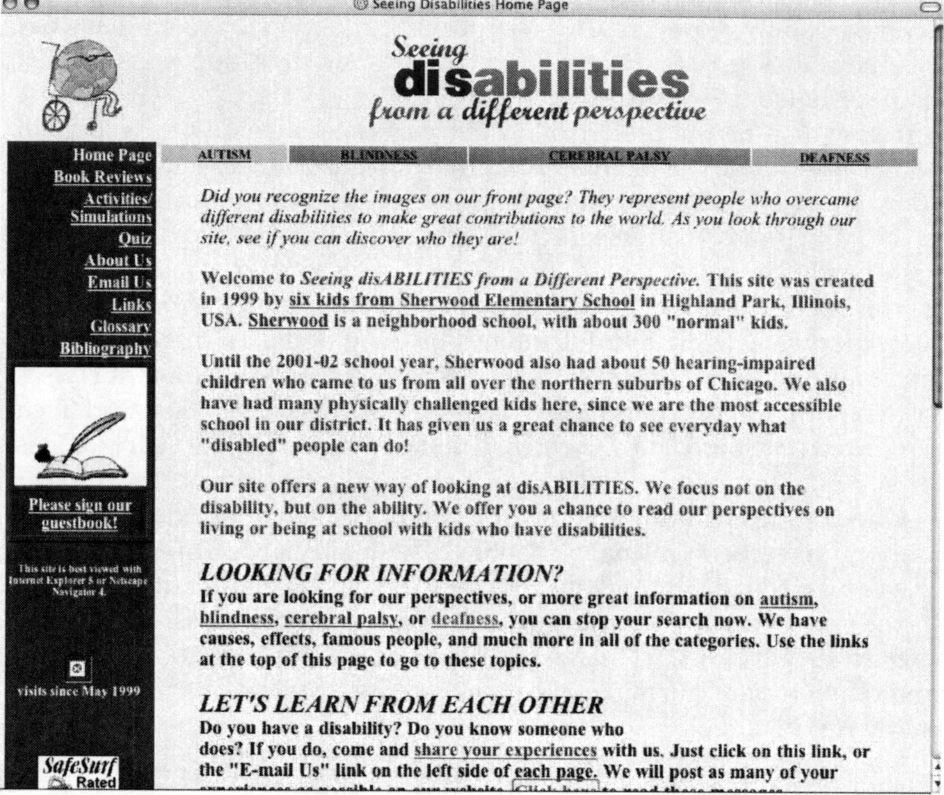

Our informal observations suggest the Internet may provide special motivational opportunities for those children who have been less successful in previous academic tasks.

Directories for Teachers of Students with Special Needs

Accommodating Internet experiences for other students in your class who have been formally identified as requiring special assistance does not differ substantially from the types of accommodations you make in other areas of your curriculum. Two ideas, though, may be useful as you seek to provide opportunities for each of your children to learn and grow.

First, our informal observations suggest the Internet may provide special motivational opportunities for those children who have been less successful in previous academic tasks. We have seen this happen enough times in school classrooms to believe something important is happening. We do not know the reason for this phenomenon. It may be that multimedia resources provide multiple sources of information (graphics, animations, audio, video, etc.) so that students are not just dependent on a single, textual, source for information that has always given them difficulty. It may be that the interactive nature of this environment and the new types of strategic knowledge that are necessary advantage certain types of children over others, children who have not been previously advantaged in non-electronic environments. Or, it may be that the Internet kindles a new spark of interest among students who have lost interest in learning. In any case, it happens often enough that we should think about taking advantage of the phenomenon.

One way to do this is to share new information about navigation strategies with students who have been less successful in school learning tasks before you share it with others. Then, have these students teach others the new information. This quickly puts students who have been less successful into a privileged position, a position these students seldom experience in classroom learning tasks. The effects of this strategy can sometimes be quite dramatic as less successful students suddenly feel empowered and become more interested in learning. We encourage you to try this strategy.

A second idea is also useful. Spend time exploring sites on the Internet that can provide you with more information about your students who have been formally identified as requiring special assistance. There are many useful ideas for instruction and many other informative resources on the Web. Exploring these sites will provide you with important assistance as you seek to include all students in your classroom activities. Directory sites we have found helpful include:

For students diagnosed with particular reading or language difficulties, creating environments that foster access to information becomes even more challenging. Fortunately, technology tools such as online text readers can enhance accessibility to the information on the Internet for all students.

- **Special Education Resources on the Internet (SERI)**—http://seriweb.com/
  This is one of the best sites on the Internet for special education resources. It contains a comprehensive and well-organized set of links to locations important for special education issues.
- **Family Village**—http://www.familyvillage.wisc.edu/
  This is an excellent site for mental retardation and other disabilities. Set a bookmark!
- **Special Education Resources from Bowling Green School District in Ohio**—http://www.bgcs.k12.oh.us/sped/spedres.html
  This site opens the door to national organizations, legal resources, educational interventions, and materials for students with particular special needs.
- **The Council for Exceptional Children**—http://www.cec.sped.org/
  A major professional organization in special education.
- **National Dissemination Center for Children with Disabilities (NICHCY)**—http://www.nichcy.org/
  This site, available in both English and Spanish, is a central source of information on laws, policies, and research-based effective educational practices for students with special needs.

Assistive Technology Tools for All Students

One of the concerns we hear most often from teachers with regard to using the Internet in their classrooms is that the reading level of the text is often too difficult for their students to read independently. For students diagnosed with particular reading or language difficulties, creating environments that foster access to information becomes even more challenging. Fortunately, technology tools such as online text readers can enhance accessibility to the information on the Internet for all students. A text-to-speech reader, also known as a screenreader, reads text out loud from webpages or any other electronic document. In the past few years, text readers have evolved from having clunky interfaces with robot-like voices into classroom friendly tools with customizable features. **Read Please** (http://www.readplease.com/rpfree.php), for example, is a free text reader available for Windows users that features natural voices and options to adjust the speed and font size. The text reader window opens next to the Internet site and text is highlighted in yellow as it is read out loud in a pre-selected natural voice. **TextAloud MP3** (http://www.nextup.com/TextAloud/) is another speech reader that converts any text from webpages, email, applications, and even program menus into MP3 audio files. It is free to download and use for thirty days, and after that, it is available for a fee (one that is considerably less than most other text-to-speech readers).

You may also be interested in the **Special Needs Opportunities Windows (SNOW) Website** (http://snow.utoronto.ca/index.html) from Toronto, Canada. From here, you can access directions on how to download the text readers **HelpRead for Windows** and **Sound Talker for Mac** (http://snow.utoronto.ca/help/read.html) as well other **audio and video players** (http://snow.utoronto.ca/help/configure.html) to enhance access to text for all students.

INTERNET FAQ

Is there anything available on the Internet for determining the reading level of text at certain websites?

Although we have not found any online tools developed specifically for this purpose, we have recently located some resources that may assist you in this area. First, you may use the **OKAPI Readability Statistics Tool** (http://www.interventioncentral.org/htmdocs/tools/okapi/okapi.shtml) as a way to help locate websites with text at a student's approximate reading level. Visit a site you'd like to test, copy and paste a few passages into the "Text to be analyzed" box of the OKAPI tool, click on "Run Readability Analysis" and you'll get an estimated reading level using either the Spache (Grades 1–3) or Dale-Challe (Grades 4 and up) readability formula. You may also explore the **Reading Level Calculator** (http://linda-andrews.com/readability_tool.htm) for a similar process. If you use the **KidsClick Searchengine** (http:/www. kids click.org), the search results are annotated with fairly accurate grade level ranges from Grades K–2, Grades 3–6, or Grades 7+, helping you to at least narrow down the range of reading levels within a certain website. Finally, the article entitled **Readability Issues to Consider** (http://www.timetabler.com/reading.html), reminds us that elements other than text level influence the actual "readability" of information for students.

Finally, we recently discovered a unique tool known as **Betsie** (http://www.bbc.co.uk/education/betsie/index.html), which stands for BBC Education Text to Speech Internet Enhancer. It's a simple computer script that creates an automatic text-only version of a website and was created to alleviate the difficulty that current text to speech systems have when they encounter images mixed in with text. Currently, the British Broadcasting Corporation (BBC) in the United Kingdom uses this filter to create an all-text version of its entire website and new websites are regularly being added to their list of "Betsie-enhanced sites." This type of technology can surely play a role in enhancing access to electronic information for all students.

Opportunities for Students Who Are Visually or Hearing Challenged

The Internet provides special opportunities for children who are visually or hearing challenged. For children who are visually challenged, a common problem is often a dependency on large print texts, texts which do not always coincide with the materials used in the classroom. Alternatively, large and bulky readers are sometimes used. Both are less than ideal solutions for many students.

Netscape, Internet Explorer, and Safari browsers offer an opportunity to enlarge the print size appearing on the computer screen to nearly any size one wishes. This allows children who are visually challenged to access a wide range of information that might otherwise be inaccessible to them.

Netscape, Internet Explorer, and Safari browsers offer an opportunity to enlarge the print size appearing on the computer screen to nearly any size one wishes. This allows children who are visually challenged to access a wide range of information that might otherwise be inaccessible to them. To do this in Netscape, select the "Netscape" item from your menu bar and then select "Preferences." Within "Preferences," select the category for "Fonts." You will see a window similar to Figure 11-3. Select the size you wish to use for both proportional and fixed fonts. You may select any size you wish. Note that one choice is "Other." This allows you to type in sizes larger than 24. To change the font size in Internet Explorer, you may also simply select View from your menu bar, and then "Text Zoom" and the percentage you prefer from the pop-up menu that appears. In the Safari browser, select "View" and then choose "Make Text Bigger" or "Make Text Smaller".

Enlarging the font size for children who are visually challenged works especially well on webpages that use a lot of text. It works less well at those sites with graphics, since graphics are not enlarged with this approach. In these situations you may wish to use software that enlarges the entire screen, not just text. With the more recent Macintosh systems, this is already available to you in *Easy Access*. If you can't locate this feature, if you need to download this software, or if you wish to read about using this software, just visit the Apple location **Access Features** (http://www.apple.com/disability/easyaccess.html). If you use a Windows system, visit the **Microsoft Accessibility Home Page** (http://www.microsoft.com/enable/) for similar solutions. You may also want to explore the large collection of accessibility freeware and shareware on both computer platforms for people with all kinds of sensory and physical disabilities at **Trace Shareware and Freeware** (http://trace.wisc.edu/world/computer_access/multi/sharewar.htm).

Figure 11-3. The preferences folder in **Netscape**, showing how to change the size of the font used to display text information on the Web.

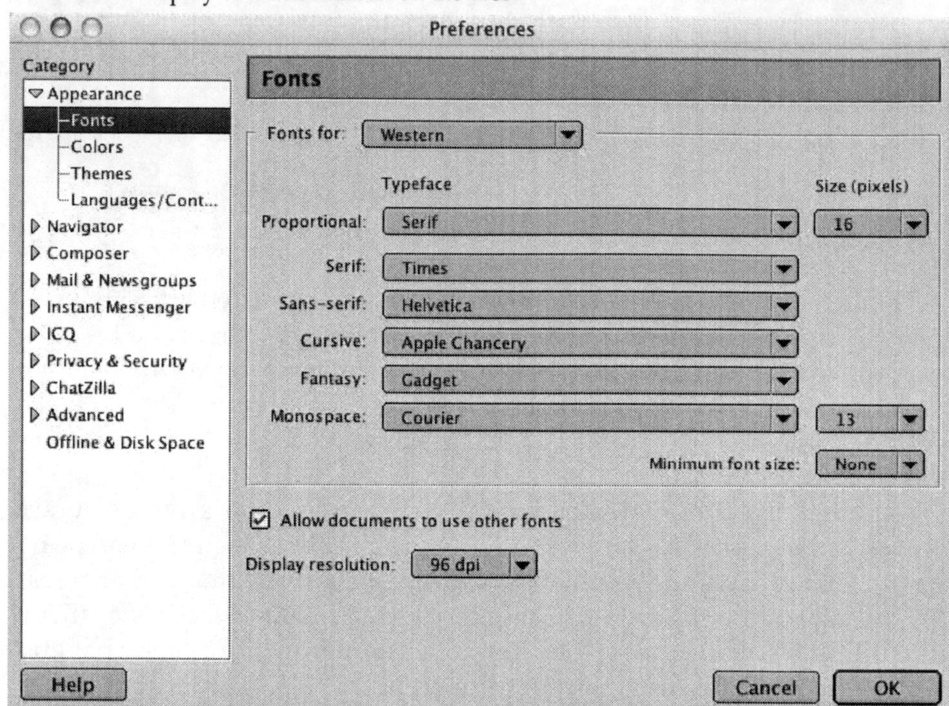

You may also wish to visit these central sites for visually challenged students to locate additional resources and instructional strategies:

- **Visually Impaired Resource Guide—**
  http://www.setbc.org/special/virg/

  Be sure to explore this guide, created by the Special Education Technology Resource Program in British Columbia. It includes a sequential framework for addressing technology options in the reading and writing curriculum for students who use Braille and for those with low vision. For each type of technology or use thereof, it lists prerequisite skills, objectives, and a list of related resources.
- **Strategies for Teaching Students with Vision Impairments**—
  http://www.as.wvu.edu/~scidis/vision.html

  Several helpful classroom tips and strategies for accommodating the needs of students who are visually challenged.
- **Blindness Resource Center—**http://www.nyise.org/blind.htm

  A great central site for visually challenged and blind individuals. Set a bookmark!

There are also locations on the Internet to support hearing challenged students. You might begin by visiting **The Deaf/Hard of Hearing** (http://www.familyvillage.wisc.edu/lib_deaf.htm) location of the Family Village site. This has links to excellent resources on the Web as well as information about chat and mailing lists for students. Another useful location is **SERI Hearing Impairment Resources** (http://seriweb.com/hearing.htm). If you or parents of your students are interested in pursuing verbal communication instead of sign language for students who have hearing difficulties, you may wish to explore **Auditory Verbal International** (http://www.auditory-verbal.org/) or **Oral Deaf Education** (http://www.oraldeafed.org/).

INTERNET FAQ

What kinds of new assistive technologies are on the horizon for my students with significant visual challenges?

One of the newest technologies we've seen for individuals with visual disabilities is a camera-based scene reader called **vOICe Sonification Browser (for PC)** (http://www.seeingwithsound.com/winvoice.htm). You can download this free video sonification software that translates arbitrary video images from a regular PC camera into sounds. It also includes advanced features such as color identification, integrated email, and an integrated browser to even hear images on the Web. This new technology may well be worth exploring to open up new worlds for some of your older students!

Several other locations may be useful for all students in your classroom. **A Basic Dictionary of ASL Terms** (http://www.masterstech-home.com/ASLDict.html) and **The American Sign Language Browser** (http://commtechlab.msu.edu/sites/aslWeb/browser.htm) provide an extensive signing dictionary. You may wish to make these sites a regular part of Internet Workshop and begin to develop the ability to sign with your hearing students. Sharing new signs during Internet Workshop helps everyone become more skilled in communicating with hearing challenged children.[10] For older students and teachers wanting to learn more, **Sound and Fury** (http://www.pbs.org/wnet/soundandfury/) is a companion website to a PBS television special about living with cochlear implants. From here, you may access information about deaf culture, the debate around cochlear implants, and online lesson plans and resources for middle and high school students to explore. The **Sign Writing Site** (http://www.SignWriting.org/) describes the process by which sign language can become a written language, providing another alternative way of fostering communication between deaf and hearing people. Finally, we found the list of tips from **Communicating Effectively with Individuals that have Visual and Hearing Difficulties** (http://www.dpa.org.sg/VH/tips.htm) to be very helpful when thinking about how to best meet each individual's diverse needs and communication styles.

Developing the ability to sign with your hearing students during Internet Workshop helps everyone become more skilled in communicating with hearing challenged children.

Here is a way to conduct a simple Internet Workshop with your younger students, developing the ability to communicate with a limited set of ASL signs. Set a bookmark or a link to **American Sign Language Browser** (http://commtechlab.msu.edu/sites/aslWeb/browser.htm). Give students a set of high frequency words that may be combined in different ways to make a variety of sentences: I, you, we, it, play, see, eat, read, baseball, funny, apple, ice cream, book, and so on. Then, using this Internet site, have them learn one sentence to share during the workshop session. Encourage students to visit this location often, learning the symbol of the day and sharing it with the rest of the class. By the end of the year, your students will have developed important, initial signing skills and started a journey to better understand and communicate with the deaf community.

Figure 11-4. A great location for all students is **American Sign Language Browser** (http://commtechlab.msu.edu/sites/aslWeb/browser.htm).

E-MAIL FOR YOU

From: Nicole Gamble <ddnrg@IX.NETCOM.COM>
Subject: Diversity

My students learned a very valuable lesson this week about diversity and empathy. We have been reading *Princess Pooh* by Kathleen Muldoon. It's a story about two sisters, one of whom happens to be in a wheelchair. After talking about what might be difficult about being in a wheelchair, we invited a first grade student who uses an electric wheelchair into our classroom to demonstrate how it works. She answered a lot of our questions and the students were very interested in what she had to share. In our discussion we found out that she was unable to use a drinking fountain in school because the only wheelchair accessible drinking fountain had been broken all year. After she left, my class asked if they could write a letter to the principal and find out about fixing the drinking fountain. They wrote the letter, took it to the principal, and the drinking fountain got fixed! The principal came into the class and told everyone that she appreciated how much they cared. It turns out that new parts for the drinking fountain had been ordered and had arrived, but the maintenance department hadn't made it a priority to fix it. What a great lesson!

Nicole Gamble

Opportunities for Students Who Are Otherwise Challenged

The Internet also provides special opportunities for other students in your class with a range of diverse learning needs. In this next section, we'll explore central resource directories and links to instructional strategies for teachers that address the specific needs of students with a learning disability or an attention deficit disorder, students with autism, and students who exhibit a range of challenging behaviors.

Meeting the Needs of Students with Learning Disabilities or Attention Deficit Disorder

One of our very favorite resources for supporting educators in making informed decisions about effective instruction for students with learning disabilities or attention deficit disorder (ADD) is **LDOnline** (http://www.ldonline.org/). This site provides a comprehensive, in-depth, and research-based series of articles, summaries of expert advice, first person stories, and instructional strategies for both regular and special educators. This resource also features an email newsletter subscription, many online discussion forums, and a weekly student Artist and Author Contest, with a winner whose work is displayed on its homepage. All educators should know about the resources available here!

You may also wish to pay a visit to the ***Center for Applied Special Technology*** *to learn more about their vision of Universal Design for Learning that uses technology to expand opportunities for all people, especially those with disabilities.*

You may also wish to pay a visit to the **Center for Applied Special Technology (CAST)** (http://www.cast.org) to learn more about their vision of Universal Design for Learning that uses technology to expand opportunities for all people, especially those with disabilities. The site is chock full of research-based materials, including their **Teaching Every Student** (http://www.cast.org/teachingeverystudent/) section that features full-text access to the book *Teaching Every Student in the Digital Age* (Rose & Meyer, 2002) as well as many articles that address issues of meeting individual learning needs with technology.

Three other central sites that provide a wealth of information to support students with learning disabilities and/or attention difficulties include the following:

- **Learning Disabilities Resource Community**—http://www.ldrc.ca/
  This community provides knowledge building and communication tools to promote learning awareness among educators striving to meet the needs of students with learning disabilities and online exercises that promote learning awareness.
- **The National Center for Learning Disabilities**—
  http://www.ncld.org/
  NCLD works to ensure early identification and advocacy for students with learning difficulties. Be sure to check out their incredible collection of **LD Fact Sheets** (http://www.ncld.org/LDInfoZone/InfoZone_FactSheetIndex.cfm) designed to help parents and educators identify and respond to specific types of learning difficulties such as dyslexia, dyscalculia, dysgraphia, dyspraxia, and visual or processing disorders.

- **Attention Deficit Disorder**—http://www.ncpamd.com/adhd.htm From here you can read many articles from a team of doctors in Maryland to learn more about important medical and educational issues associated with Attention Deficit Disorder.

Meeting the Needs of Students with Autism or Asperger's Syndrome

Neurological disorders such as autism and Asperger's syndrome present a different set of challenges for students and teachers. A few directories that provide information about the special learning needs of students with autism include the **Autism Society of America** (http://www.autism-society.org/site/PageServer), the **Autism PDD Resources Network** (http://www.autism-pdd.net/), and **Doug Flutie's Foundation for Autism** (http://www.dougflutiejrfoundation.org/) which features a comprehensive list of resources, a unique expert and virtual speaker database, and many interactive discussion boards for those seeking guidance and support in education students with autism. This site also sponsors a free online course for parents of children with autism in collaboration with **Canter Online** (http://www.Webed.com/parents/). Be sure to also explore the wealth of exceptional lessons created by special educators in Green Bay, Wisconsin at their webpage entitled **Autism: Interventions and Strategies for Success** (http://www.cesa7.k12.wi.us/sped/autism/index1.htm).

Older students with autism may enjoy working with a partner to explore, download, and add text to the visual pictures available from ***Use Visual Strategies*** *as a means of building communication skills.*

There are also a number of locations that provide opportunities for students with autism to access Internet activities that enhance learning and communication.

- The **Thinking Skills Workbook designed for Children with Autism** (http://www.autism-pdd.net/booklet/wbook1/cover.html) is a small gateway into a series of science, math, and language arts activities for younger children with autism.
- Older students with autism may enjoy working with a partner to explore, download, and add text to the visual pictures available from the site **Use Visual Strategies** (http://www.usevisualstrategies.com/pix.htm) as a means of building communication skills.The pictures can be printed out and used to assist students in their attempts to communicate their needs, feelings, and interests in the classroom, as in the examples provided at http://www.usevisualstrategies.com/success.htm.
- The online collection of **Picture Recipes** (http://www.bry-backmanor.org/picturerecipes.html) may provide another avenue for students with autism to actively participate in integrated lessons for reading, science, and math.
- Since many students with autism have difficulty recognizing how other people are feeling by their facial expressions, the **Online Feelings Game** (http://www.do2learn.com/games/feelingsgame/index.htm) is an example of an activity that could be set up as part of an Internet Workshop activity. Other online learning games and printed educational materials for students with autism are located from the main page of the **Do2Learn website** (http://www.do2learn.com/games/learningames.htm).

Using Internet Workshop

Internet Workshop is a good way to begin using the Internet in your classroom with all students. Taking time to carefully arrange opportunities for students with special needs to have access to the Internet independently or with a partner in a non-threatening environment is an important first step. Internet Workshop opportunities can include time for students to log on and join one of the many web-based communities that have been created to foster interaction with other students who have similar or unique educational, social, or medical needs. Here are several examples of online support communities suitable for classroom use that provide opportunities for students with special needs to express themselves and communicate with others in an online environment:

- **PatchWorx: Online Support Center for Kids with Illnesses or Disabilities**—http://www.patchworx.org/
  This online community offers a warm and friendly environment for children facing serious illness or disability. Students of all ages will enjoy the interactive games and posting their own stories and artwork, while older students can exchange ideas and reflections through an online chat room, bulletin board, or interactive "kid's quilt" that links to other individual's webpages. Older students are also invited to provide online leadership in this supportive community.
- **Club BraveKids**—http://www.bravekids.org/kids/index.html
  Club BraveKids recognizes the advantages of networking among individuals with chronic, life-threatening illnesses or disabilities and has designed this community to feature contests, message boards, a weekly poll, medical information, and a few interactive games for students.
- **Ability Online**—http://www.ablelink.org/public/default.htm
  This computer network is "designed to enhance the lives of children and youth with disabilities or illness by providing an online community of friendship and support." Students can share information, experiences, stories, or interests with others while learning more about opportunities for personal growth.
- **Deaf Child International**—http://www.deafchild.org/
  After registering and logging in, students and teachers have an opportunity to interact online with other individuals from around the world using various types of Information and Communication Technologies (ICT).
- **I Am Dyslexic**—http://www.iamdyslexic.com/
  This site was created by Barnaby, a 14-year-old boy with dyslexia, for other children with dyslexia. He shares unique tips and strategies for spelling, research, and typing; he hosts a daily message board with other students with dyslexia from around the world; and his KidsZone features a weekly math and spelling quiz as well as a weekly treasure hunt contest. This very active site is sure to serve as an inspiration for your own students who face the challenges associated with dyslexia.

Internet Workshop activities can also be designed to facilitate awareness among regular education students of the unique needs and experiences of students who are challenged in the classroom. You may design an entire learning unit using Internet resources that engage your students in activities and discussions about students with special needs. For example, middle and high school students may reading "Success Stories" of students like those featured by the **Special Education Technology from British Columbia (SET-BC)** (http://www.setbc.org/success/docs/welcome.html) or others featured in the online companion to the PBS Special **Misunderstanding Minds** (http://www.pbs.org/wgbh/misunderstoodminds/).

Internet Workshop activities can also be designed to facilitate awareness among regular education students of the unique needs and experiences of students who are challenged in the classroom. You may design an entire learning unit using Internet resources that engage your students in activities and discussions about students with special needs.

Other sites feature interactive games or quizzes so students can test their own knowledge of various types of disabilities. The **Disability Awareness Site for Youth** (http://www.iidc.indiana.edu/cedir/kidsWeb/) from the Center for Disability Information & Referral, for example, includes a Truth or Lie Quiz, a sign language puzzle, and an annotated list of famous people with disabilities to match up. Similarly, students can try their hand at fingerspelling by taking the **ASL Fingerspelling Quiz** (http://www.SignWriting.org/), which also provides links to a Fingerspelling Converter and an Online Fingerspelling Dictionary.

For younger children, they may enjoy the activities available from websites that feature both information and games, such as the **Braille Bug Site** (www.afb.org/braillebug/default.asp) about individuals with visual challenges, **Youth to Youth: Children with Disabilities** (http://www.childrenwithdisabilities.ncjrs.org/kids.html). You may also pa a visit to the collection of **Arthur webpages** that feature interactive games designed to encourage hearing and sighted children to become more aware of how their peers who are deaf, hard of hearing, blind, or visually impaired learn, play, and enjoy many of the same things that they do. These include:

- **Sign Design**—http://pbskids.org/arthur/print/signdesign/
- **About Face**—http://pbskids.org/arthur/games/aboutface/
- **Fern, the Effective Detective**—
http://pbskids.org/arthur/games/effectivedetective/
- **Online Braille Translator**—http://pbskids.org/arthur/print/braille/

If you wish to design a series of classroom lessons focused around Disability Awareness for younger children, take a look at the many visual simulation activities available from **Inservices to Sighted Classmates** (http://www.viguide.com/vsninsvc.htm), or the **Understanding Friends Program** (http://www.udel.edu/bkirby/asperger/faherty_friends.html) designed to educate children about differences and to foster empathy. Also be sure to share with your students the interactive sound ruler and several short video clips about **Children Who Are Deaf or Hard of Hearing** (http://www.nidcd.nih.gov/health/education/index.asp).

Using Internet Project

As we have mentioned in other chapters, Internet Project takes a little more time and planning than Internet Workshop sessions. However, these types of projects may provide opportunities to extend student awareness to unique issues outside of your classroom, should you not have the opportunity to work with students with particular special needs in your own population. These types of experiences can foster reading and writing activities, inspire new topics for research, or even provide unique experiences to build new friendships with students with special needs. Examples of some Internet projects like these include:

Internet Projects can foster reading and writing activities, inspire new topics for research, or even provide unique experiences to build new friendships with students with special needs.

- **Sign-Writing Literacy Project—**
  http://www.SignWriting.org/forums/teachers/teachers.html#anchor649325

  Participating schools in this project receive free Sign-Writing materials for deaf students in return for documented feedback about their use. Each classroom has their own webpage to share and exchange reflections, opinions, and finished student products written with sign writing. From the related **Children to Children site** (http://cyberjer.com/signkids/index.htm), you can see many more examples of stories and poems written by children using Sign-Writing. This project provides opportunities for deaf and hearing students to communicate together while expressing their own individuality.
- **Paralympics: Where Heroes Come—**
  http://www.melazerte.com/library/paralympics/index.htm

  This language arts/social studies project was created by teachers in Alberta, Canada to "develop an appreciation of the Paralympic Games as a celebration of the power of the human mind, body and spirit." Middle and high school students explore related Internet sites in small groups and synthesize their findings of these heroic athletes into a brochure or poster to share online. Participating classes even receive a free book about the Paralympics!
- **E-Buddies—**http://www.ebuddies.org/

  E-Buddies is one project of several from the Best Buddies International Program. Your students can volunteer to serve as an email buddy to another student with intellectual challenges. Participants email each other at least once a week for a year, and many students go on to serve in leadership positions with offline activities as well.

Opportunities for Inquiry for Students with Special Needs

In Chapter 9, we discussed various reasons why Internet Inquiry projects are lesson common in the primary grades, including our desire to keep children safe from the dangers of independent exploration and the need to support their emerging levels of literacy with more carefully guided activities. Still, we discovered a few examples of inspiring stories from classroom teachers eagerly exploring inquiry-based strategies in their primary school curriculum. Similarly, in our search for inquiry projects involving students with special needs, we came across a few inquiry-based learning projects, some that involve technology and others that do not. As educators, we should be open to new ideas about adapting our traditional curriculum in ways that foster the curiosity and engagement of all students, not just those who regularly excel in their studies. Opportunities for students with special needs to explore the Internet and engage in new literacies are important steps toward equity for all students. Two examples of inquiry activities that remind us that all learners have unique interests and abilities and that supported inquiry has a place at all levels of education include the following:

Opportunities for students with special needs to explore the Internet and engage in new literacies are important steps toward equity for all students.

- **Action Reflection Process: Supporting All Students in Inquiry Based Science**—http://www.edc.org/ARProcess/index.htm
  This site outlines a collaborative process of ensuring that students with disabilities succeed in an inquiry-based science education program. You can view strategies that teachers use, access a three-session virtual experience with the action reflection process from pre-assessment to post-evaluation, and explore evidence that this process makes a difference in promoting science concepts among students with special needs.
- **Multimedia and More: Help for Students with Learning Disabilities**—http://ldonline.org/ld_indepth/technology/multimedia.html
  In this unit, high school students with and without learning disabilities are motivated by the opportunity to incorporate their own brainstorms into a hypermedia template that eventually results in an interactive web-based story. Multimedia technologies capitalize on students' unique abilities and interests to support writing and inquiry in this project.

Internet Webquests Focusing on Individuals with Special Needs

When searching for webquests that consider students with special needs, we found several that serve as a motivating opportunity for students to practice new literacies such as searching and synthesizing information as part of a Disability Awareness Unit. One of our favorites is the **Kids' Quest on Disability and Health** (http://www.cdc.gov/ncbddd/kids/kidhome.htm), which was created by the National Center on Birth Defects and Developmental Disabilities. Framed around six separate quests, it includes a wealth of activities that foster discussion and thinking about people with disabilities and some of the issues related to participation in daily activities, health, and accessibility. Students can choose from learning quests related to autism, fetal alcohol syndrome, visual impairment, communication disorders, learning disabilities, and physical disabilities.

The **Disability WebQuest** (http://www.west.asu.edu/achristie/CTC/Elisa/Disabilities) presents a series of activities that encourage elementary students to explore visual and hearing disabilities on and off the Internet with an older reading buddy. If you teach Grades 6–12, you might wish students to complete the WebQuest entitled **Walk in My Shoes: How a Disability Changes Your Life** (http://www.inwave.com/schools/Parker/speced/SpEdWebQuest/WebQuest.htm). It was designed as an extension of a high school class study of Helen Keller and *The Miracle Worker* by William Gibson. Students work in small groups of four, playing the role of Internet Researcher, Interviewer, Editor, or Producer, while exploring what it would be like to have a specific disability and how it would affect their lives.

Finally, **Think-Quest Junior Information About Sign Language** (http://library.thinkquest.org/J002931/dev.thinkquest.org/sign_language.htm?tqskip1=1&tqtime=0503) serves as a model of a web-based resource created by two fifth grade girls who were interested in learning more about sign language and deafness. Your students could investigate other groups of individuals with special needs and create a similar type of learning quest. They may even want to enter it into the global **Internet Thinkquest** contest (http://www.thinkquest.org/) to share their expertise with others and maybe even win a prize!

Figure 11-5. The homepage of the **Kids' Quest on Disability and Health** (http://www.cdc.gov/ncbddd/kids/kidhome.htm), a webquest that engages students in Internet investigations about what it feels like to have difficulty learning, seeing, hearing, or communicating with others. From the CDC National Center for Birth Defects and Developmental Disabilities (http://www2.cdc.gov/ncbddd/ContactUs/frmSubmit.asp).

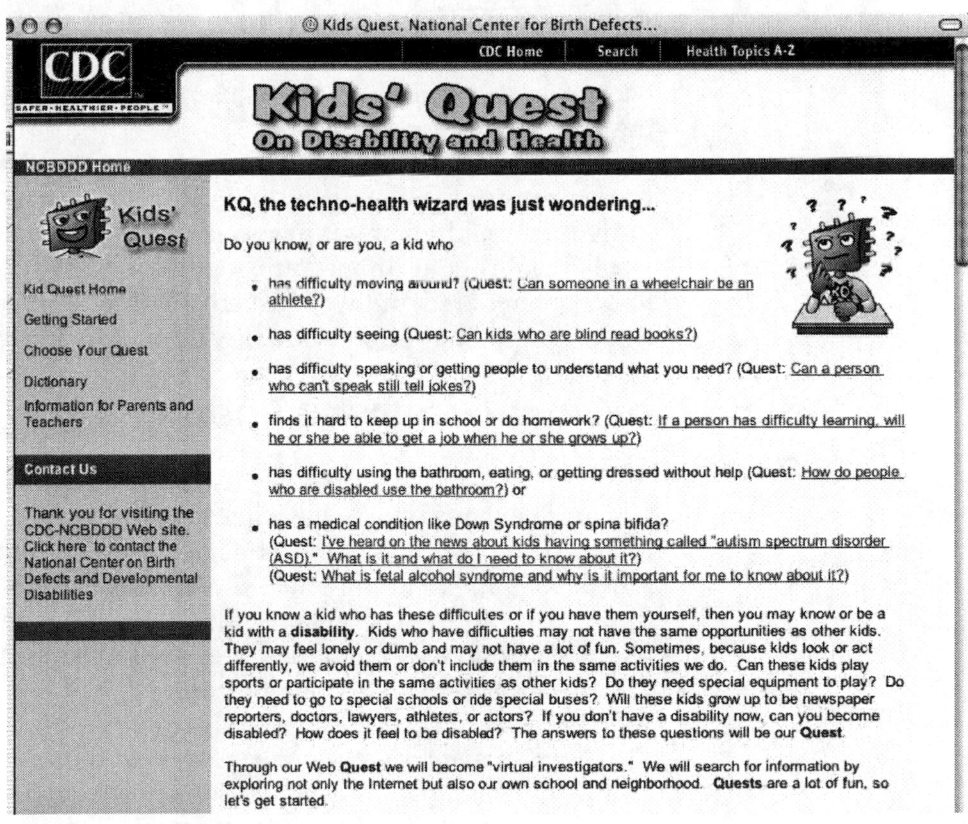

A fun activity to foster your students' appreciation of their own individual strengths and areas of challenge is to have them learn more about Howard Gardner's Multiple Intelligences while exploring various collections of resources related to each area of intelligence from the **Match Multiple Intelligences with Technology** website (http://muse.widener.edu/~kab0306/Multintell.html). They can also explore the "Intelligence Stations" compiled at **Multiple Intelligences and Technology** (http://www.creighton.k12.az.us/mi/) by elementary teachers in Arizona and then have a discussion about their particular areas of interest and strength. You may even have students with different strengths and interests pair up together and share one of their favorite resources from the list to increase an awareness of individual differences. For more lesson ideas, you may wish to explore the information available from **Teaching to the Seven Multiple Intelligences** (http://www.mitest.com/GRPWEBPG.HTM).

Special Thoughts About Special Students

As you plan instructional programming for children with special needs in your classroom, we hope you keep two ideas in mind. First, each of your students is, in fact, a child with special needs.

Each and every child has unique needs that must be recognized as you make instructional decisions. You must always consider each student's background and abilities as you use the Internet in your classroom. Nothing is more important.

Second, legal and categorical designations used for legal and administrative purposes must never limit your instructional decisions regarding individual children or your expectations for their achievement. The use of labels has brought important benefits to students whose needs have too long been ignored, but we must ensure that those labels do not prevent us from recognizing the individuality each of us expresses in our daily lives.

Visiting the Classroom: Fred Roemer's Fifth Grade Class in Florida

We're exhausted. We have just finished exploring a portion, a portion mind you, of the classroom webpage for Fred Roemer's fifth grade class in Pinellas County, Florida entitled **Mr. Roemer's Fifth Grade Polar Bears** (http://www.pb5th.com/index.htm). How does he do it? There is so much wonderful information for his students and so many resources to support their learning (see links from the homepage in Figure 11-6). We are certain we have not seen everything—and we spent several hours at this location! There are so many practical ideas for us in the work Fred and his class are doing and so many important lessons to consider.

Read the **Daily Log** (http://www.pb5th.com/Polar_Bear_Fat/vb/index.php), for example, to discover what is taking place with the Polar Bears each day. This is written daily by one of the students in his class and illustrated with digital pictures. It is a perfect language arts project for students, each of whom will end up writing six to eight descriptive narratives about something important and familiar over the course of the year. And, think of the incentive to have colleagues proof your work, to be certain it is error-free, before it goes up on the Internet for everyone to read. "Did I describe the most important events?" "Did I explain what happened clearly?" "Did I make it interesting to readers?" "Is my work error-free?" There must be continuous revision and editing conferences taking place among the members of Fred's class, just around this one assignment. We are certain it generates critical learning experiences for each classroom reporter. This is a really exciting idea all of us could use in our classrooms, especially since so many states include a descriptive essay in their state writing assessment.

Figure 11-6. Fred Roemer's 5th Grade Polar Bears Classroom Website (http://www.pb5th.com/index.shtml) is a one-stop location that illustrates the power of positive classroom community, student responsibility and communication with parents in both offline and online environments.

Another important lesson is how Fred and his class use their webpage to build community within the classroom. They begin each year by developing a class mission statement. This past year it was this: "The purpose of the polar bears is to make friends and get along, while helping each other, which all adds up to learning so we get a good career." This mission follows a set of seven principles framed around the seven Kwanzaa principles. From there, Fred and his class work hard to develop an esprit de corps that

Another important lesson is how Fred and his class use their webpage to build community within the classroom. They begin each year by developing a class mission statement.

is very special, much of it through the many webpages showing their work, their dreams, and their many wonderful accomplishments. Having a moniker, The Polar Bears, which is used in his class and throughout the class webpage also contributes to their special community, as does the fact that he "loops" with his class, having the same group for several years. But looking at their class webpage we have to believe that this is a critical piece of the puzzle.

Finally, Fred's classroom page shows all of us many new literacies we could use in our own class pages. Take just a few moments and you will encounter new literacies you could use with your classroom: a free and easy-to-use online poll that immediately generates a graph of the results; an online word search; clear descriptions of assignments with examples of formatting requirements for all to see, the results of an Internet project with KidsLink, online grade reports available to parents and students, and much more. Take a look! You will learn a lot about the potentials of the Internet for your classroom. Fred's students are fortunate to have him for their teacher.

New Literacies for Students with Special Needs

New literacies provide new opportunities for learning. They also help each student achieve their full potential as an active, informed, and valued member of our society. As a result, new literacies need to be accessible to every student in our classrooms. New literacies, however, are only developed with effective instructional approaches that permit self-discovery, socially mediated learning with peers, and instruction, all thoughtfully orchestrated by an insightful teacher.

In this book, we have illustrated how a number of instructional approaches may be used to support the development of new literacies. One especially powerful model for instruction is Internet Inquiry. This model helps students to develop independent research skills and acquire critical literacy strategies as they pursue questions that hold a special interest. Unfortunately, opportunities for authentic Internet inquiry of any type are few and far between for many students with special needs. Too often, it is assumed their learning experiences need to be limited. We believe this approach has the unfortunate result of also limiting our students' potential. All students, not just those who achieve at higher levels or who complete their work earlier than others, should have equal access to Internet Inquiry and to developing the new literacies that inquiry activities support.

You have seen how many types of assistive technologies may be used to make the powerful world of the Internet available to students with special needs. These technologies need to be combined with full access to equally powerful methods of instruction such as Internet Inquiry. The technologies and strategies that we have outlined will help you to accomplish this. Fortunately, too, the finest minds in literacy, special education, and technology are also hard at work, developing even more powerful technologies that go far beyond what we have today to assist your students with special needs. One promising example is the work taking place at the Center for Applied Special Technology (CAST). Pay a visit to **Internet Inquiry with All Students** (http://www.cast.org/udl/index.cfm?i=2619).

Here, you can learn about research that involves middle school students with and without learning disabilities who successfully use *etrekker*, a software prototype developed by CAST to support students engaged in Internet Inquiry projects. Work like this holds tremendous promise for us as we support the development of new literacies, creating new opportunities for all students.

It is important to keep in mind, however, these assistive technologies are not nearly as important as *you* are in ensuring complete access to the Internet, effective instructional approaches, and the new literacies that will be so important to their future. *You* make the important decisions in your classroom, not technology. The active role that you play in orchestrating experiences with the Internet will determine the extent to which all of your students develop the new literacies they require.

It is important to keep in mind, however, these assistive technologies are not nearly as important as ***you*** *are in ensuring complete access to the Internet, effective instructional approaches, and the new literacies that will be so important to their future.* ***You*** *make the important decisions in your classroom, not technology.*

To illustrate how important teachers are to the development of new literacies, we invite you to read an article describing the most thoughtfully conducted Internet Inquiry project we have encountered—the **Hero Inquiry Project.** This article is available online as an Adobe PDF file that you may download (http://archive.ncte.org/pdfs/subscribers-only/vm/0103-march03/VM0103Teaching.pdf). In this article you will discover how teachers carefully supported each of their students in developing questions, searching for information, critically evaluating the information they found, and then synthesizing their discoveries and sharing them with others. It is a wonderful example of good teaching with Internet Inquiry. By combining assistive technologies, knowledge about the unique needs of your students, and a powerful approach such as the one illustrated in this article, you can ensure more complete access to the special opportunities the Internet provides for each student in your classroom.

Additional Resources on the Internet for Students with Special Needs

Adobe Acrobat Solutions for Accessibility—
http://www.adobe.com/products/acrobat/solutionsacc.html

This site features a host of solutions that improve the accessibility of text files saved as Adobe PDF files such as customized font size and options to read PDF files out loud.

Apple's Disability Resources—
http://www.apple.com/education/k12/disability/macaccess.html

Here is the location for getting in touch with all kinds of information about adaptive technologies provided by Apple Computer and other companies. This location also includes many free or shareware programs to use with your computer, links to disability-related resources on the Internet, and opportunities to communicate with others about disabilities and teaching/learning issues. Set a bookmark!

Autism Resources—http://www.autism-resources.com/

A site with many links to resources related to Autism and Asperger's Syndrome including links to online discussions, mailing lists, news, treatment methods, research, and much more.

Band-Aids and Blackboards—
http://www.faculty.fairfield.edu/fleitas/contents.html
Young children and teens share stories and information about growing up with medical problems. Stories and support systems are organized into sections for young children, teens, and adults.

Behavior Homepage in Kentucky—
http://www.state.ky.us/agencies/behave/homepage.html
This site, a collaborative effort between the Kentucky Department of Education and the University of Kentucky, hosts a superb collection of resources, articles, and online supports for parents and educators interested in sharing effective practices for working with children who display challenging behaviors. Many great ideas here and lots of support!

Blindness Resource Center—http://www.nyise.org/blind.htm
A great location with extensive information about blindness and resources to inform teachers and assist students.

Brain Connection—http://www.brainconnection.com/
A really neat collection of resources, interactive lessons, games, and activities to get you and your students thinking more about how our brains impact hearing, vision, movement, reading, writing, and much more!

Center for Effective Collaboration and Practice—http://cecp.air.org/
This center is dedicated to sharing effective practices that foster the development of children or youth with or at risk of developing serious emotional disturbance. Be sure to check out their amazing collection of "Mini-Web" resources for educators.

ERIC/OSEP Special Project—http://ericec.org/osep-sp.html
A very nice listing of synthesized research and news briefs about topics in special education collected through a collaboration between ERIC Clearinghouse on Disabilities and Gifted Education and the Council for Exceptional Children (CEC).

Family Village Inclusion Resources—
http://www.familyvillage.wisc.edu/education/inclusion.html
Another nice location to provide resources for teachers interested in inclusive education. Contains links to locations to communicate with others, research, online newsletters, and websites related to inclusion.

Inclusion—http://www.uni.edu/coe/inclusion/
An outstanding collection of resources designed for the teacher who practices, or will soon practice, an inclusion model in the classroom. Links to teaching strategies, strategies to prepare for inclusion, and many supportive Internet resources.

Learning Disabilities Association of America—
http://www.ldanatl.org/
The home page for this organization with over 60,000 members. This location provides links and resources for individuals interested in learning more about learning disabilities.

Learning Disabilities—
http://www.kidsource.com/kidsource/content/learningdis.html
This website contains a booklet from the National Institutes of Mental Health. It explains learning disabilities to parents.

International Dyslexia Association—http://interdys.org/
The International Dyslexia Association (IDA) is an international, non-profit, scientific, and educational organization dedicated to the study and treatment of dyslexia. This location provides access to its many resources related to this important learning disability.

Microsoft Accessibility Home Page—
http://www.microsoft.com/enable/
This is the location for links to many accessibility technologies if you use a Windows operating system. Many free downloads and links to important resources appear here.

Network for Inclusive Education—http://www.enablinginclusion.org/
This site promotes the concept of Inclusive Education with a special focus on the Asian perspective. Information summarizes strategies for inclusion, challenges, and many other insightful perspectives.

New Horizons for Learning—http://www.newhorizons.org/
This organization seeks to implement successful change for education through electronic technologies. Many useful articles about instructional methods to help all learners achieve.

So Get Into It: A Curriculum That Breaks Barriers—
http://www.specialolympics.org/Special+Olympics+Public+Web site/English/Initiatives/Schools_and_Youth/SOGII/default.asp?ID
From here, you can download a free curriculum that celebrates the diverse gifts of every student by learning about the Special Olympics experience and all its positive messages. This program helps kids with and without disabilities learn how to make a difference in their lives.

Signs of Spring—
http://comsewogue.k12.ny.us/showcase/dematteo/dematteo.htm
These first graders invite you into their classroom to share their work related to seasons, poetry, and sign language. They construct drawings with Kid Pix and use sign language to express their feelings about Spring through a whole class performance.

Sparktop.org—http://www.sparktop.org/intro.html
Sponsored by Schwab Learning, this is an online interactive environment in which kids who learn differently can create, share, play games, and connect electronically with other kids like them.

Swan and SNAP Rating Scales for Attention Deficit Disorder—
http://ADHD.net/
These two scales, developed by Dr. James Swanson at the University of California, Irvine to identify and evaluate extreme behaviors related to Attention Deficit Disorder and/or Hyperactivity, are available for download from this site. You can also read research papers about the scales.

Teaching Students with Autism: A Guide for Educators—
http://www.sasked.gov.sk.ca/k/pecs/se/docs/autism/autism.html
Visit this site to download a free 77-page teacher's guide of activities for students with autism developed by educators in Saskatchewan, Canada.

Parents and Teachers of Explosive Kids—
http://www.explosivekids.org/

A very nice collection of tips and strategies from experts using collaborative problem solving to assist students with challenging behaviors. Be sure to visit the online message board here as well.

Perky Duck Free Braille Emulator—
http://www.brl.org/perkyduck.html

From here, you can access a free computer-based, six-key Braille emulator program designed specifically for distance learning programs to help students create Braille files using Windows or Macintosh systems. You'll also find a unique collection of online Braille reference tools.

World Around You: A Magazine for Deaf Teens—
http://clerccenter.gallaudet.edu/worldaroundyou/index.html

Gallaudet University publishes this free magazine for deaf and hard of hearing teens and a teacher's guide three times a year. The magazine also features a yearly essay contest with scholarship awards for high school students.

You Can Handle Them All—
http://www.disciplinehelp.com/behindex/default.htm

This is an extremely helpful list of solutions to 117 of the most common misbehaviors, including those associated with seeking attention, power, revenge, or self-confidence. Each solution outlines the behavior's description, effects, actions, common management mistakes, and links to related behaviors. A true lifesaver for any teacher or parent!

Zigawhat—http://www.nichcy.org/kids/index.htm

An interactive website for learning, connecting, and having fun for young people with disabilities and their peers created by the National Information Center for Children and Youth with Disabilities (NICHCY).

Online Communities for Including All Students on the Internet

Behavior Discussion Forum

A forum to discuss and comment on issues concerning children with behavioral issues

Homepage: http://ebd.coe.uky.edu/Interaction$/behavior/

CHATBACK

A discussion group on special education. Follow typical listserv procedures to subscribe.

Subscription Address: listserv@sjuvm.stjohns.edu

DEAFKIDS

A discussion group for children who are deaf. Follow typical listserv procedures to subscribe.

Subscription Address: listserv@sjuvm.stjohns.edu

DIS-FORUM

A discussion list from the United Kingdom for disabled students and their support staff. Many local topics are relevant to special educators from any country.

Subscription Address: DIS-FORUM@JISCMAIL.AC.UK

Archives: http://www.jiscmail.ac.uk/lists/dis-forum.html

INCLUSIVE-EDUCATION

An inclusive education discussion list. Follow typical listserv procedures to subscribe.

Subscription Address: mailbase@mailbase.ac.uk

KidSource Forums

Here is a directory of several forums for teachers and parents sponsored by KidSource online. Two particularly relevant forums are those focusing on children with learning and other disabilities and gifted children.

Homepage: http://www5.kidsource.com/forums

List of Lists

A list of mailing lists related to special needs issues.

Homepage: http://www.med.stanford.edu/touchstone/listserv.html

SPECED-L

A special education discussion list.

Subscription Address: speced-l@uga.cc.uga.edu

12 Developing A Homepage for your Classroom

We are nearing the end of our journey together. You have accomplished much in a short period of time. There is one final topic we want to share with you: developing a classroom homepage on the Web. You have already seen many outstanding examples of classroom homepages by teachers featured in this book. If you have not already begun to develop your own classroom homepage, now is a wonderful time to begin your own journey in this area. This isn't that hard to do. Really! It will take you less than 30 minutes to acquire the new literacies required to create a classroom homepage.

As you develop a homepage for your class, it projects an important image of professionalism to the public—teachers embracing new literacies and using these in powerful ways to guide students' learning.

Learning the new literacies necessary to develop a homepage is what we call a "four-for," something that gives you *four* important results *for one* activity. In a life where time is always a precious commodity, any "four-for" should be treasured. What are the four important results a homepage will achieve?

First, developing a homepage helps your students learn. It provides a location for publishing student work and it allows you to organize safe links to Internet locations. This enables students to easily access the information you want them to use. Second, developing a homepage also helps others. As you develop instructional materials and links to information resources, you will find other classrooms visiting your page, benefiting from your instructional ideas. Third, developing a homepage enables you to forge a tighter link between home and school. As more computers enter the home, parents can use your homepage to see what is taking place in your classroom and communicate with you about their children. Finally, developing a homepage helps the teaching profession. As you develop a homepage for your class, it projects an important image of professionalism to the public—teachers embracing new literacies and using these in powerful ways to guide students' learning. We hope you take the time to develop a homepage for your class. It will be useful for your students, other teachers, parents, and our profession.

After reading this chapter, you should be able to:

1. Locate other teachers' classroom homepages to see how they integrate the new literacies of the Internet into their classrooms.
2. Develop a homepage on the Internet for your own classroom.
3. Integrate the most common and most useful elements into your classroom homepage.
4. Continue your own development, adding your own ideas about new literacies to the growing community of educators who are online.

Teaching with the Internet: Tama Forth's Class

It was 8:35 A.M. in Room 102.

"And I wanted to tell you that we are going to be adding a new section to our classroom homepage with links to information about California missions. We will be studying the California missions next month and I have posted a workshop assignment in the computer center."

Tama Forth pointed to the workshop assignment:

> Internet Workshop
>
> Conduct a search for the two best sites about the missions of early California using Yahooligans or Kids Click. Add the titles of these sites, along with their URL, to the document "Mission List" located on the desktop. Put your name next to your sites.
>
> Be careful! Let's avoid commercial sites if possible. Come to Internet Workshop prepared to tell us why you believe the information you found is accurate and the sites you selected are the very best that you can find. Also, be prepared to tell us two helpful search strategies that you used to locate your sites. We will be making a list of good search strategies.

Tama Forth was in the middle of the morning announcements to her class before her class got underway.

"I also wanted to remind you that since this is Friday, you should be certain to write a short message to your parents or guardians. Do this with email or on the word processor. Tell them something special that you have done this week. If they have an email address, send it with my email account and remind them to visit our classroom homepage on the Internet. You can also type your message and print it out to take home. I would like to check your messages before you send them out or take them home."

Tama made this assignment each Friday. She found these little notes forged a new type of home–school connection, initiating important conversations at home about what was taking place at school. This helped her students.

"We have received three new messages to our weblog from students and teachers who visited our homepage yesterday. One was very impressed with our wildlife poems we did at the beginning of the year. Also, a student in Germany wanted to know if we could provide her with more information about the Battle of Lexington and Paul Revere's ride. Could you respond to this message, Katherine? You might want to send her a copy of your report. Please use my email account. There was also a message from a teacher in Prince Rupert, Canada telling us how much he liked our homepage. I posted a copy of each message on our *Email Around the World* board next to the computer. Read these new messages about the great work you are all doing in this class."

At the beginning of the year, Tama had taken a workshop with other teachers at her school on developing a classroom homepage on the Internet. Most of their work was done independently. They worked their way through a simple online tutorial, **Creating a New Web Page** (http://wp.netscape.com/browsers/using/newusers/composer/pagecreate.html), on the use of Composer, the free web editor within the Netscape browser. After they completed this tutorial, they worked their way through another online tutorial that was a bit more advanced, **Designing Web Pages with Netscape Composer** (http://courses.aims.edu/~composer/index.htm). Every week they got together to share new ideas and questions that had emerged. The professional development class used a model very similar to Internet Workshop. This week, they had learned how to add graphics to their homepages.

Tama was surprised at how simple it was to create a webpage with Composer. This made developing a homepage for the Web as easy as typing with a word processor. She wondered why no one had told her before how easy this was to do. Somehow, she had thought developing a webpage required many years of experience and a lot of technical training. She quickly discovered that if you know how to use a word processor, you do not need any additional skills to be able to use a webpage editor such as Composer; all you need is a curious mind.

"If I can do this, anyone can."

As Tama had told her colleagues, "If I can do this, anyone can." She had concluded that all someone really needed was a few minutes to play around with a web editor such as Composer and a location on the Internet to place your homepage. The workshop and the tutorial were nice, but not even necessary.

Tama had set up several sections on the first version of her classroom homepage. One contained the wildlife poems they did earlier, another contained a set of links she used for Internet Workshop, another displayed the research they had done on the Battle of Lexington during the Revolutionary War, and another contained photos and a description of the field trip they recently took to Bunker Hill. She also put her email address on the homepage so parents could get in touch with her or send messages to their children when they wanted to surprise them at school. Clicking on this address immediately opened an email message window with her address in the "To" box. This was just the first draft of her classroom homepage, however. Her instructor told her that homepages continue to evolve over time.

Figure 12-1. The homepage for **Creating a New Web Page** (http://wp.netscape.com/browsers/using/newusers/composer/pagecreate.html), one of the many excellent tutorials for creating a webpage.

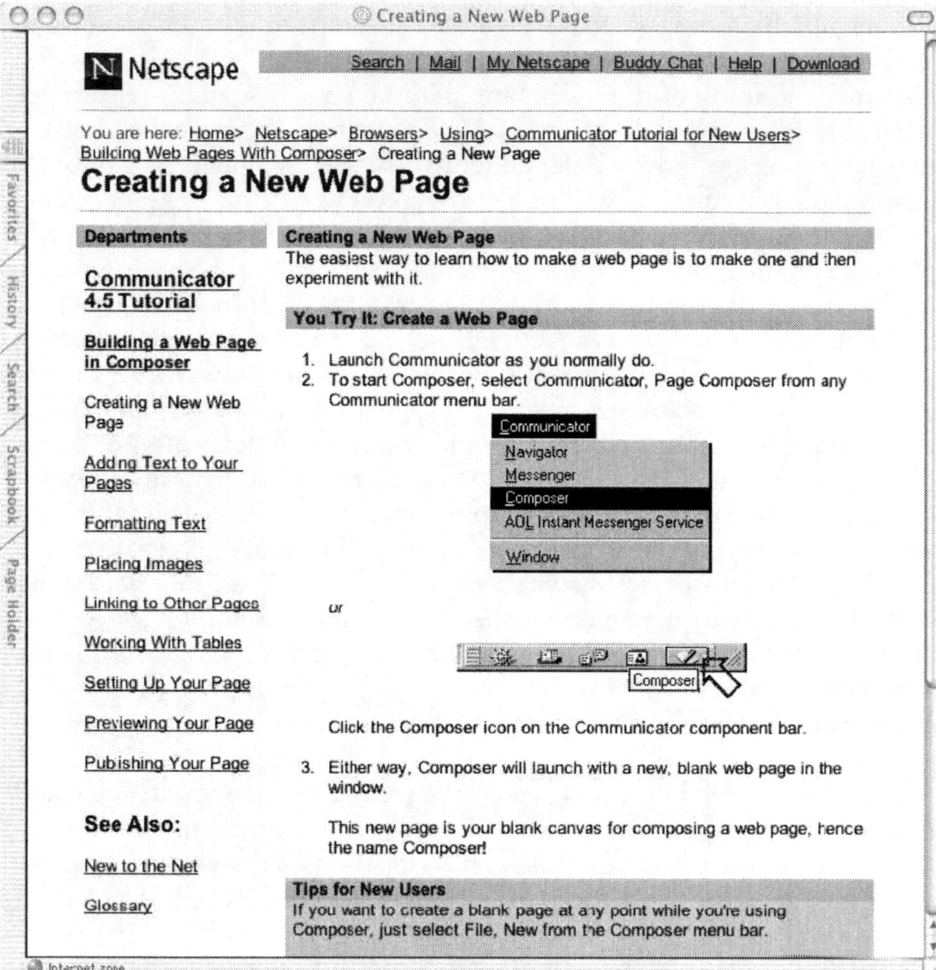

Developing a homepage is not all that complex if you already are familiar with basic word processing. The new HTML editors appearing with Internet browsers make it easy to create a classroom homepage.

Lessons from the Classroom

This episode in Tama Forth's class illustrates several important lessons about developing and using a classroom homepage on the Internet. First, it shows that developing a homepage is easy to do if you already are familiar with basic word processing. Web editors are now available with Internet browsers and they make it simple to create a classroom homepage. Anyone can do this.

This episode also shows how a homepage helps to organize Internet resources for classroom instruction. Tama used her homepage to organize each unit. She simply created a page for each unit during the year and added useful links. She included each of the instructional models that she had used in her classroom: Internet Workshop, Internet Project, Internet Inquiry, and WebQuest. The nice thing about a webpage was that she could reuse the units the following year without much additional effort. Setting up organized sets of links in this fashion also assisted her Internet safety program. Tama always previewed the sites she included to be certain they would not lead her students off into areas of the Internet that they should not be exploring.

Third, the episode shows how a homepage may be used to publish work that students complete in a classroom. Tama always had a writing project for each thematic unit. These projects went through each phase of the writing process. In the final phase, students published their work on the classroom homepage so that everyone in the class could read it and so that others around the world might see their wonderful writing. The most avid readers of the website, Tama discovered, were the students themselves and their parents. Several times at the local library, she found a student showing work to parents on the Internet computer located there. She also knew that some parents viewed this work from home because several parents had left her messages. And a few told her they liked to show off their child's work to others in their office.

A homepage may be used to publish the work that students complete in a classroom.

Also, notice how a homepage for your class assists other classrooms. Often, you will develop a unit that other teachers may wish to use. Or, sometimes another teacher will send you an email message, asking questions about your unit. One of the more powerful aspects of the Internet in school classrooms is that it allows teachers to develop curriculum that is immediately available to others throughout the world. This potential will be exploited with increasing regularity in the future.

Home–school relationships are also strengthened when you develop a classroom homepage. While not all families have immediate access to the Internet, this is rapidly changing as increasing numbers of families are coming online or using Internet connections at your school or local library. Having a homepage allows your parents to view their children's work and all the fine things you are doing in the classroom. It also provides an opportunity for parents and guardians to drop you an email message when they have a question. The Internet provides many new opportunities to work with the families of students in your class.

Parents who see your classroom homepage become more aware of the many wonderful things you do to support their children's development.

Finally, a homepage for your classroom accomplishes another important goal—it projects an important image of teachers as professionals. Parents who see your classroom homepage become more aware of the many wonderful things you do to support their children's development. We are used to many members of the tax-paying public thinking that anybody can teach children. Putting up a homepage, displaying your students' work, and inviting parents into your electronic classroom displays the many talents we all have as teachers. This is of central importance when school systems rely on taxpayers to support their efforts, especially in a period when individuals who are unfamiliar with what we do and what we know sometimes criticize the teaching profession.

E-MAIL FOR YOU

From: Doug Crosby (kiwi@digisys.net)
Subject: Using the Internet in First Grade

Greetings!

Spring had finally arrived in Montana after a particularly long and cold winter. It was time to take our first grade field trip, this year we were off to a local biological station.

All year, we had been publishing class books using a variety of media but we wanted to make our field trip report something special. Our school had recently posted a homepage on the Internet so we decided to publish our field trip report for all the world to see.

It was kind of a gray day with showers threatening but we had already postponed the trip once so off we went with our digital camera in hand. It turned out to be a wonderful day with a great variety of learning activities taking place. We snapped away with our camera; there were the aquatic insects, the stream, the microscopes, and of course the big log where we all sat to eat lunch!

After returning to school, we all sat around the computer to view the photos and within a short time we had come up with a whole class report, which was typed directly on the screen. It looked great once we posted it on our webpage. We have had a lot of fun reading email from people around the world who have come across our report (http://www.digisys.net/cherry/Mr.Crosbyfield_trip.htm) and just dropped a note to say well done.

This has been a wonderful experience for my first graders in electronic publishing and a great introduction into the world of their futures.

Doug: The Kiwi at Cherry
Cherry Valley School
Polson, Montana
http://www.polson.k12.mt.us/cherry/teachers/crosby/crosby.site/index.html

Examples of Classroom Homepages

You can find many more homepages by simply doing a search with ***Google*** *(http:// www.google.com) or another search engine.*

Before looking at strategies for developing a classroom homepage, it might be useful to see what outstanding teachers are doing with their own homepages. Throughout this book you have seen many outstanding classroom homepages and learned important lessons from the teachers who have created them. You can find many more homepages by doing a search with **Google** (http://www.google.com) or another search engine. Simply do a search for the terms that often appear on classroom homepages. These include one item from each set of items below:

- Ms., Mr., or Mrs.
- classroom
- homepage or home page

If you are looking for examples of classroom homepages for a particular grade level, just add an additional keyword for that grade level: sixth grade, kindergarten, fourth grade, and so on. If you are looking for a classroom homepage for a particular subject at the middle or high school level, just add a keyword for the subject area: earth science, biology, geometry, American history, physics, and so on.

The results of a search like this will yield many examples of classroom homepages to explore. These will generate exceptional ideas about what to include in your own classroom homepage and how to organize the information most effectively. They will also provide you with links to resources that may prove useful. In fact, we have learned that some of the best classroom resources may be found by following links from well-designed and thoughtfully organized classroom homepages. Classroom teachers on the Internet have much to teach all of us about these new literacies. A good homepage is a gold mine for all of us.

Classroom homepages at each level of the K-12 continuum tend to share certain qualities.

Classroom homepages at each level of the K-12 continuum tend to share certain qualities. If you explore the world of preschools and kindergartens, you will find published student work as well as important information for parents. You will not find many curriculum assignments or links to other academic resources. Classroom homepages at these beginning levels celebrate the learning of young children in developmentally appropriate ways—through photographs of them at work and images of their drawings. In addition, because these levels usually provide the first contact with a school system for parents, teachers use homepages to communicate information about school policies and the beginning-of-school experience. This helps to inform parents about the school experience and supports them in this important transition. Often, teachers also provide parents with links to useful information about parenting and the developmental processes their young children are experiencing. Thus, classroom homepages, at the very earliest levels, often serve the needs of parents more than they serve the needs of children.

Your search at the preschool or kindergarten level may yield classroom homepages such as **Ms. Kristine's Class Page** (http://homepage.mac.com/whiteb/sas_preschool/Menu20.html). This is a preschool site and you will see how images of students at work and play dominate the site, informing parents of the exciting experiences their children are having. Or, you may find the kindergarten classroom homepage at **Mrs. Emmons Kindergarten** (http://home.cfl.rr.com/emmons/). In Figure 12-2, you can see how an area is devoted to "Parent Pages." These resources help parents to better understand the school's policies and procedures.

If you are interested in including digital photography as part of your classroom experiences, and want to use photos at your classroom homepage you may wish to pay a visit to **1001 Uses for a Digital Camera in Educational Settings** (http://pegasus.cc.ucf.edu/~ucfcasio/qvuses.htm). To find many more ideas, do a Google search using these keywords: "using a digital camera in the classroom." Surround the words with quotation marks so that only sites with this exact phrase will show up in the results list. Keep in mind that each district will have their own policies regarding digital photos of students. Be certain to find out what your district's policy is. For child safety reasons, no district will permit you to use both first and last names. Some districts permit you to use photos, but only if group photos are used without any names identifying individuals. Some do not permit you to use photos, even without names. In this later situation, teachers in the primary grades will sometimes post drawings by students of themselves and scan these to digitize them.

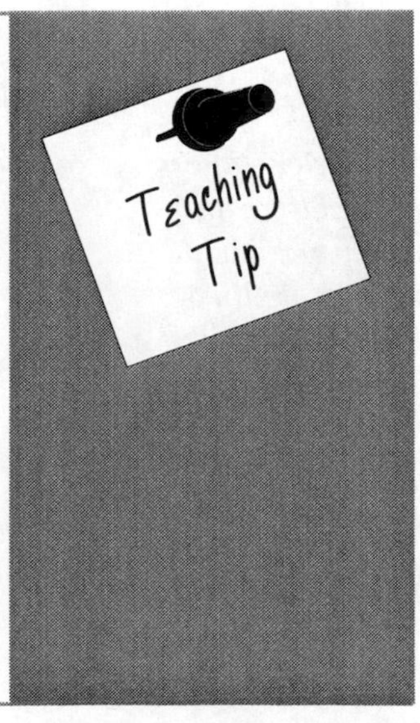

Figure 12-2. Mrs. Emmons Kindergarten (http://home.cfl.rr.com/emmons/), the classroom homepage created by Joyce Emmons in Florida for her kindergarten class. Note the separate sections for parents and children.

At the elementary level, classroom homepages include many more links to curriculum resources on the Internet.

At the elementary level, classroom homepages include many more links to curriculum resources on the Internet. There is a greater focus on using information on the Internet for units of study. Classroom homepages are frequently used to organize sites the teacher wishes students to use during assignments. In addition, elementary pages often include student work and information for parents. Some of the better ones have regular newsletters for parents. An example of a classroom homepage at the elementary level is **Mrs. Bogucki's Third Grade Class** (http://hbogucki. staffnet.com/aemes/default.htm). Here you will find all kinds of great links for study at the third grade level. You will also find published student work as well as information for parents.

Weblogs are beginning to appear at some classroom homepages, keeping the world informed about the events taking place in a class on a daily basis. This is an important new tool and a wonderful development for classrooms. You can find examples of class weblogs by searching for classroom homepages as you did above but also adding the word weblog or blog as a keyword. You will discover that some teachers are beginning to experiment with this new technology. In some cases weblogs (blogs) are beginning to replace classroom homepages, providing a more interactive experience for visitors. Take a look at these locations to see the emergence of the new literacies of blogs appearing at classroom homepages:

- **Mary Kreul's 4th Grade Blog**—
  http://marykreul.teacherhosting.com/blog/
- **Blogging with Partners: Mrs. Contner's 4th Grade Blog**—
  http://contner.weblogger.com/
- **Mainville Elementary Blog**—
  http://www.littlemiamischools.com/hm/
- **Using Weblogs in Literature Circles**—http://mustangblog.typepad.com/

Figure 12-3. Mrs. Bogucki's Third Grade Class
(http://hbogucki.staffnet.com/aemes/default.htm), an exceptional homepage for the elementary grades.

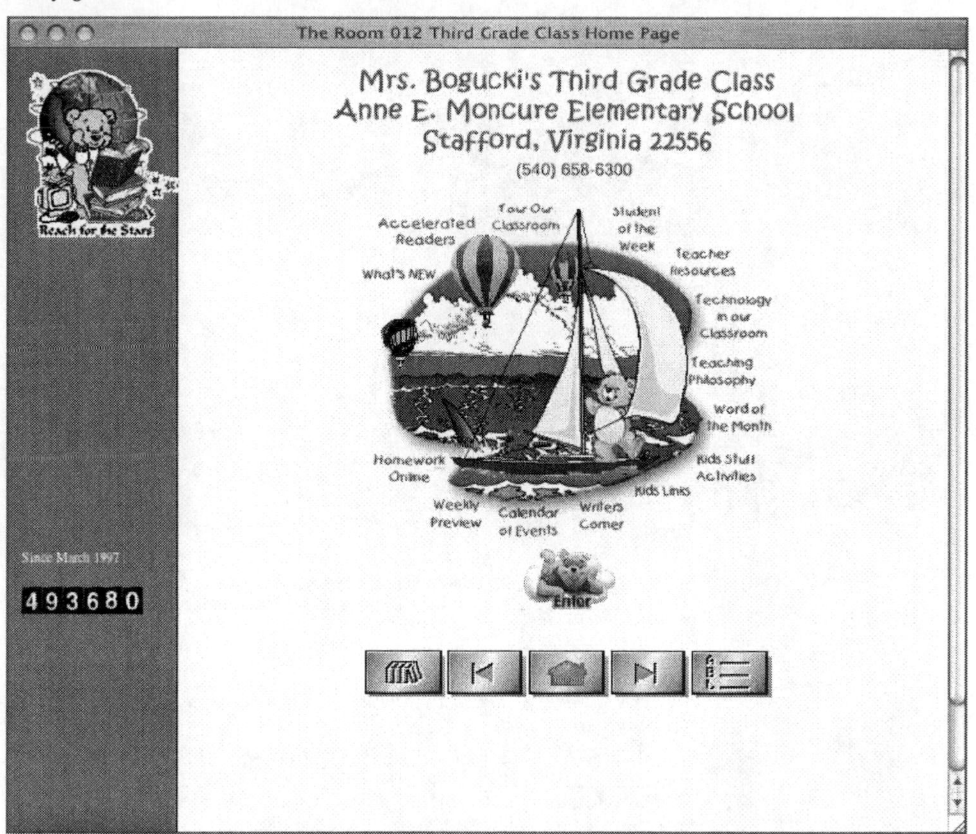

Middle and high school classroom homepages also have their distinctive style. Generally, homepages at this level focus more directly on the content that is expected to be mastered. As a result, you will find lecture and study notes for classes, assignments, and sometimes even an online grade book. Since teachers at this level often teach several classes, they will often have a main page with links to each of the classes that they teach. A nice example of a classroom homepage for middle or high school levels may be seen at **Ms. B's Home Page** (http://www.arps.org/users/hs/blaunerp/index.html). Ms. Blauner teaches physics. Other exceptional examples include:

- **Mr. Patch's Quilt Club**—
  http://www.smfc.k12.ca.us/technology/mrpatch/
- **Palo Alto High School Spanish**—
  http://www.paly.net/~cmerritt/spanishteach.html
- **Chemistry Geek.com**—http://www.chemistrygeek.com/
- **Mr. M's Grade 8 Page**—http://www.hpedsb.on.ca/bayps/mrozewski/
- **Mrs. Adams' High School English**—
  http://www.studyguide.org/index.htm

Middle and high school classroom homepages also have their distinctive style. Generally, homepages at this level focus more directly on the content that is expected to be mastered.

Figure 12-4. Physics, one of several course websites located at **Ms. B's Home Page** (http://www.arps.org/users/hs/blaunerp/index.html), the classroom homepage of Ms. Blauner, a high school physics teacher in Amherst, Massachusetts. Note the different type of content compared to an elementary classroom homepage.

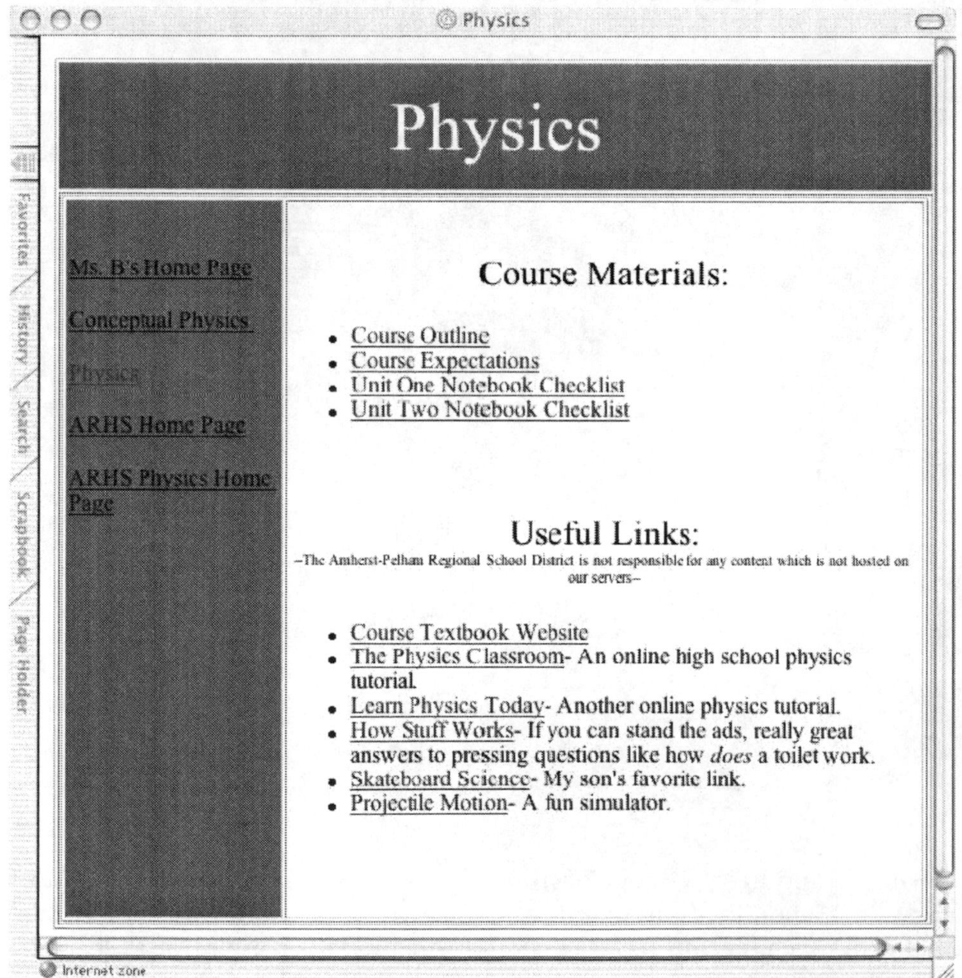

Creating Your Own Classroom Homepage

Developing a homepage may seem intimidating. After all, a programming language, HTML (Hypertext Mark-up Language) is used to create pages on the Web. Fortunately, though, new tools are appearing that make this easy. Today, knowing this programming language is not as necessary as it once was. To develop a homepage, all you really need to know is how to type with a word processor. If you also know how to copy and paste graphics, that is an added bonus. We will show you how to make a classroom homepage in just 30 minutes! Maybe less.

To develop a homepage, all you really need to know is how to type with a word processor.

HTML is the programming language used most often to design homepages on the Internet. You may see a few lines of HTML code in Figure 12-5. HTML code such as this is behind every webpage that you see on the Internet. Browsers such as Internet Explorer, Netscape Navigator, and Safari read this code and turn it into what you see on your screen. So, if a browser read the HTML code in Figure 12-5, it would appear as in Figure 12-6. This is what happens each time you view a page on the Web. To demonstrate this, all you have to do is to open up any page on the Web with your browser and, if you know how, you can view the HTML code used to develop that page. Each browser has a slightly different procedure to view the underlying HTML code. Follow these directions:

- In Netscape Navigator, go to the menu item called "View" and select the item "page source." This will open up the HTML file used to create the page you were just viewing.
- In Internet Explorer, go to the menu item called "View" and select the item "source." You will see HTML code similar to what you find in Figure 12-5.
- In Safari, go to the menu item called "View" and select the item "View source."

INTERNET FAQ

I have heard that people often "borrow" code after viewing the HTML source code at a page they admire. They say that they "borrow" images, animations, pictures, and other elements from several pages by copying and pasting and adding these to their own. Is this illegal?

This, unfortunately, is all too common. Copyright issues are still being defined in this area. Still, it appears that webpage owners possess copyright to all of the elements at their location, as long as it is original work. This means you need to request permission from a web owner before "borrowing" original text, images, or anything else from a page's source code. If you wish to read more about copyright issues on the Web, you may wish to pay a visit to the **U.S. Copyright Office Homepage** (http://www.copyright.gov/) or **Copyright Internet Resources** (http://lcweb.loc.gov/copyright/resces.html). You may also refer to the section on citing sources in Chapter 3 and the Teaching Tip on detecting plagiarism in Chapter 2.

Figure 12-5. An example of HTML (Hypertext Mark-up Language)

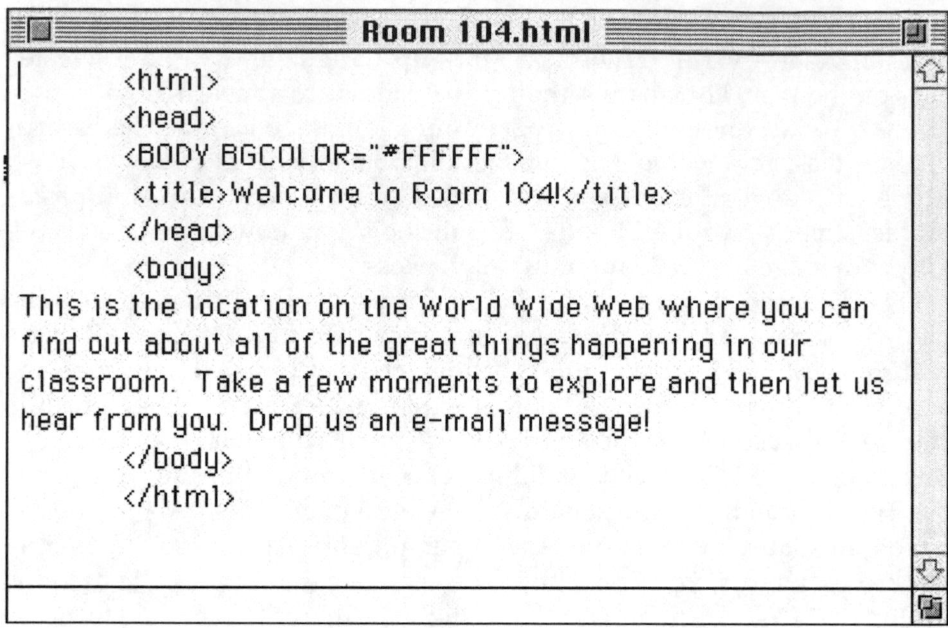

Figure 12-6. What the information in Figure 12-5 looks like when it is read by a web browser such as Netscape.

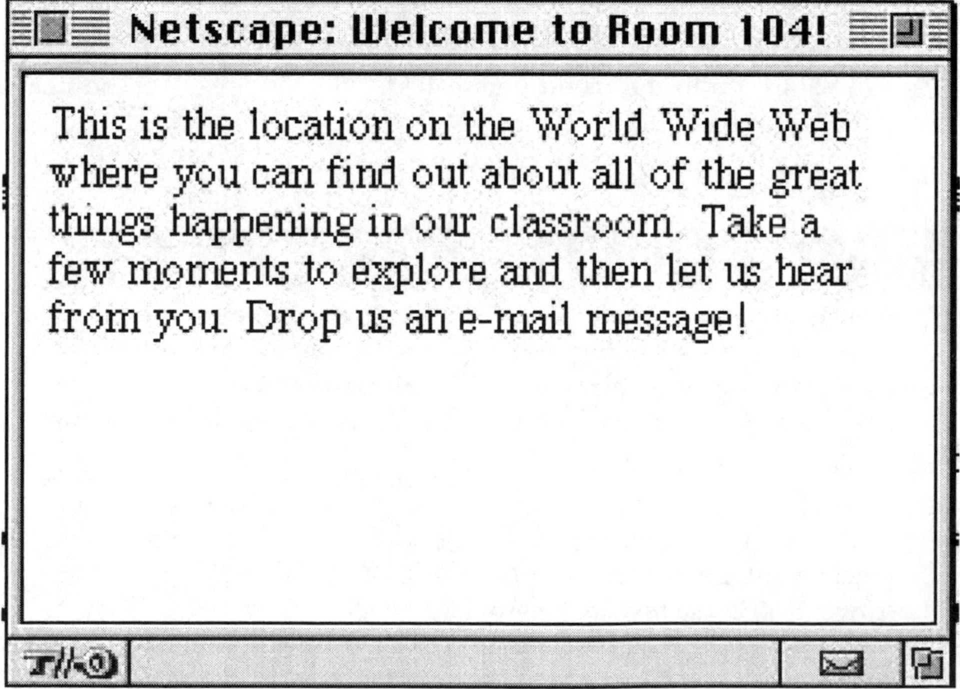

There are two strategies for developing a classroom homepage in HTML. The easiest way to develop a homepage for your classroom is to independently explore the features of any simple web editor. A web editor allows you to develop your page using a program similar to a word processor. The program will automatically convert the pages you type into HTML code and you will never even see the code. Thus, all you do is type up your classroom page until it looks the way you wish it to appear. During the process, the HTML code will always be there, behind the scenes, even though you may never see it. There are several fine programs that enable you to do this.

If you are using Netscape 4.0 or higher your program comes with a free web editor already built in called Netscape Composer. Figure 12-7 shows an image of this program as a teacher quickly developed an initial version of a homepage in just ten minutes. To access this web editor, you simply click on the pencil icon in the bottom of the software window. This launches Composer, a web editor. Like all web editors, Composer requires little explanation. It works similarly to a word processor. Just begin typing away in the window for Composer and explore the formatting tools that allow you to design your page the way you wish it to look. You can type text, format text, insert a graphic, make a link to another page, set text to blink on and off, add color, and use many additional functions as you design your page. Simply explore each of the editing tools at the top of the Composer window and in the menu items. You will have a first draft of a classroom homepage in just 30 minutes . . . or less!

The easiest way to develop a homepage for your classroom is to use an HTML editor. This will allow you to develop your page using a program similar to a word processor.

Figure 12-7. The beginnings of a homepage being developed with an HTML editor, Netscape Composer.

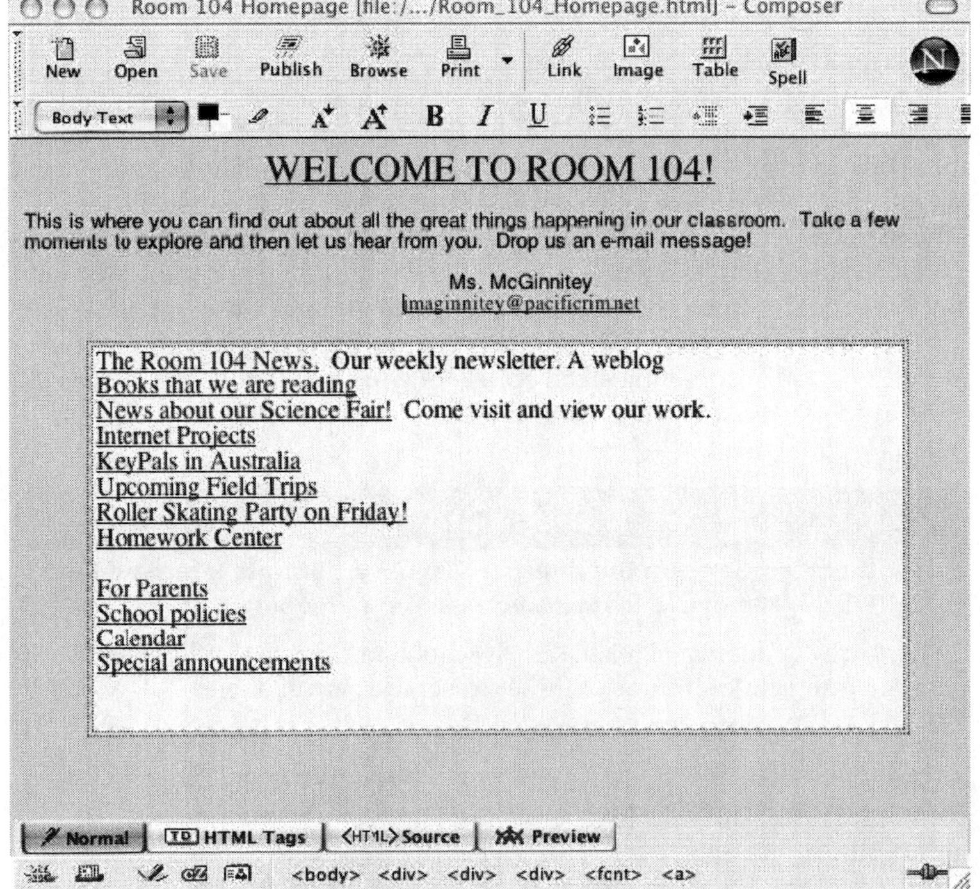

Save your new homepage as a file on your hard drive. Then, select "Open file" from your menu bar and locate the file on your hard drive containing your homepage. It will appear as if it was on the Internet. Or, you can just click on the "Preview" button at the bottom.

INTERNET FAQ

I am viewing my homepage. Why do I see a big red X in the location where I inserted a graphic onto my homepage?

This happens whenever an image for a webpage has been saved outside of the folder where the webpage is located. To ensure that all images will appear with your webpage, be certain to include each image within the same folder as your webpage.

You now have a webpage that you may view. Others, though, will not be able to view your home page since it only resides on your hard drive. To make your homepage available to everyone else out on the Internet, you need to move it to a server and obtain a URL (uniform resource locator; a www address) for its location. Your district may have a server you can use. You should check with your technical support to see if this is available to you and what procedures are required to place your homepage on the district's server. If you have a separate Internet Service Provider (ISP) at a home account, it is likely that they also provide server space for any webpages that you develop. You may wish to also check with your home ISP about the procedures to follow.

Or, you may wish to purchase space on a commercial site designed to host webpages. There are many on the Internet. Simply do a search using these keywords: free web hosting. A number of commercial locations will appear that provide free space on a server for your webpages. In return, however, these companies will place ads at your site. You may wish to try a location on a temporary basis. But, since you do not control the ads and since students will use this site, you never wish to make this a permanent solution. At most of these free locations, you may pay a small amount each month to avoid ever having an ad appear at your site. If you intend the site to be used by students, you will want to explore this option.

INTERNET FAQ

Are there locations on the Internet that have a simple template for me to use to make a classroom homepage?

There are commercial sites that host school and classroom homepages on the Internet. Visit three of these to see what is available:

- **TeacherWeb**—http://teacherweb.com/
- **MySchoolOnline**—http://www.myschoolonline.com/golocal/
- **Scholastic**—http://teacher.scholastic.com/homepagebuilder/monthly_tips.htm

A second, more structured, approach for developing a classroom homepage is to spend a little time going through one of several fine tutorials on the Internet that will teach you how to create a webpage. There are many that exist. You may wish to begin with one of these:

A second approach for developing a classroom homepage is to spend a little time going through one of several fine tutorials that exist on the Internet.

- **Creating a New Web Page—** http://wp.netscape.com/browsers/using/newusers/composer/pagecreate.html
- **Designing Web Pages with Netscape Composer—** http://courses.aims.edu/~composer/index.htm
- **Netscape Tutorial Introduction—** http://www.mwc.edu/training/inte/internet/composer/index.htm
- **Netscape Composer Introduction—Basics 101—** http://www.valsvisions.com/html/index.html

These take you step-by-step through everything you need to know to develop a webpage.

E-MAIL FOR YOU

From: Mary Lou Balcom (mlbalcom@aol.com)
Subject: Classroom Homepages and Internet Use

I've been exploring the Internet and still feel awestruck by the wealth of information available. The Internet has provided me with current information on topics I teach, actual lesson plans that I have used, great ideas to try in my classroom, and lots of interesting sites that relate to my curricula. I am excited by the avenues that will be open to my students. I feel that I will play the role of a facilitator as I guide and structure my students' use of the Web.

I share the concerns of many colleagues regarding both the appropriate use and optimal use of the Web. I plan to include my students in the development of appropriate use guidelines for the Web the same way that I have typically developed classroom rules. My experience with class rules has been that students traditionally include the basics that most teachers would incorporate, and I think I will guide the process for Internet access in the same fashion.

My biggest concern is that students may waste the precious little time they have access to the computer on pointless meanderings around the Web. One of the ways to avoid this is to initially give very structured assignments to ensure that students will have successful and meaningful experiences. It is also beneficial to design your own homepage that organizes the topics you are studying. I recently took a class to learn how to design a homepage. At first I was overwhelmed by the process, but by the end of the week had made a very simple page based on our study of ancient Egypt. I would expect the page to evolve as my students study Egypt and I would update the page. The page could change to reflect the current topic of study.

I think I'm ready to take on the challenge of using the Web in my classroom to enhance my students' learning.

Mary Lou Balcom, Sixth grade teacher
Edward Smith Elementary School
Syracuse, NY

Which Elements Should I Include in my Classroom Homepage?

The design elements you include in your classroom homepage will inevitably reflect your grade level, your teaching style, and the culture of your classroom. You may, however, wish to consider elements such as the following:

- a location where parents and others can send you and your class an email message;
- a location where students may publish their work;
- a location where due dates for major assignments are posted;
- a location for organizing links to sites in various units; and
- a location where you or your students can publish a newspaper of classroom events and opinions.

The design elements you include in your classroom homepage will inevitably reflect your teaching style and the culture of your classroom.

It is important to think of your homepage as a window through which the rest of the world may see your class. Thus, you will want to provide an opportunity for others to communicate with you and your students. This can be easily done on a homepage. You can quickly make a link that will open up an email message window containing your address. To do this, follow these steps:

1. Using a web editor, type your name on your webpage.
2. Highlight your name.
3. Select the "make a link" function.
4. Type in the "mailto:" command followed by your email address when you create the link (e.g., mailto:donald.leu@uconn.edu).
5. Save the webpage.

Now, whenever someone clicks on your name, a message window containing your address will appear. This makes it easy for parents and others to get in touch with you and your students.

You should also consider using your homepage as a location where students may publish their work. This allows others to see what you are doing. It also makes material and information available for others to read and enjoy. Stories, poetry, descriptions of classroom events, responses to literature....your homepage will provide countless opportunities to allow your students to show off their best writing and art. And, a web editor makes all of this very easy. Here are a few examples:

- **The Fourth Grade Times**—
  http://home.dstream.net/~tksmith/news/planet.htm
- **Fred Roemer's Daily Log**—
  http://www.pb5th.com/Polar_Bear_Fat/vb/forumdisplay.php?s=&forumid=43

You might also wish to have a bulletin board listing due dates for major classroom assignments. Often, parents appreciate knowing when assignments are due. This is especially important in the older grades.

Another important function for your homepage may be to organize links on the Web for the various units you cover during the year. You can save students much time by placing these at a single location where they are easy to access.

Finally, if you teach in the elementary grades, think about including a student newspaper on your homepage. This can be a wonderful source for many writing activities. You may wish to appoint an editor for each two-week period and make this person responsible for soliciting articles and seeing that they are revised and edited to meet the standards of your homepage. These provide students, parents, and others with a real understanding of all the great things that take place in your classroom.

INTERNET FAQ

Do you have any other good suggestions for developing a classroom homepage?

Sure. We encourage you to read the following two documents. The first is a personal set of recommendations to teachers about to develop their classroom homepage by Mrs. Bogucki, **Creating a Classroom Web Page** (http://hbogucki.staffnet.com/aemes/resource/webpage.htm). The second is **Designing a Classroom Web Page** (http://www.enc.org/features/focus/archive/realworld/document.shtm?input=FOC-000883-index). Both of these will give you lots of additional ideas.

Visting the Classroom: Heather Renz's Fourth Grade Class in Oregon

An exceptional model for all of us to consider is the classroom homepage of Heather Renz and her fourth grade students in Redmond, Oregon. A tour of **Mrs. Renz's 4th Grade Class** (http://www.redmond.k12.or.us/patrick/renz/index.html) will provide you with an exceptional picture of all that takes place in her classroom. Take a look at: their web buddies (other classrooms at the fourth grade level who are also online and exchange information with her class), the Word of the Day site, the daily schedule, the parent corner, and many other exciting resources. You can even take a photo tour through her classroom to see how it is organized.

Heather Renz's students also have a location on this classroom homepage where they make and manage their own webpages, sharing important work during the year with the rest of the world. One gets the sense that there must be an extraordinary exchange of new literacies that takes place throughout this classroom.

All of the elements that any good classroom webpage should contain are here. Plus, there is so much more. Pay a visit to Heather's class to discover all of the many ways that she integrates the new literacies of the Internet and other ICT into her curriculum. You will discover that this opens many new windows to the world for Heather and her students, bringing them into closer contact with other people around the world. We know a visit to this class will give you many new ideas for your own classroom.

Figure 12-8. The classroom homepage of **Mrs. Renz's 4th Grade Class** (http://www.redmond.k12.or.us/patrick/renz/index.html)

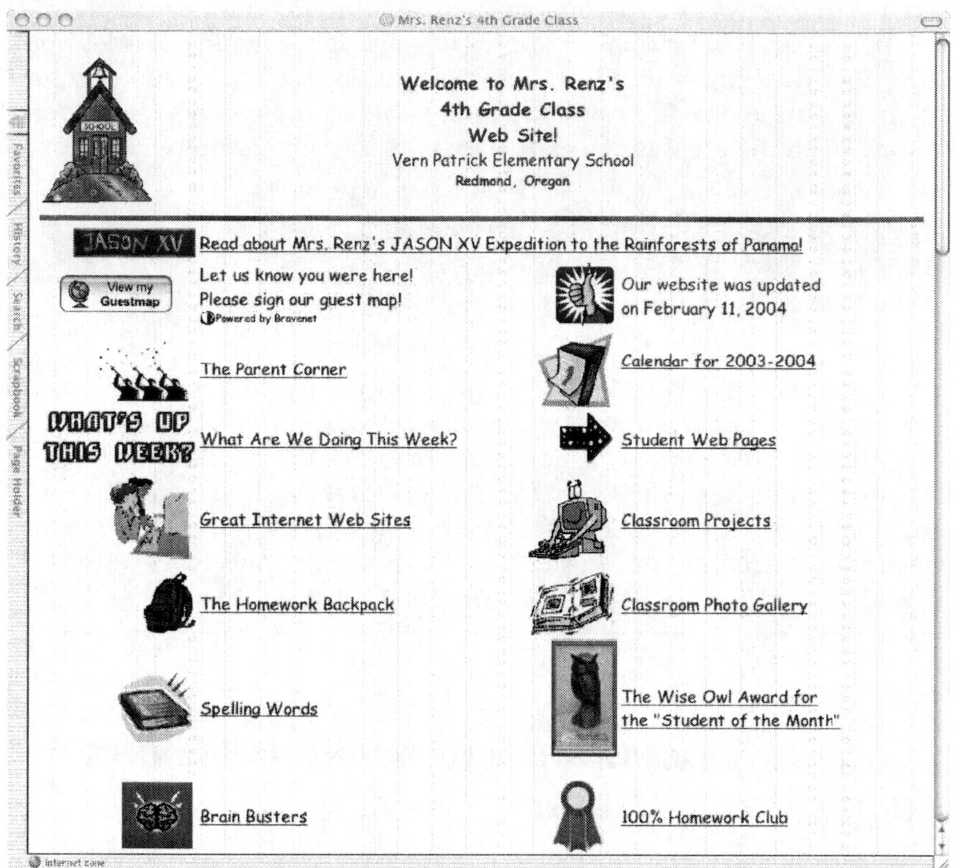

E-MAIL FOR YOU

From: Heather Renz <hrenz@redmond.k12.or.us>
Subject: Harnessing the Power of the Internet for Classroom Instruction

I have been a classroom teacher for over 23 years, teaching 1st, 4th, 5th and middle school math. I currently teach 4th grade in a rural Oregon community of 16,000 people. In my years of teaching, I have never found a more valuable tool than web applications for teaching.

During the summer of 2000, as a personal enrichment activity, I purchased a copy of Front Page, a web editor, and began exploring the world of web-based learning. Self taught, I developed my initial webpage to document class activities, act as a classroom-learning tool, and serve as a parent notification system.

Since that time, my site has been discovered and used as a resource for teachers across the country and around the world. In the short time since its introduction, the website has received numerous awards and has been termed a major education portal.

Despite the recognition my site has received, it remains a tool for students. It allows students to utilize technology to access a web of scientists, teachers, experts, and resources enabling them to extend and enrich their classroom experiences beyond our rural community. Students use my website

cont.

not only at school, but at home as well. Students stay focused on sites I have chosen to include on my website, sites which are focused towards reinforcing grade level standards.

As educators, we can share our passion for teaching through our websites. The rewards are many. Students are proud to see their work showcased on their individual webpages and take pride in achieving the best result possible. I cannot imagine teaching without a classroom website and access to technology.

In closing, by integrating my fourth grade classroom activities with my passion for the Web, the power of technology and the Internet has been harnessed to facilitate and enhance learning for my rural students. The students of today are the work force of the future, and their future success depends on their technological literacy.

Good luck on your journey!
Heather Renz

The New Literacies of a Classroom Homepage

Creating a classroom homepage permits you to communicate with your students, the parents of your students, and the rest of the world. It says: This is who I am and this is what we do. It is, we believe, one of the most profound statements that you can make about the important work that you accomplish every day in your classroom. A classroom homepage demonstrates to the world all of the new literacies that you have acquired and are passing along to your students.

Why is this? You will recall the five major functions of a new literacies perspective from Chapter 1:

1. *identify* important questions;
2. *navigate* information networks to locate relevant information;
3. *critically evaluate* the usefulness of information that is found;
4. *synthesize* information to answer the question or solve the problem; and
5. *communicate* the answer to others.

A classroom homepage allows you to share with others the entire story of your new literacies journey. As a result, your classroom homepage represents, in a very real way, the culmination and the application of *all* the new literacies that you have acquired. It shows the world what you have done to: *identify important questions* about teaching and learning; *navigate information networks* to locate relevant information; *critically evaluate* the usefulness of information you located; *synthesize information* to answer your questions; and, of course, *communicate* the answers that you have found on your journey. Your classroom homepage tells the central story of your new literacies journey.

And, as you regularly update your classroom homepage, perhaps by adding a guestbook, a calendar of important upcoming events, or a photo tour of your classroom, you will also be demonstrating to the world that you continue to grow and acquire additional new literacies on your journey. By networking with other teachers and classrooms you will continuously be learning new literacies and representing many of these on your classroom homepage. Yes, your classroom homepage does all of this, capturing the essence of what it means to be a new literacies educator.

The End Of Your Journey

We are firmly convinced that the world awaiting our students is one where each of them has more potential to grow and to learn than at any time in history

No. This isn't the end of your journey. It is really just the beginning as you discover additional new literacies, new resources on the web, new friends from around the world, and new sources of inspiration for the important work that you do with the students in your classroom.

We are firmly convinced that the world awaiting our students is one where each of them has more potential to grow and to learn than at any time in history. We also believe your role will be central to their success, especially with these new technologies. As we indicated in the first chapter, Internet resources will increase, not decrease, the central role you play in orchestrating learning experiences for your students. Each of us will be challenged to thoughtfully guide students' learning about new literacies within information environments that are richer and more complex than traditional print media, presenting new and more powerful learning opportunities for both you and your students. We hope you have found the ideas we have shared useful in the important work you do to prepare children for all of their tomorrows. Best wishes on your journey!

Additional Resources on the Internet for Developing a Classroom Homepage

Backgrounds Archive—http://www.backgroundsarchive.com/
Find a number of free backgrounds for your homepage here.

Educational Web Design—
http://www.oswego.org/staff/cchamber/webdesign/edwebdesign.htm
Go here first if you are beginning your webpage journey. Cathy Chamberlain in Oswego, New York has made it easy for all of us. This is a one-stop shopping center for anyone who wants to learn how to make a classroom homepage.

Graphics Automat—http://www.webdiner.com/alpha/alpha.htm
Are you looking for great new graphics and fonts to jazz up your website? That is what you will find at the Graphics Automat. Take a look.

How Do They Do That With HTML?—
http://www.tashian.com/htmlguide/
Have you ever seen a great webpage and wondered how they were able to use a special background pattern, animations, background sounds, or other tricks? Here is the page that explains everything and shows you how to include these and many other useful features in your classroom homepage. Set a bookmark!

Links for Web Page Design—
http://home.att.net/~sociologyclassroom/webpagedesign.html
A great collection of resources designed to help teachers who are creating webpages.

Lisa Explains HTML for Kids—
http://www.lissaexplains.com/index.shtml

An 11-year-old, now 17, started this site long ago. She will help kids, as well as adults, with the new literacies of HTML webpage construction. A wonderful demonstration of new literacies at work.

Media Builder—http://mediabuilder.com/

Many free samples for backgrounds, clip art, fonts, and other elements for your homepage are located here.

Resources for Icons, Images, and Graphics—
http://www.aphids.com/susan/imres

Another nice location to obtain great visual elements for your classroom homepage.

TalkFrontPage Forum—http://www.talkfrontpage.com/

A forum for people who use FrontPage, another web editor, to create webpages.

Tutorial on Creating Web Pages with FrontPage Editor—
http://www.siec.k12.in.us/~west/online/website/index.html

A great, easy to follow, tutorial that takes you step by step in using this popular web editor.

Web Adventure—http://www.webdiner.com/webadv/index.htm

A nicely structured series of tutorials for learning how to develop webpages. It takes you from the very simple things to the most advanced. Take your time and learn all there is to learn about making webpages.

Web Design—http://www.uni.edu/profdev/teachnet/four/eval_g4.html

Here is a great location containing extensive rubrics for evaluating any web page that you create.

Web Page Design and Layout—
http://dir.yahoo.com/Arts/Design_Arts/Graphic_Design/Web_Page_Design_and_Layout/

The mother of all directories for web design. So much to learn and so little time!

Online Communities for Developing a Classroom Homepage

Designers' Café

Enter into conversations with webpage designers at all levels and learn from others on this journey.
Homepage: http://ellington.nmailer.com/mailman/listinfo/cafe

Web Design Forums

This site has a number of forums to help kids develop webpages. Join in and these kids will be happy to help you. Over 17,000 members.
Homepage: http://www.lissaexplains.com/vbindex.php

References

Aaronson, E. (1978). *The jigsaw classroom.* Beverly Hills, CA: Sage Publications.

Alvermann, D. E., Moon, J. S., & Hagood, M. C. (1999). Popular culture in the *classroom: Teaching and researching critical media literacy.* Newark, DE:

International Reading Association & Chicago, IL: National Reading Conference.

Bahktin, M. M. (1981). *The dialogic imagination* (C. Emerson & M. Holquist, Trans.). Austin: University of Texas Press.

Burke, J. (2002). The Internet Reader. *Educational Leadership, 60,* 38–42.

Coiro, J. (2003, February). Reading comprehension on the Internet: Expanding our understanding of reading comprehension to encompass new literacies. *The Reading Teacher, 56*(6). Available: http://www.readingonline.org/electronic/elec_index.asp?HREF=/electronic/RT/2-03_column/index.html

Eagleton, M. B., Guinee, K. & Langlais, K. (2003). Teaching Internet literacy strategies: The hero inquiry project. *Voices from the Middle,* 10, 28–35.

Eagleton, M. B., Guinee, K. (2002). Strategies for supporting student inquiry. *New England Reading Association Journal,* 38, 39–47.

Freedman, M. (1998). Don't blame the Internet for Plagiarism. *Education Week, 18,* 36–40. Available: http://www.edweek.org/ew/1998/14freed.h18

Graves, D. (1983). *Writing: Teachers and children at work.* Portsmouth, NH: Heinemann.

Guinee, K., Eagleton, M. B., & Hall, T. (2004). Adolescents' Internet search strategies: Drawing upon familiar cognitive paradigms when accessing electronic information sources. *Journal of Educational Computing Research, 29*(3), 363–374.

Gilster, P. (1997). *Digital literacy.* New York: John Wiley.

Hollan, J., Hutchins, E., & Kirsch, D. (2001). Distributed cognition: Toward a new foundation for human-computer interaction research. In J. M. Carroll (Ed.) *Human-computer interaction in the new millennium,* New York: ACM Press, pp. 75–94.

Hollan, J., Hutchins, E., & Kirsch, D. (2001). Distributed cognition: Toward a new foundation for human-computer interaction research. In J. M. Carroll (Ed.) *Human-computer interaction in the new millennium,* New York: ACM Press, pp. 75-94.

Hynds, S. (1997). On the brink: Negotiating literature and life with adolescents. New York: Teachers College Press.

International Reading Association (IRA). (2002). *Integrating literacy and technology in the curriculum: A position statement*. Newark, DE: International Reading Association.

Johnson, D. W. & Johnson, R. (1984). *Circles of learning: Cooperation in the classroom*. Alexandria, VA: Association of Supervision and Curriculum Development.

Jonassen, D. H., Howland, J., Moore, J., & Marra, R. M. (2003). *Learning to solve problems with technology: A constructivist perspective*, 2nd Ed. Columbus, OH: Merrill/Prentice-Hall.

Jonassen, D. H. (Ed., in press). *Handbook of research for educational communications and technology*, 2nd Ed. Mahwah, NJ: Lawrence Erlbaum Associates.

Lankshear, C. and Knobel, M. (2003). *New literacies: Changing knowledge in the classroom*. Buckingham & Philadelphia: Open University Press, UK.

Lebo, H. (2003). *The UCLA Internet report: Surveying the digital future*. Los Angeles UCLA Center for Communication Policy. Retrieved December 15, 2003 from http://*www.ccp.ucla.edu*

Leu, D. J., Jr. (2002). The new literacies: Research on reading instruction with the Internet and other digital technologies. (pp. 310–336). In J. Samuels and A. E. Farstrup (Eds.). *What research has to say about reading instruction*. Newark, DE: International Reading Association.

Leu, D. J., Jr. (2002, February). Internet Workshop: Making time for literacy [Exploring Literacy on the Internet department]. *The Reading Teacher*, *55*(5). Available: http://www.readingonline.org/electronic/elec_index.asp? HREF=rt/2-02_column/index.html

Leu, D. J., Jr. (2001, March). Internet Project: Preparing students for new literacies in a global village. *The Reading Teacher*, *54*(6). Available: http://www.readingonline.org/electronic/elec_index.asp?HREF=/electronic/RT/3-01_Column/index.html

Leu, D. J., Jr. (2000a). Developing new literacies: Using the Internet in content area instruction. In M. McLaughlin & M. Vogt, (Eds.). *Creativity and innovation in content area teaching* (pp. 183–206). Norwood, MA: Christopher-Gordon.

Leu, D. J., Jr. (2000b). Literacy and technology: Deictic consequences for literacy education in an information age. In M. L. Kamil, P. Mosenthal, P. D. Pearson, and R. Barr (Eds.) *Handbook of Reading Research, Volume III* (pp. 743–770). Mahwah, NJ: Erlbaum.

Leu, D. J., Jr. (1996). Sarah's secret: Social aspects of literacy and learning in a digital information age. *The Reading Teacher*, *50* (2), 162–165.

Leu, D. J., Jr. & Kinzer, C. K. (2002). *Effective literacy instruction*, 5th Ed. Upper Saddle River, NJ: Prentice Hall.

Leu, D. J., Jr. & Kinzer, C. K. (1999). *Effective literacy instruction*, 4th Ed. Upper Saddle River, NJ: Prentice Hall.

Leu, D. J., Jr., Kinzer, C. K., Coiro, J., Cammack, D. (2004). Toward a theory of new literacies emerging from the Internet and other information and communication technologies. In R. B. Ruddell & N. Unrau (Eds.), *Theoretical Models and Processes of Reading, Fifth Edition* (1568-1611). Newark, DE: International Reading Association. Available: http://www.readingonline.org/newliteracies/lit_index.asp?HREF=/newliteracies/leu

McGee, L. M., & Richgels, D. J. (1990). *Literacy's beginnings: Supporting young readers and writers*. Boston: Allyn & Bacon.

McMahon, S. I., Raphael, T. E., Goatley, V. J. & Pardo, L. S. (Eds.). (1997). *The book club connection.* New York: Teachers College Press.

Meyer, D. K. (1993). What is scaffolded instruction? Definitions, distinguishing features, and misnomers. In D. J. Leu, Jr. and C. K. Kinzer (Eds.) *Examining central issues in literacy research, theory, and practice.* Forty–second Yearbook of the National Reading Conference. Chicago: National Reading Conference.

Mikulecky, L., & Kirkley, J. R. (1998). Changing workplaces, changing classes: The new role of technology in workplace literacy. In D. Reinking, M. McKenna, L. D. Labbo, & R. Kieffer (Eds.), *Handbook of literacy and technology: Transformations in a post-typographic world* (pp. 303–320). Mahwah, NJ: Erlbaum.

Muspratt, A., Luke, A. & Freebody, P. (Eds.) (1998). *Constructing critical literacies.* Sydney: Allen & Unwin.

Negroponte, N. (1995). *Being digital.* New York: Knopf.

National Center for Education Statistics (2002). *Internet access in public schools and classrooms: 1994–2000.* Available: *http://nces.ed.gov/pubsearch/pubsinfo.asp?pubid=2002018*

Ogle, D. M. (1989). The know, want to know, learn strategy. In K.D. Muth (Ed.) *Children's comprehension of text* (pp. 205–223). Newark, DE: International Reading Association.

RAND Reading Study Group. (2002). *Reading for understanding: Toward an R&D program in reading comprehension.* Santa Monica, CA: RAND. Available: http://www.rand.org/publications/MR/MR1465/

Reich, R. (1992). *The work of nations.* New York: Vintage Books.

Schmar, E. (2002, December). *Reading on the Internet: What we have learned from print–based text, what we can learn from electronic text.* Paper presented at the annual meeting of the National Reading Conference, Miami, FL.

Short, K. (1993). Intertextuality: Searching for patterns that connect. In D. J. Leu, Jr. & C. K. Kinzer (Eds.), *Literacy research, theory and practice: Views from many perspectives.* Chicago: National Reading Conference.

Smolin, L. I. & Lawless, K. A. (2003). Becoming literate in the technological age: New responsibilities and tools for teachers. *The Reading Teacher, 56,* 570–577.

Spires, H. A. & Estes, T. (2002). Reading in web-based learning environments. In C. Collins Block & M. Pressley (Eds.), *Comprehension instruction: Research-based best practices* (pp. 115–125). Guilford Press: New York.

Snyder, I. (2001). A new communication order: Researching literacy practices in the network society. *Language and Education: An International Journal, 15,* 117–131.

Sutherland–Smith, W. (2002). Weaving the literacy web: Changes in reading from page to screen. *The Reading Teacher, 55,* 662–669.

The New London Group. (2000). *Multiliteracies: Literacy learning and the design of social futures.* London: Routledge.

Thoman, E. (1999). Skills and strategies for media education. *Educational Leadership, 56* (5), 50–54.

U.S. Department of Commerce: National Telecommunications and Information Administration (2002). *A nation online: How Americans are expanding their use of the Internet.* Washington, DC: U.S. Department of Commerce.

Vygotsky, L. S. (1978) *Mind in society: The development of higher psychological processes*. (M. Cole, V. John–Steiner, S. Scribner, E. Souberman, Eds.). Cambridge, MA: Harvard University Press.

Glossary

acceptable use policy (AUP)
A written agreement signed by parents/guardians, students, and teachers that specifies the conditions under which students may use the Internet, defines appropriate and unacceptable use, and defines penalties for violating items in the policy.

bookmark
The feature used in Netscape Navigator and some other browsers to mark a location on the Internet so that you may quickly return there at a later time without having to do another search.

browser
A software program installed on your computer that allows you to locate and view pages on the Internet. It can also be used to organize and manage your favorite Internet resources. Many browsers include email and news features. There are several different browsers; Netscape Navigator, Internet Explorer, and Safari are three of the most popular. Most browsers are available in at least two platforms: Windows and Macintosh.

classroom homepage
A location on the Internet created and maintained by a teacher to communicate with students and parents, display work the class is doing, and organize links to useful resources for students, parents, and other teachers.

cookies
Electronic requests for information from website administrators, which enable them to gather and record information about you from your computer whenever you visit their sites. Sometimes this information is used to direct you to locations you visit most often. Sometimes it is used for statistical purposes, such as determining how many people visit a site.

directory
A location on the Internet with extensive and well-organized links to websites dealing with a content area or important subject. Most are located at stable sites that do not change location often. Examples include: **History/Social Studies for K-12 Teachers** (http://members. cox.net/dboals/boals.html), **Children's Literature Web Guide** (http://www. ucalgary.ca/~dkbrown/index.html), and **Math Forum** (http://math forum.org/).

directory strategy
Teachers often find that a directory strategy is effective for locating useful instructional resources. Instead of using a search engine, they locate a directory in a subject area, set a bookmark, and then use this location to locate useful resources.

Favorites
The feature used in Internet Explorer to mark a location on the Internet so that you may quickly return there at a later time without having to do another search.

filters
Software programs that cause a computer to deny access to locations where certain words appear. Teachers and parents may edit the list of words used in this blocking software. Two of the most popular filtering tools include **Cyber Patrol** (http://www.cyberpatrol.com) and **Net Nanny** (http://www.netnanny.com).

homepage
The main page of an Internet website that directs users to information, features, and links found at that location.

HTML (HyperText Mark-up Language)
HyperText Mark-up Language, or HTML, the programming language used to design webpages on the Internet.

HTML editor
A software program that allows you to design a webpage in the way you wish it to appear while automatically converting your design into HTML code. Netscape's Composer and Adobe's PageMill are examples.

hypertext link
Words or icons that take you to the location on the Internet that is linked to that item when you click it. A key element of Internet navigation.

Internet Workshop
An instructional practice often used by teachers who are getting started with using the Internet in their classrooms. It usually includes these steps: locating a site or sites on the Internet with content related to a classroom unit of instruction and setting a bookmark for the location(s); developing an activity requiring students to use the site(s); assigning this activity to be completed during the week; having students gather together to share their work, questions, and new insights about content and new literacies in a workshop session, often at the end of the week.

Internet Inquiry
An instructional practice using the Internet in a student-directed fashion. It usually contains five phases: developing a question, searching for information, evaluating the information, composing an answer to the question, and sharing the answer with others.

Internet Project

An instructional practice that uses a collaborative approach to classroom use of the Internet. Generally, Internet projects follow these steps: planning a collaborative project for an upcoming unit in your classroom and writing a project description; posting the project description and timeline several months in advance at one or several project registry locations, seeking collaborative classroom partners; arranging collaboration details with teachers in other classrooms who agree to participate; completing the project, most often using Internet Workshop as a forum in your own class for working on the project; and exchanging information with your collaborating classrooms.

Internet activity page

A page developed by teachers to help students organize the tasks in an Internet activity. Students complete the activities on the page and then bring it to Internet Workshop for discussion about what they have learned, new questions they have, and new literacies they have encountered.

Internet driver's license

A "license" or document showing that a student is qualified and has permission to use the Internet. To obtain a license, students usually take one or more online interactive quizze. These quizzes present various situations and then ask students to make choices about which response would be the most ethical, appropriate, and safe. When students complete the quiz successfully, they earn a license and the right to use the Internet in their classroom.

menu

A list of browser functions or features. You may select items such as File, Edit, View, and Help from the main toolbar menu. There are also pull-down menus that appear on screen when you select an item from the main menu. For example, if you click File on the main menu, you may then select from options such as New, Open, Close, and Print in the pull-down menu.

netiquette

Internet etiquette—basically the good manners, common courtesy, and knowledge of generally accepted online practices that allow successful electronic communication to take place.

new literacies

The new literacies of the Internet include the skills, strategies, and dispositions necessary to successfully use and adapt to the rapidly changing information and communication technologies and contexts that continuously emerge in our world and influence all areas of our personal and professional lives. These new literacies allow us to use the Internet and other ICT to identify important questions, navigate to locate information, critically evaluate the usefulness of that information, synthesize information to solve problems, and communicate the solutions to others.

online community

A group of people who use electronic communication technology such as mailing lists, newsgroups, bulletin boards, and forums to discuss and ask questions about a topic of mutual interest. Some groups make their postings available to anyone who wants to participate while others require subscription or membership in a sponsoring organization.

plug-in

A software program you can download from the Internet allowing you to read, view, or play multimedia features on a webpage.

search engines

Computers on the Internet that help you locate information by searching for sites containing words or phrases that you specify. There are numerous examples, such as Ask.Com, Google, and Yahoo for older students and adults; and Ask Jeeves for Kids, KidsClick, and Yahooligans for younger students.

server

A server is a computer in a network, containing information or programs that are often shared with other computers. A webpage on the Internet is always located on a server.

startup page

A startup page is the page that appears first on your screen each time students connect to the Internet. You may select a startup location of your choice by setting a preference, usually from the Preferences item in your browser's main menu.

Student-to-Student Activity

During a Student-to-Student Activity, students first identify a useful Internet location related to their studies. Then they develop a learning experience for other students to complete using that website. This is often used as a culminating activity for Internet Inquiry or thematic units.

toolbar

A row of icons and/or labels appearing in a bar on a browser. Items in the toolbar let you access and use various features of your browser. The main toolbar often includes items such as "Back," "Forward," "Refresh," "Home," "Search," "Go," "Print," and "Stop." Other toolbars may include icons for mail, an address book, or instant messaging.

website Internet project

A website Internet project is a more permanent Internet project with its own webpage. Website projects are ongoing or restart periodically, and are often coordinated by an individual who can be contacted through the website.

URL (Uniform Resource Locator)

The address of a location on the Internet. For example, the URL for the website that accompanies this book is: (http://www.sp.uconn.edu/~djleu/fourth.html).

weblog (blog)

This definition is still evolving, but generally, *weblog* refers to a frequently updated website that contains reverse chronological postings of links to interesting sites and news articles on the Internet; usually created and maintained by a single author. Blogs are often focused around a theme and usually include comments from the site's creator and from readers. A small but growing number of teachers have created class weblogs or are using weblog technology to create classroom homepages.

WebQuest

An instructional practice, originally developed by Bernie Dodge, that has students answer a query by using pre-defined Internet resources to complete a specified task. Today, thousands of webquests are being created by teachers and students from around the world. They may use a variety of formats, but most quests include the following elements: an introduction including a query, the task definition, a description of the process, a list of Internet (and other) resources, guidance in organizing information obtained from those resources, and a concluding activity.

Index

About the Authors

Donald J. Leu holds the John and Maria Neag Chair in Literacy and Technology at the University of Connecticut. He started his teaching career in the Peace Corps, teaching English as a Second Language. Later, he taught in the Bay Area of California where he also worked as a reading specialist. Don completed his Masters degree at Harvard in Reading and Human Development and his Ph.D. at Berkeley in Language and Literacy. He is the author of more than 100 books, articles, and software in literacy education and electronic learning environments. He is a frequent speaker on new literacies, having lectured at Harvard and Berkeley as well as keynote addresses in Europe, Australia, Asia, South America, and North America. Don is President-Elect of the National Reading Conference and is a Fellow in the National Conference on Research in Language and Literacy. He enjoys flyfishing, backpacking, and spending time with his family.

Deborah Diadiun Leu began her teaching career as a Peace Corps volunteer in the Marshall Islands of Micronesia. Her passion has always been working in the classroom to help her students become more proficient in English and literacy. Over the years, she has worked with many populations of English Language Learners (ELL) including elementary and middle school students, immigrants, and language teachers. For the last twenty years at Syracuse University's English Language Institute, she taught international university students and business professionals using a variety of electronic media. She has given presentations on this topic at a number of conferences and forums. Deborah received her Masters degree in Linguistics and English as a Second Language from Syracuse University. Recently retired, she looks forward to reading, exploring new cultures, and spending time with family and friends.

Julie Coiro is a certified teacher with eight years of classroom teaching experience and a Masters degree in Curriculum and Instruction. She has taught in preschool, elementary, and middle school classrooms, and has also worked as a reading specialist and software consultant. Currently, Julie provides professional development opportunities for educators in the areas of technology integration, curriculum development, and literacy skills and strategies. She has completed her third year in the doctoral program in literacy and technology at the University of Connecticut. Her areas of interest include reading comprehension, critical reading strategies, and effective practices for technology integration and professional development. Julie has published work in *The Reading Teacher*, the *New England Reading Association Journal*, *Theoretical Models and Processes of Reading, 5th Edition*, and has an upcoming chapter in *The Handbook of Literacy and Technology, 2nd Edition*. Julie enjoys writing, traveling, and spending time with her husband and two daughters.